THIS ASTOUNDING CLOSE

MARK L. BRADLEY

THIS ASTOUNDING CLOSE

THE ROAD TO BENNETT PLACE

The University of North Carolina Press   Chapel Hill & London

© 2000

The University of North Carolina Press

All rights reserved

Set in New Baskerville by Tseng Information Systems

Manufactured in the United States of America

The paper in this book meets the guidelines for permanence and
durability of the Committee on Production Guidelines for Book Longevity
of the Council on Library Resources.

Library of Congress Cataloging-in-Publication Data

Bradley, Mark L.

This astounding close: the road to Bennett Place / Mark L. Bradley.

p.   cm.

Includes bibliographical references (p.   ) and index.

ISBN 0-8078-2565-4 (cloth: alk. paper)

1. North Carolina—History—Civil War, 1861–1865—Campaigns.

2. North Carolina—History—Civil War, 1861–1865—Social aspects.

3. Sherman's March through the Carolinas.   4. United States—History—
Civil War, 1861–1865—Social aspects.   5. United States—History—Civil
War, 1861–1865—Campaigns.   6. United States—History—Civil War,
1861–1865—Peace.   I. Title.

E477.7 .B73   2000

973.7′38—dc21   00-025564

04   03   02   01   00   5   4   3   2   1

To my wife, Nancy

*Once before in my life the accomplishment of hopes long
and anxiously dwelt on, ever present, and which entered into
all my thoughts, left me without even the power to express or give
utterance to the joy & thankfulness which filled my heart. Something
similar is the effect upon me of* THIS ASTOUNDING CLOSE *of the
most terrible contest of modern times. At last, Peace, blessed God-given
Peace, is so near that we can hear her gracious voice and her gentle
foot-fall over fields too long drenched with fraternal blood. . . . God
be praised! God help us all, "loyal" and "rebel" alike, to take to
heart the terrible lessons of the last five years, and alike to shun
the errors, the follies and the crimes, which brought upon
us all such discipline.*

Maj. Henry Hitchcock to his wife, Mary, April 16, 1865

CONTENTS

ILLUSTRATIONS

MAPS

PREFACE

When I began this project ten years ago, I knew the road would lead to Bennett Place, but I assumed little else. I intended to tell the story of Sherman's campaigns in North Carolina, bearing in mind that as the year 1865 opened, Northern victory and Southern defeat appeared imminent, but none of the participants could predict when and how the end would come, or how much death and destruction would occur in the meantime. My first objective was to convey that sense of foreboding and uncertainty in describing the final month of the war in North Carolina.

During my research, I discovered that only part of the Bennett Place story has been told. Most previous studies have treated the end of the Civil War in North Carolina as a brief episode within a larger narrative framework, thereby omitting many important details of the military operations in central North Carolina, the effect of those operations on the Bennett Place conferences, Gen. Joseph E. Johnston's role in those negotiations, and the final days of Johnston's Army of Tennessee. A few unpublished studies investigate the morale of the Confederate forces facing Sherman's army during the last year of the war, but they do not provide a detailed profile of Johnston's army during its final weeks. The closing chapter in the tragic saga of the Army of Tennessee deserves to be told.

I have discovered that in April 1865 the Army of Tennessee was larger, better equipped, and better supplied than has generally been thought and that morale remained surprisingly good. Confederate muster rolls indicate that the fall of Richmond and Lee's surrender at Appomattox Court House caused some desertions but did not break the army's spirit. Only when rumors of its own surrender began to spread on the afternoon of April 16 did the Army of Tennessee collapse.

Johnston also deserves more credit for his accomplishments in April 1865. By keeping his army intact and as much as eighty miles from Sherman's, the Confederate commander was able to negotiate from a position of strength. Sherman knew that Johnston could have led his army on a march into the Deep South and prolonged the war indefinitely, and this knowledge contributed to his decision to offer his adversary generous terms. When Sherman's original surrender agreement was disapproved in Washington, a persistent Johnston still managed to obtain better terms for his troops than Lee's soldiers had received at Appomattox.

Sherman's role is less crucial than is generally thought. It was Lee's surrender, not Sherman's half-hearted pursuit, that induced Johnston to negotiate with his Federal counterpart. Though Sherman's role as peacemaker should not be dismissed, it was Johnston who initiated the negotiations and dictated the first proposed terms, which no doubt influenced Sherman's own first agreement.

I perceive this book as a necessary sequel to my study on the Battle of Bentonville, which told only the first half of the story. My keenest regret in completing this project is that I am taking leave of some compelling characters. William T. Sherman and Joseph E. Johnston remain embroiled in controversy to this day. Few characters in our history inspire such extremes of hatred and admiration as "Uncle Billy." "Old Joe" has also come under fire from historians in recent years, but his star now appears to be in the ascendant. For all the vicissitudes their reputations have undergone, however, Sherman and Johnston formed a lifelong bond during the Bennett Place negotiations.

In striking contrast, the mutual enmity of Confederate cavalry commander Wade Hampton and his Union counterpart, Judson Kilpatrick, resulted in a heated confrontation outside the Bennett farmhouse. Other memorable characters include Governor Zebulon B. Vance, the remarkable "War Governor" of North Carolina; Union general John A. "Black Jack" Logan, who prevented a mob of his soldiers from burning Raleigh, North Carolina; Lieutenant Walsh of the 11th Texas Cavalry, whose rashness jeopardized the Tar Heel capital and cost him his life; Federal secretary of war Edwin M. Stanton, whose machinations so infuriated Sherman; and railroad conductor Dallas Ward, who participated in the Vance peace mission to Sherman and witnessed both the Confederate evacuation and the Federal occupation of the state capital. Presidents Abraham Lincoln and Jefferson Davis also make several brief but crucial appearances in the story.

The epigraph is from a letter written by Sherman staff officer Maj. Henry Hitchcock in response to news that Johnston had agreed to meet Sherman to discuss surrender terms. Johnston's reply arrived at Sherman's headquarters on April 16, two days after Lincoln's assassination, but one day before the news reached Raleigh. Hitchcock hoped that God would enable "loyal" and "rebel" alike to profit from the terrible lessons of the war; the quotation marks imply that there were no longer Yankees and Rebels, but only Americans. As Lincoln had noted in his second inaugural address, both regions shared guilt for the war and atoned for it with their blood. Both Lincoln and Hitchcock described the outcome of the war as "astounding"—a word that connotes neither triumph nor defeat, but rather awe and astonishment.

ACKNOWLEDGMENTS

This study has benefited from the help and advice of many people. I owe a debt of gratitude to Edwin C. Bearss for taking time to read the manuscript. Despite a hectic schedule that lends new meaning to the word "retirement," Ed returned each chapter promptly and with many helpful suggestions. My thanks also to William C. Harris of North Carolina State University for finding time in his busy schedule to read the manuscript. His comments were invaluable. Thanks to Chris E. Fonvielle of the University of North Carolina at Wilmington, John F. Marszalek of Mississippi State University, and Stephen Middleton of North Carolina State University for reading portions of the manuscript. I am also grateful to Gary W. Gallagher, editor of the University of North Carolina Press Civil War America series, for his advice and comments. A special thanks to Richard M. McMurry for his painstaking critique of the manuscript.

I wish to thank Bennett Place State Historic Site manager Davis Waters and assistant manager Kent McCoury for all their help. I particularly benefited from the many hours of discussion with Kent regarding the final weeks of the Civil War in North Carolina. Thanks also to Bentonville Battleground State Historic Site manager John C. Goode and assistant manager Frederick Burgess. I am equally grateful to former site employee Lynn Bull and past Bentonville Battleground Historical Association president Lauren Cook Burgess.

Many thanks to supervisor Jerry C. Cashion and researcher Michael Hill of the Research Branch of the North Carolina Division of Archives and History for their assistance. I am particularly grateful to Mike for providing me with several valuable documents from his own work. To Stephen E. Massengill of the Archival Services Branch, a special thanks for his help in locating many excellent illustrations for the book.

I am grateful to Raymond L. Beck, the North Carolina state capitol historian, for giving my wife, Nancy, and me a private tour of the capitol.

That marvelous old edifice has a knowledgeable and devoted caretaker in Ray Beck.

My thanks to Elizabeth Reid Murray, author of Wake County's definitive history, and Nancy Carter Moore, coauthor of the second volume, for their encouragement and assistance. Whatever they do not know about North Carolina's capital county is either lost or not worth knowing.

My appreciation to Nat Hughes of Chattanooga, Tennessee, for his advice and encouragement.

Thanks also to David E. Roth, publisher of *Blue and Gray* magazine; Theodore P. "Ted" Savas of Savas Publishing Company; Walt Smith and Sion H. "Si" Harrington III of the Averasboro Battlefield Commission; Lt. Col. Al Aycock of the John F. Kennedy Special Warfare Center and School at Fort Bragg, North Carolina; James B. Clary of Cary, North Carolina; Mac Wyckoff of Fredericksburg, Virginia; Thomas P. Nanzig of Ann Arbor, Michigan; E. Chris Evans of Heath, Ohio; Col. Michael J. Brennan and the Grand Army of the Cussewago; and the U.S. Army, U.S. Special Operations Forces, and U.S. Marine Corps staff ride groups I have been fortunate enough to have led.

To Marvin Sanderman and Curt A. Carlson of the Chicago Civil War Round Table, thank you for taking Nancy and me to the Chicago Historical Society, and otherwise rolling out the red carpet.

I am grateful to Alan and Nancy Bruns of Fredericksburg, Virginia, for their hospitality and for providing a photograph of their ancestor, Brig. Gen. Thomas M. Logan.

Many thanks to the University of North Carolina Press staff for the care they have lavished on my book. I am especially grateful to editor-in-chief David Perry, project editor Pamela Upton, copyeditor Mary Reid, assistant editor Mark Simpson-Vos, and graphics coordinator Jackie Johnson.

My thanks to Ethel S. Arnett, John G. Barrett, Burke Davis, John M. Gibson, Joseph T. Glatthaar, Howard O. Hendricks, Arthur C. Menius III, Noah Andre Trudeau, and William M. Vatavuk for their work on the final month of the Civil War in North Carolina.

To my good friend and historian-cartographer extraordinaire, Mark A. Moore, my thanks for his advice and support.

I am grateful to my parents, John and Audrey Bradley, as well as my brothers, Bill and Jim, for their support and encouragement. A special thanks to my grandfather, James Jackson Hagan, for making the long-ago Civil War come alive.

To my wife, Nancy, special thanks for her help as editor and research assistant, and for her faith, encouragement, and support.

Finally, without the helpful assistance of staff members at numerous libraries and archives, I could not have written this book. For going far above and beyond the call of duty, special thanks to Richard J. Sommers and David A. Keough of the United States Army Military History Institute, Carlisle Barracks, Pennsylvania; Susan Ravdin of the Bowdoin College Library, Brunswick, Maine; Margaret Lee of the Johnston County Public Library, Smithfield, North Carolina; Mark E. Thomas of the Cincinnati Historical Society, Cincinnati, Ohio; Joanne Hohler of the State Historical Society of Wisconsin, Madison, Wisconsin; Hampton Smith and Alissa Rosenberg of the Minnesota Historical Society, St. Paul, Minnesota; DeAnne Blanton of the National Archives, Washington, D.C.; and William B. Tubbs of the Illinois State Historical Library, Springfield, Illinois.

THIS ASTOUNDING CLOSE

CHAPTER 1

NO SUCH ARMY SINCE THE DAYS OF JULIUS CAESAR

On December 22, 1864, Maj. Gen. William T. Sherman concluded his March to the Sea by presenting the city of Savannah, Georgia, to President Abraham Lincoln as a Christmas gift. For all its significance in the popular imagination, Sherman regarded the march as a mere change of base. With characteristic foresight, he had already conceived a second and far more devastating sword thrust into the Confederacy's vitals: a march taking him northward through the Carolinas to Richmond, Virginia, the Confederate capital. In comparing the two campaigns, Sherman would later write: "Were I to express my measure of the relative importance of the march to the sea, and that from Savannah northward, I would place the former at one, and the latter at ten, or the maximum."[1]

But the Union general-in-chief, Lt. Gen. Ulysses S. Grant, had other plans for Sherman's army. For the past eight months, the forces under Grant's immediate command, the Army of the Potomac and the Army of the James, had failed to crush Gen. Robert E. Lee's Army of Northern Virginia. The two sides remained deadlocked around Richmond and Petersburg, with no prospect of a Union breakthrough in the foreseeable future. Believing that Sherman's veteran troops would tip the balance in his favor, Grant directed that they be boarded on ships at Savannah and transported to the Virginia theater as rapidly as possible. Sherman objected to Grant's plan and advocated a march through the Carolinas instead. "[W]e can punish South Carolina as she deserves, and as thousands of the people in Georgia hoped we would do," he wrote Grant. "I do sincerely believe that the whole United States, North and South, would rejoice to have [my] army turned loose on South Carolina, to devastate that State in the manner we have done in Georgia, and it would have a direct and immediate bearing on the campaign in Virginia." Sherman argued that his marauding army would cut Lee's supply lines to the Deep South and induce many Confederate soldiers from that region to desert. If his army traveled to Virginia by sea, however, neither objective would be accomplished, and his troops' morale and conditioning could be damaged by the long ocean voyage. Meanwhile, Grant learned that the transfer of Sherman's army by sea would take at least two months, about the time needed to march that distance. The general-in-chief considered Sherman's proposed plan in this light and gave his approval.[2]

Sherman received Grant's revised instructions on Christmas Eve and was delighted with the change in orders. "I feel no doubt whatever as to our future plans," he told Grant. "I have thought them over so long and well that they appear as clear as daylight." Sherman would divide his army into two wings, as he had done on the March to the Sea. At the outset, he would feint toward Augusta, Georgia, and its gunpowder works to the west, and toward Charleston, South Carolina—the so-called Cradle of Secession—to the east, forcing the Confederates to divide their forces to defend the two important points. He would then advance via Columbia, South Carolina, to the coast—preferably Wilmington, North Carolina—to refit his army before resuming the march to Raleigh in early spring. "The game is then up with Lee," Sherman wrote, "unless he comes out of Richmond, avoids you and fights me, in which case I should reckon on your being on his heels."[3]

On January 2, 1865, Sherman directed his two wing commanders, Major Generals Oliver O. Howard and Henry W. Slocum, to advance their armies into South Carolina. In mid-January, Howard's Army of the Tennessee secured a lodgment at Pocotaligo, while Slocum's Army of Georgia, preceded by Bvt. Maj. Gen. Judson Kilpatrick's Third Cavalry Division, began crossing the Savannah River at Sister's Ferry. As on the March to the Sea, Howard's command was the grand army's right wing and Slocum's the left wing. Before Slocum could complete his crossing, the winter rains set in; the ensuing flood carried off a portion of the Army of Georgia's pontoon bridge and transformed the roads into quagmires. The flooding of the Savannah River compelled Sherman to postpone the opening of his campaign until February 1.[4]

While Sherman waited impatiently for the flood waters to subside, Fort Fisher in North Carolina fell to a Federal amphibious force on January 15, thus closing Wilmington, the Confederacy's last major blockade-running seaport. Grant initially was lukewarm concerning plans to seize Wilming-

Maj. Gen. William T. Sherman (North Carolina Division of Archives and History)

ton, but once Sherman selected the port as a possible objective, the Union general-in-chief regarded its capture as a high priority. As Grant studied his map of North Carolina, however, he noticed an even more desirable objective from Sherman's standpoint. Goldsboro lay about 450 miles north of Savannah. As the inland junction of two coastal railroads, the Wilmington and Weldon and the Atlantic and North Carolina, Goldsboro provided rail connections with both Wilmington and Morehead City; it was an ideal location for Sherman's army to refit. Grant directed Maj. Gen. George H. Thomas, the Union commander at Nashville, Tennessee, to transfer Maj.

Gen. John M. Schofield's Twenty-third Corps to North Carolina, where it would join forces with Maj. Gen. Alfred H. Terry's Provisional Corps, the captors of Fort Fisher. As commander of the newly reestablished Department of North Carolina, Schofield was to advance on Goldsboro—either from Wilmington, once the latter had fallen, or from Federal-held New Bern—and secure the inland rail junction for Sherman. After receiving Grant's letter explaining these dispositions, Sherman chose Goldsboro as his ultimate destination.[5]

When Sherman began his Carolinas campaign on February 1, 1865, his grand army—or "army group," as it would be called today—numbered 60,079 officers and men. The core of this army consisted of veteran volunteers who had enlisted during the first two years of the war and then reenlisted in 1864 after their two- and three-year terms had expired. These campaign-toughened veterans were the survivors of what one soldier called "a rigorous weeding-out process" effected by Rebel bullets, hardship, and disease. Moreover, prior to both the Savannah and Carolinas campaigns, Sherman directed the Medical Department to examine all soldiers with health problems and ship out those deemed unfit for active campaigning. As a result, the army that Sherman led into South Carolina was a seasoned fighting force that in the closing months of the war had no equal.[6]

Sherman's grand army consisted of four infantry corps and one cavalry division—the Fifteenth Corps and Seventeenth Corps in the Army of the Tennessee, the Fourteenth Corps and Twentieth Corps in the Army of Georgia, and the Third Cavalry Division. Most regiments were of western origin, although many Twentieth Corps units had served in the Army of the Potomac before their transfer to the western theater in the fall of 1863. Since September 1864, Sherman's grand army had captured Atlanta and Savannah and had marched unchecked through the rich farming region of Georgia, encountering only weak and scattered opposition. By early 1865, the faith of the soldiers in "Uncle Billy" Sherman was absolute. "[T]here never was such a man as Sherman or as they call him (Crazy Bill)," wrote one Fifteenth Corps veteran, "and he has got his men to believe they cant be whiped."[7]

Prior to the march north, Sherman stripped his army down to fighting trim, reducing the number of wagons to 2,500 and the ambulances to 600. The ordnance wagons carried an ample supply of ammunition, but the commissary wagons hauled just seven days' forage and twenty days' hard bread, coffee, sugar, and salt. The army would have to rely on provisions foraged from the countryside. As for baggage, Sherman permitted just one wagon per regiment. Even the commanding general usually slept under a tent fly, reserving his large wall tent for clerical work. Sherman also re-

No Such Army

duced the number of cannon to sixty-eight, or about one field piece for every 1,000 men. Despite these Spartan measures, even on good roads the marching column of each wing often stretched out for ten miles. To reduce straggling, the four corps marched on separate roads whenever possible. The long Federal columns would have been vulnerable to hit-and-run raids by Confederate cavalry had it not been for the protective screen provided by Kilpatrick's horsemen and the army's numerous foraging details.[8]

As Sherman swept into South Carolina in early February, his armies cut a swath more than forty miles wide. His tactic of feinting on Charleston to the east and Augusta to the west made it almost impossible for the Confederates to determine where the Federals were headed, enabling Sherman to advance between the forces of his divided and outnumbered opposition.

Opposing the Union advance through South Carolina was a heterogeneous array of Confederate forces led by Gen. Pierre Gustave Toutant Beauregard, the commander of the Military Division of the West. On February 2, Beauregard held a council of war near Augusta. The Creole and his lieutenants debated whether they should attempt to concentrate their forces and offer battle to Sherman, but Beauregard dismissed the idea as impractical. He believed that the success of the upcoming peace negotiations might hinge on defending Charleston and Augusta for as long as possible, the former for its symbolic value and the latter for its logistical importance. Beauregard therefore divided his meager forces to defend the two towns, intending to reunite his command at Columbia, if necessary, in time to contest Sherman's advance through the interior of the Palmetto State.[9]

The peace negotiations in which Beauregard placed his faith came to be known as the Hampton Roads Conference. Held aboard the steamer *River Queen* on the morning of February 3, the four-hour meeting passed amicably but was inconclusive. President Lincoln would settle for nothing less than restoration of the Union, while the Confederate representatives were empowered to negotiate solely on the basis of an armistice that President Jefferson Davis believed would lead to an independent Confederacy. The failure of the Hampton Roads Conference meant that Beauregard's decision to defend Charleston and Augusta played into Sherman's hands, for the divided Confederate forces were unable to unite in sufficient numbers to oppose the Federal army's advance through South Carolina.[10]

Perhaps Beauregard had counted on the innumerable South Carolina swamps and inclement weather to halt Sherman's progress. Gen. Joseph E. Johnston, who lived in Columbia at the time, later recounted how Lt. Gen. William J. Hardee, the commander at Charleston, had assured him that Sherman's army could never pass through the swamps bordering the

Salkehatchie River. Hardee's complacency soon proved to be unfounded. "[W]hen I learned that Sherman's army was marching through the Salke-hatchie swamps, making its own corduroy road at the rate of a dozen miles a day or more, and bringing its artillery and wagons with it," Johnston confessed, "I made up my mind that there had been no such army in existence since the days of Julius Caesar." When Sherman's modern-day legions reached the outskirts of Columbia on February 16, the city was de-fended by a small Confederate force consisting of cavalry commanded by Maj. Gen. Joseph Wheeler, elements of Lt. Gen. Stephen D. Lee's Corps from the Army of Tennessee, and Maj. Gen. Matthew C. Butler's cavalry di-vision, recently arrived from Virginia. Beauregard and native son Lt. Gen. Wade Hampton, another recent arrival from the Old Dominion, directed operations. Also present was General Johnston, without a command since President Davis had dismissed him from the Army of Tennessee the previ-ous July.[11]

After encountering only token opposition, Sherman's army captured Columbia on February 17. By the next morning, much of the South Caro-lina capital lay in ashes, the result of a conflagration caused by high winds, burning cotton—initially set afire by Hampton's cavalry—and drunken Federal soldiers. Meanwhile, Hardee's command evacuated Charleston under orders from Beauregard, who realized that the loss of Columbia ren-dered the port city untenable.[12]

On February 19, Sherman resumed his advance in the direction of Winnsboro, and once again Beauregard misjudged his intentions. Sup-posing that the Federals were heading toward Petersburg via Charlotte, Greensboro, and Danville, Beauregard ordered Hardee to board his troops on trains for Greensboro via Wilmington, oblivious to the fact that Scho-field's Union forces were on the verge of capturing the latter town. On February 21, Gen. Braxton Bragg, the Confederate commander at Wil-mington, warned Hardee that the Federals had cut the Wilmington and Manchester Railroad, necessitating a change of route to Cheraw, South Carolina. Wilmington fell to Schofield on the following day, February 22. Meanwhile, Sherman's army suddenly shifted its line of march and threat-ened to beat Hardee to Cheraw.[13]

By now it was clear to the Confederacy's newly appointed general-in-chief, Robert E. Lee, that Beauregard could not stop Sherman. "Genl Beauregard makes no mention of what he proposes or what he can do, or where his troops are," a frustrated Lee wrote President Davis. "He does not appear from his despatches to be able to do much." A subsequent dis-patch from Beauregard outlining a scheme in which the Confederate army

No Such Army

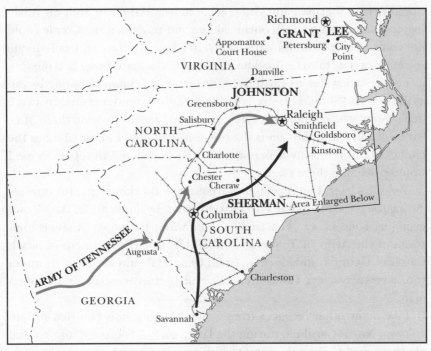

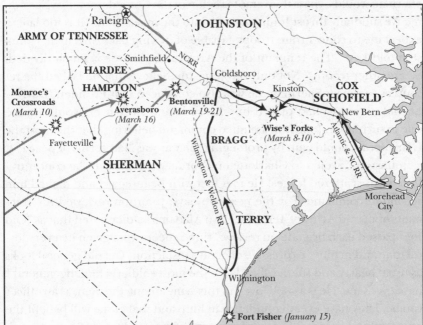

Map 1. The Carolinas campaign, January–March 1865

would defeat Sherman and Grant separately and then "march on Washington to dictate a peace" convinced Lee and Davis that the Creole could not come to grips with military reality. In a letter to the new Confederate secretary of war, John C. Breckinridge, Lee had already broached the subject of replacing Beauregard, using Beauregard's rumored failing health as the reason. "Should his strength give way, there is no one on duty in the department who could replace him, nor have I any one to send there," Lee wrote. "Genl J. E. Johnston is the only officer whom I know who has the confidence of the army & people, & if he was ordered to report to me I would place him there on duty." [14]

Two days later, Lee repeated his request to Breckinridge, this time securing the secretary of war's permission—and, by implication, Davis's own grudging consent. On February 22, Lee wired Johnston: "Assume command of the Army of Tennessee and all troops in Department of South Carolina, Georgia, and Florida. Assign General Beauregard to duty under you, as you may select. Concentrate all available forces and drive back Sherman." [15]

Like many other refugees from Columbia, Johnston had fled to Lincolnton, North Carolina, during the latter part of February, hoping that Sherman would bypass this remote region of the Confederacy. But Lee's directive suddenly thrust Johnston back into the maelstrom. "It is too late to expect me to concentrate troops capable of driving back Sherman," Johnston told Lee. "The remnant of the Army of Tennessee is much divided. So are other troops." Not only did Johnston believe that he lacked the resources to defeat Sherman, he was also convinced that President Davis—his old nemesis—had placed him in command so that he would be the one to surrender. Johnston assumed command believing that the most the Confederacy could gain by prolonging the war was "fair terms of peace." [16]

Johnston traveled to Charlotte on February 23 to begin the concentration of his scattered forces. He met first with Beauregard and named him second-in-command. For the next two days, Johnston reviewed the remnants of his old Army of Tennessee. An Alabama soldier noted that as "Old Joe" passed each brigade on review, "three cheers were given in a very joyful tone and manner expressive of great satisfaction. The old general looks as usual hearty and soldier like. He is the most soldierly looking general I have ever seen. He is as well loved in this army among the men, as an officer can be. They have every confidence in him, and that alone will benefit the army and the service." Though Johnston appreciated the enthusiastic welcome from the Army of Tennessee veterans, the reviews merely confirmed what he had suspected about his army's condition. On February 25, Johnston informed Robert E. Lee that his small army was "too weak to cope with

Gen. Joseph E. Johnston (North Carolina Division of Archives and History)

Sherman." Altogether, the Army of Tennessee contingent, Hardee's command, and Wade Hampton's cavalry numbered fewer than 25,000 soldiers; according to Hampton, "it would scarcely have been possible to disperse a force more effectually."[17]

As Sherman swept through South Carolina, Johnston's scattered command attempted to concentrate and offer battle. Following its rout in the Battle of Nashville, the Army of Tennessee had fallen back into north-eastern Mississippi and established winter camp at Tupelo. "If not in the strict sense of the word, a disorganized mob, it was no longer an army," observed inspection officer Col. Alfred Roman. In January 1865, President Davis had ordered Beauregard to transfer most of the remnant to South Carolina to oppose Sherman's advance. The soldiers traveled the 500 miles from Tupelo to Augusta on foot, by boat, and by train. Only a few arrived in time to dispute Sherman's march through the Palmetto State; the remainder marched on roads west of the Federals. Discipline was uncertain at best: a Texan branded his comrades "a set of thieves," noting that they "behaved shamefully all the way around from Tupelo, Mississippi," yet he explained that their plundering compensated for lost pay and nonexistent whiskey and tobacco rations. Beauregard's quartermaster, Capt. John M. Goodman, called the Army of Tennessee "a complete mob. I have never witnessed so much demoralization in my life. I have feared for my life in contending with our own troops and in the attempt to keep them in some kind of discipline." Goodman expressed a hope shared by many other Confederates: that General Johnston would soon restore the army's discipline and morale.[18]

While the Army of Tennessee concentrated at Charlotte, Hardee's Corps, evacuating from Charleston, raced Sherman's army to Cheraw. Most of Hardee's soldiers were former coastal artillerymen or garrison troops unaccustomed to hard marching. At first they welcomed the march as a relief from the monotony of picket duty, but "[o]ur feet soon became blistered and sore," recalled Cpl. A. P. Ford, a South Carolinian in Hardee's command. "[M]any of us had no shoes, but trudged along in the cold and mud as best we could." Hardee's troops quickly learned an invaluable lesson: travel light. "Our men had started on this march with as much baggage as they . . . could carry," Corporal Ford added, "but soon began to throw aside the impedimenta and settle down to . . . one blanket per man and the suit of clothes each actually wore. For some miles both sides of the road were strewn with knapsacks, articles of clothing, etc., . . . and the highway appeared as if fleeing troops in panic had passed along."[19]

According to Hardee's chief of staff, Lt. Col. Thomas B. Roy, a "[g]reat many desertions" occurred on the march from Charleston. "Some art[illery] companies [were] almost disbanded by desertion," Roy reported. Corporal Ford echoed Roy's observation: "All along the line of march large numbers of men were constantly deserting. Nightly, under cover of darkness, many would sneak from their bivouacs and go off, not to the enemy, but to their homes. . . . The most influential cause of desertion was the news that reached the men of the great suffering of their wives and children at home, caused by the devastations of Sherman's army." On Febru-

No Such Army

ary 22, Hardee consolidated his three divisions into two, having lost about a quarter of his command since the evacuation of Charleston. The attrition resulted from straggling and desertion as well as the recall of several state militia units by South Carolina governor Andrew Magrath.[20]

After marching to St. Stephen's Depot, forty miles north of Charleston, Hardee's footsore soldiers boarded trains for Cheraw. At first Hardee doubted that all of his command could reach Cheraw before he would be forced to evacuate. "This [rail]road, like all others in the Confederacy, is wretchedly managed," an exasperated Hardee wrote Johnston on February 28. "With proper management I ought to have had everything here by this time. . . . A rapid march of the enemy will bring him here tomorrow." Hardee's luck soon improved, however, as the rest of his infantry began arriving that afternoon and incessant winter rains finally stalled Sherman's army. With the Federals occupied for nearly a week in crossing the rain-swollen Catawba River and Lynch's Creek, Hardee's Corps was able to reach Cheraw before Sherman.[21]

While "Uncle Billy" fretted, he learned that Joe Johnston was back in command. Outwardly, Sherman remained as confident and unperturbed as before. Responding to rumors that Johnston was in Cheraw, Sherman wrote: "Big generals may be there but not a large force." Yet the Union commander later admitted: "I then knew that my special antagonist, General Jos. Johnston, was back with part of his old army; that he would not be misled by feints and false reports, and would somehow compel me to exercise more caution than I had hitherto done."[22]

Sherman was right—Johnston would not be as easily misled as Beauregard. On March 1, Johnston wrote Lee, discounting Beauregard's and Hampton's reports that Sherman appeared to be heading toward Charlotte: "The route by Charlotte, Greensboro, and Danville is very difficult now, as you remark," Johnston noted. "It would also leave your army exactly between those of General Grant and General Sherman. It seems to me, therefore, that . . . General Sherman ought not to take it. His junction with General Schofield is also an object important enough . . . to induce him to keep more to the east. Such a course would render his junction with General Grant easier."[23]

Johnston told Lee that he intended to combine Hardee's command with the Army of Tennessee. "These forces united may impede the march of the Federal army," Johnston explained, "and even find opportunities to strike heavy blows, or at least prevent it from gathering food." If Johnston's show of confidence gave Lee a flicker of hope, the next sentence must have extinguished it: "Would it be possible to hold Richmond itself with half your army, while the other half joined us near [the] Roanoke [River] to crush

Sherman? We might then turn upon Grant." Lee no doubt found Johnston's proposal sadly reminiscent of Beauregard's impractical schemes.[24]

On March 3, Hardee evacuated Cheraw, closely followed by the Federal
right wing. After receiving confusing and contradictory instructions from
several superiors, Hardee finally received Johnston's orders to march to
Fayetteville, which also happened to be Sherman's next objective. Screen-
ing the rear of Hardee's column was Butler's cavalry division. To the west,
Wheeler's cavalry corps shadowed the Federal left wing and Kilpatrick's
cavalry.[25]

Once it appeared that Sherman would enter the Old North State, Lee
assigned Gen. Braxton Bragg's Department of North Carolina troops to
Johnston's command. When Bragg received word, he fired off a letter to
President Davis: "I beg that you will relieve me from [this] embarrassing
position. I seek no command or position, and only desire to be ordered
to await assignment to duty at some point in Georgia or Alabama. The
circumstances constraining me to make this request are painful in the extreme, but I cannot blindly disregard them." Bragg had good reason to
be alarmed. As Davis's chief of staff eight months before, he had recommended Johnston's removal from command. Bragg therefore found his
new subordinate relationship to Johnston awkward, to say the least. Davis
refused to intercede for Bragg, however, forcing the general to make the
best of the situation.[26]

Meanwhile, Johnston traveled from Charlotte to Fayetteville to be nearer
Sherman's line of march. Encouraged by the Federals' difficult South Carolina river crossings, Johnston planned to unite the Army of Tennessee contingent with Hardee's Corps in time to strike part of Sherman's army as it
crossed the Cape Fear River. But Bragg, whose small force was concentrating near Kinston, saw a better opportunity on his front and asked Johnston
to divert the Army of Tennessee troops to him.[27]

Advancing inland from New Bern was the Federal Twenty-third Corps,
commanded by Maj. Gen. Jacob D. Cox, whose objective was to secure
Goldsboro for Sherman. Bragg, however, intended to defeat Cox and prevent the Twenty-third Corps's junction with Sherman's army. On March 6,
Bragg asked Johnston to send him the Army of Tennessee troops earmarked for Fayetteville. "A few hours would suffice to unite [those] forces
. . . with mine and insure a victory," Bragg promised. Abandoning his plan
of striking Sherman at Fayetteville, Johnston granted Bragg's request but
instructed him to send the Army of Tennessee troops to Smithfield as soon
as possible for use against Sherman.[28]

The troop transfer led to an uneasy alliance between Bragg and Maj.
Gen. Daniel Harvey Hill, the commander of the Army of Tennessee contin-

gent. The two men had been bitter enemies since Hill's dismissal at Bragg's hands eighteen months earlier. Johnston closed his dispatch ordering Hill to join Bragg with a plea "to forget the past for this emergency." Hill swallowed his pride and reported to Bragg. Besides Hill's Army of Tennessee contingent, Bragg's command included Maj. Gen. Robert F. Hoke's Division and the North Carolina Junior Reserves Brigade.[29]

On March 8, Cox's Federals collided with Bragg's Confederates at Wise's Forks four miles east of Kinston. As the battle opened, the Southerners routed a portion of the Union forces, capturing one cannon and 800 men. The remainder of Cox's troops dug in during the night, and after desultory skirmishing the next day, the Confederates resumed the offensive on March 10. The well-entrenched Federals repulsed the Southerners' assaults easily. Learning that Cox had been reinforced, Bragg withdrew to Kinston that night. Once again the ill-starred Bragg had seen an apparent victory end in retreat.[30]

While Bragg fell back toward Kinston and Goldsboro, Johnston resumed preparations for opposing Sherman. In this endeavor he enjoyed the considerable advantage of the North Carolina Railroad, which formed a 220-mile-long arc from Charlotte to Goldsboro. Unfortunately for Johnston, a 120-car backlog of troops, artillery, and supplies accumulated at Salisbury, while another sixty-five carloads waited at Chester, South Carolina. The bottleneck occurred at Salisbury because the width of the track narrowed there, and most of the narrow-gauge rolling stock sent to Bragg had not returned. Although Bragg's monopolization of the railroad created the backlog, Johnston's failure to intercede further aggravated the problem. At stake was "Old Joe's" ability to strike Sherman with every soldier at his disposal. When the moment of truth arrived, many of Johnston's troops would still be stranded at Salisbury.[31]

Adding to Johnston's woes, Lee and Secretary of War Breckinridge informed him that subsistence stores collected in depots on the North Carolina Railroad were reserved for the Army of Northern Virginia. (Johnston later discovered that the depots held enough rations to feed a 60,000-man army for four months.) Lee told Johnston that his army must subsist on the countryside. Lacking the necessary wagons and teams, Johnston turned to Governor Zebulon B. Vance of North Carolina and Maj. Archibald H. Cole of the Confederate Quartermaster General's office for assistance. Acting with Johnston's authorization, Vance and Cole's agents impressed wagons and draft animals along the expected route of Sherman's march. By this means Johnston's army fed itself until its own wagons arrived.[32]

Johnston was further frustrated by the Richmond bureaucracy. When he sought to obtain pay for his men, Breckinridge told him that the Confederate treasury was broke and callously suggested that he should "make the best of the circumstances." When Johnston requested that a large store of supplies in Charlotte belonging to the Confederate navy (which had almost ceased to exist) be turned over to the army, Secretary of the Navy Stephen R. Mallory refused to comply. Worse yet, 1,300 of Johnston's men lacked rifle-muskets.[33]

With the Federals advancing in superior force on two fronts, the concentration of his own army hampered by delays on the railroad, and that army dependent on a sparsely settled region for subsistence, prospects appeared bleak for Johnston. On March 11, he wrote Lee: "I will not give battle with Sherman's united army . . . but will if I can find it divided." Johnston gathered his own divided army in the desperate hope that he could defeat either Sherman or Schofield before one could combine with the other.[34]

As Sherman's grand army swept into North Carolina during the first week of March, the Confederates continued to reel before the Federal juggernaut. Since the evacuation of Columbia, Wade Hampton's cavalry had fought numerous rearguard actions against Federal infantry and had skirmished with countless foraging details and cavalry patrols. Meanwhile, Hampton sought an opportunity to surprise Kilpatrick.

On March 7, Hampton discovered that Kilpatrick's cavalry had gotten between him and Hardee's Corps. "As soon as my command can be concentrated," Hampton informed Hardee, "I shall move round the left flank of the enemy to his front." This feat proved more difficult than Hampton anticipated, and Kilpatrick remained between him and "Old Reliable."[35]

On the afternoon of March 9, Kilpatrick captured some Confederate stragglers, who reported that a large force of Yankee cavalry had gotten between Hampton and Hardee. This was wonderful news to Kilpatrick, who believed that he could prevent Hampton from joining Hardee simply by blocking the roads to Fayetteville. Kilpatrick ignored Sherman's order to avoid battle for the present. In order to cover the roads Hampton was advancing on, "Little Kil" recklessly divided his command, which contained about the same number of horsemen as Hampton's cavalry. Kilpatrick was inviting Hampton to defeat him in detail, and Hampton eagerly accepted his invitation.[36]

Kilpatrick and two of his four brigades made camp at Monroe's Crossroads on the night of March 9. Torrential rains and Confederate cavalry prevented his remaining two brigades from taking up their positions, leaving the Union cavalry commander's encampment isolated and vulnerable to a surprise attack—precisely what Hampton had in mind. Throughout

No Such Army

the cold, rainy night, Confederate troopers deployed for an assault on Kilpatrick's camp. Hopes ran high among the Southerners that they would deal the Federals a stunning blow at Monroe's Crossroads and perhaps bag "Little Kil" himself.[37]

As dawn broke on March 10, Confederate cavalry burst out of the woods —shrieking the Rebel yell—and overran the Federal camp. Kilpatrick witnessed the onslaught from the porch of the house that was serving as his headquarters. His first thought was "My God, here's a Major General's commission after four years' hard fighting gone up with an infernal surprise." Clad only in his shirt, pants, and slippers, Kilpatrick fled into a nearby swamp.[38]

After a furious, seesaw struggle, the Federals drove off the Confederates and regained their camp. Even so, the Southerners had opened the road to Fayetteville and freed all of their captured comrades. The engagement at Monroe's Crossroads was a moral victory for the Confederates: waggish Union infantrymen dubbed the Rebel surprise attack "Kilpatrick's Shirt-tail Skedaddle." The Federals should have learned from Monroe's Crossroads that the Confederates still posed a considerable threat, but Kilpatrick apparently ignored this lesson, if his subsequent actions are any indication.[39]

Sherman's grand army occupied Fayetteville on March 11 and rested there for four days. Acting under "Uncle Billy's" orders, the 1st Michigan Engineers and Mechanics destroyed the Confederate arsenal on the edge of town. Meanwhile, the Federal commander plotted the final stage of his 450-mile march to Goldsboro. As usual, Sherman's plan included a feint— this time due north toward Raleigh with four divisions of Slocum's left wing in light marching order. The remaining two divisions would escort all nonessential wagons in the rear of Howard's right wing. Slocum would advance up the Plank Road to within four miles of Averasboro and then head east on the Goldsboro Road via Bentonville. Meanwhile, Kilpatrick's cavalry and an infantry division would continue feinting on Raleigh before veering off toward Goldsboro. Howard would march northeast on a direct route to Goldsboro, keeping five of his seven divisions in light marching order and ready to support Slocum. Of Slocum's march toward Bentonville, Sherman observed: "I do think it is Johnston's only chance to meet this army before an easy junction with Schofield can be effected."[40]

While Sherman's army rested at Fayetteville, Hardee's Corps halted at Smithville (not to be confused with Smithfield), about five miles south of Averasboro. Since the evacuation of Charleston in mid-February, Hardee had lost half of his 13,000 troops to straggling, desertion, and Governor Magrath's militia recalls. The general realized that he must either fight or

The Confederate arsenal, Fayetteville (Frank Leslie's Illustrated Newspaper, *1865*)

face the final disintegration of his demoralized command. Hardee also hoped to buy time for the concentration of Johnston's army. He deployed his corps in three lines, placing the relatively inexperienced soldiers of Brig. Gen. William B. Taliaferro's Division on the first two lines and entrusting the third and main line to the more seasoned troops of Maj. Gen. Lafayette McLaws's Division.

Sherman's army resumed the advance on March 15. The left wing headed up the Raleigh Plank Road with Kilpatrick's cavalry in the lead. About mid-afternoon, Kilpatrick's advance regiment collided with Confederates from Hardee's command, and after a brief skirmish, the two sides dug in for the night. "Hardee is ahead of me and shows fight," Sherman wrote early on March 16. "I will go at him in the morning with four divisions and push him as far as Averasborough before turning toward Bentonville and [Goldsboro]."[41]

The Battle of Averasboro began at dawn on March 16, amid a steady rain that lingered for most of the day. Throughout the morning Kilpatrick's cavalry and the Union Twentieth Corps deployed and probed Hardee's first line for weaknesses. About noon Sherman ordered Slocum to send a brigade around the Confederate right flank. Slocum chose Col. Henry Case's Twentieth Corps brigade, whose surprise flank attack routed the Confederates of Col. Alfred M. Rhett's Brigade manning the first line. "The Johnnies showed their heels as fast as God would let them," wrote an Illinois soldier who participated in the assault. Soon afterward, the Federals drove back the second line held by Brig. Gen. Stephen Elliott's Brigade. As Brig. Gen. James D. Morgan's division of the Union Fourteenth Corps advanced on the left in an effort to outflank Hardee's third line, two small divisions of

Wheeler's cavalry arrived just in time to plug the gap. With Hardee's line now stretching from the Cape Fear River on his right to the swamps bordering the Black River on his left, Sherman decided to postpone making a general assault until the next morning. Unknown to the Federals, however, Hardee began evacuating his position at nightfall. When Union skirmishers advanced at dawn on March 17, they discovered that the Confederates had retreated.[42]

Hardee's delaying action at Averasboro had succeeded in checking Sherman's advance for one day, buying Johnston invaluable time to concentrate his forces. "Old Reliable" had also given his green troops their first taste of field combat and boosted their sagging morale. For his part, Sherman had driven Hardee toward Smithfield and Raleigh, opening the road to Goldsboro.[43]

On the eve of the Battle of Averasboro, Johnston had traveled to Smithfield, where his army was converging. Several days beforehand, the general had received heartening news from his friend and political ally, Texas senator Louis T. Wigfall, in Richmond. "You are mistaken as to the motive which induced your being ordered to the command," Wigfall told Johnston. "It was out of confidence & kindness & a real desire to obtain the benefit of your ability in this crisis." Wigfall then named the man responsible for Johnston's reinstatement: "It was Lee & not Davis. . . . For God's sake communicate with Lee fully & freely & with kindness & confidence & give him the full benefit of your judgment in this hour of peril."[44]

"What you write me of Lee gratifies me beyond measure," Johnston replied. "In youth & early manhood I loved and admired him more than any man in the world," Johnston confessed, recalling his friendship with Lee in their days as cadets at West Point. "Since then we have had little intercourse & have become formal in our personal intercourse. . . . I have long thought that he had forgotten our early friendship. To be mistaken in so thinking would give me inexpressible pleasure. Be assured however, that knight of old never fought under his King more loyally than I'll serve under General Lee." Because of Wigfall's timely missive, Johnston and the Confederate War Department began working in harmony for the first time in almost four years. Johnston nevertheless feared that his appointment had come too late and that there was little he could do to stop Sherman.[45]

Johnston chose Smithfield as his point of concentration because it stood midway between Raleigh and Goldsboro, Sherman's two most likely objectives. Arriving at Smithfield were Hoke's Division under Bragg and the remnant of the Army of Tennessee, which "Old Joe" placed under Lt. Gen. Alexander P. Stewart. Johnston formed the Army of the South from the four distinct forces under his immediate command—Hardee's Corps, Hoke's Division, the Army of Tennessee contingent, and Hampton's cavalry. In mid-March, Johnston had 20,000 troops in the field.[46]

After the Battle of Averasboro, Hardee marched toward Smithfield to join Johnston's army. "Old Reliable" told his chief that he believed Sherman's destination was Goldsboro. On the evening of March 17, Johnston notified Hardee that the time had come to act. "Something must be done to-morrow morning," Johnston wrote, "and yet I have no satisfactory information as to the enemy's movements. Can you give me any certain information of the force you engaged yesterday?" Hardee's reply is lost, but it probably indicated that Hampton was better informed as to the enemy's position and strength. Johnston ordered Bragg and Stewart to prepare to march at dawn. He then sent a message to Hampton: "Please send by the bearer all the information you have of the movement and position of the enemy, the number of their columns, their location and distance apart, and distance from Goldsborough, and give me your opinion whether it is practicable to reach them from Smithfield on the south side of the [Neuse] river before they reach Goldsborough."[47]

Hampton replied that the two Federal wings were indeed advancing on Goldsboro and were widely separated. He stated that the Union column marching up the road from Averasboro was more than a day's march from his headquarters at the Willis Cole plantation. The cavalry commander suggested that the plantation would make an excellent site for a surprise attack and assured Johnston that he could delay the Federal advance long enough to enable the Confederate army to arrive from Smithfield.[48]

Johnston received Hampton's reply at dawn on March 18. A glance at the state map indicated to "Old Joe" that the two Federal wings were a dozen miles apart and separated by a day's march. He therefore decided to attack the nearest enemy column—Slocum's wing—as it marched up the Goldsboro Road. "We will go to the place at which your dispatch was written," Johnston wrote Hampton. "The scheme mentioned in my note, which you pronounce practicable, will be attempted." Johnston instructed Stewart and Bragg to march for Bentonville and then sent similar orders to Hardee at Elevation on the Smithfield Road.[49]

For only the third time in the war, the ever-cautious Johnston decided to launch an attack. He did so for three reasons. First, he deemed it essential to strike Sherman in detail before the Federal commander could combine with Schofield. Second, he believed that a stunning blow to Sherman would give the South greater leverage at the bargaining table. Third, having vowed that "knight of old never fought under his King more loyally than I'll serve under General Lee," Johnston was determined to do all he could to aid his old friend and comrade.[50]

Unknown to the Confederates, however, the state maps were wildly inaccurate, leading Johnston to underestimate Hardee's distance from Bentonville while overestimating the distance separating the Federal columns. Although Bragg and Stewart's column reached Bentonville at nightfall, Hardee's Corps was still six miles north of the village when it halted at 9:00 P.M.[51]

The Federals had advanced to within five miles of the Cole plantation on the afternoon of March 18. Sherman remained cautious as the Union army approached Bentonville, the two wings of his army just a few miles apart. "I think it probable that Joe Johnston will try to prevent our getting Goldsboro," Sherman wrote Howard about mid-afternoon. A few hours later, he received two messages that calmed his fears. First, Kilpatrick reported that Hardee was retreating toward Smithfield and Johnston was concentrating his army a few miles south of Raleigh (apparently "Little Kil" had forgotten the Confederates' audacity at Monroe's Crossroads). Second, a Fourteenth Corps regiment reported that the Rebels had burned the bridge spanning Mill Creek on the Smithfield-Clinton Road. According to Sherman's faulty state map, the Confederates had burned a bridge across their only approach route to Bentonville, indicating a retreat toward Raleigh. Sherman's map omitted the Smithfield-Bentonville Road—or the Devil's Race Path—the road that Bragg and Stewart were using. Sherman now believed that Johnston had conceded Goldsboro. Although several Union foraging parties returned to camp that night reporting stiff resistance from Confederate cavalry, their reports were ignored by their superiors. On the evening of March 18, the Federals' point of vulnerability was not the distance separating their columns but their growing overconfidence.[52]

While Sherman camped several miles to the southwest, Johnston conferred with Hampton at his headquarters in Bentonville. Since Johnston had arrived too late to reconnoiter the proposed battlefield, Hampton outlined a plan of attack based on his own study of the ground. Hampton's plan exploited the heavily wooded terrain surrounding the Willis Cole house, where he recommended launching the attack. The cavalryman suggested that Johnston place Hoke's Division astride the Goldsboro Road to block the Federals' advance and deploy Hardee's Corps and Stewart's Army of Tennessee contingent in the thick woods north of the road. At a prearranged time, Hardee and Stewart would burst out of the woods and rout the Union column before it could deploy. Johnston approved Hampton's plan, though he regretted that Hardee's Corps was farther from the battlefield than the Federal advance. Realizing that this might be his last opportunity to strike Sherman with any hope of success, however, Johnston directed the deployment to begin at sunrise.[53]

Sunday, March 19, dawned a beautiful spring day. The awakening Federal soldiers enjoyed the mild morning air and the sight of budding apple and peach trees. Their thoughts were far removed from battle and focused instead on reaching Goldsboro, where new shoes, clean clothes, and mail from home awaited them. "We feel in excellent spirits," Lt. John Marshall Branum of the 98th Ohio jotted in his diary. "Everything promises for a smooth entry into Goldsboro." This entry would prove to be Branum's last; within a few hours, he would be lying dead on the field of battle.[54]

Believing that the danger of a Confederate attack had passed, Sherman prepared to rejoin Howard's wing at dawn on March 19 to communicate with General Schofield. Before his departure, Sherman briefly conferred with General Slocum and other subordinates at the crossroads leading to Howard's column. During the conversation, Bvt. Maj. Gen. Jefferson C. Davis said that he thought his Fourteenth Corps would encounter more than the usual cavalry opposition. "No, Jeff," Sherman told him. "There is nothing there but Dibbrell's cavalry. Brush them out of the way. . . . I'll meet you tomorrow morning at Cox's Bridge." With that, Sherman led his staff and escort down the road toward Howard's wing, unaware that Slocum's wing would not reach Cox's Bridge for another four days.[55]

At first the Federal advance, consisting of Brig. Gen. William P. Carlin's division of the Fourteenth Corps, easily drove back the Confederate cavalry in its front. The Southerners' resistance stiffened at the Cole plantation, where Carlin collided with a force far larger than Col. George G. Dibrell's small cavalry division. Carlin deployed all three of his brigades and still met with fierce opposition. Ignoring Carlin's plight, Slocum informed Sherman that he was merely skirmishing with Confederate cavalry and needed no assistance from Howard. An impatient Slocum then ordered Carlin to launch an attack to develop the Rebel position. About noon Carlin assaulted the Confederate line at several points, only to meet with a bloody repulse.

Undaunted, Slocum brought up Morgan's Fourteenth Corps division on Carlin's right and was preparing to deploy the Twentieth Corps on the same line in a more ambitious attempt to outflank Johnston's position. But a Union prisoner of war who had made his escape during Carlin's attack brought Slocum some startling intelligence: Johnston's army was on the field, and Joe Johnston himself had told his troops that they would crush one wing of Sherman's army at Bentonville and then fall upon the other wing and destroy it as well. If Slocum required further convincing of his predicament, he received it from a staff officer who reported: "Well, General, I have found something more than Dibrell's cavalry—I find [Confederate] infantry intrenched along our whole front, and enough of them to give us all the amusement we shall want for the rest of the day."[56]

Slocum received the staff officer's report at 1:30 P.M. and immediately shifted to the defensive. The left wing commander kept his two Fourteenth Corps divisions at the front to absorb the shock of the expected Confederate attack while deploying his two Twentieth Corps divisions on more defensible ground at the Reddick Morris farm a mile to the rear. Slocum also sent Sherman a far more accurate assessment of his situation. As the afternoon wore on, Slocum's messages to his chief became increasingly urgent and were invariably accompanied by appeals for reinforcements from Howard's wing.[57]

For Johnston, the morning of March 19 was fraught with aggravating delays. Because the Confederates had only one approach route to the battlefield, their deployment "consumed a weary time." When Carlin launched his probing attack at noon, only Hoke's Division and the Army of Tennessee contingent were in position, while Hardee's Corps was just marching onto the field. Carlin's noontime attack further delayed Johnston's own assault and induced General Bragg, the commander of Hoke's Division, to request reinforcements. Johnston sent McLaws's Division of Hardee's Corps, which proved to be "Old Joe's" worst blunder of the day. By the time McLaws reached Bragg's position, Hoke had already repulsed the Federal attack. Bragg held the division in reserve for most of the afternoon, depriving Johnston of one-quarter of his infantry. When McLaws's Division finally entered the fight at dusk, it was deployed piecemeal and accomplished nothing.[58]

Despite the frustrating delays, Johnston finally launched his assault at 2:45 P.M. Hardee led Johnston's right wing, consisting of Taliaferro's Division of Hardee's Corps along with the Army of Tennessee contingent. An onlooker thought that the Confederate advance "looked like a picture and was truly beautiful." He also found it "painful to see how close their battle flags were together, regiments being scarcely larger than companies." Despite its depleted ranks, Hardee's wing overran Carlin's position north of the Goldsboro Road. "[We] stood as long as man can stand," wrote a Michigan soldier in Carlin's division, "& when that was no longer a possibility [we] run like the duce." During the rout, Hardee's men captured two cannon of the 19th Indiana Battery and drove off Carlin's troops south of the road. Thus far the Confederate grand assault was an unqualified success.[59]

The Confederates' success might have been greater still had Bragg's wing, consisting of Hoke's and McLaws's Divisions, attacked when ordered. Instead, Bragg waited until 4:00 P.M., more than an hour after the time designated by Johnston. Perhaps Bragg delayed his assault pending the outcome of Hardee's charge, but such a course is indefensible since it would have been in disobedience of Johnston's orders. In any event, Bragg gave the Federals of Morgan's division a precious extra hour to strengthen their log fortifications.

Morgan's stand south of the Goldsboro Road proved to be the turning point of the March 19 battle at Bentonville. Attacked in quick succession by Hoke's Division along their front and left flank and by several brigades of the Army of Tennessee from their rear, Morgan's Federals stubbornly clung to their swampy salient. In the course of the struggle, the bluecoats fought on both sides of their log works. Aided by the timely arrival of Bvt. Brig. Gen. William Cogswell's Twentieth Corps brigade, Morgan's troops repulsed the Confederates and turned the tide in favor of the Federals.

The Confederates' final assaults of the day were launched against the Twentieth Corps's position on the Morris farm. Spearheaded by troops from Taliaferro's Division and Cheatham's Corps of the Army of Tennessee, the attacks constituted the Confederate army's high-water mark at Bentonville. Advancing several times to within thirty yards of the Union line, the Southerners braved a blistering fire before Johnston finally called off the assaults and ordered his army to return to its jumping-off point. The Union line at Bentonville had held.[60]

Meanwhile, Sherman received Slocum's appeals for reinforcements and ordered Howard's column to march to the left wing's support. Early on the morning of March 20, the Union right wing marched west on the Goldsboro Road toward the Confederate rear. Johnston utilized his cavalry to delay the Federals' advance and swung back Hoke's and McLaws's Divisions on a new left flank that angled northeast toward Bentonville. The right wing's vanguard reached the vicinity of Bentonville at noon. Johnston now faced a Union army three times the size of his own. The Confederates' new position was a tenuous, four-mile-long bastion that defended their sole line of retreat across Mill Creek at Bentonville.

Sherman was surprised that Johnston—contrary to his usual cautious behavior—held his ground. "I cannot see why he remains," Sherman wrote Slocum, "and still think he will avail himself of night to get back to Smithfield. I would rather avoid a general battle if possible, but if he insists on it, we must accommodate him." Why *did* Johnston remain at Bentonville? Having failed to crush one wing of Sherman's army, did he expect to fare better against both wings? Johnston offered two reasons for remaining.

No Such Army

Two views of the Battle of Bentonville. The top view depicts the Confederate high tide at Bentonville—the March 19 assault against the Federal position on the Reddick Morris farm. Union batteries (foreground) played a crucial role in repulsing the Confederate attacks. The bottom view depicts the Fifteenth Corps of Howard's wing skirmishing on the afternoon of March 20. Both views were sketched by Harper's *artist William Waud.*
(Harper's Weekly, *1865*)

First, he intended to evacuate his wounded before retreating, and second, he hoped that Sherman might attempt a costly frontal assault against his well-entrenched line. Perhaps Johnston had a third reason as well—his army's morale. By standing toe to toe with Sherman's larger army while evacuating his wounded, Johnston would achieve a moral victory, whereas if he abandoned the field following the first day's battle, he would concede defeat. Johnston doubtless believed that his army's morale was worth the risk of remaining at Bentonville.[61]

Johnston's decision to hold his ground nearly proved to be his undoing, however. On the morning of March 21, the First Division of the Seventeenth Corps deployed on the extreme right of the Union line. The division was commanded by Sherman's most aggressive general, Maj. Gen. Joseph A. Mower. Although under orders to avoid a general engagement, "Fighting Joe" Mower intended to attack the Confederates, perhaps hoping to draw Sherman into the pitched battle he did not want. Facing

Mower turning the Confederate left at Bentonville (Frank Leslie's
Illustrated Newspaper, *1865*)

Mower's division was Hampton's cavalry, spread out in a vain attempt to
cover the Confederates' vulnerable left flank.

Mower began his attack about noon in a downpour. His two attacking brigades struggled through the briar-infested swamp separating them
from Hampton's position and easily drove back the outnumbered Confederates. Meanwhile, Hampton reported the breakthrough to Johnston,
who assigned Hardee the task of repulsing the attack. At stake was Johnston's only avenue of retreat across Mill Creek. Fortunately for the Confederates, Mower halted his main line even as his skirmishers overran Johnston's headquarters at Bentonville, enabling Hardee to counterattack with
a hastily assembled force. One of the regiments was the 8th Texas Cavalry
—or Terry Rangers—whose newest recruit was General Hardee's only son,
sixteen-year-old Willie Hardee. The youth was mortally wounded while
charging in the Rangers' front rank. The Confederates succeeded in repulsing Mower's charge, but "Fighting Joe" was preparing to attack again
when Sherman sent him orders to halt. Johnston's army had survived to
fight another day.

During the night of March 21–22, the Confederates retreated across Mill
Creek bridge and marched toward Smithfield. Except for some skirmishing the next day, the Battle of Bentonville was over. The culminating event

No Such Army

of Sherman's march from Savannah, the Battle of Bentonville nevertheless proved indecisive. Although the Federals had opened the road to Goldsboro, Sherman had failed to crush Johnston's army, and though Johnston had won a moral victory, he had failed to defeat Slocum's wing. The stage was now set for the next phase of Sherman's Carolinas campaign.[62]

CHAPTER 2

AS GOOD AS A PICNIC
AND THREE CIRCUSES

On the afternoon of March 21, 1865, Brig. Gen. Charles J. Paine's Federal division reached the charred ruins of Cox's Bridge, which the Confederates had burned the previous day. The bridge had spanned the Neuse River about ten miles south of Goldsboro. Paine's division consisted of nine regiments of U.S. Colored Troops and was attached to Maj. Gen. Alfred H. Terry's Provisional Corps.[1]

The Provisional Corps had marched northward from Wilmington to join forces with Sherman's grand army. Terry's men first came within hearing of Sherman on March 20. "His big guns sounding some eighteen miles distant told us we were nearing the great champion," wrote Chaplain Henry M. Turner of the 1st U.S. Colored Troops, who heard noise from the Battle of Bentonville. "Our army was much fatigued, and everyone felt quite exhausted, until the sound of his artillery gave us new life. We all longed to be there. The consequence was that we now marched more swiftly, and took longer strides."[2]

On the morning of March 21, Turner and his anxious comrades first encountered the track of Sherman's army—or, more precisely, that of his foragers. "And here we just began to learn what destruction was," Turner noted. Houses were burnt and fences demolished, and the woods for miles around were ablaze. The few inhabitants who remained were left with little more than the clothes on their backs; some stood on their porches, vacant-eyed and haggard, watching Terry's troops march past their empty pastures and farmyards. "We thought our men had been doing outrageously," Turner commented, "but now we were convinced that we were all good fellows."[3]

On the evening of March 21, the 58th Indiana Pontoniers laid a pontoon bridge across the Neuse at the site of Cox's Bridge. Once again Turner heard the din of battle: "All the afternoon and part of the night, amid a heavy falling rain, did the terrific roar of cannon and musketry [at Bentonville] keep up an unbroken clamor. . . . Never did I hear such musketry before, except at Petersburg, on the night of the 18th of June, 1864, when Grant and Lee, with more than fifty thousand men on each side, were kicking up a dust over that doomed city."[4]

Paine's troops had their first glimpse of Sherman's veterans on March 22, during the latter's crossing of the pontoon bridge en route to Goldsboro. "We all desired to see Sherman's men," Turner wrote, "and they were anxious to see colored soldiers, particularly 'the colored heroes of Petersburg,' as they called us. Therefore you may be sure they were not passing very long before our boys thronged each side of the road."[5]

At first Paine's soldiers "made the mistake of thinking when they first saw us that we were also Negroes," one of Sherman's men recalled. "This was not surprising as we were certainly as black as they were." As the ragged, filthy column filed past, one of Paine's troops exclaimed, "Sherman's men are a hard lookin' set, *sure*." Hoosier chaplain John J. Hight noted that some of the white soldiers were "a little disposed to twit the negroes," but the black troops proved adept at trading insults. General Paine heard one of Sherman's grizzled veterans shout, "O you nigger!"—to which a black soldier replied, "You ain't the man to talk till you wash yo face." A Wisconsin private admitted that "the black soldiers had the best of the joke."[6]

Sherman's troops were just as eager to glimpse Paine's men, for many had never seen black soldiers. Capt. William F. Allee of the 22nd Indiana admitted that Paine's troops "made a much finer display than we did." Sgt. Rice Bull of the 123rd New York concurred: "While in the matter of complexion we might resemble our colored comrades, in other ways we presented a strange contrast. Their uniforms were new and well fitted, bright and clean, their shoes were new, black, and shining; their guns were the Springfield latest model and sparkled with brightness. The men looked fat and sleek, showing the good care and food they had received. Their officers were splendidly dressed, with buttons shining and wearing new unfaded sashes. What a contrast they did present to Sherman's veterans."[7]

The contrast extended even to Sherman's generals, whom Chaplain Turner thought "looked worse than our second lieutenants." Turner's observation was certainly apt in the case of Twentieth Corps commander Alpheus Williams, as "Old Pap" confessed in a letter to his daughters:

I doubt if your worthy "Pop" would have made a very presentable appearance in a drawing room. His pants, which were originally of light-colored corduroys, had assumed a very dirty and burnt-black color. The coat, torn in numerous places and badly patched, would have been an excellent "habit" in the *Beggar's Opera*. The vest had lost all but two buttons, and the shirt of brown woolen had undergone a three weeks' wear and tear. The hat, which was new in Savannah, having braved forty severe rain storms, had lopped down all round and the yellow cord turned to a dingy yellow gray. His beard, of a three-months' growth, never once in that time reflected from a looking glass, really seemed frightfully grizzly as first seen from a farmhouse mirror.[8]

The strange and comical procession of Sherman's tatterdemalion army into Goldsboro began on March 23 and continued the next day. "I doubt if at any time the troops of the rebel army were more ragged than we," recalled U. H. Farr of the 70th Indiana. "Probably one man in a dozen had a full suit of clothes, but even this suit was patched and full of holes." The commander of the 70th Indiana, Lt. Col. Samuel Merrill, told his wife: "It would make you laugh & cry both to see the poor fellows with their bare heads, bare feet & bare—well, it won't do to describe them too minutely." According to Henry Weltay, adjutant of the 68th Ohio, thirty-five men in his regiment were barefoot, forty-three bareheaded, and 270 wearing at least one article of civilian clothing. A reporter for the *New York Tribune* saw "men strutting in mimic dignity in old swallowtailed coats, with plug hats, the tops knocked in; there a group in seedy coats and pants of Rebel grey, with arms and legs protruding beyond all semblance of fit or fashion; short jackets, long tailed surtcoats, and coats of every cast with broadtails, narrow tails, no tails at all—all of them [in] most antiquated styles. Some wore women's bonnets, or young ladies' hats, with streamers of faded ribbons floating fantastically in the wind."[9]

Perhaps the most picturesque sight in Sherman's columns was that of the foragers, also known as "bummers," "smokehouse rangers," or "dough-boys." Thomas Christie, a forager for the 1st Minnesota Battery, described the appearance of his detail:

The picture should represent a man, dressed in a nondescript suit part blue part homespun grey or Butternut, with a white hat . . . and perhaps barefooted, with his Belt & cartridge box on (for we always go well armed), his trusty carbine by his side, and a revolver stuck in his Belt. When you have the man drawn out according to these directions, you must mount him in a splendid Buggy in which the aristocrats of the plantation used to take the air. . . . The Buggy is to be hauled by the

"Bummer's" old long eared, tail shorn mule. . . . Here you have the forager and his conveyance—now for the plunder. First and foremost you will observe that the carriage is piled full of hams . . . , and on top of these you will see three or four sacks of meal or flour, while around and behind hang clusters of turkeys. . . . If you will enlarge your picture so as to include three or four of these equipages with the same number of mounted men in the advance, and a dozen darkeys bringing up the rear mounted on captured horses and mules, you will have a very good idea of how my train looks.[10]

During the crossing of the pontoons, the bummers in Howard's wing were ordered to surrender their horses and mules. Several sources indicate that many men refused to comply. Their independent spirit is well conveyed in a story of an encounter between one such bummer and General Sherman. According to Col. Charles Sheldon of the 18th Missouri, Sherman was dissatisfied with the slow progress of his column at the bridge and "frequently expressed his feelings in language more forcible than polite." At one point, a soldier mounted on a rawboned mule rode up to "Uncle Billy," saluted, and addressed him as follows: "General Sherman, the chief of the Bummers sends his compliments, and has the honor to inform you that he has a d——d sight better bridge than yours, about half a mile above, which is entirely at your service." With that, the bummer again saluted and then melted into the crowd of marching soldiers. Colonel Sheldon noted that a bridge was indeed found, "composed of barges used in the transportation of rosin, etc., which was planked over with boards from houses that had been torn down."[11]

A second witness, Pvt. William Evans of the 27th Ohio, stated that bummers had built the bridge to continue their foraging raids without interference from higher authority. "Then they sent the provost marshal a note," Evans wrote, "giving their compliments, & stating that they would not be under any obligations to him for his bridge, they having one of their own." A detail was sent to arrest the culprits, who easily eluded capture and continued to forage in defiance of orders.[12]

The procession of Sherman's army into Goldsboro was hardly less comical for the absence of these bummers. Having occupied the town two days beforehand, soldiers of Schofield's Twenty-third Corps "lined the road as spectators, cheered uproariously and laughed till the tears ran down their faces whenever the panorama of raggedness became unusually ludicrous," recalled one of Sherman's veterans. "It was as good as a picnic and three circuses," quipped a Minnesotan in Schofield's command. Some Twenty-third Corps soldiers exclaimed, "Why, it's Sherman's greasers!" Sherman's troops responded by calling Schofield's men "white gloves and paper collars," among other things. Despite the name-calling, "it seemed as if old friends and acquaintances were meeting," wrote Kentuckian Henry Clay Weaver, a veteran of the Twenty-third Corps who recalled his service with Sherman during the Atlanta campaign.[13]

General Sherman placed his own stamp on this bizarre procession by ordering a review of his passing troops. "This was a little too much," recalled one soldier, "and mutterings were heard on every hand." Particularly galling was the contrast between the men in Schofield's command, in their "exceptionally clean and comfortable attire," and Sherman's tattered ranks. According to Brig. Gen. Manning F. Force, Sherman stood by the roadside without his sword, looking "like any casual spectator." Consequently, half the soldiers failed to recognize the commanding general and did not salute him, much to the chagrin of their officers. During the review, Seventeenth Corps commander Maj. Gen. Frank P. Blair turned to Sherman and said, "See those poor fellows with bare legs." "Uncle Billy" replied, "Splendid legs! Splendid legs! I would give both of mine for any one of them!" That night Sherman wrote his wife, Ellen: "I would like to march this army through New York just as it appears today with its wagons, pack mules, cattle, niggers and bummers." Yet according to one veteran, "the review was the joke of the army for a season."[14]

In truth, the review demonstrated how desperately Sherman's men needed rest and supplies. A soldier in the Seventeenth Corps noted that he and his comrades were "nearly in a nude state." The inspector general of the Seventeenth Corps supported the Ohioan's statement, reporting that 5,023 men lacked uniform pants, 3,888 needed boots or shoes, 2,726 were without regulation hats or caps, and 2,298 were missing uniform coats. As pressing as the need for clothing and footgear was, though, Sherman's first priority was to feed his men. On March 22, "Uncle Billy" had instructed his chief commissary officer, Bvt. Brig. Gen. Amos Beckwith, to hurry forward enough rations to feed the army, but the abundance of supplies that Sherman had expected to find at Goldsboro had not yet arrived. A thoroughly disappointed Sherman told Grant that he suspected negligence. On March 23, Sherman informed his chief quartermaster, Bvt. Brig. Gen. L. C. Easton: "I have constantly held out to the officers and men to bear patiently the want of clothing and other necessaries, for at Goldsborough awaited us everything. If you can expedite the movement of stores from the sea to the army, do so, and don't stand on expenses." Sherman urged Easton to detail work crews around the clock to expedite the flow of supplies and sent similar orders to Col. W. W. Wright, who supervised the rebuilding of the railroads from Morehead City and Wilmington.[15]

As Good as a Picnic

Despite its ragged and filthy appearance, the army that marched into Goldsboro was a healthy one. The army's medical director, John Moore, reported that no more than 2 percent of the men were sick at any time during the campaign. Moore attributed the good health of his charges to "open air, freedom from drunkenness and other vices inseparable from garrison life, but most of all the novelty and excitement of an active campaign." Most of the wounded resulted from the battles near Averasboro and Bentonville. Surgeon Moore characterized their gunshot wounds as "of an unusually grave character" because the firing was generally short-range, but he noted that the sturdiness of the wounded often ensured a rapid recovery.[16]

Perhaps the best example of the toughness of Sherman's men is the case of Sgt. Benjamin Hunter, the color-bearer for the 79th Ohio. Hunter was wounded in the Battle of Averasboro on March 16. Several of the sergeant's comrades carried him back to a house serving as a Union army hospital. One of Hunter's comrades, Pvt. J. B. Newburry, asked a surgeon to examine the sergeant's wound. After noting that Hunter was shot through both lungs, the doctor left to tend another patient. When Newburry asked if anything could be done for his comrade, the surgeon ordered a steward to give the wounded sergeant a large dose of morphine. "I knew what that was for," Newburry recalled, "to stupefy him so he could die easy." Newburry and his comrades bade farewell to Hunter and returned to their regiment, certain they had seen him alive for the last time.

Hunter was loaded into an empty supply wagon and jolted for several days over miles of corduroy road before being transferred to an ambulance. The sergeant found the ambulance ride no less bumpy, however, and now had to share his cramped quarters with two other severely wounded men. Meanwhile, he kicked off his pants because they were stiff with clotted blood and infested with lice, or "graybacks." On the night of March 22, Hunter was lifted out of the ambulance and placed on cold, damp ground near the site of Cox's Bridge. The next morning, his wounds were dressed, one week after his wounding. The sergeant also ate his first solid food in a week.

Hunter's ordeal was far from over, however. On March 24, he was loaded back into an ambulance and taken to Goldsboro, where he and other wounded comrades were placed inside a tent on damp ground, "so close that we could not spit without spitting on each other." Conditions improved for the sergeant and his tentmates when several orderlies fashioned pallets for them from fence rails, but Hunter's recovery was slow and painful. For more than a month the sergeant was too weak to combat the persistent graybacks, nor could he muster enough strength to venture out of

View of Goldsboro. The four-story building (right of center) is the Goldsboro Female College,
*used as a Union army hospital. (*Frank Leslie's Illustrated Newspaper, *1865)*

bed until May 25 (having been transferred to a New York City hospital
in the meantime). On June 20, Hunter finally returned home to Martins-
ville, Ohio, in time to welcome his old comrade, J. B. Newburry, upon *his*
return.[17]

According to Surgeon Moore's estimate, Hunter was but one of 2,888
sick and wounded men arriving with Sherman's army at Goldsboro. As
many convalescents as possible were placed in tents in the countryside.
"Every year's experience tends to prove the advantage of treating wounded
men in tents," the medical director noted, "where they can enjoy the venti-
lation almost of the open air." Since the practice of antisepsis was then unknown, Moore doubtless assumed that his patients enjoyed a high recovery
rate because of their exposure to fresh air. He was partly right, though he
was unaware that overcrowded hospital buildings were far more likely to
serve as incubators for infectious diseases than tents in the open. Nevertheless, Moore was forced to place many patients in buildings—including
the Goldsboro Female College—because the Medical Department lacked
tents to accommodate all of the wounded.[18]

While the wounded were moved into the college building, Sherman
established his headquarters at the Richard Washington house a few blocks
away. The general reportedly gave the septuagenarian Washington and his
large household of children and grandchildren only a few hours' notice
to vacate the premises. Once settled in, Sherman wrote a steady stream of
letters, dispatches, and orders. "I write as usual very fast," he told his wife,
"& can keep half a dozen clerks busy in copying."[19]

On March 23, General Sherman released Special Field Orders No. 35,
congratulating his officers and men for beating on their "chosen ground
the concentrated armies of our enemy," and calling the result of the campaign "a glorious success." Sherman noted: "After a march of the most extraordinary character, near 500 miles, over swamps and rivers, deemed
impassable to others, at the most inclement season of the year, and draw-

As Good as a Picnic

ing our chief supplies from a poor and wasted country, we reach our destination in good health and condition." The Union commander promised: "You shall now have rest and all the supplies that can be brought from the rich granaries and store-houses of our magnificent country before again embarking on new and untried dangers." Sherman relied on Generals Easton and Beckwith and Colonel Wright to fulfill his promise.[20]

"Thus was concluded one of the longest and most important marches ever made by an organized army in a civilized country," Sherman later declared. In a letter to his wife, the general boasted: "It [was] far more difficult and important than the Savannah march. . . . I almost fear the consequences of the reputation this will give me among military men." Based on his stated objectives, the march from Savannah to Goldsboro was an unqualified success. Having led his grand army 450 miles through a hostile country in mid-winter, Sherman now stood within ten days' march of Grant's forces at Richmond and Petersburg. His army had combined with Schofield's two corps, and Goldsboro provided the Union commander with a crucial rail junction linking him to coastal supply bases at Morehead City and Wilmington.[21]

Moreover, Sherman's march through the Carolinas caused the desertion of thousands of Confederate soldiers—men desperate to return home after receiving graphic accounts of the Yankees' wholesale devastation of the countryside. Sherman had also cut Lee and Johnston's supply lines to the Deep South, rendering them dependent on desolate and sparsely settled regions in Virginia and North Carolina for subsistence. Perhaps most important, Sherman's march demonstrated the Confederacy's inability to defend its heartland, thereby dealing a stunning blow to Southern morale on the home front.

Nevertheless, Sherman exercised poor judgment at the conclusion of his campaign in not crushing Johnston's army at Bentonville. Although subsequent events in Virginia would render his decision wise and prudent, Sherman himself later admitted that he had erred in not overwhelming Johnston. But would the destruction of Johnston's army at that late date have shortened the war? Viewed from the modern historian's distant perspective, such an outcome appears unlikely. Yet on the morning of March 22, 1865, neither Sherman nor Johnston assumed that the fighting in their theater had ended. Both commanders expected to fight at least one more battle, possibly involving Grant's and Lee's armies as well. Perhaps General Lee stated the case best in a March 14 dispatch to President Jefferson Davis: "The greatest calamity that can befall us is the destruction of our armies. If they can be maintained, we may recover from our reverses, but if lost we have no resource." Because of its escape from Bentonville,

Johnston's army remained a factor that Grant and Sherman had to consider in plotting their joint strategy for ending the war.[22]

The missed opportunity at Bentonville was far from Sherman's mind as he worked to refit his army. While Colonel Wright's crews rebuilt the railroads from Morehead City and Wilmington, the first wagons bearing shoes, clothing, and rations for Sherman's army rolled out of Kinston. (During the Battle of Bentonville, Sherman had instructed Slocum and Howard to send all of their empty wagons to Kinston.) The ranking quartermaster at Kinston, Col. Michael C. Garber, assured the commanding general that enough supplies were arriving by boat that he could refit the army without the railroads. Despite Garber's optimism, Sherman perceived the present system as no more than a temporary expedient.[23]

While supplies rolled in, Sherman's 90,000-man army settled into camp. Cox's Twenty-third Corps bivouacked south and west of Goldsboro, Slocum's Army of Georgia to the north and west, and Howard's Army of the Tennessee to the north and east. Kilpatrick's three cavalry brigades camped at Mount Olive, fifteen miles south of Goldsboro, and Terry's Provisional Corps at Faison's Depot, seven miles south of Mount Olive. The soldiers soon received orders to fortify their camps. Although some men grumbled that a large army had no need for breastworks, most veterans understood the value of strong entrenchments. The soldiers still regarded Johnston's army as a considerable threat, borne out by the Confederates' March 24 attack on Paine's division.[24]

By March 23 (before their move to Faison's Depot), the soldiers of Paine's division had dug a semicircular line of entrenchments about 300 yards north of the 58th Indiana's pontoons. "That night," wrote Capt. Solon Carter, the division adjutant, "an alarm was raised that Johnston's army was . . . moving down on us." Soon afterward, Confederate cavalry drove several foraging details into Paine's defenses, indicating that an attack was imminent. "The troops were all put under arms and tents struck and packed," Carter continued, "ready to 'light out' if necessary. [But] Joe [Johnston] didn't come and about eleven o'clock we pitched our tents and went to sleep again."[25]

Early on the morning of March 24, all was quiet and the enemy seemed far away. "Our boys are growing impatient to take up the bridge and be off," Chaplain John J. Hight of the 58th Indiana jotted in his diary. Within a few hours, however, Paine's men heard the faint rattle of musketry, indicating that their pickets and foragers were skirmishing with Confederates. About noon cannon fire began booming in the distance. By mid-afternoon the

As Good as a Picnic

firing was loud and continuous. "The shrill assembly calls [the Federals] once more into line of battle," Chaplain Hight wrote. "In our camp, there was the usual rattle of ramrods and snapping of [percussion] caps. The tattered banners were unfurled and [the] men stood ready for action."[26]

"Our works teemed with 'smoked Yankees,' as the rebels call us," observed Chaplain Turner of the 1st U.S. Colored Troops. Several companies of black troops advanced to develop the Confederate force. After a brief exchange of musketry, the Federals withdrew to their entrenchments, having clashed with a portion of Butler's cavalry division under Wade Hampton.[27]

The Southerners began shelling the Union camp. Captain Carter was sleeping in his tent when the first Confederate shell exploded about thirty yards away. Suffering from a chill, Carter struggled to his feet and ordered all headquarters tents struck, but not before his own was torn by a shell fragment. A third shell struck under the wagon into which the headquarters servants were tossing the officers' baggage. After that, "it was with the greatest difficulty I could make them stay to pick up all our cooking utensils, baggage, etc.," Carter recalled.[28]

Paine's servants were not the only unfortunates to panic under fire. Chaplain Turner noted that "three or four bombs passed over and through my quarters. I raised up to ascertain whether they were really in earnest. At that moment, here came another. I then bargained with my feet and legs to carry my body away from that place, which they did in a hurry." As Turner dashed past a line of soldiers, the latter—momentarily ignoring the incoming shells—laughed and shouted at the fleeing chaplain. "But the chaplain," Turner coyly explained in the third person, "preferring a good run to a bad stand, charged out of range as bravely as his soldiers generally charge in, which enabled him to bury the killed with divine service, instead of being buried with it himself." When the Confederates finally withdrew, Chaplain Turner discovered that he had five killed and nine wounded souls to attend to.[29]

Although the skirmish at Cox's Bridge proved to be the only significant Confederate assault on Federal camps near Goldsboro, Union foragers often had to fight—or run—for their lives. The less fortunate were either killed or captured. On March 23, foragers from the 33rd Indiana were captured by Maj. Gen. Joseph Wheeler's Special Scouts company, commanded by Capt. A. M. Shannon. A forager named Matt Collins recalled that he and his comrades were relieved of their valuables and then condemned to be hanged. Fortunately for the captive Hoosiers, one of Shannon's men refused to carry out the captain's sentence. Though Shannon repeated the order several times, the private remained adamant. The enraged captain finally ordered his command to escort the prisoners to headquarters and let a higher-ranking officer decide the Yankees' fate.[30]

The prisoners were brought before Brig. Gen. William W. Allen, one of Wheeler's division commanders. Only at this point in his narrative did Private Collins confess that he was captured wearing a Confederate uniform. The private was fortunate that he was not hanged on the spot. General Allen merely stated that if the gray-clad Collins had been captured near a Confederate camp, he would have been tried as a spy. When the Federal prisoners were presented to Wheeler, "Fighting Joe" ordered them sent to Raleigh. From there, Private Collins and his comrades were transported to Richmond's Libby Prison. The move was fortuitous, for the Confederate capital fell within days of their imprisonment, rendering them free men once more.[31]

In contrast to the often precarious existence of the foragers, camp life around Goldsboro was routine. After digging entrenchments, the soldiers' next task was to lay out their camps and pitch their tents. Many built "she-bangs," as they called their hybrid shelters of wooden walls and canvas roofs. "Having nothing else to write about I will let you know what kind of residence I have to live in now," Maj. William C. Stevens of the 9th Michigan Cavalry wrote his sister. "I boarded up three sides of a square about four feet high and put up the poles with a crow bar, the same as for a tent. (You are enough of a soldier to know what I mean.) I stretched a tent fly over the crow bar for a roof, leaving the front of my house entirely open. I used a shelter tent to stop up the rear of my residence above where it was boarded. It is considerable longer than an ordinary wall tent and is much better for this season of the year. Our furniture consists of a bedstead, table and two chairs." "Our parlor furniture has not come on yet," the major dryly added, "and I have made up my mind not to get a piano *this* spring." [32]

Lt. Edward Allen of the 16th Wisconsin noted that his Seventeenth Corps division had no sooner reached its campsite than the men began gathering material for their shebangs. "Near by there was a house with the usual number of barns or shanties," Allen wrote, "so, knowing we were to stay here the Division charged on them and [within] about 15 minutes there was nothing left but the house, which might have gone too but for the guard." Allen observed that "it was labor in vain," for the division soon received orders to move elsewhere.[33]

In late March, Sherman's army experienced a religious revival. Outdoor services were often attended by huge congregations, unlike anything the preachers had seen at home. "It was a strange but impressive scene," recalled Capt. J. B. Brant, the acting chaplain for the 85th Indiana, "to look down upon a thousand or more stalwart veterans, worshipping in a camp lighted by burning pitch pine knots on a high platform covered with dirt; and [the men] seated on logs arranged in tiers in front of an extemporized platform for the speaker." At one Sabbath service, Pvt. Joseph Hoffhines of the 33rd Ohio saw seventy-five men take communion, and at another, he witnessed twenty-five baptisms, "mostly by Emersion." [34]

The soldiers engaged in less exalted activities as well. Some read books or newspapers or wrote letters to family and friends; others took part in horse races, pitched horseshoes, or played baseball or cards; still others attended cock fights between contestants with such colorful nicknames as "Billy Sherman," "Joe Johnston," and "Bobby Lee." Goldsboro's red-light district was a favorite gathering place for Sherman's men. "Houses containing certain classes of women were surrounded by large gangs which had to be continually dispersed," wrote a soldier who served in the town's provost guard. [35]

The return to a more settled existence also meant the resumption of unit drills, dress parades, and inspections—none of which Sherman's men liked. The chief inspector of the Seventeenth Corps, Lt. Col. Andrew Hickenlooper, noted that the first time the troops of his command were assembled for inspection at Goldsboro, he and his assistants subjected the soldiers' quarters to an even more rigorous examination. "The result was the collection of the largest and most heterogeneous mass of booty ever gathered together by pilfering soldiers," Hickenlooper recalled. "There were probably 25,000 different articles, embracing everything that mind can conceive, from a paper of pins to a woman's night-dress. Some, such as watches, rings and jewelry, were of considerable value, but the great mass of the find [was] stuff for which the possessor could have no earthly use either present or prospective." [36]

The wholesale plundering was largely the result of Sherman's Special Field Orders No. 120, issued just before the army had begun the March to the Sea. The order stipulated that the army must "forage liberally on the country." Each brigade had a foraging detail under a commissioned officer. Because the numerous foraging parties ranged far from the main column, discipline often proved unreliable. The order also permitted soldiers in the main column to gather food while in camp or at rest. In short, Sherman sacrificed strict discipline to enable his army to live off the land. Although his orders forbade the troops from entering houses and restricted destruction of property to the discretion of his army and corps commanders, the commanding general often winked at his soldiers' excesses, believing that his "hard war" policy was hastening final victory by eroding the enemy's morale.[37]

At least one general in Sherman's army condemned the foragers' excesses. "I regret that I have to except any one from praise and credit," Brig. Gen. James D. Morgan noted in his official report,

> but I have some men in my command . . . who have mistaken the name and meaning of the term foragers, and have become under the name highwaymen, with all their cruelty and ferocity and none of their courage; their victims are usually old men, women, and children, and negroes, whom they rob and maltreat without mercy, firing dwellings and outhouses even when filled with grain that the army need[s], and sometimes endangering the trains by the universal firing of fences. These men are a disgrace to the name of soldier and the country. I desire to place upon record my detestation and abhorrence of their acts.[38]

More scrupulous Federals also profited from the march through the Carolinas. Lieutenant Colonel Hickenlooper admitted that he too was "a beneficiary of the spoils of war," having captured a Confederate detail escorting several prized racehorses, including the celebrated thoroughbred Kemper. Hickenlooper claimed the horse and later sold it for $3,000—a considerable sum in 1865.[39]

For most officers, the return to camp life at Goldsboro was no holiday, for they had to lead daily drill and parade exercises and contend with mountains of paperwork. "Since our arrival here, I do not believe that a moment has been unemployed," complained Capt. John Safely of the 13th Iowa. "I never had as much business pressing my attention with so few facilities for its transaction." Even the generals were not exempt from this flurry of activity, as Twentieth Corps commander Alpheus Williams explained:

> Reflect how much my mind is constantly engrossed with the care of nearly 20,000 men. No sooner do I reach camp after a most arduous campaign than my labors begin in making preparation for the next. Everything from wagon grease to the armament of artillery has to be attended to. With all the agents and assistance I have, I am still responsible that it is all done and done right. It must all be supervised. If it fails, or is neglected, I am the responsible man. In consequence, my mind is never at rest. My anxieties never cease. I dream of the work at night and I ponder and inquire and sometimes fret all day. I doubt if these stops to rest are not more harassing to me than the actual campaign.[40]

As Good as a Picnic

Early on the morning of March 25, the shrill whistle of Col. W. W. Wright's construction train alerted the waking soldiers that repairs on the railroad from Morehead City were nearly complete. Lt. Edward Allen rode into Goldsboro—which he called "a miserable tumble down affair"—to watch the laborers drive the last few spikes into place. While there he heard the good news that two or three trains were expected to arrive that afternoon. The lieutenant galloped back to his tent to put the finishing touches on his journal, hoping to send it home on the first train. Other visitors included Lt. Charles Brown of the 21st Michigan, who described Goldsboro as "a little 7 × 9 sort of hole." Pvt. Alfred Rigby of the 24th Iowa was even more scathing than Allen or Brown. "We would suppose at least some refinement among the fair sex from the fine edifice [of the Goldsboro Female College] erected for their culture," Rigby declared. "But on an average they are a fair specimen of clay eating snuff suckers." Though the judgment of Rigby and other Federals regarding Goldsboro and its citizenry was harsh, it was amply reciprocated by those same inhabitants. "I think," wrote H. M. Dewey of Goldsboro, "that the unanimous voice of the people of Goldsboro & vicinity is that the number of *gentlemen* in Sherman's army is exceedingly small."[41]

If the residents of Goldsboro had few kind words for Sherman's troops, they had mostly praise for the conduct of Schofield's men—particularly the 9th New Jersey. Because it was the first Federal regiment to enter Goldsboro, the 9th received the honor of serving as the town's provost guard. The New Jersey soldiers earned the gratitude of the locals by maintaining law and order. The 9th's historian noted that whenever some of Sherman's troops came into town wanting "to paint things red," the New Jersey men swiftly rounded them up and tossed them into jail. As a result, when rumors spread that the 9th was to be relieved of provost duty, hundreds of citizens signed a petition urging General Schofield to reconsider. Much to the townspeople's satisfaction, the 9th New Jersey remained at its post until the army's departure.[42]

An enterprising soldier from the regiment, Cpl. Charles Hinton, assumed control of the local printing office when he learned that the proprietor had fled town. With the help of a comrade skilled in typesetting, the corporal soon had the shop in working order. Replacing the ardently secessionist *Goldsboro State Journal* with the *Loyal State Journal*, Hinton printed issues featuring staunchly pro-Union material. According to Hinton, the newspapers sold "like hot cakes," and at almost any price he cared to name. Lacking more conventional stock, Hinton printed the *Journal* on wallpaper stripped from deserted houses. Hinton and his partner also "did a thriving jobbing business," printing poems and songs submitted by literary-minded soldiers. Before their departure, the two bluecoat publishers sent for the print shop owner (whose profit motive apparently overcame his fear of Yankees) and split the proceeds with him.[43]

Corporal Hinton was only one of many entrepreneurs in town. Although peddling was forbidden, "on almost every street corner were boys of Sherman's army selling tobacco, watches, silver, etc., captured in the late march," observed Edmund Cleveland of the 9th New Jersey. Cleveland also noted that many of the town's citizens were selling "little notions from their front porches." One such merchant was the mayor of Goldsboro, James H. Privett, who had a tobacco stand in his front yard. An onlooker observed that every soldier-salesman peddled his goods "as though his livelihood depended on success," and in a sense it did. The army paymasters had not yet arrived at Goldsboro, and even General Sherman had to borrow money to send home to his family.[44]

With the first train from Morehead City came the soldiers' first mail. "Hurrah! Hurrah! Hurrah!" Lt. Edward Allen scribbled in his diary on March 25. "It has come at last—such piles of letters & packages. Two months fasting sharpens a persons appetite for mail. Such shouting & rejoycing as one opens a well directed Valentine or goodie from home." Although Sherman placed severe restrictions on the use of railroad rolling stock, he saw to it that his men received their mail, for he recognized its importance to morale. "We can endure short rations of bread, meat and coffee," wrote Sgt. Francis McAdams of the 113th Ohio, "but when the mail fails us we are despondent and unhappy." Though notoriously security-conscious, Sherman kept his capable superintendent of mails, Col. Absalom H. Markland, up to date concerning the army's movements so that his men would receive their mail without undue delay.[45]

With the railroad to Morehead City open, Sherman prepared to travel to City Point, Virginia, to confer with Grant. Before leaving, he summoned his army commanders—Schofield, Howard, and Slocum—and outlined his plan for the coming campaign. Sherman staff officer Maj. Henry Hitchcock noted: "It was like watching sheet lightning playing [on] the horizon thro' a bank of clouds to hear him. . . . He predicted that this spring 'will see the d——est fighting there ever was on the continent, or else no fighting at all.'" Sherman also placed Schofield in command in his absence.[46]

On the afternoon of March 25, "Uncle Billy" took the first train to Morehead City. He stopped at New Bern for the night and was met at the station by hundreds of soldiers demanding a speech. "I'm going up to see Grant for five minutes," Sherman told them, "and have it all chalked out for me,

As Good as a Picnic

and then I'll come back and pitch in again. I only want to see him five minutes, and won't be gone but two or three days." The remark about having
things "all chalked out" was a trifle disingenuous, for Sherman already had
conceived a plan for the next campaign. He hoped to obtain Grant's approval, and, if necessary, persuade the general-in-chief to postpone his own
campaign until the army in North Carolina was ready to march.[47]

Sherman also hoped to secure Maj. Gen. Philip H. Sheridan's assistance
in cornering Johnston's army. Recalling his futile chase of Gen. John Bell
Hood the previous autumn, Sherman feared that Johnston could likewise
outmarch him. The swiftness of Sheridan's cavalry would offset whatever
advantage Johnston's smaller and more mobile army enjoyed. Moreover,
Sherman's confidence in Kilpatrick had faltered since the latter's near disaster at Monroe's Crossroads. Soon after that incident, Sherman had received a dispatch from Schofield informing him that Sheridan appeared to
be heading in his direction. "I am delighted that Sheridan is slashing away
with his cavalry," Sherman exulted. "He will be a disturbing element in the
grand and beautiful game of war, and if he reaches me I'll make all North
Carolina howl. I will make him a deed gift of every horse in the state, to
be settled for at the day of judgment." On March 22, Grant had informed
Sherman that he was planning to send Sheridan on a mission to cut the
South Side and Danville Railroads, leaving it to the cavalryman's discretion whether to continue southward and join Sherman in North Carolina.
Though Grant's letter encouraged Sherman to believe that he could count
on "Little Phil" to supplant "Little Kil," he would soon be disabused of that
notion.[48]

The visit to City Point would also afford Sherman an opportunity to re-
late the tale of his marches and catch up on unfinished business with his
old friend Grant, whom he had not seen in a year. Most important, Sherman and Grant could plan the campaign that would deliver the death blow
to the Confederacy.[49]

On the morning of March 26, Sherman reached Morehead City and
boarded the steamer *Russia*. On his arrival at Fort Monroe, Virginia, early
the next day, the general telegraphed his brother, Senator John Sherman
of Ohio, inviting him to come down from Washington for a few days. After
transferring from the *Russia* to the *Blackbird*, Sherman then sailed up the
James River to City Point, arriving at 6:00 P.M. "City Point was a busy
place," recalled an eyewitness, "the river crowded with gunboats, moni-
tors, transports, &c., [and] the quartermaster's docks lined with vessels of
every sort, unloading stores and munitions for the army." Among the ships
docked at City Point was the presidential steamer *River Queen*, with President and Mrs. Lincoln on board.[50]

Waiting for Sherman at the bustling wharf were General Grant and several of his aides, among them Lt. Col. Horace Porter. "How d' you do, Sherman!" the general-in-chief called out, to which Sherman replied, "How are you, Grant!" The two men clasped hands, "uttering earnest words of familiar greeting," Porter noted. "Their encounter was more like that of two school-boys coming together after a vacation than the meeting of the chief actors in a great war tragedy."[51]

After paying his respects to Mrs. Grant at headquarters, Sherman sat down by the campfire and—surrounded by Grant and his staff—regaled his audience with stories of his marches through Georgia and the Carolinas. "Never were listeners more enthusiastic," Porter recalled, "never was a speaker more eloquent. The story, told as he alone could tell it, was a grand epic related with Homeric power." Sherman occasionally descended from the Homeric to the humorous, as in the tale of a bummer who was "a little more 'previous' than the rest" of the army in reaching Goldsboro. When an officer in Schofield's command spied the fellow up a telegraph pole hacking away at the wires with a hatchet, he yelled, "What are you doing there? You're destroying one of our own telegraph lines." The man glared at his interrogator and said, "I'm one o' Billy Sherman's bummers, and the last thing he said to us when we started out on this hunt was: 'Be sure and cut all the telegraph wires you come across, and don't go to foolin' away time askin' who they belong to.' "[52]

At length, Grant reminded Sherman that President Lincoln was anxious to see him. The two generals walked down to the wharf, boarded the *River Queen,* and met the president in the ship's saloon. Sherman later recalled that Lincoln "remembered me perfectly" from their first meeting four years earlier. "Uncle Billy" described the president's demeanor: "When at rest or listening, his legs and arms seemed to hang almost lifeless, and his face was care-worn and haggard, but the moment he began to talk, his face lightened up, his tall form, as it were, unfolded, and he was the very impersonation of good-humor and fellowship." Lincoln peppered Sherman with questions about "the Great March" but also expressed concern that some misfortune would befall the army in North Carolina during the general's absence. Sherman assured Lincoln that the army was in General Schofield's capable hands and was resting and drawing supplies in preparation for the next campaign.[53]

After making "a good, long, social visit," the generals returned to Grant's quarters for dinner. When Julia Grant asked her husband if he had paid his respects to Mrs. Lincoln, Grant replied that he had not, and Sherman volunteered that he did not know she was on board. "Well, you are a pretty pair!" Mrs. Grant scolded, adding that their neglect was inexcusable. The lieutenant general promised his wife that he would make amends for the unintended slight the next morning.[54]

Later that evening, several high-ranking officers from the army and navy came to pay their respects to Sherman, including Brig. Gen. Marsena R. Patrick, the Army of the Potomac's provost marshal-general. "He looks remarkably well," Patrick observed, "better than he did when he was about Washington in 1861—so full of fun and cracking jokes, especially with Admiral Porter." Like Grant, Union naval hero David Dixon Porter was an old friend of Sherman, the two men having served as joint commanders in several combined operations on the Mississippi River. Aside from "Uncle Billy," Porter's unbridled contempt for army officers brooked few exceptions. The admiral would accompany Grant and Sherman on their visit to Lincoln the next morning.[55]

When the socializing ended, Sherman, Grant, and several staff officers retired to the general-in-chief's cabin. The men seated themselves around a large map that Sherman used to outline his next campaign. As midnight approached, General Sheridan appeared, his arrival having been delayed by a railroad accident. Following a brief exchange of greetings, Sherman announced that he planned to march from Goldsboro on April 10, and, unless circumstances changed in the meantime, he would join Grant in an all-out effort against Lee. "Uncle Billy" intended to march toward Weldon and Gaston while feinting on Raleigh. After crossing the Roanoke River, he would either seize the junction of the South Side and Danville Railroads at Burke's Station to block Lee's remaining supply routes or join Grant near Richmond and Petersburg. Encouraged by Grant's March 22 dispatch, Sherman then suggested that Sheridan join him near the Roanoke after striking the South Side and Danville lines.[56]

With mounting anger, Sheridan listened as Sherman explained the cavalryman's role in the final campaign. This was a sore subject for Sheridan, because just the day before, Grant had presented him with discretionary orders to join Sherman in North Carolina. Sheridan had argued then "that it would be bad policy" for him to assist Sherman in defeating Johnston and then allow Sherman to assist Grant in defeating Lee. "Such a course would give rise to the charge that [Grant's] own forces around Petersburg were not equal to the task, and would seriously affect public opinion in the North," Sheridan had contended. Grant had assured his cavalry commander that the proposed move into North Carolina was merely a contingency should the coming offensive fall short of complete success. Sheridan had thus left Grant's headquarters greatly relieved that he would not have to join Sherman in North Carolina.[57]

That peace of mind would be short-lived. On the afternoon of March 27,

Sheridan learned that Sherman was en route to City Point, and he feared the worst. From experience, "Little Phil" knew Sherman's powers of persuasion when pleading his case to Grant. He therefore rushed to City Point, determined to prevent Sherman from swaying the general-in-chief.

No one at Grant's headquarters was surprised that the feisty Sheridan "dissented emphatically" when Sherman suggested that the cavalry commander join him in North Carolina. Grant sought to mollify "Little Phil" by repeating his assurance of the day before. Undeterred by this setback, Sherman then suggested that Grant postpone the opening of his campaign to mid-April. The lieutenant general replied that he intended to begin his next offensive in a few days by attacking Lee's position at Dinwiddie Court House.

"A big banter! A big banter!" Sherman exclaimed, attempting to conceal his disappointment by making light of Grant's next move. "But *we* can make things perfectly sure."

"Well," said Grant, "if we don't succeed here, probably I can keep [Lee] from drawing back till you come up." The discussion ended on this inconclusive note, and the generals retired for the night.[58]

Sheridan left Grant's headquarters satisfied that he and Grant had made it clear that his cavalry would remain in Virginia. But Sherman was nothing if not persistent. Early the next day, he paid a visit to Sheridan, who was still in bed. Once more Sherman mentioned having "Little Phil's" cavalry join his army in North Carolina, and once more Sheridan rebuffed him. "Uncle Billy" wisely steered the conversation in another direction and left soon afterward. Thus far, Sherman had failed to accomplish his two key objectives for this visit: securing Sheridan's cavalry for his own operations and persuading Grant to postpone his campaign until mid-April.[59]

Sherman may have been distracted from these sobering truths by the arrival of Maj. Gen. George Gordon Meade, the Army of the Potomac's commander. Ignoring the rumor that Sherman had been summoned to City Point to supersede him, General Meade was eager to meet his western counterpart. As Meade and his aide, Lt. Col. Theodore Lyman, approached Grant's log hut, "there suddenly issued from the house a tall figure who jerked himself forward, pulled suddenly up, and regarded the landscape with an inquisitive and very wrinkled expression. This was the redoubtable Sherman himself." Lyman described the Union commander:

> He is a very remarkable-looking man, such as could not be grown out of America—the concentrated quintessence of Yankeedom. He is tall, spare, and sinewy, with a very long neck, and a big head at the end of the same. The said big head is a most unusual combination. I mean

As Good as a Picnic

that, when a man is spare, with a high forehead, he usually has a con-
tracted back to his head; but Sherman has a swelling "fighting" back
to *his* head, and all his features express determination, particularly the
mouth, which is wide and straight, with lips that shut tightly together.
He is a very homely man, with a regular nest of wrinkles in his face,
which play and twist as he eagerly talks on each subject; but his expression is pleasant and kindly. But he believes in hard war. I heard him say:
"Columbia—pretty much all burned; and burned *good!*" [60]

In addition to Meade, several other high-ranking generals met Sherman
at City Point on the morning of March 28, including Maj. Gen. Edward
O. C. Ord, the Army of the James's commander, and Brig. Gen. Rufus
Ingalls, Grant's chief quartermaster. "I saw Sherman, Grant, Meade, and
Sheridan, all together," Lieutenant Colonel Lyman noted. "A thing to
speak of in after years!" [61]

The generals chatted briefly, until Grant reminded Sherman and Porter
that Lincoln was expecting them. The three boarded a tug and steamed
out to the *River Queen*, where they were met by the president himself. In the
ship's saloon, Grant asked after Mrs. Lincoln, as he had promised his wife
he would do. Lincoln went to the first lady's stateroom but soon returned
to say that his wife was unwell and begged to be excused. [62]

Grant opened the discussion by briefing the president on his new campaign. He said that Sheridan's cavalry was crossing the James River to
strike General Lee's remaining supply routes: the Boydton Plank Road and
the Danville and South Side Railroads. The general-in-chief stated that
the decisive moment was at hand. As the day for launching his offensive
approached, Grant feared that Lee would abandon his fortifications and
move southward. "With Johnston and him combined, a long, tedious, and
expensive campaign, consuming most of the summer, might become necessary," Grant conjectured. So long as the Confederacy's two principal field
armies could unite, they would pose a viable threat to final Union victory.
Though Grant never doubted achieving ultimate success, he agonized over
how long it might take and how much it might cost. [63]

Seeking to calm Grant's apprehensions, Sherman said that his army
could contend with Lee and Johnston's combined forces until Grant's arrival. But if circumstances permitted him a few more weeks to refit, Sherman would march up to Burke's Station and cut the South Side and Danville Railroads, forcing Lee to fight in the open or starve inside his trenches.
Grant, however, said that he was eager to attack and would wait no longer.
Because of Sherman's presence, Grant left unsaid his desire to defeat Lee
without "Uncle Billy's" help, so that the eastern army would not have to

The Peace Makers, *chromolithograph. Artist George P. A. Healy's rendering of the March 28, 1865, City Point Conference aboard the* River Queen *between (from left) William T. Sherman, Ulysses S. Grant, Abraham Lincoln, and David D. Porter. According to Sherman, the scene depicted is the moment he declares, "[I]f Lee would only remain in Richmond till I could reach Burkesville we would have him between our thumb and fingers" (W. T. Sherman to I. N. Arnold, November 28, 1872, Isaac N. Arnold Papers, Chicago Historical Society). (Courtesy of Chicago Historical Society)*

share the laurels with the western army. "I mean to end the business here," the Union general-in-chief had earlier confided to Phil Sheridan.[64]

Though differing on how to win the war, Grant and Sherman agreed that they would have to fight at least one more battle. Lincoln exclaimed that enough blood had been shed and asked if another battle could possibly be avoided. Sherman replied that the decision rested with the enemy: he supposed that "both Jeff. Davis and General Lee would be forced to fight one more desperate and bloody battle." Sherman stated that he expected to fight the final battle somewhere near Raleigh. Grant replied that he would soon be ready to pursue Lee in the event of a breakout. Once again, Lincoln said that he was uneasy about Sherman being away from his army, and once more, Sherman assured the president that Schofield was capable of commanding in his absence, adding that he planned to start back for Goldsboro in a few hours.[65]

Sherman abruptly shifted the conversation from military to political

As Good as a Picnic

matters when he asked Lincoln if he was "all ready for the end of the war."
"What was to be done with the rebel armies when defeated?" the general
inquired. "And what should be done with the political leaders, such as Jeff
Davis? Should we allow them to escape?" Lincoln replied that he was "all
ready." He now desired the swift defeat of the Confederate armies to get the
Southern men home as quickly as possible. As for Davis, Lincoln admitted
that he was not at liberty to speak his mind fully. The president indicated
that he thought the Rebel leader "ought to clear out, 'escape the country,'"
Sherman recalled, "only it would not do for him to say so openly." Lincoln
illustrated his point in a story: "A man once had taken the total-abstinence
pledge. When visiting a friend, he was invited to take a drink, but declined,
on the score of his pledge; then his friend suggested lemonade, which was
accepted. In preparing the lemonade, the friend pointed to the brandy-
bottle, and said the lemonade would be more palatable if he were to pour
in a little brandy; when his guest said, if he could do so 'unbeknown' to
him, he would not object." From this story Sherman inferred that Lincoln
wanted Davis to escape—"unbeknown" to him, of course.[66]

The accounts of the principals vary greatly regarding the president's
statements. Lincoln himself left no record of this meeting, as he had of
the Hampton Roads Conference. In all probability, he regarded the meeting with Grant, Sherman, and Porter as an informal discussion meriting
no such memorandum. He could not have foreseen that this would be his
final opportunity to discuss his plans with them. Grant was circumspect on
the subject of the so-called City Point Conference, saying only that Sherman had met with Lincoln and was aware of the president's statement to
the Confederate representatives at the Hampton Roads Conference. There
Lincoln had insisted that before negotiations could begin the Confederates must agree upon two points: preservation of the Union and no concessions on the emancipation issue as it stood at that time. Concerning all
other issues within his power, Lincoln had assured the Southern commissioners that he would act in a spirit of generosity.[67]

Sherman and Porter were far more specific than Grant in their recollections—and far more contradictory. Porter depicted Lincoln as so anxious
for peace that he was prepared to grant almost any terms to attain it. In
fact, however, Lincoln regarded preservation of the Union and no concessions on the emancipation issue as fixed principles beyond the realm of
compromise.[68]

Porter's grasp of the military situation in North Carolina was no surer
than his understanding of Lincoln's conditions for peace. According to
Porter, when Lincoln advised Sherman to offer Johnston the same generous terms Grant intended to give Lee, Sherman demurred, saying that he

had his adversary "cooped up where he could not get away." Porter noted that he had never seen Sherman more emphatic than when arguing this point with Lincoln. The admiral quoted Sherman as saying, "Mr. President, there is no possible way for Johnston to escape as he is now situated. I can command his unconditional surrender." According to Porter, Sherman used a map to show his position at Goldsboro and Johnston's at Smithfield, demonstrating his ability to "dictate his own terms to General Johnston." By Porter's account, Lincoln then said that he feared Johnston would escape southward by rail, but Sherman answered, "I have him where he cannot move without breaking up his army, which, once disbanded, can never again be got together; and I have destroyed the Southern railroads, so that they cannot be used again for a long time." Grant asked, "What is to prevent their laying the rails again?" To which Sherman replied, "Why, my bummers don't do things by halves. Every rail, after having been placed over a hot fire, has been twisted as crooked as a ram's horn, and they never can be used again." [69]

Porter's account appears accurate at first glance, but it overlooks several inconsistencies that Lincoln and Grant apparently recognized, judging from their pointed questions. A brief study of Sherman's map of North Carolina may have convinced the president and general-in-chief that "Uncle Billy" lacked the means to demand Johnston's unconditional surrender. They might have noted that Smithfield lay twenty-five miles northwest of Goldsboro—almost a two-day march separated Sherman from Johnston. They may also have noted that the Confederates still enjoyed the use of the North Carolina Railroad from Smithfield to Charlotte and realized that Johnston could still retreat westward on that railroad, either to form a junction with Lee near Danville or to retreat southward beyond Sherman's reach. [70]

Porter is even less convincing when contending that Lincoln "insisted that the surrender of Johnston's army must be obtained on any terms," given the president's inflexible stance on the preservation of the Union and the abolition of slavery. Porter maintained that, in the end, "Sherman, as a subordinate officer, yielded his views to those of the President," but the admiral did not specify the terms that Lincoln authorized Sherman to grant Johnston. [71]

Although Sherman later stated that he recalled his conversation with Lincoln from memory, whereas Porter relied on contemporaneous notes, Sherman nevertheless remembered the discussion in far greater detail than Porter. "Mr. Lincoln was full and frank in his conversation," Sherman wrote, "assuring me that in his mind he was all ready for the civil reorganization of affairs at the South as soon as the war was over; and he distinctly

As Good as a Picnic

authorized me to assure Governor Vance and the people of North Carolina that, as soon as the rebel armies laid down their arms, and resumed their civil pursuits, they would at once be guaranteed all their rights as citizens of a common country; and that to avoid anarchy the State governments then in existence, with their civil functionaries, would be recognized by him as the government *de facto* till Congress could provide others." [72]

That Lincoln had a firm Reconstruction policy for North Carolina is debatable; that he would have recognized Governor Vance and the secessionist legislature of the Old North State contradicts his stated policy of refusing to recognize the Confederate government in any form. This account also conflicts with a previous statement Sherman made in a letter to Isaac N. Arnold, a friend and biographer of Lincoln. "I ought not and must not attempt to recall the words of that conversation," Sherman wrote. "Though I cannot attempt to recall the words spoken by any one of the persons present, on that occasion I know we talked generally about what was to be done when Lee & Johnstons armies were beaten and dispersed." Sherman recalled that Lincoln "contemplated no revenge—no harsh measures, but quite the contrary, and that [the Rebels'] suffering and hardships in the war would make them the more submissive to Law—I cannot say that Mr. Lincoln or any body else used this language at the time, but I know I left his presence with the conviction that he had in his mind, or that his cabinet had, some plan of settlement, ready for application the moment Lee & Johnston were defeated." [73]

At best, Sherman left City Point with a general impression of Lincoln's intentions concerning the defeated South. Regarding Lincoln, he wrote: "I know, when I left him, that I was more than ever impressed by his kindly nature, his deep and earnest sympathy with the afflictions of the whole people, resulting from the war. . . . In the language of his second inaugural address, he seemed to have 'charity for all, malice toward none'. . . . Of all the men I ever met, he seemed to possess more of the elements of greatness, combined with goodness, than any other." [74]

As Sherman and the president parted at the gangway of the *River Queen,* Lincoln's last words were that he would feel much better once the general was with his army at Goldsboro. Sherman later told his wife that Lincoln "was lavish in his good wishes." Oddly enough, Sherman did not mention his conversations with Lincoln to his wife or his father-in-law, Thomas Ewing, until much later. Writing Ellen on March 31, Sherman said only that he had just returned from "a hasty visit to City Point," where he conferred with Grant "on points of importance." On the same day, he mentioned his visit to Grant in a letter to Ewing, hastening to assure him: "You need not fear my committing a political mistake, for I am fully conscious of the fact that I would imperil all by any concessions in that direction. I have and shall continue to repel all advances made me of such a kind." Judging from his statement to Ewing, Sherman left City Point with the intention of hewing to a strictly military surrender and leaving political matters to the politicians. It would seem that Sherman was focused on defeating the Confederates and would reflect on his discussions with Lincoln at City Point only later, when he prepared to negotiate surrender terms with his adversary Johnston.[75]

At 4:00 P.M. on March 28, Sherman boarded the steamer *Bat,* which Admiral Porter had provided for the return trip. The general reached Fort Monroe at 10:00 that night and was met by his brother, Senator John Sherman, and Edwin Stanton, the secretary of war's son. Also awaiting him was an uncharacteristically effusive message from the elder Stanton: "God speed you; and that He may have you in his keeping, shield you from every danger, and crown you with victory, is my earnest prayer."[76]

At midnight the general resumed his journey, accompanied by his brother and the younger Stanton. On March 30, the *Bat* broke down within ten miles of New Bern, forcing the party to switch to a rowboat in a driving rain. At New Bern they dined at the headquarters of Brig. Gen. Innis Palmer before boarding a train for Goldsboro, arriving at midnight.[77]

Sherman was pleased to find "all things working well" upon his return. Supplies continually rolled in from the coast, and his army was beginning to look like an army once more. "The fellows who passed in review before me with smoke black faces, dirty and ragged, many with feet bare or wrapped in cloth," Sherman wrote his wife, "now strut about as proud as young chicken cocks with their clean faces and bright blue clothes." Most of the soldiers also noticed the startling transformation. "Our Regt has not made as fine an appearance as they do now since the summer of 1863," wrote John D. Inskeep of the 17th Ohio. "Really the change from the ragged, barefooted, dirty, weary battalion that reached this place on the 23rd [of March] to the neat, clean, well-clothed, well-fed & contented one that we had on Dress parade this evening seems almost magical." In answer to a petition from two of his corps commanders requesting that chief quartermaster Easton and chief commissary officer Beckwith be sacked on the grounds of "utter incompetency and inefficiency," Sherman wrote, "All has been done that was possible, and I will not reflect on officers who have done so much and done it well." Only a week earlier Sherman had suspected negligence on the part of Easton and Beckwith, but now he was chiding the commanders for failing to take into account "the difficulties arising from mud banks, storms at sea, difficulties of navigation, &c."[78]

As Good as a Picnic

Despite the influx of supplies at Goldsboro in late March, much of Sherman's army was still ragged and clothed in civilian attire, as the commanding general's brother discovered. "Most of the troops had received their new uniforms and equipments," Senator John Sherman recalled, "but outlying regiments were constantly coming in, ragged, with tattered hats, shoes and boots of every description, almost black from exposure and the smoke of the pine woods, and as hardy a looking set of men as one could conceive of. They had picked up all kinds of paraphernalia, 'stove pipe' hats being the favorite."[79]

While the commanding general and the senator scrutinized the army, Pvt. Sylvester "Vett" Noble, a clerk at "Uncle Billy's" headquarters, compared the brothers Sherman. "Their features are a good deal alike," Noble observed, "but the Generals hair is sandy—or tow-color—while Mr.'s is dark—now almost grey—both are very tall and of slight build—look as if they were dryed, like old, shrivelled up men—won't get fat!" Senator Sherman and the younger Stanton stayed at Goldsboro for only a day, returning home late on March 31 aboard the repaired *Bat*.[80]

While at City Point, Sherman had secured from Grant an outlay of tugboats and barges for hauling supplies from the coast to Kinston via the Neuse River. This move was fortuitous, for upon his return to Goldsboro, Sherman learned that repairs to the Wilmington and Weldon Railroad were not yet completed. "Uncle Billy" had also arranged for the railroad department in Virginia to send him additional locomotives and rolling stock compatible with the track used in North Carolina, but instead he received equipment for the larger gauge used in the Old Dominion. This logistical blunder might have impeded Sherman's efforts to supply his army, but the level countryside from Morehead City to Goldsboro enabled the trains to haul more than double the load that Sherman had calculated based on his experience in the more rugged terrain of Tennessee and Georgia. Although Confederate raiding parties succeeded in destroying several cargo ships on the Neuse River and tearing up some railroad track, their efforts failed to hinder the flow of Federal supplies.[81]

During his visit to City Point, Sherman had arranged the reorganization of his grand army with Grant. While retaining the right wing, or Army of the Tennessee, under Howard and the left wing, or Army of Georgia, under Slocum, Sherman designated Schofield's new command the center, or Army of the Ohio. Sherman also received authorization for creating Slocum's Army of Georgia by detaching two corps from the Army of the Cumberland. The order was a mere technicality, insofar as the Army of Georgia had been an accomplished fact since the previous autumn. Each of Sherman's three armies consisted of two corps: the Fifteenth and Seventeenth in Howard's Army of the Tennessee, the Fourteenth and Twentieth in Slocum's Army of Georgia, and the Tenth (formerly the Provisional Corps) and Twenty-third in Schofield's Army of the Ohio. Sherman's mounted arm, the Third Cavalry Division, remained under Kilpatrick.[82]

Sherman made one change in his corps commanders, replacing Twentieth Corps chief Alpheus Williams with Joe Mower, which sparked some controversy. At Bentonville, Mower had disobeyed orders by launching an assault with his Seventeenth Corps division, but instead of being reprimanded, "Fighting Joe" was promoted. Though rumor had it that Mower benefited from Sherman's favoritism, it is equally probable that Sherman wanted to make maximum use of his most aggressive general. "I had specially asked for General Mower to command the Twentieth Corps," Sherman later explained, "because I regarded him as one of the boldest and best fighting generals in the army. His predecessor, General A. S. Williams, . . . had commanded the corps well from Atlanta to Goldsboro, and it may have seemed unjust to replace him at that precise moment; but I was resolved to be prepared for a most desperate and, as then expected, a final battle, should it fall on me." Sherman's rationale for promoting Mower thus refutes the argument of Sherman apologists that the Federal commander did not engage Johnston in a decisive battle at Bentonville because he regarded the Confederates as already defeated.[83]

Many of "Pap" Williams's troops resented having their commander superseded by an outsider. "This seemed but a poor return for the long and admirable service which General Williams had performed," recalled one disgruntled Twentieth Corps veteran. Conversely, some of the men in Mower's old command rejoiced at the news of his departure. "Maj. Gen. Mower has been relieved from the command of our division and assigned to the 20th army Corps," Pvt. William H. Pittenger of the 39th Ohio wrote. "We are glad of this as we consider him rather an imprudent general [though] desperately brave." A disappointed Williams lamented: "This is about the fortieth time that I have been foisted up by seniority to be let down by rank!" Yet Williams found Mower to be "a very pleasant, gentlemanly man of the old army." Once again, "Old Pap" would command the First Division of the "Star Corps," which he had previously led for more than three years. His disappointment must have been eased when his three brigade commanders—Brig. Gen. James S. Robinson and Colonels William Hawley and James L. Selfridge—formally welcomed him back on behalf of their troops.[84]

While Sherman reorganized his grand army, thousands of volunteers, conscripts, and returning veterans streamed into Goldsboro. The new recruits were criticized by their veteran comrades for waiting until the war

As Good as a Picnic

was nearly over to join the army and collect their cash bounties. "The boys are pestering these 'bounty grabbers' shamefully," noted the 104th Ohio's Sgt. Joseph W. Gaskill, on whose shoulders his lieutenant had placed the burden of drilling their company's six recruits. "Almost any kind of a man passes examination and is accepted," Gaskill wrote. "Buck-kneed, bow-legged, and warped spinal columns, and two who are well up into their forty's—too old to learn new tricks—are sent to fill up the ranks and paid for by men with more money than patriotism." Gaskill felt somewhat repaid for his efforts as drillmaster during the manual of arms, for "I enjoy the pounding they give to each other's corns when coming to an order arms," though he regretted that his lieutenant's corns "are not within reach of these bombardments."[85]

The Union army's three-week halt at Goldsboro saw the convening of numerous courts-martial. One of the accused was a soldier in the 48th Illinois who was convicted of rape. As punishment, the man's head was shaved and then marked in red ink with the letters "D R," stigmatizing him as a deserter and a rapist. He was led down the length of his regiment at bayonet point while the colonel followed at his heels, shouting, "You dirty hog, you!" This was done in full view of the soldier's Fifteenth Corps division. He was then marched beyond the army's picket line and warned that if he was found within Union lines, he would be shot. In another case, during his first—and final—week with the army, a cavalryman murdered a civilian and was tried, convicted, and executed by firing squad. It was later discovered that he had made his living as a bounty jumper, enlisting in a regiment to collect a cash bounty, then deserting and repeating the process with another regiment.[86]

Of all incidents occurring in late March, the execution of Pvt. James Preble of the 12th New York Cavalry aroused the most comment. Preble was convicted of rape and sentenced to be shot on March 31. On that morning, Pvt. William Bircher and his comrades of the 2nd Minnesota received orders to assemble at 1:00 P.M. to witness Preble's execution. "I need hardly say that this was most unwelcome news," Bircher wrote. "Nobody wished to see so sad a sight. Some of the men begged to be excused from attending, and others could not be found when the drums beat the 'assembly'; for none could well endure, as they said, 'to see a man shot down like a dog.'" At the appointed hour, Bircher and his comrades marched to an open field outside Goldsboro and formed three sides of a hollow square two ranks deep, facing inward. On the fourth side, a freshly dug grave lay in plain view.[87]

Scarcely had the men gotten into formation when they could hear the doleful strains of the "Dead March." Private Bircher recalled seeing "a long procession marching sadly and slowly to the measured stroke of the drum." The band appeared first, followed by the firing squad and then the condemned soldier's pine coffin, borne by four men. Preble came next in an ambulance, flanked by two army chaplains. Bringing up the rear were several arrested men under guard: it was hoped that Preble's execution would exert a salutary influence on the prisoners. The ambulance halted before the open grave, and Preble was led around the square. He marched with a firm step, though keeping his head bowed. Preble halted before his grave. The commander of the firing squad read the charges against the condemned man, followed by the sentence.[88]

Sgt. William B. Miller of the 75th Indiana was filling out his regiment's payroll records when he heard the sound of muffled drums outside his tent. Dropping his work, he followed the procession to an open field. Miller noted that Preble was asked if he had anything to say. The condemned man exhorted his comrades not to do as he had done, but to be good soldiers. Preble regretted that he had to die this way because of his mother, and he forgave all who took part in his trial and execution. The cavalryman knelt before his coffin and was joined by the two chaplains, who prayed with him for several minutes. Meanwhile, the firing squad stepped forward. Preble briefly looked about and was then blindfolded. Moments later, the orders came in rapid succession—"Ready! Aim! Fire!"—and Private Preble fell to the ground dead. "I don't think I will ever witness another such a horror if I can get away from it," Sergeant Miller wrote. "I have seen men shot in battle, but never in cold blood before. He died brave like [the] soldier that he was." A Federal soldier noted that several hundred Confederates witnessed the execution from a creek 300 yards away, yet no shots were fired.[89]

On the following day, April 1, "All Fools' Day was noisily observed in camp," recalled a soldier in the 55th Illinois. "Every man who did not stay close in quarters and hold his peace became sooner or later the victim of some ridiculous joke. Discipline for a time was abandoned, even the officers joining in the frolic to the loss of all authority." At nightfall came the ever-welcome call: "Come and get your mail!" The soldiers of the 55th gathered around the postmaster and eagerly grabbed their letters as their names were cried out. Only when they reached their quarters and tore open envelopes bulging with blank paper did the men realize that the postmaster had duped them. By then it was too late to retaliate, "for the cruel joker was safe in concealment."[90]

Also on April 1, eighteen-year-old Elizabeth Collier went to General Schofield's headquarters and requested that her family be allowed to pass through Yankee lines. Schofield "very politely said he would," she noted in

As Good as a Picnic

her diary. Elizabeth and her family had recently arrived at Goldsboro as refugees. Their home was at Everittsville about a dozen miles to the south. Since the arrival of Union foragers on March 20, the Colliers had lived in constant terror. Although the family eventually received a safeguard, they lost all of their provisions and livestock and most of their personal possessions. After staying with the town doctor for a few days, the terrified family fled to Goldsboro, having been branded "*damned rebels*" by the last foraging party they encountered.

Early on April 2, Elizabeth and her family rode out to the Federal picket post under a flag of truce. Schofield's provost marshal, Lt. Col. Philip C. Hayes, examined the family's baggage and told Elizabeth and her mother that they could keep only two trunks, "but I was too thankful to be rid of this hateful presence at any cost," Elizabeth later wrote. The women rode off and soon found themselves among friends. "I really do not think I was ever so happy in all my life, as I was when I first *saw our men—rebel soldiers in their gray jackets,*" Elizabeth rejoiced. "Their bright, open, cheerful countenances were such a striking contrast to the mean, low miserable looking Yankees."[91]

The repairs to the railroad from Wilmington were completed on April 4, providing Sherman with an additional supply line for his grand army, which no longer needed it. Now that supplies had ceased to concern him, Sherman shifted his attention to the grand movement northward. There never seemed to be any doubt as to the commanding general's ultimate objective. At the outset of the March to the Sea five months earlier, a private had called out to the general: "Uncle Billy, I guess Grant is waiting for us at Richmond!" As Sherman later noted, "Indeed, the general sentiment was that we were marching for Richmond, and that there we should end the war."[92]

On April 5, Sherman released Special Field Orders No. 48 to his army and corps commanders. The plan was a classic Sherman maneuver, employing feints on Raleigh to the northwest by Slocum's left wing and on Weldon to the northeast by Kilpatrick's cavalry. Schofield's army would follow Slocum in the center, ready to support the latter since his wing would be nearest Johnston's army at Smithfield. Meanwhile, Howard's right wing would march in the rear of Kilpatrick to the east. Sherman's grand army would converge on Warrenton about eighty miles north of Goldsboro. From Warrenton, Sherman intended to strike the junction of the South Side and Danville Railroads at Burke's Station, cutting Robert E. Lee's two remaining rail supply lines. Though seizing Burke's Station fell far short of capturing Richmond, Sherman perceived this as the best means of preventing Johnston from combining forces with Lee, which he understood to be his first objective.[93]

As the day for resuming the march approached, Sherman grew increasingly anxious at the general-in-chief's silence. In a dispatch accompanying Grant's copy of Special Field Orders No. 48, Sherman wrote: "I get nothing from you—not a word since I left [City Point]—and am of course impatient to know what Lee proposes to do." Sherman also confessed that he had no intelligence regarding Johnston's army at Smithfield. "We find Wade Hampton's cavalry on the roads to Weldon and Raleigh," he continued, "but evidently only watching us. They have made no effort to strike our railroads anywhere." Sherman told Grant that he expected to hear from him before starting out on April 10, but that he would not wait for a reply.[94]

April 5 was a day of nagging uncertainty for everyone from Sherman to the men in the ranks. As a result, rumors flew about camp regarding the situation at Richmond and Petersburg. General Howard wrote to the commanding officer at Morehead City: "Please inform me what news there is from General Grant. . . . A rumor of a severe battle has reached us, but nothing definite." While eagerly awaiting news from Virginia, the 90,000 Federals encamped near Goldsboro had no choice but to go about their daily routine.[95]

As Good as a Picnic

CHAPTER 3

THE SKELETON ARMY

On March 22, Gen. Joseph E. Johnston's Army of the South marched from Bentonville toward Smithfield, fifteen miles to the north. The soldiers were bone tired after fighting a three-day battle against Sherman's army. One Confederate found the army's route "in terrible condition[;] wagons bogged down, [and] roads seemed to have no bottom." In a letter headed "On the road to Somewhere," Pvt. Charles W. Hutson of Stuart's South Carolina battery noted that he and his comrades "plunged almost knee deep at every step." After slogging through mud for most of the day, the exhausted Southerners camped a few miles west of Smithfield. That night, Maj. Gen. Daniel Harvey Hill slept in a bed "for the first time in thirty nights," he later informed his family, "& I was so tired that I did hardly struggle to pull off my coat." Hill noted that he slept "a good deal" and now felt better than he had in months. Alluding to the fighting at Bentonville, the general wrote: "I was sick Sunday, but the battle made me well."[1]

The army rested on March 23, much to the soldiers' delight. "It is a treat that we are permitted to-day to wash up and put on clean clothes," wrote Capt. Bromfield Ridley of Lt. Gen. A. P. Stewart's staff. On reaching camp, the Rebel soldiers bore a striking resemblance to the enemy. "You would hardly know me now," William Johnson of the 1st South Carolina Artillery wrote his sweetheart. "I am so weather beaten in face, shabby in clothing and . . . begrimed with smoke. On the march we often do not get a chance to wash our faces for two days together, and the smoky atmosphere of the camp, when we halt at night, makes us look like the Yankee prisoners in the 'bull pen.'"[2]

Some of the soldiers took the opportunity to inform their loved ones that they were alive and well. "I have just returned from an expedition to Bentonville against Sherman which has been satisfactory on the whole,"

Duncan Campbell wrote his wife. "We killed some few, caught some few and brought off as trophies two cannon." Although he feared that his letter would not get through, Lt. Benjamin Williams of the 47th Georgia wrote his mother anyway, telling her that he and his brother were "getting along finely." Williams assured his mother that he was getting "plenty to eat," including bacon, corn bread, and "a good deal of flour." He also noted that his comrades had been "getting pretty low spirited," but since Johnston had assumed command, they had "brightened up considerably." Williams believed that Johnston's presence "has been worth 20 thousand men to the Army."[3]

On March 24, Johnston's army resumed the march, crossing the Neuse at Turner's Bridge and passing through Smithfield. But instead of pressing on toward Raleigh or Weldon—as many soldiers had expected—the Confederates halted three miles north of Smithfield, near Mitchener's Station on the North Carolina Railroad. There they camped, and there they would remain until Sherman decided to march. Johnston established his headquarters at the Pharaoh Richardson house, once again making Smithfield his base because of its central location. The Confederate commander assumed that Sherman's next objective would be Richmond, via either Raleigh or Weldon; regardless of Sherman's route, Johnston could obstruct his advance. To monitor the enemy's movements, "Old Joe" ordered Wade Hampton to post Butler's Division west of Goldsboro and Wheeler's Corps to the north.[4]

Although his assignment was a passive one, Hampton assumed the offensive on March 24. Leading elements of Butler's Division, the South Carolinian attacked the Union force defending the pontoons at the site of Cox's Bridge. Though repulsed, Hampton nevertheless convinced the Federals to abandon their isolated position. He also learned from Union prisoners that Sherman planned to remain at Goldsboro for several weeks. Hampton relayed this information to Johnston and urged his superior to attack other Federal camps. Instead, Johnston adopted a watch and wait posture in the face of the numerically superior Union army. If Sherman intended to rest his army for the next few weeks, then Johnston would do likewise.[5]

Once his army was safely ensconced near Smithfield, Johnston sent a message urging Robert E. Lee to abandon Richmond and Petersburg and join forces with the Army of the South. "Sherman's course cannot be hindered by the small force I have," Johnston told Lee. "I respectfully suggest that it is no longer a question whether you leave present position; you have only to decide where to meet Sherman. I will be near him." Along with his letter, Johnston sent Lt. Gen. Theophilus H. Holmes to discuss his proposal

The Skeleton Army

with Lee. In a second dispatch to the general-in-chief, "Old Joe" reported that Sherman and Schofield had united at Goldsboro and that Sheridan was expected to join Sherman soon. Johnston supposed that Sherman intended to cross the Roanoke River at Weldon and recommended attacking him in North Carolina. "I will impede his march if possible," Johnston wrote, "and keep in his front to join you should you wish to fight Grant first."[6]

Lee agreed with his subordinate's supposition that Sherman would take the Weldon route but dismissed Sheridan's expected junction with Sherman as mere rumor. As to the idea of attacking Grant first, Lee saw only disaster in such a move. Ultimately, the discussion of strategic combinations gave way to harsh reality. According to his March 24 troop returns, Johnston's infantry numbered only 13,900, and as Lee informed President Davis, such a small force "would add so little to [my] army as not to make it more than a match for Sherman, with whom to risk a battle in the presence of Grant's army would hardly seem justifiable." Lee estimated that Grant's and Sherman's armies outnumbered his and Johnston's forces by 100,000 men. "I fear now it will be impossible to prevent a junction between Grant and Sherman," Lee wrote, "nor do I deem it prudent that this army should maintain its position [at Richmond and Petersburg] should the latter approach too near." In short, Lee was preparing Davis for the inevitable—the evacuation of the Confederate capital. Such was the bleak strategic picture confronting the Southern high command in late March 1865.[7]

The logistical situation appeared to be no better: Johnston's army desperately needed small arms and shoes, among other supplies. On March 29, 908 of "Old Joe's" soldiers lacked rifle-muskets, and a March 28 report indicated that more than a quarter of the men in the Army of Tennessee contingent either were barefoot or likely to become so soon. While appealing to the quartermaster general in Richmond for 5,000 pairs of shoes, Johnston released this order: "No privilege or exemption from duty whatever will be granted to barefooted men merely on account of their being without shoes." Adding insult to injury, the Treasury Department announced that its coffers were empty and the soldiers could not be paid. Secretary of the Treasury George A. Trenholm appealed to the soldiers' "intelligence and patriotism to bear these additional trials with fortitude," promising that "every effort shall be made to give them relief, and no claim upon the Treasury shall have preference over theirs." Having served for months or even years without pay, the soldiers met this disappointment with stony silence.[8]

Short rations were another of the Confederates' woes. Sgt. W. H. Andrews of the 1st Georgia Regulars recalled paying a dollar for a roasting ear at Smithfield. Andrews nonetheless felt "extremely lucky" to get the corn, though cognizant that it had probably "been stolen from some poor old horse that needed it as bad as I did, but hunger does not make a man feel very charitably inclined." To supplement their meager rations, soldiers fished or seined the Neuse River for shad. A few lucky Tar Heels such as Maj. Walter Clark of the Junior Reserves received food packages from home.[9]

Thanks largely to area farmers, Johnston's troops received enough to subsist on, for like the Federals, the Confederates lived off the land. Raleigh attorney Bartholomew F. Moore complained that Confederate foragers took his "only milch cow," and he knew a poor farmer who lost his "last plough horse" by the same means. "I could not pray for the success of a govt which habitually endorses such conduct," an infuriated Moore told his brother. From Hillsborough, J. W. Norwood wrote: "We have now here a large force of reserve Artillery, 80 Guns, who are impressing grain and forage, & stripping the country very bare." Norwood noted that until recently, the artillerymen had also impressed horses. A Johnston County farmer named Goodin reported that a detail from Law's cavalry brigade plundered his stores "without mercy." The Confederates unroofed Goodin's corncribs "like a hurricane," loading most of the corn into their wagons.

The Skeleton Army

Then they descended on his poultry yard and "robbed him of ducks, geese, chickens and eggs." Goodin's account appeared in the March 28 *Raleigh Confederate* under the heading, "The Want of Discipline." The correspondent conceded that General Johnston could not be expected to "bring up the debris of armies and organize and discipline them in a moment" but noted that "the ravages upon the loyal and good people of Johnston County, by our own troops, have not only shocked the public sense, but have almost reduced to beggary some of the warmest friends of the country." From Raleigh, former North Carolina governor Charles Manly declared: "The horrid deeds perpetrated by the Yankees in Fayetteville & the not less lawless & atrocious acts of our people in Johnston & Wake [Counties] exceed the enormities of Barbarians. Between the two fires desolation, plunder, & actual starvation await us. God help the country."[10]

North Carolina governor Zebulon B. Vance informed General Johnston that excessive impressments were causing "much distress" around Raleigh, with "officers often taking every horse a farmer has." Vance urged the general to "order all horses so taken to be returned." Johnston assured the governor: "If the perpetrators of illegal impressments are pointed out they shall be punished. If the property so impressed is identified it shall be restored. . . . I am anxious to protect citizens against robbery." In fairness to Johnston, not all details were as they claimed: marauding deserters posing as "Wheeler's men" did nothing to improve the reputation of Joe Wheeler's much-maligned cavalry.[11]

The Confederate high command took stringent measures to prevent pillaging and plundering. "I have been and am laboring most earnestly to detect and punish the rascals who are committing outrages in the country," Wade Hampton informed Johnston. "I hope my efforts have checked their offenses in some measure, and I promise you to do all in my power to check them altogether." The crimes committed by soldiers against civilians indicated an even greater crisis: the increase in desertion and straggling. To remedy the problem, Maj. Gen. Lafayette McLaws ordered all companies in his division to make five roll calls per day, and he sent out patrols to arrest soldiers absent without leave. Despite his reputation as a "soldier's general," Johnston was a stern disciplinarian who dealt harshly with deserters and stragglers. During the halt at Smithfield, "Old Joe" issued orders minimizing straggling and refused to commute several deserters' death sentences.[12]

The Confederate army's high desertion rate stemmed from sinking morale. Immediately following the Battle of Bentonville, morale had been high, for the soldiers took pride in checking Sherman's numerically superior army. Most would have agreed with McLaws's March 23 declaration to his wife: "I believe Gen'l Sherman will be chased out of the state." They also trusted and respected their army commander. "Everyone is delighted at Johnston's being put in command," wrote Augustine Smythe, a South Carolinian in Hardee's Corps. "We feel that he can be a match for Sherman." By early April, however, Southern spirits began to flag. Capt. John Swain of the 17th North Carolina advised his brother not to join the army, but to remain at home where he was more useful. "There is a dark cloud hanging over our country," Swain warned, "and every passing breeze comes laden with the din of war, devastation, and death." David Copeland of the 3rd South Carolina noted that "a great many" of his comrades "are on French furloughs as we caul them which in other words have runaway from their Regt without any furlough." Another South Carolinian, Charles Hutson of Stuart's Battery, spent much of his time "trying to talk good cheer into the hearts of the despondent, for I am sorry to say there are some badly whipped men around me."[13]

One of the army's worst cases of low morale may have been Gen. Braxton Bragg, whose command—the Department of North Carolina—was stripped from him until he was left with little more than his headquarters in Raleigh and a title. His March 26 letter to President Davis fairly oozes with pessimism and self-pity:

I have retired to this point, where I have nothing to do but mourn over the sad spectacle hourly presented of disorganization, demoralization, and destruction. No language, Mr. President, can paint the condition of our military affairs in this quarter. . . . Officers seem paralyzed, men indifferent to everything but plunder, and the people . . . [appear] disgusted and dismayed. This state of things cannot last, and no one is so blind as not to see the inevitable result. . . . You hear of victories & routs. I see disasters, disorderly retreats, and utter confusion on our front, with combinations and numbers against us which must prevail. . . . With no duty to perform, I shall remain quietly here awaiting events, and fall back towards the south as necessity may require. My position is both mortifying and humiliating, but with your example before me, I shall bear it with all the patience I can command. You should permit yourself to hope for nothing in the present condition of our mil[itary] affairs; and in your movements, official & personal, [you] should be governed accordingly. This is intended for your eye only, but it may suggest the propriety of sending someone to look for you and report officially.

I am, dear sir, yours, as ever,

BRAXTON BRAGG

Having fired his parting salvo, Braxton Bragg receded into the background, joining a growing number of discarded Confederate commanders in North Carolina who had once led armies in the field, only to serve as pencil-pushing functionaries at the end of the war.[14]

Yet for every such harbinger of doom in Johnston's army, there was another who was prepared "to die in the last ditch." "I have always felt confident of our great destiny," Charles Hutson declared, "and nothing less than total ruin will ever shake that confidence." In a letter to his mother, Maj. Walter Clark of the North Carolina Junior Reserves stated: "It is beyond my ken to see any end to the War, but while I am able for service I intend to stand by the cause while a banner floats to tell where Freedom [lives] and freedom's sons still support her cause." For every deserter there was another who was hurrying to rejoin his comrades at the front. From mid-March to early April, several thousand troops from the Army of Tennessee under the command of Lt. Gen. Stephen D. Lee traveled from Augusta to Smithfield—"only to surrender," prophesied the ubiquitous diarist Mary Chesnut. She described their procession through the streets of Chester, South Carolina: "They march with as airy a tread as if they still believed the world was all on their side, and that there were no Yankee bullets for the unwary. What will Joe Johnston do with them now?"[15]

What Johnston did was to marshal his forces and await a decision to act from either Lee or Sherman. On March 31, Johnston's army numbered 25,011 present for duty, a substantial increase since the Battle of Bentonville, but not enough to offset Sherman's 90,000 soldiers. The Army of the South was stronger than "Old Joe" chose to admit. Johnston cited the effective strength of his army—21,119—which comprised only soldiers with their units, whereas the "present for duty" tally also included dismounted cavalry and men on detached service or on the sick list, who were still capable of serving on the firing line. Johnston's total also excluded remote detachments able to join the army on short notice. On March 31, "Old Joe" could have fielded about 28,000 troops—double the 13,900 "effective infantry" cited on March 24. Though Lee and Johnston were incapable of stopping Sherman individually, their combined strength of about 80,000 front-line troops would have presented a formidable obstacle. But the question remained: Could Lee steal a march on Grant and combine with Johnston?[16]

While Johnston prepared to meet Sherman in his front, he learned of a threat to his rear. The commander at Salisbury, Brig. Gen. Bradley T. Johnson, warned that Maj. Gen. George Stoneman's Union cavalry division, about 4,000 strong, was advancing toward his position on the North

Carolina Railroad. Soon afterward, a conflicting report arrived claiming that Stoneman's raid was "all bosh," and the raiders were actually a band of "tories and deserters." Although Governor Vance vouched for the latter source, "Old Joe" wisely acted on Johnson's warning. He delegated the task of stopping Stoneman to General Beauregard at Raleigh. On March 31, the Creole flooded the telegraph wires with messages to the commanders at Hillsborough, Greensboro, and Chester, transferring troops to Salisbury to oppose Stoneman's cavalry. On April 1, Beauregard traveled to Salisbury, but Stoneman had already veered north toward Greensboro. A few days later, the elusive Federal raiders entered Virginia and threatened Danville. By April 5, Stoneman had ceased to concern Beauregard, who informed Johnston that he no longer required assistance from Wheeler's cavalry.[17]

As Beauregard prepared to oppose Stoneman's raiders, Johnston found himself under attack by a former protégé. On March 30, the *Raleigh Confederate* began reprinting Gen. John Bell Hood's report for the Atlanta and Tennessee campaigns. Copies of the newspaper reached Johnston's headquarters on the same day and circulated throughout the army. Hood had succeeded Johnston as commander of the Army of Tennessee on July 18, 1864, on the outskirts of Atlanta, which fell to Sherman's army six weeks later. Hood blamed Johnston for the loss of the city, and the latter believed himself falsely accused. Most soldiers in the Army of Tennessee contingent sided with "Old Joe" in the controversy. A staff officer noted that Hood "abuses a great many for tardiness and dereliction of duty, and I think some unjustly." Another officer called Hood's report "a vindictive paper," and a third accused the general of making "a great many erroneous assertions." Capt. William D. Gale refused to "cast stones at Hood," however. Although Gale termed Hood's report "indelicate and unfortunate," he conceded that it contained "what every man in the army recognizes as the truth."[18]

On the heels of Hood's report, Johnston's friend and political ally, Senator Louis T. Wigfall, arrived in Smithfield. Congress having adjourned in Richmond, Wigfall was en route to his home in Texas. Accompanying the senator was his son Halsey, who, by a twist of fate, had served on Hood's staff. Johnston obliged the senator by appointing Halsey to his own staff. The fiery Wigfall had denounced Hood's report on the Senate floor and doubtless advised the proud and punctilious Johnston to seek redress. In any event, two days after Senator Wigfall's arrival, Johnston informed the adjutant general's office: "I have read General Hood's report, and will prefer charges against him as soon as I can find leisure. Please inform him." On April 4, Johnston notified Hood directly, but by then, time had almost run out for the Confederacy. The two men would have to wait until after

The Skeleton Army

the war when—by means of their memoirs—they could argue their case before the court of public opinion.[19]

Johnston was only one of several high-ranking Confederates nursing a grudge against Hood. Beauregard had been Hood's superior during the Tennessee campaign and, in a letter to the adjutant general, was sharply critical of his former subordinate. The worst imbroglio, however, involved General Hardee, who had served under Hood during the Atlanta campaign. Hardee and Hood exchanged belligerent correspondence over an insult that might have caused a duel had not spotty Southern mail service intervened. The dispute began with an article that appeared in the *Augusta Daily Constitutionalist* under the initials "G.W.S."—for Gustavus W. Smith, a Confederate general and relative of Hood. The author condemned Hardee's generalship while praising Hood's, and Hardee accused Hood of complicity. In his final letter to Hardee, Hood demanded an apology, to which "Old Reliable" replied there was no need for one. Because of the poor Southern mail service just after the war, Hardee's reply probably never reached its intended recipient, and each man was thereby satisfied that he had the last word in the affair.[20]

On April 1, Johnston engaged Robert E. Lee in correspondence of a far different sort. "Do you think that conference between us would be advantageous?" he inquired. "If so, I'll go to your headquarters." Lee answered: "I think what you propose advisable if you can come on." Circumstances would prevent them from meeting, however, and force them to act independently—a situation they had sought to avoid at all costs.[21]

All Fools' Day proved to be as raucous in the Confederates' camps as it was in the Federals'. "Many are the attempts to 'fool' some unsuspecting brother," Col. William C. P. Breckinridge wrote his wife. "Being no great respecter of rank or person, they have tried various tricks upon me—thus far I have been too watchful." Breckinridge decided to play a trick of his own and allowed rumors to circulate that another officer was to assume command of his cavalry brigade. "The tale was gravely told," Breckinridge noted. "[T]he couriers mournfully confirmed hints & innuendo—I gave some encouragement to it! & the April fool was believed; and for two hours a great commotion stirred the camp. It proved in some degree my own standing with the command."[22]

Camp life varied little between Smithfield and Goldsboro—with the difference that supplies were more varied and plentiful at the latter place. For most Confederates, soap and new uniforms and accoutrements were rare luxuries. Yet state warehouses in Raleigh bulged with goods reserved for Tar Heel soldiers, most of whom served in Virginia. Many of the Confederates complained that the Smithfield area "is not verry good country to soldier in." They found the region flat, marshy, and thinly settled, with long stretches of pine barren. "'Tis a sad thought to have to spend a lovely spring in such a desolate country," lamented a nature-loving Tennessean. "[S]carcely a bird is to be seen or heard—not a flower, not even a wildflower unlocks its fragrant store—no beautiful lawns through which to walk—no broad meadows—nothing to elicit admiration." For some soldiers, the absence of beautiful scenery was the least of their complaints. "Soldiering in these piney woods is more disagreeable than any I have yet experienced," complained one soot-begrimed officer. Texan Robert Hughes noted: "We are all nearly as black as negroes from the pine smoke. The whole country has been burned of[f] since we came here. Everything is as black as tar." [23]

For all their complaining, the Confederates enjoyed their three-week halt at Smithfield. One veteran recalled that "[h]orse racing now was the order of the day," with men of all ranks and from all branches of service participating. The horses varied as much in size and station as their riders, ranging from burly draft animals to the sleek, splendid mounts of generals. "Out in a large old field every day thousands of soldiers and civilians, with a sprinkling of the fair ladies of the surrounding country, would congregate to witness the excitement of the race course." The competition was fierce: "Confederate money by the handfuls changed owners every day." [24]

Card playing was another popular pastime. "Our gambling went on night and day," wrote Lt. R. M. Collins of Granbury's Texas brigade. "Fires made of those big, fat pine-knots gave lots of good light, and we would sit around on the ground in squads of two and four, and stack up our Confederate money at poker like lords." Collins noted that Confederate money was "plentiful," though almost worthless. Much to the delight of Collins and his fellow Texans, resin was no less plentiful in the pine woods surrounding their camp. "We all nearly wore ourselves out chewing 'rosum,'" Collins recalled. "It was the first time we had ever found it in bewildering profusion, and we just chewed like sheep." [25]

The halt near Smithfield also saw the resumption of revival meetings. Many troops spent their free time reading books and newspapers. Victor Hugo's *Les Misérables* was a particular favorite among the soldiers, who inevitably dubbed it "Lee's Miserables." Among other pastimes, some men swam or bathed in the Neuse River, some sang in glee clubs, and a lucky few went on leave to Raleigh. [26]

Extended rest also meant the resumption of unit drills, inspections, and reviews. The exercises were thought to improve unit cohesion and bolster morale, but one review convinced Capt. Bromfield Ridley that the end was

The Skeleton Army

near. "I witnessed to-day the saddest spectacle of my life," Ridley noted on April 4,

> the review of the skeleton Army of Tennessee, that but one year ago was replete with men, and now filed by with tattered garments, worn out shoes, bare-footed and ranks so depleted that each color was supported by only thirty or forty men. . . . The march was so slow—colors tattered and torn with bullets—that it looked like a funeral procession. The countenance of every spectator . . . was depressed and dejected, and the solemn, stern look of the soldiery was so impressive—Oh! It is beginning to look dark in the east, gloomy in the west, and like almost a lost hope when we reflect upon the review of to-day!

David Copeland of Kennedy's South Carolina brigade also witnessed the review: "I think a great many of our men are low in spirits[,] for the army of Tenesee is in bad condition for the present campaign. [O]ur Brigade I believe has moor life in it than all of the Tenesee army."[27]

Many Confederates, however, did not regard the cause as irretrievably lost, and some even saw a solution to the Confederacy's manpower shortage: recruiting black soldiers. A congressional bill authorizing the arming of slaves (and their conditional emancipation) had narrowly passed one month before. On this issue the troops were more in accord than the Southern politicians, many of whom grudgingly conceded the necessity—while dreading the consequences—of arming blacks to fight the Yankees. "A wonderful change upon the subject is going on all over the army," wrote Colonel Breckinridge of Wheeler's cavalry, "& the soldiers are not only becoming willing but advocates. . . . I have declared from the first that between success without slavery or failure with slavery I had no hesitation in choosing." Lt. W. A. Johnson of the 2nd South Carolina took a similarly pragmatic view: "Guess we had as well let the negroes fight on our side for their freedom, as for the enemy to let them fight on their side for the same purpose." Although Maj. Walter Clark of the Junior Reserves had opposed the bill, he regarded it as his duty to support the new law. "Let Negro fight negro," Clark coldly reasoned.[28]

Confederates such as Lt. R. M. Collins perceived the arming of slaves as a means for advancement. Believing that he had earned a colonel's commission by virtue of having commanded a company for most of the war, Collins applied to the secretary of war for authorization "to raise a regiment of North Carolina Confederate buck negroes." Johnston suggested to Lee that the first black recruits be used as substitutes for extra duty men, adding that he "should be very glad to get some thousands" for that purpose. Unfortunately for Johnston, Collins, and the rest of the Confederacy, the war would end before their requests could be acted upon.[29]

On April 4, Beauregard (who was then at Greensboro) learned from President Davis that Richmond and Petersburg had fallen. Wiring from Danville, Davis informed Beauregard that he had not heard from Lee since the evacuation of the Confederate capital two days before. Word soon spread to Raleigh and Smithfield. Oddly enough, Johnston learned from a press dispatch rather than through official channels. He wired Secretary of War John C. Breckinridge for confirmation but received instead a message from his old nemesis, President Davis, informing him that Breckinridge was not at Danville, and that Davis had not heard from Lee since the evacuation. The president knew only that Lee was heading toward Amelia Court House. "We have had rumors of hard fighting," Davis wrote. "No official intelligence has reached me." The president had sent a courier to Lee and expected to hear from the general soon. Meanwhile, Davis suggested, Johnston should govern his army's movements according to his knowledge of Lee's plans. But "Old Joe" was as ignorant of Lee's intentions as Davis. Johnston also had to remain focused on Sherman, who was certain to march to Grant's assistance. It now appeared that Lee and Johnston must combine near Danville or face destruction in detail.[30]

News of the Confederate capital's fall caused morale to plummet in Johnston's army. *"Bad news from Richmond!"* was staff officer Maj. John Johnson's terse comment. "The affairs of the Confederacy are in worse plight than ever," lamented William Johnson of the 1st South Carolina Artillery. "The only consoling thought, in viewing them, is that the affair must soon be settled, and my candid opinion is that, without foreign aid, we are ruined." Capt. Bromfield Ridley's reaction was scarcely less despairing: "The shades of sorrow are gathering upon us—horrible rumors! We, today, have heard of the distressing news that the fall of Richmond took place the [second] day of the month. . . . Heavens, the gloom and how terrible our feelings!" Some soldiers expressed relief, however, for they believed that the Confederate capital had been held longer than was prudent. "I wish [Richmond] had been given up long since," wrote Surgeon D. G. Godwin, who nevertheless conceded that "the moral effect for the present, is all that I dread." Yet a Tennessee cavalryman in Wheeler's Corps noted a more positive reaction among his comrades. "The spirit of our troops, so far as my observation extends, is in no wise depressed by our late disaster in Virginia, if indeed it is a disaster," he contended. "The boys say, now that Richmond is gone up, we will quit trying to hold any one place to

The Skeleton Army

the sacrifice of every other consideration—that our armies will be concentrated, and under the lead of our two great Generals, Lee and Johnston, will march to victory." Lt. W. A. Johnson of the 2nd South Carolina reacted to the news with grim defiance: "The capture of Richmond seems to be conceded. [But] we are not whipped yet."[31]

Johnston now expected Sherman to march immediately for Virginia. "Old Joe" alerted Hampton and ordered him to damage the railroads as close to Goldsboro as possible. In case Sherman advanced up the Weldon Railroad, Johnston ordered the bridges across the Roanoke at Gaston and Weldon burned. He also directed his impressment and commissary officers to sweep the region of livestock and provisions. For four years, the area between Goldsboro and Weldon had remained relatively untouched by "the hard hand of war," and the fact that the inhabitants were suffering at the hands of their own soldiery made their misfortune even more difficult to bear. "[T]his forced patriotism is not the thing," wrote Catherine Edmondston, whose family's Halifax County plantations were visited by several collection details. "[It] is not the way to treat a free & generous people, & ere long hearts will be alienated away from the Government & system that thus tramples on our rights, our feelings, & our sacred honor." The bitter irony of the Edmondstons' "forced patriotism" was that Sherman bypassed their neighborhood.[32]

More bad news reached Smithfield on April 6 in the form of a dispatch announcing the fall of Selma, Alabama. Still there was no word from Virginia. "What are General Lee's position and condition?" a frustrated Joe Johnston asked Brig. Gen. H. H. Walker at Danville. "I hear nothing of him."[33]

"Great rejoicing among us tonight—Victory! Victory!" Federal staff officer C. C. Platter jotted in his diary on April 6. Allan Morgan Geer of the 20th Illinois noted: "Glorious news Richmond ours at last. We believe Sherman would have taken it sooner, but all hail to Grant for his 25,000 prisoners and 500 [captured] guns." Though disappointed at not taking part in the capture of Richmond, few of Sherman's troops begrudged the victory to their comrades in the eastern army. "We had all hoped we would be sharers in the glory of the fall of the Rebel Capital & strong hold," wrote Charles Brown Tompkins of the 55th Illinois, "but it is much better as it is, for the western army can boast of enough victories without this one and the bitter feeling among eastern troops against western ones would have been increased if we had been participants in *their* glory of taking Richmond." Many Twentieth Corps veterans "were especially rejoiced that the Army of the Potomac won the crowning glory of the war," wrote Capt. Julian W. Hinkley of the 3rd Wisconsin, for they regarded the eastern army as their "alma mater," having served in its ranks earlier in the war.[34]

Surprisingly, some officers and men in Sherman's army expressed disappointment in the fall of Richmond. "I do not feel much rejoiced," wrote Twentieth Corps division commander Alpheus Williams. "I think if Lee had held on a little longer it would be better for us, as we should have made a junction with Grant. Now the whole Rebel army, I fear, will get between us." An officer in the 10th Illinois noted that one of his men "says he's getting scared; the war will soon be over, and he'll be out of a job!" Others were at first skeptical. "Our regiment drew a barrel of beans over the victory, but the news was too good to be true and was . . . not generally credited," observed a private in the 47th Ohio. Most Federals overcame their initial skepticism, however. A soldier in the 12th Wisconsin noted that "[t]ime and again" he and his comrades had heard the announcement that Richmond was taken, only to learn that the rumor proved false. "But . . . this time there seemed no doubt about the matter," he recalled. "[I]t was just what we expected."[35]

Sgt. Francis McAdams of the 113th Ohio noted that Brig. Gen. John G. Mitchell read the news to his brigade, which responded with "such cheering as seldom vibrates on mortal ears. The men are in a state of excitement bordering on insanity." Rufus Mead of the 5th Connecticut described the army's celebration for his "Dear Folks at Home": "Such cheering, shouting, gun firing, band playing, &c I never heard before. Every body was wild most & some being particularly 'Oh be joyful' [that is, drunk] kept the country awake with their cheers till long after I was asleep." The celebrating continued throughout the night of April 6 and into the next morning. Using long fuses, soldiers exploded canteens they had filled with powder and buried in the ground, and launched colorful signal rockets into the nighttime sky. "Not one day sufficed to express the sentiments of general joy," recalled William McIntosh of the 22nd Wisconsin. "All next day bursts of music were interrupted by spontaneous cheers, and again the humid night air was burdened by outcries and the thunder of cannon."[36]

Despite the festive atmosphere, some veterans regarded April 6–7 as an occasion for somber reflection. "Three years ago today," Lt. Col. Peter Ege of the 34th Illinois wrote on April 7, "the [34th] was in its first action—the name of Shiloh will ever be remembered by those who were there with me—how many alas are now on earth no more. Since then . . . the Regt. has been in many Battles and Skirmishes—but two of the old officers remain, myself & Capt. Slaughter."[37]

If the army's highest-ranking veteran of Shiloh—General Sherman—

reflected on the anniversary of that battle or what had transpired since, he left no record of it, probably because he was too preoccupied with the upcoming campaign. After receiving news of Richmond's capture on the morning of April 6, Sherman plotted a new route for his grand army. "Uncle Billy" echoed General Williams in wishing that Grant had moved "a few days later or I a few days sooner," for he now feared that his adversary might slip off to the south. "I feel confident we can whip Joe Johnston quick if he stops," Sherman wrote, "but he may travel back towards Georgia and I don't want to follow him again on that long road." Scrapping his original plan, the Union commander shifted his destination from Richmond to Raleigh. He now supposed that Lee and Johnston would succeed in combining near the Virginia line.[38]

On April 7, Sherman outlined his revised plan to Howard, Slocum, Schofield, and Kilpatrick. At daybreak on April 10, Slocum's wing would take the direct road to Smithfield and Raleigh, while Howard's wing would march to the north via Pikeville, Lowell's Factory, Whitley's Mill, and Pine Level, reinforcing Slocum if the enemy opposed him at Smithfield. Kilpatrick's cavalry would swing out to the south and west via Bentonville and Elevation and then cross the Neuse River. Once across, Kilpatrick would damage the North Carolina Railroad near Gulley's Station "to prevent its use for a day or so—and then act against the flanks of the enemy should he retreat on Raleigh." Sherman urged his cavalry commander to "act boldly and even rashly now"—provocative words for the impetuous Kilpatrick—"for this is the time to strike quick and strong. We must get possession of Raleigh before Lee and Johnston have time to confer and make new combinations forced on them by the loss of their capital and the defeat of their principal army about Petersburg." Schofield's Tenth Corps would follow Kilpatrick and his Twenty-third Corps would accompany Slocum.[39]

Although Sherman deemed it to be of the utmost importance "to strike quick and strong," he remained at Goldsboro until April 10, believing that Johnston would wait for him at Smithfield. Regardless of Johnston's plans, by waiting in Goldsboro for three days Sherman gave his enemy the very breathing room he intended to deny him. The Union commander had no logistical reason to wait, because provisions could easily have been forwarded to the army. It would appear that Sherman remained at Goldsboro in slavish adherence to his timetable instead of pursuing Johnston.[40]

On April 7, Sherman learned that Grant was pursuing Lee toward Burke's Station and Danville. An even more encouraging message from Grant arrived the next day. That evening, a crowd of several thousand soldiers gathered before Sherman's headquarters, "cheering loud and long," noted Sgt. Henry Clay Weaver of the 16th Kentucky. When their commander finally stepped outside, the men yelled, "Uncle Bill, make us a speech!" "Tell us the latest news!" Sherman replied that soldiers do not make speeches; the men refused to be put off, however, insisting that generals were notorious speechmakers. Sherman told them to "wait until the close of the war," when he would make "a good long speech." "Boys," he said, "I haven't got time to make you a speech, but I will have the latest dispatch from General Grant read to you."[41]

Sherman motioned one of his staff officers forward. Dispatch in hand, the officer mounted the gatepost and read:

> All indications now are that Lee will attempt to reach Danville with the remnant of his force. Sheridan, who was up with him last night, reports all that is left, horse, foot, and dragoons, at 20,000, much demoralized. We hope to reduce the number one-half. I shall push on to [Burke's Station] and if a stand is made at Danville will in a very few days go there. If you can possibly do so push on from where you are and let us see if we cannot finish the job with Lee's and Johnston's armies. Whether it will be better for you to strike for Greensborough or nearer to Danville you will be better able to judge when you receive this. Rebel armies are now the only strategic points to strike at.
>
> U. S. GRANT,
> *Lieutenant-General*

The crowd responded by cheering for ten minutes. "Believe me there was no sleep in camp that night," recalled Daniel Baker of the 1st Missouri Engineers.[42]

Sherman wrote a long reply to Grant, promising to "bear in mind your plain and unmistakable point that 'the rebel armies are now the strategic points to strike at.'" He intended to pursue Johnston toward Greensboro and then force him north toward Danville. "It is to our interest to let Lee and Johnston come together," Sherman noted, "just as a billiard player would nurse the balls when he has them in a nice place." He made yet another attempt to secure "Little Phil's" cavalry: "If Sheridan don't run his horses off their legs and you can spare him for a week or so let him feel down for me, and I think he can make a big haul of horses. Tell him I make him a free gift of all the blooded stock of North Carolina, including Wade Hampton, whose pedigree and stud are of high repute." Later that night, Sherman sent an urgent dispatch to Morehead City: "Get a message to General Grant, at any cost, that I will push Joe Johnston to the death."[43]

On the morning of April 7, Raleigh buzzed with news that General Johnston was holding a grand review near Smithfield. Among those planning

The Skeleton Army

to attend was the editor of the *Daily Confederate,* Duncan Kirkland McRae. A former attorney, the forty-six-year-old McRae had once enjoyed a reputation as the most formidable trial lawyer in the state. He had served as a U.S. consul in France during the Franklin Pierce administration and later ran unsuccessfully for governor of North Carolina against John W. Ellis. In 1861 Ellis appointed him colonel of the 5th North Carolina. McRae led his regiment at Manassas and Williamsburg—in the latter battle, two-thirds of his command fell in a courageous but futile charge. He commanded the remnant of the 5th during the Seven Days campaign and assumed command of Garland's Brigade at South Mountain. McRae's hard-luck brigade was outflanked both there and at Sharpsburg, where he was wounded. Suffering from ill-health and disappointed at not receiving a general's star, McRae resigned his commission in the fall of 1862. Governor Vance utilized McRae's diplomatic skills by sending him to England as a purchasing agent for the state's blockade-running trade. In 1864 McRae returned to North Carolina and established the *Raleigh Confederate,* the Old North State's foremost pro-Davis daily.[44]

In addition to McRae, a few dozen young ladies from Raleigh—"among them several of the most beautiful and attractive"—boarded the train to Smithfield. By far the most noteworthy passenger was Governor Vance himself, who in postwar years would be remembered as the "War Governor of the South." Like McRae a lawyer by training, Vance was an adept politician, having served in the North Carolina House of Commons and the U.S. House of Representatives before he was thirty. Now one month shy of his thirty-fifth birthday, Vance was serving his second term as governor. He brought a spirit of boundless energy and enthusiasm to his high office. The youthful governor had little patience with those unable or unwilling to keep pace with him, once vowing to "cut loose from some of the old fogies" and rely upon "men nearer my own age & notion of things."[45]

Much of Vance's political success was due to his brilliance as a stump speaker. A staunch Union Whig before the war, Vance had used his considerable oratorical skills to plead for restraint in his home state during the secession crisis the winter of 1860–61. When the critical moment arrived, however, his transformation from Unionist to Secessionist was instantaneous. While addressing "a large and excited crowd" in April 1861, Vance had thrust his arm upward, "pleading for peace and the Union of our Fathers." But at that moment, the news arrived that Fort Sumter had been fired on and President Lincoln had called for 75,000 volunteers to put down the rebellion. "When my hand came down from that impassioned gesticulation," Vance noted, "it fell slowly and sadly by the side of a Secessionist."[46]

Governor Zebulon B. Vance
(North Carolina Division of
Archives and History)

With war now certain, Vance abandoned the stump circuit and returned to his native Buncombe County to enlist as a private in the "Rough and Ready Guards." Soon after his enlistment, Vance's company elected him captain, and on August 27, he became colonel of the 26th North Carolina. Vance led the 26th in the 1862 battles of New Bern and Malvern Hill. On June 16 of that year, he agreed to become the Conservative Party candidate for governor and went on to win a landslide victory over his Confederate Party opponent. As governor, Vance proved to be both an able administrator and an adroit politician, steering a difficult course between supporting the Confederate government's conscription, impressment, and tithing programs and defending Tar Heels whose rights were violated by the Davis administration. Thanks to the Old North State's blockade-running efforts —Vance having arranged the purchase of shares in several blockade runners—North Carolina soldiers ranked among the best-equipped in the Confederate army. Vance also won the gratitude of his constituents by providing food and other necessities to needy soldiers' families.[47]

In the gubernatorial race of 1864, Vance's opponent was the man most responsible for his election two years earlier: William W. Holden, the editor of the *Raleigh Standard* and the Peace Party candidate. As the war dragged on through 1862, Holden had concluded that the South could not win the struggle on the battlefield. By 1863 an outspoken peace advocate,

The Skeleton Army

Holden denounced the Davis administration for failing to negotiate with the North, and in early 1864 he called for a state convention to discuss peace terms. Although Holden never specified the terms, it appeared to Vance and his supporters that the *Standard* editor would settle for less than Southern independence. At first Vance hesitated to repudiate his former ally, but in February 1864 he began a statewide speaking tour against Holden. While Vance appealed directly to the people, Holden attacked Vance in the pages of the *Standard,* mindful that he could not match his more charismatic opponent on the hustings. The 1864 election was an even more decisive victory for Vance than the 1862 contest had been; the governor now had his mandate to fight on.[48]

No sooner had Vance received that mandate than the fall of Atlanta convinced him of an awful truth. "It shows what I have always believed," Vance wrote his friend and mentor, David L. Swain, "that the great *popular heart* is not now & never has been in this war." Vance cited the failure of Georgia civilians to disrupt Sherman's 500-mile line of communications, and their apparent submission to the enemy. "It was a revolution of the politicians not the people," Vance continued. "[It] was fought at first by the natural enthusiasm of our young men, and has been kept going by State & sectional pride assisted by that bitterness of feeling produced by the cruelties & brutalities of the enemy."[49]

As 1865 opened, Vance realized that the war was lost. "I frankly confess to you," he wrote Georgia governor Joseph E. Brown, "that I regard as our chief aim at this time to hold the demoralized and trembling fragments of society and law together and prevent them from dropping to pieces until the rapidly hastening end of our struggle shall be developed." The end was indeed approaching. On January 15, Fort Fisher fell, closing Wilmington to blockade-running traffic and severing the Confederacy from the rest of the world. On February 1, Sherman began his inexorable advance through South Carolina. Reports of widespread destruction and pillaging soon reached the Old North State, terrorizing the populace. Meanwhile, rumors of a peace conference between Union and Confederate representatives buoyed Southerners' spirits, particularly in North Carolina, where many hoped that a negotiated settlement would enable their state to avert the fate of South Carolina. All such hopes crumbled, however, when news arrived of the failure of the Hampton Roads Conference.[50]

On February 14, Governor Vance responded by drafting "A Proclamation to the People of North Carolina." The failure of peace negotiations resulted from Lincoln's refusal to compromise, Vance declared, indicating that submission to Northern rule would lead only to subjugation, death, and destruction. The governor painted a bleak picture of a conquered

South: millions of former slaves would be "turned loose at once in our midst; our lands confiscated and sold out to pay the cost of our subjugation . . . ; our women, children, and old men reduced to beggary . . . ; our mutilated and diseased soldiers starving in rags from door to door . . . , whilst the gallows grows weary under the burden of wisest statesmen and bravest defenders." Vance condemned those who wanted to surrender: "Great God! Is there a man in all this honorable, high spirited, and noble Commonwealth so steeped in every conceivable meanness, so blackened with all the guilt of treason, or so damned with all the leprosy of cowardice as to say: 'Yes, we will submit to all this; and whilst there yet remains half a million men amongst us able to resist.' " Exhorting the people to "lay down all party bitterness" and close ranks against the common foe, Vance suggested that they convene county meetings "and let the whole world, and especially our enemies, see how a free people can meet a proposition for their absolute submission to the will of their conquerors." A small but vocal minority of North Carolinians responded to Vance's appeal, holding meetings even as Sherman entered the state. The governor spoke at several of the rallies.[51]

Despite the modest success of the county meetings, Vance encountered increasing evidence of demoralization and disaffection in the Old North State. A petition signed by nearly 500 women begged the governor to take immediate steps "for the establishment of peace. Let this horrible war end! Let blood cease to flow!" In late February, General Lee requested Vance's cooperation in stemming Tar Heel desertions, which had reached an alarming rate. Lee believed the problem was "occasioned to a considerable extent by letters written to the soldiers by their friends at home."[52]

Vance also had his critics, the most vocal of whom were Holden and the peace advocates and McRae and the "destructives" (so-called by Holden because they favored Davis's suicidal pro-war policy). Whereas Holden accused Vance of supporting a war that could not be won, McRae criticized the governor for opposing such necessary war measures as suspension of the writ of habeas corpus. Despite the two-front journalistic assault, Vance enjoyed the support of his own party organ, the *Raleigh Conservative,* and the grudging respect of the "destructives," who conceded the governor's good intentions.[53]

Although Vance was committed to fighting to the bitter end, North Carolina's elder statesman, Confederate senator William Alexander Graham, hoped to negotiate his state out of the war. The sixty-year-old Graham was a former U.S. senator, governor of North Carolina, secretary of the navy, and Whig vice presidential candidate. He first broached the subject of peace with Vance on March 20. The senator had left Richmond on

The Skeleton Army

March 17 convinced that Southern independence was "perfectly hopeless," that the Davis administration offered no prospect of peace so long as it could wage war, and that state governments must, therefore, initiate their own peace negotiations. According to Graham, he told a "surprized" and "incredulous" Vance

> that Richmond would fall in less than thirty days, and would be followed probably by a rout, or dispersion of Lee's army for want of food, if for no other cause; that the Confed. Gov't had no plan or policy beyond this event, although it was generally anticipated; that I had reason to believe Gen'l Lee was anxious for an accommodation; that Johnston had not, and could not raise a sufficient force to encounter Sherman; that I had conferred with the Pres't and found him, though in an anxious frame of mind, constrained by the scruple that he could not "commit suicide" by treating his government out of existence.

Davis had also told Graham that the Federal government refused to specify peace terms for individual Southern states.[54]

Graham said that most of his congressional colleagues were "anxious for a settlement" but hesitated to act out of "false pride" or for fear of betraying earlier promises. Rather, they hoped that someone else might take the initiative—a suggestion Vance refused to heed. Graham likened the situation to the dilemma facing a besieged fortress: was it better "to capitulate on terms, or hold out, & be put to the sword, on a false point of honor?" Though shaken by Graham's candid assessment, the governor opposed taking separate action and promised only to convene the Council of State.[55]

Graham next met with Vance on April 6. The governor said that the Council of State could not agree on a course of action, but that Tar Heel congressman John A. Gilmer had recommended communicating with Sherman. Graham told Vance to notify Davis first, but he advised the governor to remain "in a position to act independently of the President." The senator also suggested that Vance call an emergency session of the General Assembly, but once again, Vance promised only to consult the Council of State. Although the governor still hesitated to take the first step toward a separate peace, Graham believed that "since the fall of Richmond he has a truer conception of the situation."[56]

Vance invited Graham to attend the grand review the next day, but the senator declined, "not seeing any good to be accomplished there." Though Graham respected Johnston, he dismissed most of the general's subordinates as "drunken men of desperate fortunes, who have no idea but to continue the war indefinitely."[57]

On the morning of April 7, the train carrying Vance, McRae, and the young ladies arrived at its destination. The party boarded ambulances for the ride to General Hardee's headquarters. McRae noted that their unannounced appearance surprised the general, "not so much so, however, as to be forced to retreat—though enough so to prevent *our* repulse," the editor joked. After a brief rest, the civilians followed Hardee and his staff to the reviewing field. The command on review was Hardee's Corps, with Johnston and Vance presiding. This proved to be the second review of the corps in five days. "I thought it rather too much of a good thing to be paraded twice in a week," wrote Lt. Col. James Welsman Brown of the 2nd South Carolina Artillery, "but the sight of the girls soon drove such unsoldierly thoughts away." The young women cheered loudest for the Tar Heels of Hoke's Division, who in turn gave Vance three rousing cheers. McRae called the review "a fine martial display. No eye could look without emotions of pride upon the hardy and bronzed veterans, with their pierced and tattered banners, with precise step and head erect . . . passing before their favorite commander." Many onlookers thought the review of Hardee's Corps a far greater success than the Army of Tennessee's review on April 4. "This shows what drilling will effect," Lieutenant Colonel Brown boasted.[58]

After the review, the generals and their guests attended a reception given by Hardee, where they were served ham biscuits, ginger cakes, and brandy and ice while a military band serenaded them. McRae noted that the guests included Generals Cheatham, Hill, Hoke, McLaws, and Taliaferro. Lieutenant Colonel Brown also attended and, much to his delight, was introduced to several of the young ladies from Raleigh.[59]

After an hour or so, the party moved to General Hoke's headquarters, where Vance addressed the boys of the North Carolina Junior Reserves Brigade. "On this occasion he surpassed himself," McRae wrote of the governor's speech. The editor noted that the Junior Reserves "particularly relished" Vance's oratory. Boy soldier Ruff Collie later recalled that Vance exhorted his young audience to "fight till Hell freezes over!" Collie found this an unfortunate turn of phrase, for he and many comrades believed that the infernal regions were already a bit icy around the edges.[60]

Following Vance's speech, the governor's party traveled to a nearby farmhouse for a cotillion before returning to Raleigh. That night, Lieutenant Colonel Brown wrote in his diary: "This has been a notable day in my field experience." It would be the last grand review of the Confederate army, although few participants believed the end was so near.[61]

The end, in truth, was at hand. As Vance urged the boy soldiers to "fight till Hell freezes over," Grant was asking Lee to surrender "that portion of

The Skeleton Army

the Confederate States army known as the Army of Northern Virginia." While soldiers and civilians danced inside a Smithfield farmhouse, Lee replied: "I have received your note of this day. Though not entertaining the opinion you express on the hopelessness of further resistance on the part of the Army of Northern Virginia, I reciprocate your desire to avoid useless effusion of blood, and therefore before considering your proposition, ask the terms you will offer on condition of its surrender."[62]

Johnston knew nothing of the situation in Virginia. On April 8, he asked Gen. Samuel Cooper at Danville for news concerning Lee. "When you can communicate [with Lee] ask him how I can cooperate with him," Johnston wrote. "It is important that I be informed before Sherman moves." Presidential aide John Taylor Wood's reply indicated that there was still no official word from Lee. "All private accounts cheering," Wood noted, "and represent the army in good condition and spirits. Little straggling." He reported that Maj. Gen. Fitzhugh Lee's cavalry had defeated a large Federal force, capturing 1,000 prisoners. A subsequent dispatch from Secretary of War Breckinridge was less encouraging: "Straggling has been great and the situation is not favorable." Breckinridge stated that though Lee's army had met with "a serious reverse" on the afternoon of April 6, it apparently had put the Appomattox River between itself and the enemy, for he had heard "little firing" for the past two days. Breckinridge indicated that Lee still hoped to maneuver into North Carolina but could not determine "what route circumstances would permit him to take." This was Johnston's first intimation that Lee had encountered serious difficulty. Given the Davis party's apparent lack of concern, Johnston had no reason to suppose that "General Lee had been *driven* from the position he had held many months with so much skill and resolution."[63]

Meanwhile, a proclamation from President Davis appeared in the April 7 *Raleigh Confederate* and circulated through the camps near Smithfield. The tone was defiant and optimistic: "We have now entered upon a new phase of the struggle, the memory of which is to endure for all ages." No longer would the Confederacy be bound to defend its cities, "important but not vital" to its success. Davis exhorted his fellow Southerners to fight on until the Yankees abandoned the struggle. "Nothing is now needed to render our triumph certain, but the exhibition of our own unquenchable resolve. . . . Let us but will it, and we are free." The soldiers, no doubt weary of high-flown rhetoric, said little in regard to Davis's proclamation.[64]

Though unmoved by proclamations, the men found a more tangible reason for hopefulness: on April 7, the Army of the South numbered 30,424 officers and men—a one-week increase of about 5,500. Johnston commanded an army that was larger by half than the one that had fought at Bentonville three weeks earlier. Even so, Sherman's army also had increased by one-half and still outnumbered Johnston's three-to-one. But the knowledge that the armies of Lee and Johnston might yet combine encouraged most soldiers at Smithfield to remain with the colors.[65]

In early April, Johnston reorganized his army, which he renamed—to no one's surprise—the Army of Tennessee. The three infantry corps were commanded by Lieutenant Generals William J. Hardee, Alexander P. Stewart, and Stephen D. Lee, with Lt. Gen. Wade Hampton retaining command of the cavalry. The consolidation of numerous regiments and brigades left dozens of high-ranking officers without commands. A South Carolina soldier complained that the consolidation merely succeeded in "throwing out some of our best and bravest officers." Among the supernumeraries were four veteran division commanders: Generals Bate, Clayton, McLaws, and Taliaferro. Johnston also ordered the overhauling of his reserve artillery at Hillsborough, which was supervised by Hardee's capable chief of artillery, Col. Ambrosio J. Gonzales, a Cuban revolutionary-turned-Confederate. By consolidating the best draft animals and ordnance from a pool of sixteen batteries, Gonzales formed seven field-ready, four-gun batteries. Since the army's consolidation occurred on April 8–10, at the onset of a new campaign, most soldiers scarcely noticed the changes.[66]

Of far greater interest to Johnston's men were reports that Sherman's army was preparing to march. On April 8, Hampton informed Johnston that Sherman would advance toward Raleigh by the 10th. On the afternoon of April 9, "Old Joe" ordered his corps commanders to prepare to move the next day. When Hampton's expected warning arrived on the morning of April 10, Johnston notified Breckinridge: "Sherman is moving toward Raleigh, and we [are] falling back." Still there was no word from Lee and the Army of Northern Virginia.[67]

CHAPTER 4

THE FINAL SCENE OF THE DRAMA
IS AT HAND

On Monday, April 10, reveille sounded at 4:00 A.M. in the camps of Col. James L. Selfridge's Federal brigade. The men ate breakfast, took down their tents, packed their knapsacks, and by 5:30 were on the march for Raleigh. Led by the 123rd New York, Selfridge's four regiments had the advance of the Twentieth Corps column, which left its bivouac at Scottsville and passed through Goldsboro, heading west on the Neuse River Road. The day dawned cool and cloudy—a pleasant enough morning, though rain threatened.[1]

About four miles to the north, the Fourteenth Corps marched on the Stage Road. Brig. Gen. John G. Mitchell's brigade was the vanguard. The half-dozen regiments in Mitchell's command were well stocked with stores plundered from their sutler, Nick White, the evening before. "The sutler fought bravely," noted Edwin Payne of the 34th Illinois, "but after having one of his own cheeses bursted over his head and his eyes filled with sand, yielded to the inevitable and consoled himself with such philosophy as he could command."[2]

An onlooker in the Fourteenth Corps watched as General Slocum's headquarters train rumbled past with its splendid-looking teams and new wagon covers bearing the freshly painted legend, "HEADQUARTERS ARMY OF GEORGIA." On the congested backcountry roads, the march was stop-and-go much of the way. "The most tiresome thing in the world is to march a quarter of a mile & then stand & wait & wait until ones heart sinks into ones boots," lamented Lt. Col. Samuel Merrill of the 70th Indiana, a Twentieth Corps regiment near the rear of the column. "The rising at three & the retiring late is not so hard as the vexatious hitching halting poking

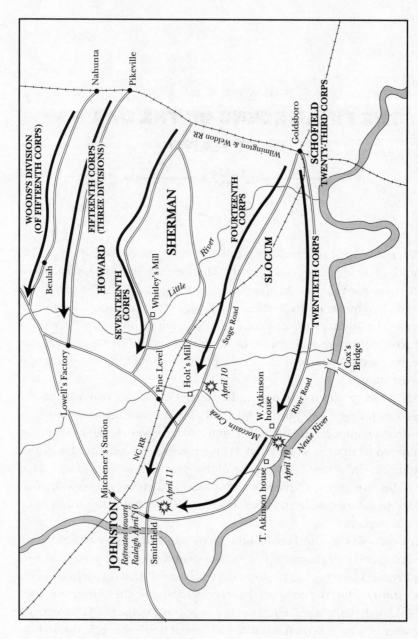

Map 2. Howard's and Slocum's wings advance from Goldsboro, April 10–11, 1865

along at a pace that would try the patience of a snail." To make matters worse, a light rain fell for most of the day. Merrill noted that his regiment finally crawled into camp at midnight, "wet & weary," having marched just ten miles.[3]

While the Fourteenth and Twentieth Corps of Slocum's wing crept west toward Smithfield, the Fifteenth and Seventeenth Corps of Howard's wing advanced northward at a similar pace along the Wilmington and Weldon Railroad. Howard's column had to wait two hours for the Twentieth Corps to pass, and then further delays ensued as the pioneers corduroyed long sections of muddy road. Most of the soldiers were loaded down with supplies they had drawn in preparation for the new campaign. "[W]e was positively ordered to draw two suits all around and even woolen blankets," complained Pvt. Hiram Matthew of the 66th Indiana, who preferred marching light. "[T]hey even told me i had to draw two pair of drawers and Caray [carry] them along. . . . they can make me draw them but they cant make me wear them."[4]

Once the road cleared, Charles Woods's division of the Fifteenth Corps marched to Nahunta, a village on the Weldon Railroad ten miles north of Goldsboro. General Howard had sent the division forward to screen the rest of his wing. Woods's advance skirmished occasionally with detachments of Wheeler's cavalry but met no determined resistance. The other three divisions of the Fifteenth Corps marched to Pikeville, a few miles south of Nahunta. The Seventeenth Corps, after marching northward in the rear of the Fifteenth Corps, turned west on the Little River Road to Whitley's Mill, where it bivouacked at 3:00 P.M. The Seventeenth Corps's advance skirmished with elements of Wheeler's cavalry but encountered no more opposition than had Woods's vanguard.[5]

Unfortunately for the advance units of Slocum's wing, the Confederate cavalry disputing their progress was far more stubborn and resourceful. At 9:30 A.M., after marching ten miles, the 123rd New York heard the familiar rattle of musketry in its front and was ordered to halt. Federal scouts soon galloped into sight with news of Rebel cavalry that refused to budge. Selfridge ordered Col. James C. Rogers of the 123rd New York to deploy two of his companies as skirmishers and resume the advance. The enemy's pickets were concealed behind trees at the far end of an open field, about a half-mile away. As the 123rd's skirmish line swept across the field, the Confederates opened fire and then fell back, nevertheless remaining within range of the advancing New Yorkers. After retreating a few miles, the Confederates halted at Moccasin Creek, forcing Colonel Rogers to deploy his entire regiment as skirmishers. Selfridge's remaining three regiments—the 141st

New York, 5th Connecticut, and 46th Pennsylvania—followed in line of battle.[6]

The 123rd New York faced the 1st South Carolina and 6th North Carolina cavalry regiments under the command of Col. John Logan Black. A thirty-four-year-old West Pointer who did not graduate, Black had led the 1st for most of the war and now found himself in his first independent command. Black had come full circle, for he and his regiment had served in Wade Hampton's Brigade in Virginia, Maryland, and Pennsylvania before their transfer to Charleston in March 1864. Following the evacuation of Charleston one year later, Black rejoined Hampton in North Carolina, and the 1st South Carolina Cavalry was attached to Logan's Brigade of Butler's Division. Black characterized the morale of his men as "not bad," which proved good enough for the Carolinians to offer the New Yorkers a respectable fight.[7]

Colonel Black also commanded Capt. Edwin L. Halsey's Battery of four twelve-pound Napoleons, which he posted on the west bank of Moccasin Creek, near his headquarters at the Thomas Atkinson house. Black had earlier ordered some of his troopers to construct a barricade on the east bank, near the home of William Atkinson, Thomas's twin brother. Black's skirmishers made a brief stand at the barricade before withdrawing across the creek, tearing planks from the two bridges as they fell back. The Confederate colonel also directed his men to break the milldam on his left to flood the creek and surrounding swamps.[8]

Meanwhile, the 123rd New York trotted into view, the men winded and sweating from their two-mile pursuit across fields, through thickets, and over fences while carrying full packs. In obedience to Colonel Rogers's orders, they waded the swamp, the cold water coming up to their waists. When the New Yorkers reached the first channel of the creek, they discovered that it was too deep to ford. Braving a hot fire, the men crossed the bridge on whatever loose planks they could find. Then they plunged into the swamp again, the water proving so deep that some had to cross with their cartridge boxes slung over their shoulders. At the second channel, the Federals repeated their perilous bridge crossing. As they plunged once more into the swamp for the final dash to the west bank, the men of the 123rd cheered before splashing onto dry ground, driving the Confederates before them. By this time, one gun of Capt. Thomas S. Sloan's Battery E, Pennsylvania Light Artillery, had unlimbered on the east bank and opened fire on the retreating Southerners. Colonel Black ordered Halsey's Battery to reply in kind and instructed his troopers to withdraw to the artillery at Thomas Atkinson's house. Black then directed his command to fall back toward Smithfield, ending the skirmish at Moccasin Creek.[9]

Black was proud of his 800-man cavalry force for delaying the progress of the Twentieth Corps. Even so, the Federal advance made fifteen miles by the end of the day. According to Colonel Rogers of the 123rd New York, the Confederates lost two men killed and eight wounded in the skirmish; Rogers reported his own loss as one killed and three wounded, and division commander Alpheus Williams noted that a member of his escort was mortally wounded. The lone fatality of the 123rd, Pvt. William H. Toohey of Company K, was one of the two last infantrymen in Sherman's army to be killed in action.[10]

While the 123rd New York skirmished with Colonel Black's troopers along the River Road, the Fourteenth Corps's advance clashed with a second contingent of Butler's Division on the Stage Road several miles to the north. The Confederates fell back to Holt's Mill on Moccasin Creek and dared the Yankees to cross. John Mitchell's brigade of Morgan's division had the lead. Mitchell sent forward the 108th Ohio, closely followed by the 113th Ohio. Much as Colonel Black had done, the Southern troopers cut the dam at Holt's Mill and flooded the creek. When the Federal skirmishers began crossing the stream, a section of Rebel artillery treated them to a volley of case shot. The shrapnel overshot its mark and headed straight for the 34th Illinois, which had just reached the crest of a hill overlooking the creek. Before the startled Illinoisans could react, the deadly projectiles screamed past them. "What a relief it was," recalled Sgt. Lyman Widney of the 34th, "to realize . . . that no holes had been shot through our bodies and that our heads and limbs still remained in their proper position." While the Confederate gunners frantically reloaded their pieces, Lt. Col. Peter Ege ordered the men of the 34th to seek cover in the woods to the right of the road and behind the brow of the hill. When the Rebel guns fired a second volley, the case shot rattled harmlessly against the trees above the Federals' heads.[11]

Second Division commander Brig. Gen. James D. Morgan soon appeared at the front, accompanied by his staff. The men of the 34th Illinois were relieved to learn that Morgan had ordered Brig. Gen. William Vandever's brigade to the right to outflank the Rebels while Mitchell held them in check. As Mitchell's other regiments arrived, Sergeant Widney noted the solemn faces of the men in the ranks, who, unaware of Vandever's flanking maneuver, thought they were being deployed for a frontal assault. "Not a careless or indifferent countenance was to be seen," Widney observed. "The silence that pervaded the ranks, and the tightly compressed lips, indicated the thought that oppressed each heart, the thought of falling at the very threshold of peace." A somber-looking lieutenant marched past, and seeing General Morgan, thought he had better make a good impression.

Turning to his slow-moving company, the lieutenant shouted, "Come, buck along men, buck along." The order was followed by an explosion, Widney recalled, not of shell, but of Morgan's laughter. "Did you ever hear such a command in your life?" the general howled. According to Widney, "the lieutenant had passed out of sight long before [Morgan] recovered his war visage."[12]

Meanwhile, left wing commander Henry Slocum rode to the front to investigate the delay and was pleased to find that Morgan had the situation well in hand. "Hope to take tea at Smithfield to-morrow," Slocum informed Sherman, who was traveling with the Twentieth Corps.[13]

Outnumbered and outflanked, the Confederates retreated, but not before inflicting several casualties (two killed and five wounded) on the Yankees. The two fatalities were Capt. Franz Fleischmann of Company H, 108th Ohio (probably the last infantry officer in Sherman's army killed in action), and Pvt. John Bensell of Company A, 113th Ohio, who vies with William Toohey of the 123rd New York for the unhappy distinction of being the last of Sherman's infantrymen to die on the firing line.[14]

On the west bank of Moccasin Creek, Sergeant Widney and several of his men came to a cabin that had stood between the opposing skirmish lines. The pine boards were perforated with bullet holes. Inside they found a mother and her three small children huddled in a corner of the cabin, expecting a renewal of the fight at any moment. The terrified woman told Widney that when the shooting started, she used her body as a shield to protect her children while bullets whistled past and splinters flew in all directions. It took considerable effort on the part of the Illinois sergeant to persuade the woman that the skirmish was over.[15]

In contrast to the vanguard of Howard's and Slocum's wings, the left—or southern—flank of Sherman's grand army passed a quiet day on the march. Kilpatrick's cavalry left its camps around Mount Olive at daylight and marched twenty-five miles to Bentonville, using the same roads it had traveled on three weeks before. One of Kilpatrick's brigade commanders, Bvt. Brig. Gen. Smith D. Atkins, noted that the countryside he passed through was desolate, most of the inhabitants having fled after the Battle of Bentonville. Kilpatrick intended to strike the North Carolina Railroad between Raleigh and Smithfield, damage the road, and, if possible, cut off a portion of Johnston's retreating army.[16]

Following Kilpatrick was the Tenth Corps of General Schofield's Army of the Ohio, commanded by Maj. Gen. Alfred H. Terry. Breaking camp at Faison's Depot, the Tenth Corps set out amid loud cheering and the music of several brass bands, accompanied by hundreds of refugees—white as well as black.[17]

Terry's corps passed through the Bentonville battleground on April 11. "The marks of bullet, shot and shell were thick on shrub and tree," recalled Surgeon James Mowris of the 117th New York. "[A]t a certain height from the surface, there was scarcely a twig or bough that did not present its transverse groove, or its abrupt termination." Chaplain Turner of the 1st U.S. Colored Troops thought he could discern a marked superiority in Federal as opposed to Confederate earthworks. "If Johnston's military genius as displayed at Bentonville constitutes him a great general, then I know I am a greater one," Turner commented. Surgeon Mowris noted that Bentonville consisted of "scarcely a dozen small unpainted weather-beaten buildings." Several homes sheltered Confederate soldiers wounded in the March battle. The Tenth Corps rested at Bentonville until mid-afternoon while pioneers rebuilt the Mill Creek bridge, which had been destroyed by Confederate cavalry. That night, Terry's command camped a few miles above the village.[18]

The Twenty-third Corps of the Army of the Ohio followed Slocum's wing on the Neuse River Road. The commander, Maj. Gen. Jacob D. Cox, reported that his column started at 1:00 P.M., marching just eight miles. Lt. Redmond Laswell of the 120th Indiana noted that the march was stop-and-go most of the way, much as Lieutenant Colonel Merrill had described the Twentieth Corps's progress. "Marched for two or three hundred yards & stoped and then the same thing over until after dark," Laswell scrawled in his diary. "[T]hen we halted and had thirty minutes to get supper in & eat it." No sooner had Laswell and his Hoosier comrades begun eating than the bugle sounded the assembly, forcing them to wolf down their food while on a march that took them only a half-mile in two hours. The army's tradition of "hurry up and wait" seems to be a time-honored one.[19]

General Sherman traveled with the Twentieth Corps of Slocum's wing because it was nearest to Johnston's army at Smithfield. The Union commander led a force totaling 88,948 officers and men, the largest number under his immediate command since the Atlanta campaign. Estimating his enemy's strength at no more than 45,000, Sherman expected Johnston to offer only token opposition. Deeming it unlikely that the Confederates would make a stand at Smithfield or Raleigh, "Uncle Billy" intended to cut off Johnston's escape route south and force him north toward Danville. Although this scenario coincided with Johnston's objective of combining forces with Lee near the Virginia border, Sherman regarded the junction of Lee's and Johnston's armies as preferable to a pursuit of Johnston's swifter force through South Carolina and Georgia.[20]

Despite the difficulties of getting his 90,000-man army under way, Sherman had advanced to within a dozen miles of Smithfield and forty miles

Sherman and his generals, 1865. The generals (and their commands as of April 10, 1865) are, from left, Oliver O. Howard (Right Wing), John A. Logan (Fifteenth Corps), William B. Hazen (Second Division, Fifteenth Corps), Sherman, Jefferson C. Davis (Fourteenth Corps), Henry W. Slocum (Left Wing), Joseph A. Mower (Twentieth Corps), and Frank P. Blair Jr. (Seventeenth Corps). The commander of the Center, John M. Schofield, and his two corps commanders, Alfred H. Terry (Tenth Corps) and Jacob D. Cox (Twenty-third Corps), are not pictured. (Barnard, Photographic Views of Sherman's Campaign, *pl. 1)*

of Raleigh. On the evening of April 10, General Cox noted in his journal: "[E]verything indicates that the final scene of the drama of the Confederacy is at hand."[21]

Reveille sounded in the Army of Tennessee's camps at dawn on April 10, and at 9:30 A.M., Johnston's headquarters alerted the army's three corps commanders to prepare to move out. The march toward Raleigh began at 11:00, with Stewart's Corps and Lee's Corps taking the Louisburg Road east of the Neuse River. Their route led to the crossing of the Neuse at Battle's Bridge, ten miles southeast of Raleigh. Meanwhile, General Hardee proceeded with Hoke's Division of his corps through Smithfield, crossed the Neuse, and then marched northwestward on the Raleigh Road beside the North Carolina Railroad. Hardee's remaining two divisions followed Stewart and Lee.[22]

The Final Scene of the Drama

As was the case with Sherman's army, many units in the Army of Tennessee did not march until mid-afternoon. "[W]e were roused for an early start," wrote Charles Hutson of Stuart's South Carolina battery, "our [tent] flies put away on the caissons, & our bodies left waiting impatiently in the rain for orders to move. We got drenched to the skin, but did not march until 3 in the evening. We marched deep into the night, halting within an hour or so of daylight. Of course we are not much refreshed this morning, having had so little sleep." The rumor soon spread that Lee's army had met with disaster, which did nothing to improve morale. Despite the all-night march, Johnston's army advanced only ten miles toward Raleigh. "Old Joe" was dissatisfied with the progress of his columns and was determined to push his men even harder on April 11.[23]

Johnston and his staff were among the last Confederates to break camp on April 10. At mid-afternoon their horses were saddled and waiting at army headquarters when a deputation from Kennedy's South Carolina brigade arrived to present a petition to Johnston, requesting that the commanding general commute the sentences of four soldiers scheduled to be executed by firing squad the next day. One of Johnston's adjutants, Maj. Joseph Cumming, received the petition and brought it before the general, who was sitting on the veranda of the Pharaoh Richardson house, deep in thought. "He had a way when thus preoccupied of jerking his head from side to side as if he had a very mild case of the palsy," Cumming noted. The staff officer "knew that it was not well to interrupt him at such times, but the occasion was such that I felt I must approach him, though I did so with much trepidation and many misgivings as to my reception." Cumming acknowledged that the rumor of Lee's surrender was very much on his mind when he approached the general.[24]

It was appropriate that this unpleasant task should fall on Major Cumming's shoulders, for, in addition to other duties, he was responsible for reviewing the army's court-martial records and reporting their results to Johnston. The adjutant informed the general that four men in Kennedy's Brigade were sentenced to be shot the next day for desertion, that he had in his hand a petition signed by the officers of that brigade requesting that the sentence be commuted or suspended, and that several of those officers were present, awaiting the general's answer. Cumming handed the petition to Johnston, who refused to take it, but the general did ask the adjutant whether he had reviewed the record. When Cumming replied that he had, Johnston asked,

"Is not the record correct?"

Cumming said that it was.

"Has anything new occurred since?"

"Not to my knowledge," the major answered.

"Have I not then ordered the sentence to be carried out?"

Cumming replied that the general certainly had. Johnston resumed his previous train of thought, while the adjutant stood before him, petition in hand, waiting in vain for positive orders. At last Cumming broke the silence:

"General, I beg pardon for interrupting you, but this is a matter of life and death. I have not had your answer to this petition, and I ought not to assume the responsibility of giving an answer to the officers who brought it, and I beg that you will tell me definitely what I shall say to them."

"Tell them the sentence must be carried out," Johnston curtly replied.[25]

There the matter ended—for the time being. Soon afterward, Johnston and his staff left the Richardson house and rode to Battle's Bridge on the Neuse, where they encamped after dark. The general slept under a tent fly, while his chief of staff, Col. Archer Anderson, retired to a nearby house along with Major Cumming and several other officers. Cumming lay down on the floor and soon fell asleep. When the hardness of the floor caused the major to awaken during the night, he noticed that Anderson was seated at a table before a dim light, hard at work on what Cumming assumed was a cipher dispatch announcing the surrender of Lee's army.[26]

Cumming soon discovered that his hunch was correct. The fateful dispatch from President Davis had reached Johnston at 1:00 A.M. on April 11. "A scout reports that General Lee surrendered the remnant of his army near to Appomattox Court-House yesterday," the message read. "No official intelligence of the event but there is little room for doubt as to result."[27]

At daylight Johnston summoned Cumming to his tent; within minutes, the major was standing before the commanding general. Johnston asked the adjutant to whose corps the condemned soldiers' brigade belonged. Cumming replied that it was Stewart's Corps.

"Write an order at once to General Stewart," Johnston said, "to suspend the execution until further orders."

The major scribbled a dispatch to A. P. Stewart. Meanwhile, Johnston summoned a courier and ordered him to ride with all possible speed to Stewart's headquarters and deliver the note to the general personally. "Then I knew," Cumming recalled, "was positively certain, that the war was over. I knew that General Johnston, on the one hand, would not relent so long as there was a necessity for preserving discipline, and that, on the other hand, he would not sacrifice a life unnecessarily. I was confident . . . that he had heard of Lee's surrender, [and] that there would be no prolongation of the struggle."[28]

The Final Scene of the Drama

Johnston made no official announcement of Lee's surrender. He may have chosen this course because the intelligence was unofficial, though even President Davis conceded its reliability. It is more likely that Johnston, having already witnessed the devastating effect of the news of Richmond's fall, feared that word of Lee's surrender might cause his army to degenerate into a mob or disintegrate altogether. "Old Joe" believed that his first duty now was to surrender his army on the best possible terms, which he could accomplish only if that army remained intact. Johnston realized that his men would eventually learn of Lee's surrender, but he doubtless resigned himself to the notion that it would be better if they learned of it later rather than sooner.

Johnston's army resumed the march on April 11. The day was sultry, the men were out of marching condition after their long rest at Smithfield, and there was much straggling. "I was never more wearied in my life," wrote Capt. Alfred Fielder of the 2nd Tennessee Consolidated, "and my old wounds hurt me very much." In Elliott's Brigade of Maj. Gen. Patton Anderson's Division, only 214 men out of 1,499 answered the evening roll call after their twenty-mile march. The brigade commander, Lt. Col. James Welsman Brown, called it "the most severe march we have had." General Anderson, a longtime veteran of the Army of Tennessee, remarked that he had never seen a march to equal it. Fortunately for Anderson, most of his stragglers reached camp during the night.[29]

Like most of his comrades in Anderson's Division, Charles Hutson of Stuart's Battery was a straggler on April 11. He had dropped out at Raleigh to beg "in cool shamelessness for something to eat." The young South Carolinian found plenty to eat, and while in town, he heard a rumor that France had recognized the Confederacy. "Of course no one believes it," Hutson wrote his mother, though he conceded that "it may possibly be true." Hutson found Raleigh to be "a beautiful town" and noted that "the ladies were very kind." Indeed, women lining both sides of Fayetteville Street handed out meat, bread, and tobacco to the passing soldiers. Lt. W. A. Johnson of the 2nd South Carolina "saw many pretty girls" during his tramp through town. "Lucky to see *something* pretty," he jotted in his diary.[30]

Without question the soldiers' favorite stopping place in Raleigh was St. Mary's School, which stood in a shady grove on the western edge of town. Dozens of young ladies gathered by the roadside, doling out food, water, and words of encouragement to the passing troops. Capt. Bromfield Ridley noted that "the beautiful school girls greeted us warmly. Each one had a pitcher of water and goblet. We drank, took their addresses, and had a big time." When the order came to move on, Ridley had "a terrible time" tearing his fellow staff officers away. The North Carolina Junior Reserves

Brigade was a particular favorite of the young women. "Why, girls, these are all *young men*," one student cried out to her friends, to which a boy soldier replied, "Yes, ladies, and we are all looking for wives!"[31]

As the Confederate columns wound through the streets of Raleigh, regimental bands struck up "Dixie," and the troops made an effort to appear as soldierly as possible, despite their faded and tattered uniforms. "[T]heir careworn faces, however, told the sad tale," recalled an eyewitness, "and silently they wended their way westward." Mary Bayard Clarke was cheering the passing soldiers when the woman standing next to her turned and cried out, "My God! This is the funeral procession of the Southern Confederacy!"

"What do you mean?" Mrs. Clarke asked.

"Lee has surrendered to Grant!" The woman explained to her dumbfounded neighbor that one of the passing soldiers had whispered the terrible news to her while pausing for a drink. And that was not all: with the rumors of Lee's surrender came warnings that Sherman was close at hand.[32]

Since mid-March the people of Raleigh had dreaded Sherman's arrival. Residents had flown into a frenzy when news of Fayetteville's occupation reached the state capital. "Raleigh is in a bustle," Capt. James A. Blackshear wrote on March 15. "Every thing and every body running. Some people no doubt will run to welcome the Yankees as some are running to make ready for them." When the Union juggernaut veered to Goldsboro instead, the citizens of Raleigh breathed a sigh of relief and then resumed their preparations for Sherman's arrival. Governor Vance noted that many Raleighites were "going up the spout" or—to use another popular expression of the time—were "refugeeing." Those who chose to remain buried their valuables or sent them to friends and family west of the capital. On April 9, Raleigh attorney Bartholomew F. Moore informed his friend, University of North Carolina president David L. Swain, that he was sending him a package for safekeeping. "The city is being disencumbered of its warlike materials . . . in anticipation of its being uncovered," Moore informed Swain. "Johnson will move tomorrow if Sherman will let him. And Raleigh will be Sherman's by the last of the week. God save us from the retreating friend & the advancing foe."[33]

In anticipation of Sherman's arrival, University of North Carolina trustee and former governor Charles Manly buried a packet of valuable university papers and personal effects in a forest near Raleigh. Trusting no one else to do the job, Manly dug the hole himself, hauled off the excess dirt, and covered up his hiding place. "It was a terrible job," the seventy-year-old Manly wrote, "I laid down on the ground perfectly ex-

The Final Scene of the Drama

hausted before I could gain strength to mount my horse." In an April 8 letter to President Swain (himself a former governor of North Carolina), Manly lamented: "I don't know what to do. I think it pretty certain that Johnston & Sherman will both pass over this place. Utter & universal devastation & ruin will follow inevitably. There is no difference in the two armies as to making a clean sweep wherever they go of provisions, stock & every thing dead or alive."[34]

While Moore and Manly indulged in hand-wringing, two other North Carolinians were planning to save the state from further devastation. On the day that Manly wrote him, Swain wrote Senator Graham, suggesting that they meet Governor Vance in Raleigh. "Since the organization of our State government in December 1776," Swain began, "North Carolina has never passed through an ordeal more severe than that which we are about to undergo." Swain predicted that unless something were done to prevent it, "suffering, privation and death—death on the battlefield, and death in the most horrible of all forms, the lingering death of famine, is imminent to thousands, not merely men, but helpless and innocent women and children."[35]

Graham received Swain's dire missive later that day and replied immediately. Convinced that the cause of Southern independence was hopeless and that President Davis would never sue for peace so long as he had the means to wage war, Graham believed that the Old North State should act independently. The senator conjectured that Swain might persuade Vance to treat with Sherman and that the governor might ask Swain to participate. Graham urged Swain to confer with Vance on the subject but saw no point in taking part himself, since he had failed to sway the governor in a similar discussion on April 6. Nevertheless, Graham invited Swain to visit him at his home in Hillsborough so that they could discuss their plan more fully.[36]

Swain traveled to Hillsborough on Sunday, April 9. In the course of a long conversation, the two men agreed that a separate peace constituted North Carolina's best hope. As a basis of action, the senator suggested that the General Assembly should meet to pass resolutions calling for an end to the war and inviting other Confederate states to do likewise. The legislature should also elect commissioners to negotiate with the Federal government and report to a state convention given special powers to deal with the crisis. Graham also recommended that Vance send a commission to Sherman requesting a suspension of hostilities to facilitate negotiations. The senator then put his proposal in writing.[37]

Swain arrived in Raleigh on the morning of April 10 and discussed Graham's plan with Vance over dinner. The governor remained noncommittal, telling Swain that he would seek General Johnston's opinion before deciding.[38]

While Vance considered Graham's proposal, two prominent Raleigh citizens were hatching their own plan to induce the governor to seek peace. On the morning of April 11, Kenneth Rayner and Bartholomew F. Moore attended the funeral of a mutual acquaintance. During the procession that followed, Rayner and Moore discussed in hushed tones the necessity of taking immediate action to prevent the destruction of the capital at the hands of Sherman's army. "Rayner," Moore told his friend, "the time has come when every man that has any influence . . . should make an effort to save his country from ruin." Bringing up the rear of the funeral procession, the two men waited at a street corner until the other mourners had passed out of sight. When they resumed their discussion, Rayner and Moore decided to find Swain, believing him to be the only man able to persuade the governor to negotiate with Sherman. Indeed, since his days as a law student at the University of North Carolina, Vance had regarded Swain as his mentor.[39]

Rayner also knew that Swain planned to leave Raleigh that day and might already have done so. "He *must not* go," Moore insisted, "there is not a moment to be lost. . . . You go to the Capitol and try to intercept Gov. Swain, and I will go to the depot, and keep watch for him there." Rayner found Swain, carpetbag in hand, on his way to the depot. After some hesitation, Swain agreed to accompany Rayner to the capitol, where they met Vance in his office. The governor had just received a telegram from President Davis. Having heard the rumor of Lee's surrender, Vance had wired Davis for confirmation. In making his reply, Davis chose to conceal from the governor what he had revealed to Johnston. "I have no official report," Davis's message read, "but scouts, said to be reliable, . . . represent the disaster as extreme. I have not heard from General Lee since the 6th instant, and have little or no hope from his army as an organized body." Finding the president's reply "vague and indefinite," Vance assumed the worst. "This of course put an end to the war," he later wrote of Lee's surrender. At that moment, Vance decided to send a flag of truce to Sherman.[40]

Swain and Rayner had no difficulty convincing Vance of the necessity for communicating with the Federal commander. During the discussion, General Johnston arrived to inform the governor that he was evacuating the capital. Vance asked Johnston whether the general thought it advisable for him to remain in Raleigh and negotiate with Sherman. Johnston said that Vance should obtain the best terms from Sherman that he could. Having received Johnston's blessing, Vance deemed himself free to communicate with Sherman. The choice of commissioners was obvious: Graham and Swain. His course of action now decided, Vance urged Graham to hurry to Raleigh. "This place will not be held longer than tomorrow," the governor wrote.[41]

Not satisfied merely with goading Vance into action, Rayner and Moore agreed on a second plan to save the capital. After meeting with Swain and Vance, Rayner called on Raleigh mayor William H. Harrison, urging him to appoint a committee to surrender the town. Otherwise, Rayner warned, Raleigh would share the fate of Columbia. Not one to shrink from the limelight, Rayner suggested that Harrison appoint him spokesman of the committee. Although Rayner was quick to take credit for suggesting a formal surrender to Harrison, the mayor and the capital's Board of Commissioners had discussed the idea a day or two previously.[42]

While Moore and Rayner did all they could to save Raleigh, Vance and Johnston attempted to save the remaining supplies in the capital city. Since mid-March, state and Confederate stores had been sent westward to various points on the North Carolina Railroad in anticipation of Sherman's advance. In addition to state monies, stocks, securities, and departmental records, Vance had transferred to Graham, Greensboro, and Salisbury thousands of blankets, overcoats, uniforms, shoes, and boots, as well as medical supplies, tons of provisions, and a stockpile of arms and ammunition. On April 11, all that remained were some commissary stores and essential daily records under the joint control of the state adjutant general, R. C. Gatlin, and the state treasurer, Jonathan Worth. The Confederate army still had a large quantity of supplies to evacuate, however, for on the afternoon of April 11, Johnston ordered Beauregard at Greensboro to send 100 freight cars to Raleigh at once.[43]

At 5:00 P.M. on the same day, Johnston received a message from President Davis summoning him to Greensboro. Johnston acknowledged Davis's dispatch and directed General Hardee to take temporary command of the army and continue the westward retreat. After Johnston and Hardee dined together at the home of Rufus Tucker in Raleigh, the Confederate commander left for Greensboro at midnight.[44]

On the morning of April 12, the long gray and butternut columns of Johnston's army resumed their procession through the streets of Raleigh. The Confederates marched up New Bern Street toward the east facade of the statehouse in the center of Capitol Square. Turning left, they entered Wilmington Street and then swung right onto Morgan Street. On their right loomed a bronze statue of George Washington, dwarfed by massive oaks. The soldiers passed close by the iron railing bordering the square to steal a closer look at the statue and the statehouse. The domed granite

Lt. Gen. William J. Hardee. Johnston's senior corps commander, Hardee briefly led the Army of Tennessee in "Old Joe's" absence. (Massachusetts Commandery, Military Order of the Loyal Legion Collection, U.S. Army Military History Institute)

structure reminded a Tennessean of his home state's capitol in Nashville, but he thought the Tar Heel version "not near so large or so fine." The troops filed right onto Salisbury Street and then turned left onto Hillsborough Street, heading west. "Have no idea where we are going," admitted Pvt. Thomas Sullivan of the 9th Mississippi Consolidated. But Sullivan was certain of at least one thing: "Think the Yankee flag will soon be flown on the Capital of N. Car."[45]

The soldiers who passed through Raleigh on the morning of April 12 found no handkerchief-waving crowds lining the sidewalks to greet them—in sharp contrast to the rousing reception accorded the Confederates the day before. Most of the residents' doors were shut, "and the inmates were only to be seen through the windows and generally upstairs," wrote Capt. Alfred Fielder of the 2nd Tennessee Consolidated. "I suppose they felt bad or it might have been from prudential motives." Indeed, Raleigh had already assumed the appearance of a conquered town.[46]

At dawn on April 11, Sherman's army resumed the march toward Raleigh, and once again, Hampton's cavalry harried the Federal columns. The warmest skirmish of the day occurred on the Stage Road to Smithfield, where the 75th Indiana, the lead regiment of the Fourteenth Corps, maintained a running fight with elements of Butler's Division led by Wade Hampton. The Confederates had built a series of barricades across the road, to which they fell back in succession whenever the Hoosiers threatened to outflank them. Two companies of the 75th Indiana advanced in skirmish formation, the remainder following in line of battle. The Southerners' resistance stiffened on the outskirts of Smithfield, which the 75th reached at noon. Fighting dismounted behind their log barricades or any other available shelter, Hampton's troopers pinned down the Hoosier skirmishers in an open field. In order to dislodge the Confederate rear guard, the commander of the 75th, Lt. Col. William O'Brien, sent three more companies under Capt. Mahlon H. Floyd onto the skirmish line.[47]

The augmented skirmish line of the 75th Indiana soon pressed the Confederate troopers back into the streets of Smithfield. But the retreating Southerners gave ground stubbornly, enabling their comrades at the Neuse River bridge to prepare it for burning. During the Federals' advance through town, Captain Floyd was climbing over a high fence into a garden when a bullet struck the board he was astride, toppling him over with such force that he appeared to have been hit. Fearing that the captain was dead, several of the skirmishers ran over to his motionless form and were relieved to find that he was merely stunned. One of Floyd's skirmishers, Pvt. Daniel Herron, was not so fortunate. He was wounded in the hip— the last man in the 75th Indiana to fall on the firing line. In the Battle of Chickamauga, Herron had been saved by a pack of cards in his breast pocket, which had stopped a bullet that might have killed him. Until today, Herron's comrades had believed that he led a charmed life.[48]

Sgt. William B. Miller of the 75th Indiana supposed that a conspicuous Rebel officer riding a white horse must have enjoyed a "charmed life," for he had seen the man in the thick of the fight and assumed that every soldier on the skirmish line had shot at him at least once. The gallant officer may have been General Hampton or the ubiquitous Col. John Logan Black, the commander of the rear guard at Moccasin Creek. Black and Hampton were the last two mounted Confederates to cross the covered bridge spanning the Neuse. A squad of dismounted men followed, setting fire to the bridge as they passed through it. Fed by piles of pine shavings spread across the flooring, flames soon engulfed the wooden structure. The Confederates thus succeeded in stalling the Federal pursuit for the rest of the day.[49]

Although the 75th Indiana had failed to save the bridge, the regiment enjoyed the honor of capturing the town. The Hoosiers took full advantage of their elevated status. One of the men discovered three barrels of applejack under a pile of rubbish. Calling for help, he and several comrades rolled the barrels into the 75th's camp on the outskirts of town. The head of one barrel was knocked in and the soldiers of the 75th filled their cups and canteens. They drank a toast to their benefactor and then proceeded to drink some more, until everyone—officers and men alike—felt "glorious," recalled Pvt. Lew Ginger. "I believe [only] one man in the regiment was sober," Ginger wrote. "He was on guard at the Quartermaster's a half-mile away."[50]

The men stumbled into town and had a rollicking good time. They found a building that housed the Odd Fellows and Sons of Malta lodges. Donning ornate masks and gowns that constituted the Odd Fellows' regalia, the drunken Hoosiers took to the streets "and scared some of the darkies nearly to death," Sergeant Miller noted. At this point, the Hoosiers' division commander, Bvt. Maj. Gen. Absalom Baird, appeared. In a fatherly tone, Baird told the Hoosiers "that they had done well that day, and that they might consider themselves privileged characters," recalled Private Ginger. Baird then told the men "to have all the fun they wanted," so long as they did not destroy any property. A crowd of the 75th Indiana gathered in the shade of the Odd Fellows building, where they swapped stories, sang songs, and sipped applejack from their canteens.[51]

Meanwhile, a soldier in the 75th found a large box in the top-story room of the Odd Fellows building. He tore off the lid and gave a yell—before him lay a grinning skeleton, strung together with wire. The Hoosier soon regained his composure and called out to several of his comrades, "Here is a d——d rebel hiding from us. Let's send him down among the boys." Seizing the skeleton, the soldier ran to the window and hurled it through, sending a shower of human bones, broken glass, and wood splinters down on the unsuspecting revelers, who scattered for cover. Private Ginger had seen these men hold fast in battle while their comrades fell on every side, but a falling skeleton caused them to panic. "What happened after this some of the other boys will have to tell," Ginger confessed, "for it was my first tussle with applejack, and he got the heels of me."[52]

Chaplain John J. Hight of the 58th Indiana was laboring under no such disadvantage, however. He strolled through town, noting the sorry state of the Odd Fellows building, though admiring the beautiful elm and hackberry trees that shaded the wide streets. The chaplain entered the Johnston County Court House and saw the archives scattered about the floor; finding the churches open, he observed that they too had been rifled. The damage extended to the town commons. "Even in Smithfield the public stocks 'went up,'" punned Maj. Henry Hitchcock of Sherman's staff, "visibly— for some of 'the boys' set fire to them. I refer to the wooden stocks near

The Final Scene of the Drama

the jail, a comfortable institution for the improvement of criminals which the conservative old North State has retained from colonial times." Yet not all of the bluecoat visitors who left their mark in Smithfield were vandals. In the Methodist Church Sabbath School record book, a Federal soldier penciled an admonition to the parishioners:

> The members of this church must still Worship God and pray that the war will soon come to a close and let this war be a lesson for you never take up arms again against the best Goverment in the world, the country that our forefathers fought for and established and now you are fighting to tair it down. I am Sore [sorry] to see this church and Books Missused so, but you must look over it, you must bare and [bear in] mind that there is some Rootless [ruthless] men in the army that dont cear [care] any thing for them Selves nor any body Else.[53]

The Twentieth Corps's advance arrived in Smithfield soon after that of the Fourteenth Corps, but the rear of the column did not reach camp until midnight. "Day hot and sultry," wrote First Division commander Alpheus Williams, whose comments echoed those of his Confederate counterparts. "Men more fatigued than I have seen them for months." Sherman established his headquarters at the courthouse and Slocum at the Methodist church a few blocks away. That afternoon, the Federals laid two pontoon bridges across the Neuse at Smithfield. Meanwhile, Sherman received word from Howard that the Fifteenth Corps was camped at Folk's Bridge and Lowell's Factory and the Seventeenth Corps at Pine Level, several miles northeast of Smithfield. Howard asked Sherman whether his "wishes with regard to destroying factories, mills, &c., remain the same," for Fifteenth Corps commander John Logan requested instructions for dealing with Lowell's Factory. "You need not have the Lowell Factory destroyed," Sherman replied—perhaps the first tangible evidence that he regarded the war as all but over. "You may instruct General Logan to exact bonds that the factory shall not be used for the Confederacy. Of course the bond is not worth a cent, but if the factory owners do not abide by the conditions they cannot expect any mercy the next time."[54]

In Special Field Orders No. 53, Sherman directed Howard's wing to continue marching along the east bank of the Neuse, crossing at Battle's and Hinton's Bridges near Raleigh. Slocum's wing—"the column of direction"—would cross at Smithfield and take the two direct roads to the North Carolina capital. Schofield's two corps would advance on Slocum's left to outflank Johnston's army should it halt at Raleigh. (The Twenty-third Corps would have to cross the Neuse on pontoons because the Confed-

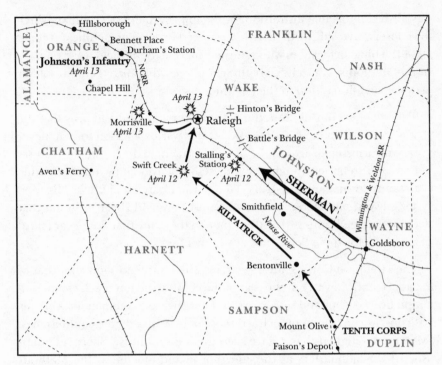

Map 3. Sherman's pursuit of Johnston, April 10–13, 1865

erates had burned Turner's Bridge near Smithfield.) To facilitate pursuit, Sherman enjoined his army commanders to leave their supply trains well to the rear.[55]

Sherman also heard from his cavalry commander on April 11. Kilpatrick reported that he was at a "Mr. Moore's house" on Middle Creek (about ten miles west of Smithfield); he had been forced to make a wide detour to the left because the enemy had burned several key bridges across Black Creek. "My command is not sufficiently well up, owing to the long march and bad roads," "Little Kil" wrote, "to make a successful dash on the enemy's columns, even if I was within striking distance."[56]

Sherman searched in vain on his map for "Moore's on Middle Creek." "Please hereafter in reporting your position, to use names on our map," "Uncle Billy" chided his cavalry commander. "I don't think Hampton has 2,000 cavalry with him, and this is your chance. I will push all the column[s] straight on Raleigh. I don't care about Raleigh now, but want to defeat and destroy the Confederate army; therefore you may run any risk." The next day Kilpatrick would seize the chance Sherman offered and attempt to return the favor that Wade Hampton had bestowed on him at Monroe's Crossroads.[57]

The Final Scene of the Drama

Far to the rear of Slocum, Jacob Cox's Twenty-third Corps spent the morning crossing Moccasin Swamp, which was flanked by the estates of Thomas and William Atkinson. Finding the roads in "a horrible condition," Cox reported that his command marched just three miles before noon and ten miles in all, the head of the column reaching the Whitley house, eight miles south of Smithfield, at 6:00 P.M.[58]

The Atkinson brothers suffered grievously at the hands of Yankee bummers. Ohio surgeon George A. Collamore spent the night at William Atkinson's house on the Goldsboro side of Moccasin Creek. He called it the "finest house" he had seen since leaving Goldsboro and observed that the troops preceding him had "utterly ruined every article of furniture in the house, and attempted to burn it." Sgt. Adam Furnas noted that mattress feathers littered the yard, and so many men had tramped through the house that an inch of mud caked the floors.[59]

The home of William's identical twin, Thomas, stood four miles farther on. Thomas Atkinson realized what was in store for him when he recognized his brother's carriage piled high with family heirlooms among the Union army wagons that passed his estate. Unfortunately, Thomas would be the victim in a case of mistaken identity that might have been comical had it not had such tragic consequences. The Federals mistook Thomas for his twin brother, believing that William Atkinson had covered the four miles to Thomas's house to spy on the Yankees there. It did not help Thomas's plight that he—like his brother—was hard of hearing and therefore slow to answer his Yankee inquisitors' questions. The soldiers accused Thomas of being a Rebel conscription agent and threatened to lynch him. Fortunately, someone suggested that they send a detail back to William's house to verify his brother's story. In the end, Federal soldiers spared Thomas Atkinson's life but burned his house to the ground.[60]

Angered by the burning of the Thomas Atkinson house and several others, General Cox issued the following circular to his corps on April 12:

> Since we left Goldsboro there has been a constant succession of house burning in rear of this command. This has never before been the case since this corps was organized, and the prospect of speedy peace makes this more than ever reprehensible. Division commanders will take the most vigorous measures to put a stop to these outrages, whether committed by men of this command or by stragglers from other corps. Any one firing a dwelling-house, or any building in close proximity to one, should be summarily shot.[61]

Whether Cox's circular saved any houses is uncertain. Surgeon Collamore observed that the order did not prevent the destruction of property entirely, though he noted fewer destroyed buildings on April 12 than on the day before. Another eyewitness, Sgt. Adam Furnas, saw several columns of smoke, but he could not tell whether they denoted burning structures or merely turpentine stills.[62]

The Federals might have dealt more harshly with a Johnston County widow had it not been for the intervention of a former schoolmate, now a Union officer. On the afternoon of April 11, Maj. Henry A. Gildersleeve of the First Division, Twentieth Corps, was riding at the head of the column when a scout rode up to confer with General Williams. As Williams's provost marshal, Gildersleeve thought it a good idea to eavesdrop. The major overheard the scout tell Williams that a widow who lived up the road claimed to be a loyal New Yorker in need of protection for herself and her children. A New Yorker himself, Gildersleeve asked General Williams if he could help the woman. Williams consented, and Gildersleeve galloped off with the scout.[63]

When they reached the widow's house near Smithfield, Gildersleeve dismounted, went to the door, and knocked. He held out his hand to the woman who opened the door and said, "Why, how do you do?" She stared at him and said nothing. "Do you not remember Gildersleeve?" the officer asked. "We went to school together." The woman, Fannie Secor Mitchener, at last recognized her former schoolmate from the Claverack Institute in Columbia County, New York. The twenty-five-year-old Mrs. Mitchener had lived in New York until 1859, when she moved to North Carolina to teach at a private school partly financed by Agrippa Mitchener, a wealthy Johnston County planter. The young woman had married Mitchener soon after her arrival, but he died less than a year after their marriage. Widowed at twenty-one, Fannie Mitchener suddenly found herself in charge of an extensive plantation and two small children by Mitchener's first wife. When war came, she remained at the Mitchener estate rather than forfeit her right to live there under the terms of her husband's will.[64]

Doubtless Fannie Mitchener could not believe her good fortune. Standing before her was a former schoolmate—now a Federal officer—who promised to furnish a safeguard. When Army of the Ohio commander John Schofield arrived at the house, Gildersleeve introduced her as a loyal Northern woman and an old friend. General Schofield made the Mitchener home his headquarters on the evening of April 11, and for that night at least, the young widow could sleep soundly.[65]

The following day proved to be a different matter. After the passing of the main column, bummers overran the Mitchener plantation. They burned the barn and gin house, along with 60,000 pounds of cotton and 5,000 pounds of forage, and then rode off with the three remaining horses.

The Final Scene of the Drama

Fannie Mitchener later estimated her total loss at $14,365. (Nearly three decades later, she would petition the U.S. Congress to reimburse her for her losses. Descendants claim that she received full compensation, but there are no records to substantiate this.) Despite their losses, Mitchener and her stepchildren still had a roof over their heads and an ample supply of corn hidden inside the hollow columns fronting the house. They were in far better condition than the Atkinsons at Moccasin Creek.[66]

Prior to Schofield's departure on the morning of April 12, momentous news arrived at the Mitchener house. About 5:00 A.M., two riders had galloped up to Sherman's headquarters at Smithfield and delivered a dispatch from General Grant announcing Lee's surrender. "I hardly know how to express my feelings, but you can imagine them," Sherman wrote Grant. "The terms you have given Lee are magnanimous and liberal. Should Johnston follow Lee's example I shall of course grant the same." Sherman added that he was pursuing Johnston toward Raleigh, twenty-seven miles to the northwest. "Roads are heavy, but under the inspiration of the news from you we can march twenty-five miles a day." Once more Sherman requested the services of Grant's cavalry chief: "I shall expect to hear from General Sheridan in case Johnston does not surrender at Raleigh. With a little more cavalry I would be sure to capture the whole army." When Schofield received word of Lee's surrender, he ordered a lantern hung from the balcony of the Mitchener house in honor of the event. "The news from Grant is glorious beyond parallel," Schofield wrote Sherman. "I hope Johnston will follow Lee's sensible example in a few days."[67]

Sherman now regarded the end of the war as a matter of time, for he knew that Johnston's army was no match for his. As the Federal commander saw it, only two questions remained. Would Johnston surrender, or would he continue to fall back and allow his army to disperse into guerrilla bands? Believing that Johnston could retreat faster than the Federals could pursue him, Sherman feared that if his adversary chose the latter course, the war would be prolonged indefinitely—hence his repeated requests for Sheridan's cavalry to help him corner Johnston. These doubts did not cloud Sherman's thoughts until after the celebrations on the morning of April 12, however.[68]

The day began like so many others as Bvt. Maj. Gen. William T. Ward's division of the Twentieth Corps tramped into Smithfield at first light. But to everyone's surprise, General Ward ordered the head of the column to halt when it reached Sherman's headquarters in the courthouse square. "Uncle Billy" himself stepped forward and read Grant's dispatch to the men. "[Y]ou had ought to have seen the excitement," a Federal soldier wrote his wife. "[O]ur band was at the head of the collum[.] [W]e played

Johnston County Court House, Smithfield. Sherman established his headquarters in the courthouse square on the afternoon of April 11 and announced the news of Lee's surrender to his troops there the next morning. (North Carolina Division of Archives and History)

all the National airs, [and] the soldiers threw up their hats and chreed [cheered] with all their might. [T]hey got a negro on a blanket and threw him ten feet." Major Hitchcock watched as "brigade after brigade came along by our HdQrs and were told the news. . . . Imagine the billows of tumultuous cheering which rolled along the lines. . . . [M]eanwhile, band after band . . . made the little old town echo with music as beautiful as it was patriotic."[69]

Staff officer George W. Balloch watched Sherman "pacing nonchalantly back and forth" while his adjutant, Maj. Lewis M. Dayton, read the news to each passing brigade. The Federal commander "was smoking a cigar," Balloch recalled, "apparently the most unconcerned man in the army" amid a "perfect pandemonium." Sherman's seeming lack of concern was feigned, however. When General Williams reached the crowded courthouse square, he heard someone shout his name. Dismounting, Williams looked about and saw a beaming "Uncle Billy" waving at him. The commanding general "almost shook my arm off," Williams wrote his daughters. "I have never seen Sherman so elated."[70]

The news shot like an electric current through Sherman's grand army. As an excited courier raced down the Twenty-third Corps's column shouting, "Lee has surrendered! Lee has surrendered!" one wag yelled after him:

The Final Scene of the Drama

"Great God! You're the man I've been looking for these last four years." Lt. Charles Brown of the 21st Michigan noted that his entire Fourteenth Corps division was assembled to receive the news. "You can imagine the noise made by 15 Regts giving three times three & a tiger," Brown wrote his family. "By jove I never thought men had such lungs—beat the yell with which we charged at Bentonville all to nothing." During a rest halt, Bvt. Brig. Gen. Thomas J. Henderson's Twenty-third Corps brigade sang such patriotic songs as "The Battle Cry of Freedom," "Marching through Georgia," and "When Johnny Comes Marching Home," accompanied by several brass bands. The 1,500-voice choir then closed its impromptu concert with "Old Hundred." "Thoughts of meeting wives, children, and friends from whom they had been so long separated by the long struggle, occupied the minds of all," recalled left wing commander Henry Slocum. "A happier body of men never before surrounded their camp-fires than were to be found along the roads leading to Raleigh." The reaction of many women on the line of march was no less demonstrative. An Ohio lieutenant recalled seeing a young mother kneel down and embrace her children. "Thank God!" she cried. "The war is over. Now your father can come home."[71]

In an army as large as Sherman's, there were bound to be a few who were unwilling—or unable—to join in the revelry. When Lt. Col. William O'Brien read the news to the men of the 75th Indiana, most of them cheered, though there was at least one exception. "I tried to, but couldn't," recalled Pvt. Lew Ginger, who was nursing an applejack-induced hangover. "Hats went up into the air; mine would not stay on anyhow. In fact, it was several sizes too small for me." Others in Sherman's army greeted the news with skepticism, calling it "a pack of d——d lies," one they had heard so often "that it was played out now." But the skeptics were a conspicuous minority.[72]

One incident that occurred on April 12 presents a stark contrast to the day's celebrations. Four men belonging to the escort of Bvt. Maj. Gen. Giles A. Smith (a Seventeenth Corps division commander) were captured, lined up, and shot in the back of the head by a detail of Butler's cavalry. A fifth man, Pvt. William C. Crockett of the 11th Illinois Cavalry, survived and related the story. The incident harkened back to executions that had occurred in South Carolina two months earlier, when several dozen Union foragers and cavalrymen were found with their throats cut and signs pinned to their chests that read, "Death to all foragers." In this case, the Federal high command chose not to retaliate as it had done in South Carolina.[73]

While Sherman's infantry celebrated news of Lee's surrender, Kilpatrick's cavalry led the drive on Raleigh, opposed by Hampton's horsemen.

Hampton ordered Wheeler to burn Battle's Bridge and cover the remaining eastern approaches to Raleigh, while the South Carolinian established a defensive line at Swift Creek several miles south of town. The Jeff Davis Legion of Young's Brigade, commanded by Col. Joseph Frederick Waring, manned this line. Waring's Georgians and Mississippians were fighting dismounted behind fence rails and inside rifle pits. At 10:30 A.M., the 92nd Illinois Mounted Infantry of Atkins's brigade collided with "the Jeff." Finding the planks torn from the bridge spanning Swift Creek, the Federals filed off the road and deployed into line of battle. The men of the 92nd whooped and hollered as they splashed across the creek, having just received word of Lee's surrender. The Illinoisans brandished seven-shot Spencer repeating rifles—mementos of their days as part of Col. John T. Wilder's "Lightning Brigade."[74]

Knowing that the 92nd Illinois would be most vulnerable while crossing the stream, the commander of Young's Brigade, Col. Gilbert J. "Gib" Wright, ordered the Phillips Legion to attack. The Georgians charged with drawn sabers and momentarily stalled the Illinoisans' advance, but their steel was no match for the 92nd's Spencers. Once the Phillips Legion had galloped out of harm's way, "the Jeff" opened fire on the 92nd, which responded by launching a charge of its own. A small detachment of Cobb's Legion rode up to protect "the Jeff's" open right flank, but the 92nd Illinois overran the Confederates, cutting off numerous Rebels from their commands. Lt. Wiley Howard of Cobb's Legion suddenly found himself "in one of the hottest encounters in the range of my experience." Closely pursued by the Illinoisans, Howard and three of his comrades raced for their lives. Bullets from the 92nd's Spencers "rained like hail," Howard thought, and claimed two of his comrades—one of whom was his best friend, Lt. Tom Dunnahoo. Defying the onrushing enemy, Howard galloped back to his fallen friend. "I came across [Dunnahoo]," Howard recalled, "and raised his head on my lap, his horse and mine standing there, and he gasped his last breath. [T]he blood flowing from his bosom had bespattered the picture of his little motherless daughter which he carried there." With a comrade's help, Howard lifted Dunnahoo's body and draped it across his saddle; he then fell back with the rest of Cobb's Legion.[75]

Kilpatrick's cavalry pursued the Confederates up the North Carolina Railroad, while skirmishers from Brig. Gen. George S. Greene's Fourteenth Corps infantry brigade clashed with another body of Southern cavalry near Stalling's Station, twelve miles south of Raleigh. And just a few miles south of the capital, Atkins's cavalry brigade and a section of the 23rd New York Battery repulsed another charge of Wade Hampton's rear guard, cutting it off from the main body. The Yankees surrounded Hampton, presenting

The Final Scene of the Drama

"Little Kil" with an ideal opportunity to exact revenge for his "Shirt-tail Skedaddle" at Monroe's Crossroads.[76]

In the midst of the action, the Federals glimpsed a retreating locomotive and passenger coach. Flying a white flag above the solitary coach, the train appeared incongruous amid the clouds of gunpowder smoke and the converging lines of battle. Whatever General Atkins's thoughts were at that moment, he could not have guessed that the train carried his future father-in-law.[77]

CHAPTER 5

WE ARE NOT ENEMIES,
I HOPE?

Senator Graham stood knocking on the front door of the Governor's Palace before sunrise on Wednesday, April 12. Upon receiving Vance's telegram of the previous day urging him to come to Raleigh, Graham had taken the first train, leaving Hillsborough at 11:00 P.M. He arrived in Raleigh four hours later, weary but determined to do what he could for the governor. Ushered inside, Graham met Swain and Vance, the latter at his desk writing dispatches by candlelight. Aside from Col. James G. Burr of the governor's staff, they were the only occupants of the executive mansion. Vance had sent his wife, Hattie, and their four sons, along with most of the furniture, west to Statesville.[1]

The four men had breakfast and then rode to the capitol, where Vance drafted a letter to General Sherman. The governor was at last taking the step so strongly urged upon him by Graham and Swain. "Understanding that your army is advancing on this capital," the letter began, "I have to request, under proper safe-conduct, a personal interview, in such time as may be agreeable to you, for the purpose of conferring upon the subject of a suspension of hostilities, with a view to further communications with the authorities of the United States, touching the final termination of the existing war. If you concur in the propriety of such a proceeding I shall be obliged by an early reply." Colonel Burr recalled that Vance signed the document and then bowed his head down on the desk, "completely unmanned."[2]

Vance instructed his two commissioners to deliver his letter to Sherman and "learn upon what terms I could remain & exercise the functions of my office." The governor directed two of his aides, Colonel Burr and Maj. John

Devereux, to accompany the commissioners. Catching wind of the scheme, the state surgeon general, Dr. Edward Warren, went to Vance and volunteered his services. "I believe, Warren," the governor quipped, "you would volunteer to go to the devil if an expedition were started for the domains of his Satanic Majesty." Only Swain and Graham knew the objective of their mission; Burr, Devereux, and Warren assumed they were merely seeking protection for the capital (although the three must have had an inkling of the commissioners' instructions). The governor next obtained General Hardee's permission to send a flag of truce through his lines, as well as a written order to that effect. At 10:00 A.M., the commissioners and their three-man escort boarded the train and were on their way to Sherman's headquarters. Because the Union advance was reported to be just fourteen miles from Raleigh, Vance expected the party's return by no later than 4:00 that afternoon.[3]

Vance spent a hectic day at his office in the capitol. Dozens of Raleighites sought the governor's advice. He invariably told them to remain at their homes, for their presence was the best means of protecting their families and property. Several visitors, including Bartholomew Moore, Kenneth Rayner, and former governor Thomas Bragg, were no less eager to advise Vance. Another self-appointed counselor, Duncan K. McRae, editor of the pro-Davis *Raleigh Confederate,* burst into Vance's office demanding to know if the governor had taken leave of his senses. McRae had just learned from Kenneth Rayner that Graham and Swain were en route to Sherman's headquarters to surrender the Old North State.[4]

"Governor," McRae said, "if you contemplate being engaged in such a transaction, before you enter on it you had better get some friend to take a grapevine and hang you by the neck until you are dead, for you will thereby avoid a great infamy."

"Why, McRae," Vance replied, "I have no thought of such a thing. . . . I mean to stand on Confederate soil as long as there is ground enough to pirouette on one toe, and under the Confederate flag while there is a rag left to flutter in the breeze." With that, McRae left Vance's office, satisfied that the governor had no intention of treating with the enemy.[5]

McRae soon realized that *something* was afoot, for as he left Capitol Square, another acquaintance greeted him with news of the Graham-Swain peace mission. The editor believed that the two former governors had to be stopped at once. He went to the office of General Johnston's chief of staff, Col. Archer Anderson, and apprised him of the situation. The two men hurried to the telegraph office, where Anderson sent a message addressed to Johnston and President Davis at Greensboro. "I am reliably informed Vance is sending Graham and Swain to Sherman with proposal

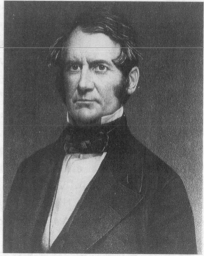

The peace commissioners: President David L. Swain of the University of North Carolina (left) and Senator William A. Graham of North Carolina (right). (North Carolina Division of Archives and History)

for armistice and assembly of legislature," Anderson wrote. "I have tele-graphed General Hampton not to let them pass till he hears from you."[6]

The commissioners' train crept southward from Raleigh because the conductor, nineteen-year-old Dallas Ward, believed that a slow-moving object was less apt to be fired on than a fast one. Inside the coach, the passengers exchanged only a few whispered words, keenly aware of the danger ahead. The commissioners and their escort knew that, despite the white flag fluttering above their car, they might suddenly find themselves under fire from either friend or foe. Near Auburn, several miles southeast of town, General Hampton stopped the train. The general boarded and met Graham and Swain, who presented Hardee's safe-conduct and Vance's letter. After reading the documents, Hampton remarked that although Hardee was his superior and orders were orders, he had grave doubts as to the propriety of the mission. Hampton then wrote a dispatch to Sherman, accompanied by a note from Graham and Swain requesting a conference. The general sent a courier under flag of truce with the letters and directed the train to advance slowly pending Sherman's reply.[7]

The train had advanced about a mile when a staff officer from Hampton galloped up and ordered it to halt. The officer informed the commissioners that Hampton had just received instructions from Johnston to cancel the safe-conduct and return the train to Raleigh. Graham replied that such

We *Are Not Enemies, I Hope?*

an order should be given by Hampton himself, and, in the meantime, the train would remain where it had stopped. Hampton soon arrived and read the dispatch he had just sent Sherman, informing the Union commander that Graham and Swain were returning to Raleigh. The two commissioners expressed their disappointment at this sudden turn of events. The engine was reversed, and the mission to Sherman appeared to have ended before it had properly begun.[8]

The train had retired a short distance when the rattle of small arms fire heralded the approach of Union cavalry. "They piled down upon us like wild Indians," Dallas Ward recalled. Dr. Warren was standing on a platform behind the tender when a squad of Yankee troopers, "with wild yells and leveled weapons," rushed the train and opened fire on him. Had Warren not crouched down behind the tender, he might have had an opportunity to test Vance's theory regarding an expedition to the infernal regions. Terrified, Warren thrust his handkerchief skyward in token of surrender.[9]

The train halted, surrounded by several hundred troopers of the 9th Michigan Cavalry and the 92nd Illinois Mounted Infantry of Atkins's brigade. Several of the "cursing and hooting" cavalrymen poked their weapons into the car and yelled, "Come out of that coach!" Putting on a brave front before the cocked rifles and carbines, Warren demanded to see the Federals' commanding officer. Moments later, the doctor found himself standing face-to-face with Lt. Col. George L. Godfrey of Kilpatrick's staff. "I will conduct you to headquarters," Godfrey told Warren. "But you must keep near to me, for these are a wild set of fellows, and it is difficult to control them." While Warren descended from the front of the train (taking care to stay close to Godfrey), the rest of the party exited from the back. General Atkins rode up in the meantime and informed the commissioners that he was sending them under escort to Kilpatrick's headquarters. While the others were led away, young Ward and the engineer were detained at gunpoint. The youth was promptly relieved of his watch and $2,200 in Confederate money, and Graham lost his carpetbag and personal effects when some Federals ransacked the coach. Ward recalled that his captors also "enjoyed making sport of me and calling me 'little Johnny Rebel.' "[10]

The commissioners and their escort were taken by carriage to Kilpatrick's headquarters at the home of a Mr. Fort. The Federal cavalry commander greeted them politely and then read Hardee's safe-conduct and Vance's letter to Sherman. "It is true, gentlemen," Kilpatrick said, looking up from the papers, "that you came under the protection of a flag of truce, and are the bearers of important dispatches to my Commanding General, but that gave you no right to cross my skirmish line while a fight was going on." Under the circumstances, "Little Kil" observed, he had every right

Bvt. Maj. Gen. Judson Kilpatrick, Sherman's cavalry commander and the man "Uncle Billy" allegedly called "a hell of a damned fool." (Library of Congress)

to consider the commissioners prisoners of war—which right he had no intention of exercising. Graham replied that the circumstances explained themselves, for the party obviously had not intended to ride into a cross-fire.[11]

Kilpatrick abruptly concluded the debate by saying, "Well, as you had started to see General Sherman, see him you should." The cavalry commander told the commissioners that any man who willingly shed blood

We Are Not Enemies, I Hope?

from that time forward was a murderer. He then read them Sherman's Special Field Orders No. 54:

> The general commanding announces to the army that he has official notice from General Grant that General Lee surrendered to him his entire army on the 9th instant at Appomattox Court-House, Va. Glory to God and our country, and all honor to our comrades in arms, toward whom we are marching. A little more labor, a little more toil on our part, the great race is won, and our Government stands regenerated after four long years of bloody war.

Graham and Swain were thunderstruck. They had heard the rumors and seen Davis's telegram to Vance, but this was the first conclusive intelligence of the catastrophe. Because the commissioners were in the presence of an enemy, they reacted to the news with all the stoic indifference they could muster. Kilpatrick ordered them taken to a safe place while he communicated with Sherman.[12]

Graham, Swain, and their escort walked about a mile to the rear in full view of Kilpatrick's men, who subjected them to innumerable "jibes and jeers and ribald jests," remembered Colonel Burr, who found the Yankees' insults "irritating almost beyond endurance." The former governors were the "especial butts and targets" of the troopers' barbs, recalled Dr. Warren, "as they were dressed in long-tailed coats and tall beaver hats, *ante-bellum* relics, which they had especially donned for the occasion." The two commissioners passed the jeering bystanders "with measured tread and the dignity of Roman Senators, [though] indignant to the last degree." The doctor was amused by the ludicrous scene and found himself unable to repress an occasional outburst of laughter. "Every now and then [the soldiers] gave me a shot as well," Warren admitted, "but having less dignity to support . . . , I only smiled in return and let them have their fun." The commissioners were taken to a house near the railroad and kept there for about an hour, until Kilpatrick summoned them back to his headquarters. He spared their wounded pride further injury by providing a carriage for the return trip.[13]

Upon their return, Kilpatrick informed the commissioners that he would send them to Sherman's headquarters as soon as their locomotive was ready. The Union cavalry commander ordered his band to entertain his guests in the meantime. Colonel Burr expected to hear Kilpatrick request "Yankee Doodle," but after a moment's reflection, "Little Kil" turned to the bandmaster and said, "Play 'Dixie' for these gentlemen." Burr thought the band rendered it "most admirably" and recalled that he could "scarcely keep from shouting and tossing my hat up in the air."[14]

At length the commissioners were escorted to their train and sent down to Sherman's headquarters at Gulley's Station, accompanied by Kilpatrick's adjutant, Maj. L. G. Estes, and an escort of forty men stationed inside and atop the coach. As the train traveled southward, a wall of blue converged on either side of the track, cheering the flag of truce and the peace it portended. Railroad conductor Dallas Ward recalled that it was dark enough to see the glow of campfires in every direction.[15]

General Sherman and his staff were waiting at Gulley's Station when the commissioners' train pulled in. The Union commander greeted his guests warmly and took them to his headquarters for dinner. Sherman assured the commissioners that they were *not* his prisoners, though privately he agreed with Kilpatrick that they were not entitled to a flag of truce. In the interest of peace, however, Sherman respected their intentions. Major Devereux was surprised to find Sherman a courteous host—in contrast with Kilpatrick, whom he characterized as "a happy compound of braggart and brute."[16]

Graham presented Vance's letter to Sherman and asked him if the governor could remain in office during Federal occupation. The general was receptive to Vance's propositions and was willing to let him continue as governor. Sherman wrote a reply to Vance, enclosing a safeguard for the governor and other state officials who wished to remain in Raleigh: "I would gladly have enabled you to meet me here, but some interruption occurred to the train, by the orders of General Johnston, after it had passed within the lines of my cavalry advance, but as it came out in good faith it shall be returned in good faith, and will in no measure be claimed by us." The Union commander doubted the feasibility of an immediate suspension of hostilities between his army and Johnston's, but he assured the governor: "I will aid you all in my power to contribute to the end you aim to reach, the termination of the existing war."[17]

By permitting Vance to remain in the capital, Sherman was repeating the experiment he had attempted the previous September, when he had invited Governor Joseph E. Brown of Georgia to meet him in Atlanta to discuss peace terms. Sherman had proposed to pay for his army's provisions and forage and cease his policy of destruction if Brown ordered the withdrawal of all Georgia troops from the Confederate army. Although Brown never responded, Sherman believed that the Georgia governor desired to cooperate but hesitated for fear of reprisal. Remembering Lincoln's enthusiastic response to the Brown peace overture, Sherman now felt free to act on his own judgment. He hoped to persuade Vance to do what Brown would not—withdraw his state's troops from the Confederate army.[18]

At the conclusion of their discussion, the general, his staff, and his guests

We *Are Not Enemies, I Hope?*

sat down to supper. During the meal Swain remarked that before the war he and Sherman had been engaged in the same profession. Noting that he had indeed been president of the Louisiana Seminary of Learning and Military Academy, Sherman said he knew that Swain was president of the University of North Carolina. "Two or three of your boys were with me for a time," Swain said. "Yes," the general answered, "and many more of yours have been with me during the war, who came, poor fellows, before they were men, and when they ought to have remained with you. And they too frequently helped to fill my hospitals. I think, however, when they return, they will do me the justice to tell you I treated them kindly." Swain asked after a former student of his, Maj. Gen. Frank Blair, who commanded the Seventeenth Corps in Howard's wing. Replying that Blair was no more than a few hours' ride from Gulley's Station, "Uncle Billy" noted that he had read some accounts in a Raleigh newspaper of the destruction Blair had wreaked in Fayetteville. "I will turn Frank over to you to answer for it in the morning," Sherman joked.[19]

The conversation abruptly took a darker turn when Swain mentioned the burning of Columbia. Sherman angrily denied responsibility, stating that he and his lieutenants had "strained every nerve" to put the fire out: "I declare in the presence of my God that Hampton burned Columbia, and that he alone is responsible for it." The Union commander insisted that the fire started when glowing embers from the cotton Hampton had burned in the streets were scattered throughout the town by high winds.[20]

Colonel Burr observed that, aside from this brief outburst, Sherman "maintained a courtesy of manners that I did not expect." Burr noted that, while the general's actions opened him to the "severest condemnation," Sherman nevertheless impressed him "as a man of quick perception, resolute will and prompt action, a rough unpolished man, who fought for himself and [w]ould not brook opposition to his opinions."[21]

After a long conversation, Sherman remarked that the hour was late and it was time to retire. He informed the commissioners that their locomotive was undergoing repairs but would be ready by dawn tomorrow. Though dubious as to the reason for their detention, Graham and Swain resigned themselves to the situation. For all their disappointment, common sense indicated that they would be safer returning in the morning.[22]

The commanding general invited Graham to share his tent, while Swain received an invitation from an unexpected source. One of Sherman's staff officers, Maj. Henry Hitchcock, introduced himself to Swain, noting that his mother often referred to a childhood playmate, "Davie Swain of Buncombe County." Swain was delighted at this coincidence and rattled off several anecdotes about Hitchcock's mother that caused the major to feel he had known Swain all his life. After some polite disagreement, Hitchcock succeeded in turning over his tent to his mother's old friend.[23]

On the night of April 12, Sherman's grand army camped on an arc extending a dozen miles to the south and east of Raleigh. The Fourteenth Corps of Slocum's wing had advanced to Gulley's Station, fourteen miles southeast of Raleigh on the Smithfield Road, while the Twentieth Corps had marched to within the same distance on the Elevation Road to the west. The Fifteenth Corps of Howard's wing halted at Pineville, a few miles east of the Fourteenth Corps, while the Seventeenth Corps bivouacked two miles north of Mitchener's Station after a grueling ten-mile march over muddy roads that had proved virtually impassable. Far to the rear, Schofield's Army of the Ohio stopped at Middle Creek. At Fifteenth Corps commander John Logan's behest, the 29th Missouri Mounted Infantry rode ahead to Battle's Bridge to secure the crossing. But the commander of the 29th, Col. Joseph S. Gage, discovered that Wheeler's cavalry had burned that bridge before crossing the Neuse at Hinton's Bridge, several miles to the north.[24]

As Wheeler was slipping into Raleigh from the east, Hampton had found his escape route south of town blocked by Atkins's brigade of Kilpatrick's cavalry. "Little Kil" intended to capture his adversary or drive him into the Neuse, thus avenging his "Shirt-tail Skedaddle." But the resourceful Hampton dashed into town at nightfall, proving as slippery on the outskirts of Raleigh as Kilpatrick had been at Monroe's Crossroads.[25]

Meanwhile, the Army of Tennessee's infantry camped on a line stretching from Page's Station, eight miles west of Raleigh, to Durham's Station, twenty-six miles west of the capital. Division commander Patton Anderson reported that the wholesale straggling of April 11 had been virtually eliminated, thanks to "extraordinary exertion and slow marching" on the part of his troops. On April 13, Lee's Corps and Stewart's Corps would continue up the Hillsborough Road, while Hardee's Corps, under the temporary command of Maj. Gen. Frank Cheatham, would turn left at Morrisville and take the Chapel Hill Road. Hardee would remain in command of the army during Johnston's absence and would travel with Stewart and Lee.[26]

To the east, Joe Wheeler's cavalry rode through Raleigh—albeit not quickly enough for some residents. Among Southern civilians, "Wheeler's men" had almost as unsavory a reputation as Sherman's dreaded bummers—a reputation sometimes deserved. Mrs. J. L. Pennington, the wife of the editor of the *Raleigh Progress*, complained that a handful of Wheeler's troopers had dug up her garden in a vain search for her silverware and had

We Are Not Enemies, I Hope?

left only because of a warning that Sherman's army was on the outskirts of town.[27]

The villainous stereotype of "Wheeler's men" proved difficult to overcome, as Georgia cavalryman William W. Gordon discovered. During a soiree at the home of Kenneth Rayner, Gordon was asked by Rayner's daughter Sally: "Captain, is it true what we hear, that Wheeler's cavalry, after being entertained by citizens, carry off the silver or any other small articles of value?" Wearing a deadpan expression, Gordon replied, "Certainly they do." Since the quizzical expression on Sally Rayner's face indicated that this was not the answer she expected, the mischievous Gordon added, "After a while I'll show you." Later, Gordon grabbed a handful of silverware and, with a broad gesture, stuffed it into his coat pocket. "Miss Rayner," he exclaimed, "this is the way we take things." When Sally turned around and saw the half-concealed silver, she gave a startled cry. All eyes suddenly focused on the gleaming silverware in Gordon's pocket. The embarrassed captain explained that he was merely playing a joke on Miss Rayner, but he believed that several people in the room suspected him of darker motives.[28]

The wild and profoundly unmilitary character of Wheeler's cavalry made a lasting impression on many residents of the capital. Margaret Devereux recalled witnessing a squad of troopers literally fall out in the middle of the street when ordered to halt, sleeping wherever they happened to collapse and forcing passersby to step over them. One cavalryman exclaimed as he pointed to the weathercock atop the steeple of Christ Episcopal Church that it was the first and only time he had seen a chicken that Joe Wheeler's boys could not catch. Some of the troopers plundered the commissary and quartermaster stores and several other establishments in town. The poet Mary Bayard Clarke saw a squad of Wheeler's horsemen galloping down the street, tossing everything from handkerchiefs to hoop skirts at female bystanders while shouting, "Take 'em, ladies! Take 'em! The Yankees'll get 'em if we don't." Clarke assumed that these sundry articles had *not* been issued to Wheeler's cavalry by the Confederate government and concluded that they must have been stolen. Railroad executive Kemp P. Battle watched the troopers ride through town and noted their faded and tattered uniforms. Despite their downtrodden appearance, they looked as defiant as ever, Battle observed, and their horses appeared to be in good condition. Several of the riders called out to him: "We've got 'em where we want 'em, haven't we, old man!" Battle interpreted this comment to mean that "they were making fun of the bragging 'stay at homes'"—civilians such as himself who left the fighting to others. For the first time in his life, Battle carried a revolver with the expectation of using it. "General Wheeler may have been [unfairly] maligned," Battle noted, "but the lawless conduct of some of his soldiers was generally credited." [29]

As Johnston's army evacuated Raleigh, state treasurer Jonathan Worth and state adjutant general R. C. Gatlin transferred the state's remaining stores and archives. Since removing the army's supplies took first priority, the state's train did not get under way until 9:00 P.M. on April 12, accompanied by Worth, Gatlin, and their assistants. Many wounded Confederates were also loaded into cars and sent west. Joining the westward exodus were some of the capital's more outspoken citizens, including editor Duncan K. McRae, who chose to flee with Johnston's army or the state train rather than place themselves at the mercy of Sherman's soldiery. [30]

There was no more anxious person in Raleigh than Governor Vance, who awaited word from his commissioners. After learning that Johnston had ordered their return to Raleigh, Vance heard nothing of them until nightfall, when Wheeler reported the capture of their train. Concluding that his peace mission had failed, Vance decided to leave the capital that night, unwilling to surrender himself unconditionally to the Federals. The governor wrote Sherman, indicating that he had authorized Mayor Harrison to surrender the town and requesting that the citizens, capitol, and state institutions be protected. Vance waited until midnight for the commissioners' return and then rode eight miles west to Hoke's camp near Page's Station. The governor was accompanied by two volunteer aides, Captains George P. Bryan and J. J. Guthrie, but other subordinates were conspicuously absent. "Many of my staff officers basely deserted me," Vance later contended. "I rode out of Raleigh . . . without a single officer of all my staff with me! Not one. I shall hit the deserters some day, *hard*." [31]

The governor's hopes of remaining in the capital and obtaining a separate peace for his state had evaporated. Vance later maintained that he was grateful for this result, because it "kept the N C troops to their colors and . . . enabled me to say that whilst there was a soldier in the field I stood with him." It also saved him the embarrassment of having to explain why he had undertaken separate negotiations with Sherman. Yet Vance felt compelled to justify himself to President Davis on the afternoon of April 12, when he received word that Johnston had recalled the commissioners' train. The governor explained that his letter to Sherman "requesting an interview" had met with Johnston's and Hardee's approval, and that he had no intention of doing "anything subversive of your prerogative or without consultation with yourself." Davis replied that he "could not attribute to you such purpose as you disclaim" but observed that Vance's

We Are Not Enemies, I Hope?

"military experience and good judgment" should have told him that he had acted without proper authority.[32]

The coming weeks would prove to be a trying time for Vance. Finding himself relegated to figurehead status, the Tar Heel governor could only look on while others determined the fate of his state and its people.

Swain, Graham, and their escort left Sherman's headquarters at daybreak on April 13. Seeing them off at Gulley's Station were the commanding general and Major Hitchcock. As the North Carolinians boarded the coach, Swain shook hands with Hitchcock, saying, "Goodbye Major—*we are not enemies, I hope?*" On the way to Raleigh, their train stopped at Kilpatrick's headquarters, five miles south of town. The commissioners presented Sherman's letter and safeguard to the cavalry commander, who "received the order with very great dissatisfaction," thought Major Devereux. Kilpatrick told Swain and Graham that they were free to continue on their way, but he issued a stern warning: "If you show any resistance, *we will give you hell.*" [33]

The day dawned cold and cloudy, with a light rain falling. A mile from the capital, the commissioners spotted a thick column of smoke, which they took to mean that the railroad depot was on fire. By the time they reached the station house, the flames had spread to the track, forcing them to stop. They walked to the farther end of the depot in hopes of finding another train for their journey to Hillsborough, but to no avail. After sending Devereux and Warren to inform General Wheeler that the city would be formally surrendered, Swain and Graham searched for a horse and carriage. The two younger men soon found Wheeler and showed him a copy of Sherman's safeguard. The cavalry commander promised to withdraw his forces at once.[34]

Meanwhile, Graham, Swain, and Burr looked in vain for transportation. The commissioners walked from the Governor's Palace at the foot of Fayetteville Street to the capitol without meeting anyone. At the statehouse, Graham and Swain learned that Governor Vance had left Raleigh after hearing that the commissioners had been captured, and that he was en route to Hillsborough. The two former governors decided on a new course of action: Graham and Burr would make their way to Hillsborough, while Swain awaited the Federal advance at the capitol. The senator and the colonel began their journey on foot, following Wheeler's cavalry.[35]

With the caretaker's help, Swain opened the doors and shuttered windows of the governor's office; then, with Sherman's safeguard in hand, he took his station at the south entrance of the capitol. At that moment, strag-

Maj. Gen. Joseph Wheeler, Wade Hampton's second-in-command. A courageous soldier and a superb horseman, Wheeler lacked his superior's outstanding leadership skills. (Massachusetts Commandery, Military Order of the Loyal Legion Collection, U.S. Army Military History Institute)

glers from Wheeler's cavalry dismounted at the head of Fayetteville Street and began looting several stores. Swain warned the men that Sherman's advance was close at hand and that any "show of resistance might result in the destruction of the city." The commissioner was joined by a citizen who added his own plea for restraint, but the cavalrymen were unmoved: "D——n Sherman and the town too," one of the pillagers shouted.[36]

More than thirty years before, Swain had stood on this site and watched the old State House burn to the ground; one year later, he had been present at the dedication of the new capitol, which he now sought to protect. He knew that if the stragglers fired on Sherman's advance, the result could make the conflagration of thirty-four years ago seem mere child's play.

Swain saw the head of Kilpatrick's column swing into view at the far end of Fayetteville Street. He shouted a warning to the stragglers, who dashed out of stores, mounted their horses, and sped off—except for the "chivalric leader," as Swain contemptuously dubbed him. The lone rider calmly awaited the Yankees' approach, grasping his horse's bridle rein with one hand and his revolver with the other. Swain admired the Confederate's courage, but he also feared that Raleigh's fate might rest in the nameless rider's hands.[37]

At first light a detail of ten Federal horsemen had filed into the Raleigh Road near Gulley's Station. Passing the camps of Kilpatrick's cavalry, the riders advanced cautiously into the no man's land bordering the town. Two of the men rode far to the front, while the remainder followed in single file at wide intervals. As dawn broke, they glimpsed several church spires and the dome of the capitol. To all appearances they could have been a band of bummers eager for provisions and plunder. Yet these men were on a different errand: they were under orders to capture the capital of North Carolina in the name of the First Brigade, First Division, Fourteenth Corps. The detail consisted of five staff officers and five orderlies. On the evening of April 12, Bvt. Brig. Gen. Harrison C. Hobart had summoned the five officers—Maj. James T. Reeve, Captains Daniel W. Benham, James E. Stuart, and B. J. Van Valkenburgh, and Lt. Charles A. Whittaker—to his headquarters for an unusual assignment. Hobart was anxious to beat the Twentieth Corps and Kilpatrick's cavalry into Raleigh, but with the former marching on a parallel road and the latter squarely in his front, the conventional method of sending out a strong skirmish line would only guarantee failure. Instead, Hobart directed his five officers and their orderlies to ride forward and determine whether the state capital was held in force. If possible, they were to dash into town and capture it for the Fourteenth Corps.[38]

Within two miles of Raleigh, the Federal detachment met a Confederate delegation carrying a flag of truce in the form of a white silk handkerchief tied to a cavalry saber. The commanding officer bore a dispatch from Wade Hampton stating that the Confederate army had uncovered Raleigh and the mayor wished to make a formal surrender. The Federal officers briefly conferred and decided that they should send for Kilpatrick, who was with his lead regiment a mile to the rear. "Little Kil" soon arrived and directed the Confederate flag of truce to lead the way. A Southern officer accompanying the flag later described the language of the Union cavalry commander as " 'By God' & 'God-damn' all the time."[39]

The Federal party had proceeded another half mile when it was met by a second flag of truce before the toll gate on Holleman Road. Waiting in carriages were Mayor Harrison and a special committee consisting of eight civic commissioners and private citizens, including the spokesman, Kenneth Rayner. In a brief speech to Kilpatrick and other Federals, Rayner formally surrendered the town, pledging that the Confederate army would offer no resistance and the citizens would submit quietly. He then requested protection for the inhabitants and their property. Kilpatrick promised to furnish guards for both public buildings and private homes. At the conclusion of the ceremony, the Union cavalry commander sent his provost marshal, Capt. William H. Day, and an aide, Capt. Edward M. Hayes, into Raleigh with General Hobart's ten-man detachment. The delegation was accompanied by several newspaper reporters eager for a story; they would not be disappointed.[40]

On entering the capital, the party passed a line of earthworks that ringed the town and saw several siege guns left behind by the retreating Confederates. The first person they met was a woman—"well-dressed and fine-looking," thought Major Reeve—who bid them, "Welcome to Raleigh." The detail then headed up Fayetteville Street toward the capitol, well in advance of the main body of Kilpatrick's cavalry. They saw a solitary rider in blue stationed in the middle of the street before the statehouse. "Well, there is a bummer who has gotten in ahead of us," said one disappointed officer. When the Federals approached to within "easy pistol range," Reeve noted, the so-called bummer drew a revolver and opened fire on them. After emptying his pistol, the blue-clad Confederate spurred his horse and sped west down Morgan Street, hoping to overtake his comrades on Hillsborough Street one block to the north. The Federals soon recovered from their confusion and galloped off in pursuit.[41]

Fortune now deserted the lone Confederate. He came to a dead end on Morgan Street at the North Carolina Railroad cut and was forced to backtrack. Turning the corner at West Street, both the rider and his mount tumbled headlong when his saddle girt broke. The cavalryman picked him-

We Are Not Enemies, I Hope?

self up and continued on foot while his horse dashed ahead to the Confederates at the Hillsborough Street bridge. Federal pursuers captured the unfortunate Southerner within sight of his comrades and escorted him back to Capitol Square. The prisoner identified himself as Lieutenant Walsh of the 11th Texas Cavalry. He was brought before Kilpatrick, who sentenced him to be summarily executed for violating Raleigh's surrender. The Texan reportedly asked for five minutes to write to his wife but was refused. He was then taken to Lovejoy's Grove a few blocks from the capitol and hanged. In the weeks following Walsh's execution, several young ladies of the town decorated his grave with flowers, "little aware how nearly the city may have been on the verge of devastation," contended Swain, "from this rash act of lawless warfare." [42]

Shortly after Walsh's sentencing, a second Confederate captive was brought before Kilpatrick. He was Lt. Theodore Calhoun James, the acting commandant and provost marshal of the Post of Raleigh. A veteran of Lee's Army of Northern Virginia, James had served as the adjutant of the 3rd North Carolina until he lost his right arm in the Battle of the Wilderness. He had remained in the capital to prevent the depredations of Wheeler's stragglers and to say farewell to several female friends. James was captured while trying to bluff a Union cavalryman into surrendering; his captors soon discovered that the one-armed Confederate was also unarmed. Kilpatrick was in a foul mood when James was brought before him and seemed inclined to deal as harshly with the North Carolinian as he had dealt with the Texan. But James proved equal to the occasion.

"Do you know what we do with such men as you?" Kilpatrick asked his prisoner.

"No," James said, "and I don't know that I care."

"We hang them."

"Very well," James replied. "You will have to hang me then. I cannot help myself." [43]

Kilpatrick did not hang the defiant James, having learned that the lieutenant was not associated with Wheeler's stragglers. Instead, he had James imprisoned in the county jail, where the Tar Heel remained for several weeks, refusing to take the loyalty oath as a condition of his release. The Union provost marshal serving as James's jailer developed a grudging respect for his Rebel prisoner and was pleased to inform him one morning that he was a free man. According to an eyewitness, by the time James was set free his cell was "a perfect bower of roses," thanks to numerous gifts of flowers from female admirers. [44]

While Kilpatrick dealt with the two Confederate prisoners, his cavalry took possession of Raleigh. Col. Michael Kerwin's brigade enjoyed the

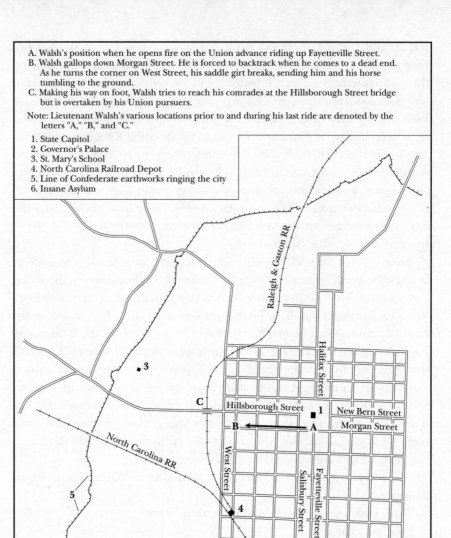

A. Walsh's position when he opens fire on the Union advance riding up Fayetteville Street.
B. Walsh gallops down Morgan Street. He is forced to backtrack when he comes to a dead end. As he turns the corner on West Street, his saddle girt breaks, sending him and his horse tumbling to the ground.
C. Making his way on foot, Walsh tries to reach his comrades at the Hillsborough Street bridge but is overtaken by his Union pursuers.

Note: Lieutenant Walsh's various locations prior to and during his last ride are denoted by the letters "A," "B," and "C."

1. State Capitol
2. Governor's Palace
3. St. Mary's School
4. North Carolina Railroad Depot
5. Line of Confederate earthworks ringing the city
6. Insane Asylum

Map 4. Map of Raleigh showing the last ride of Lieutenant Walsh, April 13, 1865

honor of entering the North Carolina capital first. Brigade adjutant Lew McMakin immediately posted guards from the 5th Ohio Cavalry throughout the town, and not a moment too soon, for bummers were already busy at their work. When an indignant woman demanded a safeguard before the Yankees pillaged her house, McMakin told her that he would see to it at once. Attempting to soothe her frazzled nerves, the adjutant assured her that she need not worry much longer, for the war was almost over. But his ploy backfired. "That's a nasty, dirty, Yankee lie!" she retorted, slamming the door in McMakin's face amid the laughter of his comrades.[45]

The Stars and Stripes and the Third Cavalry Division's guidon soon fluttered above the capitol, hoisted by a squad from the 13th Pennsylvania Cavalry. "We done some tall old Cheering as we passed the Capitol and saw our . . . Flags floating from the dome," wrote the 9th Pennsylvania Cavalry's Maj. George Shuman. At the south entrance of the statehouse, Swain presented Sherman's safeguard to the officer commanding the flag-raising detail. Swain was later joined by several state and civic officials, including Dr. Warren and Mayor Harrison, who answered the questions of Kilpatrick's provost marshal, Captain Day, concerning Raleigh's layout. Among the trophies taken by Kilpatrick's troopers were some Union and Confederate flags found inside the capitol.[46]

Raleigh soon teemed with Federal cavalry. A citizen recalled seeing row after row of blue-clad horsemen riding up Fayetteville Street, their rubber ponchos glistening in the rain. The Union cavalrymen met with an enthusiastic reception from numerous black residents, who danced about them while shouting words of welcome. Women stood at their doors and windows waving handkerchiefs and greeting the Federals as they passed. When General Atkins reached St. Mary's School on the western outskirts of town, he ordered his brigade to halt and had his band from the 92nd Illinois Mounted Infantry serenade the young ladies.[47]

Kilpatrick's cavalry rested in the capital for an hour before resuming its pursuit of the Confederate rear guard. Following the cavalry came the 21st Wisconsin of Hobart's Fourteenth Corps brigade, the first regiment of Sherman's infantry to enter the town. In close succession, left wing commander Slocum, Fourteenth Corps commander Davis, and commander in chief Sherman galloped past the 21st, each general accompanied by his staff and escort. The Wisconsinites marched to Capitol Square, where they found the three generals lined up before the statue of George Washington. Railroad conductor Dallas Ward noted that Sherman was standing on the same spot occupied by General Johnston just two days before, during the review of *his* troops. Ward also remarked on the contrast between the Federals' bright new uniforms and the faded and torn clothing of the Confederates. The 21st Wisconsin stacked arms on the lawn and then fell out to make camp. Within minutes, the colors of the 21st were flying above the capitol dome.[48]

Beaten in the race for Raleigh, the Twentieth Corps found the Fourteenth Corps already at the railroad crossing where their routes converged several miles south of town. Since his division had the Twentieth Corps's advance, Alpheus Williams directed his pioneers to build a new road to the left of the main thoroughfare occupied by the Fourteenth Corps. Angered by the "unprecedented straggling" of his division the day before, Williams ordered roll calls during halts of ten minutes or longer. Any soldier found "absent without proper authority" would be fined one month's pay for each infraction. The failure of an officer to enforce this punishment would result in his "dishonorable dismissal from Service." As a result of this order, straggling in Williams's division ceased to be a problem on April 13.[49]

The Twentieth Corps reached Raleigh about noon. As the 154th New York of Bvt. Maj. Gen. John W. Geary's division tramped into the suburbs, a small boy on the roadside remarked that he had stood there all morning and watched the Yankees pass, and he had yet to see one with horns on his head. A wit in the 154th replied that *he* had seen some with horns—horns of whiskey, that is. Several black bystanders told the New Yorkers that the Rebels had warned them the Yankees "would kill them all," but their presence indicated that they took such tales with a good deal of skepticism. The Twentieth Corps camped on the southwestern edge of town near the Insane Asylum, while the Fourteenth Corps bivouacked within the capital and on its northern and western fringes.[50]

The Federal right wing halted near the Neuse River on the afternoon of April 13, the Fifteenth Corps after crossing Hinton's Bridge (which Wheeler's cavalry had left intact) and the Seventeenth Corps upon reaching the smoldering ruins of Battle's Bridge, where it would lay its pontoon the next morning. The two corps camped ten miles east of Raleigh, while Schofield's Army of the Ohio bivouacked on a line extending from Smithfield to the capital.[51]

While the left wing marched into Raleigh, General Sherman left Capitol Square and established his headquarters at the Governor's Palace. "This is the fourth State Capitol he has walked into," marveled Sherman staff officer Henry Hitchcock. "It's a way he has." About 3:00 P.M., Swain and Graham paid a visit to the Union commander. The senator had just rejoined Swain at the capitol, having abandoned his attempt to reach Hillsborough. Graham had managed to persuade one of Wheeler's horsemen to let him ride double, but when Kilpatrick's advance suddenly appeared and opened fire, he prudently dismounted. The Federal cavalry had arrived none too

We Are Not Enemies, I Hope?

soon as far as Colonel Burr was concerned, for several of Wheeler's rear guard had just robbed him of his watch and were threatening to do worse. Moments later, Graham and Burr found themselves in the hands of the Yankees, the two men having survived a blistering crossfire—their second such close call in two days.[52]

Swain and Graham delivered the statehouse keys to Sherman, who assured them that he would protect the capital and its citizens. Expressing regret that the governor had fled, the Union commander wrote a safe-conduct for Vance and other government officials, which he entrusted to the commissioners. Sherman also furnished Graham and Swain with a horse and carriage and wrote another safe-conduct permitting them to return to their homes. The commissioners remained at the Governor's Palace as Sherman's guests for the evening. They were joined by Swain's daughter Eleanor, who presented the commanding general and his staff with a bouquet of flowers. The general's clerk, Sylvester "Vett" Noble, was quite smitten with "Ellie" Swain; he would not be the only Federal to fall under her spell. After staying overnight in Raleigh, Graham and Swain began their journey home the next morning.[53]

By mid-afternoon of April 13, it appeared that Raleigh would be spared the disaster that had befallen Columbia and would enjoy instead the relative peace and security that had marked Sherman's occupation of Savannah. While a long list of North Carolinians, including elder statesmen Graham and Swain, Mayor Harrison and his Board of Commissioners, and private citizens Kenneth Rayner and Bartholomew F. Moore, deserve praise for their courageous peacemaking efforts, the lion's share of credit for the quiet entry of Sherman's army into Raleigh should nevertheless go to the officers and men of that army. Without their cooperation, no amount of good intentions on the part of the civilian peace commissioners could have saved the North Carolina capital from catastrophe. The army that is so often remembered for its violent excesses exercised remarkable discipline and restraint at Savannah and Raleigh. Even so, the severest trial was yet to come for the Tar Heel capital and the Federal army that occupied it.

In contrast to Sherman's peaceful occupation of Raleigh, Kilpatrick's pursuit of Hampton was swift and unrelenting. "I will hunt him to the death," "Little Kil" vowed as he set out after his adversary. At 8:30 A.M. on April 13, the 13th Pennsylvania Cavalry struck Wheeler's rear guard behind barricades two miles west of Raleigh and a warm skirmish developed. While Lt. L. B. Manning's section of the 23rd New York Battery provided cover fire, the 13th Pennsylvania led the assault on the barricades, driving the Confederate rear guard back on the main body. The Federals' sudden onslaught took Wheeler's cavalry by surprise. Having drawn some corn from the North Carolina Railroad depot before it was burned, the Southerners were resting and feeding their horses when the bugles sounded "Boots and Saddles." As the dazed Confederates saddled and bridled their mounts, the Pennsylvanians burst in among them, panicking horses and riders and scattering them in all directions. "It was the worst stampeed that I ever saw—every man had to take care of himself," recalled O. P. Hargis, a trooper with the 1st Georgia Cavalry of Col. Charles C. Crews's Brigade. Rallying his men, Crews launched a countercharge against the 13th Pennsylvania. The Georgians blunted the Federals' momentum, enabling the rest of Wheeler's command to re-form and fall back in good order. Its objective accomplished, Crews's Brigade retreated westward, supported by Hagan's Alabama brigade.[54]

The Federals maintained a running fight with the Confederates for several hours. Meanwhile, Kilpatrick sent the 8th Indiana and 9th Pennsylvania cavalry regiments of Bvt. Brig. Gen. Thomas J. Jordan's brigade forward in relief of the 13th Pennsylvania. About four miles west of Raleigh the Hillsborough Road forked, compelling Hampton to divide his forces to cover both routes. He sent Butler's Division under Brig. Gen. Evander M. Law on one road and Wheeler's command on the other. Kilpatrick pressed Wheeler's column harder, for near Asbury Station two miles farther west, "Fighting Joe" was compelled to deploy his entire force, whereas Law required only the 10th Georgia Cavalry to hold off his pursuers. The two Confederate columns reunited at a crossroads near Page's Station, eight miles west of Raleigh, and then fell back another four miles to Morrisville, with the Federals in close pursuit. Halting on a hill just east of the village, the Union advance observed a long wagon train and a string of freight cars. General Kilpatrick ordered Lt. Joseph Kittinger's section of the 23rd New York Battery to unlimber and open fire on the retreating Confederates.[55]

A newcomer to Kilpatrick's division, the 23rd was a large field battery by Civil War standards, consisting of four two-gun sections. Kittinger's section was attached to Jordan's brigade and consisted of thirteen of the 23rd's veteran artillerymen and thirty-one cavalrymen detailed from Jordan's ranks. Their two three-inch rifled guns had changed hands twice during the past year. Originally the property of the 24th Indiana Battery, the cannon fell into Confederate hands when Maj. Gen. George Stoneman surrendered to Colonel Crews at the close of the failed McCook-Stoneman raid during the Atlanta campaign. Four months later, Kilpatrick's 8th Indiana and 3rd Kentucky recaptured the guns at Lovejoy's Station, Georgia. Since then, the guns had remained with "Little Kil's" cavalry. One of the targets of Kittinger's two cannon was Crews's Brigade, commanded by the man who had

We Are Not Enemies, I Hope?

accepted Stoneman's surrender and whose Georgians had hauled off the very guns now being used against them.[56]

After reaching the front at the gallop, Kittinger's section fired percussion shell and spherical case at the retreating Confederates, who dashed into houses and dived behind hastily built barricades. The village erupted with rifle and carbine fire as the Rebel horsemen attempted to silence the Federal battery. But weatherboarding and fence rails proved to be inadequate cover against shell and case shot, so the Southerners grudgingly fell back before the Union artillery's overwhelming fire.[57]

While Kittinger's two guns transformed Morrisville into kindling, the 9th Pennsylvania and 8th Indiana charged a locomotive as it left the depot. Just beyond the fleeing locomotive was a slow-moving troop train filled with wounded Confederates from Raleigh, including Brig. Gen. Daniel H. Reynolds, who noted that numerous "threats were made to kill the Conductor" if he allowed them to fall into enemy hands. The Federals galloped to within 100 yards of the rear locomotive, but Wheeler's cavalry repulsed them and enabled the troop train to escape—doubtless earning the gratitude of the conductor.[58]

After briefly skirmishing with the Federals to ensure the train's safe withdrawal, the Confederate cavalry uncovered Morrisville. Wheeler's command took the Chapel Hill Road and Law's two brigades continued up the Hillsborough Road, with the 8th Indiana pursuing Wheeler's rear guard for two miles. At Morrisville the Federals captured two dozen freight cars, some wagons filled with provisions, and several of Wheeler's cavalrymen, to whom they broke the news of Lee's surrender. "I have been scattering Wheeler's cavalry all day," Kilpatrick boasted in a mid-afternoon dispatch to Sherman. "His cavalry is totally demoralized." Sherman instructed "Little Kil" to rest his command the next day and resume operations on April 15.[59]

Sherman plotted the next stage of his campaign in Special Field Orders No. 55. His objective was to cut off Johnston's southerly line of retreat via Salisbury and Charlotte. The Federal grand army's point of concentration was Asheboro, about twenty-five miles south of Greensboro and forty miles east of Salisbury. On April 14, lead elements of the three Federal armies would begin the westward march, followed by the main body on April 15 and 16. Kilpatrick's cavalry would feint toward Hillsborough and Graham on the army's extreme right, supported by a division from Howard's right wing. The remainder of the right wing would advance via Pittsboro, the center under Schofield via Haywood, and the left wing under Slocum via Carthage.[60]

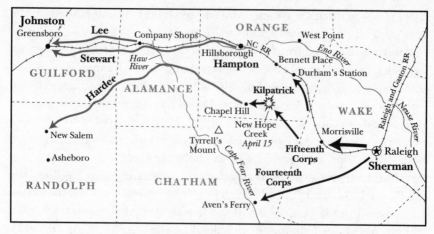

Map 5. The Army of Tennessee's line of retreat, April 13–16, 1865

The Federal commander instructed his lieutenants to deal kindly with the inhabitants. Anticipating "an early reconciliation" with the South, he forbade the destruction of railroads, mills, cotton, and produce without specific orders from an army commander. Sherman nevertheless permitted his troops to continue foraging, though he suggested that they take care "not to strip the poorer classes too closely."[61]

Unfortunately for Sherman and his grand army, the Confederates had a substantial head start. On the evening of April 13, Stewart's Corps and Lee's Corps camped at Hillsborough, and Hardee's Corps bivouacked two miles west of Chapel Hill. If Sherman hoped to win the race to Salisbury, his forces at Raleigh would have to cover 105 miles to the Confederates' 80—a race that Johnston's army could easily win, given that Sherman's pursuit was not the "push to the death" he had promised Grant. Nevertheless, "Uncle Billy" expected to play his trump card by having Phil Sheridan sweep down from Danville and turn Johnston's position at Greensboro. This scenario would have been feasible had Sheridan been poised to strike, but that was not the case. Contrary to Sherman's expectations, Sheridan and his three cavalry divisions were resting at Nottoway Court House, seventy-five miles northeast of Danville.[62]

Despite Sherman's careful planning, the outcome rested in Joseph E. Johnston's hands. The Confederate commander could march southward and make his escape, but he chose not to. Nor did Johnston intend to fight his adversary, for aside from the overwhelming odds he would have faced, he now regarded fighting another pitched battle as tantamount to murder. He could have dispersed his army and avoided surrendering, but he regarded this alternative as cowardly and destructive. Rather, Johnston

We Are Not Enemies, I Hope?

hoped to obtain fair terms for his men, and, if possible, for the Southern people in general. He realized that to negotiate from an advantageous position, he must keep his army intact and prevent it from being surrounded as Lee's had been at Appomattox Court House. Before he could open negotiations with Sherman, however, Johnston had to overcome a familiar obstacle in the form of his old nemesis, President Jefferson Davis.[63]

CHAPTER 6

TO OBTAIN FAIR TERMS
OF PEACE

On Palm Sunday, April 9, the day of Lee's surrender to Grant at Appomattox Court House, Maj. Gen. George Stoneman Jr. and his cavalry division made their second foray into North Carolina. Their return following a successful raid into southwestern Virginia took the Confederates in the Old North State by surprise, enabling the Federals to strike with devastating effect. Stoneman's objective was to destroy supplies, bridges, and railroads on Lee's and Johnston's probable routes of retreat—until Lee's surrender made Johnston's army the sole target. Stoneman, however, was unaware of this crucial shift in the Confederacy's fortunes when he struck in North Carolina.[1]

At Germanton, Stoneman directed Col. William J. Palmer's brigade to strike Salem, a dozen miles to the south, and then proceed twenty-five miles east to Greensboro, destroying railroad bridges and supply depots on his route. Meanwhile, Stoneman led his other two brigades toward Salisbury, the main target of his raid. Colonel Palmer reached Salem on the afternoon of April 10 and burned 7,000 bales of cotton. That night, Palmer divided his brigade into four detachments and sent them to the south and east. At noon the next day, the first detachment destroyed the Piedmont Railroad's bridge spanning Reedy Fork, ten miles north of Greensboro. Unknown to the Federal raiders, the train carrying President Jefferson Davis and his cabinet had crossed that bridge barely an hour beforehand. When apprised of his close call at Reedy Fork, Davis remarked, "A miss is as good as a mile." Nevertheless, the destruction wrought by other details of Stoneman's cavalry would prevent the Davis party from traveling beyond Greensboro by rail.[2]

Palmer's second detachment made a bold feint on Greensboro. After routing the 3rd South Carolina Cavalry in a surprise attack, the Federals rode to within two miles of Greensboro, where they cut a telegraph line and burned the North Carolina Railroad bridge across Buffalo Creek. The third detachment attacked Florence and Jamestown, about fifteen miles southwest of Greensboro, burning a gun factory, some Confederate cotton and commissary stores, and the North Carolina Railroad bridge spanning Deep River. Palmer's fourth detachment struck at High Point, a few miles southwest of Jamestown, burning 1,700 bales of cotton and two trains loaded with medical and commissary supplies. Having completed its work of destruction, Palmer's brigade rejoined Stoneman's main column on April 12. Palmer's four-pronged strike wreaked untold havoc on the enemy, but Stoneman could not judge his raid a success until he captured Salisbury.[3]

George Stoneman was fortunate to be leading this raid. He had been a conspicuous failure both as the Army of the Potomac's chief of cavalry during the Chancellorsville campaign and as commander of a cavalry division in Sherman's army during the Atlanta campaign. In December 1864, both Secretary of War Edwin M. Stanton and General Grant had recommended shelving Stoneman. Only the intervention of John M. Schofield, then commander of the Department of the Ohio, saved the cavalryman from reassignment to a desk job. Stoneman repaid Schofield's unwavering confidence in him by leading a successful raid into southwestern Virginia during the final weeks of 1864. Two months later, Stoneman was named commander of the District of East Tennessee. He was eager to launch a raid into South Carolina in support of Sherman's march, but several delays forced him to abandon that undertaking and shift his focus to Virginia and North Carolina.[4]

All that remained to make Stoneman's final raid of the war his greatest triumph was the capture of Salisbury. The town had both strategic and symbolic importance: it was the junction of the North Carolina and Western North Carolina Railroads; it boasted a foundry, an arsenal, and several warehouses containing state and Confederate goods; and it was the site of a notorious military prison. The capture of Salisbury would also go far in avenging Stoneman's disastrous raid on Macon and Andersonville, which had resulted in his surrender and subsequent humiliation.[5]

When Stoneman reached Salisbury on the morning of April 12, the town was defended by a scratch force of three light artillery batteries, a handful of frontline troops en route to their regiments, several hundred Home Guardsmen and state reservists, and a few companies of "galvanized Yankees"—Union captives who had agreed to serve in the Confederate army rather than rot in Southern prisons. Ironically, most of the regular

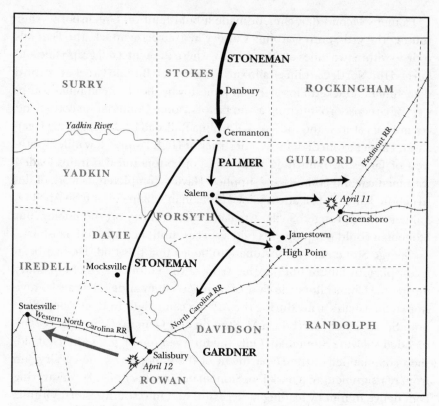

Map 6. Stoneman's last raid: North Carolina, April 9–13, 1865

Salisbury garrison was at Greensboro because the Confederates believed it was Stoneman's main target. William M. Gardner, a journeyman brigadier general, commanded the motley force defending Salisbury. Overseeing Gardner's artillery was Lt. Col. John C. Pemberton, an erstwhile lieutenant general whose Civil War career was as checkered as Stoneman's. After Pemberton's surrender to Grant at Vicksburg, President Davis had sought a new command for the general commensurate with his rank, but it soon became evident that he was the only man in the Confederacy who still valued the Pennsylvania-born Rebel. Pemberton therefore resigned his general's commission and agreed to serve as the commander of the Richmond artillery defenses. In January 1865, he was named the Confederate army's inspector of artillery and ordnance.[6]

General Gardner established his defensive position at Grant's Creek, about two miles west of Salisbury, spreading his meager force on a tenuous four-mile line to cover the incoming roads. At dawn, Stoneman deployed his two available brigades and launched a general assault, routing the Confederates and capturing 1,364 prisoners and all eighteen of their

To Obtain Fair Terms of Peace

field pieces. At Salisbury the Federals destroyed four cotton factories and 7,000 bales of cotton, as well as four magazines containing a large stockpile of arms, ammunition, and gunpowder. They also burned several buildings and a passenger train of the Western North Carolina Railroad and damaged ten miles of the North Carolina Railroad's track. The raiders confiscated thousands of gray uniforms and blankets and tons of forage, provisions, and medical supplies. The Federals threw most of the goods into the street for the townspeople. Stoneman found no Union prisoners to liberate, however, for two months earlier they had been transferred to Richmond and Wilmington for exchange. The general had to settle for burning the prison buildings, which now housed machinery from Raleigh and Richmond. That night the fires were seen for fifteen miles, and the resulting explosions reached the volume of a pitched battle.[7]

On the afternoon of April 13, Stoneman left Salisbury for his base at Greeneville, Tennessee. He had accomplished his objective, but critics— General Grant foremost among them—have contended that Stoneman's last raid served no strategic purpose, for the war was almost over. This viewpoint (endowed as it is with infallible hindsight) overlooks the fact that the Confederates in North Carolina apparently had no intention of surrendering. Even as Stoneman's raiders attacked Salisbury, President Davis was informing his cabinet and two of his highest-ranking generals that the war was far from lost.[8]

In the spring of 1861, Greensboro was a quiet village on the North Carolina Railroad numbering 2,000 inhabitants. After four years of war, it had mushroomed into "quite a city," according to an officer stationed there in early 1865. Important in the transformation was the opening of the Piedmont Railroad from Danville in May 1864, making Greensboro a vital rail hub linking Virginia, the Atlantic Coast, and the Deep South. A resident noted that "huge trains of cars swept through almost hourly," hauling badly needed supplies to Lee's army in Virginia. As Sherman's juggernaut advanced into North Carolina, long troop trains headed east for a showdown with "Uncle Billy." In late March, hundreds of Confederates wounded in the Battle of Bentonville arrived, occupying the Guilford County Court House, the Edgeworth Seminary, the Odd Fellows Hall, the Methodist and Presbyterian churches, and other buildings. Since early 1862, refugees from threatened areas in Virginia and coastal North Carolina had flocked to Greensboro. In February 1865, Sherman's invasion of the Carolinas had prompted an influx of refugees from the south as well.[9]

In early April, several regiments of Confederate troops and Home Guardsmen arrived in response to Stoneman's raid, further crowding

Greensboro. They were supported by field artillery from Hillsborough, including Bachman's South Carolina battery, whose brief stay proved to be a bonanza. As the artillerymen rode into town, they discovered a store of Confederate tobacco. On the following day, the South Carolinians happened upon the destruction of Confederate medicinal whiskey, a detail knocking in the heads of barrels and pouring the liquor on the ground. Determined to prevent some of that good "medicine" from going to waste, the artillerymen dipped as much as they could from a small lake that had formed, before an officer stopped them. The experience of Bachman's Battery was an innocent foreshadowing of more violent attempts to seize public property in Greensboro. The town's military warehouses would cause some of the last bloodshed of the war in North Carolina.[10]

In April 1865, Greensboro was bustling and ramshackle. An eyewitness recalled:

> The streets were swimming in mud, and the houses were in a deplorable condition. "Tramp, tramp, tramp" was heard at all hours, day and night. . . . The drum and fife and bugle were heard giving out their discordant sounds wherever a group of "gray-jackets" could be seen, and the nightly camp-fires sparkled and blazed from every hill top and on every street in and around the town. The rumbling of passing cannon, the neighing of frightened horses, the jingling of spurs and clashing of sabres, the shrill whistle of the coming engines, the movement of wagons, the rushing to and fro of citizens and soldiers . . . all presented a scene and sound never before witnessed or heard in this inland town.[11]

Amid this chaos, the train bearing President Davis and his cabinet officers pulled into the station at Greensboro on the afternoon of April 11. No civic officials and cheering crowds greeted the president, as they had during a brief stop the previous September. The empty railway platform probably resulted from rumors of Lee's surrender and warnings that Stoneman's cavalry was approaching. The Davis party was met, however, by John Motley Morehead, a former governor of the Old North State and the first president of the North Carolina Railroad. Ignoring other cabinet members, Morehead invited the ailing secretary of the treasury, George A. Trenholm, to stay with him. According to presidential aide Burton Harrison, Morehead hoped to persuade Trenholm to convert his worthless Confederate bonds into "Treasury gold." In any event, Mrs. Trenholm noted that the former governor treated them "most hospitably" during their stay. Morehead and several others also invited the president to stay with them, but Davis reportedly declined their hospitality because of the trouble it might cause if the Federals occupied the town. The president instead stayed in a

To Obtain Fair Terms of Peace

room provided by his nephew and aide, Col. John Taylor Wood, who was renting a small house for his family.[12]

The people of Greensboro have long been castigated for their chilly reception of the Davis party. It is said they were anxious to see Davis go, fearing the Yankees' retaliation for harboring the fugitive Rebel leader. Critics note that many townspeople were reluctant secessionists and retained strong Unionist sympathies—accusations frequently leveled against Tar Heel Confederates. Such criticism is misleading, however. Starting with Beauregard, many Confederate soldiers praised the townspeople for their kindness and generosity. Moreover, the hundreds of sick and wounded in Greensboro's homes and public buildings are often overlooked by the critics. When the relative condition of the convalescents and the Davis entourage is weighed in the balance, the hardships endured by the latter shrink to insignificance.[13]

Most of the Davis retinue spent the next four days inside their passenger coaches at the railroad yard, beside the freight cars that constituted General Beauregard's headquarters. Beauregard had arrived at Greensboro on the night of April 10. As Johnston's troubleshooter, he had been shuttling between Raleigh, Greensboro, and Salisbury. For greater mobility, Beauregard had three boxcars outfitted as his traveling headquarters. One car housed himself, a second his staff, and a third served as a stable for their horses.[14]

Shortly after his arrival, President Davis summoned Beauregard to his coach. Upon opening the door, the general stood face-to-face with the Confederate hierarchy. There was gruff old Samuel Cooper, the Confederacy's highest-ranking general, but a War Department bureaucrat who had never led troops in the field; nearby sat Secretary of State Judah P. Benjamin, whose ever-present smile contrasted sharply with Cooper's perpetual scowl. Like Benjamin, the other cabinet officers on board were lawyers by training. There was the Texas frontiersman-turned-politician, Postmaster General John H. Reagan; the urbane Floridian, Secretary of the Navy Stephen R. Mallory; the solemn North Carolinian, Attorney General George Davis; and a dozen lesser officials. They were a capable lot, but Beauregard was struck by their "helpless appearance." They gave the Creole a warm welcome and bombarded him with questions.[15]

The president soon appeared and greeted Beauregard. The two men retired to an empty corner of the car, where Davis questioned the general on current military affairs. Speaking in hushed tones, Beauregard gave the president "a gloomy account" of the situation facing the Confederacy. He stated that Sherman was advancing toward Raleigh while Stoneman was damaging railroad track and other property from the state line to

President Jefferson Davis (National Archives)

Salisbury. From Georgia, Maj. Gen. Howell Cobb reported that Federals in Alabama had captured Selma and were advancing on Montgomery and Atlanta. From Alabama, Lt. Gen. Richard Taylor indicated that the fall of Mobile was imminent. Beauregard told Davis that he deemed it his duty to prepare the president "for the inevitable."[16]

Despite his bleak assessment, Beauregard failed to convince the presi-

To Obtain Fair Terms of Peace

dent that the cause was lost. Davis acknowledged the Confederacy's recent setbacks but remained optimistic. He asserted that the war could still be won by utilizing the South's remaining resources, and, if necessary, by continuing the struggle in the Trans-Mississippi, where Gen. Kirby Smith still fielded a large army. Though Beauregard admired Davis's unshakable confidence, he found the president utterly lacking in sound judgment—an accusation that, ironically, Davis had leveled at the Creole general more than once during the war.[17]

After conferring with Beauregard, Davis summoned Johnston to Greensboro; Johnston's train left Raleigh at midnight. Meanwhile, the president slept in his room at Colonel Wood's house, and the cabinet members on board the "leaky, dilapidated passenger car" sought ways for "a man of six feet to sleep upon a car seat of four," recalled Stephen Mallory. On the morning of April 12, procuring breakfast took precedence over such weighty matters as "state sovereignty, secession, foreign intervention & recognition, finance & independence." Mealtime inspired Mallory to give free reign to his powers of description:

> The Navy store supplied bread & bacon, & by the active foraging of Paymaster [James] Semple & others of the party, biscuits, eggs & coffee were added; & with a few tin cups, spoons & pocket knives, & a lib-

eral use of fingers, & capital appetites, they managed to get enough to eat. . . . Here was the astute "Minister of Justice" [George Davis], a grave & most exemplary gentleman, with a piece of half-broiled middling in one hand & a hoe cake in the other, his face bearing unmistakable evidence of the condition of the bacon. There was the clever Secretary of State [Benjamin], busily dividing his attention between a bucket of stewed dried apples & a haversack of hard boiled eggs; here was the Postmaster General [Reagan] sternly & energetically running his bowie knife through a ham, as if it were the chief business of life, and there was a Secretary of the Navy [Mallory] swallowing his coffee scalding hot that he might not keep the venerable Adjutant General [Cooper] waiting too long for the coveted tin cup.[18]

While the cabinet officers breakfasted, Johnston arrived in Greensboro, his seventy-five-mile trip on the rickety North Carolina Railroad having taken most of the night. Beauregard met the commanding general at the station and took him to his headquarters car. The generals assumed that Davis sought Johnston's advice on whether to continue the war. Though crediting unofficial reports of Lee's surrender, Johnston and Beauregard agreed that it was pointless to discuss the military situation with Davis until they had official word on the fate of Lee's army.[19]

The president sent for the two generals at noon. They called on Davis in his room at Colonel Wood's house. Johnston recalled that Benjamin, Mallory, and Reagan were also present. The irony of this gathering was not lost on anyone in the room, especially Davis and Johnston, for whom it must have been a tense and awkward reunion. The president now had to place his trust in two generals in whom he had long since lost all confidence and who regarded him in the same light.[20]

The generals assumed that they had been summoned to brief Davis on the military situation. "But the President's object seemed to be to give, not to obtain information," Johnston recalled. Davis launched into his scheme of raising a large field army in a matter of weeks by recalling the thousands of men who either had deserted or evaded conscription. Finding the president's scheme "inexpressibly wild," Johnston argued that it would be impossible to induce deserters and shirkers to rejoin or enter the army "upon mere invitation" when the cause appeared lost. Davis abruptly adjourned the meeting without consulting the generals. As Johnston and Beauregard rose to leave, the president informed them that Secretary of War Breckinridge was expected to arrive that evening with news of Lee's army. The meeting ended on this inconclusive note, and the generals no doubt left the room wondering why Davis had sent for them.[21]

To Obtain Fair Terms of Peace

Breckinridge arrived as expected, reporting that Lee had surrendered at Appomattox Court House on April 9. After hearing this stunning—albeit expected—news, Johnston and Beauregard agreed that "the Confederacy was overthrown." Since assuming command in February 1865, Johnston had believed that the most he could accomplish was "to obtain fair terms of peace," and Lee's surrender indicated that the time for negotiations had arrived. "Old Joe" told Breckinridge that the president had "but one power of government left in his hands—that of terminating hostilities." Johnston offered to so advise Davis if Breckinridge provided him with an opportunity. The secretary promised to arrange a conference for the next day.[22]

On the morning of April 13, Johnston and Beauregard were summoned to the president's quarters, presumably at Breckinridge's request. When they arrived, Davis was already conducting a meeting with his cabinet. All the ministers were present except Trenholm, the ailing secretary of the treasury. Postmaster General Reagan described the atmosphere as "solemnly funereal." Yet President Davis behaved as if unaware of the mood and indifferent to the disasters befalling the Confederacy. He resumed his old habit of breaking the ice by recounting several anecdotes unrelated to the business at hand. In the past, Mallory had found this to be a "very happy & pleasing" way to open their meetings, but now it seemed wholly inappropriate.[23]

The president at last turned to General Johnston and said, "I have requested you & General Beauregard to join us, that we may have the benefit of your views upon the situation of the Country. Of course, we all feel the magnitude of the moment, the late disasters are terrible; but I do not think we should regard them as fatal. I think we can whip the enemy yet if our people will turn out. We must look at matters calmly, however, & see what is left for us to do. Whatever can be done must be done at once. We have not a day to lose." In short, Davis did not want the generals' opinion on whether he should sue for peace. Rather, he wanted their advice on the best means of continuing the war.[24]

The room fell silent. The generals and most of the cabinet officials were stunned by Davis's assessment of the present situation, which struck Johnston and Beauregard as a flight from reality bordering on madness. While the others saw a Confederacy on the verge of collapse, Davis envisioned large armies in the field, numerous depots filled with supplies, and vast expanses of fertile Southern land on both sides of the Mississippi peopled by an unvanquished citizenry. The president was therefore unprepared for what Johnston had to tell him.[25]

Davis had to coax "Old Joe" into speaking his mind. Once prompted, Johnston launched into his reply "without preface or introduction," Mallory recalled. The general spoke in "brief, decisive sentences, [his] tone & manner almost spiteful." Johnston noted that the Union army outnumbered the Confederate eighteen to one, that his troops had only the arms in their hands and the ammunition in their cartridge boxes because the Confederacy lacked the money, credit, and factories to purchase or produce more, and that fighting on would only complete the devastation of the South without significantly harming the enemy. In short, "it would be the greatest of human crimes to continue the war," Johnston maintained. "I therefore urged that the President should exercise at once the only function of government still in his possession, and open negotiations for peace."[26]

While Johnston spoke, Davis stared at a scrap of paper which he absently folded and unfolded. When the general had finished, a long silence ensued. Still gazing at the paper, Davis said:

"What do you say, General Beauregard?"

"I concur in all Genl. Johnston has said," Beauregard replied.

The president then polled his cabinet officers and found that they too favored suing for peace—with the exception of Benjamin, who delivered a fiery speech for war. The vote was followed by a second silence. Davis finally lifted his gaze and said, "Well, General Johnston, what do you propose?

To Obtain Fair Terms of Peace

You speak of obtaining terms. You know, of course, that the enemy refuses to treat with us."[27]

Johnston replied that in such cases it was customary for military commanders to open negotiations and suggested that he be permitted to communicate with General Sherman. Davis expressed skepticism that any good could result from negotiating with the enemy, given their previous hardline stance, but he resigned himself to the view of the majority. With Mallory acting as secretary, the president dictated a letter to Sherman:

> The results of the recent campaign in Virginia have changed the relative military condition of the belligerents. I am therefore induced to address you in this form the inquiry, whether, in order to stop the further effusion of blood and devastation of property, you are willing to make a temporary suspension of active operations, and to communicate to Lieutenant-General Grant, commanding the armies of the United States, the request that he will take like action in regard to other armies; the object being to permit the civil authorities to enter into the needful arrangements to terminate the existing war.

Mallory handed the letter to Johnston, who signed it and ordered it sent at once to General Hampton for delivery to the Federals.[28]

It is significant that after dictating his letter to Sherman, Davis issued orders for establishing supply depots on Johnston's proposed route of retreat. Although he had opened communications with Sherman, Davis neither hoped nor expected to treat with the Lincoln administration, nor did he believe that Sherman and Johnston would be content to act merely as intermediaries. Contrary to his stated intentions, Davis hoped that discussions between the military commanders would break down, reinforcing his contention that negotiating with the Federals was futile. On April 14, Davis wrote a letter to his wife expressing his disappointment: "Everything is dark. I have lingered on the road and labored to little purpose."[29]

At the White House on Good Friday, April 14, President Abraham Lincoln's mood was considerably more buoyant than that of his Confederate counterpart. And if the atmosphere of Davis's cabinet meeting the day before had been "funereal," as Postmaster General Reagan noted, then Lincoln's cabinet meeting that Friday would have appeared festive in contrast. The talk was of Washington City's magnificent fireworks display the previous night, and of the flag-raising ceremony that was taking place that afternoon at Fort Sumter on the fourth anniversary of its surrender. The cabinet officers also discussed lifting trade restrictions on Southern ports, and Secretary of War Edwin M. Stanton outlined his proposal for reconstruction in the Rebel states. The president spoke seldom but listened attentively. General Grant also was present and frequently joined in the discussion.

One of the secretaries asked if there was any news from Sherman. Grant replied that he was expecting word soon. Lincoln said that he expected good news from that quarter at any moment, for his most recent dream had preceded nearly every auspicious event of the war. Secretary of the Navy Gideon Welles asked the president to describe his recurrent dream. Lincoln replied that the secretary's own element, water, figured in the dream, and that he was on a ship sailing toward some unknown shore. "I had this strange dream again last night," the president commented, "and we shall, judging from the past, have great news very soon. I think it must be from Sherman. My thoughts are in that direction, as are most of yours."[30]

While Lincoln described his recurrent dream, Sherman was at Raleigh's Capitol Square reviewing the Army of the Tennessee. After passing the capitol, the Fifteenth Corps and Seventeenth Corps marched up Hillsborough Street and bivouacked several miles west of town. "As far as [the] eye can reach is a sea of bayonets," marveled Maj. Gen. Carl Schurz, who witnessed the procession from the capitol. Hundreds of soldiers and civilians gathered in the square to watch. Standing near Schurz was a young woman who frequently dabbed her eyes with a handkerchief. "It is all over with us," she sobbed. "I see now, it is all over. A few days ago I saw General Johnston's army, ragged and starved. Now when I look at these strong, healthy men and see them coming and coming—it is all over with us!" The Fourteenth Corps of the Army of Georgia also marched on Good Friday, reaching Jones's Crossroads, fifteen miles southwest of Raleigh. The Twentieth Corps remained in camp, however. The Twenty-third Corps of the Army of the Ohio arrived that afternoon and camped south and east of town. Bvt. Brig. Gen. Israel N. Stiles's brigade served as garrison for the Post of Raleigh. The Tenth Corps's advance also reached town on Good Friday.[31]

A curious incident occurred at the rear of the Twenty-third Corps's wagon train, about fifteen miles south of Raleigh. A Confederate cavalryman dressed in a Federal lieutenant's uniform separated a portion of the train from the column by ordering it to make a detour. He halted the wagons near a house and instructed the drivers to water their horses and mules. As the teamsters unhitched their animals, Rebel cavalry burst out of the woods and overran the wagon train. A handful of guards from the 104th Ohio opened fire on the Confederates, prompting Capt. Frank Rundell to rush to the rescue with two companies of his 100th Ohio. By the time Run-

To Obtain Fair Terms of Peace

dell's men drove off the Southerners, the latter had escaped with seven wagons and fifteen mule teams and had burned eight more wagons. Worse yet, two men from the 100th and six more from the 104th were missing. Enraged over their missing comrades, some of the train guard burned a nearby house, believing that the occupant, Elizabeth Finch, had collaborated with the Rebel raiders. The Federals locked her inside the burning structure and threatened to shoot her when she opened a window to escape. "I had rather be shot than burned," she retorted before dropping to the ground. Fortunately for Finch, the soldiers did not carry out their threat, but they refused to heed her entreaties to douse the fire.[32]

In obedience to Sherman's orders, General Kilpatrick made a show of pursuit on April 14, limiting the advance of Jordan's and Kerwin's brigades to two miles on the Hillsborough Road and of Atkins's brigade to four miles on the Chapel Hill Road. "Johnston's army is deserting him in large numbers," Kilpatrick assured his superior. "One sharp fight, and he is gone. I was close on his cavalry this morning, and can break it all to pieces the moment they offer me battle."[33]

That afternoon, Sherman outlined the next stage of his campaign to Kilpatrick. "All I expect of you is to keep up a delusion," the Federal commander told "Little Kil," who no doubt was disappointed to find himself relegated to a supporting role. While Kilpatrick feinted toward Hillsborough, Chapel Hill, and Greensboro, the infantry would march to Asheboro and Salisbury to cut off Johnston's southerly escape route. If "Old Joe" chose to remain at Greensboro, Sherman would advance north from Salisbury and force his enemy to fight, surrender, or disperse his army. The Federals would begin their westward advance in earnest on April 15. Howard would march to Morrisville, Slocum to the crossing of the Cape Fear River at Aven's Ferry, and Schofield to Holly Springs behind Slocum. Sherman was relying on clever maneuvering and Sheridan's cavalry to corner his adversary. Sounding a familiar refrain, "Uncle Billy" hoped that Sheridan would close in on Johnston from the north. Despite Sherman's careful planning and undiminished optimism, only a miracle would enable him to overtake Johnston, for on Good Friday, the Confederates were gaining yet another day's march on the Federals.[34]

Johnston had left Greensboro on the evening of April 13 to rejoin the Army of Tennessee. An accident on the railroad prevented him from reaching Hillsborough until 7:00 A.M. on Good Friday. Johnston ordered Hampton to send out scouting parties on the roads leading to Pittsboro to determine whether the Federals had crossed the Haw River.[35]

"Old Joe" arrived at Hillsborough as Stewart's Corps and Lee's Corps were beginning the day's march. Although toiling up the steep hills was hard work, the men found the rolling countryside a delightful change from the flatlands to the east. Hillsborough was a colonial town nestled in a valley beside the Eno River and an old Indian trading path; several British and American armies had camped there during the Revolutionary War. Townspeople cheered the passing Confederates, and the girls of the local seminary gave their lunches to the grateful soldiers. Among the lucky recipients was South Carolina artilleryman Charles Hutson, who had adopted foraging as part of his daily routine. Since his success in Raleigh, Hutson had yet to be disappointed. At Hillsborough, Hutson's effort was richly rewarded: in addition to lunch at the seminary, the South Carolinian was treated to three glasses of milk at one house and some brandy and wine at another.[36]

On April 14, Stewart and Lee marched eighteen miles to the Haw River railroad bridge east of Graham, while Hardee's Corps under Frank Cheatham marched fifteen miles from Chapel Hill to the crossing of the Haw at Ruffin's Mill. Meanwhile, Butler's cavalry under General Law retreated to Strayhorn's farm, six miles east of Hillsborough, and Wheeler withdrew to Chapel Hill. Wheeler reported no advance of Sherman's infantry in his direction. The Confederates now enjoyed a forty-mile advantage over the Federals in the race for Salisbury. Although reports of Lee's surrender continued to dampen morale, many would have agreed with Col. Joseph F. Waring of the Jeff Davis Legion that the rumors were "all bosh."[37]

Wade Hampton established his headquarters at Strayhorn's on the evening of April 14. The general and Maj. William J. Saunders of his staff were relaxing on the veranda when a horse and carriage rode into view. Recognizing the passengers as Graham and Swain, Saunders exclaimed: "Yonder come the commissioners!" Hampton rose from his chair and walked to the front gate as the carriage came to a halt. Graham announced Lee's surrender, which the two cavalrymen refused to believe. The commissioners then recounted several incidents of their journey to Sherman's headquarters but did not mention their conference with the Union commander. Major Saunders suspected that their reticence concealed an overture from Sherman to Vance. The observant Saunders also noticed that Graham's hand was thrust deep in his coat pocket as if he were hiding something. Preoccupied with news of Lee's surrender, Hampton neglected to question Graham and Swain concerning their meeting with Sherman.[38]

Graham and Swain drove off while Hampton and Saunders returned to their seats on the veranda. Turning to his aide with a puzzled expression, Hampton asked, "What do you think of all this?" The major replied, "I expected you to ask them in."

"What do you mean?"

To Obtain Fair Terms of Peace

"Why, couldn't you see that Governor Graham had a letter in his pocket to Vance?"[39]

Assuming that Graham was acting as an intermediary in secret negotiations between Vance and Sherman, Hampton sprang to his feet and ordered Major Saunders to prepare to ride. The general went inside and scribbled two dispatches while Saunders had his horse brought from the stable. When the major returned to the house, Hampton handed him the two messages, saying that one was for Graham and the other was for Johnston. Hampton ordered Saunders to give Graham the dispatch demanding Sherman's letter to Vance. If Graham succeeded in delivering Sherman's message, the major was to arrest the senator, escort him by rail to Johnston's headquarters, and present the other dispatch to the commanding general.

Riding in a nighttime downpour, Saunders failed to overtake the commissioners' carriage. The major stopped at the railroad station to secure a locomotive and wire ahead to Johnston's headquarters. While there he met a fellow Hampton staff officer, whom he cajoled into accompanying him on his unpleasant errand.[40]

While Saunders struggled through the rainstorm, the two commissioners arrived at Graham's house in Hillsborough, where they found Governor Vance and an aide awaiting them. Graham confirmed Vance's suspicions regarding Lee's surrender and handed the governor Sherman's letter inviting him back to Raleigh. The commissioners urged Vance to return with them at once, but the governor refused, explaining that President Davis had asked to see him in Greensboro. Vance planned to inform Davis of his intentions and obtain a pass from Johnston before returning to the capital.[41]

When Major Saunders and his comrade arrived at the Graham house, they found only the senator and Mrs. Graham in their sitting room. Both Vance and Swain were out of sight. "My dear," Graham told his wife, "you had better retire, as these gentlemen doubtless wish to see me on business." Saunders then gave the senator Hampton's letter. As he read, Graham's face flushed with anger. He exclaimed, "I am ready to accompany you, sir!"

"Governor," Saunders said, "hadn't you better hand me that letter?"

"I have already delivered it to Governor Vance, sir," Graham replied, neglecting to mention that the governor was his overnight guest. Seeing the disappointment on Saunders's face, the senator laid his hand on the major's shoulder and said, "I understand, I know how you feel your position."[42]

Concluding that it was pointless to arrest Graham, Saunders nevertheless rode the eighteen miles to Johnston's headquarters to report the result of his visit. He arrived at daylight, having ridden on horseback all night in a driving rain. Soon afterward, Vance and Swain left Graham's house, the former setting out for Greensboro and the latter returning home to Chapel Hill.[43]

Major Saunders was not the only member of Hampton's staff riding on an important errand that miserable night. Following Saunders's departure, Davis's letter to Sherman requesting an armistice reached Hampton's headquarters after an unaccountable delay. Hampton ordered Capt. Rawlins Lowndes to deliver the dispatch and offered him an escort, but Lowndes insisted on taking just one private because a large party might draw Federal picket fire.

Accompanied by an orderly bearing a flag of truce, Lowndes rode in a downpour for twenty miles before reaching a Union outpost on the Hillsborough Road. An escort took Lowndes to Kilpatrick's headquarters at Morrisville. Handing the letter to "Little Kil," Lowndes said that it was from Johnston to Sherman. Kilpatrick notified "Uncle Billy," who ordered him to deliver the message at once.[44]

Johnston's dispatch reached Sherman's headquarters at midnight. The Union commander was pleased to find the message as he expected, and he wrote an immediate reply: "I have this moment received your communication of this date. I am fully empowered to arrange with you any terms for the suspension of further hostilities as between the armies commanded by you and those commanded by myself, and will be willing to confer with you to that end." Sherman would halt his infantry and expected Johnston to do likewise. "That a basis of action may be had," Sherman wrote, "I undertake to abide by the same terms and conditions as were made by Generals Grant and Lee at Appomattox Court-House, on the 9th instant." Sherman either ignored or overlooked Johnston's request for a suspension of hostilities "to permit the *civil authorities* to enter into the needful arrangements to terminate the existing war" (italics mine). He nevertheless promised to recall Stoneman's cavalry and secure a general cease-fire from Grant. "I will add that I really desire to save the people of North Carolina the damage they would sustain by the march of this army through the central or western parts of the State." Sherman sent his letter to Kilpatrick and dispatched staff officer Maj. James C. McCoy and a telegraph operator to Morrisville with orders to transmit Johnston's reply.[45]

Meanwhile, Captain Lowndes awaited Sherman's reply at Kilpatrick's headquarters. At first conversation was polite, but several of "Little Kil's" staff began chaffing Lowndes about some of the Confederate cavalry's recent setbacks. Kilpatrick himself chimed in concerning his experience at

To Obtain Fair Terms of Peace

Monroe's Crossroads, claiming that a similar fight with fair warning would have resulted more to the Federals' advantage. Kilpatrick's boast convinced the hot-tempered Lowndes that the time for talk was over. "Well, General," he said, "I make you the following proposition, and I will pledge myself that General Hampton will carry it out in every respect." Lowndes thereupon challenged Kilpatrick to a duel, but with a twist. The Confederate proposed that Kilpatrick and 1,500 men meet Hampton and 1,000 men on the field of honor. All would be armed with sabers and charge at a given signal. The outcome would determine which side was superior. Kilpatrick laughed at Lowndes's bold challenge and told him he would consider it.[46]

Sherman's reply to Johnston arrived soon afterward, along with a message to Kilpatrick stating that the letter from the Confederate commander was "the beginning of the end." Sherman ordered Kilpatrick to forward the reply to Johnston at once; in a subsequent message, he instructed "Little Kil" to limit the cavalry's advance to Chapel Hill and Durham's Station.[47]

Early on April 15 in a driving rain, Kilpatrick resumed the pursuit at the head of Jordan's and Kerwin's brigades. Arriving at Durham's Station about mid-morning, "Little Kil" established his headquarters at Dr. Richard Blacknall's house. Kilpatrick then replied to Sherman's message announcing "the beginning of the end." "I don't think Johnston can be trusted," the cavalryman warned. "I believe if he can escape he will do so." Disobeying Sherman's orders to forward his reply to Johnston at once, Kilpatrick instead sent Lt. Col. George L. Godfrey to Hampton's headquarters to arrange a truce and had his adjutant, Maj. L. G. Estes, detain Captain Lowndes and Sherman's letter at the forward outpost until Godfrey's return. Kilpatrick hoped to convince Sherman that Johnston was untrustworthy, for the longer Estes held Sherman's reply, the farther the Confederate army would march in violation of Johnston's proposed cease-fire. As a result, Sherman's reply did not reach Hampton's headquarters until that evening.[48]

While Jordan's and Kerwin's brigades rode into Durham's Station, Kilpatrick's Second Brigade under General Atkins advanced to New Hope Creek, eight miles east of Chapel Hill, where it received orders from the Federal cavalry commander to halt. The troopers built barricades and camped for the night. A battalion of the 9th Ohio Cavalry went on picket duty along the banks of the creek and soon drew the attention of a detachment of Wheeler's cavalry. The Confederates charged the Buckeye pickets, who responded with a furious fire from their new Spencer repeating carbines. In late March, the Ohioans had traded in their old single-shot Burnside carbines for seven-shot Spencers and were grateful for the opportunity to fire them before the war ended. Convinced by the racket that they faced overwhelming odds, the Southern horsemen withdrew toward Chapel Hill.[49]

Atkins responded by sending out a second battalion of the 9th Ohio in pursuit. Although the Confederates had burned the bridge over New Hope Creek, the dismounted troopers either waded the stream or crossed on fallen logs. The Federals then advanced through a swampy forest. After a brief but noisy skirmish, the outgunned and outflanked Confederates resumed their withdrawal, while the Ohioans followed at a respectful distance before returning to camp, both sides unaware that they had participated in the last reported engagement between Sherman's and Johnston's forces.[50]

The Confederates fell back to the outskirts of Chapel Hill and found their camps abuzz with word of Lee's surrender. On the morning of April 15, David L. Swain had returned bearing the sad news, which spread rapidly through town and was overheard by the chaplain of the 4th Tennessee Cavalry. When the commander of Harrison's Brigade, Col. Baxter Smith, learned that the chaplain was spreading this vile rumor, he had the unfortunate man brought to his headquarters. When Smith asked him to explain his behavior, the chaplain answered that he was only repeating what he had heard in town. Smith told him to take a seat, for he was under arrest. Fifteen minutes later, a picket presented a man who said that he had surrendered with Lee's army at Appomattox Court House. The man fished a crumpled paper from his pocket that proved to be his parole form. Smith returned the paper to the man and dismissed him; turning to the chaplain, the colonel said, "You, too, can go your way." Smith's response to Lee's surrender was similar to Johnston's: he behaved as if nothing had happened.[51]

According to Chapel Hill resident Cornelia Phillips Spencer, the reaction of Wheeler's rank and file was a good deal more demonstrative. A Tennessean buried his face in his hands and cried like a child, while a six-and-a-half-foot Kentuckian swore that he would "take his allegiance and his revolver over the water" and join the French army. "No, no," insisted a Georgia youth of nineteen, "[the Yankees] won't get me." Indeed, the consensus among the troopers was that if the end was at hand, they would ride out rather than surrender.[52]

On April 15, some of Lee's veterans passed through Hillsborough and met troopers of Law's cavalry division, which had been detached from the Army of Northern Virginia in January and sent south to contest Sherman's march through the Carolinas. One of the parolees read aloud General Orders No. 9, Lee's farewell address to his army. "[Lee] says that the army

To Obtain Fair Terms of Peace

was overwhelmed 'by superior numbers and resources,'" Col. Joseph F. Waring of the Jeff Davis Legion wrote. "God help the cause." The news struck J. W. Evans, the teenage guidon-bearer for Phillips's Georgia Legion, with the force of an electric shock. For two days Evans "rolled in the dust, kicked, cussed, and vowed, and neither ate nor slept much."[53]

While the cavalry reeled from news of Lee's surrender, Johnston's infantry crossed the Haw River. Recent floods had carried away all crossings except the railroad bridge. Lacking the Army of Tennessee's pontoon equipment, General Johnston ordered his chief engineer, Col. John J. Clarke, to make the railroad bridge passable for artillery. The improvised planking served well enough for infantry, but the dizzying height of the bridge made crossing the horses and mules of the artillery teams a perilous undertaking. Unfortunately for the drivers and their teams, the downpour of that morning had transformed the Haw into a cataract, rendering the fords impassable. The batteries had to use the railroad bridge.[54]

While Pvt. Daniel E. H. Smith of Parker's South Carolina battery waited on the east bank, he learned that the preceding battery's forge had just toppled over the side, killing the teamsters and mules. A nervous Private Smith and his comrades decided to unhitch the lead and swing teams, leaving only the wheel pair in harness. By this means, the artillerymen led their teams without mishap until the horses hauling Smith's caisson balked halfway across. After a few anxious moments, Smith and another comrade coaxed the horses to the other side.[55]

Aside from the problems encountered by the artillery, Stewart's Corps and Lee's Corps crossed the railroad bridge over the Haw with few incidents. The crossing of Hardee's Corps at Ruffin's Mill, two miles to the south, proved a far greater challenge, however. The soldiers had to wade the river—hip deep and a raging torrent. During the crossing, several boys of the Junior Reserves struggled to reach some fish traps, only to be swept to their deaths. Only a few miles farther on, the column reached Little Alamance Creek, which was almost as treacherous as the Haw. But the soldiers' most daunting obstacle lay a short distance beyond, in the form of Great Alamance Creek. The downpour had flooded the stream, rendering it virtually impassable. Soldiers at the head of Cheatham's Division tried to cross by joining hands and forming a chain, but they were swept away by the current, causing the rest to halt. Frank Cheatham soon rode up and ordered the men at the creek to cross. They refused, however, and employed some "pretty lively swearing" to emphasize their point. The fiery Cheatham grabbed one unfortunate by the scruff of the neck and rode across the creek with him in tow. The general then returned and repeated the crossing with another soldier. Seeing that two of their comrades had reached the opposite side, the men along the bank shouted and plunged in, a few of them grabbing the tail of Cheatham's horse. Many soon discovered that the water came up to their armpits.[56]

The boys of the Junior Reserves had greater difficulty crossing Great Alamance Creek than their older comrades, and many would have drowned had it not been for the lifesaving efforts of Lt. Col. W. F. French. One youth was fished out of the creek by a bigger comrade, only to plunge in a second—and then a third—time, whereupon the boy's rescuer asked him if he was trying to kill himself. "Why," said the young man, shivering and dripping water from head to toe, "my gun's down there and I'm trying to *git* it."[57]

Worse yet, Hardee's wagon train appeared unable to cross Great Alamance Creek. Several wagons were swept away by the current, inducing a frustrated "Old Reliable" (who had rejoined his corps that morning) to order the destruction of the train. Instead, a cool-headed Robert Hoke soon found a good ford at Holt's Mill a few miles downstream, and the wagons crossed there without mishap.[58]

Hardee's column then marched several miles on the Salisbury Road and camped at Alamance Battleground, where colonial militia under Governor William Tryon had defeated the Regulators on May 16, 1771. That night, the wet and weary troops dried themselves around blazing fires.[59]

A few miles to the north, Lee's Corps and Stewart's Corps marched through Graham and Company Shops (on the site of present-day Burlington); Lee then took the Greensboro Road and Stewart the Old Stage Road a mile to the south. Johnston accompanied Lee's Corps and was met by Lt. Col. David G. McIntosh's fugitive artillery battalion from the Army of Northern Virginia. McIntosh offered his services to "Old Joe," but the general replied that he already had "more artillery than he knew what to do with." Despite the rebuff, McIntosh noted that he was "much pleased" with Johnston's "quiet, gentlemanly manners."[60]

During the march, homeward-bound veterans from Virginia announced Lee's surrender to Johnston's troops. One of Lee's men fell in with Parker's Battery and broke the news to Pvt. Daniel E. H. Smith, who blurted, "You are a damned liar!" The stranger replied, "I only wish it was a lie." Meanwhile, Stewart and Stephen D. Lee marched to within fifteen miles of Greensboro before camping. That night, Maj. George Harper of the 58th North Carolina wrote in his diary: "Report of Lee's surrender confirmed." Nevertheless, many soldiers in the Army of Tennessee refused to believe the unthinkable. "Great God! Can it be true?" wrote Capt. William E. Stoney of Hagood's South Carolina brigade. "I have never for a moment doubted the ultimate success of our cause."[61]

To Obtain Fair Terms of Peace

Although Lee's surrender was a severe blow to morale, most soldiers in Johnston's army held fast to the colors. Had the general ordered his men to fight, they would have obeyed without hesitation. On April 15, the Army of Tennessee remained a viable fighting force that trusted and respected its commander.[62]

The morale at Greensboro was a different matter, as most of the soldiers there were state reservists and Home Guardsmen of doubtful reliability. "I have perceived within a day or two a material alteration in the morale of the troops occupying the lines on the west of Greensborough," Brig. Gen. Collett Leventhorpe informed Beauregard on April 14. "Desertions are becoming very numerous. About 200 men of one battalion abandoned their post last night, and the remaining men of this force state openly their intention to return to their homes." The commander of the Greensboro garrison, Brig. Gen. Alfred Iverson, reported that only 500 men remained on April 15, and most of the remnant was about to desert. "I have no longer any more troops than are barely sufficient to guard stores," Iverson wrote Beauregard. "Men are now waiting here for the opportunity to plunder."[63]

Iverson's dire assessment proved correct. On April 15, Greensboro teemed with parolees and fugitives from Lee's army and cavalrymen of Brig. Gen. George G. Dibrell's Division, newly arrived from Johnston's army. An officer found the town "in great commotion." Liquor was easy to find and many soldiers were drunk. A mob gathered on East Market Street and stormed the state and Confederate warehouses there, carrying off food, clothing, shoes, and blankets. The quartermasters in charge responded decisively. Maj. Samuel R. Chisman rushed into the Confederate warehouse with a flaming torch and threatened to ignite a powder keg if the pillagers refused to disperse. Taking the major at his word, the looters escaped through every door and window in the building.[64]

State quartermaster Maj. James Sloan appealed to Beauregard for troops to drive off the pillagers. The general dispatched Lt. Col. A. C. McAlister's Tar Heel contingent to the scene. McAlister's command comprised the 7th North Carolina and elements of eight other Tar Heel regiments. In February, they had been detached from the Army of Northern Virginia and sent to central North Carolina to round up deserters.[65]

McAlister's Tar Heels double-quicked to the state warehouses and dispersed the mob. In the looters' wake, abandoned plunder and paperwork littered the muddy streets. No sooner did the North Carolinians restore order than another mob appeared, mostly Kentuckians and Tennesseans from Dibrell's cavalry. Ignoring McAlister's order to disperse, Dibrell's men opened fire on the Tar Heels, who responded with a volley that killed one trooper and wounded three others. After a brief exchange of musketry, the cavalrymen fled "over fences, through yards and back streets, . . . rising, falling, leaping, rolling, tumbling and rapidly disappearing," recalled an eyewitness.[66]

On the afternoon of April 16, Brig. Gen. William F. Brantly's Brigade relieved McAlister's North Carolinians at the warehouses. Col. James R. Cole also replaced the elderly Major Sloan as quartermaster. Instructing Brantly to allow no one to enter the warehouses without his permission, Cole left to attend to some business. As he was returning, the quartermaster saw a mob rush around the corner toward the warehouses. A friend turned to him and said, "Cole, you are gone up."[67]

An anxious Cole was relieved to find Brantly and his troops holding their ground, the mob maintaining a respectful distance from the Confederates' leveled bayonets. Many in the crowd were women demanding that the guards stand aside like gentlemen. When it became apparent that the soldiers would not yield, the women clamored for a fair distribution of goods. Meanwhile, Cole struggled through the crowd and loudly ordered Brantly to shoot anyone who attempted to break his line. The mob dispersed soon afterward. When apprised of the warehouse riots, Governor Vance ordered the goods distributed to North Carolina units in the Army of Tennessee.[68]

All but forgotten amid the chaos were President Davis and his entourage. Believing that he could accomplish nothing in Greensboro and anxious to rejoin his family, Davis had heeded his cabinet ministers' advice to resume the journey south. Because of damage to the railroad by Stoneman's raiders, Davis was compelled to travel on horseback. At 6:00 P.M. on April 15, the Davis party set out on the Salisbury Road, escorted by Dibrell's cavalry. They rode eight miles through rain and mud before stopping at a Mr. Wyatt's for the night.[69]

After receiving Sherman's reply on Easter Sunday morning, April 16, Johnston rode into Greensboro to notify Davis. Only then did "Old Joe" learn that the president was gone, for no one in the Davis party had thought to inform the general. A perturbed Johnston decided to act without Davis's authorization. Beauregard wisely suggested that he send for Breckinridge, whose presence would shield Johnston from presidential criticism during the negotiations.[70]

After writing to Breckinridge, Johnston instructed Hampton to arrange for his conference with Sherman. The Confederate commander ordered Stewart and Lee to halt at Greensboro and Hardee at New Salem, seventeen miles to the south, where they would remain until further orders. Johnston instructed Hampton to hold Law's cavalry at Hillsborough and

To Obtain Fair Terms of Peace

order Wheeler's withdrawal to a point due south of Law; he also ordered Wheeler to determine whether the Federals were crossing the Haw River.[71]

In accordance with Johnston's orders, Wheeler's rear guard evacuated Chapel Hill at 2:00 P.M. on Easter Sunday. One of the last Confederates to leave was Tennessee cavalryman Lt. Charles Coffin, who bid a sad farewell to his alma mater, the University of North Carolina. After clearing the town of stragglers, Coffin and his comrades withdrew. "A few hours of absolute and Sabbath stillness and silence ensued," recalled Chapel Hill resident Cornelia Phillips Spencer. "We sat in our pleasant piazzas and awaited events with quiet resignation." Spencer noted that the townspeople had concealed their valuables, and few provisions remained for the Yankees to carry off. "[T]hat was one comfort," she wryly observed. "Our wardrobes were hardly worth hiding—homespun and jeans hung placidly in their accustomed places." Of greatest concern to Spencer and many neighbors was the fate of the town's libraries and the university: "[A]ll minor selfish considerations were merged in a generous anxiety for these."[72]

At sunset a squadron of the 10th Ohio Cavalry rode into Chapel Hill on the Raleigh Road. A deputation led by David L. Swain met the Federals on the edge of town; Swain informed the commanding officer that Sherman had promised to spare the town and university. Replying that his orders were the same, the officer directed his men to scout the town. The Federals encountered no Rebels but found Confederate flags fluttering on several university buildings. The commanding officer ordered the flags removed and handed over, which was promptly done. Satisfied that the Confederates were gone, the Ohioans returned to camp for the night. Chapel Hill had just earned the dubious distinction of being the last town to fall to Sherman's army.[73]

If anyone was determined to sabotage peace negotiations on this rainy Easter Sunday, it was Judson Kilpatrick. At 2:00 A.M., "Little Kil" had informed Sherman that his message had not reached Hampton's headquarters until sundown the previous day. Kilpatrick noted that his courier was presently waiting there for Johnston's reply, which probably would not arrive before 4:00 P.M. "So far as I can learn," Kilpatrick wrote, "Johnston's whole army is still marching on, and I believe this unnecessary delay in receiving and transmitting dispatches on the part of the rebels is simply to gain time." Of course Kilpatrick neglected to inform Sherman that the most recent delay was his own handiwork. "I have no faith in the rebels," the cavalryman added. "If Johnston can escape I believe he will do so." Kilpatrick later warned Sherman that Hampton had burned, or was preparing to burn, several railroad bridges near Hillsborough to cover the Confederates' retreat. "I have no confidence in the word of a rebel, no matter what his position," Kilpatrick wrote. "He is but a traitor at best." [74]

Sherman refused to be taken in by Kilpatrick. "I have faith in General Johnston's personal sincerity," the Union commander replied, "and do not believe he would use a subterfuge to cover his movements. He could not stop the movement of his troops till he got my letter, which I hear was delayed all day yesterday by your adjutant's not sending it forward." Sherman had such faith in Johnston's good intentions that he limited Howard's advance to Morrisville and Slocum's to Aven's Ferry. Sherman's faith was justified, for that evening Kilpatrick relayed a dispatch from Wade Hampton proposing a conference on April 17 between the opposing picket lines on the Hillsborough Road. The courier found Sherman as he and Maj. Henry Hitchcock were returning to headquarters after a visit to former governor Thomas Bragg. Sherman hurried to the telegraph office to wire his acceptance to Kilpatrick. As he left the office, Sherman turned to Hitchcock and blurted: "The war is over—occupation's gone!" [75]

Meanwhile, Johnston was en route to Hampton's new headquarters at Alexander Dickson's house, about one mile southeast of Hillsborough. Accompanying the general on the train from Greensboro were staff officers Maj. John Johnson and Lt. Wade Hampton Jr. From the Dickson house, Johnston would ride out to meet Sherman. [76]

During the Battle of Bentonville just one month before, someone had asked Sherman what he thought his Confederate counterpart would do next. "Johnston & I are not on speaking terms," "Uncle Billy" had gruffly replied. As of noon on April 17, 1865, those words would no longer hold true. [77]

To Obtain Fair Terms of Peace

CHAPTER 7

THE BEST I CAN DO

◀▮▶━━━━◀▮◖❀◗▮▶━━━━▮▶

At 8:00 on the morning of Monday, April 17, 1865, General Sherman and his entourage arrived at Raleigh's North Carolina Railroad depot for the trip to Durham's Station. As the Federals boarded their two coaches, the telegraph operator ran out of his office to notify Sherman that he was receiving an important cipher dispatch from Morehead City. The general held the train nearly an hour while the operator decoded the message. When completed, it read:

> Major-General SHERMAN,
>   *Commanding:*
>   President Lincoln was murdered about 10 o'clock last night in his private box at Ford's Theater in this city, by an assassin who shot him through the head with a pistol ball. . . . The assassin of the President leaped from the box, brandishing a dagger, exclaiming, *Sic semper tyrannis!* and that now Virginia was revenged. Mr. Lincoln fell senseless from his seat, and continued in that state until twenty-two minutes after 7 o'clock, at which time he breathed his last. . . .
>   EDWIN M. STANTON,
>   *Secretary of War.*

"Of course it fell on me with terrific force," Sherman later wrote of the dispatch, "but I had dealt with death in so many familiar forms that no one with me, from my words or bearing, dreamed of the contents." Dreading the reaction of his men to Lincoln's assassination, Sherman instructed the operator to tell no one until his return.[1]

The train made two stops en route to Kilpatrick's headquarters, one at Asbury Station to eject an unwanted reporter and another at Morrisville, where Sherman briefly conferred with Fifteenth Corps commander John

Logan. Sherman reached Durham's Station about 11:00 and was met at the depot by Kilpatrick. Twenty minutes later, "Uncle Billy" and his entourage headed west on the Hillsborough Road, followed by an escort of 200 troopers from Col. Michael Kerwin's brigade. Several reporters, among them Volney Hickox of the *Cincinnati Daily Commercial* and O. F. Howe of the *New York Herald,* accompanied the Federals. Sherman staff officer Maj. George W. Nichols recalled:

> As General Sherman rode past his picket line upon that sunny spring morning, the fresh breeze came laden with the fragrance of the pines, of apple blossoms, of lilacs, roses, and violets. . . . Here and there in the forest, the deep-toned evergreen of some sturdy old pine or cedar was displayed in dark relief against the fresher verdure; but the prevailing tone of earth and sky was pregnant with the loving promise of spring. The scene was symbolic of the new era of peace then just beginning to dawn upon the nation.[2]

At 10:00 A.M., General Johnston and his entourage rode east from Hampton's headquarters near Hillsborough. Johnston and Hampton were accompanied by Major Johnson and Lieutenant Hampton of "Old Joe's" staff, and by Major Saunders and Captain Lowndes of the cavalry commander's staff. Their escort consisted of sixty men from the Jeff Davis Legion commanded by Col. Joseph F. Waring. Hampton's adjutant, Maj. Henry B. McClellan, bore the flag of truce. The generals spoke briefly to the men of Brig. Gen. Thomas M. Logan's Brigade and then rode eight miles to James Bennett's farm on the Hillsborough Road. Passing the house and kitchen on their left, the Confederates had continued another half mile when flag of truce bearer McClellan met his Federal counterpart, four miles west of Durham's Station. It was twelve noon. The Union and Confederate commanders soon received word and rode forward to the flags.[3]

Although they had both served in the prewar Regular Army, Sherman and Johnston had not met until now. The two men contrasted sharply in appearance and manner. Johnston was fifty-eight and Sherman forty-five, but the younger man was far more wrinkled. "Old Joe" wore a crisp gray dress uniform buttoned to the neck, whereas "Uncle Billy's" rumpled blue coat was unbuttoned, revealing a matching vest. The gray and balding Johnston sported a neatly trimmed mustache and goatee, while Sherman had tousled auburn hair and a salt-and-pepper beard. According to journalist O. F. Howe, Sherman was "quite cheerful and at his ease, having the air of one who felt himself indubitably 'master of the situation,' " whereas Johnston appeared "quite haggard and careworn." For all their differences, the

The Best I Can Do

Generals Sherman and Johnston meeting at Bennett Place (Harper's Weekly, *1865*)

two adversaries had formed a mutual respect dating back to the Atlanta campaign.[4]

Sherman and Johnston saluted and then shook hands. They also inquired after mutual acquaintances and presented their respective subordinates. These introductions passed amicably, though neither Sherman nor Hampton wanted to meet the other. The two men blamed each other for the burning of Columbia and had recently engaged in an acrimonious correspondence regarding murdered Union foragers that had appeared in both Northern and Southern newspapers. Major Johnson recalled that Hampton's horse became "fractious" during the introductions and refused to heed its master. By the time the South Carolinian brought his mount under control, the commanders had left. Johnson implied that Hampton, a superb horseman, had engineered his difficulties to avoid shaking hands with the detested Sherman. If so, then "Uncle Billy" would have been grateful for the favor.[5]

The commanding generals had moved because Sherman suggested they find a private place to talk. Johnston replied that he had passed a nearby farmhouse that would serve their purpose. The two men rode up a slight incline, stopped at the gate, and dismounted. Before them stood two modest wood frame buildings—the Bennetts' house and kitchen. They walked to the door of the house, knocked, and were met by James and Nancy Bennett, who permitted them to use their home for a conference. The Bennetts then retired to the kitchen.[6]

The Best I Can Do

Once inside, Sherman sent an orderly after his saddlebags, which contained maps, documents, paper, pens, and ink. Sherman also reserved a pocket for a bottle of whiskey and some shot glasses. He recalled finding two beds, some chairs, and a table in the Bennetts' main room, which a reporter described as "scrupulously neat, the floors scrubbed to a milky whiteness."[7]

As soon as his orderly had left, Sherman handed Johnston the telegram announcing Lincoln's assassination. "Uncle Billy" studied "Old Joe" closely as he read. "The perspiration came out in large drops on his forehead," Sherman recalled, "and he did not attempt to conceal his distress." Johnston reportedly said that he believed "the event was the greatest possible calamity to the South," yet the Confederate commander himself remembered his reaction as having been more restrained. Sherman also recalled mentioning Jefferson Davis as a possible accessory, whereas Johnston insisted that the Federal commander would not have been so rude. In any event, Sherman remembered saying that he had not yet announced the news to his army and dreaded the reaction of his troops. "Mr. Lincoln was peculiarly endeared to the soldiers," Sherman noted, "and I feared that some foolish woman or man in Raleigh might say something or do something that would madden our men, and that a fate worse than Columbia would befall the place." Johnston agreed that Sherman's situation was "extremely delicate" indeed.[8]

Speaking in a tone that Johnston believed "carried conviction of sincerity," Sherman said that he wanted to spare the South further devastation. The Federal commander observed that Johnston's army was hopelessly outnumbered and Lee's surrender had rendered his own capitulation honorable and proper. Sherman thereupon offered Johnston the terms that Grant had given Lee at Appomattox Court House. Reminding Sherman of his April 13 dispatch, "Old Joe" said that he regarded their conference as a means of initiating negotiations between *civilian authorities*. But "Uncle Billy" objected on the grounds that the U.S. government refused to acknowledge the Confederacy or anyone purporting to represent it.[9]

In truth, Johnston welcomed the opportunity to negotiate with his Federal counterpart. "Old Joe" acknowledged that the Appomattox terms were generous and that further bloodshed would be "the highest possible crime." Johnston also noted that Lee had been surrounded, whereas he and Sherman were a four days' march apart. The Confederate commander then played his trump card, proposing that they "make one job of it" by negotiating the surrender of *all* remaining Confederate armies. When Sherman asked how he intended to arrange such a surrender, Johnston replied that he would obtain President Davis's authorization.[10]

The Best I Can Do

The two men discussed the terms of Johnston's proposed surrender. Sherman related Lincoln's wish to end the war without further bloodshed. According to Johnston, Sherman also said that Lincoln's first priority had been to preserve the Union. "Old Joe" inferred that all else—with the possible exception of emancipation—was negotiable. Sherman assured his Confederate counterpart that the Northern people harbored no vindictive feelings against the Southern soldiery, although they felt far less charitable toward Davis and other civilian leaders of the South.[11]

Johnston noted that he and Sherman agreed to terms with one important exception—the Federal commanders's refusal to include Davis and his cabinet in a general amnesty. Sherman, however, recalled that his only concern was whether Johnston could secure Davis's approval of the terms. The generals ended their conference at 2:30, to give Johnston time to communicate with Davis and enable Sherman to reach Raleigh before word of Lincoln's assassination could spread. They agreed to return to the Bennett house at noon the next day.[12]

While Sherman and Johnston conferred inside the house, the Union and Confederate troopers outside kept their distance at first, watering and feeding their horses. "The Yanks were in splendid and handsome uniforms of blue," recalled one Southern horseman, "the 'Johnny Rebs' in torn and sodden suits of gray." Before long the Federals began to mingle with the Southerners, though some of the latter remained openly hostile. Several of Hampton's staff officers refused their Federal counterparts' offers of wine and cigars, while one Confederate private responded to a Union trooper's invitation to share some coffee by insisting that the Yankee take a drink to see if it was poisoned. But the commander of the Confederate escort, Colonel Waring, impressed the Federals with his courteous manner. As Waring and Kilpatrick's adjutant, Maj. L. G. Estes, recounted their battles, Estes remarked that "it seemed like meeting old friends." Waring noted that it was a "queer expression for a man who is ready to cut my throat when we next meet on the field." "But he is a good fellow," Waring said of Estes, "[even] if he is my enemy."[13]

It was inevitable that the two cavalry commanders, Wade Hampton and Judson Kilpatrick, should meet. During the conference, Hampton and his son, Wade Jr., spent most of their time lounging on a carpenter's bench that rested against the Bennett house. At forty-seven, the ruddy-faced Hampton had the dark brown mustache and beard of a much younger man. The South Carolinian was dressed in his finest uniform and wore a black felt hat adorned with gold braid. His gauntlets were new and his boots brightly polished. In lieu of a sword, Hampton carried only a freshly cut switch, as if eager to thrash some impudent Yankee soldier. If so, he need not

The confrontation between Generals Hampton and Kilpatrick at Bennett Place.
Although Leslie's artist James Taylor failed to faithfully render his two principal figures
(center), he has doubtless captured the spirit of their encounter. (Frank Leslie's
Illustrated Newspaper, *1865)*

have looked far, for Kilpatrick soon found him. According to an onlooker, "Wade Hampton looked savage enough to eat 'little Kil,' " while the latter "returned his looks most defiantly." [14]

Like Waring and Estes, the two generals rehashed their old campaigns, but with considerably more vitriol. As tempers flared, Hampton rose from his seat to reply to one of Kilpatrick's taunts. A strapping six-footer, the South Carolinian towered over "Little Kil." "Well," Hampton said, pausing for emphasis, "you never ran *me* out of Headquarters in my stocking feet!" This was an obvious reference to Kilpatrick's "Shirt-tail Skedaddle" at Monroe's Crossroads, and in the words of a Union cavalryman who overheard it, Hampton's barb "was a home thrust and too true to be funny." Kilpatrick replied that Hampton had had to leave faster than he came, and then "words grew hot," recalled an eyewitness, "both parties expressing a desire that the issue of the war should be left between the cavalry." At that point, Sherman and Johnston, having just concluded their conference, intervened and separated their cavalry commanders. [15]

The two sides parted for the day, the Federals returning to Durham's Station and the Confederates to Hillsborough. As soon as Sherman reached Kilpatrick's headquarters, he read the telegram announcing Lincoln's assassination to his cavalry commander. Sherman cautioned "Little Kil" to watch his men closely. Among the first Federals to receive the news were troopers of the 5th Ohio Cavalry on guard duty near Kilpatrick's head-

The Best I Can Do

quarters. "The effect upon the men," recalled Pvt. J. R. Keyes, "as they sat upon their horses with sabres still at 'present' was similar to that produced by a stunning blow upon the head." Several cavalrymen burst into tears while the rest sat in stunned disbelief. A carefree German private spoke first: "I vonder if I gits my money since Uncle Sam vas det." Grief soon succumbed to rage, the Ohioans declaring their intention to avenge Lincoln's murder.[16]

Before returning to Raleigh, Sherman stopped at Morrisville to inform General Logan and at Jones's Station to notify Bvt. Maj. Gen. Giles A. Smith, a division commander in the Seventeenth Corps. At Jones's, Pvt. Edward A. Rowley and several comrades of the 1st Minnesota Battery chanced to see "Uncle Billy." "[H]e looks careworn and we pitty him," Rowley scrawled in his diary.[17]

Upon his arrival at Raleigh, Sherman discovered that news of Lincoln's assassination had already spread throughout the capital. A crowd of angry soldiers met him at the depot, shouting: "Don't let Johnston surrender! Don't let the Rebels surrender!" That evening, Maj. Charles Wills of the 103rd Illinois wrote in his diary: "The army is crazy for vengeance. If we make another campaign it will be an awful one. . . . We hope Johnston will not surrender. God pity this country if he retreats or fights us."[18]

As soon as he reached the Governor's Palace, Sherman penned Special Field Orders No. 56, announcing "with pain and sorrow" the assassination of President Lincoln. "Thus it seems that our enemy, despairing of meeting us in open, manly warfare, begins to resort to the assassin's tools." The Union commander believed that while the "great mass of the Confederate army would scorn to sanction such acts," the assassination was "the legitimate consequence of rebellion against rightful authority." Sherman warned the enemies of the Union: "We have met every phase which this war has assumed, and must now be prepared for it in its worst shape, that of assassins and guerrillas; but *woe* unto the people who seek to expend their wild passions in such a manner, for there is but one dread result." Fortunately, Sherman's order did not appear until April 18, for its inflammatory language would have whipped an infuriated Federal army into an even greater frenzy.[19]

Sherman strengthened the guard patrolling Raleigh, posted pickets on all roads into town, and ordered all unauthorized soldiers found in the capital arrested and jailed. The Union commander also spent the night riding through the surrounding camps, calming his men. He later claimed that without his efforts, Raleigh would have been destroyed.[20]

At least one more name should be added to the growing list of Raleigh's saviors—Maj. Gen. John A. "Black Jack" Logan. When Sherman informed

"Black Jack" Logan saving Raleigh (Dawson, Life and Services
of General John A. Logan)

him of Lincoln's assassination, Logan expected trouble and immediately
rode into Raleigh. Soon after the general's arrival, a breathless private
rushed into his headquarters reporting that a mob of several thousand men
from the Fifteenth Corps was advancing toward the capital.[21]

Logan confronted the mob on the outskirts of town. "Black Jack" at
first tried to reason with his men, telling them that the people of Raleigh
were not responsible for Lincoln's murder. But the soldiers continued to
press forward amid shouts that Raleigh was "a Rebel hole and ought to
be cleaned out." Pointing with his sword to an artillery battery that had
unlimbered behind him, Logan warned the soldiers that if they did not
disperse, he would order the cannon to open fire. The men realized they
were beaten and returned to camp. "General Logan saved the City, and it
owes him a debt it can never pay," wrote eyewitness Sgt. Theodore F. Upson
of the 100th Indiana.[22]

Yet for the anxious citizens of Raleigh, the night of April 17–18 was far
from over. Earlier, Union soldiers had gathered on street corners, loudly
cursing the town and threatening to destroy everything in sight. Fearing
a reprise of the burning of Columbia, many Raleighites remained awake
all night, armed with basins and buckets of water. When the fire alarm bell
sounded at 9:00 P.M., the townspeople feared that it was the signal for a
night of burning and pillaging. Fortunately, the fire was confined to a de-

The Best I Can Do

serted machine shop on the edge of town and appeared to be accidental. During the night, however, the provost guard filled the jail with soldiers who had stolen into town against orders. The prisoners received a stern reprimand from General Sherman before their release the next morning.[23]

Sunrise revealed that the North Carolina capital had emerged unscathed from the longest night in its history. When Northern papers dated April 12 arrived in Raleigh on April 18, the absence of news concerning Lincoln's assassination led many Federal soldiers to dismiss it as a hoax. After all, Special Field Orders No. 56 mentioned April 11 as the date of the shooting. This false hope was soon dashed, however, for the Raleigh papers ran the correct date—April 14—in their afternoon editions.[24]

Mayor Harrison and other leading Raleigh citizens were understandably eager to issue a public statement condemning Lincoln's murder. At 4:00 P.M. on April 18, the mayor convened a special meeting in the Wake County Court House—"one of the largest ever held by our citizens," reported the *Raleigh Standard*. A committee of five, including Bartholomew F. Moore and Kenneth Rayner, drafted three resolutions "to express our utmost abhorrence of the atrocious deed." The document noted that "such a deed at any time would deserve the indignation of civilized men," but that it was "peculiarly unfortunate and calamitous," coming at "the close of a long continued struggle in arms." The resolutions were unanimously adopted and helped to assuage the Federal soldiers' anger. General Cox nevertheless warned that "if active operations were to commence again it would be impossible to restrain the troops from great outrages."[25]

The Union army's reaction to Lincoln's assassination indicated the necessity of an immediate and all-embracing surrender. Sherman's lieutenants advised securing Johnston's surrender quickly because they dreaded pursuing a "dissolving and fleeing army." The generals recommended offering liberal terms to Johnston—one even suggested providing a seagoing vessel to facilitate Jefferson Davis's escape. In light of the furor over Lincoln's murder and the unlikelihood of trapping Johnston's army, Sherman decided that he must obtain "Old Joe's" surrender without further delay— and he was prepared to grant generous terms to secure it.[26]

Upon his return to Hampton's headquarters, Johnston wired Breckinridge at Greensboro, requesting the secretary of war to join him that evening. Given Breckinridge's influence with President Davis, Johnston regarded the war minister's cooperation as essential to the success of his negotiations with Sherman. Accompanying Breckinridge were Postmaster General Reagan and Governor Vance. They rode to Hampton's headquarters in a freight car, arriving sometime after midnight. Although their rail-

Alexander Dickson house, near Hillsborough. The Dickson house served as Wade Hampton's headquarters during the latter part of April 1865. The April 18 conference between Johnston, Hampton, Breckinridge, and Reagan was held in the back room on the left. The house was later moved from its original site, about one mile southeast of town (where it had fallen into disrepair), to downtown Hillsborough. It has been renovated and is now open to the public. (North Carolina Division of Archives and History)

way accommodations were less than luxurious, the feast that awaited the weary travelers at the Dickson house more than compensated for their inconvenience. The pièce de résistance was a twenty-five-pound turkey served with elegant china and silverware, courtesy of the Cadwallader Jones family of Hillsborough.[27]

After the late-night supper was finished and the table cleared, Hampton confronted Vance regarding his embassy to Sherman and accused the governor of treating with the enemy. Hampton opposed negotiations of any kind with the Federals. He had told Kilpatrick at the Bennett house: "[H]ad I the writing of the terms of agreement they should never be written, [for] I never could bring myself to live again with a people who have waged war as you have done." The South Carolinian also had condemned the Graham-Swain mission to Sherman, saying that "it was a matter of perfect indifference" to him "how much *such men* as the Raleigh commis-

The Best I Can Do

sioners were fired upon" by Kilpatrick's troopers. Even more embarrassing to Vance than Hampton's accusation, however, was the awkward silence that followed, for no one spoke up in the governor's defense. Instead, Johnston asked him to leave the room while the generals and cabinet officers discussed the surrender terms.[28]

The governor went out to the lawn and lay down beside Major Saunders, the Hampton staff officer who had been ordered to arrest Senator Graham several nights previously. Saunders had earlier introduced himself to Vance as a fellow Tar Heel. The night air was chill, inducing the governor to pull Saunders's blanket over his own stocky frame. Vance may have thought back to a speech he had made at Hillsborough a few months before, in which he had exhorted his audience to "fight 'til Hell freezes over, then continue the fight on skates!"—much as he had addressed the Junior Reserves near Smithfield. Those words would have mocked him now and made falling asleep even more difficult.[29]

The governor awoke at daybreak and ate breakfast; he then asked Saunders to take a walk with him. Once they were beyond earshot of the others, Vance poured out his heart to the staff officer. "I came here to explain the Sherman letter," he said, the tears rolling down his face, "and they wouldn't hear me. Me in communication with the enemy, me making terms for my State unknown to the authorities! Of all men, sir, I am the last man they can accuse of such infamy!" As Saunders watched Vance sob uncontrollably, he "felt all the bitterness of resentment" toward the men who had insulted the governor, "and for the first and only time, I, a soldier of the Confederacy, was untrue and disloyal to its colors."[30]

During the late-night conference inside the Dickson house, Johnston had announced the news of Lincoln's assassination and urged everyone to say nothing until the negotiations were concluded. "Old Joe" then related the details of his conference with Sherman, noting that the Federal commander had refused to grant amnesty to Davis and his cabinet—a matter of obvious concern to Breckinridge and Reagan. At the conclusion of Johnston's briefing, Reagan offered to write down the surrender terms. Johnston dictated the terms to Reagan and then suggested that everyone get a few hours' sleep. Later that morning, Reagan was making a fair copy of the terms when Johnston announced that he was leaving for the Bennett farm. Ignoring "Old Joe's" admonition, Breckinridge informed Vance of Lincoln's murder and said that he and Johnston were riding out to meet Sherman. Soon afterward, Vance borrowed a horse and rode to Graham's house, where he spent the day awaiting Johnston's return.[31]

Leaving Reagan behind to complete his memorandum, Johnston and Breckinridge rode off for the Bennett farm at 10:00 A.M., escorted by fifty

officers and men of Col. Zimmerman Davis's 5th South Carolina Cavalry. Wade Hampton chose to remain at his headquarters.[32]

As he rode out to meet Sherman for the second time, Johnston did not know that his army was disintegrating. On the afternoon of April 16, an order to halt the Army of Tennessee's march pending further instructions convinced the men that surrender negotiations were under way. Filled with fear and uncertainty, the soldiers had mobbed their commanders' headquarters, demanding the truth. But the officers were as much in the dark as their troops and could only tell them to be patient. "Various rumors have just come into camp regarding the surrender of this army," Col. Baxter Smith wrote Wheeler, "which has already induced some men to leave, and it is probable that others will do so in the course of the night." On April 17, Hardee asked Beauregard if the rumors were true. Replying that he was not at liberty to say, Beauregard told Hardee to keep his troops "well in hand for a rapid movement" should one become necessary. That night, many of Hardee's troops made a rapid movement on their own responsibility—"taking French leave," as their comrades called it—and stole some draft animals to speed their homeward journey.[33]

A South Carolinian in Hardee's Corps, Capt. William E. Stoney, noted that rumors of being surrounded and the sight of deserting cavalry caused Hardee's troops to panic. "Disorganization was complete," Captain Stoney wrote. "Horses and mules were everywhere taken without the least regard to ownership. . . . The division supply train was thoroughly stripped. The flags of the brigade were burned by the men in certainty of surrender." According to Stoney, "with that day [April 17, 1865], the army perished—a mob remained."[34]

Nowhere was demoralization more evident than in the North Carolina units, which lost hundreds of men to desertion in mid-April. The most telling statistic involves Ellis's Battery of the 3rd North Carolina Battalion, whose adjutant kept a careful record of desertions. On April 1, Ellis's Battery numbered eighty-nine officers and men. The battery suffered five desertions the next day, three on April 14, and four more on April 15. But the night of April 16 saw thirty-one men desert the ranks. The following morning, only forty-six officers and men were present at morning roll call. Because most Tar Heel soldiers were closer to home than their out-of-state comrades, the temptation to desert was greater, but the example of Ellis's Battery reflects the demoralization that now gripped all units in Johnston's army as rumors of their surrender spread.[35]

The Army of Tennessee suffered three devastating blows to its morale in April 1865. The first was dealt by news of the fall of Richmond, the second by the report of Lee's surrender. As severe as these shocks were, the men recovered from the first and appeared to shake off the second, but rumors concerning their own surrender struck the third and fatal blow to the Confederates' morale. "From that moment," Georgia cavalryman William W. Gordon wrote, "it was impossible for General J[ohnston] to back out from his negotiations with S[herman], never mind what terms S[herman] dictated, because [Johnston's] Army would no longer fight." Although it had not yet surrendered or disbanded, the Army of Tennessee had nonetheless ceased to exist. As of April 18, 1865, Johnston commanded an army in name only.[36]

On Tuesday, April 18, Sherman and his entourage arrived at Durham's Station about 11:00 A.M. While they waited at Kilpatrick's headquarters for their horses to be saddled, they were serenaded with martial airs by the band of the 3rd Kentucky Cavalry. As on the previous day, they basked in a glorious spring day.[37]

At 11:15, Sherman left Kilpatrick's headquarters for the Bennett farm. Hundreds of Federals converged on either side of the road to catch a glimpse of "Uncle Billy." Riding beside Sherman was Kilpatrick, resplendent in his dress uniform, sword, and sash. The escort consisted of 200 troopers from Bvt. Brig. Gen. Thomas J. Jordan's brigade.[38]

The flags of truce met before the Bennett house at noon. Sherman noted that Johnston had left his escort several hundred yards to the rear to prevent the men from mixing with the Federals, but many Union troopers strolled down to the Confederate picket line to talk to their counterparts. At the Bennett house, a Union staff officer asked after Hampton. The South Carolinian's adjutant, Major McClellan, replied that the general "did not see fit to be present today," much to the amusement of the Federals who overheard him.[39]

Sherman and Johnston shook hands and then entered the Bennett house. Johnston said that he now had the authority to surrender all remaining Confederate forces but wanted Sherman's assurance that the constitutional rights of his soldiers would be protected. Sherman stated that Lincoln's amnesty proclamation of 1863 guaranteed a full pardon for all soldiers below the rank of brigadier general, and the Appomattox terms embraced all general officers, including Robert E. Lee. Nevertheless, Johnston insisted on specific guarantees for his men, for they were extremely uneasy regarding their rights.[40]

The Confederate commander also requested that Breckinridge be allowed to participate in the negotiations, since he was responsible for the comprehensive surrender. Sherman refused at first because the Kentuckian was a member of Davis's cabinet, but Johnston observed that he was also a major general in the Confederate army. "Uncle Billy" thereupon decided that, although Breckinridge the cabinet minister was persona non grata, Breckinridge the army officer was acceptable. Johnston sent a staff officer for the secretary, who was waiting at the picket line. The former U.S. vice president arrived at the Bennett house a few minutes later. Reporter Volney Hickox recognized the "tall, commanding figure" with the distinctive handlebar mustache, whose "large, cold, gray eyes [met] with . . . defiance, the hundred questioning glances" of bluecoat onlookers.[41]

Sherman and Johnston repeated the main points of their discussion to Breckinridge, who reinforced Johnston's assertion that the Confederate soldiers desired some guarantees concerning their political status. The two Southerners conceded that slavery was dead, and Johnston laughed as he noted that the Confederacy had done its part in killing "the peculiar institution" by recruiting black troops. During the conversation, a packet of papers arrived from Hampton's headquarters. Among them was Reagan's memorandum, which Johnston and Breckinridge read and commented on in whispers. Johnston then read the document aloud, noting that it differed from the terms discussed only insofar as it granted universal amnesty. Sherman was unimpressed, finding Reagan's paper "so general and verbose" that he deemed it "inadmissible." Johnston nevertheless handed him the paper to study.[42]

Sherman called for his saddlebags and broke out his whiskey, much to the delight of Breckinridge, who poured a glass and refreshed himself. Thus inspired, the Kentuckian waxed eloquent in advocacy of the Reagan document for six or eight minutes before Sherman finally blurted, "See here, gentlemen, just who is doing this surrendering, anyhow? If this thing goes on, you'll have me sending a letter of apology to Jeff Davis." Breckinridge received no more of "Uncle Billy's" whiskey. The Kentuckian was so furious at not getting a second glass that he later told Johnston: "General Sherman is a hog. Yes, sir, a hog. . . . [N]o Kentucky gentleman would have taken away that bottle. He knew we needed it, and needed it badly." (This anecdote should be taken with a grain of salt. It appears in the reminiscences of John Wise, who was not present at the Bennett house during the surrender negotiations. Wise claimed to have heard the story from General Johnston fifteen years after the fact.)[43]

At the conclusion of Breckinridge's speech, Sherman took out pen and paper. Recalling his conversations with Lincoln at City Point—and having Reagan's document on the table before him—the Union commander wrote his "Memorandum or Basis of Agreement." Johnston noted that Sherman wrote so rapidly that he apparently had come prepared to grant the very terms in Reagan's paper. "Old Joe" gazed out the window as Sherman wrote and even went outside for a few minutes to examine a Federal's Spencer repeating carbine. Soon afterward, Sherman looked up and said, "Gentlemen, this is the best I can do." As the two Confederates read the terms, they must have realized that not only was it the best Sherman could do, it was better than they had any right to expect.[44]

Reagan's memorandum (see Appendix A) proposed that in return for disbanding the Confederate armies and recognizing the Constitution and authority of the U.S. government, the Southern states would receive the following guarantees:

1. The incumbent Southern state governments would be retained.
2. The personal, political, and property rights of the Southern people would be preserved under the authority of the constitutions of the United States and of the individual states.
3. The Southern people would receive universal amnesty for their

participation in the war. According to Johnston, this had been the one point that Sherman would not agree to during the first day's conference, because he refused to grant a blanket pardon to President Davis and his cabinet.

4. There would be a general suspension of hostilities during the negotiations.[45]

Although Sherman had dismissed Reagan's memorandum as too verbose, his own document (see Appendix B) proved to be twice the length of the Texan's, for in addition to granting the above terms, Sherman's proposal offered the Confederates a good deal more:

1. Like Reagan, Sherman proposed an armistice pending negotiations, to which he added the proviso that either of the commanders would be required to give the other forty-eight hours' notice before resuming hostilities.

2. The units comprising the remaining Confederate armies were to proceed to their respective state capitals and deposit their arms in the state arsenals. The arms and ammunition thus collected were to be used solely to maintain order within state borders, and the quantity stored was to be reported to the chief of ordnance in Washington, D.C. The officers and men were also required to file an agreement to cease all acts of war.

3. The president of the United States would recognize the various Southern state governments, provided their officers and legislators took the oaths prescribed by the U.S. Constitution. Cases involving conflicting state governments established during the war would be decided by the U.S. Supreme Court (this condition goes far beyond Reagan's guarantee of existing Southern state governments).

4. The Federal court system would be reestablished in the Southern states.

5. The president would guarantee the Southern people their personal, political, and property rights as defined by the constitutions of the United States and of the individual states.

6. The president would grant general amnesty to the Southern people for their part in the war so long as they lived in peace and obeyed the laws in force in their respective states. Although he had not consciously intended to, Sherman was thus granting a full pardon to *all* Southerners, including President Davis and his cabinet officers, which no doubt delighted Johnston and Breckinridge.

7. Sherman's final condition was a summation of the preceding six. According to the terms of agreement, the war would cease and a

The Best I Can Do

general amnesty would follow once the Confederate armies disbanded and the officers and men composing those armies resumed their peaceful pursuits.[46]

Sherman realized that he had delved into political matters beyond his authority as a military commander. He therefore inserted a clause at the end of his memorandum stating that he and General Johnston pledged to obtain the prompt approval of their "respective principals" before carrying the terms into effect.[47]

Why did Sherman involve himself in the political issues regarding the Confederates' surrender after he had promised his father-in-law, Thomas Ewing, that he would steer clear of politics and had repeatedly assured Grant that he would give Johnston the same terms that Lee had received at Appomattox Court House? Sherman took this perilous step for four reasons. First, the notion of ending the war "by one single stroke of the pen" appealed to Sherman's flair for the dramatic. Second, Sherman believed that he was fulfilling Lincoln's wishes as expressed to him at City Point. Although they probably did not discuss specific terms, Sherman inferred that Lincoln had favored a conciliatory policy enabling the Southern states to resume their peacetime status as soon as possible. Lincoln also had encouraged Sherman's efforts to communicate with Georgia governor Joseph E. Brown the previous September, indicating that the late president would have approved of "Uncle Billy's" decision to negotiate with Johnston on political as well as military matters. Moreover, Sherman had recently learned of Maj. Gen. Godfrey Weitzel's call of the Virginia legislature, permitting that body to meet while Richmond was under Federal occupation. The call indicated that Lincoln had favored retaining Confederate state governments, at least until others could be elected or appointed. Third, Sherman dreaded the prospect of pursuing Johnston's army, only to see it break up into guerrilla bands. By granting generous terms, Sherman hoped to obviate the need for extensive mopping-up operations in the South.[48]

The fourth reason involved Sherman's view of the South and his opinion of the politicians in Washington. Sherman had enjoyed living in the South prior to the war and had come to like and admire its people, but he knew that crushing the South's home-front morale was essential to restoring the region to the Union. Yet he repeatedly had said that as soon as the Confederates laid down their arms, he would be the first to come to their aid. Sherman's terms fulfilled his promise to the South. "Uncle Billy" also believed that by virtue of his superior sense and greater practical experience, he was better qualified than most Washington politicians to decide

Memorandum or basis of agreement made this 18th day of April A.D. 1865, near Durham's Station in the State of North Carolina, by and between General Joseph E. Johnston, commanding the Confederate army, and Major General William T. Sherman, commanding the army of the United States in North Carolina, both present:

First: The contending armies now in the field to maintain the "Status quo", until notice is given by the commanding General of any one to its opponent, and reasonable time, say forty-eight hours, allowed.

Second: The Confederate Armies now in existence to be disbanded and conducted to their several State Capitals, there to deposit their arms and public property in the State Arsenal: and each officer and man to execute and file an agreement to cease from acts of war, and to abide the action of both State and Federal authority. The number of arms and munitions of war to be reported to the Chief of Ordnance at Washington city, subject to the future action of the Congress of the United States, and in the meantime to be used solely to maintain peace and order within the borders of the States respectively.

Third: The recognition by the Executive of the United States of the several State Governments, on their officers and Legislatures taking the oaths prescribed by the Constitution of the United States: and where conflicting State Governments have resulted from the war, the legitimacy of all shall be submitted to the Supreme Court of the United States.

Sherman's "Memorandum or Basis of Agreement," April 18, 1865. Fair copy in Pvt. Arthur O. Granger's hand, signed by Generals Sherman and Johnston. (Library of Congress)

upon what terms the South should reenter the Union. Sherman perceived the Radical Republican faction in Congress as eager to rebuild the South to suit its own interests, whereas he felt that the best means of securing a lasting peace was to let the Southerners determine their own fate.

Johnston's contribution to the Bennett Place negotiations is often over-

Fourth: The re-establishment of all the Federal Courts in the several States, with powers as defined by the Constitution and laws of Congress.

Fifth: The people and inhabitants of all the States to be guaranteed, so far as the Executive can, their political rights and franchises, as well as their rights of person and property as defined by the Constitution of the United States and of the States respectively.

Sixth: The Executive authority of the Government of the United States not to disturb any of the people by reason of the late war, so long as they live in peace and quiet, abstain from acts of armed hostility, and obey the laws in existence at the place of their residence.

Seventh: In general terms, — The war to cease: — a general amnesty so far as the Executive of the United States can command, on condition of the disbandment of the Confederate Armies, the distribution of the arms, and the resumption of peaceful pursuits by the officers and men hitherto composing said armies.

— Not being fully empowered by our respective principals to fulfil these terms, we individually and officially pledge ourselves to promptly obtain the necessary authority and to carry out the above programme.

W. T. Sherman
Maj Genl Comdg
Army U.S. in N.C.

J. E. Johnston
General Comdg
C.S. Army in N.C.

looked, as if he were a mere onlooker. Nothing could be further from the truth. Johnston initiated negotiations with Sherman and insisted on a comprehensive surrender based on terms derived from Reagan's memorandum bearing "Old Joe's" unmistakable stamp. Johnston later noted that Sherman's paper differed from Reagan's only in being more detailed. "[Sherman] had accepted, virtually, the terms I had offered in writing,"

Bennett Place, drawn by Theodore R. Davis (Harper's Weekly, *1865)*

Johnston boasted three years later. "They included general amnesty without naming individuals or classes." Viewed in this light, the true victor at the Bennett farm on April 18 was Joe Johnston.[49]

After the two commanders signed the agreement, Sherman stepped to the doorway and called for his clerk, Pvt. Arthur Granger. Sherman ordered the private to make two copies of the document. Granger recalled hearing the generals converse freely, making him wish he could put down his pen and listen. When Granger was finished, Sherman summoned Maj. Henry Hitchcock to assist in proofreading the copies.[50]

The Union soldiers outside the house now realized that Sherman and Johnston had reached an agreement. Officers and men standing in the Bennetts' yard plucked strawberry and cherry blossoms as well as sprigs from privet bushes as souvenirs. Federal general Thomas J. Jordan made a rough sketch of the Bennett house, while *Harper's* artist Theo Davis limned a more finished view, adding the kitchen to the right of the house, a large white oak tree in the yard, and some Union cavalrymen feeding their horses.

Then it was Davis's turn to answer Sherman's summons. After introductions, Sherman and Johnston sat down at the table where the surrender document had been written and signed. Thanks to years of hard-earned experience as a battlefield artist, Davis drew rapidly and soon had a detailed representation of the two generals inside the Bennetts' main room.

The Best I Can Do

Theodore R. Davis. A true rarity among journalists, Theo Davis was a trusted member of Sherman's military family. (North Carolina Division of Archives and History)

Years later, Johnston visited Davis's studio and, while viewing the sketch, remarked that posterity would construe the bottle on the table to be whiskey, and since it stood nearer to him, "down to history" that bottle would go as his. When Davis asked Sherman afterward if he remembered the bottle, the general replied that he did, and that "it was good whiskey, some of my own." And so down to history the bottle goes as Sherman's.[51]

When the copies had been proofread and signed, Sherman, Johnston, and Breckinridge emerged from the Bennett house. It was 4:00 P.M. As the three men parted at the gate, Sherman advised Breckinridge to flee the country, for his status as a former U.S. vice president made him a marked man. The Kentuckian replied that he intended to escape and never return.[52]

As the two commanders shook hands, Col. Orlando M. Poe, Sherman's chief engineer, parted with Johnston's engineering officer, Maj. John Johnson. Poe and Johnson had spent the afternoon talking shop under the tall oak tree. Major Hitchcock also had chatted with Johnson, and as Hitchcock passed through the Bennetts' front gate, Johnson said, "Good-bye, Major—hope we shall meet again!" to which he added in a low voice, "*in the right way.*"[53]

The Federals set out for Durham's Station at a "fast lope," Volney Hickox

The Best I Can Do

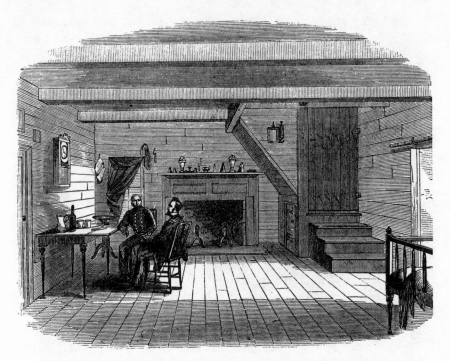

Interior view of the Bennett house, by Theodore R. Davis. This sketch portrays Sherman and Johnston seated at the table where they conducted their negotiations. Note the much ballyhooed bottle of whiskey. (Harper's Weekly, *1865*)

noted. As the column rode into view of Kilpatrick's headquarters, cavalrymen streamed down to the road from all directions to learn if Johnston had surrendered. The railway village erupted with cheering as the news spread. "All the troops are jubilant and talking of going home," wrote Lt. Joseph Kittinger of the 23rd New York Battery. "God be praised for the glorious termination of this War." Few of "Little Kil's" men knew that the agreement required the approval of Presidents Andrew Johnson and Jefferson Davis.[54]

Sherman and his staff ate dinner at Kilpatrick's headquarters before returning to Raleigh. Late that night, Sherman sent Major Hitchcock to Washington with the surrender document and a letter addressed to Grant and army chief of staff Maj. Gen. Henry W. Halleck. "I inclose herewith a copy of an agreement made this day between General Joseph E. Johnston and myself," Sherman wrote, "which, if approved by the President of the United States, will produce peace from the Potomac to the Rio Grande." Sherman informed Grant that Breckinridge had attended the conference as a major general—a subtle distinction in the Confederate secretary of war's status that Grant doubtless failed to appreciate—and that the Kentuckian had assured him of Johnston's ability to execute the terms of the

The Best I Can Do

agreement. "[I]f you will get the President to simply indorse the copy and commission me to carry out the terms," Sherman continued,

I will follow them to the conclusion. You will observe that it is an absolute submission of the enemy to the lawful authority of the United States, and disperses his armies absolutely, and the point to which I attach most importance is that the dispersion and disbandment of these armies is done in such a manner as to prevent their breaking up into guerrilla bands. On the other hand, we can retain as much of the army as we please. I agreed to the mode and the manner of the surrender of arms as set forth, as it gives the States the means of repressing guerrillas, which we could not expect them to do if we stripped them of all arms. Both Generals Johnston and Breckinridge admitted that slavery was dead, and I could not insist on embracing it in such a paper, because it can be made with the States in detail. I know that all the men of substance South sincerely want peace, and I do not believe that they will resort to war again during this century.[55]

In reply to Halleck's dispatch warning that an assassin might be after him, "Uncle Billy" joked that the man "had better be in a hurry or he will be too late." Once again Sherman urged Halleck to convince the president "not to vary the terms at all, for I have considered everything and believe that the Confederate armies once dispersed we can adjust all else fairly and well." To his wife, Sherman confided: "I can hardly realize it, but I can see no slip. The terms are all on our side. If approved I can soon complete the details, leave Schofield here and march my army for the Potomac[,] there to be mustered out and paid. If I accomplish this I surely think I will be entitled to a months leave to come and see you." Sherman was supremely confident that his terms would be approved. If he anticipated any objections from President Johnson and other Washington politicians, he counted on the good sense of his old army friends, Grant and Halleck, to prevail.[56]

On the evening of April 18, Sherman conferred with most of his army and corps commanders at the Governor's Palace. The Union commander recalled that several of his subordinates—including his two political generals, John Logan and Frank Blair—advised him to ratify the terms without the president's approval. Army of Georgia commander Henry Slocum was also present and heard no dissenting voices concerning Sherman's memorandum. When Slocum returned to his headquarters, he was met by his chief of staff, Maj. Gen. Carl Schurz, who was anxious to learn Sherman's terms. Earlier that day, Schurz had written his wife: "I fear that Sherman will attempt to excel Grant as mediator, since Grant has excelled him as leader in battle." As Slocum described the terms, Schurz realized that his fears were well founded. The politically astute Schurz knew at once that the agreement would not be approved, because Sherman—a mere general in the field—was dictating the Federal government's reconstruction policy. Schurz's argument must have convinced Slocum, for the latter was heard to say at Howard's headquarters the next evening that he did not think Sherman's terms would be approved. Several others, including General Logan, agreed with Slocum. The about-face at Howard's headquarters indicates that, although Sherman's subordinates supported him, they realized that his agreement was doomed to failure and were reluctant to tell him.[57]

On April 19, Sherman released Special Field Orders No. 58, announcing a suspension of hostilities pending ratification of his agreement with Johnston: "[T]he general hopes and believes that in a very few days it will be his good fortune to conduct you all to your homes." Separating the two armies was a truce line running northeast from Tyrell's Mount near the Haw River to Chapel Hill and Durham's Station, and then extending north to West Point on the Eno River.[58]

The reaction of Sherman's soldiers was comparatively subdued. "That's all. Good-bye, war," wrote Maj. Charles Wills of the 103rd Illinois. Samuel Mahon of the 7th Iowa was only somewhat more demonstrative. "[E]re this reaches you," Mahon wrote his sister, "you will have heard the glorious news of Johnsons surrender to Sherman both of his army and all the states from the Rio Grande to the Atlantic. . . . [T]he work of the Army is done[;] a few months easy duty and then like Othello our occupation will be gone." The Federals' low-key response should be no surprise, for they had recently celebrated Richmond's fall and Lee's surrender, only to be stunned by Lincoln's assassination. Many also realized that the agreement was conditional, and that there would be time enough to celebrate once the terms were ratified.[59]

When General Johnston reached the Dickson house on the evening of April 18, he ordered Major Johnson to make two copies of the surrender agreement. Meanwhile, Johnston dashed off a synopsis of the terms for Beauregard. Johnston, Breckinridge, and Reagan dined at 8:00 P.M. and then boarded their train for Greensboro. They stopped at the Hillsborough depot, but Governor Vance was not there as arranged. North Carolina Railroad president Thomas Webb was on board and instructed the engineer to blow the whistle repeatedly. After waiting forty-five minutes—by Webb's estimate—the train proceeded to Greensboro without the governor, arriving at 2:00 A.M. on April 19.[60]

Zeb Vance was furious when he learned that the train had left without

The Best I Can Do

him. The governor had waited at the depot from 4:00 P.M. (the time designated by Johnston) until 8:00 that evening, when he had returned in disgust to Graham's house. Both Breckinridge and Webb had promised to notify Vance of the train's arrival, but Webb later explained that he had no one to send after the governor. Understandably, Vance suspected he had intentionally been left behind.[61]

At midnight, Webb sent a special train from Company Shops to take the governor to Greensboro. Upon his arrival, Vance fired off an angry letter to Johnston. "Being totally uninformed of the condition of affairs in the State and being unable to obtain from any one a statement of what is going on or what the Government of the Confederate States intends to do," the governor wrote, "I respectfully request permission to send by flag of truce a letter to Genl Sherman[,] commanding forces of United States in North Carolina, which shall be submitted for your perusal. I am induced to take this course for the reason that the people of my State are now suffering all the horrors of rapine and I feel it my duty in the absence of other authority on whom it might more properly devolve to use my best exertions to protect them."[62]

Neither approving nor denying Vance's request, Johnston instead noted that the governor could have read the terms of agreement had he waited at the depot as arranged. The general promised to send Vance his copy of the terms as soon as it was returned to him. After receiving Johnston's reply, Vance wrote a second letter to the general. The governor complained of being left behind at Hillsborough, though hastening to add that he did not blame Johnston. Vance then mentioned the late-night conference at Hampton's headquarters. "I was invited by General Breckinridge to go down to where you were to participate in the consultation there to take place," Vance wrote, "and as I supposed and desired, to accompany the flag of truce to a conference with General Sherman, thinking, very naturally, that I was entitled to know something of and participate in proceedings which were more immediately to affect my people than those of any other State in the Confederacy." Having been excluded from those negotiations, Vance continued, he had written his letter requesting a parley with Sherman to make "such provision as remained in my power for the welfare of the State."[63]

In his second reply to Vance, Johnston explained that "as a mere military officer arranging the terms of an armistice" (the general was downplaying his role to the point of absurdity), he did not think it proper for civilians to take part in the negotiations. "Old Joe" assured the governor that had the terms been his to write, "there would have been no gentleman whose aid I would have sought more gladly than yours." With more than a little duplicity, Johnston informed Vance that he was limited to acting on "the views of the President." Referring to the copy of the terms enclosed with his letter, Johnston assured Vance that it contained "all the information to be had on the subject." The general assumed that once Vance had read the document, he would have no desire to contact Sherman.[64]

By the time Vance received Johnston's second letter, his temper had cooled. "I regret, general, that the correspondence should have assumed the phase of a mere personal complaint on my part," Vance wrote, "though I felt so acutely what I thought to be exceedingly uncourteous treatment on the part of some one [Wade Hampton] toward myself, that I perhaps improperly referred to it in a letter." The governor admitted his embarrassment at being excluded from the conference at Hampton's headquarters, which was compounded by being left behind at Hillsborough. "You are correct in supposing that after reading the paper which you inclosed me yesterday, containing a memorandum of the basis of agreement written by yourself and General Sherman for the termination of the war, I would not desire to communicate with the latter," Vance conceded. "I am content, of course, to await the issue of those negotiations."[65]

April 19 was a trying day for Johnston, and not solely because of Vance's importunate letters. The general was visited by Lt. Gen. Stephen D. Lee, who was anxious to learn the terms of agreement. General Lee had brought most of his staff with him and read the terms aloud for their benefit. As Lee read, Maj. J. W. Ratchford noticed that tears welled up in "Old Joe's" eyes and then "burst bounds and trickled down his cheeks." Though Johnston had secured "fair terms of peace," they fell far short of the goal for which the Confederate commander had fought—Southern independence.[66]

For all his despondency, Johnston presented a brave front to his troops, most of whom were demoralized. Reports from his corps commanders indicated that desertion rates were epidemic. Johnston therefore did what he deemed necessary to keep the men in the ranks—he denied the obvious. "General Johnston learns with pain that an impression that negotiations were pending for the capitulation of this army has extensively prevailed and produced much desertion," read an April 19 circular from Johnston's headquarters. "He begs that you will instantly make it known that the general order for this day published discloses the whole object of the recent conferences under flag of truce." The document referred to, General Orders No. 14, announced a suspension of hostilities "pending negotiations between the two Governments"; in the meantime, the two armies would maintain their present positions.[67]

Some hopeful Confederates inferred from the phrase "the two governments" that peace based on Southern independence was at hand. They

The Best I Can Do

conjectured that the United States was at war with France over Mexico and was willing to recognize the Confederacy if it consented to an alliance. But as the terms of agreement became generally known, this forlorn hope was dashed. "We must be in a sorry plight when our leaders agree to such terms," wrote Sgt. Maj. Alexander Marshall, for whom Southern independence was the only satisfactory condition for ending the war. A disappointed Pvt. J. M. J. Tolly of the 24th Alabama commented: "It is a sad thought with me when I think of the many noble soldiers that has been Slane [slain] and for nothing." Lt. W. A. Johnson of the 2nd South Carolina observed that the army was "completely demoralized." Johnson's camp stood by the roadside, and all day he watched a steady stream of men "going home without orders." At one point, he saw Lt. Gen. A. P. Stewart plead with a group of deserters "to return to their commands, but they only laugh and mock him." The officers were scarcely less demoralized than their men. "The report of our having to capitulate is now believed, & it is immense desertion to avoid the humiliation & would that I were not in command of this Brig[ade] I would set out also," Lt. Col. James Welsman Brown of Elliott's Brigade confided to his diary. Even so, a few diehards such as Colonel Waring of the Jeff Davis Legion still believed that "[t]he army will again revive. *The South will yet be free.*" But most of Johnston's soldiers would have conceded the truth of Georgia private Hezekiah McCorkle's statement: "The sentiment seems to prevail throughout the entire army that the war is over."[68]

CHAPTER 8

CONQUERED BUT NOT SUBDUED

At 8:00 A.M. on April 17, while Sherman was boarding a train thirty miles to the east for his first conference with Johnston, Atkins's brigade of Kilpatrick's cavalry division was entering Chapel Hill. Meeting General Atkins on the edge of town was a citizens' committee led by David L. Swain, who assured the general that Wheeler's cavalry was gone. Atkins replied that his men had orders to respect all private property. Committee member Charles P. Mallett then told the general that he had seen some Union horsemen steal into town ahead of the main body. Atkins ordered Col. George S. Acker to ride into Chapel Hill with his 9th Michigan Cavalry and provide safeguards for all citizens who requested them. The 9th Michigan soon established order and won the respect if not the affection of the townspeople. Chapel Hill resident Cornelia Phillips Spencer found the Michigan troopers to be "a decent set of men, who . . . behaved with civility and propriety." According to Mallett, April 18 "dawned upon us after as quiet a night as I have ever known at Chapel Hill."[1]

News of Lincoln's assassination arrived on April 18 but resulted in no reprisals by Atkins's cavalry. The night was unsettled nonetheless, as dozens of former slaves stole away from their erstwhile masters, their departure heralded by the barking of dogs. The next morning, Mallett learned that most of his neighbors' servants had left; he suspected that his remained only because one of the women was too ill to travel.[2]

Later that day, Sherman's order announcing a suspension of hostilities arrived at Atkins's headquarters. Of greater interest to the Union troopers were rumors that Hampton and Wheeler refused to surrender, for the Federals knew they would be ordered to hunt down the Rebel diehards regardless of the outcome of negotiations.[3]

In preparation for the Yankees' arrival, many Chapel Hill residents had concealed their food stores and valuables, only to see their efforts defeated. Thinking there were no amateur astronomers in Sherman's army, Professor Charles Phillips and his father hid their watches in the university telescope, where they were promptly discovered by a stargazing Union soldier. Much to the Phillips's surprise, the Federals eventually returned their watches. Judge William H. Battle buried his silver service under a maple tree behind his house and then forgot which tree marked the spot. The absentminded Battle's silver was accidentally discovered by workmen several years later. One of Charles Mallett's neighbors complained that a Yankee had pitched his tent on the ground where her bacon lay buried. Mallett regretted burying so many of his possessions, for his guard would have rendered them safer above ground.[4]

Like the rest of the town, the university was well guarded and sustained minimal damage. Several of the buildings, however, served as the cavalry's stables, prompting townspeople to remark that General Atkins had the best educated horses in the Union army. In late April, there were only a dozen students in attendance—364 fewer than the student body of 1860–61. Only one of them, senior William C. Prout, would graduate that year. The bell summoning the handful of students to prayer was rung each morning and evening, spurring Charles Mallett to condemn President Swain and his faculty. "I feel provoked to hear the College bell sounding on as though the College was in full blast," Mallett wrote. "A miserable set—*not one* true man among them and they desire to hand it down to History that the dear Yankees did not interfere with the regular exercises of the College—when in truth there were not five students here when Wheeler left us."[5]

The countryside surrounding Chapel Hill fared much worse than the town. Federal foragers often stripped the outlying farms of all the Confederates had left. In a letter to Sherman, Swain stated that a longtime neighbor could not feed his family after losing all of his animals and most of his provisions. Swain noted that other families in the area suffered under similar hardship. "I am satisfied from my own knowledge of your character and the impression made upon me during our recent interview," Swain wrote, "that you have no disposition to add to the horrors of war by availing yourself of the utmost license which writers on this subject deem admissible, but that, on the contrary, you are disposed to treat the peaceful tillers of the soil with no unnecessary harshness or severity." Swain hoped that the suspension of hostilities would enable Sherman to relax the severity of his orders. Below Swain's signature, Atkins wrote that his command had taken animals that he would return if no future operations were contemplated. Under Atkins's note, General Kilpatrick jotted this comment: "The horses and mules referred to cannot be returned without dismounting men."[6]

Sherman assured Swain that "the moment war ceases, and I think that time is at hand, all seizures of horses and private property will cease on our part, and it may be we will be able to spare some animals for the use of the farmers in your neighborhood." Once peace was made, "we will accept it and be the friends of the farmers and working classes . . . , as well as actual patrons of churches, colleges, asylums, and all institutions of higher learning and charity." Meanwhile, the Union army would live off the land. Attempting to lessen the severity of his occupation, Atkins issued orders forbidding the confiscation of buggies, the use of black servants as foragers, and the pasturing of cavalry animals in grain fields.[7]

The region west of Chapel Hill was hardest hit, for both armies' foragers swept the area. Federals and Confederates met often in this no man's land, sometimes gathering corn from the same crib. An Illinois trooper noted that a squad of Rebels even offered to collect meat for his detail when informed that it was off-limits to Yankees. Maj. William C. Stevens of the 9th Michigan Cavalry observed a similar détente in the streets of Chapel Hill. "There are quite a number of confederate Officers here from Lee's army," Stevens wrote his sister, "and could you see them visiting and riding out with our Officers you would hardly believe they had been opposed to each other in deadly warfare for four years." The major hoped that the absence of ill feeling between the two sides indicated that they would be reunited "with greater harmony than before the war."[8]

For days the "gray, dusty and haggard" veterans of Lee's army tramped through Chapel Hill "in twos or threes, sometimes in little companies," recalled Cornelia Phillips Spencer, "making the best of their way toward their distant homes, penniless and dependent on wayside charity for their food." Many citizens opened their homes to "Lee's men," feeding them from their scanty stores and treating them as conquering heroes. "This was a work which stirred our inmost souls," Spencer wrote, "and has left a tender memory which will outlast life."[9]

The young women of Chapel Hill soon overcame their fear of Yankees, and many assumed an air of defiance. Delia White recalled that she and her sister Laura were asked by their family's guard to sing some songs at the piano. The girls could scarcely sing for laughing as they launched into one patriotic ditty after another, including "Dixie," "The Southern Girl," and "The Homespun Dress." The sisters' laughter abruptly ceased when the Yankee soldier interrupted their concert to tell them how much he liked their songs, and that he never realized "how dearly the Southern girls loved their Dixie land." Swain's daughter Eleanor expressed her pro-Southern sentiments to the tune of "Maryland, My Maryland": "Atkins' boys are marching through—Hide your mules, O hide your mules!" Nevertheless, a disapproving Charles Mallett noted that several local girls had become "quite sociable" with the Yankees, going on walks or riding trips with them. In Mallett's opinion, the Federal occupation of Chapel Hill was no laughing matter. "I feel conquered but not subdued," he confided to his son. "Might has overcome right—my thoughts and feelings are the same and will go down with me to the grave."[10]

The attitude of Charles Mallett and others prompted Michigan cavalryman William Stevens to call Chapel Hill "one of the rankest Rebel towns" he had seen. Yet he found the people "very pleasant" and the town itself "beautiful." Major Stevens noted that the village "was more like home than any place I have been in the south," and he thought the university buildings finer than those back home in Ann Arbor. Adding to Chapel Hill's appeal were the charms of a "splendid young lady" staying at the house where Stevens was billeted. In a letter to his sister, the major confessed: "I don't know but I would lose my heart if we were to remain here long enough, though it is a pretty hard thing for an old bachelor like myself to lose."[11]

Stevens was not the only "old bachelor" in Chapel Hill in danger of losing his heart. One April afternoon, General Atkins paid a social call at former governor Swain's house. During the visit, Swain offered to show the general Lord Charles Cornwallis's letter book. When Atkins assented, Swain entered the adjoining room and asked his daughter Eleanor to get the volume. Bearing the book under her arm, "Miss Ella" glided into the room with her head thrown back, determined to confront the Yankee general with all the hauteur at her command. While her father made the obligatory introduction, however, Eleanor's eyes met the general's—from that moment, Atkins called on Ellie Swain as often as duty would permit. According to Cornelia Phillips Spencer, the general's courtship of "Miss Ella" caused Swain and his wife "as much uneasiness and apprehension as anything short of a death in their family could have done." Realizing that he was powerless to influence his headstrong daughter, Swain told his wife that he would not inquire as to Eleanor's intentions until Atkins had left Chapel Hill.[12]

Meanwhile, Swain checked Atkins's background and found him capable and reliable. A lawyer with a flourishing practice in Freeport, Illinois, before the war, thirty-year-old Smith Atkins was also handsome and well mannered—an ideal son-in-law, provided he had hailed from south of the Mason-Dixon line.[13]

General Atkins's courtship of Eleanor Swain upset soldiers and civilians alike. Charles Mallett observed that "Miss Ella's" conduct scandalized Chapel Hill. Tongues wagged when she received a riding horse from the general as a gift, for everyone assumed the horse was stolen. The soldiers of Atkins's old regiment, the 92nd Illinois Mounted Infantry, resented the fact that their general had neglected them for a Southern belle. One night the 92nd and its band called on Atkins at his headquarters and, finding he was out, proceeded to Swain's house. The band serenaded the general and his lady, and then the men called upon Atkins for a speech. The general stepped onto the front porch and said: "Soldiers, I am making a speech to a young lady here tonight, and I have no eloquence to waste—she requires it all. The war, as I told you it would at Mount Olive, has played out, and in less than the ninety days I then named. I think speech-making has played out also, except to the young ladies." Atkins then ordered his men back to their quarters. The soldiers of the 92nd Illinois returned to camp, sullen and disappointed. One man called Atkins's brief address of that night "the most unpopular speech the General ever made."[14]

When Atkins left Chapel Hill on May 3, Eleanor Swain made the long-anticipated—or long-dreaded—announcement in a note to her parents: she and the general intended to marry. Eleanor also reminded her parents that she was over twenty-one and free to make her own decisions. Cornelia Phillips Spencer called the match a victory for true love and immortalized the occasion of General Atkins's "surrender" by writing a poem. The final quatrain reads:

> The best artillery is found to be the oldest,
>   And peace hath conquests too, by no means narrow;
> The wisest soldier & perchance the boldest,
>   Yields to a pair of blue eyes, and a bow & arrow.

The couple was married in Chapel Hill on August 23.[15]

While Atkins wooed Eleanor Swain, Kilpatrick was conducting a somewhat different affair at Durham's Station. When the cavalry commander arrived there in mid-April, he made Dr. Richard Blacknall's home his headquarters, reserving the east end and center of the house for himself and his adjutant, Major Estes, and the west end for the Blacknall family. Accompanying the two officers were their "wives," or so the men told Blacknall. The doctor suspected otherwise, however, when the two women appeared in privates' uniforms and answered to the names of "Charley" and "Frank." The women respected neither the Blacknall family's privacy nor the clothing of the doctor's two daughters, which they wore on their rides about Durham's. Blacknall described the women as "vulgar, rude and indecent, but fitting companions for a man of General Kilpatrick's character." "Little Kil's" two "orderlies" no doubt were the talk of the town.[16]

Conquered but Not Subdued

In 1865, Durham's Station was a railroad village of about 200 inhabitants, but during April of that year, its population swelled into the thousands. The camps of Jordan's and Kerwin's brigades dotted the countryside, while a multitude of blacks from nearby plantations gathered at the station in the desperate hope of catching a train to Wilmington and then sailing north to a new start. During the truce, the area around Durham's Station was neutral ground. Federals and Confederates met there to swap horses, run foot races, and shoot at targets during the day, and to sit around campfires at night and tell stories of hairbreadth escapes. Many peacemaking Yankees and Rebels smoked tobacco plundered from John R. Green's factory. Although Green deemed the loss of his tobacco stock catastrophic, it proved to be an extraordinary advertising coup. When the soldiers of the two armies started home that spring, they carried supplies of Green's smoking tobacco. As the year progressed, orders for more of the bright-leaf tobacco flooded the postmaster's and railroad agent's offices at Durham's Station. Green's "Durham Smoking Tobacco" scored the most complete victory of the war, conquering thousands of soldiers from Maine to Texas.[17]

If Green's success sprang from the ashes of misfortune, Paul Carrington Cameron's vast wealth enabled him to weather the storm. Cameron owned one of the largest plantations in the state, a 30,000-acre complex about ten miles north of Durham's Station. For most of the war Cameron's plantation had operated with few disturbances, but in April 1865, it was overrun by Confederates and Federals alike. From Fairntosh, the Cameron family home, Rebecca Cameron Anderson wrote her aunt in Raleigh: "[W]e have been subjected to raids from stragglers, who have plundered & ransacked what they please, notwithstanding we are on neutral ground & they have no right to cross the Eno river for any purpose." In fact, Fairntosh did not attain neutral status until the establishment of Sherman's truce line on April 19. In any event, the bummers began their depredations on Sunday, April 16.[18]

"There is not a horse mule wagon or cart upon these plantations," Rebecca Anderson wrote, "& we have only one ham . . . that we know of." She told her aunt that several bummers were drunk and went from "top to bottom" of her family's house, breaking open trunks and rifling them and loudly threatening to burn the place down. Anderson tried to save some of her clothing and her late husband's papers by giving them to the slaves for safekeeping, but the bummers plundered their cabins as well, carrying off most of the clothes and burning her husband's letters (her husband, Walker Anderson, had been killed in the Battle of the Wilderness). "I have not a word in his handwriting except my name in my Bible," Rebecca Anderson lamented. "This is very hard to bear, & I feel as if I could never be reconciled to it—but I try to feel that God has sent this bitter pill to me to swallow, & I try to believe it is for the best & some wise end." Anderson's mother, Anne Cameron, wrote to General Kilpatrick requesting a safeguard, which the family received on April 21. After that, the bummers' depredations at Fairntosh abruptly ceased. The house, barns, and cabins were thus spared, but most of the former slaves left, and the few who remained refused to work. In time, Paul Cameron and his erstwhile slaves would reach a contractual agreement, enabling work on the plantation to resume. The Cameron family would survive the economic depression that gripped the postwar South, and Paul Cameron would remain the wealthiest man in North Carolina.[19]

Two plantations near Raleigh owned by Charles Manly and Jonathan Worth were similarly ransacked. Since the arrival of Sherman's army, Worth had lost all of his cattle and sheep and his best hogs. His slaves were robbed of food and clothing, his hand tools were stolen, and some of his farm machinery was vandalized. "In short, everything stolen—nothing burned," Worth informed his son. Former governor Manly described the devastation of his plantation as "thorough and unsparing." His slaves fared no better than Worth's, losing most of their provisions and clothing. Manly's country house was plundered, most of his farm property was stolen or vandalized, and nearly all of his livestock and provisions were carried off. According to Raleigh resident George Mordecai, the losses sustained by Manly and Worth were typical. "Immediately around Raleigh the farms have been completely despoiled of everything in the shape of provisions & forage, so as to leave literally nothing for the support of man or beast," Mordecai wrote Swain. "[I]n many instances the houses have been either burned or torn to pieces."[20]

Contrary to his experience in the countryside, Worth found Raleigh "as well protected as possible." Manly, however, complained that the Federals camping on his town property behaved "in a most insolent and riotous manner." Yet the former governor reserved a few kind words for one of his Union boarders—Col. Orlando M. Poe, Sherman's chief engineer—who was quartered in Manly's law office. Fearing that bummers would unearth the box of valuables he had buried, Manly asked Poe to help him recover it. The Federal officer responded "with promptness and alacrity," Manly wrote, driving him out to the burial site in his carriage and bringing along an escort. The soldiers dug up the box, and an overjoyed Manly "brought it home in triumph." Henceforth, Poe was "a frequent & welcome visitor" to the Manly home.[21]

During the armistice, Army of the Tennessee commander Oliver O. Howard attempted to soften the hardships imposed on inhabitants by his foraging details. Howard published General Field Orders No. 15, prohibiting the taking of animals or provisions from civilians without authorization from corps or division commanders. "Great disregard has been shown in many instances to the orders heretofore issued on this subject," the document read, "and many of the poor people of the surrounding country are entirely deprived of their provisions and of their animals, which are worthless to us, but are invaluable to them." Howard enjoined his subordinates to prevent the robbery of civilians by holding officers in charge of foraging details strictly accountable. He also ordered the arrest of all men found outside camp without permission and offered to provide guards for citizens living within five miles of Raleigh. In another order issued the same day, General Howard instructed his chief commissary officer to furnish provisions to families whose means of subsistence were taken.[22]

Like Howard, Army of Georgia commander Henry W. Slocum extended a helping hand to civilians, ordering his commissary to distribute rations to several state institutions. On April 19, Slocum redistributed his General Orders No. 8 to the army and ordered the Raleigh newspapers to print it. The order had first appeared on March 7, as the army was entering the Old North State after cutting a destructive swath through South Carolina. The document noted that North Carolina was one of the last states to secede and had retained a strong Unionist element. "It should not be assumed that the inhabitants are enemies to our government," the order read, "and it is hoped that every effort will be made to prevent any wanton destruction of property or any unkind treatment of citizens." Slocum's clemency also appears in a circular issued by Twentieth Corps commander Joseph A. Mower. The bulletin notified regimental commanders that foraging was temporarily suspended and that troops would henceforth receive full rations from the corps commissary. The order also stipulated that pickets should permit no one through their lines without a pass from a division commander or higher. A subsequent order permitting foraging under special circumstances required the issuance of vouchers for animals, forage, and provisions.[23]

The Twentieth Corps's proximity to supplies at Raleigh enabled Slocum to adopt a "no foraging" policy in its case. But the twenty-five miles separating Bvt. Maj. Gen. Jefferson C. Davis's Fourteenth Corps from the state capital compelled the resumption of foraging by that corps after a brief hiatus. Fourteenth Corps commissary officer Dexter Horton was "sad to see the system of *Bummy* commence again," for he knew the hardships foraging would impose on the local populace. Although Slocum ordered General Davis to ensure that his foragers exercised "great care" in dealing with inhabitants, the Fourteenth Corps soon cleaned out the sparsely settled region between Aven's Ferry and Holly Springs. The orders from Slocum and Howard indicate that the Federal high command attempted to prevent the wholesale pillaging and robbery of North Carolina civilians. Unfortunately, the commanders' influence extended only as far as the picket line, and efforts to curb infractions beyond that point largely failed.[24]

With few exceptions Sherman's soldiers were forbidden to venture into the countryside, yet most were permitted to visit Raleigh. By virtue of their circuit through the Confederacy, the Federals regarded themselves as experts on Southern towns, and Raleigh ranked high in their estimation. General Cox called the North Carolina capital "the most attractive [town] I have seen in the South." Huge oaks and elms canopied Raleigh, and tall magnolias grew in long rows down the middle of some of its principal streets. Despite the war's rigors, many homes had green, well-tended lawns and large flower gardens in full bloom—several of the finer residences even boasted greenhouses. The capital's natural splendor inspired a Federal soldier to address an encomium to "Beautiful Raleigh, City of Oaks." The second of the poem's nine stanzas reads:

> War might have blighted thy fair face,
>   And for a time held thee enthraled;
> But like a Phoenix, arising again in its place,
>   So appears the loved city again to the world.[25]

Captain George Pepper thought the stores that lined Fayetteville Street as elegant as any in New York City, and the homes along Hillsborough Street reminded journalist William Anderson of Torresdale, an exclusive neighborhood in Philadelphia. But the capitol—a domed granite structure standing three stories high—received mixed reviews. One Union soldier called it "the finest state edifice I ever saw." Lt. Col. Samuel Merrill of the 70th Indiana wrote his wife: "Our old brick & plaster State House will have to come down when we get home, for it won't do to be surpassed in architecture by the poor state of North Carolina." Reporter Anderson noted that thousands of Federals toured the capitol each day, adding: "[I]t is well worth a visit." On the other hand, Surgeon George Collamore of the 100th Ohio called the building "no very great shakes of an edifice," while the Union army's quartermaster general, Montgomery C. Meigs, found its interior "gloomy" and the dome "too small for effect." If Meigs's judgment seems unduly harsh, he came by his high standards honestly. While serving in the army's Corps of Engineers before the war, Meigs had supervised construction on the U.S. Capitol.[26]

The state capitol's first-floor offices served as headquarters for the post

Conquered but Not Subdued

commander, Bvt. Brig. Gen. Israel N. Stiles, and the town's provost marshal, Col. Willard Warner. On the evening of April 13, Twenty-third Corps signal officer Lt. George C. Round established his station atop the capitol dome. From his high perch, Round enjoyed a breathtaking twilight view of Raleigh and the surrounding countryside. Round's peaceful reverie ended abruptly when he stepped onto what appeared in the shadows to be the smooth copper surface of the dome but was actually the glass skylight, which shattered beneath him and crashed nearly 100 feet to the stone floor of the rotunda. The lieutenant was saved by a thin wire mesh that held him until he pulled himself up to the platform. Round emerged shaken, cut, and bruised but otherwise unhurt.[27]

The senate chamber of the capitol witnessed the birth of the Society of the Army of the Tennessee, a veteran officers' organization that would meet annually into the twentieth century. The capitol also was the site of a caucus of Ohio soldiers who gathered to elect delegates for the upcoming Republican state convention. Dismissing the affair as "a big fizzle," Maj. Oscar Jackson of the 63rd Ohio noted that every Buckeye general regarded himself as a potential candidate for governor. A private "threw a bombshell into camp" by asking whether the convention purported to represent the views of *all* Ohio soldiers, since most enlisted men could not enter the capital city without a pass from their division commanders. The meeting adjourned with the resolution that the Ohio delegation would take no further action at present, but a disgusted Jackson had heard enough officers speak to conclude that most believed they were entitled to the state's political offices.[28]

Capitol Square served as both a Federal campground and a resting place for Confederates from Lee's and Johnston's armies on their way home. Raleigh resident Laura Craven noted that the square was "ruined" as a result, and that the surrounding streets had a "hot dusty sultry look" because the grass usually carpeting them each spring was trampled underfoot. Yankees and Rebels alike gathered under the shade of the oaks and elms to talk, the bluecoats often sharing their rations with the men in butternut and gray. Whether standing on the steps of the capitol or on a tree stump in camp, politically ambitious generals such as Carl Schurz and future U.S. president Benjamin Harrison eagerly exploited opportunities to address crowds of potential voters.[29]

The Insane Asylum was another favorite stop on the Union soldiers' tour of the Tar Heel capital. Many Federals amused themselves by gathering under the grated windows and talking to the inmates. A young man named Allston Lavender struck the soldiers as different from the rest and was pronounced "too smart for a Lunatic." A native of Philadelphia, the

Three views of the North Carolina state capitol, Raleigh. The image above is a rare wartime stereoscopic view of the west facade; the stovepipe-hatted figure in the center foreground is former North Carolina governor David S. Reid. The top view at right, also of the west facade, dates from around 1890 and features the capitol dome. Note the wrought-iron railing and the carriage drive, both of which are long gone (the railing now encloses the Raleigh City Cemetery). The bottom right view is a close-up of the dome, where Lt. George C. Round established his signal station on April 13, 1865. (Top and middle views, North Carolina Division of Archives and History; bottom view, Round, "The Last Signal Message of the War")

twenty-nine-year-old Lavender told the crowd of Union troops beneath his window that his father had arranged his incarceration because he refused to join the Rebel army and wanted to return to the North instead. Lavender apparently convinced his listeners, for he was given an examination by a board of army surgeons that declared him sane. He was released from the hospital and went north with Sherman's army.[30]

At least one other inmate petitioned for his own release, though without Lavender's success. When Sherman visited the hospital, he was accosted by a resident who demanded his "walking papers." The general spoke soothingly to the man: "When your papers come up to me in regular shape I will attend to them. Meanwhile you must be quiet and put your faith in God."

"In God?" the man asked.

Conquered but Not Subdued

"Yes, in God. You certainly believe in Him and his power to take care of us."

The fellow pondered Sherman's statement for a moment and then said: "Well, I think I do believe in a sort of Divine Providence, but when it comes to the question of power, it strikes me that for a man who has been walking about over the country whipping these cursed Rebels, you have a d——d sight more power than anybody I know of!"[31]

The Institute for the Deaf, Dumb, and Blind also attracted many curious soldiers who were impressed by the students' accomplishments. On one occasion, unfortunately, an anonymous prankster arranged for the 4th Minnesota's brass band to serenade a group of the institution's deaf pupils, resulting in a comedy of errors that subjected the band members to considerable chaffing from their comrades.[32]

Yet another stop on the soldiers' itinerary was the modest birthplace of President Andrew Johnson. Few Raleighites expected mercy from their former townsman, who made no secret of his hatred for "Southern traitors." In General Howard's opinion, the capital's citizens believed that, with Lincoln's death and Johnson's ascendancy, they had "passed into severer hands."[33]

When the soldiers tired of touring Raleigh, they spent their free time much as they had at Goldsboro—reading books and newspapers, writing letters to family and friends, playing baseball, building shelters, swimming or fishing in the Neuse River, attending church and camp revivals, loafing, or seeking out the "fair sex." At first the Federals found the young women of Raleigh polite and sociable, but the soldiers soon discovered that beneath this friendly exterior there lurked a grim defiance. Capt. Orville T. Chamberlain of the 74th Indiana was briefly quartered in the home of former *Raleigh Confederate* editor Duncan K. McRae, who had fled town on the Federals' approach. McRae's wife and daughters had remained behind, however, and the statements of one of the girls would have made her father proud. She told Chamberlain: "If you or any other Yankee were lying at the point of death, and I could save your life by giving you a cup of water, I would not give it. I would not even give it to relieve your dying agonies." As they became better acquainted, Miss McRae's opinion of the Federal captain improved to the extent that she told him: "After thinking the matter over, I have concluded that if you were all mangled and torn to pieces by a Rebel missile, I *would* give you a cup of water to soothe your dying agonies, and as you are a Yankee, *I wish I had the opportunity to do so.*"[34]

The soldiers' demand for the latest news was satisfied by two local dailies, the *Progress* and the *Standard,* both of which resumed publication within a few days of the Federals' entry into Raleigh. The pro-Vance *Conservative* and

Conquered but Not Subdued

President Andrew Johnson's birthplace, Raleigh (Harper's Weekly, 1865)

the pro-Davis *Confederate* were less fortunate: their offices were wrecked, and their type scattered in the muddy streets. The co-owner of the *Progress,* W. R. Richardson, also discovered that it was no longer business as usual. One April afternoon he received a terse message from the commanding general:

> To the Proprietors of the *Progress:*
> You are hereby ordered to suspend your paper and report at once to headquarters.
> W. T. SHERMAN

Richardson later confessed that as he hurried to the Governor's Palace, "the ghost of the unfortunate Texan flitted before me, and the casemated walls of Fortress Monroe angrily frowned in prospect." With the possibility of hanging or imprisonment looming up in his imagination, Richardson was understandably agitated when he met Sherman.[35]

The Union commander opened the meeting by saying, "So you are an editor."

Richardson replied that he was.

"There is one thing I want you newspapermen to understand," Sherman continued, "and that is you are not conducting a newspaper in Massachusetts or New York, but in a conquered territory. And I'll have you to under-

The Governor's Palace, Raleigh, pen and ink drawing by Theo Davis, 1865. Zebulon B. Vance was the last governor to reside here. After his abrupt departure, the building served as General Sherman's headquarters. (Courtesy of Chattanooga Regional History Museum)

stand that if you can't carry on your papers without reflecting on my army, I am determined that they shall be suspended."

When Richardson inquired as to the reason for the suspension, Sherman replied that a recent editorial in the *Progress* had criticized him for failing to compensate a civilian for the use of his house. The newspaper owner promised not to repeat his mistake, and Sherman let him off with a warning.[36]

On April 19, Johnston asked Sherman to notify his subordinates in South Carolina and Georgia of the cease-fire. Sherman had already sent word through Johnston's lines to Stoneman and had ordered Maj. Gen. Quincy A. Gillmore, the commander of the Department of the South, to suspend operations in South Carolina. Sherman's courier to Washington, Maj. Henry Hitchcock, also bore a message for the Army of the Potomac's commander, General Meade. But Sherman doubted that he could prevent his "impetuous and rapid" subordinate, Bvt. Maj. Gen. James H. Wilson, from wreaking further havoc in central Georgia. To save time, Sherman sent Johnston several copies of Special Field Orders No. 58 and a message notifying Wilson of the truce and ordering him to cease operations. As Sherman feared, however, Wilson captured Macon before word could reach him. Sherman also sent Johnston a newspaper announcing Weitzel's

Conquered but Not Subdued

call of the Virginia legislature, indicating the Federal government's recognition of a former Confederate governing body.[37]

On April 21, Sherman wrote Johnston concerning his terms of agreement. In view of Weitzel's invitation to the Virginia legislature, Sherman believed that his agreement would encounter "no trouble on the score of recognizing existing [Confederate] State governments." Yet he suspected that several other terms might require elaboration:

It may be the lawyers will want us to define more minutely what is meant by the guaranty of rights of person and property. . . . I wish you would talk to the best men you have on these points and if possible let us in the final convention make these points so clear as to leave no room for angry controversy. I believe, if the South would simply and publicly declare that slavery is dead, that you would inaugurate an era of peace and prosperity that would soon efface the ravages of the past four years of war. Negroes would remain in the South and afford you [an] abundance of cheap labor which otherwise will be driven away, and it will save the country the senseless discussions which have kept us all in hot water for fifty years. Although strictly speaking, this is no subject for a military convention, yet I am honestly convinced that our simple declaration of a result will be accepted as good law everywhere.[38]

Though conceding a few points requiring clarification, Sherman expected his agreement to be approved because both Northern and Southern leaders would regard it as the best means of reuniting the country. The Union commander betrayed his optimism in an order directing his chief quartermaster, General Easton, to send only enough clothing to meet the army's immediate needs, as he had "made terms with Johnston that will close the war and leave us only to march home."[39]

While Sherman awaited Washington's response to the agreement, Col. W. W. Wright's construction crews completed repairs to the railroad from Goldsboro to Raleigh. Except for the burning of the Neuse River bridge, damage was minimal, enabling the first train to reach the state capital on the evening of April 19. Sherman later claimed that he arranged the cease-fire to buy time for rebuilding the railroad, but the task was completed on the day he announced the truce. Sherman also urged the superintendent of the Wilmington and Weldon Railroad to repair the telegraph line from Raleigh to Petersburg by April 25 so that he could transmit the news of Johnston's surrender to the North as quickly as possible.[40]

During the truce, Sherman held daily reviews of his grand army. In addition to fostering esprit de corps and alleviating the boredom of camp life, the reviews underscored the Federal army's invincibility. "I tell you it is a splendid sight," Sherman clerk "Vett" Noble wrote, "and nothing would or does *crush the idea* of rebelling against [us] . . . as to see a Corps pass in review—which takes almost a whole day—and then the next day see the same of another Corps." Sherman reviewed the Tenth Corps on April 20, the Twenty-third Corps on April 21, and the Twentieth Corps on April 22. Because Sherman's field uniform could scarcely be called regulation, the Union commander wore his dress uniform for the reviews. "Uncle Billy" even created something of a sensation by replacing his old weather-beaten hat with a crisp new chapeau adorned with gold braid. "Pop Sherman is getting proud now the war is over," muttered one grizzled veteran. "Well," retorted his neighbor, "I reckon he's earned a new hat, ain't he?" Paine's division of the Tenth Corps stole the show, however, probably because most bystanders (including Sherman) had never seen a column of several thousand armed and uniformed black men marching in perfect step. General Slocum thought the scene "one of the most impressive of the war."[41]

While Sherman reviewed his troops, Johnston watched his army melt away. The Confederate commander estimated that during the armistice about 4,000 infantry and artillery troops and a large number of cavalrymen deserted the ranks. "Old Joe" believed they did so to avoid being sent to prisoner-of-war camps, but there were other reasons. Some deserted to avoid the stigma of surrendering or to fight on elsewhere, but most deserted because they regarded the war as over and wanted to return home.[42]

Few officers could maintain discipline with the troops who remained in the ranks. According to Sgt. W. H. Andrews of the 1st Georgia Regulars, discipline in his regiment became "a thing of the past" on the evening of April 19. When the sergeant ordered several men in his company to fall in for guard duty, they refused. Andrews reported their insubordination to the company commander, Capt. James R. DuBose, but the soldiers told the captain that they had performed their last guard detail. Andrews noted that similar scenes occurred in other companies of the regiment. He believed that regimental commander Col. Richard A. Wayne "would make trouble for the boys," for Wayne had earned a reputation as a tough—but fair—disciplinarian. Much to Andrews's surprise, Wayne reasoned with the skulkers, telling them they were placed on guard duty to maintain order, not as punishment. Yet even the colonel failed to persuade them, and for the first time in its four-year history, a camp of the 1st Georgia Regulars lacked a guard detail.[43]

The collapse of discipline in the Army of Tennessee meant that no man's property was safe and few comrades could be trusted. Morale had so de-

Conquered but Not Subdued

teriorated that thieves raided Johnston's headquarters and rode off with several horses belonging to the commanding general's staff. Meanwhile, Johnston received a barrage of letters from Governor Vance complaining that his soldiers were plundering state warehouses from Graham to Salisbury and his quartermasters were seizing state goods earmarked for North Carolina troops. "I confess I am getting tired of it," Vance wrote. "Having shown every disposition to be liberal & patriotic in dividing my reserves I should be much pleased to be permitted to dispose of the remainder as I see proper." The governor demanded restitution for the stolen goods. "North Carolina having done five times more than any other State for the clothing of the army," Vance claimed, "I think I can appeal the more strongly to you to protect her against plunder & pillage." The governor also denounced the Army of Tennessee's impressment of civilian property. He called it "a system of the most complete and outrageous robbery of private citizens" and suggested that Johnston had the means to prevent depredations.[44]

In answering Vance's charges, Johnston exercised considerable patience and tact—qualities he had seldom displayed in prior dealings with civilian authorities. Although Johnston replied that every other Confederate state had an equal claim to the army's property, he admitted: "Great outrages are committed on your people by Confederate soldiers, I know." But he blamed the crimes on "the disbanded men of the Army of North^n Va," claiming that they also stole from his troops. Johnston's answer no doubt left Vance dissatisfied, but the governor could take solace from "Old Joe's" presentation of several hundred substandard wagons and teams to the Tar Heel State.[45]

Johnston received some rare good news from his chief commissary officer, Maj. W. E. Moore, who informed the general that his agents had gathered more than 700,000 rations in depots from Washington, Georgia, to Charlotte. Johnston had originally planned to use the rations in case of a southward retreat, but he now needed them to feed his men on their homeward journey. Even this good news proved short-lived, however, for marauding soldiers and civilians emptied the depots by the end of April.[46]

In any event, Johnston's men managed to eat during the truce. "We were supplied with a fine supper, refreshed by the presence of butter in abundance," Charles W. Hutson of Stuart's South Carolina battery wrote. "This is a noble country & the people cannot be surpassed in kindness." Sgt. W. H. Andrews recalled seeing tree branches in the 1st Georgia Regulars's camp groaning under the weight of bacon sides. Tobacco was no less plentiful. Andrews noted that most of the provisions were plundered from boxcars on a nearby railroad siding. Alcohol also found its way into camp. Soldiers of the 1st Texas Consolidated discovered two barrels of apple brandy buried at the base of a pine tree blown down in a recent storm. One of the barrels was tapped and the Texans helped themselves. "[O]f course some get funny," wrote Capt. Samuel T. Foster, "some get tight some get gentlemanly drunk and some get dog drunk[;] of this latter class are all the officers from our Maj up." According to Texan Lt. R. M. Collins, even the regimental chaplain "got as drunk as an English lord." "Kept up a noise nearly all night," Foster noted, "but no one gets mad—all in a good humor."[47]

The Confederates grudgingly resigned themselves to the inevitable. "For the last four days we have been expecting Genl. Johnston to surrender the army," wrote a soldier who signed himself "Henry." "There is no other hope for it but to surrender eventually. I am firmly convinced of that fact." Though the men needed percussion caps to fire their rifle-muskets, many were now placing their caps on railroad tracks to hear the staccato of loud pops as train wheels ran over them. Sergeant Andrews of the 1st Georgia Regulars doubted that there were enough left to carry one brigade through a pitched battle. (The army in fact had considerably more caps than Andrews realized.) Many soldiers contemplated the war's end with conflicting emotions. "Some seem delighted at the idea of peace, while others are very sad at the thought of returning to the Union," observed Thomas Sullivan of the 9th Mississippi Consolidated. "As for myself, I am very glad to have peace, but dislike to return home with the rest as a whipped people, but think we are getting off very well considering the advantages the Yankees now have of us."[48]

Amid various camp rumors came news of Lincoln's assassination. "In the recklessness of the times some of the masses rejoice," Capt. Bromfield Ridley wrote, "yet our thinking gentry regard it as most unfortunate." Many Confederates regarded Lincoln as a moderate who would have protected them from the more radical members of his party.[49]

As they had done before in times of crisis, soldiers in Johnston's army called on their commanders for speeches. Veteran generals such as A. P. Stewart, William B. Bate, Frank Cheatham, and William W. Loring advised their men to be patient and promised to lead them home when the time came. Though an old leg wound forced him to hobble about on crutches, General Bate remained defiant to the end. "I might have to present my sword hilt foremost to my enemies," Bate told his troops, "but I will tell them when I do that [they] but get back what I, like a man, wrested from [them] at Manassas in 1861."[50]

Perhaps the briefest—and most emotional—speech was made by Maj. Gen. Joseph Wheeler. Sgt. William E. Sloan of the 5th Tennessee Cavalry copied Wheeler's address to Ashby's Brigade in his diary. The cavalry commander began by stating that Generals Sherman and Johnston had come to terms, and that the consequence was the loss of Southern independence. "Fellow soldiers," Wheeler said, "the cause for which you have been fighting is lost! The government you have been defending is no more!" Sloan noted that Wheeler was overcome by emotion at this point and had to stop. When the general resumed speaking, tears streaked his face. "I hardly know what advice to give you. I promised you some days ago that in case of an unconditional surrender I would lead you out of the country, but they do not call this a surrender—they call it peace! Besides, where could you go? I will venture to advise you to go home to your families, who are sadly in need of your protection and subsistence. Be peaceable citizens and live for those you love. I will keep you posted in regard to the pending negotiations, and will here say that I desire to shake hands with every one of you before we finally part." "We are all overcome with sadness," Sloan noted in his diary. In a later speech to the Georgians of Anderson's Brigade, Wheeler once more became "Fighting Joe." The general declared that he would never surrender and promised to lead out all who shared his conviction.[51]

As for Wade Hampton, there was "no surrender in him" either, to quote Colonel Waring of the Jeff Davis Legion. On April 19, the South Carolinian wrote President Davis: "My own mind is made up as to my course. I shall fight as long as my Government remains in existence; when that ceases to live I shall seek some other country, for I shall never take the 'oath of allegiance.' I am sorry that we paused to negotiate, for to my apprehension no evil can equal that of a return to the Union. . . . If you will allow me to do so, I can bring to your support many strong arms and brave hearts—men who will fight to Texas, and who, if forced from that State, will seek refuge in Mexico rather than in the Union."[52]

While Hampton communicated with Davis, cabinet members Breckinridge and Reagan experienced the difficulty of rail travel from Greensboro to Charlotte. The eighty-mile trip took them more than three days because of the destruction of the Deep River bridge at Jamestown, a break in the railroad near Salisbury, and the hijacking of their train near Concord. On the morning of April 22, the weary cabinet members delivered the Sherman-Johnston agreement to Davis at Charlotte.[53]

Davis requested his cabinet to submit written opinions concerning the terms. The ministers unanimously advised Davis to ratify the agreement; even Secretary of State Benjamin conceded the Confederacy's downfall. Reagan offered the most compelling reasons for approval, noting that the agreement guaranteed the continuance of existing Southern state governments, the provisions of the U.S. Constitution and Southern state constitutions, the preservation of political and property rights, and immunity from prosecution for war crimes. "It is also to be observed," Reagan noted, "that the agreement contains no direct reference to the question of slavery, requires no concession from us in regard to it, and leaves it subject to the Constitution and the laws of the United States and of the several States just as it was before the war." The agreement even opened the door for payment of the Confederate war debt. Though doubtful that President Johnson would ratify terms so favorable to the South, Davis deferred to his advisors and wired his approval to Johnston.[54]

While the president and his cabinet mulled over Sherman's terms, Governor Vance arrived at Charlotte. Davis was delighted to see Vance, assuming that the governor had come to join him. In actuality, Vance came to say that he regarded the Confederacy as fallen and would thereafter focus his efforts on aiding the people of North Carolina. But before the governor could speak, Davis launched into his plan to join Kirby Smith in the Trans-Mississippi, saying that he hoped Vance and many Tar Heel troops would accompany him. Several others in the room voiced their agreement. Much to Vance's relief, Breckinridge said that he "did not think they were dealing candidly" with the governor. Breckinridge suggested that "I should return to my position and its responsibilities," Vance recalled, "do the best I could for my people, and share their fate, whatever it might be."[55]

Davis conceded that perhaps Breckinridge was right. After a brief explanation of his intentions, Vance offered his hand to the president in farewell. Davis shook the governor's hand "long and warmly," saying, "God bless you, sir, and the noble old state of North Carolina." Their poignant parting contrasted sharply with former clashes over policy. "With feelings I am not able to describe," Vance later said of his conflicting emotions, "I thus bade farewell to the Southern Confederacy." That night, Vance boarded a train to Greensboro with the intention of seeking Sherman's permission to return to Raleigh and resume his official duties.[56]

Even as Vance planned his return to the state capital, Sherman notified Johnston of an unforeseen complication: the new commander in Richmond, Maj. Gen. Edward O. C. Ord, had withdrawn permission for the Virginia legislature to meet, boding ill for the article guaranteeing existing Southern state governments. Sherman realized that the North's mood following Lincoln's assassination was less conciliatory than he had supposed, but he still believed that there was "enough good sense left on this continent" for order to prevail. Although Sherman doubted the Confederate army's involvement in Lincoln's murder, he noted that Northern newspapers accused Jefferson Davis and other Southern civilian authorities of complicity in the assassination plot. Sherman warned Johnston that "the

Conquered but Not Subdued

changed feeling about Washington arising from this new and unforeseen complication" might delay ratification of the terms.[57]

Gone was the confident tone of Sherman's previous messages to Johnston. Although the Federal commander remained hopeful that his terms would be approved, he also steeled himself for their rejection. Sherman expected the authorities in Washington to regard his agreement as a well-meaning attempt to reunite the country in a spirit of conciliation. Unaware of the furor gripping the nation's capital after Lincoln's assassination, Sherman never guessed that his intentions would be viewed in a different light.

CHAPTER 9

DO YOU BRING BACK
PEACE OR WAR?

At 10:30 P.M. on April 18, Maj. Henry Hitchcock left Raleigh carrying Sherman's terms of agreement and dispatches for Grant and Halleck. Hitchcock bore instructions to deliver the papers to Grant, Halleck, or Stanton and return with their orders as quickly as possible, saying nothing to "greedy newspaper correspondents" en route. The major rode a train to Morehead City and boarded a waiting steamer. At noon on April 20, Hitchcock reached Fort Monroe, where he wired ahead to Grant before continuing up the Chesapeake Bay.[1]

Although at thirty-four one of the older members of Sherman's staff, Henry Hitchcock had seen the least military service. In 1861, he was dissuaded from joining the army by his uncle, Brig. Gen. Ethan Allen Hitchcock, a high-ranking War Department bureaucrat. In September 1864, the younger Hitchcock decided to see the secretary of war about a commission. Although the elder Hitchcock introduced his nephew as "a young man spoiling for a fight," Stanton offered Henry, a lawyer, the post of judge advocate at St. Louis, his hometown. The younger Hitchcock refused Stanton's offer and insisted on serving at the front. Realizing that the young man would not be swayed, the secretary relented. General Hitchcock soon found a place for his nephew at Sherman's headquarters, and Major Hitchcock reported for duty on October 31, 1864. Historians of Sherman's final campaigns owe much to Hitchcock, for his letters and diaries rank among the best firsthand accounts of those often misunderstood and always controversial operations.[2]

On Friday, April 21, Hitchcock's steamer sailed up the Potomac River, reaching Washington at 4:00 P.M. The major entered a city still in mourning for Lincoln, whose remains had just begun the long journey from the nation's capital to Springfield, Illinois. Hitchcock delivered Sherman's papers to Grant at his headquarters. Reading the terms with growing concern, the lieutenant general realized that he must notify Stanton at once.[3]

Grant reached the War Department about 6:30 and learned that Stanton had left. The general-in-chief dashed off a note informing the secretary that Sherman's terms had arrived and suggesting that a cabinet meeting be arranged at once. Stanton returned to the War Department a half hour later. He read Sherman's agreement, briefly conferred with Grant, and then summoned the other cabinet members to an 8:00 P.M. meeting at President Johnson's temporary quarters.

Stanton and Grant next called on Johnson. While Grant remained with the president, Stanton left to get Secretary of the Navy Gideon Welles before returning to his War Department office to dictate a memorandum on Sherman's agreement. The secretary spoke so rapidly that his poor scribe could not keep pace with him. Uttering several choice oaths, Stanton snatched the paper from the clerk's hands and scribbled a list of nine reasons for disapproving Sherman's terms. The war minister read the draft aloud and handed it back to the clerk, who made a clean copy. The agitated Stanton paced back and forth, occasionally glancing over the copyist's shoulder. As the young fellow handed the copy to Stanton, the secretary apologized for his brusqueness, explaining that he had lost his temper because of his indignation at Sherman.[4]

President Johnson and his cabinet met at 8:00 P.M. as scheduled. Secretary of State William H. Seward was absent, having been severely wounded on April 14 by would-be assassin Lewis Paine. Stanton announced that Grant had just received important dispatches from Sherman. Grant read aloud Sherman's letter stating that he had drafted terms that, if approved, would "produce peace from the Potomac to the Rio Grande." The general then read Sherman's "Memorandum or Basis of Agreement." Everyone in the room was stunned, for Sherman had recently assured Stanton and Grant, "I will accept the same terms as General Grant gave General Lee, and be careful not to complicate any points of civil policy." Yet Sherman had done precisely what he said he would *not* do. The president and cabinet unanimously rejected Sherman's proposed agreement, and, according to Grant, both Johnson and Stanton denounced Sherman himself in "very bitter terms." An outraged Stanton counted off his objections on his fingers:

*Secretary of War Edwin M. Stanton
(Library of Congress)*

1. Sherman had no authority to enter into such an arrangement, and he conceded as much when he sent his terms to Washington for approval.
2. The document was "a practical acknowledgment of the Rebel government."
3. It provided for the re-establishment of Rebel state governments and placed an immense quantity of arms and ammunition in their state arsenals.
4. It would enable the Rebels to re-establish slavery in the Southern states.
5. It might render the Federal government liable for the Rebel debt.
6. It placed in dispute several loyal Southern state governments and the recently formed state of West Virginia.
7. It virtually abolished the confiscation laws and relieved the Rebels of all "pains and penalties" for their crimes.
8. It granted terms "that had been deliberately, repeatedly, and solemnly rejected by President Lincoln, and better terms than the Rebels had ever asked in their most prosperous condition."
9. "It formed no basis of true and lasting peace" but rather enabled the Rebels to renew their efforts to overthrow the U.S. government at a later time.[5]

Although Stanton may not have cited all nine of his objections at the meeting (Secretary Welles recalled hearing only four), he immediately sent off his memorandum for publication in the *New York Times,* where it appeared on April 23. In any event, Stanton dominated the meeting and

Do You Bring Back Peace or War?

established that, for the moment, he held the reins of power in Washington.[6]

Why did Stanton react so strongly to Sherman's agreement? The secretary of war was an excitable man given to panicking under stress, and events of the past week had pushed him to the breaking point. The overwrought Stanton viewed Sherman's terms as a betrayal of all the North had fought for, and he intended to punish "Uncle Billy" for overstepping his authority. Before the war, Stanton had been one of the finest trial lawyers in the country; he would now utilize his legal skills to build an unshakable case against his wayward subordinate. The Northern press would serve as judge and jury.[7]

Stanton instructed Grant to notify Sherman that his terms were disapproved and that he must resume hostilities as soon as possible. Grant informed Sherman in a letter, adding that he had read the agreement before submitting it to the president and "felt satisfied that it could not possibly be approved. My reasons for these views I will give you at another time in a more extended letter." That letter was never written, for the lieutenant general soon received instructions from Stanton to "proceed immediately to the headquarters of General Sherman and direct operations against the enemy."[8]

While Grant wrote his wife, Julia, to tell her of his trip to Raleigh, Major Hitchcock sat in an adjoining room writing *his* wife, Mary. The major urged her not to read aloud the part of his letter relating to General Grant's journey, for it was a closely guarded secret — between husbands and wives, at least.[9]

Grant's party set out for Raleigh just before midnight on April 21. Accompanying the general-in-chief were the Union army's quartermaster general, Bvt. Maj. Gen. Montgomery C. Meigs, Hitchcock, three staff officers, and Grant's servant. They waited three hours for the *M. Martin* to be prepared when the steamer awaiting them was deemed unsuitable. Hitchcock called the substitute craft "one of the swiftest and handsomest, if not indeed the handsomest steamer I ever was on."[10]

The ship reached Fort Monroe at 3:30 P.M. on April 22. Grant informed Halleck (the new commander of the Military Division of the James in Virginia) that Sherman's truce would be suspended upon his arrival at Raleigh. The lieutenant general also directed Halleck to send Sheridan's cavalry and an infantry corps toward Greensboro as soon as possible. Sherman, however, no longer desired Sheridan's cooperation. Sheridan told Halleck that he planned to advance on April 24 and combine with Bvt. Maj. Gen. Horatio G. Wright's Sixth Corps just north of Danville.[11]

Grant and his party resumed their journey to Morehead City aboard the steamer *Alhambra*. For the past day, Hitchcock had studied Grant closely, and what he found was "Uncle Billy's" opposite. "He is very quiet & taciturn," Hitchcock wrote, "with none of Sherman's vivacity of appearance or manner & none of his off-hand, ready, entertaining conversation." The major noted that recent photographs gave a correct idea of Grant's face, though the general appeared younger and sterner-looking than he had expected. Grant asked Hitchcock only a few questions about the situation in North Carolina: one concerned a report that Sherman had Vance in his custody. The major explained that Sherman had received Vance's commissioners, but the governor had fled. "I'm glad of it," Grant said. The general's laconic reply told Hitchcock all he needed to know regarding the fate of Sherman's terms. The major proudly informed his wife that he was the only member of Grant's party who did not succumb to seasickness; Hitchcock enjoyed his meals as well as an after-dinner "segar," which even the general-in-chief had to forgo.[12]

The *Alhambra* docked at Morehead City on the evening of April 23. Hitchcock notified Sherman of his arrival, but at Grant's direction, he did not mention the lieutenant general's presence. This was perhaps the only security precaution taken on Grant's journey to Raleigh. Contrary to all notions of security, the party began the trip on a flatbed car; the major nonetheless found the starry night and the cool rush of air "exhilarating." At New Bern they switched to safer and more comfortable quarters—a freight car outfitted with beds for the generals and chairs for the staff officers and servant. Hitchcock slept soundly, awaking upon their arrival in Raleigh at 6:00 A.M. on April 24.[13]

Grant's appearance at the Governor's Palace both "surprised and pleased" Sherman, but the Union commander was neither surprised nor pleased to learn that the president had rejected his terms and ordered him to resume hostilities. After "Uncle Billy" shut the door to his office, Grant showed him Stanton's letter ordering the general-in-chief to "direct operations," which rankled Sherman. Grant then showed him another dispatch bearing the secretary of war's signature:

> WAR DEPARTMENT,
> March 3, 1865.
> Lieutenant-General GRANT:
> The President directs me to say to you that he wishes you to have no conference with General Lee, unless it be for the capitulation of General Lee's army or on some minor and purely military matter. He instructs me to say that you are not to decide, discuss, or confer upon any political question. Such questions the President holds in his own hands, and

will submit them to no military conferences or conventions. Meantime you are to press to the utmost your military advantages.

EDWIN M. STANTON,
Secretary of War.

Sherman later remarked that had Stanton sent him the dispatch sooner, it "would have saved a world of trouble." Since Grant chose not to mention the uproar "Uncle Billy's" agreement had provoked among the president and cabinet, Sherman assumed that Stanton's dispatches ended the matter as far as Washington was concerned. He could not have been more mistaken.[14]

While Sherman and Grant conferred, Major Hitchcock found himself in great demand for news from Washington, though he was almost as much in the dark as his inquisitors were. To a staff officer who asked, "Well, Major—do you bring back peace or war?" Hitchcock replied, "I brought back Genl. Grant!"[15]

Sherman sent Johnston two dispatches, the first ending the truce in forty-eight hours as agreed upon, and the second announcing that Sherman had received orders to undertake no civil negotiations and to limit the troops affected to Johnston's immediate command. "I therefore demand the surrender of your army on the same terms as were given General Lee at Appomattox, . . . purely and simply," Sherman wrote. At noon he received word that the Confederates had his dispatches, so he designated noon, April 26, as the end of the truce. Sherman announced the resumption of hostilities in Special Field Orders No. 62.[16]

Pleased with Sherman's handling of the situation, Grant disregarded Stanton's orders to "direct operations." He even planned to leave Raleigh on April 25, confident that his lieutenant now knew what was expected of him. In a letter to Stanton, Grant explained that Sherman had thought he was following Lincoln's wishes as embodied in Weitzel's call of the Virginia legislature and the terms given to Lee at Appomattox Court House. The general-in-chief noted that as soon as Sherman learned that Weitzel's call was canceled, he warned Johnston of the implications. Grant could not have known that his conciliatory letter was a wasted effort.[17]

On the morning of April 24, Grant and Sherman reviewed the Seventeenth Corps; the following afternoon, they participated in an inspection of the Fifteenth Corps. As the veterans of the Seventeenth Corps passed the reviewing stand, some could not resist the temptation to turn their heads as they recognized their former commander. Many assumed that Grant had superseded "Uncle Billy." The general-in-chief was nonetheless welcomed with three cheers at each stop on his inspection tour of the

Fifteenth Corps, but his appearance at a camp on the front lawn of St. Mary's School resulted in an embarrassing encounter with some young ladies looking on from their dormitory windows. General Howard noted that as the men cheered Grant, the students made faces and shook their fists at him behind his back. As the eyes of the men shifted toward the dormitory, Grant also looked and caught the girls mocking him.[18]

Following the inspections on April 25, Sherman returned to the Governor's Palace and wrote Grant concerning his terms. In truth, Sherman intended his letter for Stanton, as it responded to several of the secretary's objections, which "Uncle Billy" no doubt had learned of from the general-in-chief. Sherman stated that he was "well pleased" Grant was in Raleigh to observe that he had the situation under control. He explained that he had written his agreement "under the influence of the liberal terms" that Grant had given Lee and of Weitzel's call of the Virginia legislature. "I have not the least desire to interfere in the civil policy of our Government, but would shun it as something not to my liking," Sherman noted, "but occasions do arise when a prompt seizure of results is forced on military commanders not in immediate communication with the proper authority."[19]

Sherman admitted his failure to clarify that the amnesty clause applied only to Confederate soldiers but defended his recognition of incumbent Southern state governments as "the very best possible means" of securing the South's "complete submission to the lawful authority of the United States." The general argued that his agreement neither recognized "the so-called Confederate Government," assumed the Confederate debt, nor granted the Rebels immunity. Sherman noted that he had merely attempted to restore law and order in the South and warned that disapproval of his terms would lead to anarchy and guerrilla warfare.[20]

Sherman also wrote Stanton directly: "I admit my folly in embracing in a military convention any civil matters, but unfortunately such is the nature of our situation that they seem inextricably united, and I understood from you at Savannah that the financial state of our country demanded military success, and would warrant a little bending [as] to policy." Sherman again cited the Appomattox terms and Weitzel's call as his guiding precedents, though—for obvious reasons—he neglected to give due credit to Reagan's "Basis of Pacification." "I still believe the Government of the United States has made a mistake," Sherman contended, "but that is none of my business." The general then mentioned Stanton's order to Grant to "direct operations": "I had flattered myself that by four years' patient, unremitting, and successful labor I deserved no reminder such as is contained in the last paragraph of your letter to General Grant."[21]

While Sherman awaited Johnston's reply, his grand army prepared to march in accordance with Special Field Orders No. 55 (see Chapter 5). On April 25, the Seventeenth Corps advanced to Jones's Station, ten miles west of Raleigh, and the Twentieth Corps to Jones's Crossroads, thirteen miles southwest of the capital. The Tenth Corps, Fifteenth Corps, and Twenty-third Corps would march the next day. Kilpatrick's cavalry waited at Chapel Hill and Durham's Station, the Fourteenth Corps at Aven's Ferry and Holly Springs. "Everybody anticipates, and I think everybody regrets, another march," observed Major Hitchcock. "I cannot but hope even yet, as I do most earnestly, that Johnston's reply *may* be such as to obviate the necessity of our again 'sallying forth'; but I confess it is hope rather than expectation."[22]

At 5:00 P.M. on April 24, Johnston received President Davis's approval of Sherman's terms. Barely an hour later, Sherman's dispatches arrived ending the truce, rejecting the agreement, and demanding the Confederates' surrender in accordance with the Appomattox terms. Johnston immediately wired Breckinridge for instructions, but the Confederate commander was at no loss for a course of action: "We had better disband this small force to prevent devastation to the country."[23]

This was the last piece of advice Davis wanted from his ranking field commander. The president expected Johnston to maintain his army so long as the Federals refused to grant acceptable terms. Davis therefore instructed Breckinridge to order the resumption of the army's retreat. Mindful that Johnston would probably ignore a peremptory order, the secretary of war issued a proposal instead: "Does not your suggestion about disbanding refer to the infantry and most of the artillery?" The Kentuckian suggested that if Johnston found it necessary to disband the infantry and artillery, he should instruct the soldiers to retain their small arms and rendezvous at a designated point. The cavalry, joined by some artillery and mounted infantry, should head for the Trans-Mississippi.[24]

After receiving Breckinridge's dispatch, Johnston summoned Beauregard and his corps and division commanders to his headquarters for a conference at 10:00 A.M. on April 25. The meeting would be the Army of Tennessee's final council of war. Johnston asked his lieutenants to assess Breckinridge's proposal and the present condition of their forces. The consensus was that the troops would no longer fight and the secretary of war's plan was "impracticable." Johnston notified Breckinridge: "We have to save the people, spare the blood of the army, and save the high civil functionaries. Your plan, I think, can only do the last. We ought to prevent invasion, make terms for our troops, and give an escort of cavalry to the President, who ought to move without loss of a moment." "Old Joe" also reported the loss of Macon and Mobile.[25]

Johnston instructed his corps commanders to prepare to resume the march toward Salisbury at 11:00 A.M. on April 26. (Although Sherman had designated noon as the end of the truce, Johnston understood it to be an hour earlier.) "Old Joe" also directed Maj. Gen. Matthew C. Butler—who had resumed command of the cavalry division briefly led by General Law—to monitor the enemy's westward movements. "The supposition is that as we can't run out of this place[,] we must fight out," wrote Capt. Samuel T. Foster of the 1st Texas Consolidated, who believed the rumor that Johnston's army was surrounded. "We had talked peace so long in camp and had made so many calculations [as to] how we are going home &c that it is up hill business to go to fighting again." Yet Foster remained optimistic: "We have been very loose in discipline here of late, but that will come out all right in a few days of hard marching and some fighting." On the other hand, Captain Ridley noted that "the eagerness of the men to get to their homes now is beyond picture," and Captain Stoney observed that soldiers in his command were "still leaving in crowds."[26]

On the morning of April 25, Johnston acknowledged receipt of Sherman's first dispatch and proposed another armistice to resume negotiations. In reply to Sherman's second dispatch, he noted that the Appomattox terms were inadequate: "The disbanding of General Lee's army has afflicted this country with numerous bands having no means of subsistence but robbery, a knowledge of which would, I am sure, induce you to agree to other conditions."[27]

Sherman received Johnston's first dispatch at 6:15 P.M. on April 25. "I will meet you at the same place as before, to-morrow at 12 o'clock noon," he replied. Major Hitchcock responded: "Everybody is in hopes tonight that Johnston will surrender tomorrow, after all. God grant it! I cannot bear to think of this army marching any further through the country in a hostile attitude; its simple passage and subsistence, aside from the commission of any violence or outrage, would be a terrible blow to the people of the State." Johnston's second message arrived early on April 26, but Sherman saw no alternative to demanding the Appomattox terms. Although Grant remained in Raleigh, having decided not to leave for Washington until after Johnston's surrender, he did not accompany Sherman to meet Johnston. Instead, Sherman brought Generals Schofield, Howard, and Blair. For the third time, Sherman rode a train to Durham's Station and proceeded under flag of truce to James Bennett's farmhouse. On the way a

Do You Bring Back Peace or War?

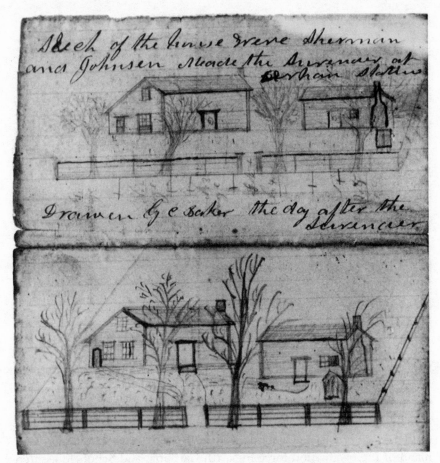

Bennett Place, as drawn by a corporal in the 9th Pennsylvania Cavalry. The caption on the upper drawing reads: "Skech of the house were Sherman and Johnsen made the surrender at Durham Statin. Drawn by C[ornelius] Baker the day after the surrender." (Courtesy of John W. Rowell)

courier overtook him with a message stating that Johnston had been delayed by an accident on the railroad and would be late.[28]

Johnston arrived at the Bennett farm at 2:00 P.M. The two commanders shook hands and entered the Bennett house. Their third conference began inauspiciously. Sherman offered the Appomattox terms, but Johnston called them inadequate and requested additional guarantees for his men. Though he conceded the necessity of supplementary terms, Sherman doubted they would be approved in Washington. After further discussion proved fruitless, "Uncle Billy" summoned Schofield to resolve their dilemma.[29]

Schofield suggested drafting a surrender document virtually identical to

Maj. Gen. John M. Schofield, Sherman's second-in-command and the drafter of the final surrender terms. After Sherman's departure in late April 1865, Schofield briefly commanded the occupation forces in North Carolina. (Massachusetts Commandery, Military Order of the Loyal Legion Collection, U.S. Army Military History Institute)

the Appomattox agreement and a second document specifying Johnston's terms. "I think General Schofield can fix it," "Old Joe" remarked. Sherman instructed his lieutenant to draft the "new" terms. Once Schofield had completed the surrender agreement, the generals discussed supplementary terms. Sherman then announced that he was leaving Schofield in command of the occupation force in North Carolina, and Schofield assured Johnston that he would fulfill the conditions of their agreement.[30]

Schofield's "Terms of a Military Convention" (see Appendix C) closely resemble the terms Grant had offered Lee at Appomattox Court House (see Appendix D):

1. Johnston's command was to cease from all acts of war.
2. Its arms and public property were to be deposited at Greensboro.
3. Rolls of all officers and men were to be in duplicate, one copy to be retained by Johnston and one copy given to an officer designated by Sherman. Each soldier in Johnston's army was to pledge in writing not to take up arms against the U.S. government until released from that obligation.
4. The officers could retain their side arms, baggage, and horses.
5. All officers and men could return to their homes, not to be disturbed by the U.S. government so long as they observed their paroles and the laws in force where they resided.[31]

Do You Bring Back Peace or War?

Sherman ordered his clerk, Pvt. Arthur Granger, to make two copies of Schofield's terms. As the generals signed the documents, Johnston said: "I believe that is the best we can do." Yet the terms comprised only the first part of their agreement.[32]

On April 27, Johnston would draft a list of eight "Supplementary Terms" based on his discussion with Schofield and Sherman at the Bennett house. After reading Johnston's draft, Schofield wrote a revised version consisting of six "Supplemental Terms" (see Appendix C):

1. Field transportation would be loaned to the Confederates for their use. Artillery horses could be retained as field transportation.
2. Each brigade or other separate unit could retain one-seventh of its small arms. The soldiers were to deposit their arms at their respective state capitals according to the instructions of the generals commanding those departments.
3. Soldiers could retain their horses and other private property.
4. Troops from Arkansas and Texas would be transported by water from Mobile or New Orleans at the discretion of Maj. Gen. Edward R. S. Canby, the commander of the Military Division of West Mississippi.
5. Paroles of all officers and men were to be signed by their immediate commanders.
6. Naval forces within Johnston's command would be included in the convention.

Surprisingly, the authorities in Washington raised no objection to the second article, which allowed the Confederates to retain one-seventh of their small arms (Johnston had proposed retaining one-fifth) and resembled one of Sherman's more controversial provisions. The sixth article regarding Confederate naval personnel would provide an odd postscript to Johnston's surrender.[33]

The Bennett Place surrender was the largest of the war, embracing almost 90,000 Confederates stationed in North Carolina, South Carolina, Georgia, and Florida. Yet Johnston's soldiers were by no means the last Rebels to surrender. Lt. Gen. Richard Taylor's command in Alabama, Mississippi, and East Louisiana surrendered on May 4, Gen. Edmund Kirby Smith's Trans-Mississippi forces capitulated on May 26, and Brig. Gen. Stand Watie's Indian Territory troops held out until June 23.

Regarding it "the greatest of human crimes to continue the war," Johnston surrendered in defiance of President Davis. Davis refused to concede that Lee's surrender spelled the end of the Confederacy, even though Lee had written the president advising him to capitulate.[34]

Brig. Gen. Thomas Muldrop Logan, a brigade commander in Butler's division of cavalry. Although the twenty-four-year-old Logan's boyish appearance led Sherman to believe that he must be the youngest general in either army, on April 28, 1865, that distinction went to twenty-year-old Bvt. Maj. Gen. Galusha Pennypacker of the Union army. (Courtesy of Alan and Nancy Bruns, Fredericksburg, Virginia)

After the signing on April 26, Sherman and Johnston invited James Bennett and their lieutenants to join them in a toast (the teetotaling Howard doubtless quaffed something less potent than "Uncle Billy's" whiskey). The commanders then introduced their respective subordinates. Among the Confederates were South Carolina cavalryman Matthew Butler—whose slight limp betrayed his artificial foot, a souvenir of Brandy Station—and one of Butler's brigade commanders, twenty-four-year-old Brig. Gen. Thomas Muldrop Logan. Reporter Volney Hickox described the two Confederates as youthful, slender, and so mild-mannered as to belie their profession. Noting "Mully" Logan's boyish face, Sherman remarked that he must be the youngest general in either army. Informed that Logan desired a train ride to his home in South Carolina, Sherman offered him a seat on the train to Raleigh. A surprised Logan stammered his thanks but told "Uncle Billy" that he was not quite ready to leave. "Very well," Sherman replied, "Just come to Kilpatrick here any time. He will see that you get to me, and I will help you all I can."[35]

Sherman presented Private Granger with the pen and inkstand used to draft and sign the terms. Granger tried to buy the table cover, but Bennett refused to sell it. After the generals' departure, souvenir hunters descended on the Bennetts' property. Journalist William Anderson reported

Do You Bring Back Peace or War?

that the Bennett house was "being carried off piecemeal" and "in due time there will be an excavation to mark the spot where the disappearing Bennett cottage now stands."[36]

On April 28, Capt. William H. Day, Kilpatrick's provost marshal, sent a detail after Bennett's drop-leaf table and its cover. The Federals offered Bennett $10 and a "first rate horse" for the table but said they had orders to take it even if he refused. Bennett accepted Day's offer. The next morning, Bennett walked to Durham's Station to collect payment for his table. Day told him that the horse was gone but would return shortly. Bennett waited all day, but his horse did not appear. When he went back to Durham's the next morning, he discovered that Day had left. Five years later, Bennett sought restitution for his table—which he learned had fetched $3,000 —and other stolen goods. He wrote Governor William W. Holden twice but received no reply. In 1873 Bennett petitioned the Southern Claims Commission, which barred his claim because he had supported the Confederacy. The hapless Bennett never received compensation for his stolen property.[37]

On the morning of April 26, the Federal army had held its position pending further orders. The Confederates, however, resumed their retreat at 11:00 A.M.—those who remained with the army, that is. "May I ever be spared such a sight as I witnessed when the order to move was given," wrote a captain in Hoke's Division. "Whole regiments remained on the [camp]ground, refusing to obey." Colquitt's Brigade left 200 men behind and Hagood's Brigade forty, the captain noted, but losses in these two brigades were comparatively light because the men were Georgians and South Carolinians marching homeward. In far worse condition were Hoke's Tar Heel units. Maj. William A. Holland deserted with most of his command, leaving only the surgeon, the quartermaster, and three privates of the 36th North Carolina and thirty-one of the 40th North Carolina. Since April 6, the two regiments had lost 264 officers and men to desertion. On March 17, the North Carolina Junior Reserves Brigade had numbered 1,213 officers and men (or boys), the largest such unit in Johnston's army. On April 26, the brigade mustered barely 200. Hoke's other Tar Heel brigades suffered comparable losses. In their haste to return home, many North Carolinians chose to leave without paroles. In striking contrast to Johnston's plight, Sherman instructed his chief quartermaster to hold 1,150 newly arrived soldiers at New Bern because he no longer needed them.[38]

Sgt. W. H. Andrews of the 1st Georgia Regulars recalled witnessing a mere rabble on the march. The springtime heat and dusty roads caused much straggling, and hundreds tossed away their rifle-muskets, littering the roadside with abandoned firearms. When Beauregard learned that the truce was renewed, he halted the retreat at 1:30 P.M. Soon afterward, the men were told that those without rifle-muskets would be arrested. When this threat failed to motivate them, orders filtered down that only soldiers with rifles could draw rations, precipitating a stampede of unarmed men back to the road in search of a weapon.[39]

Meanwhile, President Davis had received Johnston's telegram stating that he was on his way to confer with Sherman. Concluding that Johnston intended to surrender, Davis decided to leave Charlotte at once, rejoin his family in South Carolina, and press on to the Trans-Mississippi. Davis announced his decision in what would prove to be the last full meeting of the Confederate cabinet. The conference was held in the home of William Phifer, where the bedridden Secretary Trenholm was staying. During the meeting, Attorney General Davis and General Cooper resigned. Though they maintained a defiant pose for the president's sake, the remaining cabinet members were more intent on fleeing the country than fighting in the Trans-Mississippi.[40]

Wade Hampton, however, was determined to fight on. On April 25, Hampton had met Davis and obtained his permission to assemble an expeditionary force. The president suggested that Hampton turn over his cavalry corps to Wheeler before returning to Charlotte. Davis soon learned that this was impossible, for Wheeler arrived on April 26 to volunteer for the expedition himself. A delighted Davis asked Wheeler how many troopers would follow him, but his delight darkened into disappointment when "Fighting Joe" said that most of his men regarded the war as over and wanted to return home. The president's face brightened again, however, when Wheeler offered to recruit volunteers from his command.[41]

About noon on April 26, President Davis and his entourage resumed their flight. The streets of Charlotte teemed with Confederate deserters and parolees. Demoralization quickly spread to Davis's cavalry escort, consisting of Dibrell's two brigades under Colonels William C. P. Breckinridge and William S. McLemore and the brigades of Brigadier Generals Basil W. Duke, Samuel W. Ferguson, and John C. Vaughn. Presidential aide John Taylor Wood noted that the makeshift command was "committing many depredations" along the way. Beholding the chaos about him, Wood commented: "So we are falling to pieces."[42]

Sherman and Johnston left the Bennett house at 5:00 P.M. on April 26, "Old Joe" returning to Butler's headquarters at the Dickson house and "Uncle Billy" to Kilpatrick's headquarters at Durham's Station. After wiring

Do You Bring Back Peace or War?

Grant that Johnston had surrendered, Sherman ate dinner with Kilpat-rick and his staff. When the Union commander returned to the Governor's Palace at 9:00, Grant read and approved the terms and complied with Sherman's request to sign the document. "Uncle Billy" now believed that the troublesome matter "was surely at an end."[43]

Major Hitchcock stood on the crowded portico of the Governor's Palace and listened to a brass band play national airs and operatic tunes. He peered into the parlor window and saw Grant and Sherman seated at the center table, busy at their writing, one or both pausing occasionally to talk to other generals in the room. Though Hitchcock rejoiced that the war was over, his thoughts were tinged with sadness, for he had a sudden longing to be home. "It will be a hundred times harder for me now to remain in the service than when we were deep in the mud & swamps of South Caro-lina or in front of an enemy near Averysboro & Bentonville," Hitchcock wrote his wife. "There was something like a definite object there; for the sort of occupation I look forward to now I confess I have no relish, espe-cially the loafing part of it. However, the war is over now, thank God, . . . and it cannot be long before I see your dear face again."[44]

News of Johnston's surrender soon reached signal officer Lt. George Round at his station atop the capitol dome. The excited lieutenant ob-tained permission from his commanding officer to expend half his stock of signal rockets in proclaiming the news. From the dome, Round set off rocket after colorful rocket, until one failed to ignite. The lieutenant struck another match and reached out to relight the fuse when the rocket sud-denly streaked into the night, shooting flames and sparks into Round's up-turned face. Overcome with pain, Round released his grip on the railing and lost his balance. As he teetered over the edge, the lieutenant somehow regained his footing and grasped the lightning rod. For the second time in two weeks, Round had narrowly escaped falling to his death.

Once he had caught his breath, the lieutenant took stock of his condi-tion. His eyes were unharmed, but he now lacked a set of eyebrows and eyelashes, some of his hair, and "the down I then called whiskers." To his shock, Round later discovered that his face was as red as "a boiled lobster." The lieutenant found the pain of his burns less bothersome than the fact that for several days he would not be "presentable to the fair daughters of Raleigh."

After a lengthy pause "not provided for in the 'Manual of Sig-nals,'" Round resumed broadcasting his message. "Everything now worked smoothly," he recalled. "Rocket after rocket sped away to the zenith." Though the hour was late, Round heard a faint murmur in the camps, suggesting that his message was being read and understood. Then a distant shout arose as the last rocket soared into the heavens: "PEACE ON EARTH, GOOD WILL TO MEN."[45]

On the evening of April 26, Johnston traveled to the Dickson house and then boarded a waiting train for Greensboro. Troopers of Butler's Division camping nearby were the first Confederates to learn of the surrender. Most wondered what they were to do. Only the day before, the rumor had spread among members of Young's Brigade that the army's surrender was unconditional and that they would be treated as prisoners of war. As a result, several men deserted, and the rest were preparing to ride out when their commander, Col. Gilbert J. Wright, appeared in camp. "He promised us that we would not be surrendered without our consent," recalled Sgt. Charles P. Hansell of the 10th Georgia Cavalry. "Gib" Wright appealed to the soldiers of his command not to disgrace themselves by deserting, warning that they would have to do so over his dead body. "That settled it," wrote Sergeant Hansell, "for the whole brigade was more afraid of him than of the Yankees." Thanks to Wright's fiery speech, the April 25 desertions abruptly ceased.[46]

Late on April 26, the troopers of Butler's Division received orders to march. They broke camp, saddled their horses, and headed west. Hansell recalled hearing the Old Town Clock chime the hour as he rode through the dark and deserted streets of Hillsborough. The Confederates reached Company Shops at daybreak, and "Gib" Wright ordered his men to dismount. Wright announced that they now had a thirty-mile head start on "Mr. Kilpatrick's critter company," their wagons were loaded with ammunition and provisions, and all who refused to surrender could follow him to the Trans-Mississippi. As Wright addressed his men, Wade Hampton and his escort galloped up from the east.[47]

After his conference with Davis on April 25, Hampton had returned to Greensboro, where he learned of the army's surrender. Writing to Johnston, Hampton maintained that the surrender did not include him because of his absence during negotiations and a War Department order assigning him to duty in South Carolina, but he assured Johnston that he would let Breckinridge decide the matter. The South Carolinian then traveled to the Dickson house, where he discovered that Butler's Division had deserted its post and was marching west. A distraught Hampton overtook his command at Company Shops.[48]

Hampton ordered Butler's two brigades to follow him a few miles toward Greensboro, probably because their presence at "the Shops" had drawn unwanted attention. Addressing hundreds of his veterans, Hampton re-

Do You Bring Back Peace or War?

called the dangers they had faced, the hardships they had endured, and the glory they had won. The general explained that he was leaving under presidential directive and urged his men to honor the surrender rather than follow him as outlaws. By the end of Hampton's speech nearly everyone was in tears. Colonel Waring of the Jeff Davis Legion had advocated fighting to the death, but he now deemed himself "honor-bound" to obey Hampton and advised his men to do likewise. After a brief rest, Hampton pressed on to Greensboro, closely followed by Butler's Division.[49]

Hampton's procession at the head of Butler's Division aroused the curiosity of Brig. Gen. Robert H. Anderson, commanding a brigade of Wheeler's cavalry at Company Shops. Anderson notified Johnston's headquarters, prompting an angry Johnston to order the immediate return of the division to Hillsborough. An hour later, Johnston's chief of staff instructed General Anderson to occupy Butler's former position, since Hampton had not yet responded to Johnston's order. Anderson also received orders to inform Wheeler that Johnston wanted him to send a second brigade to Hillsborough, but "Fighting Joe" had vanished.[50]

Throughout April 27, the army's two senior cavalry commanders and one of their divisions defied the commanding general, raising grave doubts in Johnston's mind. Would the cavalry abide by the terms, or would it ride off in defiance and break up into bands of desperadoes? Johnston had relied on Hampton and Wheeler to control the cavalry, but they were failing him. Their abandonment of responsibility infuriated "Old Joe."[51]

Hampton found a stinging rebuke from Johnston awaiting him at Greensboro. In his letter to Johnston, the South Carolinian had referred to the Army of Tennessee's "surrender," which nettled the commanding general. An indignant Johnston wrote Hampton to explain that his agreement with Sherman was a *convention*, not a surrender. (Johnston chastised several other subordinates for failing to make this distinction. As late as 1887, "Old Joe" insisted that his army was not surrendered because his soldiers were not treated as prisoners of war.) Hampton apologized for his error and enclosed a revised letter to replace the first. The cavalryman also explained his dilemma: "If I do not accompany [the president], I shall never cease to reproach myself, and if I go with him I may go under the ban of outlawry. I choose the latter, because I believe it to be my duty to do so." Hampton thus took leave of Johnston and the Army of Tennessee.[52]

As Hampton penned his explanatory letter, Johnston attempted to locate the South Carolinian's elusive second-in-command. "Old Joe" finally found Wheeler at Salisbury and sent him a directive: "You must obey my orders, unless you have contrary orders from higher authority." Wheeler indeed possessed orders from above and — unlike Hampton — sought men "willing to stand by Jefferson Davis to the death." "Fighting Joe" raised about 600 volunteers from his five brigades. But Georgia cavalryman William W. Gordon refused to join Wheeler: he regarded the volunteer band as "no better than pirates" for riding out in defiance of the surrender.[53]

When Wheeler issued his farewell address on April 29, Sgt. William E. Sloan of the 5th Tennessee Cavalry noted that his comrades had scant use for its fine phrases. "Gen. Wheeler's act of running away at this time to escape surrender is being criticized by many of the soldiers," Sloan observed. "They see no good reason why he should not remain and share their destiny in the last hour, since nothing can be gained by his effort to fly the country, even if successful." Wheeler also left without notifying Johnston.[54]

Johnston did not mention the loss of Hampton and Wheeler in his memoirs, but their decision to accompany Davis was a crushing disappointment. "Old Joe" needed their assistance more than did the president, who already had a large and well-led escort. The cavalry commanders' first duty was to share the fate of their men. Hampton had been Johnston's ablest subordinate; his irresponsible action blemishes an otherwise superb record. Wheeler's conduct, however, confirms Col. Alfred Roman's assessment that "Fighting Joe" was unequal to the responsibilities of high command. In any event, Hampton and Wheeler never reached Davis.[55]

On April 27, Johnston issued General Orders No. 18, announcing his agreement with Sherman and outlining its terms. "The object of the convention is pacification to the extent of the authority of the commanders who made it," Johnston explained. "Events in Virginia, which broke every hope of success by war, impose on its general the duty of sparing the blood of this gallant army and saving our country from further devastation and our people from ruin." The soldiers' reaction ran the gamut of emotions. "Some raved and swore that they would never submit to it," recalled Lt. Edwin H. Rennolds of the 3rd Tennessee Consolidated. Others "wept like children," while a few met the news with stoic resignation. "All is confusion and unrest," noted Captain Ridley, "and the stern realization that we are subdued and ruined is upon us. . . . Oh! how is it in the Yankee camps tonight? Rejoicing, triumphing and revelling in the idea of glory. Think of it, the big dog has simply got the little dog down."[56]

The following day, April 28, Johnston ordered his corps commanders to make out their muster rolls in duplicate and to collect all cannon, limbers, caissons, forges, and draft animals, as well as four-fifths of the soldiers' small arms, ammunition, and accoutrements (he did not receive Schofield's stipulation to collect six-sevenths of the arms until April 30). For the final time, the Army of Tennessee lurched into action, as long lines of troops stacked arms and headquarters staffs filled out rolls. The bugler

Do You Bring Back Peace or War?

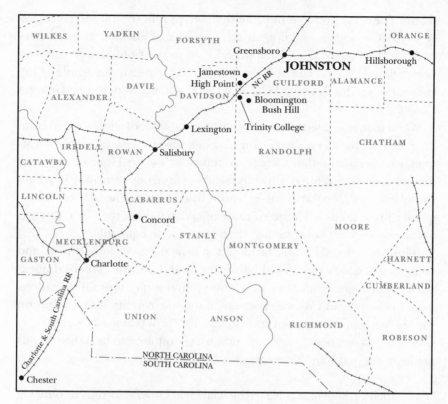

Map 7. The last encampments of the Army of Tennessee, April 26–May 3, 1865

blew "Assembly" one last time for the crews of Havis's Battery. The men fell in as they had for the past three years. Their commander, Capt. M. W. Havis, read General Orders No. 18 and instructed the men to take their usual positions beside the gun carriage wheels at the order, "Cannoneers, to your posts, march!" When the crews had helped the horses get under way, Havis gave the order, "By piece from the right, forward, march!" Instead of marching beside their guns, however, the gunners were told to halt and let them pass. As Pvt. William R. Talley watched his cannon roll by, tears came to his eyes. "I was [as] sad and sorrowful as if I had lost a loved one," Talley recalled. "We did love our guns. They had been our companions for three years and we would have died in their defense." In contrast to the surrender at Appomattox Court House, few Confederates in central North Carolina stacked arms before Federal troops.[57]

The Army of Tennessee's soldiers also drew their last pay. In mid-April, Johnston had received $39,000 in silver specie from President Davis; the commanding general ignored Davis's subsequent order to return the coin, citing his desire to pay the army. Johnston distributed the silver in equal shares. The army's returns indicate that 32,174 officers and men received $37,679.96 in specie, yielding an average share of just over $1.17 (the reduced total resulted from an appropriation to the Confederate commissary general). "It was the only pay I received for nearly the whole of my last year of service," recalled Col. Charles H. Olmstead of the 1st Georgia Consolidated.[58]

When money is divided into so many shares, someone is bound to complain that he has been shortchanged. Such was the case of Frank Cheatham, who accused fellow division commander Robert Hoke of receiving more than his fair share of silver by falsifying his troop returns. Cheatham complained to General Hardee, who refused to challenge Hoke; subsequent rumors accused Hardee himself of taking most of the silver. Rumors to the contrary notwithstanding, most shares were equitable.[59]

Johnston ordered his quartermaster to issue the men cloth, thread, and cotton yarn, which they could barter for food. "Old Joe" received unexpected assistance from Sherman, who offered a quarter-million rations from his Morehead City warehouses, on the sole condition that Johnston use his own trains to transport the provisions. "Now that war is over, I am as willing to risk my person and reputation as heretofore to heal the wounds made by the past war," Sherman wrote.[60]

On April 27, Sherman released Special Field Orders No. 65, announcing "a further suspension of hostilities and a final agreement with General Johnston which terminates the war as to the armies under his command." "Uncle Billy" placed Schofield in charge of the parole arrangements, enjoining him to execute the terms in a spirit of generosity. Sherman also permitted his army commanders to issue surplus wagons, draft animals, and supplies to needy citizens. "Foraging will forthwith cease," Sherman declared, but if necessity required its resumption, disbursing officers would pay cash or provide vouchers. Sherman enclosed a copy of the order with his letter offering Johnston the quarter-million rations. "The enlarged patriotism manifested in these papers reconciles me to what I had previously regarded as the misfortune of my life—that of having had you to encounter in the field," a grateful Johnston replied. "The enlightened and humane policy you have adopted will certainly be successful."[61]

Sherman's Special Field Orders No. 66 outlined the dispositions of his army. The Tenth Corps, Twenty-third Corps, and Kilpatrick's cavalry would remain in North Carolina under Schofield. The Army of the Tennessee under Howard and the Army of Georgia under Slocum would march to Washington "slowly and in the best of order," an injunction the unfortunate foot soldiers would soon wish their commanders had heeded.[62]

Do You Bring Back Peace or War?

Schofield issued two orders of his own on April 27. General Orders No. 31 announced an end to the war in North Carolina; Schofield urged soldiers and civilians to coexist in peace, promising rations, wagons, and draft animals for all who needed them. General Orders No. 32 declared all slaves in North Carolina free by virtue of the Emancipation Proclamation. Schofield exhorted former slaveowners to pay their freedmen a fair wage and advised erstwhile slaves to continue working for their former masters. Should this prove impossible, Schofield warned, the freedmen must find work elsewhere, for they would "not be supported in idleness."[63]

Even before Sherman and Schofield's orders appeared, news of Johnston's surrender "spread like magic," reported the *Raleigh Daily Progress*. On the morning of April 27, "shout after shout" erupted, church bells pealed, bands played patriotic tunes, rockets streaked through the air, rifles and cannon were fired, and countless canteens were filled with gunpowder and exploded.[64]

News of the surrender traveled slowly from Raleigh to the Fourteenth Corps's camps at Holly Springs and Aven's Ferry. "[W]e are here by ourselves and don't get any knews," complained Ohioan James R. Milner, "don't even know what 'we are doing ourselves.'" Given their relative isolation, it is not surprising that when some Fourteenth Corps soldiers were awakened by a burst of musketry on the night of April 27, they assumed the Rebels were attempting to cut their way out. Several regiments doublequicked to the sound of the guns, but they soon contributed to the noisy festivities as word of Johnston's surrender spread. The Fourteenth Corps's mischievous First Division commander, Brig. Gen. Charles C. Walcutt, later requested casualty reports for the "engagement."[65]

General Grant and his small party quietly slipped out of Raleigh on the morning of April 27. The general-in-chief was en route to Washington with copies of the April 26 terms. Just before his departure, Grant had received a telegram from Stanton stating that the first agreement between Sherman and Johnston "meets with universal disapprobation. No one of any class or shade of opinion approves it. . . . The hope of the country is that you may repair the misfortune occasioned by Sherman's negotiations." Grant pocketed the message and said nothing to Sherman about it. During a brief stop at Goldsboro, however, Grant discovered the futility of his efforts to conceal from Sherman the government's reaction to his first terms. He saw several Northern newspapers and was shocked by the harsh treatment Sherman was receiving from Stanton and the press. Grant realized the "great indignation" this would arouse in Sherman and no doubt dreaded the consequences.[66]

Having settled affairs in North Carolina, Sherman planned to travel to

Hilton Head and Savannah to confer with General Gillmore and Bvt. Maj. Gen. Cuvier Grover. On April 28, the day of his departure, Sherman received a copy of the April 23 *New York Times*. The following headlines arrested his eye:

Sherman's Action Promptly Repudiated.

The President and All His Cabinet Rebuke Him.

Gen. Grant Gone to North Carolina to Direct Our Armies.

Possible Escape of Jeff. Davis With His Gold.[67]

Sherman doubtless scanned the headlines with mounting anger, which must have blossomed into rage as he read Stanton's accompanying dispatch. It began with a brief report of the meeting in which the president and cabinet unanimously rejected Sherman's terms, immediately followed by Lincoln's March 3 instructions to Grant to undertake no political negotiations with Lee. Noting the close pairing of the two items, many readers inferred that Sherman had read Lincoln's dispatch and had defied the late president's wishes. Yet Sherman later stated in his official report that he had neither seen Lincoln's message nor "had one word of instruction" from Washington until Grant's arrival. "Uncle Billy" found it odd that "every bar-room loafer in New York can read in the morning journals 'official' matter that is withheld from a general whose command extends from Kentucky to North Carolina."[68]

Stanton's dispatch then noted that Sherman's orders for Stoneman to withdraw from Salisbury and join him near Raleigh would probably enable Jefferson Davis to flee to Mexico or Europe with his "plunder." "[R]espectable parties" in Richmond indicated that Davis possessed a "very large" quantity of specie and intended to arrange his escape with Sherman or another Federal commander. Anyone who read between the lines would have concluded that Sherman's order for Stoneman's withdrawal resulted from a Rebel bribe. "Uncle Billy" bristled at Stanton's insinuation, explaining that Stoneman was actually at Statesville, about twenty-five miles west of Salisbury, and might have collided with Davis had he headed east as ordered.[69]

Sherman's "Memorandum or Basis of Agreement" appeared next, followed by Stanton's nine reasons for its rejection. The first stated that Sherman had exceeded his authority and had acknowledged that fact by making his arrangement conditional. In his response, Sherman called his terms "glittering generalities" that the president could approve, reject, or modify. Sherman dismissed reasons two through seven as legalistic hairsplitting,

Do You Bring Back Peace or War?

though he later admitted that he should have declared slavery dead and limited amnesty to Confederate soldiers. The eighth reason, asserting that Sherman's terms were more generous "than the rebels had ever asked in their most prosperous condition," ignored the Rebels' repeated insistence on Southern independence as a sine qua non of peace negotiations, Sherman claimed. The ninth reason maintained that Sherman's agreement "formed no basis of a true and lasting peace"; "Uncle Billy" noted that only time would tell if Stanton was right.[70]

Before his departure on the evening of April 28, Sherman briefed his army and corps commanders at the Governor's Palace, but his remarks soon degenerated into a diatribe against Stanton. While the generals and staff officers stared in astonishment, Sherman "paced up and down the room like a caged lion," calling Stanton a "mean, scheming, vindictive politician who made it his business to rob military men of their glory." "Uncle Billy" also lashed out at the press—an old and familiar enemy—declaring that "the fellows who wielded too loose a pen" ought to be put behind bars.[71]

Sherman's outburst at the Governor's Palace reminded Slocum aide Lt. Joe Foraker of a similar gathering under far different circumstances, when the Battle of Bentonville had just ended in victory for Sherman's army and the triumphant conclusion of the Carolinas campaign was at hand. Sherman was surrounded on that occasion by dozens of well-wishing generals and staff officers. "All congratulated General Sherman in the heartiest manner," Foraker recalled, "and spoke in the most glowing terms of the high place he would hold in history." One of the generals told Sherman that his successes might put him in the White House. "Uncle Billy" was unimpressed, however, replying that he had no ambition for public office, nor any faith in his popularity, for Americans were "as mercurial in political temperament as the French; they would exalt one day and tear down the next, and do it with a wicked viciousness that indicated they enjoyed it." Sherman's statement at Bentonville now struck Foraker as prophetic.[72]

Stanton's artfully edited news bulletin ensured the unanimity of the Northern press in condemning Sherman's terms. Many hostile newspapers declared open season on the general himself. They had dared not risk attacking Sherman while he rode the crest of military success but jumped at the opportunity now that he was in disfavor. Some papers dredged up the old charge of insanity, others claimed that Sherman had been duped by Johnston and Breckinridge, and a few even accused him of treason.[73]

Even Ellen Sherman thought her husband had been too lenient in his treatment of "perjured traitors." And on April 27, the general's brother, Senator John Sherman, wrote Stanton that he "was distressed beyond measure at the terms granted Johnson by Gen. S[herman]. . . . There should be literally no terms granted." Yet the senator maintained that his brother had been done a "gross injustice," especially by the press. "The most that can be said against him is that he granted the rebels too liberal terms."[74]

Even as Senator Sherman wrote Stanton, the Northern press was softening its position. The *Cleveland Plain Dealer* cautioned its readers to "wait for the facts" before judging Sherman. And after declaring on April 24 that the general had "sealed his fate," the *Philadelphia Inquirer* stated five days later that "the temporary spot upon his reputation is already washed away."[75]

Sherman also benefited from the support of family and friends. His brother, Senator Sherman, defended him in the *Washington Chronicle,* and his father-in-law, Thomas Ewing, did likewise in the *Cincinnati Daily Commercial.* But "Uncle Billy's" broadest base of support originated in his legions. Most of his soldiers were furious at Stanton and the Northern press for slandering him. "This whole army was annoyed & indignant at the attack made by Stanton in the newspapers of the 24th on Genl. Sherman," Seventeenth Corps commander Frank Blair wrote. "If President Johnson wants to make himself odious to every soldier & officer in this army he has only to retain Stanton in office." One of Blair's brigade commanders, Brig. Gen. Charles Ewing (who was Sherman's brother-in-law), warned: "If Stanton should happen to fall into the hands of the army he would have a sorry time of it—he is cursed from one end of the army to the other & will feel it before his day is over." An officer in Ewing's brigade, Lt. Frank Putney of the 12th Wisconsin, urged his father not to join in "the hue and cry" against Sherman. Putney denounced the "*pot-gutted patriots*" of the Northern press for accepting Stanton's dispatches at face value. "These valiant quill-drivers ignore the fact that Stanton has long been considered as hostile to Sherman, and, fearing him as a future political antagonist, watched for an opportunity to give him a stab."[76]

Many other Sherman sympathizers suspected that Stanton had a private agenda for disgracing the general. They believed that Stanton viewed the politically conservative Sherman as a potential threat to Radical Reconstruction plans. The secretary of war was even rumored to fear that the victorious Sherman intended to establish a dictatorship at the head of his army. If so, Stanton failed to realize that, regardless of Sherman's political opinions, the general had no political aspirations whatsoever. "I see my name occasionally alluded to in connection with some popular office," Sherman had written a friend in late March. "You may tell *all* that I would rather serve in Sing Sing Penitentiary than in Washington & believe I would come out a better man. If that aint emphatic enough use stronger expressions and I will endorse them." Stanton also viewed Sher-

Do You Bring Back Peace or War?

Maj. Gen. Henry W. Halleck
(Library of Congress)

man's terms as a betrayal of the Northern cause and an abandonment of all its gains. Whereas Senator Sherman attributed his brother's action to misplaced generosity, Stanton viewed that action as treasonous.[77]

The truth lies far closer to Senator Sherman's perception. "Uncle Billy" had written his terms thinking that the war had sufficiently punished the South and that the sooner the region resumed its former status, the better it would be for the nation. The general believed that he was acting in the spirit of Lincoln's conciliatory attitude toward the South.[78]

Yet Sherman was not entirely blameless. As he entered James Bennett's farmhouse on April 18, Sherman should have realized that the mood in Washington following Lincoln's assassination would render negotiations on political issues a veritable minefield. In addition to overreaching his authority, Sherman was out of his depth in matters of statesmanship. Lawyers on both sides skillfully dissected his hastily written terms, revealing a "skeleton" agreement—to use "Uncle Billy's" own phraseology—that the president could ratify only by repudiating the Emancipation Proclamation, recognizing Rebel state governments while challenging the legitimacy of several Union state governments, and opening the door for payment of the Confederate war debt. Sherman's crowning misconception was his belief that, after four years of fratricidal warfare, he could induce the two sides to overcome their differences in the interest of peace and mutual prosperity.

After the meeting at the Governor's Palace, Sherman and several staff

officers left for Wilmington. During an early-morning stopover at Goldsboro, Sherman wrote Grant's chief of staff, Bvt. Maj. Gen. John A. Rawlins:
"I doubt not efforts will be made to sow dissension between Grant and myself on a false supposition that we have political aspirations, or, after killing
me off by libels, he will next be assailed. I can keep away from Washington, and I confide in his good sense to save him from the influences that
will surround him there." Then Sherman's anger spilled onto the page: "I
have no hesitation in pronouncing Mr. Stanton's compilation a gross outrage on me, which I will resent in time." Unbeknownst to Sherman, Grant
inadvertently forwarded his letter to Stanton.[79]

Sherman arrived at Wilmington on April 29, sailed to Hilton Head the
following day, and traveled to Savannah on May 1. Returning to Hilton
Head on May 2, Sherman received another shock. The April 28 *New York
Times* carried a dispatch from his old friend, Maj. Gen. Henry W. Halleck,
informing Stanton that he had ordered Meade, Sheridan, and Wright to
"pay no regard to any truce or orders of General Sherman." Halleck also
suggested that Stanton should instruct General Wilson in Georgia to disregard Sherman's orders. In an amusing slip of the pen, "Old Brains" reported that Jefferson Davis's specie train was moving south from Goldsboro—which had been in Union hands since March 21 (Halleck apparently
meant Greensboro)—hauling an estimated "six to thirteen millions."[80]

Sherman failed to see any humor in the dispatch, for Halleck's betrayal
hurt as much as it angered him. The two men had been friends since the
late 1830s; early in the war, Halleck had supported Sherman while nearly
everyone else dismissed him as "insane." "I confess I owe to you all I now enjoy of fame," Sherman had written Halleck just after the capture of Atlanta,
"for I had allowed myself in 1861 to sink into a perfect 'slough of despond,'
and I do believe if I could I would have run away and hid from the dangers and the complications that surrounded us." Sherman credited Halleck
with enabling him to recover "from what might have proved an ignoble
end," yet Halleck's "perfidious and infamous order" was unforgivable. "I
will attend to him in time," Sherman vowed.[81]

At a time when he should have been savoring the fruits of victory, Sherman found himself publicly humiliated by two men he had trusted and respected. "To say that I was merely angry at the tone and substance of these
published bulletins of the War Department, would hardly express the state
of my feelings," Sherman wrote ten years later. "I was outraged beyond
measure, and was resolved to resent the insult, cost what it might." As peace
returned to the land, Sherman declared war on Stanton and Halleck.[82]

Do You Bring Back Peace or War?

CHAPTER 10

SLIDE BACK INTO
THE UNION

When Governor Vance returned to Greensboro after his meeting with Davis, he occupied the law office of W. L. and Levi M. Scott. On April 27, the governor requested a meeting with Sherman, explaining that he had been unable to contact him sooner. Vance assumed that Sherman would no longer honor his April 12 offer of safe-conduct: "I shall therefore be obliged to you, if you will either renew the safe conduct or grant me an interview under a Flag of Truce, at as early a day as practicable." The governor recommended "the immediate convening of the Legislature of the State & the adoption of prompt measures to save the people from a condition of anarchy which now threatens them." Vance also requested that state treasurer Jonathan Worth be permitted to return the state archives to Raleigh.[1]

Treasurer Worth arrived at the capital and obtained permission to transfer the archives, but otherwise he had disappointing news for the governor: Sherman had left the state, and Schofield was now in command. Although Schofield refused to see Vance in Raleigh, the commander suggested that they meet in Greensboro. The governor realized that the political climate had changed since Sherman's offer of safe-conduct and assumed the Federals now regarded him as persona non grata. Nevertheless, Vance decided to meet Schofield before rejoining his family in Statesville.[2]

On April 28, Vance issued a proclamation to the people of North Carolina. He declared that Lee and Johnston's surrender rendered further resistance "a useless waste of blood." Warning that lawless bands roamed the countryside, Vance advised civilians to remain at home and urged returning soldiers to form posses to stop the outlaws' depredations. The governor pledged to do all "in my power to settle the government of the State, to restore the civil authority in her borders, and to further the great ends of peace, domestic tranquility and the general welfare of the people."[3]

Meanwhile, Johnston notified Schofield that most of his cavalry was riding off in defiance of the convention and he was powerless to stop them. Schofield replied, "I apprehend that the failure of so large a portion of your troops, especially cavalry, to comply with the terms of the convention will give us no little trouble, and keep the country in a disturbed condition for a long time. But we must deal with them as best we can."[4]

The two generals arranged the distribution of paroles and the collection of arms. On April 30, Schofield would send staff officers and parole forms to designated sites on the North Carolina Railroad. He stipulated that the obligation, or parole text, be written on the front of each muster roll and signed by the unit's commanding officer and one of Schofield's officers. Every officer and man in Johnston's army would receive a parole form signed in the same manner as the muster rolls. Brigade commanders would retain the paroles of their men for as long as possible to preserve a semblance of organization during the journey home.[5]

On the morning of April 30, Schofield's inspector general, Bvt. Brig. Gen. William Hartsuff, and nine other staff officers left Raleigh to distribute the Confederates' paroles. Hartsuff found the Confederates scattered 130 miles from Hillsborough to Charlotte, the main body camping around Greensboro. Dropping off his assistants at several points on the railroad, Hartsuff rode to Johnston's headquarters. Accompanying the inspector general were Capt. John M. Payne, Capt. Gideon A. Lyon, and Lt. William J. Nelson, who would inventory the Confederates' ordnance and quartermaster stores at Greensboro.[6]

At 8:00 on the morning of May 1, Hartsuff opened his paroling office in Greensboro's Britton House hotel. The first Confederate to enter was Rear Adm. and Brig. Gen. Raphael Semmes, who had arranged his appointment through Johnston the previous evening. The fifty-five-year-old Semmes had good reason to be anxious about obtaining his parole. As the former skipper of the Confederate commerce raider *Alabama*, Semmes was denounced as a pirate in the North, and he feared being tried as such.[7]

Semmes and his so-called naval brigade had joined Johnston's army on April 26. His path from naval hero to army brigadier had been a tortuous one. After the *Alabama* was sunk off Cherbourg, France, on June 19, 1864, the wounded Captain Semmes underwent a long recuperation in England and then made a roundabout journey to Richmond. In February 1865, he was promoted to rear admiral and given command of the James River squadron. When the Confederate capital fell on April 2, Semmes received

Slide Back into the Union

Bvt. Brig. Gen. William Hartsuff. As Schofield's inspector general, Hartsuff supervised the distribution of paroles to Johnston's army. (Massachusetts Commandery, Military Order of the Loyal Legion Collection, U.S. Army Military History Institute)

orders to destroy his ships and transfer his command to Danville. He commandeered a train and reached his destination on the evening of April 4. On the way, Semmes's force of 500 sailors shrank to 400, most of the deserters jumping off at their homes. At Danville, President Davis transferred Semmes's command to the army and made the admiral a brigadier general. Semmes's sailors-turned-soldiers formed a brigade of two small regiments.[8]

On April 14, Semmes and his rapidly dwindling command were ordered to Greensboro, but their arrival was delayed by a week-long stint guarding the Piedmont Railroad. On April 21, Semmes requested permission to lead his force to the Trans-Mississippi, but Johnston denied the request on the grounds that a truce was in effect. When Semmes reached Greensboro on April 26, Beauregard authorized him to escape, but before the admiral-general had left the Creole's tent, a telegram arrived announcing the resumption of the armistice. Semmes thereupon resigned himself to the inevitable.[9]

Semmes introduced himself to Hartsuff and the Confederate representative, Lt. Col. A. P. Mason of Johnston's staff, and placed his muster rolls on the table. The two generals counted the names — 239 in all — and then signed the rolls. Hartsuff counted out an equal number of parole forms (see Appendix E) and handed them to Semmes. "You have only to fill up one of these for each officer and soldier of your command, with his name and rank, and sign it and hand it to him," Hartsuff told Semmes. "I have already signed them myself. You can fill up the one intended for yourself in like manner." Semmes replied that he preferred to fill out his own parole in

Rear Adm. and Brig. Gen. Raphael Semmes. Semmes arranged to be the first Confederate to receive his parole from General Hartsuff, a move doubtless motivated by the notoriety he had earned as the skipper of the Confederate commerce raider Alabama. *(Massachusetts Commandery, Military Order of the Loyal Legion Collection, U.S. Army Military History Institute)*

Hartsuff's presence. The Federal called for an aide and had Semmes dictate his name and rank: "R. Semmes, Rear-Admiral, and Brigadier-General, C. S. Navy, and C. S. Army, commanding brigade." Semmes then signed his parole in the same way. Semmes's parole thus absolved him from prosecution for acts of war he had committed as either an army or a naval officer. "I am now satisfied," Semmes told Hartsuff as he tucked his parole into his pocket. Semmes's precaution would serve him well.[10]

The process of examining the naval brigade's muster rolls, counting out forms, and preparing Semmes's parole consumed forty-five minutes. Afterward, Semmes returned to camp. Because his men hailed from several different states and would not be traveling together, Semmes distributed their paroles and disbanded them on the spot. That afternoon, Semmes set out for his home in Mobile, arriving on May 28. Seven months later, he was arrested and charged with violating his status as a prisoner of the U.S. Navy by escaping from the sinking *Alabama*. Semmes maintained that his arrest violated his parole permitting him "to return to his home, not to be disturbed by the United States authorities so long as he observe this obligation and obey the laws in force where he may reside." Federal authorities reluctantly arrived at the same conclusion and released Semmes on April 7, 1866.[11]

Fortunately, the process of examining muster rolls and issuing parole

Slide Back into the Union

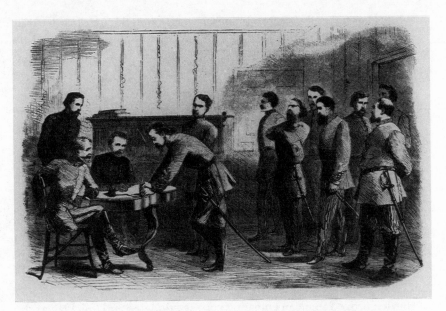

Confederate officers in Greensboro receiving their paroles (Harper's Weekly, *1865*)

forms went more quickly for subsequent Confederate commanders than it had for Semmes. One officer remarked that he had done his *"very best"* in serving the Confederacy and would henceforth be "equally zealous" in striving to be "a good American citizen." Not all Confederates were reconciled to their fate, however. "I never felt so mortified in my life as this morning when I went into the presence of the Yankee officers to sign my parole," wrote Lt. Col. Cornelius Irvine Walker of the 19th South Carolina Battalion. Several of Walker's comrades shook hands with the Federals, but the South Carolinian "would have been shot" before doing so. Instead, Walker saluted stiffly in an effort "to look as dignified as possible." He later declared that although the U.S. government had forced him to yield, "[I] have not changed my feelings towards it in the slightest degree. I feel and will always feel the same hatred to [the Yankees], however events may compel me to hide it." [12]

By the afternoon of May 1, Hartsuff realized that he needed more parole slips. He commissioned journeyman printer James Albright, a veteran of Lee's army, to print 15,000 forms. The Federals supplied Albright with all the paper he needed and instructed him to finish the job as quickly as possible. Albright and his brother "went to work with a will," cranking out thousands of paroles on an old hand press. The Albright brothers completed their task to Hartsuff's satisfaction and were paid handsomely for their work—$125 in U.S. greenbacks. [13]

While Hartsuff and his subordinates paroled Confederates, Hardee traveled to Raleigh at Johnston's behest to discuss the supplemental terms with Schofield. Accompanied only by his chief of staff, Lt. Col. Thomas B. Roy, Hardee arrived on the afternoon of May 1. After meeting with Schofield at the Governor's Palace, "Old Reliable" stayed overnight as the Federal's guest. The next morning, Hardee and Roy rode to Durham's Station and ate breakfast with Kilpatrick before resuming their journey back to Greensboro. The Confederates were joined by Theodore C. Wilson, a *New York Herald* reporter who had obtained permission to interview Johnston.[14]

Following close behind was a train carrying Schofield, Cox, and the 104th Ohio, a Twenty-third Corps regiment. The Union generals were en route to Greensboro to confer with Johnston and study the situation there. During a brief stop at Hillsborough, the Federals became uneasy when they noticed that Confederate cavalrymen surrounded their train. Meanwhile, Hardee and Roy boarded the Federals' coach to chat with Schofield and Cox.[15]

Hardee proved to be an engaging conversationalist and quickly put the anxious Northerners at their ease. "Old Reliable" admitted with a laugh that he had been "one of the hot Southerners who shared the notion that one man of the South could whip three Yankees," but that he had since been disabused of that notion. For the past two years, Hardee admitted, he had believed that, short of a miracle, the war was lost, but he had continued to fight as if certain of success. Cox noted that Hardee "seemed not to have the slightest bitterness about the result." As the old enemies conversed, their journey to Greensboro passed pleasantly and uneventfully—a noteworthy event on the decrepit North Carolina Railroad.[16]

The generals' train arrived at Greensboro about 4:00 P.M. The 104th Ohio remained at the depot, while the generals, staff officers, and journalist Wilson rode to Johnston's headquarters. "Old Joe's" tent stood beneath the shade trees in Ralph Gorrell's front yard near the railroad. Rumor had it that Johnston had refused several offers of hospitality in consideration of the homeowners, who might later suffer for their generosity. But the general's staff officers claimed that he actually preferred sleeping outdoors.[17]

Cox noted that the Confederate commander's encampment "was not quite so regular and trim as our own custom required. The wall tents did not sit quite so squarely upon the ground, and the camp was not laid out with regularity." Acknowledging the indifferent appearance of his camp, Johnston explained that an army on the eve of disbandment could not be expected to maintain a high degree of discipline. There was additional evidence of the army's disintegration: unable to trust their own headquarters

Slide Back into the Union

guard, Johnston's staff officers stood sentinel over their horses — only the commanding general was exempt from guard duty.[18]

At first glance, Cox thought the soft-spoken Johnston appeared less impressive than the flamboyant Hardee. Johnston was smaller than his lieutenant, his uniform was less showy, and his manner was quieter. But it soon became evident that Johnston was the man in command. "His quiet tones were clear," Cox recalled, "his gravity was full of conscious power, and the deference shown him by his subordinates was earnest and respectful."[19]

Schofield assured Johnston that he would fulfill Sherman's promise of a quarter-million rations, let the Confederates keep their wagons and teams, and furnish them with railroad transportation wherever possible. Hoping to provide Hartsuff with an estimate of parole forms needed, Schofield asked Johnston how many officers and men he had. "Old Joe" said that he could not be altogether certain, for his latest morning report included neither stragglers nor men on detached duty. He remarked that the refusal of Hampton and much of his cavalry to honor the convention rendered troop estimates even more unreliable. Although Johnston's final morning report tallied only 16,000 officers and men, paroles were eventually issued to more than double that number.[20]

Johnston and Hardee stated that the Confederates were laying down their arms with the intention of keeping their paroles in good faith. The generals denounced the assassination of Lincoln as a terrible crime that would result in harsher punishment for the South. Cox left the meeting convinced that Johnston "would have taken a very high place among us" had he not chosen "the wrong side in this terrible rebellion."[21]

On May 2, Johnston issued General Orders No. 22 — his farewell address to the Army of Tennessee. He urged his men to abide by the terms of the convention and

> discharge the obligations of good and peaceful citizens at your homes as well as you have performed the duties of thorough soldiers in the field. By such a course you will best secure the comfort of your families and kindred and restore tranquillity to your country. You will return to your homes with the admiration of our people, won by the courage and noble devotion you have displayed in this long war. I shall always remember with pride the loyal support and generous confidence you have given me. I now part with you with deep regret, and bid you farewell with feelings of cordial friendship and with earnest wishes that you may have hereafter all the prosperity and happiness to be found in the world.[22]

That night, Schofield and Cox stayed at former governor Morehead's home. Meeting them at Blandwood was Zeb Vance. Schofield informed Vance that the U.S. government did not recognize him or other state officials, but the news came as no surprise. After urging Schofield to protect the state's citizens and their property, Vance surrendered himself. The general had no orders for Vance's arrest, however, and said that he was free to go. In that case, Vance replied, he would rejoin his family at Statesville and remain there should Schofield wish to summon him.[23]

While the generals relaxed at Blandwood, the 104th Ohio spent a harrowing night on guard duty near the depot. Cox had brought a small force to Greensboro in deference to Johnston, who feared that a large Federal presence might result in bloodshed. As they stepped off the train, the Ohioans were quickly surrounded by a sea of men in butternut and gray eager to glimpse the Yankees. The Buckeyes' fear gave way to pity when they noticed that many Rebels wore rags and appeared underfed. As the Ohioans made their rounds that night, they heard continuous yelling and gunfire and saw numerous drunken Rebels wandering the streets. A few stray minié balls zipped past some nervous Federal guards, but the night passed without serious incident.[24]

On the morning of May 3, the 104th Ohio received orders to relieve the town's Confederate garrison, precipitating some of the oddest ceremonies of the war. First, the Confederate commandant, Brig. Gen. John D. Kennedy, formally turned over the Post of Greensboro to the commander of the 104th Ohio, Lt. Col. William J. Jordan. Then, as details of the 104th arrived at their new posts, they were met by soldiers from Kennedy's South Carolina brigade, the South Carolinians stacking arms while the Ohioans looked on in silence. At the conclusion, the Federals and Confederates shook hands and wished each other well, though there were a few grumblers on each side. Afterward, the Ohioans surveyed the property in their care. A large field on the edge of town held 119 cannon, several warehouses bulged with weapons, ammunition, and accoutrements, and the railroad yard was jammed with locomotives and rolling stock. Colonel Jordan concluded that there was too much matériel for one regiment to guard and appealed for help.[25]

Meanwhile, Schofield returned to Raleigh, leaving General Cox in command at Greensboro. Cox immediately summoned another Twenty-third Corps regiment, the 9th New Jersey, to support the 104th Ohio. The rest of the Twenty-third Corps and two brigades of Kilpatrick's cavalry were en route but would not begin arriving for several days. Although Hartsuff had finished paroling the Army of Tennessee, he noted that thousands of Confederates remained in Greensboro and were "raising the devil." On

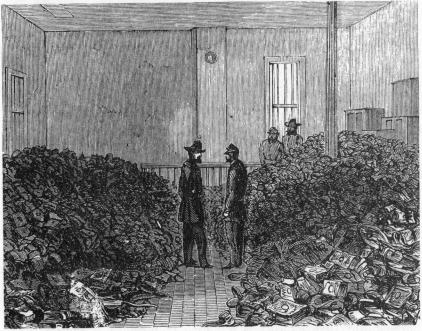

Two views of Confederate arms and accoutrements stored in Greensboro warehouses
(Harper's Weekly, *1865*)

May 3, stragglers from Lee's and Johnston's armies streamed into town to obtain paroles, compelling Hartsuff to reopen his office. The situation in Greensboro remained potentially explosive.[26]

Nevertheless, the thoughts of most Confederates were directed homeward. The Guilford County Court House was crowded with men using string and pieces of straw to measure the distance to their homes on a large wall map. Many units began their homeward journey on the morning of May 3. Leaving their encampments at Greensboro, High Point, Jamestown, Bush Hill, Bloomington, and Trinity College, they proceeded south on the Salisbury Road, hauling Federal rations in their wagons. The order to fall in "was received by the troops with a deafening shout," Georgia veteran Hezekiah McCorkle noted. "After turning in our guns and getting our parols, we feel relieved," wrote Texan Samuel T. Foster. "No more picket duty, no more guard duty, no more fighting, no more war. It is all over, and we are going home. *Home* after an absence of four years from our families and friends."[27]

On the other hand, William Andrew Fletcher of the 8th Texas Cavalry regarded this period as "the blankest part" of his life. For several days Fletcher simply existed, oblivious to past, present, and future. Then he received some sage advice from a North Carolina soldier that jolted him out of his depression. Late one night, Fletcher and his comrades rode past a column of foot soldiers and asked them where they were from. The strangers said they were North Carolinians. "Tar Heel! Tar Heel!" the Texans chanted in reply.

The noise startled Fletcher, who was nodding in his saddle. He heard one of the Tar Heels drawl, "Boys, have you got any bacon?"

The Texans said that they did.

"Well, grease and slide back into the Union."

Fletcher and his fellow Texans burst out laughing. As Fletcher rode on, he pondered the North Carolinian's unorthodox advice and realized that the world had not ended after all. Once more the future held promise, but like most of his comrades in the 8th Texas Cavalry, Fletcher would "slide back into the Union" without his parole.[28]

Many Confederates marched to Lexington on May 3 and pressed on to Salisbury the next day. At Salisbury, Tennessean Alfred Fielder saw his old division commander, Frank Cheatham, for the last time. As Cheatham rode past his former soldiers, tears streamed down his face. "Farewell, boys, farewell!" he cried, and then he was gone. From Salisbury, units from the Atlantic seaboard and Gulf Coast states continued south on the Charlotte Road, while units from Tennessee, Texas, and Arkansas headed west on the Morganton Road.[29]

Slide Back into the Union

Most commands carried out their flags in violation of the convention, and a few even marched with their colors flying. In some cases, flags were cut into small pieces and given to unit members. Perhaps the standard that met the strangest fate was the 4th Tennessee Cavalry's flag. The banner was carried home by the regiment's last color-bearer, James Nance, whose wife made it into an apron for their daughter. Many Confederates did not stack their weapons and accoutrements, burying or destroying them instead, and more than one veteran presented an overjoyed Tar Heel lad with a free rifle-musket. Johnston disapproved of these breaches and even returned a small headquarters flag to Cox with an apology on behalf of the staff officer who had kept it.[30]

On May 4, "Old Joe" said farewell to his staff and headed south to observe the situation at Salisbury and Charlotte. On the way, he stopped at Blandwood to say goodbye to former governor Morehead and his family. "Never can I forget the scene when the brave and grand Joseph E. Johnston called to say farewell, with the tears running down his brown cheeks," recalled Morehead's daughter, Letitia Walker. "Not a word was spoken, but silent prayers went up for his preservation."[31]

Meanwhile, the 9th New Jersey arrived at Greensboro and immediately went on guard duty to assist the 104th Ohio. At dawn on May 5, two companies of the 9th New Jersey boarded a train for Salisbury and Charlotte, the first Federals sent to either point. Lt. David Kille's Company I reached Salisbury at 10:30 A.M. to collect Confederate arms and ammunition. Kille's command completed its task in a few days and returned to Greensboro. Capt. Morris C. Runyan's Company G traveled on toward Charlotte and soon found its task far more difficult than Company I's had been.[32]

Captain Runyan and his company had to abandon their train at a creek just north of Concord because Stoneman's raiders had destroyed the bridge. The Federals also discovered that the raiders had cut the telegraph lines to Salisbury and Greensboro. As they crossed the creek, Runyan and his men knew they were on their own.[33]

When Runyan reached Charlotte on the evening of May 7, he found the town in a state of chaos. Bands of lawless Confederates roamed the streets, terrorizing the citizens. Assuming command of the Post of Charlotte, Runyan immediately posted guards at the powder magazine and warehouses, formed around-the-clock patrols, issued provisions to starving soldiers and civilians, and banned the sale of alcohol.[34]

On May 9, Runyan made a startling discovery. The captain entered an abandoned warehouse expecting to find provisions or ammunition but instead uncovered stacks of U.S. flags and regimental colors and dozens of boxes containing Confederate documents. Learning that General Johnston was in town and had keys to the building, Runyan asked "Old Joe" to meet him.[35]

The next day, one of Runyan's soldiers informed the captain that "a little old man" insisted on seeing him at once. As Runyan admonished the private to learn the unknown gentleman's name, the "little old man" entered the captain's office. Runyan recalled that the man wore civilian clothes and had a "remarkably striking face." The visitor introduced himself as General Johnston. A startled Runyan apologized for the private's rudeness, but Johnston waved him off with the remark that the man was only doing his duty.[36]

Johnston informed the captain that the boxes in question contained papers of the Confederate War Department and admitted to hoping that the material "might have fallen into friendly hands." Runyan assured "Old Joe" that he appreciated the documents' importance and would protect them. Johnston had also reported the abandoned records to Schofield, who sent his quartermaster to Charlotte for the flags and documents, which filled eighty large boxes.[37]

On May 12, Col. Minor T. Thomas's brigade of the Twenty-third Corps relieved Company G of the 9th New Jersey. Runyan and his command could reflect on their week in Charlotte with pride, for they had established order there quietly and without bloodshed. The captain also deserves the thanks of countless Civil War historians for preserving a priceless treasure trove of source material.[38]

At Company Shops, troopers from Kilpatrick's cavalry discovered a treasure trove of their own. While clearing away some brush to make camp, several men in Companies B and K of the 10th Ohio Cavalry found about $100,000 in gold buried in boxes and sacks marked, "Commercial Bank of New Berne, N. C." The finders wisely divided the money with several of their officers and claimed the coin as spoils of war. New Bern bank officials appealed to Kilpatrick, arguing that the gold was theirs because the war was over. Kilpatrick agreed and ordered Capt. Edwin R. Brink of the 10th Ohio Cavalry to recover the gold. Meanwhile, Schofield learned of the affair and termed Captain Brink's recovery effort "a farce." In a letter to Kilpatrick, Schofield noted that Brink had admitted to accepting a $2,000 bribe from the finders. "How is it that no effective steps have been taken to do justice in the matter?" Schofield asked. He ordered Kilpatrick to arrest all suspects and recover the money: "Do not let the disgrace of such an affair as this attach to your command."[39]

Kilpatrick arrested three troopers who allegedly had buried $30,000 of the specie at several points between Hillsborough and Company Shops; he released them when they agreed to reveal the location of their buried

Slide Back into the Union

treasure. Although the suspects wasted no time escaping, Kilpatrick informed Schofield that he had recovered $10,000 and would soon locate the remainder. Despite "Little Kil's" assurances, most of the gold was never recovered—at least not officially. Rumors indicated that veterans of the 10th Ohio Cavalry recovered most of the gold and that farmers plowed up the remainder.[40]

A second incident involving the theft of precious metal proved embarrassing for Kilpatrick's First Brigade commander, Bvt. Brig. Gen. Thomas J. Jordan. While traveling from Durham's Station to Greensboro, Jordan stayed at the home of Rebecca Jones in Hillsborough. Several days later, Jones informed Kilpatrick that Jordan's servants had stolen some of her silver plate. A chagrined Jordan searched in vain for the missing silver; he finally sent his brother to Hillsborough armed with a letter of apology and greenbacks to pay for the stolen property.[41]

The main body of the Twenty-third Corps and Kilpatrick's cavalry began arriving at Greensboro on May 5. Meanwhile, General Cox had transferred his headquarters from Blandwood to Dunleath, the home of Judge Robert P. Dick. The judge's estate was on the northern end of town, "out[side] the dust and confusion" of the Salisbury Road, which was still choked with departing Confederates. Cox impressed nearly everyone in Greensboro, including Letitia Morehead Walker, who called him "a most courteous and elegant man." The town's Presbyterian minister, Dr. Jacob Henry Smith, and his wife found Cox "intelligent, cultivated, reasonable, and just." The townspeople's opinion regarding Mrs. Cox was also favorable, though she struck some as more formal and less amiable than her husband.[42]

Nothing could have placed the town's reaction to the Coxes in starker relief than the frosty reception accorded Kilpatrick and his bizarre retinue. "Little Kil" established his headquarters at Rose Villa, the home of Alexander P. Eckels. In addition to his two orderlies, "Charley" and "Frank," Kilpatrick was accompanied by a young mulatto woman named Molly, who was, to borrow the euphemism of an eyewitness, "in the family way." Molly confided to one of the Eckels's servants that Kilpatrick had "done her so and now was trying to go back on her," but she was determined to "stick to" the general, since the baby was his.[43]

During the first two weeks of May, Greensboro teemed with thousands of former Confederate soldiers, former slaves, and local citizens, including women "laying around the streets in perfect vulgarity," observed Lt. Redmond Laswell of the 120th Indiana. "Evry thing is very quiet in Camp but not so in town. There are so many country women laying around on the streets that it keeps a continual uproar with the [Confederate] soldiers."

Maj. Gen. Jacob D. Cox. Commander of the Twenty-third Corps in Schofield's Army of the Ohio, Cox proved to be a popular occupation commander in postwar Greensboro. (Massachusetts Commandery, Military Order of the Loyal Legion Collection, U.S. Army Military History Institute)

Laswell complained that he and other Federals could not meet the women because they were continually thronged by Confederates. He also resented the fact that many Rebels "were a getting some of Uncle Sams grub to live on after trying to kill all of his boys inother day." [44]

Believing it wiser to exercise restraint than rule with an iron fist, Cox furnished safeguards and provisions to those who requested them, encouraged local businesses to reopen, and urged civic officials to resume their duties. Cox also ordered Greensboro's streets cleaned and swept, contracting unemployed blacks to do the work; many townspeople contributed by tidying up their yards and homes. The general counseled former slaves to return to their farms and shops and admonished their erstwhile masters to pay them a fair wage. Cox found the people resigned to the present situation and obedient to the Federal soldiers. [45]

By mid-May, General Schofield's occupation force covered much of the Old North State. The Tenth Corps and Heath's (formerly Kerwin's) brigade of Kilpatrick's cavalry under General Terry held the eastern half, while the Twenty-third Corps and Jordan's and Atkins's cavalry brigades under General Cox occupied the western half. On the coast, Brig. Gen. Joseph R. Hawley commanded the District of Wilmington and Brig. Gen. Innis N. Palmer the District of Beaufort. Schofield had plenty of occupation troops,

Slide Back into the Union

but he lacked instructions from Washington. "I hope the Government will make known its policy as to organization of State governments without delay," Schofield wrote Sherman.

> Affairs must necessarily be in a very unsettled state until that is done. The people are now in a mood to accept almost anything which promises a definite settlement. What is to be done with the freedmen is the question of all, and it is the all-important question. It requires prompt and wise action to prevent the negro from becoming a huge elephant on our hands. If I am to govern this State it is important for me to know it at once. If another is to be sent here it cannot be done too soon, for he will probably undo the most of what I shall have done.

Although Schofield's questions deserved prompt answers, they were not forthcoming. During his six-week stint as commander in North Carolina, Schofield functioned primarily as a glorified police chief. The fate of the Old North State would rest in other hands.[46]

On Sunday, April 30, the Army of Georgia began its 275-mile trek to Washington, D.C., followed by the Army of the Tennessee on Monday, May 1. As the columns filed into the road, bands struck up "Home Sweet Home." Sherman's troops were homeward bound and passing through country virtually untouched by the war. The armies marched in two wings as usual, but foraging was forbidden and the men carried only five rounds in their cartridge boxes rather than the usual forty. The ordnance wagons no longer hauled ammunition but were loaded instead with rations for the final march. As they tramped through villages and hamlets north of Raleigh, the Yankees were greeted by the novel sight of the Stars and Stripes fluttering from several homes. Crowds of former slaves gathered by the roadside to cheer the passing Federals, and many white citizens also watched the procession, though usually from their porches or doorways.[47]

For Anna Fuller of Louisburg, the sight of thousands of Yankee soldiers marching through town indicated that she and her neighbors were "a subjugated people." Several brass bands passed her house blaring forth national airs. "The music, I suppose, was good," Fuller wrote, "but it did not stir in my breast a single emotion of patriotism or pleasure. I felt *indignant.*" At Louisburg, soldiers of the Fifteenth Corps discovered that Sherman's orders prohibiting foraging and pillaging had teeth. As the troops marched down one tree-lined street, they saw three soldiers tied to a board fence, a piece of paper pinned to each man's chest proclaiming him a "PILLAGER."[48]

For the first several days, the army marched about twenty miles per day.

Despite the springtime heat, "Uncle Billy's" veterans managed this with little difficulty. When the army crossed into Virginia, however, the daily average increased to twenty-seven miles. As a result, many men straggled, some dropped from heat exhaustion, and a few unfortunates died. One angry private characterized their deaths as "simply murder." Rumor had it that the blistering pace resulted from a bet between corps commanders as to who would enter Richmond first.[49]

As his grand army toiled northward, General Sherman completed his southern tour by visiting Charleston and then sailing past the Cape Fear River defenses near Wilmington. Sherman reached Morehead City on the evening of May 4 and met Supreme Court chief justice Salmon P. Chase, who was embarking on a southern tour of his own. A fierce gale forced the two men to remain in port for several days. They passed the time discussing many things, including Chase's proposal to extend the vote to blacks, which Sherman feared might rekindle old animosities if introduced too hastily. Accompanying Chase was an old acquaintance of Sherman's, Whitelaw Reid, a former journalist with the *Cincinnati Gazette*. Reid noted that the general was as "nervous and restless as ever," bursting with pride at the work of his army and boiling over with anger at the insults heaped upon him for his first agreement with Johnston. Sherman complained that the government had not outlined its policy to him, compelling him to act as he thought best. "Uncle Billy" illustrated his dilemma by repeating Lincoln's City Point "lemonade anecdote." "And that," Sherman exclaimed, "is all I could get out of the Government as to what its policy was concerning the Rebel leaders, till Stanton assailed me for Davis' escape!"[50]

The storm finally subsided on May 7, enabling Sherman to sail north after his army while Chase continued south. During the voyage, Sherman wrote his wife, telling her that the treachery of Stanton and Halleck "puts them at my mercy, and in a few days look out for breakers." At Fort Monroe on May 8, Sherman replied to a telegram from Halleck inviting him to stay at his headquarters in Richmond. "After your dispatch to the Secretary of War," Sherman wrote, "I cannot have any friendly intercourse with you. I will come to City Point to-morrow and march with my troops, and I prefer we should not meet." Sherman thus struck the first blow in his war of retribution. Given that Halleck was a senior officer, Sherman's message was impolitic, but he was determined to have his revenge, "cost what it might."[51]

Arriving at City Point on the morning of May 9, "Uncle Billy" wrote his report for the final campaign. His clerk, "Vett" Noble, aptly described the thirty-three-page document as "a scorcher." Sherman devoted considerable space to defending his first agreement with Johnston and condemning

Slide Back into the Union

Halleck's orders to disregard his truce. "I was bound in honor to defend my own truce . . . even at the cost of many lives," Sherman contended, suggesting that he would have attempted to block Halleck's pursuit of Johnston's army. That afternoon Sherman rode a train to Manchester, across the James River from Richmond; arriving at 4:00 P.M., he found his grand army in camp. When Sherman learned that Halleck had ordered the Army of Georgia to pass in review through Richmond, he exploded. "I never before saw [Sherman] in such a towering passion," recalled Lt. Col. Andrew Hickenlooper, "and never believed that he was capable of using such scathing and denunciatory language as he did in reference to General Halleck." Once Sherman had cooled down, he informed "Old Brains" that the review would not occur. Sherman later explained: "All the army knew of the insult that had been made me by the Secretary of War and General Halleck, and watched me closely to see if I would tamely submit." Sherman justified his conduct toward Halleck from the standpoint of personal honor and because the respect of his troops hung in the balance. "This army has stood by me in public and private always," Sherman wrote his wife, "and I must maintain my hold on it till it ceases to exist."[52]

Sherman's men exacted their own retribution against Halleck, who had issued a peremptory order forbidding them to enter Richmond except as part of a marching column. Determined to visit the former Confederate capital, angry soldiers from the Seventeenth Corps stormed the James River bridge and routed the guard with a volley of clenched fists and flung stones.[53]

Realizing that he was on the verge of losing a friendship more important to him than Stanton's fleeting approval, Halleck responded to Sherman's missive by extending the olive branch. "You have not had during this war nor have you now a warmer friend and admirer than myself," Halleck wrote. "If in carrying out what I knew to be the wishes of the War Department in regard to your armistice I used language which has given you offense it was unintentional, and I deeply regret it. If fully aware of the circumstances under which I acted I am certain you would not attribute to me any improper motives. It is my wish to continue to regard and receive you as a personal friend. With this statement I leave the matter in your hands."[54]

Unfortunately for Halleck, the damage as Sherman saw it was irreparable. In his reply to "Old Brains," Sherman compared the "deadly malignity" of Halleck's telegram to Stanton with the "friendly expressions" of his conciliatory letter and told Halleck that he could not reconcile the two. Nor could he "consent to the renewal of a friendship I had prized so highly till I can see deeper into the diabolical plot than I now do." Sherman intended to march his army through Richmond quietly and in good order, but he warned Halleck: "I beg you to keep slightly perdu, for if noticed by some of my old command I cannot undertake to maintain a model behavior, for their feelings have become aroused by what the world adjudges an insult to at least an honest commander. If loss of life or violence result from this you must attribute it to the true cause—a public insult to a brother officer when he was far away on public service, perfectly innocent of the malignant purpose and design." From rudeness and disrespect Sherman descended one step lower, issuing threats to a senior officer. Yet he believed that Halleck's conduct toward him both justified and demanded this course of action. "Tomorrow I march through Richmond with colors flying & drums beating as a matter of right and not by Halleck's favors[;] no notice will be taken of him personally or officially," Sherman wrote his wife. "I dare him to oppose my march. He will think twice before he again undertakes to stand between me and my subordinates." Sherman's army passed through Richmond on May 11 without incident, and Halleck wisely remained out of sight.[55]

The next stage of the march took the two wings through the battlefields of eastern Virginia. A hush fell on the Seventeenth Corps as it passed the stone wall at Fredericksburg where Lt. Gen. James Longstreet's Confederate defenders had mowed down wave after wave of Maj. Gen. Ambrose E. Burnside's Federal attackers. "The ground, as well as the buildings on either side of our line of march, bore silent witness to the fearful storm of shot and shell under which [more than] 10,000 of Burnside's noble men went down," recalled M. B. Loop of the 68th Ohio.[56]

The Twentieth Corps marched through the battlefield of Spotsylvania Court House, where soldiers gathered souvenirs, including splinters said to be from the famous oak tree at the Bloody Angle that was cut down by minié balls. As they roamed the battlefield, the men saw hundreds of uniformed skeletons lying half-buried or unburied. On the night of May 14, the "Star Corps" camped at Brock Road, the scene of desperate fighting during the Battle of the Wilderness.

The next day the Twentieth Corps marched into what was for many veterans the terrible, familiar battleground of Chancellorsville. They had served in the Eleventh Corps and Twelfth Corps of the Army of the Potomac before being transferred to the western theater in the autumn of 1863. Now they had come full circle. The men were permitted to fall out and revisit the battlefield. For Sgt. Rice Bull of the 123rd New York, this was an opportunity to return to the log works where he and his comrades had made a futile stand. He found the spot on the line where he had been wounded and the old log house where he was later captured. For a few hours Bull

Slide Back into the Union

relived those unforgettable days of terror and suffering, but his memories were neither bitter nor sorrowful. "I felt a great sense of gratitude to God that I had not only survived my wounds at Chancellorsville," Bull recalled, "but during the two years of active service since that time I had escaped unscathed, and rejoiced that I was alive and homeward bound."[57]

Sherman's army reached Alexandria on May 19 and went into camp. "Uncle Billy" was on the outskirts of the nation's capital, which he recently had denounced as "corrupt as Hell" while vowing to "avoid it as a pest house." But contact with Washington and its denizens now appeared unavoidable, for Sherman was summoned to appear before the congressional Joint Committee on the Conduct of the War regarding his first agreement with Johnston, and President Johnson invited him to the White House. "Send me all orders and letters you may have for me," Sherman instructed Grant's chief of staff, "and let some one newspaper know that the vandal Sherman is encamped near the canal bridge half way between the Long Bridge and Alexandria to the west of the road, where his friends, if any, can find him. Though in disgrace he is untamed and unconquered."[58]

Having humiliated Halleck, Sherman focused his ire on the secretary of war. "Stanton wants to kill me because I do not favor the scheme of declaring the negroes of the South, now free, to be loyal voters," he told his wife, "whereby politicians may manufacture just so much pliable electioneering material." Sherman stated that he was looking for a "good opportunity" to insult the secretary of war. That opportunity materialized when he received orders from the army's adjutant general to lead his four corps in a grand review down Pennsylvania Avenue before the president, Grant, and dozens of other dignitaries, including Stanton.[59]

Sherman called on President Johnson at the White House and met several cabinet ministers there as well, though the secretary of war was conspicuously absent. Johnson assured the general that he only learned of Stanton's two bulletins by reading the morning paper, and Sherman received similar assurances from the cabinet members. "Uncle Billy" also visited his brother, Senator John Sherman, and Grant, both of whom offered to arrange a rapprochement with Stanton. Sherman refused them both.[60]

On May 21, Sherman wrote an old friend, Bvt. Maj. Gen. Stewart Van Vliet, on the subject of his breach with Stanton and Halleck. The account that "Uncle Billy" gave Van Vliet employed a new twist. He claimed that until his assassination, Lincoln had blocked the schemes of Stanton and Halleck, who now sought to ruin Sherman because he was "strictly, literally following" the late president's policy. Sherman even claimed to possess official documents that "not only justify but made imperative" his first agreement with Johnston. "Thus far I have violated no rule of official secrecy, though severely tempted," Sherman wrote, "but so much the worse for [Stanton and Halleck] when all becomes revealed."[61]

Sherman's golden opportunity to "reveal all" came the next day, when he testified before the Joint Committee on the Conduct of the War. When questioned about Lincoln's influence on his terms, Sherman cited the precedent of Weitzel's call of the Virginia legislature as well as the late president's encouragement of his overtures to Georgia governor Joseph E. Brown and Confederate vice president Alexander H. Stephens. Regarding his conferences with Lincoln on board the *River Queen*, Sherman stated that he had discussed "nothing definite" with the president concerning peace terms. In short, Sherman's testimony offered no stunning revelations, but the general nevertheless insisted, "Had President Lincoln lived, I know he would have sustained me."[62]

Sherman was, of course, mistaken in this assessment. Lincoln would never have approved an agreement that perpetuated slavery, recognized Rebel state governments while calling several Union state governments into question, and raised the possibility for paying the Confederate war debt. Yet the president probably would have avoided publicly humiliating Sherman while instructing him to demand the Appomattox Court House terms.

The revelations that Sherman promised Van Vliet were the figment of an agitated mind. In asserting his innocence to an old friend, Sherman simply overstated his case. Much has been made of the Van Vliet letter because Sherman wrote it one day prior to his appearance before the Joint Committee. Because the letter promised revelations that Sherman failed to deliver in his testimony, some historians have wrongly concluded that the general elected not to identify Lincoln as the architect of his first agreement with Johnston. This erroneous conclusion ignores Sherman's repeated assurances to Grant (who would have heard Lincoln's instructions) that he would offer Johnston the Appomattox terms, and it contradicts Sherman's oft-repeated contention that he received no presidential instructions—except Lincoln's "lemonade anecdote"—before April 24. In any event, Sherman knew that he had acted in good faith, and he believed that Stanton had maliciously impugned his motives and must therefore suffer the consequences.[63]

The Grand Review of the Army of the Potomac occurred on May 23. Sherman and his lieutenants watched from the reviewing stand and enjoyed the pageantry, but they were determined to see their own troops outdo the easterners the next day. That evening "Uncle Billy" and his sub-

Slide Back into the Union

ordinates met to plan their review. Conceding that the easterners could not be beaten for smartness of appearance and precision of drill, they decided that the western army should appear as it had on the march—with bummers, pioneers, black refugees, wagons, pontoons, and mascots. Sherman nevertheless cautioned his lieutenants to maintain strict marching formation.[64]

Wednesday, May 24, dawned clear and pleasant. A crowd even larger than the one for the Army of the Potomac's review lined both sides of Pennsylvania Avenue. Spectators also watched from rooftops, balconies, open windows, and specially built grandstands. Though many had watched the eastern army for seven hours the day before, they were still eager to view the western army, which they had only heard and read about.[65]

Sherman took his place at the head of the column forming behind the Capitol. Beside him rode General Howard, the newly appointed director of the Freedmen's Bureau. For the Grand Review, Sherman had asked Howard to yield his place at the head of the Army of the Tennessee to General Logan. In July 1864, Sherman had chosen the West Pointer Howard to command the Army of the Tennessee instead of the political general Logan, who had been a fixture in that army since its inception. Though cognizant of Logan's still-wounded pride, Howard had intended to ride at the head of the army until Sherman appealed to his sense of Christian charity. Sherman knew his man, for the devout Howard was incapable of resisting such an appeal and yielded his place to Logan.[66]

At 9:00 A.M. a cannon was fired, signaling the review to begin. At the order "Right shoulder arms! Forward, March!" the column lurched into motion, drummers beating time and brass bands striking up patriotic tunes. As he rode onto Pennsylvania Avenue, Sherman kept his eyes front, not daring to look behind him. Perhaps he dreaded seeing a repetition of the comic review at Goldsboro. Following him was his old rough-and-tumble Fifteenth Corps, more renowned for its fighting qualities than its parade-ground polish. As he approached the Treasury building, however, "Uncle Billy" yielded to the temptation to look back. "[T]he sight was simply magnificent," he recalled. "The column was compact, and the glittering muskets looked like a solid mass of steel, moving with the regularity of a pendulum." Years later Sherman would remember this moment as the happiest of his life.[67]

Sherman's men were determined to beat their eastern rivals, whether on review or in one of the many street fights or barroom brawls in which they had recently come to blows. As one division prepared to march onto Pennsylvania Avenue, officers passed the word to their troops: "Boys, remember it's 'Sherman' against the 'Potomac'—the west against the east

*The Grand Review of Sherman's army, May 24, 1865. This image, showing units
of the Twentieth Corps marching down Pennsylvania Avenue, was taken at the Treasury
building, near the point at which General Sherman turned in his saddle to view his army.
(Library of Congress)*

today." The differences between the soldiers of the two armies were striking. The western troops were generally taller and more muscular than their
eastern counterparts, and their marching stride was longer and more ath-
letic. Sherman's men also favored the wide-brimmed slouch hat as opposed
to the close-fitting kepi worn by the soldiers of the Potomac army. Many
westerners had not received new uniforms for the review and bore the appearance of veteran campaigners—appropriate for soldiers of whom Joe
Johnston had said, "[T]here had been no such army since the days of Julius
Caesar."[68]

Slide Back into the Union

Following each division were representations of the army's marches through Georgia and the Carolinas. First came the sobering spectacle of six ambulances advancing two or three abreast, each with a bloodstained stretcher hanging from either side. The ambulances were followed by a motley procession: bummers mounted on rawboned horses and mules; black cooks leading pack animals loaded down with kettles, frying pans, coffee pots, hams, and sides of bacon; brawny black pioneers carrying axes, picks, and shovels at right shoulder shift; crowds of black women and their children. Each regiment appeared to have at least one mascot, including dogs, raccoons, squirrels, and gamecocks. There were also cattle, hogs, goats, chickens, and sheep. The bystanders greeted the exotic procession with laughter and loud applause.[69]

By the time Sherman halted before the reviewing stand, he and his horse were covered with floral wreaths. As Sherman walked up the steps, the cheers and applause became deafening. Among those who greeted him were his wife, Ellen, his son, Tom, his father-in-law, Thomas Ewing, and his brother, Senator Sherman, along with President Johnson, Grant, and Stanton. The secretary of war extended his hand as Sherman approached but hastily withdrew it when "Uncle Billy" ignored him and shook hands with Grant instead. "No man, I don't care who he is, shall insult me or arraign my motives," Sherman wrote after the review. "[T]he howl against me is narrowed down to Halleck and Stanton, and I have partially resented both." There was nothing "partial" about Sherman's snubbing of Stanton, for it was witnessed by thousands of curious spectators. Sherman then took his place at the left side of the president and, for the next six hours, watched his grand army pass in review. He could hardly contain his pride: "It was, in my judgment, the most magnificent army in existence."[70]

On May 30, Sherman issued his farewell address. "Our work is done," he told his soldiers. "[A]rmed enemies no longer defy us." "Uncle Billy" proudly recalled his army's progress from Lookout Mountain to Raleigh and offered bright prospects for all the men: "[O]ur favored country is so grand, so extensive, so diversified in climate, soil, and productions, that every man may find a home and occupation suited to his taste." Sherman closed with a flourish: "Your general now bids you all farewell, with the full belief that as in war you have been good soldiers so in peace you will make good citizens, and if unfortunately new war should arise in our country 'Sherman's Army' will be the first to buckle on its old armor and come forth to maintain the Government of our inheritance."[71]

While Sherman traveled to Chicago with his family, his grand army was dismantled. The western regiments were transferred to Louisville, Kentucky, by boat and rail, whereas most eastern regiments were sent to their respective state capitals for mustering out. The westerners resented the delay, but by late July most were either home or en route.[72]

The 123rd New York made its final camp on the outskirts of Albany, New York. A few days later the men were mustered out—free to return to a world once familiar, but for which they now felt unprepared. Some suffered from crippling wounds or broken health, and most were volunteers who had sacrificed three years for their country. For the last time, the men of the 123rd received the order to fall in. Many already wore civilian clothing. Sergeant Bull recalled his captain choking out a final farewell to the company, after which the men gathered around him and wished each other well. "Surely we all rejoiced that the end had come, that victory was ours and home was near," Bull noted. "But there was after all a sadness deep down in our hearts in this parting hour. We boys had been together for three years; we had formed close friendships; we had slept under the same blanket; we had faced the enemy shoulder to shoulder on the firing line; we had marched side by side; we had borne danger, hardship, and privation alike; thus a comradeship had grown as only such conditions could form. So it was hard to separate and say goodby, one with the other; but we shook hands all around, and laughed and seemed to make merry, while our hearts were heavy and our eyes ready to shed tears."[73]

The homeward trek of Johnston's veterans presented a stark contrast to that of Sherman's. No grand review before a grateful public awaited them, and for all their anxiety to rejoin their loved ones, the Southerners dreaded returning to a homeland devastated by four years of war. Despite their paroles, many former Confederates also feared exile or imprisonment.

For Capt. Samuel T. Foster and his comrades of Granbury's Texas brigade, the journey home took six weeks. From the Texans' starting point in central North Carolina, the distance must have appeared insurmountable, as it did to a geographically challenged Tar Heel who asked Foster where he lived.

"Texas," Foster replied.

"Does Texas jine North Carliner?" the Tar Heel asked.

Foster told him that it did not.

The man asked Foster how far it was to his home.

"About 2,000 miles."

"Whew!" the gentleman exclaimed. "If I was that far from home I would just sit down and never try to get [there]."[74]

Foster and his comrades were made of sterner stuff. In mid-May they tramped across the Blue Ridge Mountains and into Tennessee. At one

Slide Back into the Union

point, Foster complained that his old leg wound was hurting him "very bad again." As the Texans passed through Greeneville, Tennessee, they saw President Johnson's old tailor shop and had their first encounter with black men dressed in Union blue. The two groups traded insults until the Federals were ordered back to camp. Shortly after this encounter, Foster had an experience that altered his view of blacks.[75]

The Texans had to wait several days at Greeneville for a train to Nashville. One morning, Foster met a black girl on her way to school. He observed that she was neatly dressed and had several books under her arm. Foster asked to see her grammar textbook. Turning to one of the lessons, he asked her several questions, which she answered correctly. He tried the same experiment using her geography and math textbooks, with the same result. "I was never more surprised in my life!" Foster admitted. This was a revelation of astounding proportions: a person's knowledge or skill—not skin color—was what mattered now. "The smartest man will win—in every department of life," the Texan reasoned. "Our children will have to contend for the honors in life with the negro . . . [a]nd the man that is the best mechanic[,] lawyer, doctor or teacher &c will succeed."[76]

On May 22, Foster and his comrades boarded a train for Nashville. Soon afterward, they learned that the train ahead of them had wrecked, killing or injuring many Arkansas men on board. As the Texans passed the site, they counted a dozen fresh graves near the roadbed and considered themselves fortunate. They rode through Knoxville and saw miles of zigzagging earthworks on the outskirts; they also passed through Chattanooga and Murfreesboro before arriving at Nashville early on May 26. As Union soldiers escorted the Texans through town, the state penitentiary loomed up before them. A rumor spread that the Federals planned to imprison them there until Kirby Smith's surrender. *"But!"* a relieved Foster noted, "we didnt go in the Penitentiary after all, but are halted out side on a grassy place—and have rations issued to us—and rest about 2 hours."[77]

The Texans then journeyed by steamboat via the Cumberland, Ohio, and Mississippi Rivers. During a brief stop at Memphis, members of a Christian society boarded and handed out Bibles, "as if we were a lot of heathens," a disgusted Foster wrote. The men next traveled to New Orleans, where they waited ten days for a ship to Galveston. During the voyage, Foster became seasick and had to endure considerable chaffing from less susceptible comrades.

After a brief delay, the Texans' ship passed through the Federal blockade at Galveston. On June 13, Foster set foot on solid ground, but the earth itself seemed to rock, rendering him sick once more. The next day, the Texans rode a train to Houston and spent the night at a soldiers' home. After

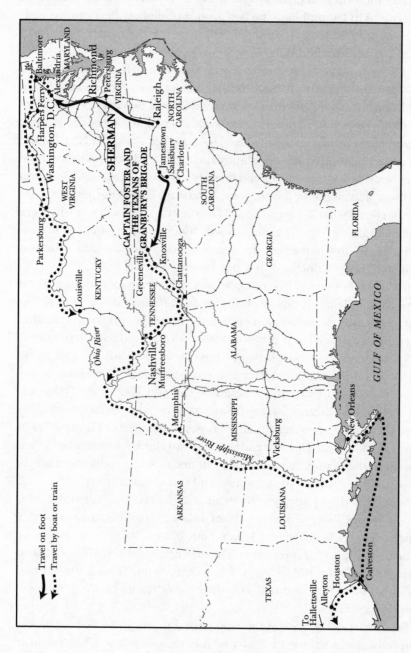

Map 8. The final march of Sherman's army and the homeward journey of Capt. Samuel T. Foster and Granbury's Texas brigade, May–June 1865

breakfast, Foster and his comrades said their farewells. "Men who have stood by each other in times of danger, men who endured the hardships of the Confederate war together, men who have marched, eat[en], slept, laughed[,] s[u]ng, cried and in fact soldiered together all through the war are now separating perhaps for life—never [to] see each other again," Foster wrote. "Ah! But the prospects of seeing all the loved ones at home, is uppermost in our minds and we are in a hurry to separate."

Foster traveled by train to Alleyton on the morning of June 15 and then rode all night on the roof of a crowded stagecoach to Hallettsville, his hometown. Arriving about sunup, he located his mother and brothers, who directed him to his family. "[S]o I go on until I find her who has been my guiding star in all my travels," Foster wrote, "my wife." He had journeyed 1,800 miles to reach his home and family.[78]

On May 6, David L. Swain had written William A. Graham concerning the situation at Chapel Hill. Since the occupation, there had been no mail service, and an occasional issue of a Raleigh newspaper was the town's only window to the outside world. Most former slaves had run off or refused to work. The farmers were destitute, and few had the means to plant a crop. The countryside had been foraged "barbarously," Swain wrote, and, according to Charles Manly, the area around Raleigh had suffered at least as much. Manly had been "very low down" over his losses, Swain reported, but he had since recovered his sense of humor, if nothing else, joking that the only living thing left on his plantation was a rat, and "the Yankees are in hot pursuit after that."[79]

Yet Swain was pleased that the town of Chapel Hill and the university remained "remarkably preserved." Of the Federal occupation, Swain wrote: "I have known the time when my [college] boys could create more disturbance, noise and confusion in an hour, than Gen'l Atkins' brigade have exhibited in a week." The town was currently guarded by a company of the 10th Ohio Cavalry, whose commander impressed Swain as "genteel, accommodating and energetic." Details patrolled the streets at night, and safeguards were provided to citizens who requested them. Swain believed that the harshest cruelties committed in the vicinity of Chapel Hill were "tender mercies" compared to the hardships endured by inhabitants of Georgia, South Carolina, and other parts of North Carolina.[80]

Although Swain was relieved to see the reestablishment of law and order, he feared for the economic future of the Old North State. All property in slaves, all state bonds issued since May 1861, all Confederate cash and bonds, and most state bank stock had been wiped out. The state's railroads were in a decrepit state, and there was no capital to finance their repair. "Our forebodings at the beginning of the contest were very gloomy, but neither of us recognized the extent to which we suffered and have yet to endure," Swain wrote Graham. "May God have mercy on the Country and upon us."[81]

Five days later, Graham reported that Hillsborough had suffered no more than Chapel Hill. Several of Graham's former slaves had left, and he had lost a mule, several hogs, and his forage and corn to the Confederate army—a trifling loss when compared to those of many others. Most of all, Graham was thankful that his five sons had returned home without permanent injury. Yet recent political developments caused Graham to dread the future. The Federals had removed Governor Vance from office and placed the Old North State under military rule. They had also rejected Vance's proposal to send a commission headed by Graham to confer with President Johnson. Graham called this rebuff "a gross indignity to the State, and an indication that rude conduct and harsh measures may be expected."[82]

Graham's words were prophetic. On May 13, a squadron of the 9th Pennsylvania Cavalry rode into Statesville to arrest Zeb Vance. It was Vance's thirty-fifth birthday. The former governor was eating dinner with his family when the Federals surrounded his house. Vance went outside to see what the trouble was and was met by Maj. John M. Porter and Capt. Edward M. Hayes, who informed him that he was under arrest. However, Porter allowed Vance to spend the night with his family.[83]

About 9:00 the next morning, Vance rode out of Statesville in a carriage driven by a neighbor, Samuel Wittkowsky. A detail of Federal horsemen surrounded the buggy. During the ride Vance burst into tears, but he soon regained his composure, telling Wittkowsky that he cared less about his own fate than that of his family and the Old North State. Vance also resolved to present a brave front to his captors.[84]

Vance's usual high spirits returned, and he began regaling the Federals with jokes and anecdotes. Major Porter allowed Vance to ride on horseback to relieve the monotony of the journey, and he permitted the former governor to enter Salisbury without an escort. While in town Vance collected $65 from friends. He needed the money because his destination was Washington's Old Capitol Prison, where inmates paid for their meals. Vance said goodbye to Wittkowsky and boarded a train for Raleigh, where he collected an additional $40. Vance entered Old Capitol Prison on May 20, sharing a cell with former Virginia governor John Letcher. From his quarters, Vance could have heard the hoopla of the Grand Review, the Federals forming ranks under his very nose.[85]

Meanwhile, *Raleigh Standard* editor William W. Holden called on President Johnson at the latter's invitation. Believing that Holden had been a

Slide Back into the Union

wartime Unionist, Johnson appointed him provisional governor of North Carolina. Had the president desired to infuriate and alarm North Carolinians across the broadest possible political spectrum, he could not have made a better choice. Former Vance Conservatives and diehard Confederates alike denounced Holden for his presumed treachery as the leader of the Old North State's wartime peace movement, and they shared a similar revulsion for the "I told you so" tone the *Standard* editor had taken since the occupation of Raleigh. Holden had declared that "[i]f a Convention had been called twelve months ago, as we desired, North Carolina could have been saved from the calamity of invasion, arrangements might have been made by which the State could have returned to its allegiance to the Union with its existing government, and the gradual emancipation of slaves might have been secured. But now it is too late." Holden blamed Vance for the misfortunes befalling the state: "Our people must now, on account of his folly, or stupidity, or wickedness, or want of ordinary foresight, rise from the dust of subjugation to which he has reduced them, and take steps to place themselves where they were in 1860. They desire to do this as *Unionists*, with new men and under new forms, and they do not wish to be further embarrassed or oppressed by Gov. Vance and his exploded oligarchy." On May 9, Holden called for a $25,000 reward for Vance's capture.[86]

Most North Carolinians resented being told that they had erred in trusting Vance, and they despised Holden for gloating over his downfall. They also knew that the *Standard* editor was maneuvering to supplant the man who had routed him at the polls the year before. Calling Vance's landslide victory the result of "force and fraud," Holden argued that neither the governor nor the legislature reflected the will of the people. But Holden's appointment as provisional governor struck many Tar Heels as a truer reflection of those words. "Already the tyranny has commenced," wrote Elizabeth Collier, a young woman from the Goldsboro area. "Holden for governor— how low we are fallen!" Catherine Edmondston, the wife of a wealthy Halifax County planter, contended that the Federals had "taken the lowest, most abject, & degraded man they could find amongst us—one Holden— and exalted him to the post of provisional Governor—a base born bastard with neither the breeding or the instincts of a gentleman, is placed over us—and in utter defiance of the fact that six months since we utterly rejected him as not fit to be our exponent & head." In any event, Holden was the man the president had chosen to pave the way for North Carolina's readmission to the Union.[87]

On July 6, Vance was paroled from Old Capitol Prison. The reason for his release remains as mysterious as the reason for his arrest, but Vance was probably freed to care for his ailing wife. Soon after his release, Vance applied to Holden for a presidential pardon, but the provisional governor refused to intercede, thus eliminating a powerful political rival and settling an old score. Although Vance had to wait two years to receive a pardon, his political fortunes revived in the 1870s: he served again as governor and later as U.S. senator.[88]

The two ranking generals in North Carolina privately disagreed with Vance's arrest and imprisonment. John Schofield thought it "wiser to treat [Vance and other state officials] with contempt than to make lions of them," whereas Jacob Cox believed that a general amnesty was the best means of pacifying the South. But orders were orders and had to be obeyed. Neither Schofield nor Cox would participate in Reconstruction in North Carolina, but both men would play crucial roles elsewhere, Schofield overseeing Reconstruction in Virginia and Cox serving as governor of Ohio.[89]

Shortly before his departure from the Old North State, Cox visited the Guilford Court House battlefield near Greensboro. On March 15, 1781, American soldiers under Maj. Gen. Nathanael Greene had fought British and German troops commanded by Maj. Gen. Charles, the Earl Cornwallis. Cox noted that the Revolutionary War battle was a British victory resulting in so many British casualties that Cornwallis abandoned the campaign. A few dilapidated buildings remained to indicate the site of the old courthouse. Armed with General Greene's official report, Cox and his companions embarked on a staff ride of sorts. As the officers traced the progress of the battle, they soon realized from Greene's report that the topography had barely changed. "We could see the reasons for the movements on both sides," Cox recalled, "and how the undulations of surface, and the cover of woods and fences, were taken advantage of by either commander." As they excitedly tramped across the old battlefield, pointing to landmarks mentioned in Greene's report, the veteran officers glimpsed their own immortality:

> Military principles being the same in all times, we found ourselves criticizing the movements as if they had occurred on one of our own recent battlefields. It brought the older and the later war into startling nearness, and made us realize, as perhaps nothing else could have done how the future visitor will trace the movements in which we have had a part, and, when we have been dust for centuries, will follow the path of our battalions from hill to hill, from stream to stream, from the border of a wood to the open ground where the bloody conflict was hand to hand, and will comment upon the history we have made.[90]

Slide Back into the Union

Deeming it his duty to oversee the dispersal of his army, Joseph E. Johnston remained in North Carolina until the end of May. He was impressed with the conduct of the Federal occupation force, noting that the soldiers treated the North Carolinians as if they were New Yorkers or Ohioans. (Only later, when the Federal government under congressional Reconstruction established its presence in the South, would Johnston find cause to complain.) Now that his army was disbanded and the Confederate archives were in safe—if not desirable—hands, "Old Joe" felt free to resume his own life. Johnston had obtained Grant's permission to travel to Canada, but his wife's poor health induced him to take her to a Danville resort instead.[1]

Johnston could leave the Old North State with the satisfaction of having done his full duty. Thanks to the general's persistence at the bargaining table, his men enjoyed numerous advantages over the parolees of Lee's army. Johnston's veterans could take home their draft animals and field transportation and one-seventh of their rifle-muskets. Soldiers from the Trans-Mississippi enjoyed the benefits of rail and river travel. The men also carried Confederate salt, thread, and yarn with which to barter, and rations provided by the Union army. Each man had at least one silver dollar in his pocket—a pittance from an economic standpoint, but of inestimable symbolic value. In short, Johnston had provided for his men and thus minimized the depredations they committed on their homeward journey.

When Johnston assumed command in February 1865, he believed the most the Confederacy could gain by continuing the war was "fair terms of peace." Even so, "Old Joe" assembled his scattered forces in four hectic weeks and fought them at Bentonville with uncharacteristic boldness. No other Confederate general—not even Robert E. Lee—could have accomplished more with so few resources and in such a brief span.[2]

At Smithfield Johnston thoroughly overhauled his motley command, transforming it into a viable field army numbering more than 30,000 officers and men. Had Johnston's and Lee's armies combined, they would have presented a daunting challenge to Sherman and Grant. After Lee's surrender, Johnston kept his army well beyond the reach of Sherman's larger force, hoping to use this to his advantage at the bargaining table. By April 16, Johnston enjoyed a substantial head start on Sherman in the race to the Deep South. Had he chosen to, Johnston could have protracted the war indefinitely by slipping southward, but he realized that such a course would only further devastate the region without offering hope of success. Johnston also refused to scatter the Army of Tennessee or fight another pitched battle, believing that the former course would result in anarchy and the latter was tantamount to murder.

Johnston understood the necessity for opening negotiations with Sherman, even if President Davis and many of his troops steadfastly refused to concede that Lee's surrender meant the war was lost. "Old Joe" bore in mind that the Confederacy was hopelessly outnumbered, its morale shattered, its resources exhausted, and its commerce and industry almost nonexistent. He demonstrated considerable ability as a negotiator and on April 18 obtained terms that, according to Confederate attorney general George Davis, would enable the former Confederate states to "re-enter the Union on the same footing on which they stood before seceding from it." When Sherman's first agreement was rejected, Johnston insisted on a compromise: supplementary terms that softened the hardships of Southern soldiers and civilians alike. In defiance of President Davis, Johnston secured fair terms of peace for his army. During the final weeks of the war in the Old North State, Johnston's qualities as commander shone forth in their most favorable aspect.[3]

After spending several weeks in Chicago and his hometown of Lancaster, Ohio, William T. Sherman traveled to Louisville for a Fourth of July barbecue with his troops. By mid-July, "Uncle Billy" was ensconced at St. Louis as the commander of the Military Division of the Mississippi—retaining his old title, but receiving a new command. Upon his arrival, Sherman found a map of his march through the Carolinas awaiting him. He spread out the map on his desk and traced the routes of his grand army from Savannah to Goldsboro, represented by blue lines for each of his four infantry corps and his cavalry. But where were the routes leading from

Epilogue

Goldsboro to Raleigh, Durham's Station, Chapel Hill, and Aven's Ferry? Sherman made a mental note to add those to the next edition.[4]

He failed to realize that their inclusion would merely illustrate the futility of the Federal army's march from Goldsboro to Raleigh. Having allowed Johnston to escape from Bentonville, Sherman was later forced to chase a smaller and more mobile army that enjoyed a twenty-five-mile advantage—which increased to seventy-five miles after a week-long pursuit. This gap explains Sherman's repeated requests for Sheridan's cavalry to aid him in cornering Johnston's army. Fortunately for both Sherman and the people of central North Carolina, Lee's surrender induced Johnston to open negotiations, rendering further pursuit unnecessary. As a result, Sherman's final operations in North Carolina succeeded virtually by default.

The issue is not whether Sherman should have employed a more vigorous pursuit (he should have), but whether his final campaign should have been necessary. Had Sherman crushed Johnston at Bentonville on March 21, the war in his theater of operations would have ended that day. Some historians claim that Sherman exercised great restraint at Bentonville by *not* attacking, but was this restraint justified by the situation on the afternoon of March 21? Lee's army remained entrenched around Richmond and Petersburg, and the Confederacy was pinning its hopes (however desperate) on the concentration of Lee's and Johnston's armies. Had Sherman eliminated Johnston from the strategic picture, Lee would have found his remaining options even bleaker than before.

It is tempting to argue that subsequent events proved Sherman's restraint at Bentonville to be a humane course, as it spared the lives of hundreds, possibly thousands, of men on both sides. Perhaps this is true, but it is impossible to know how the elimination of Johnston's army would have affected the outcome of the war had it occurred on March 21. We do know that many men were killed or wounded in subsequent fighting in Virginia and North Carolina. Sherman indicated that his restraint was motivated by tactical and logistical factors rather than humanitarian concerns, and he even admitted his mistake in not crushing Johnston's army at Bentonville. Sherman's statements regarding the likelihood of at least one more pitched battle, his promotion of "Fighting Joe" Mower, and his repeated requests for Sheridan's cavalry all underscore his conviction that Bentonville was not his last battle. Sherman's so-called restraint at Bentonville was merely his native caution reasserting itself: given the choice between risking a pitched battle and allowing his enemy to escape, Sherman chose the safer course. Had Grant made such a choice during his pursuit of Lee's army after the fall of Richmond, the war might have been prolonged indefinitely.

For all his faults as a battlefield tactician, Sherman possessed boldness and originality as a strategist, as his marches through Georgia and the Carolinas amply demonstrate. By virtue of their devastating effect on Confederate logistics and morale, Sherman's marches hastened the South's collapse in the spring of 1865. The march from Savannah to Goldsboro demonstrates Sherman's freedom from contemporary military dogma, particularly in his confident maneuvering of a large army without supply lines through a hostile territory in mid-winter. During the Civil War, only Sherman's army executed such an operation on so grand a scale.

Sherman was equally bold in offering generous surrender terms that extended into the political realm. Although his first terms were rejected by the president and cabinet, Sherman remained convinced that they offered the best means of reuniting the country. When the U.S. government abandoned its Reconstruction policy in 1877, Sherman believed that his conciliatory course was at last vindicated.

The final days of the war in North Carolina saw Union and Confederate armies still maneuvering and fighting a week after Lee's surrender. Two generals transformed a surrender negotiation into an attempt to heal their divided nation and oversaw the largest troop surrender of the war, involving two armies separated by a distance of eighty miles. The drama of these events underscores their historical significance: truly this was an astounding close to the nation's bloodiest and most divisive conflict.[5]

APPENDIX A

Postmaster General John H. Reagan's
"Basis of Pacification," April 18, 1865

As the avowed motive of the Government of the United States for the prosecution of the existing war with the Confederate States is to secure a reunion of all the States under one common government, and as wisdom and sound policy alike require that a common government should rest on the consent and be supported by the affections of all the people who compose it, now in order to ascertain whether it be practicable to put an end to the existing war and to the consequent destruction of life and property, having in view the correspondence and conversation which has recently taken place between Maj. Gen. W. T. Sherman and myself, I propose the following points as a basis of pacification:

First. The disbanding of the military forces of the Confederacy; and,

Second. The recognition of the Constitution and authority of the Government of the United States on the following conditions:

Third. The preservation and continuance of the existing State governments.

Fourth. The preservation to the people of all the political rights and rights of person and property secured to them by the Constitution of the United States and of their several States.

Fifth. Freedom from future prosecution or penalties for their participation in the present war.

Sixth. Agreement to a general suspension of hostilities pending these negotiations.

General Johnston will see that the accompanying memorandum omits all reference to details and to the necessary action of the States and the preliminary reference of the proposition to General Grant for his consent to the suspension of hostilities, and to the Government of United States for its action. He will also see that I have modified the first article, according to his suggestion, by omitting the reference to the consent of the President of the Confederate States and to his employing his good offices to secure the acquiescence of the several States to this scheme of adjustment and pacification. This may be done at a proper subsequent time.

JOHN H. REAGAN

[*Source: OR* 47(3): 244–45, 806–7.]

APPENDIX B

Maj. Gen. William T. Sherman's
"Memorandum or Basis of Agreement," April 18, 1865

Memorandum or basis of agreement made this 18th day of April, A.D. 1865, near Durham's Station, in the State of North Carolina, by and between General Joseph E. Johnston, commanding the Confederate army, and Maj. Gen. William T. Sherman, commanding the army of the United States in North Carolina, both present.

First. The contending armies now in the field to maintain the status quo until notice is given by the commanding general of any one to its opponent, and reasonable time, say forty-eight hours, allowed.

Second. The Confederate armies now in existence to be disbanded and conducted to their several State capitals, there to deposit their arms and public property in the State arsenal, and each officer and man to execute and file an agreement to cease from acts of war and to abide the action of both State and Federal authority. The number of arms and munitions of war to be reported to the Chief of Ordnance at Washington City, subject to the future action of the Congress of the United States, and in the meantime to be used solely to maintain peace and order within the borders of the States, respectively.

Third. The recognition by the Executive of the United States of the several State governments on their officers and legislatures taking the oaths prescribed by the Constitution of the United States, and where conflicting State governments have resulted from the war the legitimacy of all shall be submitted to the Supreme Court of the United States.

Fourth. The re-establishment of all the Federal courts in the several States, with powers as defined by the Constitution and laws of Congress.

Fifth. The people and inhabitants of all the States to be guaranteed, so far as the Executive can, their political rights and franchises, as well as their rights of person and property, as defined by the Constitution of the United States and of the States, respectively.

Sixth. The Executive authority of the Government of the United States not to disturb any of the people by reason of the late war so long as they live in peace and quiet, abstain from acts of armed hostility, and obey the laws in existence at the place of their residence.

Seventh. In general terms, the war to cease, a general amnesty, so far as the Executive of the United States can command, on condition of the disbandment of the

Confederate armies, the distribution of the arms, and the resumption of peaceful pursuits by the officers and men hitherto composing said armies.

Not being fully empowered by our respective principles to fulfill these terms, we individually and officially pledge ourselves to promptly obtain the necessary authority and to carry out the above programme.

W. T. SHERMAN,
Major-General, Comdg. Army United States in North Carolina.

J. E. JOHNSTON,
General, Commanding. C.S. Army in North Carolina.

[*Source: OR* 47(3): 243–44.]

APPENDIX C

Maj. Gen. John M. Schofield's "Terms of a Military Convention" and "Supplemental Terms," April 26, 1865

Terms of a military convention entered into this 26th day of April, 1865, at Bennett's house, near Durham's Station, N.C., between General Joseph E. Johnston, commanding the Confederate Army, and Maj. Gen. W. T. Sherman, commanding the United States Army in North Carolina.

1. All acts of war on the part of the troops under General Johnston's command to cease from this date.

2. All arms and public property to be deposited at Greensborough, and delivered to an ordnance officer of the United States Army.

3. Rolls of all the officers and men to be made in duplicate, one copy to be retained by the commander of the troops, and the other to be given to an officer to be designated by General Sherman, each officer and man to give his individual obligation in writing not to take up arms against the Government of the United States until properly released from this obligation.

4. The side arms of officers and their private horses and baggage to be retained by them.

5. This being done, all the officers and men will be permitted to return to their homes, not to be disturbed by the United States authorities so long as they observe their obligation and the laws in force where they may reside.

W. T. SHERMAN,
Major-General, Commanding U.S. Forces in North Carolina.

J. E. JOHNSTON,
General, Commanding C.S. Forces in North Carolina.

RALEIGH, N.C., April 26, 1865.
Approved:

U. S. GRANT,
Lieutenant-General.

Military Convention of April 26, 1865.—Supplemental Terms.

I. The field transportation to be loaned to the troops for their march to their homes, and for subsequent use in their industrial pursuits. Artillery horses may be used in field transportation if necessary.

II. Each brigade or separate body to retain a number of arms equal to one-seventh of its effective total, which, when the troops reach capitals of their States, will be disposed of as the general commanding the department may direct.

III. Private horses and other private property of both officers and men to be retained by them.

IV. The commanding general of the Military Division of West Mississippi, Major-General Canby, will be requested to give transportation by water from Mobile or New Orleans to the troops from Arkansas and Texas.

V. The obligations of officers and soldiers to be signed by their immediate commanders.

VI. Naval forces within the limits of General Johnston's command to be included in the terms of this convention.

J. M. SCHOFIELD,
Major-General, Commanding U.S. Forces in North Carolina.

J. E. JOHNSTON,
General, Commanding C.S. Troops in North Carolina.

[*Source: OR* 47(3): 313, 321, 482.]

APPENDIX D

Lt. Gen. Ulysses S. Grant's Terms of Agreement Entered into with Gen. Robert E. Lee at Appomattox Court House, Virginia, April 9, 1865, and Supplementary Terms, April 10, 1865

General R. E. Lee,
Commanding C.S. Army:

GENERAL: In accordance with the substance of my letter to you of the 8th instant, I propose to receive the surrender of the Army of Northern Virginia on the following terms, to wit: Rolls of all the officers and men to be made in duplicate—one copy to be given to an officer to be designated by me, the other to be retained by such officer or officers as you may designate; the officers to give their individual paroles not to take up arms against the Government of the United States until properly exchanged, and each company or regimental commander sign a like parole for the men of their commands. The arms, artillery, and public property to be parked and stacked, and turned over to the officers appointed by me to receive them. This will not embrace the side-arms of the officers, nor their private horses or baggage. This done, each officer and man will be allowed to return to their homes, not to be disturbed by United States authority so long as they observe their paroles and the laws in force where they may reside.

Very respectfully,
U. S. GRANT

Agreement entered into this day in regard to the surrender of the Army of Northern Virginia to the United States authorities.

1st. The troops shall march by brigades and detachments to a designated point, stack their arms, deposit their flags, sabers, pistols, &c., and from thence march to their homes under charge of their officers, superintended by their respective division and corps commanders, officers retaining their side arms, and the authorized number of private horses.

2nd. All public horses and public property of all kinds to be turned over to staff officers designated by the United States authorities.

3rd. Such transportation as may be agreed upon as necessary for the transportation of the private baggage of officers will be allowed to accompany the officers, to be turned over at the end of the trip to the nearest U.S. quartermasters, receipts being taken for the same.

4th. Couriers and mounted men of the artillery and cavalry, whose horses are their own private property, will be allowed to retain them.

5th. The surrender of the Army of Northern Virginia shall be construed to include all the forces operating with that army on the 8th instant, the date of commencement of negotiation for surrender, except such bodies of cavalry as actually made their escape previous to the surrender, and except also such pieces of artillery as were more than twenty miles from Appomattox Court-House at the time of surrender on the 9th instant.

JOHN GIBBON,
Major-General of Volunteers.

CHAS. GRIFFIN,
Brevet Major-General, U.S. Volunteers.

W. MERRITT,
Brevet Major-General.

J. LONGSTREET,
Lieutenant-General.

J. B. GORDON,
Major-General.

W. N. PENDLETON,
Brigadier-General and Chief of Artillery.

[*Source: OR* 46(3): 665, 685–86.]

APPENDIX E

Text of Parole Issued to Confederate Soldiers
in North Carolina

[This is a copy of the parole issued to Lt. Col. Joseph B. Starr,
commander of an artillery contingent in the Army of Tennessee.]

Greensboro, North Carolina.
May 1, 1865.
In accordance with the terms of the Military Convention entered into on the twenty-
sixth day of April, 1865, between General JOSEPH E. JOHNSTON, Commanding the
Confederate Army, and Major-General W. T. SHERMAN, Commanding the United
States Army in North Carolina,

       J. B. Starr, Lt. Col., 13th N. C. Battn. Lt. Artillery

has given his solemn obligation not to take up arms against the Government of the
United States until properly released from this obligation; and is permitted to return to his home, not to be disturbed by the United States authorities so long as he
observe this obligation and obey the laws in force where he may reside.

Wm. Hartsuff	J. B. Starr
Brevet Brig. Genl. & A.I.G., U.S.A.,	Lt. Col., C.S.A.,
Special Commissioner.	*Commanding.*

[*Source:* Parole of Lt. Col. Joseph B. Starr, May 1, 1865, Joseph B. Starr Papers,
NCDAH.]

APPENDIX F
Organization of Union Forces

ARMIES IN NORTH CAROLINA COMMANDED BY
Maj. Gen. William T. Sherman (88,948)

    Headquarters Guard
        7th Company Ohio Sharpshooters, *Lt. James Cox*
    Engineers and Mechanics
        1st Michigan, *Col. John B. Yates*
        1st Missouri (five companies), *Lt. Col. William Tweeddale*
    Artillery
        Bvt. Maj. Gen. William F. Barry

RIGHT WING (28,834)
(ARMY OF THE TENNESSEE)
Maj. Gen. Oliver O. Howard

    Escort
        5th Illinois Cavalry (Co. K), *Capt. William Duncan*
        4th Company Ohio Cavalry, *Capt. John L. King*
    Pontoon Train Guard
        14th Wisconsin (Co. E), *Capt. William I. Henry*

FIFTEENTH ARMY CORPS (15,670)
    Maj. Gen. John A. Logan

    First Division
        Bvt. Maj. Gen. Charles R. Woods

    First Brigade
        Bvt. Brig. Gen. William B. Woods
        12th Indiana, *Col. Reuben Williams*
        26th Iowa, *Maj. John Lubbers*

27th Missouri, *Col. Thomas Curly*

31st/32nd Missouri (six companies), *Lt. Col. Abraham J. Seay*

76th Ohio, *Lt. Col. Edward Briggs*

Second Brigade

Col. Robert F. Catterson

26th Illinois, *Lt. Col. Ira J. Bloomfield*

40th Illinois, *Lt. Col. Hiram W. Hall*

103rd Illinois, *Lt. Col. George W. Wright*

97th Indiana, *Lt. Col. Aden G. Cavins*

100th Indiana, *Maj. Ruel M. Johnson, Capt. John W. Headington*

6th Iowa, *Lt. Col. William H. Clune*

46th Ohio, *Lt. Col. Edward N. Upton*

Third Brigade

Col. George A. Stone

4th Iowa, *Maj. Albert R. Anderson*

9th Iowa, *Maj. Alonzo Abernethy*

25th Iowa, *Lt. Col. David J. Palmer*

30th Iowa, *Lt. Col. Aurelius Roberts*

31st Iowa, *Lt. Col. Jeremiah W. Jenkins*

Second Division

Maj. Gen. William B. Hazen

First Brigade

Col. Theodore Jones

55th Illinois, *Capt. Charles A. Andress*

116th Illinois, *Lt. Col. John E. Maddux, Capt. Necolas Geschwind*

127th Illinois, *Lt. Col. Frank S. Curtiss*

6th Missouri, *Lt. Col. Delos Van Deusen*

30th Ohio, *Lt. Col. Emerson P. Brooks*

57th Ohio, *Lt. Col. Samuel R. Mott*

Second Brigade

Col. Wells S. Jones

111th Illinois, *Col. James S. Martin*

83rd Indiana, *Capt. Charles W. White, Capt. William N. Craw*

37th Ohio, *Lt. Col. Louis von Blessingh*

47th Ohio, *Col. Augustus C. Parry*

53rd Ohio, *Maj. Preston R. Galloway*

54th Ohio, *Lt. Col. Israel T. Moore*

Third Brigade

Brig. Gen. John M. Oliver

48th Illinois, *Lt. Col. Thomas L. B. Weems*

90th Illinois, *Lt. Col. Owen Stuart*

99th Indiana, *Capt. Josiah Farrar*

15th Michigan, *Lt. Col. Frederick S. Hutchinson*

70th Ohio, *Lt. Col. Henry L. Philips*

Third Division
    Bvt. Maj. Gen. John E. Smith

First Brigade
    Brig. Gen. William Clark
    63rd Illinois, *Col. Joseph B. McCown, Capt. Joseph R. Stanford*
    93rd Illinois, *Lt. Col. Nicholas C. Buswell*
    48th Indiana, *Capt. Newton Bingham*
    59th Indiana, *Lt. Col. Jefferson K. Scott, Maj. Thomas A. McNaught*
    4th Minnesota, *Col. John E. Tourtellotte, Capt. Leverett R. Wellman*
    18th Wisconsin, *Lt. Col. Charles H. Jackson*
Second Brigade
    Col. Clark R. Wever
    Col. John E. Tourtellotte
    56th Illinois, *Lt. Col. John P. Hall*
    10th Iowa, *Lt. Col. William H. Silsby*
    17th Iowa (one company), *Capt. William Horner*
    10th/26th Missouri (two companies), *Lt. Theron M. Rice*
    80th Ohio, *Lt. Col. Pren Metham, Maj. Thomas C. Morris*

Fourth Division
    Bvt. Maj. Gen. John M. Corse

First Brigade
    Brig. Gen. Elliott W. Rice
    52nd Illinois, *Lt. Col. Jerome D. Davis*
    66th Indiana, *Lt. Col. Roger Martin*
    2nd Iowa, *Col. Noel B. Howard*
    7th Iowa, *Lt. Col. James C. Parrott*
Second Brigade
    Col. Robert N. Adams
    12th Illinois, *Lt. Col. Henry Van Sellar*
    66th Illinois, *Lt. Col. Andrew K. Campbell*
    81st Ohio, *Maj. William C. Henry*
Third Brigade
    Col. Frederick J. Hurlbut
    7th Illinois, *Lt. Col. Hector Perrin*
    50th Illinois, *Lt. Col. William Hanna*
    57th Illinois, *Maj. Frederick A. Battey*
    39th Iowa, *Lt. Col. Joseph M. Griffiths*
Unassigned
    29th Missouri Mounted Infantry, *Col. Joseph S. Gage*
    110th U.S. Colored Troops, *Maj. William C. Hawley, Capt. Thomas
        Kennedy, Capt. Zac. C. Wilson, Capt. Jacob Kemnitzer*
Artillery
    Lt. Col. William H. Ross

1st Illinois, Battery H, *Capt. Francis DeGress, Lt. Robert S. Gray*
1st Michigan, Battery B, *Lt. Edward B. Wright*
1st Missouri, Battery H, *Capt. Charles M. Callahan*
12th Wisconsin Battery, *Capt. William Zickerick*

SEVENTEENTH ARMY CORPS (13,164)
Maj. Gen. Frank P. Blair Jr.
11th Illinois Cavalry (Co. G), *Capt. Stephen S. Tripp*

First Division
Maj. Gen. Joseph A. Mower
Brig. Gen. Manning F. Force

First Brigade
Brig. Gen. John W. Fuller
64th Illinois, *Maj. Joseph S. Reynolds*
18th Missouri, *Col. Charles S. Sheldon, Lt. Col. William H. Minter,*
Maj. William M. Edgar
27th Ohio, *Maj. Isaac N. Gilruth*
39th Ohio, *Lt. Col. Daniel Weber*
Second Brigade
Brig. Gen. John W. Sprague
35th New Jersey, *Col. John J. Cladek*
43rd Ohio, *Maj. Horace Park*
63rd Ohio, *Maj. Oscar L. Jackson*
25th Wisconsin, *Lt. Col. Jeremiah M. Rusk*
Third Brigade
Col. Charles H. DeGroat
Bvt. Brig. Gen. John Tillson
10th Illinois, *Lt. Col. David Gillespie*
25th Indiana, *Lt. Col. James S. Wright*
32nd Wisconsin, *Lt. Col. Joseph H. Carleton, Maj. William H. Burrows*

Third Division
Bvt. Maj. Gen. Mortimer D. Leggett

First Brigade
Brig. Gen. Charles Ewing
20th Illinois, *Capt. Henry King*
30th Illinois, *Lt. Col. William C. Rhoades, Capt. John P. Davis*
31st Illinois, *Lt. Col. Robert N. Pearson*
45th Illinois, *Maj. John O. Duer*
12th Wisconsin, *Col. James K. Proudfit*
16th Wisconsin, *Col. Cassius Fairchild*
Second Brigade
Brig. Gen. Robert K. Scott

20th Ohio, *Lt. Col. Harrison Wilson*
68th Ohio, *Lt. Col. George E. Welles*
78th Ohio, *Col. Greenberry F. Wiles, Lt. Col. Gilbert D. Munson*
17th Wisconsin, *Col. Adam G. Malloy*

Fourth Division
Bvt. Maj. Gen. Giles A. Smith

First Brigade
Brig. Gen. Benjamin F. Potts
14th/15th Illinois Battalion, *Col. George C. Rogers*
53rd Illinois, *Col. John W. McClanahan*
23rd Indiana, *Lt. Col. George S. Babbitt, Capt. John W. Hammond*
53rd Indiana, *Col. Warner L. Vestal*
32nd Ohio, *Lt. Col. Jefferson J. Hibbets*
Third Brigade
Brig. Gen. William W. Belknap
32nd Illinois, *Capt. John J. Rider*
11th Iowa, *Lt. Col. Benjamin Beach*
13th Iowa, *Lt. Col. Justin C. Kennedy*
15th Iowa, *Maj. George Pomutz*
16th Iowa, *Maj. John H. Smith*
Unassigned
9th Illinois Mounted Infantry, *Lt. Col. Samuel T. Hughes*
Artillery
Maj. Frederick Welker
1st Michigan, Battery C, *Lt. William W. Hyzer*
1st Minnesota Battery, *Capt. William Z. Clayton*
15th Ohio Battery, *Capt. James Burdick*

LEFT WING (28,063)
(ARMY OF GEORGIA)
Maj. Gen. Henry W. Slocum

Pontoniers
58th Indiana, *Lt. Col. Joseph Moore*

FOURTEENTH ARMY CORPS (15,098)
Bvt. Maj. Gen. Jefferson C. Davis

Provost Guard
Lt. Col. E. Hibbard Topping
110th Illinois (nine companies)
24th Illinois (Co. A)

Appendix F

First Division
   Brig. Gen. Charles C. Walcutt

   First Brigade
      Bvt. Brig. Gen. Harrison C. Hobart
      104th Illinois, *Maj. John H. Widmer*
      42nd Indiana, *Maj. Gideon R. Kellams*
      88th Indiana, *Maj. Lewis J. Blair*
      33rd Ohio, *Capt. Joseph Hinson*
      94th Ohio, *Maj. William H. Snider*
      21st Wisconsin, *Lt. Col. Michael H. Fitch*
   Second Brigade
      Bvt. Brig. Gen. George P. Buell
      13th Michigan, *Capt. Silas A. Yerkes*
      21st Michigan, *Lt. Col. Loomis K. Bishop*
      69th Ohio, *Lt. Col. Joseph H. Brigham*
   Third Brigade
      Col. Henry A. Hambright
      38th Indiana, *Capt. David H. Patton*
      21st Ohio, *Lt. Col. Arnold McMahan*
      74th Ohio, *Maj. Robert P. Findley*
      79th Pennsylvania, *Capt. John S. McBride*

Second Division
   Bvt. Maj. Gen. James D. Morgan

   Provost Guard
      110th Illinois (Co. B), *Capt. William R. Hester*
   First Brigade
      Brig. Gen. William Vandever
      16th Illinois, *Capt. Herman Lund*
      60th Illinois, *Maj. James H. McDonald*
      10th Michigan, *Capt. William H. Dunphy*
      14th Michigan, *Lt. Col. George W. Grummond*
      17th New York, *Maj. Alexander S. Marshall*
   Second Brigade
      Brig. Gen. John G. Mitchell
      34th Illinois, *Lt. Col. Peter Ege*
      78th Illinois, *Lt. Col. Maris R. Vernon*
      98th Ohio, *Maj. David E. Roatch*
      108th Ohio, *Lt. Col. Joseph Good*
      113th Ohio, *Capt. Otway Watson*
      121st Ohio, *Maj. Aaron B. Robinson*
   Third Brigade
      Lt. Col. James W. Langley
      85th Illinois, *Capt. James R. Griffith*

Appendix F

86th Illinois, *Lt. Col. Allen L. Fahnestock*
125th Illinois, *Capt. George W. Cook*
22nd Indiana, *Capt. William H. Snodgrass*
37th Indiana (one company), *Lt. Socrates Carver*
52nd Ohio, *Maj. James T. Holmes*

Third Division
Bvt. Maj. Gen. Absalom Baird

First Brigade
Col. Morton C. Hunter
82nd Indiana, *Lt. Col. John M. Matheny*
23rd Missouri (four companies), *Maj. John H. Jolly*
11th Ohio (detachment), *Capt. Francis H. Loring*
17th Ohio, *Lt. Col. Benjamin H. Showers*
31st Ohio, *Capt. Michael Stone, Capt. Eli Wilkin*
89th Ohio, *Lt. Col. William H. Glenn*
92nd Ohio, *Lt. Col. John C. Morrow*
Second Brigade
Col. Newell Gleason
75th Indiana, *Lt. Col. William O'Brien*
87th Indiana, *Lt. Col. Edwin P. Hammond*
101st Indiana, *Lt. Col. Thomas Doan*
2nd Minnesota, *Lt. Col. Judson W. Bishop*
105th Ohio, *Lt. Col. George T. Perkins*
Third Brigade
Lt. Col. Hubbard K. Milward
Brig. Gen. George S. Greene
74th Indiana, *Lt. Col. Thomas Morgan*
18th Kentucky, *Maj. John J. Hall, Lt. Col. Hubbard K. Milward*
14th Ohio, *Lt. Col. Albert Moore*
38th Ohio, *Capt. Charles M. Gilbert*
Artillery
Maj. Charles Houghtaling
1st Illinois, Battery C, *Lt. Palmer F. Scovel*
2nd Illinois, Battery I, *Lt. Judson Rich*
19th Indiana Battery, *Lt. Clinton Keeler*
5th Wisconsin Battery, *Capt. Joseph McKnight, Lt. Elijah Booth Jr.*

TWENTIETH ARMY CORPS (12,965)
Bvt. Maj. Gen. Alpheus S. Williams
Maj. Gen. Joseph A. Mower

First Division
Brig. Gen. Nathaniel J. Jackson
Bvt. Maj. Gen. Alpheus S. Williams

First Brigade
>   *Bvt. Brig. Gen. James L. Selfridge*
>   5th Connecticut, *Lt. Col. Henry W. Daboll*
>   123rd New York, *Col. James C. Rogers*
>   141st New York, *Lt. Col. Andrew J. McNett*
>   46th Pennsylvania, *Maj. Patrick Griffith*

Second Brigade
>   *Bvt. Brig. Gen. William Hawley*
>   2nd Massachusetts, *Capt. Edward A. Phalen*
>   13th New Jersey, *Lt. Col. Frederick H. Harris*
>   107th New York, *Col. Nirom M. Crane*
>   150th New York, *Col. Alfred B. Smith*
>   3rd Wisconsin, *Lt. Col. George W. Stevenson*

Third Brigade
>   *Brig. Gen. James S. Robinson*
>   82nd Illinois, *Lt. Col. Edward S. Salomon*
>   101st Illinois, *Lt. Col. John B. LeSage*
>   143rd New York, *Col. Horace Boughton*
>   82nd Ohio (comprising 61st and 82nd Ohio), *Maj. James S. Crall*
>   31st Wisconsin, *Col. Francis H. West*

Second Division
>   *Bvt. Maj. Gen. John W. Geary*

First Brigade
>   *Col. George W. Mindil*
>   *Bvt. Brig. Gen. Ario Pardee Jr.*
>   5th Ohio, *Lt. Col. Robert Kirkup*
>   29th Ohio, *Lt. Col. Jonas Schoonover*
>   66th Ohio, *Lt. Col. Eugene Powell, Capt. Theodoric G. Keller*
>   28th Pennsylvania, *Lt. Col. James Fitzpatrick*
>   147th Pennsylvania, *Lt. Col. John Craig*

Second Brigade
>   *Col. Patrick H. Jones*
>   33rd New Jersey, *Lt. Col. Enos Fourat, Maj. Nathaniel K. Bray*
>   119th New York, *Col. John T. Lockman*
>   134th New York, *Lt. Col. Allan H. Jackson*
>   154th New York, *Lt. Col. Lewis D. Warner*
>   73rd Pennsylvania, *Maj. Christian H. Goebel*

Third Brigade
>   *Bvt. Brig. Gen. Henry A. Barnum*
>   60th New York, *Lt. Col. Lester S. Wilson*
>   102nd New York, *Maj. Oscar J. Spaulding*
>   137th New York, *Lt. Col. Koert S. Van Voorhees*
>   149th New York, *Maj. Nicholas Grumbach*
>   29th Pennsylvania, *Col. Samuel M. Zulich*

Appendix F

111th Pennsylvania (comprising 109th and 111th Pennsylvania),
    Col. Thomas M. Walker

Third Division
    Bvt. Maj. Gen. William T. Ward

First Brigade
    Col. Henry Case
    Bvt. Brig. Gen. Benjamin Harrison
    102nd Illinois, *Col. Franklin C. Smith*
    105th Illinois, *Lt. Col. Everell F. Dutton*
    129th Illinois, *Lt. Col. Thomas H. Flynn, Col. Henry Case*
    70th Indiana, *Lt. Col. Samuel Merrill*
    79th Ohio, *Lt. Col. Azariah W. Doan*
Second Brigade
    Bvt. Brig. Gen. Daniel Dustin
    33rd Indiana, *Lt. Col. James E. Burton*
    85th Indiana, *Lt. Col. Alexander B. Crane*
    19th Michigan, *Maj. David Anderson*
    22nd Wisconsin, *Lt. Col. Edward Bloodgood*
Third Brigade
    Bvt. Brig. Gen. William Cogswell
    20th Connecticut, *Lt. Col. Philo B. Buckingham*
    33rd Massachusetts, *Lt. Col. Elisha Doane*
    136th New York, *Col. James Wood Jr.*
    55th Ohio, *Maj. Charles P. Wickham*
    73rd Ohio, *Maj. Thomas W. Higgins*
    26th Wisconsin, *Maj. Francis Lackner*
Artillery
    Maj. John A. Reynolds
    Capt. Charles E. Winegar
    1st New York, Battery I, *Capt. Charles E. Winegar, Lt. Warren L. Scott*
    1st New York, Battery M, *Capt. Edward P. Newkirk*
    1st Ohio, Battery C, *Lt. Jerome B. Stephens*
    Pennsylvania Light, Battery E, *Capt. Thomas S. Sloan*

CENTER (26,392)
(ARMY OF THE OHIO)
Maj. Gen. John M. Schofield

Escort
    7th Ohio Cavalry (Co. G), *Capt. John A. Ashbury*
Signal Corps
    Capt. Edmund H. Russell

Engineers
  15th New York (three companies), *Maj. Henry V. Slosson*
Artillery
  Lt. Col. Terance J. Kennedy

TENTH ARMY CORPS (12,099)
  Maj. Gen. Alfred H. Terry

Escort
  20th New York Cavalry (Co. I), *Capt. John J. Carroll*

First Division
  Bvt. Maj. Gen. Henry W. Birge

(First Brigade at Morehead City and Second Brigade at Wilmington.)
Third Brigade
  Col. Nicholas W. Day
  24th Iowa, *Lt. Col. Edward Wright*
  38th Massachusetts, *Lt. Col. James P. Richardson*
  128th New York, *Capt. Henry H. Sincerbox*
  156th New York, *Capt. Alfred Cooley*
  175th New York (five companies), *Capt. Charles McCarthey*
  176th New York, *Maj. Charles Lewis*
Artillery
  22nd Indiana Battery, *Lt. George W. Alexander*

Second Division
  Bvt. Maj. Gen. Adelbert Ames

First Brigade
  Col. Rufus Daggett
  3rd New York, *Lt. Col. Alfred Dunham*
  112th New York, *Col. Ephraim A. Ludwick*
  117th New York, *Capt. Edward Downer*
  142nd New York, *Col. Albert M. Barney*
Second Brigade
  Col. William B. Coan
  Col. John S. Littell
  47th New York, *Col. Christopher R. MacDonald*
  48th New York, *Capt. Van Rensselaer K. Hilliard, Col. William B. Coan*
  76th Pennsylvania, *Maj. Charles Knerr*
  97th Pennsylvania, *Lt. Col. John Wainwright*
  203rd Pennsylvania, *Lt. Col. Amos W. Bachman*
Third Brigade
  Col. G. Frederick Granger
  13th Indiana, *Lt. Col. Samuel M. Zent*

9th Maine, *Lt. Col. Joseph Noble*

4th New Hampshire, *Capt. John H. Roberts*

115th New York, *Lt. Col. Nathan J. Johnson*

169th New York, *Col. James A. Colvin*

Artillery

16th New York Battery, *Capt. Richard H. Lee*

Third Division

Brig. Gen. Charles J. Paine

First Brigade

Bvt. Brig. Gen. Delevan Bates

1st U.S. Colored Troops, *Lt. Col. Giles H. Rich*

30th U.S. Colored Troops, *Lt. Col. Hiram A. Oakman*

107th U.S. Colored Troops, *Col. William H. Revere Jr.*

Second Brigade

Bvt. Brig. Gen. Samuel A. Duncan

4th U.S. Colored Troops, *Lt. Col. George Rogers*

5th U.S. Colored Troops, *Col. Giles W. Shurtleff*

39th U.S. Colored Troops, *Col. Ozora P. Stearns*

Third Brigade

Col. John H. Holman

Bvt. Brig. Gen. Albert M. Blackman

6th U.S. Colored Troops, *Col. John W. Ames*

27th U.S. Colored Troops, *Lt. Col. John W. Donnellan*

37th U.S. Colored Troops, *Col. Nathan Goff Jr.*

Unattached

3rd U.S. Artillery, Battery E, *Lt. John R. Myrick*

TWENTY-THIRD ARMY CORPS (14,293)

Maj. Gen. Jacob D. Cox

Engineer Battalion

Capt. Oliver S. McClure

Provost Guard

9th New Jersey (Co. H), *Capt. Edward S. Pullen*

Artillery

Lt. Col. George W. Schofield

Capt. Giles J. Cockerill

First Division

Bvt. Maj. Gen. Thomas H. Ruger

First Brigade

Bvt. Brig. Gen. Israel N. Stiles

120th Indiana, *Col. Allen W. Prather*

124th Indiana, *Col. John M. Orr*
128th Indiana, *Lt. Col. Jasper Packard*
180th Indiana, *Col. Willard Warner*
Second Brigade
Col. John C. McQuiston
123rd Indiana, *Lt. Col. Dewitt C. Walters*
129th Indiana, *Col. Charles A. Zollinger*
130th Indiana, *Col. Charles S. Parrish*
28th Michigan, *Col. William W. Wheeler*
Third Brigade
Col. Minor T. Thomas
25th Massachusetts, *Lt. Col. James Tucker*
8th Minnesota, *Maj. George A. Camp*
174th Ohio, *Col. John S. Jones*
178th Ohio, *Col. Joab A. Stafford*
Artillery
Elgin Battery (Illinois), *Capt. Andrew M. Wood*

Second Division
Maj. Gen. Darius N. Couch
Brig. Gen. Joseph A. Cooper

First Brigade
Col. Orlando H. Moore
Brig. Gen. Joseph A. Cooper
26th Kentucky, *Col. Thomas B. Farleigh*
25th Michigan, *Lt. Col. Benjamin F. Orcutt*
132nd New York (with detachment of 99th New York),
Col. Peter J. Claassen
52nd Pennsylvania, *Lt. Col. John B. Conyngham*
Second Brigade
Col. John Mehringer
107th Illinois, *Maj. Thomas J. Milholland*
80th Indiana, *Lt. Col. Alfred D. Owen*
23rd Michigan, *Col. Oliver L. Spaulding*
111th Ohio, *Lt. Col. Isaac R. Sherwood*
118th Ohio, *Lt. Col. Edgar Sowers*
Third Brigade
Col. Silas A. Strickland
91st Indiana, *Lt. Col. Charles H. Butterfield*
50th Ohio, *Capt. John S. Conahan, Lt. Col. James A. Bope*
181st Ohio, *Lt. Col. John E. Hudson, Col. John O'Dowd*
183rd Ohio, *Col. George W. Hoge*
Artillery
19th Ohio Battery, *Capt. Frank Wilson*

Appendix F

Third Division
> Brig. Gen. James W. Reilly
> Brig. Gen. Samuel P. Carter

Provost Guard
> 100th Ohio (Co. F), Lt. John P. Denny

First Brigade
> Col. Oscar W. Sterl
> 12th Kentucky, Lt. Col. Laurence H. Rousseau
> 16th Kentucky, Lt. Col. John S. White
> 100th Ohio, Capt. Frank Rundell
> 104th Ohio, Lt. Col. William J. Jordan
> 8th Tennessee, Capt. James W. Berry

Second Brigade
> Bvt. Brig. Gen. John S. Casement
> 65th Illinois, Lt. Col. William S. Stewart
> 65th Indiana, Lt. Col. John W. Hammond
> 9th New Jersey, Col. James Stewart Jr.
> 103rd Ohio, Capt. Henry S. Pickands
> 177th Ohio, Lt. Col. William H. Zimmerman

Third Brigade
> Bvt. Brig. Gen. Thomas J. Henderson
> 112th Illinois, Lt. Col. Emery S. Bond
> 63rd Indiana, Lt. Col. Daniel Morris, Maj. Frank Wilcox
> 140th Indiana, Col. Thomas J. Brady
> 17th Massachusetts, Lt. Col. Henry Splaine

Artillery
> 1st Ohio, Battery D, Capt. Giles J. Cockerill, Lt. Cecil C. Reed

Third Division—Cavalry (5,659)
> Bvt. Major Gen. Judson Kilpatrick

First Brigade
> Bvt. Brig. Gen. Thomas J. Jordan
> 8th Indiana (with battalion of 3rd Indiana), Lt. Col. Fielder A. Jones
> 2nd Kentucky, Maj. Owen Star
> 3rd Kentucky, Lt. Col. Robert H. King
> 9th Pennsylvania, Lt. Col. David H. Kimmel

Second Brigade
> Bvt. Brig. Gen. Smith D. Atkins
> 92nd Illinois Mounted Infantry, Lt. Col. Matthew Van Buskirk
> 9th Michigan, Col. George S. Acker
> 9th Ohio, Col. William D. Hamilton
> 10th Ohio, Col. Thomas W. Sanderson
> McLaughlin's (Ohio) Squadron, Capt. John Dalzell

Third Brigade
>
> *Col. Michael Kerwin*
>
> *Bvt. Brig. Gen. Thomas T. Heath*
>
> 1st Alabama, *Maj. Sanford Tramel*
>
> 5th Ohio, *Maj. George H. Rader*
>
> 13th Pennsylvania, *Maj. George F. McCabe, Col. Michael Kerwin*

Artillery
>
> 23rd New York Battery, *Capt. Samuel Kittinger*

[Source: *OR* 47(1): 43, 46–59.]

APPENDIX G

Organization of Confederate Forces

Since this Confederate organization table is unorthodox, an explanation of its features is in order. I have listed regimental and battery commanders for the sake of comprehensiveness and because the *OR*'s order of battle lists incorrectly or omits several of the commanders. To the right of the regimental or battery commanders' names, I have enclosed in parentheses the numerical strength of each unit as indicated on its muster rolls or as listed on the Army of Tennessee's master tabular statement. In the case of artillery battalion, brigade, division, corps, and army commanders, the number appearing to the right of the name indicates the size of the commander's staff and escort, if those are not listed separately. To the right of the troop strength figures, I have indicated with abbreviated capitals the location of each brigade and artillery battalion as listed on its muster rolls. (A key to these abbreviations appears below.) Army and corps commanders' as well as unattached or detached units' stations are also noted. I included the numerical strength figures because the size of Johnston's army at the time of its surrender has long been a matter of dispute. The numbers tell a story of the army's final days that could not be told otherwise. I included the unit stations as a means of demonstrating how widely dispersed Johnston's army was at the time of its surrender.

I had no difficulty determining which units should be included in the Confederate organization table, since both muster rolls and other associated documents furnish the necessary information. Units that served in North Carolina only briefly, such as Duke's, Ferguson's, and Vaughn's cavalry brigades (which eventually formed the bulk of President Jefferson Davis's escort), are omitted from my organization table. Yet Dibrell's cavalry division *is* listed in my order of battle because it had seen extensive service with Johnston's army before being detached to Davis's escort. But because Dibrell's Division was not present with the army at the time of Johnston's surrender, its numerical strength is omitted from the cavalry's and the Army of Tennessee's overall totals. Although troops manning the Posts of Greensboro, Salisbury, and Charlotte were not strictly a part of the Army of Tennessee, they served in the same theater of operations and received orders from Johnston and Beauregard, so they are included in the army's total numerical strength. I chose, however, to exclude all hospital and nonmilitary personnel, hospitalized troops, and individual soldiers from Lee's and Johnston's armies who received their paroles in North Carolina, because they were not a part of an organized military body at the time of Johnston's surrender.

I was pleasantly surprised to find that only a few relevant muster rolls are missing or nonexistent. Of the 150-odd units that served in the Army of Tennessee in late April 1865, there are no muster rolls for Parker's and Wheaton's Batteries of Rhett's artillery battalion or for the 4th Tennessee, 8th Texas, and 11th Texas of Harrison's cavalry brigade. Although there are no muster rolls for Darden's Battery (Co. C, 10th North Carolina) or the 3rd Arkansas Cavalry, I found their numerical strength totals on the army's tabular statement.

Johnston's command in North Carolina was a motley agglomeration consisting of at least one detachment from every state in the Confederacy, including the border states of Kentucky, Maryland, and Missouri. Although the 1865 edition of the Army of Tennessee lacked the raw numbers to contend with Sherman's grand army, it nevertheless remained a viable fighting force until General Johnston opened negotiations for its surrender. This order of battle is offered as a tribute to the Army of Tennessee and its commander.

The following abbreviations are used for the unit stations in the organization table (all stations are in North Carolina unless otherwise indicated):

BH = Bush Hill
BLOOM = Bloomington
CHAR = Charlotte
CHES = Chester, South Carolina
CONC = Concord
GRN = Greensboro
HP = High Point
HILLS = Hillsborough
JAMES = Jamestown
LEX = Lexington
SAL = Salisbury
TC = Trinity College

ARMY OF TENNESSEE (32,440)
Gen. Joseph E. Johnston (357) GRN

Escort
Holloway's Cavalry Company (Alabama) (44)
Capt. E. M. Holloway

SECOND-IN-COMMAND
Gen. P. G. T. Beauregard (53) GRN

Escort
Jeff Davis Legion, Co. A (Mississippi) (33) GRN
Lt. R. E. Conner

Provost Marshal-General
    Detachment of Lewis's Brigade and other units
      (241) GRN
    Col. Martin H. Cofer
Signal Corps (36) GRN
    Lt. Eli Duvall

HARDEE'S CORPS (8,260)
    Lt. Gen. William J. Hardee (70) TC

    Escort and Scouts
    Raum's Cavalry Company (Mississippi) (73) TC
    Capt. William C. Raum
    Stono Scouts Company (South Carolina) (58) TC
    Capt. John B. L. Walpole, Lt. Paul T. Gervais

Brown's Division (2,375)
    Maj. Gen. John C. Brown (82)

    Smith's Brigade (1,241) HP
    Brig. Gen. James A. Smith (7)
    1st Florida Consolidated (comprising 1st, 3rd, 4th, 6th, and 7th
      Florida Infantry and 1st Florida Cavalry [Dismounted]), *Lt. Col.*
      Elisha Mashburn (402)
    1st Georgia Consolidated (comprising 1st, 57th, and 63rd Georgia
      Infantry), *Col. Charles H. Olmstead* (447)
    54th Georgia Consolidated (comprising 37th and 54th Georgia and
      4th Battalion Georgia Sharpshooters), *Col. Theodore D.*
      Caswell (385)
    Govan's Brigade (1,052) JAMES
    Brig. Gen. Daniel C. Govan (10)
    1st Arkansas Consolidated (comprising 1st, 2nd, 5th, 6th, 7th,
      8th, 13th, 15th, 19th, and 24th Arkansas and 3rd Confederate),
      Col. E. A. Howell (635)
    1st Texas Consolidated (comprising 6th, 7th, 10th, and 15th Texas
      Infantry and 17th, 18th, 24th, and 25th Texas Cavalry
      [Dismounted]), *Lt. Col. William A. Ryan* (407)

Hoke's Division (1,754)
    Maj. Gen. Robert F. Hoke (62)

    Clingman's Brigade (151) HP
    Brig. Gen. Thomas L. Clingman (8)
    8th North Carolina, *Lt. Col. Rufus A. Barrier* (25)
    31st North Carolina, *Lt. Col. Charles W. Knight* (22)
    36th/40th North Carolina (Consolidated), *Lt. Selby Hardenburgh* (36)

Appendix G

51st North Carolina, *Capt. James W. Lippitt* (46)

61st North Carolina, *Capt. A. D. Lippitt* (14), *Col. William L. Devane*

Colquitt's Brigade (736) BLOOM

> *Brig. Gen. Alfred H. Colquitt* (6)
>
> 6th Georgia, *Maj. James M. Culpepper* (152)
>
> 19th Georgia, *Maj. William Hamilton* (135)
>
> 23rd Georgia, *Col. Marcus R. Ballenger* (92)
>
> 27th Georgia, *Col. Charles T. Zachry* (229)
>
> 28th Georgia, *Lt. Col. W. P. Crawford* (122)

Hagood's Brigade (378) HP

> *Lt. Col. James H. Rion* (9), *Col. Robert F. Graham*
>
> 11th South Carolina, *Capt. B. F. Wyman* (65)
>
> 21st South Carolina, *Col. Robert F. Graham* (24), *Capt. J. A. W. Thomas*
>
> 25th South Carolina, *Capt. E. R. Lesesne* (41)
>
> 27th South Carolina, *Capt. Thomas Y. Simons* (59)
>
> 7th South Carolina Battalion, *Capt. William Clyburn* (180), *Lt. Col.*
> *James H. Rion*

Kirkland's Brigade (218) BH

> *Brig. Gen. William W. Kirkland* (8)
>
> 17th North Carolina, *Capt. Stuart L. Johnston* (46)
>
> 42nd North Carolina, *Col. John E. Brown* (72)
>
> 50th North Carolina, *Col. George Wortham* (42)
>
> 66th North Carolina/10th North Carolina Battalion (Consolidated),
> *Col. John H. Nethercutt* (50)

First Brigade Junior Reserves (209) HP

> *Col. Frank S. Armistead* (7)
>
> 1st North Carolina Reserves, *Lt. Col. Charles W. Broadfoot* (50)
>
> 2nd North Carolina Reserves, *Col. John H. Anderson* (100)
>
> 3rd North Carolina Reserves, *Col. John W. Hinsdale* (41)
>
> 1st (Millard's) North Carolina Reserves Battalion, *Capt. J. L.*
> *Eaves* (11)

Cheatham's Division (3,009)

> *Maj. Gen. Benjamin F. Cheatham* (153)
>
> *Maj. Gen. William B. Bate* (20)

Palmer's Brigade (1,998) HP

> *Brig. Gen. Joseph B. Palmer* (11)
>
> 1st Tennessee Consolidated (comprising 1st, 6th, 8th, 9th, 16th,
> 27th, 28th, and 34th Tennessee and 24th Tennessee Battalion),
> *Lt. Col. Oliver A. Bradshaw* (384)
>
> 2nd Tennessee Consolidated (comprising 11th, 12th, 13th, 29th,
> 47th, 50th, 51st, 52nd, and 154th Tennessee), *Lt. Col. George W.*
> *Pease* (441)
>
> 3rd Tennessee Consolidated (comprising 4th, 5th, 19th, 24th, 31st,
> 33rd, 35th, 38th, and 41st Tennessee), *Col. James D. Tillman* (473)

Appendix G

4th Tennessee Consolidated (comprising 2nd, 3rd, 10th, 15th, 18th, 20th, 26th, 30th, 32nd, 37th, and 45th Tennessee and 23rd Tennessee Battalion), *Col. Anderson Searcy* (689)

Gist's Brigade (838) HP
 Col. William G. Foster (5)
 46th Georgia, *Lt. Col. Abe Miles* (227)
 65th Georgia Consolidated (65th Georgia and 2nd and 8th Georgia Battalions), *Lt. Col. Zachariah L. Watters* (211)
 16th/24th South Carolina Consolidated, *Maj. B. Burgh Smith* (395)

Artillery (921)
 Col. Ambrosio J. Gonzales (8)

Artillery Battalion (340) BH
 Maj. Basil C. Manly (9)
 Bridges's Battery (Louisiana), *Capt. William M. Bridges* (98)
 Atkins's Battery (North Carolina), *Capt. George B. Atkins* (15)
 Walter's Battery (South Carolina), *Capt. George H. Walter* (149)
 Zimmerman's Battery (South Carolina), *Capt. William E. Zimmerman* (39)
 Paris's Battery (Virginia), *Lt. Thomas M. Tucker* (30)

Reserve Artillery Battalion (573) BLOOM
 Lt. Col. Del. Kemper (35)
 (There are no muster rolls for Bachman's, Barnwell's, Gaillard's, and Maxwell's Batteries, all of which were part of the Reserve Battalion as of April 10. These units probably were either transferred to South Carolina or consolidated with the batteries listed below, which would explain the absence of muster rolls bearing their names.)
 Guerard's Battery (Georgia), *Capt. John M. Guerard* (42)
 Lumpkin's Battery (Georgia), *Capt. Edward P. Lumpkin* (108)
 1st Missouri Battery, *Capt. A. W. Harris* (77)
 Charles's Battery (South Carolina), *Capt. William E. Charles* (23)
 DePass's Battery (South Carolina), *Lt. A. A. Gilbert* (54)
 C. E. Kanapaux's Battery (South Carolina), *Capt. Charles E. Kanapaux, Lt. Thomas J. Sistrunk* (60)
 Schulz's Battery (Palmetto Light Artillery, Co. F., South Carolina), *Capt. Frederick C. Schulz* (66)
 Wagener's Battery (German Artillery, Cos. A and C, South Carolina), *Capt. F. W. Wagener* (57)
 Huggins's Battery (Tennessee), *Capt. Almaria L. Huggins* (51)

STEWART'S CORPS (8,715)
 Lt. Gen. Alexander P. Stewart (108) GRN

Loring's Division (3,599)
 Maj. Gen. William W. Loring (15)

Featherston's Brigade (1,249) JAMES

Brig. Gen. Winfield S. Featherston (5)

1st Arkansas Mounted Rifles Consolidated (comprising 1st and 2nd
Arkansas Mounted Rifles [Dismounted], and 4th, 9th, and 25th
Arkansas Infantry), Col. Henry G. Bunn (542)

3rd Mississippi Consolidated (comprising 3rd, 31st, and 40th
Mississippi), Col. James M. Stigler (174)

22nd Mississippi Consolidated (comprising 1st, 22nd, and 33rd
Mississippi and 1st Mississippi Battalion), Col. Martin A.
Oatis (376)

37th Mississippi Battalion, Maj. Q. C. Heidelberg (152)

Lowry's Brigade (1,249) GRN

Brig. Gen. Robert Lowry (8)

29th Alabama, Maj. Henry B. Turner (117)

12th Louisiana, Lt. Col. E. M. Graham (288)

14th Mississippi Consolidated (comprising 5th, 14th, and 43rd
Mississippi), Col. Robert J. Lawrence (416)

15th Mississippi Consolidated (comprising 6th, 15th, 20th, and 23rd
Mississippi), Lt. Col. Thomas B. Graham (420)

Shelley's Brigade (1,086) GRN

Brig. Gen. Charles M. Shelley (21)

1st Alabama Consolidated (comprising 1st, 16th, 26th, 33rd, and
eight companies of 45th Alabama), Col. Robert H.
Abercrombie (366)

17th Alabama, Lt. Col. Edward P. Holcombe (306)

27th Alabama Consolidated (comprising 27th, 35th, 49th, 55th, and
57th Alabama), Col. Edward McAlexander (352)

45th Alabama (Cos. C and H), Lt. G. P. Bledsoe (41) LEX

Anderson's Division (1,722)

Maj. Gen. Patton Anderson (41)

Elliott's Brigade (1,132) GRN

Lt. Col. J. Welsman Brown (4)

22nd Georgia Battalion, Maj. Mark J. McMullen (363)

27th Georgia Battalion, Maj. Alfred L. Hartridge (155)

2nd South Carolina Artillery, Maj. F. F. Warley (461)

Manigault's Battalion (South Carolina), Capt. Theodore G. Boag (149)

Rhett's Brigade (549) GRN

Col. William Butler (6)

1st South Carolina (Regulars), Lt. Col. Warren Adams (259)

1st South Carolina Artillery (Regulars), Lt. Col. Joseph A. Yates (230)

15th South Carolina Battalion (Lucas's Battalion), Capt. Theodore B.
Hayne (54)

Appendix G

Walthall's Division (2,990)
    Maj. Gen. Edward C. Walthall (74)

  Harrison's Brigade (1,543) GRN
    Col. George P. Harrison Jr. (4)
    1st Georgia Regulars, *Col. Richard A. Wayne* (457)
    5th Georgia, *Col. Charles P. Daniel* (262)
    5th Georgia Reserves, *Maj. C. E. McGregor* (304)
    32nd Georgia, *Lt. Col. E. H. Bacon Jr.* (516)
  Kennedy's Brigade (1,373) GRN
    Brig. Gen. John D. Kennedy (6)
    2nd South Carolina Consolidated (comprising 2nd and 20th South
       Carolina and detachment of Blanchard's Reserves), *Col. William
       Wallace* (508)
    3rd South Carolina Consolidated (comprising 3rd and 8th South
       Carolina, 3rd South Carolina Battalion, and detachment of
       Blanchard's Reserves), *Col. Eli T. Stackhouse* (423)
    7th South Carolina Consolidated (comprising 7th and 15th South
       Carolina and detachment of Blanchard's Reserves), *Col. John B.
       Davis* (436)
  Artillery Battalion (296+) GRN
    Maj. A. Burnet Rhett (5)
    Brooks's Battery (Georgia), *Capt. John W. Brooks* (89)
    LeGardeur's Battery (Louisiana), *Capt. Gustave LeGardeur Jr.* (92)
    Parker's Battery (Marion Light Artillery, South Carolina), *Capt.
       Edward L. Parker* (?)
    Stuart's Battery (Beaufort Light Artillery, South Carolina), *Capt.
       Henry M. Stuart* (110)
    Wheaton's Battery (Chatham Light Artillery, Georgia), *Capt. John F.
       Wheaton* (?)

LEE'S CORPS (6,191)
  Lt. Gen. Stephen D. Lee (40) JAMES

  Escort
    Ragland's Cavalry Company (Georgia) (76) JAMES
    Capt. George G. Ragland

  Hill's Division (3,109)
    Maj. Gen. D. H. Hill (22)

  Sharp's Brigade (1,458) HP/JAMES
    Brig. Gen. Jacob H. Sharp (22)
    24th Alabama Consolidated (comprising 24th, 28th, and 34th
       Alabama), *Col. John C. Carter* (425)
    8th Mississippi Consolidated Battalion (comprising 5th, 8th, and

32nd Mississippi and 3rd Mississippi Battalion), *Lt. Col. J. R. Moore* (273)

9th Mississippi Consolidated (comprising 7th, 9th, 10th, 41st, and 44th Mississippi and 9th Mississippi Battalion Sharpshooters), *Lt. Col. William C. Richards* (420)

19th South Carolina Battalion (Consolidated) (comprising 10th and 19th South Carolina), *Lt. Col. C. Irvine Walker* (318)

Brantly's Brigade (1,362) GRN

Brig. Gen. William F. Brantly (9)

22nd Alabama Consolidated (comprising 22nd, 25th, 39th, and 50th Alabama), *Col. Harry T. Toulmin* (522)

37th Alabama Consolidated (comprising 37th, 42nd, and 54th Alabama), *Col. John A. Minter* (384)

24th Mississippi Consolidated (comprising 24th, 27th, 29th, 30th, and 34th Mississippi), *Col. R. W. Williamson* (328)

58th North Carolina (Consolidated) (comprising 58th and 60th North Carolina), *Lt. Col. Thaddeus Coleman* (119)

Detachment, Army of Northern Virginia (267) JAMES

Lt. Col. A. C. McAlister (1)

Contingent from Lane's Brigade (154)

7th North Carolina, *Maj. James S. Harris*

Contingent from Cooke's and Grimes's Brigades (112)

15th North Carolina (Cos. B, F, and I)

27th North Carolina (Cos. C, F, and G)

32nd North Carolina (Cos. E and K)

43rd North Carolina (Co. F)

45th North Carolina (Co. I)

46th North Carolina (Cos. B, D, G, and I)

48th North Carolina (Cos. A and B)

55th North Carolina (Cos. A and K)

Stevenson's Division (2,856)

Maj. Gen. Carter L. Stevenson (53)

Henderson's Brigade (1,402) HP

Brig. Gen. Robert J. Henderson (7)

1st Confederate (Georgia) Consolidated Battalion (comprising 1st Confederate, 25th, 29th, 30th, and 66th Georgia, and 1st Battalion Georgia Sharpshooters), *Capt. W. J. Whitsitt* (345)

39th Georgia Consolidated (comprising 34th and 39th Georgia and detachments of 52nd and 56th Georgia), *Col. Charles H. Phinizy* (365)

42nd Georgia Consolidated (comprising 36th and 42nd Georgia and detachments of 34th and 56th Georgia), *Lt. Col. L. P. Thomas* (398)

40th Georgia Consolidated Battalion (comprising 40th, 41st, and
43rd Georgia), *Lt. Col. S. D. Clements* (287)
Pettus's Brigade (1,401) SAL
Brig. Gen. Edmund W. Pettus (9)
19th Alabama, *Col. M. L. Woods* (405)
20th Alabama, *Lt. Col. James K. Elliott* (455)
23rd Alabama, *Lt. Col. Osceola Kyle* (399)
27th Alabama (Co. B), *Lt. Robert G. Hampton* (39)
54th Virginia (Consolidated) Battalion (comprising 54th and 63rd
Virginia), *Lt. Col. Connally H. Lynch* (94)
Artillery (110) JAMES
J. T. Kanapaux's Battery (South Carolina), *Capt. J. T. Kanapaux*

Independent Naval Contingent
Naval Regiment, *Flag Off. French Forrest* (64) GRN

Naval Brigade (239) GRN
Rear Adm. and Brig. Gen. Raphael Semmes (53)
1st Regiment (90)
2nd Regiment (96)

Unattached Artillery

Artillery Battalion (307) GRN
Maj. Joseph Palmer (1)
Havis's Battery (14th Battalion, Co. A, Georgia Light Artillery), *Capt.*
M. W. Havis (90)
Anderson's Battery (14th Battalion, Co. D, Georgia Light Artillery),
Capt. Ruel Wooten Anderson (119)
Yates's Battery (Mississippi), *Capt. James H. Yates* (74)
Moseley's Battery (Sampson Artillery, North Carolina), *Capt.*
Abner A. Moseley (23)
Independent Batteries
Abell's Light Artillery (Florida), *Capt. Henry F. Abell* (122) GRN
Swett's Battery (Mississippi), *Lt. H. Shannon* (56) GRN

Artillery
Lt. Col. Joseph B. Starr (9)

10th North Carolina (1st Artillery) (96) GRN
Darden's Battery (Co. C), *Lt. Alfred M. Darden* (18)
Southerland's Battery (Co. I), *Capt. Thomas L. Southerland* (78)
3rd North Carolina Battalion (134) GRN
Maj. John W. Moore (6)
Ellis's Battery (Co. A), *Capt. A. J. Ellis* (45)
Badham's Battery (Co. B), *Capt. William Badham* (63)

Sutton's Battery (Co. C), *Capt. John M. Sutton* (20)
13th North Carolina Battalion (139) GRN
    Cumming's Battery (Co. C), *Capt. James D. Cumming* (42)
    Dickson's Battery (Co. E), *Capt. Henry Dickson* (97) CHES
Kelly's Battery (Chesterfield Artillery, South Carolina),
    Capt. James I. Kelly (95) GRN

CAVALRY CORPS (4,772)
    Lt. Gen. Wade Hampton (62)
    Maj. Gen. Matthew C. Butler GRN

Butler's Division (1,483)
    Brig. Gen. Evander M. Law
    Maj. Gen. Matthew C. Butler (90)

Logan's Brigade (206) GRN
    Brig. Gen. Thomas M. Logan (6)
    1st South Carolina Cavalry, *Lt. J. A. Ratchford* (44)
    4th South Carolina Cavalry, *Capt. O. Barber* (32)
    5th South Carolina Cavalry, *Capt. George Tupper* (44)
    6th South Carolina Cavalry, *Lt. J. A. Tagart* (61)
    19th South Carolina Cavalry Battalion, *Lt. W. H. Pagett* (19)
Young's Brigade (1,010) GRN
    Col. Gilbert J. Wright (6)
    Cobb's Legion Cavalry (Georgia), *Capt. R. Bill Roberts* (317)
    Phillips Legion Cavalry (Georgia), *Maj. Wesley W. Thomas* (254)
    10th Georgia Cavalry, *Capt. Edwin W. Moise* (178)
    Jeff Davis Legion (Mississippi), *Col. J. Fred. Waring* (255)
Horse Artillery (177)
    Earle's Battery (South Carolina), *Capt. William E. Earle* (72) HP
    Halsey's Battery (South Carolina), *Capt. E. Lindsley Halsey* (105) GRN

Wheeler's Cavalry Contingent (3,227)
    (Formerly Wheeler's Cavalry Corps, Army of Tennessee)
    Maj. Gen. Joseph Wheeler
    Brig. Gen. William W. Allen (60) CONC

Escort
    1st Alabama Cavalry, Co. G (50) CONC
    Lt. James M. Smith
Scout Company
    Shannon's Special Scouts (55) GRN
    Maj. A. M. Shannon
Engineer Troop (24) CONC
    Lt. L. C. Anderson

Appendix G

Allen's Division (1,738)
>   *Brig. Gen. William W. Allen*
>   *Col. Charles C. Crews* (17)
>   (When General Allen assumed command of Wheeler's cavalry, he
>   placed Colonel Crews in command of his division—evidently
>   because General Anderson was on detached service with his brigade
>   at Hillsborough.)

>   Anderson's Brigade (871) HILLS
>   >   *Brig. Gen. Robert H. Anderson* (14)
>   >   3rd Confederate Cavalry (Georgia), *Col. P. H. Rice* (114)
>   >   8th Confederate Cavalry (Georgia), *Lt. Col. John S. Prather* (186)
>   >   10th Confederate Cavalry (Georgia), *Capt. W. H. Brazier* (258)
>   >   5th Georgia Cavalry, *Col. Edward Bird* (299)
>   Crews's Brigade (504+) SAL
>   >   *Col. Charles C. Crews*
>   >   *Col. John R. Hart* (1+)
>   >   1st Georgia Cavalry, *Lt. Col. George T. Watts* (151)
>   >   2nd Georgia Cavalry, *Lt. Col. F. M. Ison* (124)
>   >   3rd Georgia Cavalry, *Lt. Col. J. T. Thornton* (122)
>   >   6th Georgia Cavalry, *Col. John R. Hart* (47)
>   >   12th Georgia Cavalry, *Capt. James H. Graham* (59)
>   Hagan's Brigade (346) CONC
>   >   *Col. David T. Blakey* (16)
>   >   1st Alabama Cavalry, *Lt. Col. Augustus H. Johnson* (112)
>   >   3rd Alabama Cavalry, *Capt. A. P. Forney* (10)
>   >   9th Alabama Cavalry, *Lt. Asl. Blansit* (75)
>   >   12th Alabama Cavalry, *Capt. A. D. Bennett* (11)
>   >   51st Alabama Cavalry, *Col. M. L. Kirkpatrick* (122)

Humes's Division (1,300)
>   *Col. Henry M. Ashby* (14)

>   Ashby's Brigade (1,107) CHAR
>   >   *Col. James T. Wheeler* (12)
>   >   1st (or 6th) Tennessee Cavalry, *Lt. Col. James H. Lewis* (403)
>   >   2nd Tennessee Cavalry, *Lt. Col. John H. Kuhn* (213)
>   >   5th Tennessee Cavalry, *Col. George W. McKenzie* (300)
>   >   9th Tennessee Cavalry Battalion, *Maj. James H. Akin* (179)
>   Harrison's Brigade (179+) CHAR
>   >   *Col. Baxter Smith* (5)
>   >   3rd Arkansas Cavalry, *Maj. William H. Blackwell* (174)
>   >   4th Tennessee Cavalry (Smith's)
>   >   8th Texas Cavalry
>   >   11th Texas Cavalry

Dibrell's Division (800?)

> *Brig. Gen. George G. Dibrell*
>
> (Served with Wheeler's cavalry until April 15, 1865, when it was detached for special service as President Jefferson Davis's escort. Dibrell's Division therefore is *not* included in the tally for Wheeler's cavalry.)

Breckinridge's Brigade

> *Col. William C. P. Breckinridge*
>
> 1st (or 3rd) Kentucky Cavalry
>
> 2nd Kentucky Cavalry
>
> 9th Kentucky Cavalry

McLemore's Brigade

> *Col. William S. McLemore*
>
> 4th (or 8th) Tennessee Cavalry (McLemore's)
>
> 13th Tennessee Cavalry
>
> Shaw's Battalion (Tennessee)

Post of Greensboro (717)

> *Brig. Gen. Alfred Iverson*
>
> *Brig. Gen. John D. Kennedy*

Includes the following commands:

> Detachment of Lewis's Brigade (2nd, 4th, 5th, 6th, and 9th Kentucky Mounted Infantry), *Lt. J. M. McGuire* (36)
>
> Buckner Guards (2nd Kentucky Cavalry Battalion, Co. B, and 4th Tennessee Cavalry, Co. C), *Lt. Isaiah Yokum* (46)
>
> Tucker's Regiment Confederate Infantry (Pioneer Troops), *Col. Julius G. Tucker* (72)
>
> Invalid Corps (North Carolina), *Col. Frank Parker* (9)
>
> Troops from various commands (154)
>
> Maj. Gen. Lunsford L. Lomax and staff and unattached officers and men of the Army of Northern Virginia (27)
>
> All others (including Brig. Gen. John Echols and staff) (373)

Post of Salisbury (679)

> *Brig. Gen. Bradley T. Johnson* (98)
>
> (Among those serving at General Johnson's headquarters were twelve officers and men from the 2nd Maryland Infantry and the 1st Maryland Cavalry.)

Includes the following commands:

> Freeman's Battalion (North Carolina)
>
> Salisbury Prison Guard (Co. A), *Capt. C. D. Freeman* (49)
>
> Salisbury Prison Guard (Co. B), *Capt. H. P. Allen* (24)
>
> Salisbury Prison Guard (Co. C), *Sgt. W. J. Whitaker* (18)
>
> 1st Regiment Detailed Men (North Carolina) (14)

All others (excluding hospital personnel, hospitalized troops, and
units already listed elsewhere) (476)

Post of Charlotte (1,081)
Col. William J. Hoke
(Excludes hospital and nonmilitary personnel, hospitalized troops,
and units already listed elsewhere.)

[Sources: *OR* 47(1): 1061–66; *OR* 47(3): 773–74, 781–82, 844; Muster Rolls and Lists
of Confederate Troops Paroled in North Carolina, M1781, Rolls 1–7 (mf), RG 109,
NA; Given Campbell Journal, LC; Herriot, "At Greensboro, N.C., in April, 1865,"
101; Harris, *Seventh North Carolina*, 61; Joseph Mullen Jr. Diary, April 16, 1865, Diary
Collection, MOC; Walter Clark, *Histories,* 1:386, 3:79.]

NOTES

NA	National Archives, Washington, D.C.
NACB	National Archives Cartographic and Architectural Branch, Alexandria, Virginia
NCC-GPL	North Carolina Collection, Greensboro Public Library, Greensboro, North Carolina
NCC-UNC	North Carolina Collection, Wilson Library, University of North Carolina at Chapel Hill
NCDAH	North Carolina Division of Archives and History, Raleigh
OHS	Archives and Research Center, Ohio Historical Society, Columbus
OR	U.S. War Department. *The War of the Rebellion: A Compilation of the Official Records of the Union and Confederate Armies.* 128 vols. Washington, D.C.: Government Printing Office, 1880–1901. All citations are to series 1, unless otherwise indicated.
OR Atlas	U.S. War Department. *Atlas to Accompany the Official Records of the Union and Confederate Armies.* Washington, D.C.: Government Printing Office, 1891–95.
SHC-UNC	Southern Historical Collection, Wilson Library, University of North Carolina at Chapel Hill
SHSW	State Historical Society of Wisconsin, Madison
TNSLA	Tennessee State Library and Archives, Nashville
UDC	United Daughters of the Confederacy
UGA	Hargrett Rare Book and Manuscript Library, University of Georgia, Athens
UND	Archives, University of Notre Dame, South Bend, Indiana
USAMHI	Archives Branch, United States Army Military History Institute, Carlisle Barracks, Pennsylvania
USC	South Caroliniana Library, University of South Carolina, Columbia
UWA	University of Washington Libraries, Seattle
VAHS	Virginia Historical Society, Richmond
W&M	Manuscripts and Rare Book Department, Swem Library, College of William and Mary, Williamsburg, Virginia
WRHS	Western Reserve Historical Society, Cleveland, Ohio
YHS	Ypsilanti Historical Society, Ypsilanti, Michigan

CHAPTER ONE

1. Bradley, *Last Stand,* 1–2; Sherman, *Memoirs,* 2:221, 231.

2. Bradley, *Last Stand,* 2; Sherman, "Grand Strategy," 259; Sherman, *Memoirs,* 2: 206, 223–24.

3. Sherman, *Memoirs,* 2:224–25; Bradley, *Last Stand,* 2–4.

4. Sherman, *Memoirs,* 2:224–25, 255–57; Bradley, *Last Stand,* 4.

5. Grant, *Personal Memoirs,* 518; Sherman, *Memoirs,* 2:257–59; Bradley, *Last Stand,* 4–5; Fonvielle, *Last Rays,* 192–94.

6. *OR* 47(1):42; Sherman, *Memoirs,* 2:172, 269; Glatthaar, *March to the Sea,* 19–21; Bradley, *Last Stand,* 20–21.

7. Bradley, *Last Stand*, 54; Young [J. Powell] to "Friend Ellen," March 27, 1865, Ellen Aumack Papers, DU.

8. Sherman, *Memoirs*, 2:175, 176–78, 183, 192, 269, 388; Nichols, *Story of the Great March*, 130; Bradley, *Last Stand*, 21; Glatthaar, *March to the Sea*, 123.

9. Bradley, *Last Stand*, 21–22; *OR* 47(2):1079, 1084–85.

10. Bradley, *Last Stand*, 22–23; *OR* 47(1):19–20; Harris, "Hampton Roads Peace Conference,"30.

11. "Governor Cox's Speech," 116; Bradley, *Last Stand*, 23–24.

12. Bradley, *Last Stand*, 24. For the definitive study of the Columbia controversy, see Lucas, *Sherman and the Burning of Columbia*. On the same night much of Charleston also burned, the result of the firing of supply and munitions warehouses by retreating Confederates.

13. *OR* 47(2):1217–18, 1222–23; Thomas B. Roy Diary, February 19–21, 1865, photocopy in the possession of N. C. Hughes Jr., Chattanooga, Tennessee; Bradley, *Last Stand*, 24.

14. Dowdey and Manarin, *Wartime Papers of R. E. Lee*, 904, 906, 909; Bradley, *Last Stand*, 24–25; *OR* 47(2):1238.

15. Dowdey and Manarin, *Wartime Papers of R. E. Lee*, 906, 909; *OR* 47(2):1247; Bradley, *Last Stand*, 25–26.

16. Bradley, *Last Stand*, 27; *OR* 47(2):1247; Johnston, *Narrative*, 371–72; Woodward, *Mary Chesnut's Civil War*, 729, 731. In his *Narrative*, Johnston states that he received Lee's order on February 23, but his reply is dated February 22.

17. *OR* 47(2):1257, 1271, 1274; Johnston, *Narrative*, 371–72; George to Father, February 24, 1865, Civil War Soldiers' Letters: M. J. Blackwell, ALDAH; Bradley, *Last Stand*, 27–28; Hampton, "Battle of Bentonville," 701. Although Johnston did not issue the order announcing his return to command until February 25, he was already in Charlotte on February 23 organizing and reviewing his forces.

18. Bradley, *Last Stand*, 28–30; Roman, *Military Operations of Beauregard*, 2:331–32; William E. Stanton to Cousin, March 30, 1865, William E. Stanton Letters, Center for American History, University of Texas, Austin; Jno. M. G[oodman] to Sister, March 1, 1865, William T. Sherman Papers, LC.

19. Ford and Ford, *Life in the Confederate Army*, 42; Ford, "A March"; Thomas B. Roy Diary, February 25, 1865, photocopy in the possession of N. C. Hughes Jr.; *OR* 47(2):1281–82, 1288; Bradley, *Last Stand*, 30.

20. Thomas B. Roy Diary, February 20, 22, 1865, photocopy in the possession of N. C. Hughes Jr.; Ford and Ford, *Life in the Confederate Army*, 43–44; Bradley, *Last Stand*, 31.

21. Bradley, *Last Stand*, 36–39; *OR* 47(2):1290–91.

22. *OR* 47(2):631–32; Sherman, *Memoirs*, 2:292, 299; Bradley, *Last Stand*, 39. In his *Memoirs*, Sherman states that he learned of Johnston's restoration to command while at Cheraw, but he actually received the news several days beforehand.

23. *OR* 47(2):1297; Bradley, *Last Stand*, 39–40.

24. *OR* 47(2):1297–98; Bradley, *Last Stand*, 40.

25. Bradley, *Last Stand*, 58–59, 71–72, 85.

26. *OR* 47(2):1257, 1320, 1328; Bradley, *Last Stand*, 73–74.

27. *OR* 47(2):1321, 1337; Johnston, *Narrative*, 378; Bradley, *Last Stand*, 73–74.

28. Cox, *March to the Sea*, 155–56; *OR* 47(2):1334; Bradley, *Last Stand*, 74.

29. *OR* 47(2):1338–39; Bradley, *Last Stand*, 74–75.

30. I use General Cox's statement of losses; General Bragg's tally is three guns and 1,500 prisoners. *OR* 47 (1):62, 932–33, 976–79, 1078–79, 1086–88; *OR* 47(2):1354; Johnston, *Narrative*, 378–80; Cox, *March to the Sea*, 158–60; Bradley, *Last Stand*, 75.

31. Bradley, *Last Stand*, 75–77; Lash, *Destroyer of the Iron Horse*, 158, 164–65; *OR* 47(2):1374, 1388, 1406–7.

32. Bradley, *Last Stand*, 77; Johnston, *Narrative*, 374–75; *OR* 47(2):1313, 1320, 1324, 1326, 1330, 1332.

33. *OR* 47(2):1290, 1296–97, 1373–74; Johnston, *Narrative*, 374–76; Bradley, *Last Stand*, 77.

34. *OR* 47(2):1373; Bradley, *Last Stand*, 77–78.

35. *OR* 47(2):1337–38; Bradley, *Last Stand*, 85.

36. *OR* 47(1):861; *OR* 47(2):721, 786; Bradley, *Last Stand*, 86–88.

37. *OR* 47(1):861; *OR* 47(2):786; Bradley, *Last Stand*, 91–94.

38. M. C. Butler to Edward L. Wells, March 27, 1900, Edward L. Wells Correspondence, South Carolina Historical Society, Charleston; Bradley, *Last Stand*, 96. Contrary to several recent accounts, Marie Boozer was not at Monroe's Crossroads, nor did she accompany Kilpatrick from Columbia to Fayetteville. She and her mother were the guests of Maj. Gen. Oliver O. Howard and his quartermaster, Col. James T. Conklin. The evidence is in a letter that Howard wrote to his wife from Fayetteville on March 12, 1865 (undated by Howard, but easy to date after reading the text). Howard and Conklin were in Columbia, but Kilpatrick never came near that town. See Martin, *"Kill-Cavalry,"* 221–22; Bradley, *Last Stand*, 475 n. 23; O. O. Howard to Wife, [March 12,] 1865, Oliver O. Howard Papers, BC.

According to Capt. James H. Miller of the 5th Ohio Cavalry, Kilpatrick's traveling companion was named Alice. She was said to be a Northern schoolteacher whom "Little Kil" was escorting. "It was the general belief of the command that he [Kilpatrick] carried her with him for purposes less honorable than those alleged by him," Miller noted. Alice left Kilpatrick at Fayetteville, traveled to Wilmington, and then sailed north. "Alice" also happens to be the name of Kilpatrick's first wife, who died in the fall of 1863. Records Concerning the Conduct and Loyalty of Certain Union Army Officers, Civilian Employees of the War Department, and U.S. Citizens during the Civil War, 1861–1872, Box 2, RG 107, NA.

39. Bradley, *Last Stand*, 104; William D. Hamilton, *Recollections*, 199; Alonzo L. Brown, *Fourth Minnesota*, 388.

40. Bradley, *Last Stand*, 109–12; *OR* 47(1):24; *OR* 47(2):822.

41. Bradley, *Last Stand*, 114–16, 120; *OR* 47(2):867.

42. Bradley, *Last Stand*, 121–34; Thomas Y. Finley Diary, March 16, 1865, Civil War Miscellaneous Collection, USAMHI.

43. Bradley, *Last Stand*, 132.

44. Albert Q. Porter Diary, March 15, 1865, Albert Q. Porter Collection, LC; L. T. Wigfall to J. E. Johnston, February 27, March 3, 1865, JO 304 and JO 305, Joseph E. Johnston Papers, HEHL; Symonds, *Joseph E. Johnston*, 343–44.

45. J. E. Johnston to L. T. Wigfall, March 14, 1865, Louis T. Wigfall Papers, LC; Ridley, *Battles and Sketches*, 452.

46. Bradley, *Last Stand,* 136–37; Ridley, *Battles and Sketches,* 452; *OR* 47(2):1399.

47. *OR* 47(2):1410–11, 1413, 1415, 1422; Bradley, *Last Stand,* 140–42.

48. Bradley, *Last Stand,* 142; *OR* 47(1):1055–56; *OR* 47(2):1430; Hampton, "Battle of Bentonville," 701; Johnston, *Narrative,* 384.

49. *OR* 47(1):1056; *OR* 47(2):1428–29, 1435; Johnston, *Narrative,* 384–85; Bradley, *Last Stand,* 142.

50. Bradley, *Last Stand,* 143. Johnston's other two planned offensives were Seven Pines in 1862 and Cassville in 1864, but he canceled the latter attack on the advice of subordinates.

51. *OR* 47(1):1056; *OR* 47(2):1428; Johnston, *Narrative,* 385; Bradley, *Last Stand,* 143–44.

52. *OR* 47(1):172; *OR* 47(2):885–86; Sherman, *Memoirs,* 2:303; Nichols, *Story of the Great March,* 262; *Outline of the Tenth Michigan,* 25–26; Bradley, *Last Stand,* 143, 145–46, 147–48, 150.

53. Hampton, "Battle of Bentonville," 702–3; Johnston, *Narrative,* 385–86; *OR* 47(1):1056; Bradley, *Last Stand,* 148–49.

54. Branum, "Letters," June 21, 1900; Bradley, *Last Stand,* 153, 233.

55. Bradley, *Last Stand,* 154; Sherman, *Memoirs,* 2:303; *OR* 47(1):25; McClurg, "Last Chance," 391.

56. Bradley, *Last Stand,* 159, 163, 174–77, 178–79, 182–91; *OR* 47(1):423–24; Slocum, "Sherman's March," 692–93, 695; McClurg, "Last Chance," 392.

57. *OR* 47(1):423–24; Bradley, *Last Stand,* 190–91, 314, 320.

58. *OR* 47(1):1056; Johnston, *Narrative,* 386–87; Hampton, "Battle of Bentonville," 703–4; J. E. Johnston to R. F. Hoke, January 27, 1871, Robert F. Hoke Papers, NCDAH; Bradley, *Last Stand,* 179–80, 301, 303.

59. Bradley, *Last Stand,* 203–4, 216–17, 219–21; Walter Clark, *Histories,* 4:21; Chas. S. Brown to Etta, April 26, 1865, Charles S. Brown Papers, DU.

60. Bradley, *Last Stand,* 222–23, 224–60 passim, 279–95, 308.

61. Ibid., 320, 323–29, 343, 345, 347; *OR* 47(2):919.

62. Bradley, *Last Stand,* 369, 373–91, 393–95, 400–401, 406.

CHAPTER TWO

1. *OR* 47(1):57, 149, 152, 321; *OR* 47(2):916.

2. *Christian Recorder* (Philadelphia), April 15, 1865.

3. Ibid.

4. Ibid.; Stormont, *Fifty-eighth Indiana,* 503. In his report, Col. Joseph Moore wrote that his 58th Indiana Pontoniers constructed a 260-foot bridge late on March 21 and added a 240-foot bridge the next day. Meanwhile, Sherman's chief engineer, Col. Orlando M. Poe, reported three additional pontoon bridges across the Neuse. "[O]ne [is] at the Neck, and one at the 'county bridge.' Another will be finished in an hour," Poe told Sherman. "It will be at the railroad bridge." *OR* 47(1):428; *OR* 47(2):950–51.

5. *Christian Recorder,* April 15, 1865; Redkey, "They Are Invincible," 37.

6. Bauer, *Soldiering,* 233; Fleharty, *Our Regiment,* 163; Stormont, *Fifty-eighth Indi-*

ana, 502; Charles J. Paine to Father, April 1, 1865, Charles J. Paine Papers, VAHS; Bryant, *Third Wisconsin,* 326–27.

7. Allee, "A Civil War History," 2:186, MNHS; Bauer, *Soldiering,* 233. "You speak of Sherman's having enough colored troops to form a corps," General Paine wrote his father. "Many of his officers told mine they had never *seen* colored soldiers before[,] though they had heard of them." Charles J. Paine to Father, April 1, 1865, Charles J. Paine Papers, VAHS. Only one black regiment, the 110th U.S. Colored Troops, served in Sherman's army before the addition of Paine's division. But the soldiers of the 110th were detailed as pioneers and teamsters rather than as infantrymen. See Glatthaar, *March to the Sea,* 57.

8. *Christian Recorder,* April 15, 1865; Quaife, *From the Cannon's Mouth,* 376–77.

9. U. H. Farr reminiscence in Merrill, *Seventieth Indiana,* 260; S[amuel] M[errill] to Emily, March 28, 1865, Samuel Merrill Papers, INSL; Loop, "Rounding Up the Confederacy," June 27, 1901; *New York Tribune* correspondent quoted in Eleanor B. Powell, "Bedraggled Troops Paraded Here for Sherman," *Goldsboro News-Argus,* July 4, 1976.

10. Baker, *A Soldier's Experiences,* 47; Thomas D. Christie to Brother Dave, March 28, 1865, Christie Family Papers, MNHS.

11. Sargeant, *Personal Recollections.* On March 23, Army of the Tennessee commander Howard released Special Field Orders No. 69, which states: "Every person not entitled to be mounted will be dismounted and all horses and mules turned over to the corps quartermaster." *OR* 47(2) 972. According to local resident F. L. Castex, so many surplus horses and mules were shot as they were driven into the Neuse that their carcasses nearly dammed up the river. "Goldsboro during Civil War," *Goldsboro News-Argus,* April 4, 1976.

12. William D. Evans Diary, March 24, 1865, William D. Evans Papers, WRHS.

13. U. H. Farr reminiscence in Merrill, *Seventieth Indiana,* 261; Cambell, "Personal Reminiscences," 82, Cambell Family Papers, MNHS; Fleharty, *Our Regiment,* 163; Drake, *Ninth New Jersey,* 284; Edward W. Allen Diary-Letter, March 24, 1865, Edward W. Allen Papers, SHC-UNC; Henry to Nelie, March 24, 1865, Henry Clay Weaver Papers, LC; William H. McIntosh, "Annals of the 22d Wisconsin," 218, William H. McIntosh Papers, SHSW. Schofield's troops also called Sherman's soldiers "swamp angels." See M[ike] Griffin to "Friend Glyde," April 1, 1865, Samuel Glyde Swain Papers, SHSW.

14. Kerr, "From Atlanta to Raleigh," 222; Manning F. Force Letterbook-Journal, March 24, 1865, Manning F. Force Papers, UWA; Force, "Marching Across Carolina," 10; Johnson, "Through the Carolinas to Goldsboro," 75, LC; Andrew H. Hickenlooper Reminiscences, 108, *CWTI* Collection, USAMHI; W. T. S[herman] to Ellen, March 23, 1865, Sherman Family Papers, UND.

15. William H. Pittenger Diary, March 25, 1865, OHS; Andrew H. Hickenlooper Reminiscences, 108, *CWTI* Collection, USAMHI; Strong, "Extracts from Journal," March 24, 1865, William E. Strong Papers, Illinois State Historical Library, Springfield; *OR* 47(2):951, 969–70. One Union private wrote that he did not care about drawing another pair of shoes so long as he could stop marching long enough to allow some new skin to grow on the soles of his bare feet. See Theodore to Jane, March 23, 1865, Theodore E. St. John Papers, LC.

16. *OR* 47(1):189–90.

17. Hunter, "A Soldier's Reminiscence" (with additional commentary by J. B. New-burry), *CWTI* Collection, USAMHI; T. E. Smith to Brother, March 23, 1865, Thomas E. Smith and Family Collection, CINHS.

18. *OR* 47(1):190; Charles S. Norwood Sr., "A Look at the Early Years of Golds-boro," *Goldsboro News-Argus,* July 4, 1976; Drake, *Ninth New Jersey,* 283; Charles S. Brown to "My Dear Folks," n.d. [March 1865?], Charles S. Brown Papers, DU.

19. Spencer, *Last Ninety Days,* 95; Charles S. Norwood, "Bentonville Battle," *Goldsboro News-Argus,* July 4, 1976; W. T. Sherman to Ellen, April 5, 1865, Sherman Family Papers, UND.

20. *OR* 47(1):44; Sherman, *General and Field Orders,* 202–3. Although written on March 22, Special Field Orders No. 35 was not read to the men until the next day.

21. Sherman, *Memoirs,* 2:306; W. T. S[herman] to Ellen, March 23, 1865, Sherman Family Papers, UND.

22. Sherman, *Memoirs,* 2:304, 306; Dowdey and Manarin, *Wartime Papers of R. E. Lee,* 915.

23. *OR* 47(2):919, 930; *OR* 47(3):5–6, 19.

24. *OR* 47(1):79–98 passim, 101, 106, 119, 125, 126, 131, 142, 144, 146–63 pas-sim, 695; Oten to Emily, March 28, 1865, Solon A. Carter Papers, USAMHI; *Christian Recorder,* April 15, 1865.

25. *Christian Recorder,* April 15, 1865; Oten to Emily, March 28, 1865, Solon A. Carter Papers, USAMHI; *OR* 47(1):149.

26. Stormont, *Fifty-eighth Indiana,* 504–5; *Christian Recorder,* April 29, 1865.

27. *Christian Recorder,* April 29, 1865; Oten to Emily, March 28, 1865, Solon A. Carter Papers, USAMHI; Charles J. Paine to Father, April 1, 1865, Charles J. Paine Papers, VAHS; Joseph F. Waring Diary, March 24, 1865, SHC-UNC; *OR* 47(2):1452; *OR* 47(3):684.

28. Oten to Emily, March 28, 1865, Solon A. Carter Papers, USAMHI; Stormont, *Fifty-eighth Indiana,* 505.

29. *Christian Recorder,* April 29, 1865.

30. McBride, *Thirty-third Indiana,* 174. For two examples of Union scouting or for-aging parties that were virtually annihilated, see Miller, "With Sherman," 41–42, and *Christian Recorder,* April 29, 1865.

31. McBride, *Thirty-third Indiana,* 174–75.

32. William to Sister, April 2, 1865, William C. Stevens Correspondence, BL-UMI; Levi N. Green Diary, March 28, 1865, Levi N. Green Papers, MNHS; Glatt-haar, *March to the Sea,* 84–85. An Iowa soldier in the Seventeenth Corps referred to his regiment's huts as "ranches." See Olynthus B. Clark, *Downing's Civil War Diary,* 264.

33. Edward W. Allen Diary-Letter, March 24, 1865, Edward W. Allen Papers, SHC-UNC.

34. Stormont, *Fifty-eighth Indiana,* 512; McBride, *Thirty-third Indiana,* 215–16; Brant, *Eighty-fifth Indiana,* 119; J. R. Stillwell to Wife, April 6, 1865, James R. Stillwell Letters, OHS; Joseph Hoffhines to Wife, April 9, 1865, Joseph Hoffhines Papers, OHS; Glatthaar, *March to the Sea,* 93–94.

35. Glatthaar, *March to the Sea,* 98; Andersen, *Diary of Allen Morgan Geer,* 212;

McAdams, *Every-Day Soldier Life,* 148; Brant, *Eighty-fifth Indiana,* 109–10; Edmund J. Cleveland Diary, April 6, 1865, SHC-UNC.

36. Glatthaar, *March to the Sea,* 85–86; Rhoderick R. Rockwood Diary, March 25, 1865, Western Historical Manuscripts Collection, University of Missouri, Columbia; Andrew H. Hickenlooper Reminiscences, 108–9, *CWTI* Collection, USAMHI. Contrary to Hickenlooper's account, Brig. Gen. Manning F. Force, the commander of a Seventeenth Corps brigade, stated that the corps provost guard made an unannounced search of his camps in early March, but the only contraband found was some civilian clothing and tobacco. See Force, "Marching Across Carolina," 15.

For some insights into this highly controversial topic, see the chapter titled "Destruction and Pillaging" in Glatthaar, *March to the Sea,* 134–54; Royster, *Destructive War,* 342–47; Grimsley, *Hard Hand of War,* 190–204.

37. *OR* 39(2):713–14; Marszalek, *Sherman,* 302–3.

38. *OR* 47(1):487.

39. Andrew H. Hickenlooper Reminiscences, 109–10, *CWTI* Collection, USAMHI.

40. John J. Safely to Mary McEwen, April 9, 1865, McEwen Family Papers, Library and Collections Center, Missouri Historical Society, St. Louis; Quaife, *From the Cannon's Mouth,* 375–76; Glatthaar, *March to the Sea,* 85; Edward W. Allen Diary-Letter, March 25, 1865, Edward W. Allen Papers, SHC-UNC; W. T. Sherman to Ellen, April 5, 1865, Sherman Family Papers, UND.

41. *OR* 5, ser. 3, 31; Edward W. Allen Diary-Letter, March 25, 1865, Edward W. Allen Papers, SHC-UNC; Charles S. Brown to "My Dear Folks," n.d. [March 1865?], Charles S. Brown Papers, DU; Alfred A. Rigby Diary, April 10, 1865, EU; H. M. Dewey to Mrs. Spencer, March 5, 1866, Cornelia P. Spencer Papers, SHC-UNC.

42. Spencer, *Last Ninety Days,* 94–95; Drake, *Ninth New Jersey,* 282–84.

43. Charles Hinton reminiscence in Drake, *Ninth New Jersey,* 285–87; Edmund J. Cleveland Diary, April 4, 1865, SHC-UNC.

44. Edmund J. Cleveland Diary, April 5, 8, 1865, SHC-UNC; Hatcher, *Last Four Weeks,* 158–59; W. T. Sherman to Ellen, April 5, 9, 1865, Sherman Family Papers, UND.

45. Edward W. Allen Diary-Letter, March 25, 1865, Edward W. Allen Papers, SHC-UNC; Sherman, *Memoirs,* 2:408; Barrett, *Sherman's March,* 192; McAdams, *Every-Day Soldier Life,* 148; *OR* 47(3):121; Circular, March 27, 1865, Absalom H. Markland Papers, LC (this dispatch is published in *OR* 47[3]:35).

46. Henry to Uncle [Ethan Allen Hitchcock], March 26, 1865, Henry Hitchcock Papers, Library and Collections Center, Missouri Historical Society, St. Louis; Sherman, *Memoirs,* 2:324; *OR* 47(1):28; *OR* 47(3):19–20; Sherman, *General and Field Orders,* 206–7; William T. Sherman Diary, March 25, 1865, Sherman Family Papers, UND.

47. *New York Herald,* March 31, 1865; Barrett, *Sherman's March,* 194–96; Sherman, *Memoirs,* 2:324, Grant, *Personal Memoirs,* 527.

48. *OR* 47(2):803, 867, 948–49; Barrett, *Sherman's March,* 197.

49. Marszalek, *Sherman,* 335.

50. Sherman, *Memoirs,* 2:324; William T. Sherman Diary, March 26–27, 1865, Sherman Family Papers, UND; G. S. Dodge to Col. Boyd, March 27, 1865, Mili-

tary Telegram Book, Joseph F. Boyd Papers, DU; Sparks, *Inside Lincoln's Army*, 483; Barnes, "With Lincoln," 48–49.

51. Horace Porter, *Campaigning with Grant*, 417–18; Thomas, *Three Years with Grant*, 297; Manning F. Force Letterbook-Journal, March 30 [31?], 1865, Manning F. Force Papers, UWA; Pfanz, *Petersburg Campaign*, 24.

52. Horace Porter, *Campaigning with Grant*, 418–19.

53. Sherman, *Memoirs*, 1:167–68, 2:324–25, 327–28. Sherman's account of his conversations with Lincoln conflicts with that of Rear Adm. David Dixon Porter. Sherman recollected that Porter was not present at the March 27 conference, whereas Porter—who claimed to have made notes of the conversation—recalled that he was. Porter also recalled that Lincoln failed to recognize Sherman until the general reminded the president of the circumstances of their first meeting.

Sherman had left his first meeting with Lincoln less than impressed with the new chief executive. Sherman had just returned from Louisiana after the state's secession, and when Lincoln asked "how they are getting along down there," "Cump" had replied, "They think they are getting along swimmingly—they are preparing for war." "Oh, well!" said the president, "I guess we'll manage to keep house." Afterward, an angry Sherman had turned on his brother, Senator John Sherman of Ohio, and said, "You [politicians] have got things in a hell of a fix, and you may get them out as best you can." See Sherman, *Memoirs*, 1:168.

54. Horace Porter, *Campaigning with Grant*, 419–20; Sherman, *Memoirs*, 2:325.

55. Sparks, *Inside Lincoln's Army*, 483–84; Horace Porter, *Campaigning with Grant*, 421.

56. Horace Porter, *Campaigning with Grant*, 421–22; Sheridan, *Personal Memoirs*, 2: 131–32; *OR* 46(1):51–52; Benjamin P. Thomas, *Three Years with Grant*, 297; *OR Atlas*, pl. 137; Bearss and Calkins, *Battle of Five Forks*, 1.

57. *OR* 46(1):50; *OR* 47(3):234; Sheridan, *Personal Memoirs*, 2:126–29; Grant, *Personal Memoirs*, 530–31. If Grant had intended to use his discretionary orders to Sheridan as "a blind" (as he indicates in his memoirs), then he should not have misled Sherman as he did in his March 22 dispatch, which understandably led Sherman to believe that he could count on Sheridan's assistance in North Carolina. See *OR* 47(2):948.

58. Sheridan, *Personal Memoirs*, 2:131–33; Horace Porter, *Campaigning with Grant*, 421–22; Benjamin P. Thomas, *Three Years with Grant*, 297; *OR* 46(1):52.

59. Sheridan, *Personal Memoirs*, 2:133.

60. Agassiz, *Meade's Headquarters*, 327; J. R. Hamilton to Swinton, March 28, 1865, J. R. Hamilton Letter, Mss 2 H1805 a1, VAHS.

61. J. R. Hamilton to Swinton, March 28, 1865, J. R. Hamilton Letter, Mss 2 H1805 a1, VAHS; Agassiz, *Meade's Headquarters*, 327; Sherman, *Memoirs*, 2:325; Charles C. Coffin, *Boys of '61*, 488–89.

62. Sherman, *Memoirs*, 2:325; Horace Porter, *Campaigning with Grant*, 422–23.

63. Sherman, *Memoirs*, 2:325–26; Horace Porter, *Campaigning with Grant*, 423; *OR* 46(1):52; Grant, *Personal Memoirs*, 527.

64. Sherman, *Memoirs*, 2:325–26; Grant, *Personal Memoirs*, 541–42; Barrett, *Sherman's March*, 196; McPherson, *Battle Cry of Freedom*, 844.

65. Sherman, *Memoirs*, 2:326; Horace Porter, *Campaigning with Grant*, 423–24.

66. Sherman, *Memoirs*, 2:326–27; Horace Porter, *Campaigning with Grant*, 424. In his memoirs, Grant relates a similar anecdote that Lincoln told regarding Virginia governor William "Extra Billy" Smith. Like Sherman, Grant also believed that Lincoln hoped Davis would flee the country. Grant, *Personal Memoirs*, 572–73, 578.

67. Grant, *Personal Memoirs*, 569; *OR* 46(2):509. Lincoln had a third indispensable clause not mentioned by Grant: "No cessation of hostilities short of an end of the war and the disbanding of all forces hostile to the [U.S.] Government."

68. Admiral Porter left numerous accounts of the conference aboard the *River Queen*. See Sherman, *Memoirs*, 2:328–31; David Porter, *Incidents and Anecdotes*, 313–16, and *Naval History*, 794–95; Draper, *History of the Civil War*, 3:598–99; "Vice Admiral Porter Private Journal No. 2," 37, David D. Porter Papers, LC. For an incisive refutation of Porter's version of events, see Naroll, "Lincoln and the Sherman Peace Fiasco," 472–75.

69. Sherman, *Memoirs*, 2:329–30; "Vice Admiral Porter Private Journal No. 2," 37, David D. Porter Papers, LC; David Porter, *Naval History*, 794–95, and *Incidents and Anecdotes*, 314–15.

70. Johnston's routes of retreat along the North Carolina and Piedmont (Greensboro to Danville) Railroads remained intact until mid-April, when Maj. Gen. George Stoneman's cavalry struck portions of the routes, destroying bridges, track, and supply depots, while operating behind Johnston's army. For a fuller discussion of Stoneman's raid, see Chapters 3 and 6.

71. Sherman, *Memoirs*, 2:330.

72. Ibid., 327.

73. W. T. Sherman to I. N. Arnold, November 28, 1872, Isaac N. Arnold Papers, Archives and Manuscripts Department, Chicago Historical Society; [Sherman], "Unpublished Letters of General Sherman," 374.

74. Sherman, "Surrender of Gen. Johnston," 333–34, and *Memoirs*, 2:327–28; Nevins, *Organized War to Victory*, 291–92; Fellman, *Citizen Sherman*, 241–42; Barrett, *Sherman's March*, 195–96. In his testimony before the Joint Committee on the Conduct of the War, Sherman stated that "nothing definite" regarding terms for the Confederates had been discussed during his conferences with Lincoln and Grant at City Point. "It was simply a matter of general conversation," Sherman said, "nothing specific and definite." See U.S. Congress, "Sherman-Johnston," 3:13.

75. Sherman, *Memoirs*, 2:328; W. T. Sherman to Ellen, March 31, April 5, 1865, Sherman Family Papers, UND; Howe, *Home Letters of Sherman*, 338; Schofield, *Forty-six Years*, 348.

76. Sherman, *Memoirs*, 2:331–32; William T. Sherman Diary, March 28, 1865, Sherman Family Papers, UND; *OR* 47(1):28; *OR* 47(3):42; John Sherman, *Recollections*, 353–54.

77. William T. Sherman Diary, March 28–30, 1865, Sherman Family Papers, UND; Sherman, *Memoirs*, 2:331–32.

78. *OR* 47(1):28; *OR* 47(2):969; *OR* 47(3):28–29, 65; W. T. Sherman to Ellen, April 9, 1865, Sherman Family Papers, UND; John D. Inskeep Diary, April 2, 1865, OHS.

79. John Sherman, *Recollections*, 354.

80. Bub to Sis, March 31, 1865, Sylvester C. Noble Papers, YHS; *OR* 47(3):66.

81. *OR* 47(1) 29, 1134; *OR* 47(3):43, 95, 100; *OR* 5, ser. 3, 31–32; Sherman, *Memoirs*, 2:331, 341; Walter Clark, *Histories*, 3:709–10, 727.

82. Sherman, *Memoirs*, 2:332–33; Sherman, *General and Field Orders*, 214; *OR* 47(3):75. Sherman's six corps commanders were Maj. Gen. John A. Logan, Fifteenth Corps; Maj. Gen. Frank P. Blair Jr., Seventeenth Corps; Bvt. Maj. Gen. Jefferson C. Davis, Fourteenth Corps; Maj. Gen. Joseph A. Mower, Twentieth Corps; Maj. Gen. Alfred H. Terry, Tenth Corps; and Maj. Gen. Jacob D. Cox, Twenty-third Corps.

83. Sherman, *Memoirs*, 2:304, 333.

84. Bryant, *Third Wisconsin*, 328; Osborn, *Trials and Triumphs*, 207; Miles K. Lewis quoted in Cook and Benton, *"Dutchess County Regiment,"* 159–60; William H. Pittenger Diary, March 31, 1865, OHS; Quaife, *From the Cannon's Mouth*, 379–80. The Twentieth Corps was known as the "Star Corps" because of its insignia.

85. Glatthaar, *March to the Sea*, 35–36; William H. McIntosh, "Annals of the 22d Wisconsin," 220, William H. McIntosh Papers, SHSW; William D. Hamilton, *Recollections*, 200; Gaskill, *Footprints through Dixie*, 175–77.

86. Glatthaar, *March to the Sea*, 86–87; Aaron Overstreet to "Dear Wife and children," April 3, 1865, Aaron Overstreet Letters, Civil War Miscellaneous Collection, USAMHI; Edward E. Schweitzer Diary, April 2, 1865, Edward E. Schweitzer Diaries and Correspondence, *CWTI* Collection, USAMHI; George P. Metz Diary, [April 2,] 1865, George P. Metz Papers, DU; Saunier, *Forty-seventh Ohio*, 424; William D. Hamilton, *Recollections*, 200–201.

87. General Court-Martial Proceedings No. OO 3428—Pvt. James Preble, Co. K, 12th New York Vol. Cav., RG 153, NA; *North Carolina Times* (New Bern), April 4, 1865; Axel H. Reed Diary, April 1, 1865, Axel H. Reed Papers, MNHS; Bircher, *Drummer-Boy's Diary*, 176–78.

88. Bircher, *Drummer-Boy's Diary*, 178–79; Axel H. Reed Diary, April 1, 1865, Axel H. Reed Papers, MNHS; McAdams, *Every-Day Soldier Life*, 148; *North Carolina Times*, April 4, 1865; Kirwan and Splaine, *Seventeenth Massachusetts*, 360; Hatcher, *Last Four Weeks*, 81–82.

89. William B. Miller Journal, March 31, 1865, INHS; Axel H. Reed Diary, April 1, 1865, Axel H. Reed Papers, MNHS; *North Carolina Times*, April 4, 1865; Hatcher, *Last Four Weeks*, 82; Kirwan and Splaine, *Seventeenth Massachusetts*, 360.

90. Committee of the Regiment, *Fifty-fifth Illinois*, 429.

91. Elizabeth Collier Diary, April 20, 1865, SHC-UNC.

92. *OR* 47(3):100; *OR* 5, ser. 3, 32; Sherman, *Memoirs*, 2:179; Price, "Railroads of North Carolina," 185.

93. Sherman, *General and Field Orders*, 219–21; *OR* 47(3):102–3.

94. *OR* 47(3):100.

95. McAdams, *Every-Day Soldier Life*, 149; Bryant, *Third Wisconsin*, 327–28; *OR* 47(3):103.

CHAPTER THREE

1. *OR* 47(1):1055, 1057; *OR* 47(2):1453–54; Johnston, *Narrative*, 392; William Calder Diary, March 22, 1865, William Calder Papers, DU; Holmes, *Diary of Henry*

McCall Holmes, 33; C. W. Hutson to Em [Journal-Letter], March 21–22, 1865, Charles W. Hutson Papers, SHC-UNC; R. M. Collins, *Chapters,* 292; Ridley, *Battles and Sketches,* 453; D. H. Hill to Daughter, March 23, 1865, Daniel H. Hill Papers, USAMHI.

2. Ridley, *Battles and Sketches,* 453; W. A. Johnson, "Marching, Camping, Fighting," Lovic P. Thomas Scrapbooks, 2:149, Lovic P. Thomas Papers, AHS; William to Lina, April 6, 1865, William H. Johnson Papers, USC.

3. Duncan to Wife, March 22, 1865, Campbell Family Papers, SHC-UNC; B. S. Williams to Mother, March 23, 1865, Benjamin S. Williams Papers, DU.

4. Ridley, *Battles and Sketches,* 453; W. A. Johnson, "Closing Days," June 5, 1902; W. A. Johnson, "Marching, Camping, Fighting," Lovic P. Thomas Scrapbooks, 2:149, Lovic P. Thomas Papers, AHS; Holmes, *Diary of Henry McCall Holmes,* 33; John Johnson Diary, March 24, 1865, DU; Wade Hampton Jr. to "My dear Col" [William C. P. Breckinridge], April 7, [1865], vol. 240, Breckinridge Family Papers, LC; Brooks and Lefler, *Papers of Walter Clark,* 1:136; *Annals of an American Family,* 177; *OR* 47(2): 1456–57; Johnston, *Narrative,* 394.

5. *OR* 47(3):684; Joseph F. Waring Diary, March 24, 1865, SHC-UNC; Jesse R. Sparkman Diary, March 24, 1865, Box 3, Diaries, Memoirs, Etc., TNSLA; Johnston, *Narrative,* 394; William Calder to Mother, March 25, 1865, William Calder Papers, SHC-UNC.

6. *OR* 47(2):1453–54; *OR* 47(3):682; Johnston, *Narrative,* 395.

7. *OR* 47(3):687; Freeman, *Lee's Dispatches,* 341–46; Dowdey and Manarin, *Wartime Papers of R. E. Lee,* 916–18.

8. *OR* 47(3):689, 700, 708, 710, 712, 713, 715. Johnston also ordered the commander at Augusta, Georgia, to send him 10,000 pairs each of shoes and pants.

9. Andrews, *Footprints,* 177; Charles C. Jones, *Chatham Artillery,* 215; William Connell to "Dear Major," March 28, 1865, Charles W. Hutson Papers, SHC-UNC; R. M. Collins, *Chapters,* 292; W. A. Johnson, "Closing Days," June 5, 1902; W. A. Johnson, "Marching, Camping, Fighting," Lovic P. Thomas Scrapbooks, 2:149, Lovic P. Thomas Papers, AHS; Ridley, *Battles and Sketches,* 455; Brooks and Lefler, *Papers of Walter Clark,* 1:136.

10. Johnston, *Narrative,* 374–75; *OR* 47(2):1324, 1326, 1330; Bradley, *Last Stand,* 77; *Raleigh Weekly Conservative,* April 5, 1865; B. F. Moore to Alfred, March 22, 1865, Moore-Gatling Law Firm Papers, SHC-UNC; J. W. Norwood to William, March 29, 1865, Tillinghast Family Papers, DU; *Raleigh Daily Confederate,* March 28, 1865; Charles Manly to "My Dear Gov.," March 29, 1865, David L. Swain Papers, SHC-UNC.

11. Z. B. Vance to J. E. Johnston [two letters], March 28, 1865, Letterbook, vol. 7, Zebulon B. Vance Papers, NCDAH; *OR* 47(3):707–8; "Inspection Report Made by Colonel E. E. Portlock, Jr. on General Inspection Duties from War Department, March and April, 1865," in Dodson, *Campaigns of Wheeler,* 426–30; J. W. Avery to E. E. Portlock Jr., April 17, 1865, Wheeler Family Papers: Joseph Wheeler, ALDAH.

12. *OR* 47(3):688, 694, 729–30; Lafayette McLaws Order Book, March 28, 1865, Lafayette McLaws Papers, SHC-UNC; Joseph B. Cumming War Recollections, 83–84, SHC-UNC.

13. *OR* 47(1):1057; *OR* 47(3):699; Lafayette McLaws to Wife, March 23, 1865,

Lafayette McLaws Papers, SHC-UNC; Augustine Smythe to "Miss Lou," March 30, 1865, Augustine T. Smythe Papers, SHC-UNC; "General Johnston's Effect on His Soldiers," 207; Cuttino, *Saddle Bag and Spinning Wheel*, 212; J. L. Swain to Julius, April 10, 1865, John L. Swain Papers, SHC-UNC; D. T. Copeland to Mattie, April 4, 1865, David T. Copeland Papers, SHC-UNC; C. W. Hutson to Mother, April 7, 1865 [see Journal-Letter entry for April 9, 1865], Charles W. Hutson Papers, SHC-UNC.

14. Braxton Bragg to "Mr. President," March 26, 1865, Document P95, Braxton Bragg Papers in the William P. Palmer Collection, WRHS (see *OR* 53:415–16 for a somewhat different version of Bragg's letter).

Former Confederate army commanders who spent the final days of the war in North Carolina included P. G. T. Beauregard, Braxton Bragg, John C. Pemberton, and Theophilus H. Holmes (formerly the commander of the Trans-Mississippi Department). Johnston's senior corps commander, William J. Hardee, should also be included in this group because he had briefly commanded the Army of Tennessee in December 1863. Of these five, only Hardee was still holding a field command in April 1865.

15. C. W. Hutson to Mother, April 7, 1865 [see Journal-Letter entry for April 8, 1865], Charles W. Hutson Papers, SHC-UNC; Brooks and Lefler, *Papers of Walter Clark*, 1:139–40; William Calder to Mother, March 31, 1865, William Calder Papers, SHC-UNC; Woodward, *Mary Chesnut's Civil War*, 768. Maj. Joseph Cumming, who served as Lt. Gen. Stephen D. Lee's acting chief of staff, recalled the march through South Carolina with fondness. "It was beautiful spring weather," Cumming wrote. "We were passing through a fine country which had not been swept clean by the armies. Fresh eggs were plentiful and wild onions everywhere and Lucius concocted a noble *omelette aux oignons*, for every meal." Cumming also found his superior, General Lee, to be "a most agreeable gentleman." The march ended at Chester, where Lee's troops boarded cars bound for Salisbury, North Carolina. At Salisbury, the soldiers switched trains for the trip to Smithfield, arriving there in early April. See Joseph B. Cumming War Recollections, 82, SHC-UNC.

16. *OR* 47(3):731–36. In an essay on Johnston's conduct of the Atlanta campaign, historian Richard McMurry builds a similar case concerning the Army of Tennessee's troop strength in 1864. See McMurry, "A Policy So Disastrous," 230–36. For a conservative estimate of Robert E. Lee's troop strength on March 27, 1865, see Bearss and Calkins, *Battle of Five Forks*, 8–9.

17. Though Brig. Gen. Alvan C. Gillem was the Federal division commander, Stoneman was in overall command. *OR* 47(3):718–19, 722–29, 738–40, 742–47, 749–57, 760; Barrett, *Civil War in North Carolina*, 351.

18. *Raleigh Daily Confederate*, March 30, 31, and April 1, 1865 (Hood's report was published in three installments); Ridley, *Battles and Sketches*, 455; Holmes, *Diary of Henry McCall Holmes*, 33; D. G. Godwin to Bettie, April 4, 1865, D. G. Godwin Letters, Civil War Collection—Confederate, TNSLA; W. D. Gale to Wife, April 1, 1865, Gale and Polk Family Papers, SHC-UNC. Hood's report for the Atlanta and Tennessee campaigns may also be found in *OR* 38(3):628–36 and *OR* 45(1):652–62.

19. *OR* 47(3):718; *OR* 38(1):637; W. D. Gale to Wife, April 1, 1865, Gale and Polk Family Papers, SHC-UNC; "Report of Hon. L. T. Wigfall in the Senate of the Confederate States, March 18, 1865," reprinted in Johnston, *Narrative*, 588–602; rough

draft excerpt from Burke Davis's *Sherman's March* manuscript, Box 145, Folder 656, Burke Davis Papers, SHC-UNC; J[.] E[.] J[ohnston] to S[amuel] Cooper, March 31, 1865, and J. E. Johnston to J. B. Hood, April 4, 1865, Vol. 6: Telegram Book No. 3 of General Joseph E. Johnston, March 11–April 29, 1865, Joseph E. Johnston Papers, W&M. Although Johnston did not read Hood's report until late March, Wigfall had outlined it for him in a letter. See L. T. Wigfall to J. E. Johnston, February 27, 1865, JO 304, Joseph E. Johnston Papers, HEHL; Symonds, *Joseph E. Johnston,* 352–53.

20. *OR* 45(1):646–51; [P. G. T. Beauregard] to Samuel Cooper, April 15, 1865, Miscellaneous Confederate Correspondence, 1864–1865, Box 4, #450, RG 109, NA; W. J. Hardee to J. B. Hood, February 10, 1865, J. B. Hood to W. J. Hardee, March 11, 1865, W. J. Hardee to J. B. Hood, April 2, 1865, J. B. Hood to W. J. Hardee, April 8, 1865, J. B. Hood to W. J. Hardee, April 13, 1865, W. J. Hardee to Genl. Hood, May 31, 1865 (copies made in 1910 by Thomas B. Roy), William J. Hardee Papers, ALDAH; McMurry, *John Bell Hood,* 187–88.

21. *OR* 47(3):737; J. E. J[ohnston] to R. E. Lee, April 1, 1865, Vol. 6: Telegram Book No. 3 of General Joseph E. Johnston, March 11–April 29, 1865, Joseph E. Johnston Papers, W&M.

22. Wm. C. P. Breckinridge to Issa Breckinridge, April 1, 1865, vol. 240, Breckinridge Family Papers, LC.

23. W. A. Johnson, "Closing Days," June 5, 1902; W. A. Johnson, "Marching, Camping, Fighting," Lovic P. Thomas Scrapbooks, 2:149, Lovic P. Thomas Papers, AHS; R. M. Collins, *Chapters,* 292; Ridley, *Battles and Sketches,* 453–54; Walter Clark, *Histories,* 3:199; Spencer, *Last Ninety Days,* 146; Zebulon B. Vance, "Lecture—Last Days of the War in North Carolina," in Dowd, *Life of Vance,* 489–90; D. G. Godwin to Bettie, April 4, 1865, D. G. Godwin Letters, Civil War Collection—Confederate, TNSLA; Darst, "Robert Hughes," 39.

24. Dickert, *Kershaw's Brigade,* 526.

25. R. M. Collins, *Chapters,* 292.

26. Goodloe, *Some Rebel Relics,* 311; Alfred T. Fielder Diary, April 9, 1865, Tennessee Historical Society Collection, TNSLA; W. A. Johnson, "Closing Days," June 5, 1902; W. A. Johnson, "Marching, Camping, Fighting," Lovic P. Thomas Scrapbooks, 2:149, Lovic P. Thomas Papers, AHS; Joseph F. Waring Diary, March 25, 1865, SHC-UNC; C. W. Hutson, "My Reminiscences," 112, Charles W. Hutson Papers, SHC-UNC; John Johnson Diary, April 5, 1865, DU; Ridley, *Battles and Sketches,* 454–55.

27. Ridley, *Battles and Sketches,* 456; D. T. Copeland to Mattie, April 4, 1865, David T. Copeland Papers, SHC-UNC; Lafayette McLaws Order Book, March 29, 1865, Lafayette McLaws Papers, SHC-UNC; James W. Brown Diary, April 3, 7, 1865, Private Papers, Mf Drawer 187, Reel 13, GADAH.

28. Ballard, *A Long Shadow,* 9–13; Wm. C. P. Breckinridge to Issa Breckinridge, April 2, 1865, vol. 240, Breckinridge Family Papers, LC; W. A. Johnson, "Marching, Camping, Fighting," Lovic P. Thomas Scrapbooks, 2:149, Lovic P. Thomas Papers, AHS; Brooks and Lefler, *Papers of Walter Clark,* 1:140.

29. R. M. Collins, *Chapters,* 293–94; *OR* 47(3):737.

30. *OR* 47(3):750, 755, 759; Johnston, *Narrative,* 395. Johnston probably heard rumors concerning Richmond's fall on April 4. See Joseph F. Waring Diary, April 4,

1865, SHC-UNC; D. G. Godwin to Bettie, April 4, 1865, D. G. Godwin Letters, Civil War Collection—Confederate, TNSLA; D. T. Copeland to Mattie, April 4, 1865, David T. Copeland Papers, SHC-UNC.

31. John Johnson Diary, April 5, 1865, DU; William to Lina, April 6, 1865, William H. Johnson Papers, USC; Ridley, *Battles and Sketches*, 456; D. G. Godwin to Bettie, April 4, 1865, D. G. Godwin Letters, Civil War Collection—Confederate, TNSLA; Joseph F. Waring Diary, April 4, 1865, SHC-UNC; *Raleigh Daily Confederate*, April 10, 1865; W. A. Johnson, "Closing Days," June 5, 1902; W. A. Johnson, "Marching, Camping, Fighting," Lovic P. Thomas Scrapbooks, 2:149, Lovic P. Thomas Papers, AHS.

32. *OR* 47(3):755, 759, 762, 765–66; Joseph Hamilton, *Correspondence of Jonathan Worth*, 1:379; Price, "Railroads of North Carolina," 191; Mullen, "Last Days," 103–4; Crabtree and Patton, *"Journal of a Secesh Lady,"* 691–92. Historian Jeffrey Lash, a harsh critic of Johnston's misuse of Confederate rail transportation earlier in the war, praises the general's handling of rail logistics in North Carolina during the final days of the conflict. See Lash, *Destroyer of the Iron Horse*, 171–73.

33. *OR* 47(3):764–65.

34. C. C. Platter Diary, April 6, 1865, UGA; Andersen, *Diary of Allen Morgan Geer*, 211; Charlie to Wife, April 7, 1865, Charles B. Tompkins Papers, DU; J. W. H[inkley] to Wells, April 7, 1865, Julian W. Hinkley Papers, SHSW.

35. Quaife, *From the Cannon's Mouth*, 380; Jamison, *Recollections*, 325; Saunier, *Forty-seventh Ohio*, 426; Rood, *Company E, Twelfth Wisconsin*, 425.

36. McAdams, *Every-Day Soldier Life*, 149; R[.] Mead to "Dear Folks at Home," April 7, 1865, Rufus Mead Papers, LC; Slocum, "Final Operations," 755; Stormont, *Fifty-eighth Indiana*, 507; Calkins, *One Hundred and Fourth Illinois*, 310; William H. McIntosh, "Annals of the 22d Wisconsin," 221, William H. McIntosh Papers, SHSW; *OR* 47(1):936.

37. Peter Ege Daily Army Record, April 7, 1865, Peter Ege Papers, SHSW.

38. *OR* 47(3):110, 113, 129; Schafer, *Intimate Letters of Carl Schurz*, 328; W. T. Sherman to Ellen, April 9, 1865, and William T. Sherman Diary, April 6, 1865, Sherman Family Papers, UND; Sherman, *Memoirs*, 2:343.

39. *OR* 47(3):119, 121–24.

40. Barrett, *Sherman's March*, 199; Bradley, *Last Stand*, 348, 405.

41. *OR* 47(3):89–90, 99–100; Henry to Nelie, April 10, 1865, Henry Clay Weaver Papers, LC; Baker, *A Soldier's Experiences*, 48; *New York Herald*, April 14, 1865.

42. *New York Herald*, April 14, 1865; Henry to Nelie, April 10, 1865, Henry Clay Weaver Papers, LC; *OR* 47(3):99–100; Sherman, *Memoirs*, 2:343; Baker, *A Soldier's Experiences*, 48.

43. *OR* 47(3):128–29.

44. *Raleigh Daily Confederate*, April 10, 1865; Powell, *North Carolina Biography*, 4:189–90; Hill, *North Carolina*, 626–28; Hamilton and Williams, *Papers of William A. Graham*, 6:48–49; Sears, *To the Gates*, 79–81; *OR* 11(1):609–11; *OR* 11(2):639–45; *OR* 19(1):1027, 1039–43; Yates, "Vance as War Governor," 64; Rowland, *Jefferson Davis*, 9:329–30; Spencer, *Last Ninety Days*, 247–48.

45. *Raleigh Daily Confederate*, April 10, 1865; Powell, *North Carolina Biography*, 6:85–86; Yates, "Vance as War Governor," 43–44; Frontis Johnson, "Vance: A Person-

ality Sketch," 178, 187–88; Z. B. Vance to E. J. Hale, October 11, 1864, Letterbook, vol. 3, Edward J. Hale Papers, NCDAH.

46. Frontis Johnson, "Vance: A Personality Sketch," 186–87; Zebulon B. Vance quoted in Dowd, *Life of Vance,* 441; Spencer, *Last Ninety Days,* 18.

47. *OR* 9:254–57; *OR* 11(2):793; Yates, "Vance as War Governor," 47–49, 55–67; Walter Clark, *Histories,* 2:305–6.

48. Yates, "Vance as War Governor," 68–72.

49. Z. B. Vance to D. L. Swain, September 22, 1864, Letterbook, vol. 5, Zebulon B. Vance Papers, NCDAH.

50. *OR* 46(2):1093–94.

51. *OR* 47(2):1187–92. For accounts and notices of public meetings, see *Fayetteville Observer,* February 20, 27, 1865; *Raleigh Daily Confederate,* February 20, 24 (reprinted from the *Goldsboro State Journal,* n.d.), March 23, 1865; *Hillsborough Recorder,* February 22, 1865; *Raleigh Weekly Conservative,* March 15, 1865.

52. Undated document, Papers of Governor Zebulon B. Vance, State Agency Records, NCDAH; *OR* 47(2):1270–71.

53. *Raleigh Semi-Weekly Standard,* February 21, 1865; Rowland, *Jefferson Davis,* 9:330–33; Spencer, *Last Ninety Days,* 248.

54. Spencer, *Last Ninety Days,* 103–4; Powell, *North Carolina Biography,* 2:337–39; Hamilton and Williams, *Papers of William A. Graham,* 6:294.

55. Hamilton and Williams, *Papers of William A. Graham,* 6:294–95; Walter Clark, *Histories,* 5:478–79; Zebulon B. Vance quoted in Dowd, *Life of Vance,* 460; Yates, *Confederacy and Zeb Vance,* 114–15; McGehee, *Life of Graham,* 50–51.

56. Hamilton and Williams, *Papers of William A. Graham,* 6:295.

57. Ibid., 295–96.

58. *Raleigh Daily Confederate,* April 10, 1865; Ridley, *Battles and Sketches,* 456; James W. Brown Diary, April 7, 1865, Private Papers, Mf Drawer 187, Reel 13, GADAH.

59. James W. Brown Diary, April 7, 1865, Private Papers, Mf Drawer 187, Reel 13, GADAH; *Raleigh Daily Confederate,* April 10, 1865; *Smithfield Herald,* October 24, 1989; Greco, "Individual Property Form for the Everitt P. Stevens House."

60. *Raleigh Daily Confederate,* April 10, 1865; James W. Brown Diary, April 7, 1865, Private Papers, Mf Drawer 187, Reel 13, GADAH; William E. Stoney quoted in Hagood, *Memoirs,* 367; Ruffin Van Buren Collie quoted in Hoar, *South's Last Boys,* 429.

61. *Raleigh Daily Confederate,* April 10, 1865; James W. Brown Diary, April 7, 1865, Private Papers, Mf Drawer 187, Reel 13, GADAH.

62. *OR* 46(3):619.

63. *OR* 47(3):767–68; Johnston, *Narrative,* 395.

64. *Raleigh Daily Confederate,* April 7, 1865; Ridley, *Battles and Sketches,* 456; Jefferson Davis, *Rise and Fall,* 2:676–78; William C. Davis, *Jefferson Davis,* 608–9; Ballard, *A Long Shadow,* 56–57. The prevailing opinion has been that Davis was urging his fellow Southerners to resort to partisan guerrilla warfare, but historian Mark Grimsley, among others, suggests that Davis was referring to hit-and-run conventional warfare as practiced by Maj. Gen. George Washington in the 1776–77 New Jersey campaign of the American War of Independence. Grimsley, "Fighting a Lost War."

65. *OR* 47(3):754, 764, 766; Return of the Effective Strength of the Army of Ten-

nessee, April 7, 1865, Joseph E. Johnston Papers, W&M; Sherman, *Memoirs*, 2:334; Johnston, *Narrative*, 395; Ridley, *Battles and Sketches*, 556. The actual troop strength of Johnston's army was probably higher. The April 28 muster rolls for the reorganized Army of Tennessee show 29,963 officers and men, a figure that does not include the garrisons of Charlotte, Greensboro, and Salisbury. If the April 7 figure were accurate, this would indicate a loss of fewer than 1,000 in three weeks, which is far too low. See Appendix G of this volume.

66. *OR* 47(1):1061–65, 1083; *OR* 47(3):720, 773–74, 781–82; Dickert, *Kershaw's Brigade*, 527; Ridley, *Battles and Sketches*, 457; Guild, *Fourth Tennessee Cavalry*, 136–37; W. H. Andrews, "First Georgia Regulars at Johnston's Surrender," Lovic P. Thomas Scrapbooks, 1:38, Lovic P. Thomas Papers, AHS; Alfred T. Fielder Diary, April 9–10, 1865, Tennessee Historical Society Collection, TNSLA; Thomas L. Sullivan Account Book, April 10, 1865, Civil War Collection—Confederate, TNSLA; "Orders, Smithfield, N.C., April 8, 1865. Co. C Book, 45th Ala. Reg.—Co. C, 1st Ala. Vols., 1862–1865," chap. 8, vol. 4, 100, RG 109, NA; D. E. H. Smith, *A Charlestonian's Recollections*, 103–4; Charles C. Jones, *Chatham Artillery*, 215.

67. *OR* 47(3):771, 773, 776, 780; Johnston, *Narrative*, 396.

CHAPTER FOUR

1. *OR* 47(1):603; Alpheus S. Williams Diary, April 10, 1865, Alpheus S. Williams Papers, DPL; Bauer, *Soldiering*, 238; Morhous, *123rd N.Y.*, 174; Maurice S. Toler, "After Bentonville," *Smithfield Herald*, April 12, 1983; "Campaign Maps Showing the Line of March of the Army of Georgia from Goldsboro, N.C. to Avens Bridge, N.C.," H96, Map No. 1, RG 77, NACB.

2. "Campaign Maps Showing the Line of March of the Army of Georgia from Goldsboro, N.C. to Avens Bridge, N.C.," H96, Map No. 1, RG 77, NACB; "Journal of the Campaign from Goldsboro, North Carolina to Alexandria, Virginia," April 10, 1865, James D. Morgan Collection, HSQAC; Peter Ege Daily Army Record, April 9, 1865, Peter Ege Papers, SHSW; Payne, *Thirty-fourth Illinois*, 210; McAdams, *Every-Day Soldier Life*, 149; Maurice S. Toler, "After Bentonville," *Smithfield Herald*, April 12, 1983.

3. Stormont, *Fifty-eighth Indiana*, 511; S[amuel] Merrill to Emma, April 15, 1865, Samuel Merrill Papers, INSL; William H. McIntosh, "Annals of the 22d Wisconsin," 222, William H. McIntosh Papers, SHSW.

4. *OR* 47(1):210; *OR* 47(3):141, 152; Hiram Matthew to Wife, April 9, 1865, Hiram Matthew Letters, INSL; Alonzo L. Brown, *Fourth Minnesota*, 398.

5. *OR* 47(3):141, 152; Wright, *Sixth Iowa*, 446; Gage, *From Vicksburg*, 303–4; Wills, *Army Life*, 367.

6. *OR* 47(1):614, 618, 626, 630, 634; Bauer, *Soldiering*, 238; Morhous, *123rd N.Y.*, 174; Calvin Edgerton, "Ever Hear of Battle of Moccasin Swamp?" *Smithfield Herald*, April 7, 1992.

7. John L. Black, *Crumbling Defenses*, 110–11, 113–16; Krick, *Lee's Colonels*, 48; Walter Clark, *Histories*, 3:681; *OR* 47(1):626; *OR* 47(3):157, 749, 766.

8. John L. Black, *Crumbling Defenses*, 113–15; *OR* 47(1):627; Morhous, *123rd N.Y.*, 174; *Annals of an American Family*, 203.

9. Bauer, *Soldiering*, 238–39; Morhous, *123rd N.Y.*, 174–75; Brady, *Hurrah for the Artillery!*, 405; David Nichol Diary, April 10, 1865, David Nichol Papers, Harrisburg Civil War Round Table Collection, USAMHI; *OR* 47(1):627, 857; John L. Black, *Crumbling Defenses*, 115–16.

10. John L. Black, *Crumbling Defenses*, 115; *OR* 47(1):603, 627. The name is spelled "Tooley" in the reports of division commander Williams and brigade commander Selfridge. *OR* 47(3):607, 614. The casualty Williams referred to was probably Martin V. B. Ingram of the 13th New Jersey. According to the historian of the 13th, Ingram was an orderly on the staff of Twentieth Corps commander Joseph A. Mower. See Toombs, *Reminiscences*, 220.

11. "Journal of the Campaign from Goldsboro, North Carolina to Alexandria, Virginia," April 10, 1865, James D. Morgan Collection, HSQAC; Peter Ege Daily Army Record, April 10, 1865, Peter Ege Papers, SHSW; *OR* 47(3):783; Lyman S. Widney Diary-Reminiscences, chap. 46, p. 1, Lyman S. Widney Papers, KMNP; Widney, "From the Sea," September 3, 1903; McAdams, *Every-Day Soldier Life*, 149–50; Payne, *Thirty-fourth Illinois*, 210.

12. Lyman S. Widney Diary-Reminiscences, chap. 46, p. 2, Lyman S. Widney Papers, KMNP; Widney, "From the Sea," September 3, 1903.

13. *OR* 47(3):133, 155–56.

14. "Journal of the Campaign from Goldsboro, North Carolina to Alexandria, Virginia," April 10, 1865, James D. Morgan Collection, HSQAC; McAdams, *Every-Day Soldier Life*, 150.

15. Lyman S. Widney Diary-Reminiscences, chap. 46, p. 3, Lyman S. Widney Papers, KMNP; Widney, "From the Sea," September 3, 1903.

16. *OR* 47(3):132, 158; Committee of the Regiment, *Ninety-second Illinois*, 234–35.

17. *Christian Recorder* (Philadelphia), May 6, 1865.

18. Mowris, *One Hundred and Seventeenth New York*, 208–9; *Christian Recorder*, May 6, 1865.

19. *OR* 47(1):936; Redmond F. Laswell Diary, April 10, 1865, Military Archival Collection, ACHM.

20. *OR* 47(1):30, 43; *OR* 47(3):128–29, 156; W. T. Sherman to Ellen, April 9, 1865, Sherman Family Papers, UND; Sherman, *Memoirs*, 2:334.

21. *OR* 47(1):936.

22. In his *Narrative*, Johnston states that Hardee's *Corps* took the direct road to Raleigh, but two dispatches from Johnston's chief of staff, Col. Archer Anderson, indicate that only one *division* of Hardee's Corps marched on that road. The other two divisions therefore followed Stewart's and Lee's Corps on the Louisburg Road. The journal of Maj. Henry Hampton, the adjutant of Cheatham's Division of Hardee's Corps, supports this conclusion. Johnston, *Narrative*, 396; *OR* 47(1):1083; *OR* 47(3): 780, 782; William E. Stoney quoted in Hagood, *Memoirs*, 367; Thomas L. Sullivan Account Book, April 10, 1865, Civil War Collection—Confederate, TNSLA; D. E. H. Smith, *A Charlestonian's Recollections*, 104; W. A. Johnson, "Closing Days," June 5, 1902; W. A. Johnson, "Marching, Camping, Fighting," Lovic P. Thomas Scrapbooks, 2:155, Lovic P. Thomas Papers, AHS.

23. C. W. Hutson, "My Reminiscences," 124, and Charles W. Hutson to Mother, April 7, 1865 [Journal-Letter, April 11, 1865], Charles W. Hutson Papers, SHC-

UNC; D. E. H. Smith, *A Charlestonian's Recollections*, 104; Alfred T. Fielder Diary, April 10, 1865, Tennessee Historical Society Collection, TNSLA; W. A. Johnson, "Closing Days," June 5, 1902; W. A. Johnson, "Marching, Camping, Fighting," Lovic P. Thomas Scrapbooks, 1:155, Lovic P. Thomas Papers, AHS; *OR* 47(1):1083; William E. Stoney quoted in Hagood, *Memoirs*, 367–68; Thomas L. Sullivan Account Book, April 10–11, 1865, Civil War Collection—Confederate, TNSLA.

24. *OR* 47(3):782; Cumming, "How I Knew," 18; Joseph B. Cumming War Recollections, 82–83, SHC-UNC. In his reminiscences, Major Cumming notes that only one South Carolina soldier was sentenced to be executed. According to the army's court-martial records, however, four men of Kennedy's South Carolina brigade were condemned: Sgt. Jasper P. Parker, Pvt. John McClain, and Pvt. John F. Knight of the 20th South Carolina, and Pvt. Samuel Mabry of the 15th South Carolina. Six other South Carolinians were sentenced to be shot, but their sentences were commuted by the court pending President Davis's verdict. See General Orders No. 9, April 9, 1865, and General Orders No. 10, April 9, 1865, Box 81, Telegrams, Orders, Letters, and Court-Martial Proceedings, Department and Army of Tennessee—Gen. Joseph E. Johnston, RG 109, NA; *OR* 47(3):790 (in which Private McClain's name is misspelled "McJair"); W. A. Johnson, "Closing Days," June 5, 1902.

25. Cumming, "How I Knew," 18; Joseph B. Cumming War Recollections, 83–84, SHC-UNC.

26. Johnston, *Narrative*, 396; Cumming, "How I Knew," 18.

27. Johnston, *Narrative*, 396; *OR* 47(3):777.

28. Cumming, "How I Knew," 18–19.

29. William E. Stoney quoted in Hagood, *Memoirs*, 368; Alfred T. Fielder Diary, April 11, 1865, Tennessee Historical Society Collection, TNSLA; James W. Brown Diary, April 11–12, 1865, Private Papers, Mf Drawer 187, Reel 13, GADAH.

30. C. W. Hutson, "My Reminiscences," 124, and Charles W. Hutson to Mother, April 7, 1865 [Journal-Letter, April 11, 1865], Charles W. Hutson Papers, SHC-UNC; Harriet Cobb Lane Reminiscence: "For My Children," 3, NCC-UNC; Clarke, "Sherman in Raleigh," 226; W. A. Johnson, "Closing Days," June 5, 1902; W. A. Johnson, "Marching, Camping, Fighting," Lovic P. Thomas Scrapbooks, 2:155, Lovic P. Thomas Papers, AHS.

31. Ridley, *Battles and Sketches*, 457; Kate McKimmon quoted in Mrs. John Huske Anderson, *North Carolina Women*, 104; Walter Clark, *Histories*, 4:59–60.

32. *City of Raleigh*, 55, 57; Clarke, "Sherman in Raleigh," 227; [R. H. Battle] to C. P. Spencer, February 26, 1866, Cornelia P. Spencer Papers, SHC-UNC.

33. James A. Blackshear Diary, March 15, 1865, EU; [R. H. Battle] to C. P. Spencer, February 26, 1866, and Z. B. Vance to C. P. Spencer, February 17, 1866, Cornelia P. Spencer Papers, SHC-UNC; Spencer, *Last Ninety Days*, 146; B. F. Moore to "Gov. Swain," April 9, 1865, David L. Swain Papers, SHC-UNC.

34. Charles Manly to "My Dear Gov.," April 8, 1865, David L. Swain Papers, SHC-UNC.

35. Hamilton and Williams, *Papers of William A. Graham*, 6:292–93; Spencer, *Last Ninety Days*, 135–37.

36. Hamilton and Williams, *Papers of William A. Graham*, 6:294–97; Spencer, *Last Ninety Days*, 137–41.

37. Hamilton and Williams, *Papers of William A. Graham*, 6:297; Spencer, *Last Ninety Days*, 141–43; Yates, "Governor Vance and the End of the War," 328.

38. Spencer, *Last Ninety Days*, 143.

39. B. F. Moore to K. Rayner, May 10, 1867, and K. Rayner to B. F. Moore, May 13, 1867, Kenneth Rayner Papers, SHC-UNC.

40. B. F. Moore to K. Rayner, May 10, 1867, and K. Rayner to B. F. Moore, May 13, 1867, Kenneth Rayner Papers, SHC-UNC; Z. B. Vance to C. P. Spencer, February 17, 1866, Cornelia P. Spencer Papers, SHC-UNC; Zebulon B. Vance to "My dear friend" [Cornelia P. Spencer], January 8, 1867, David L. Swain Papers, SHC-UNC; *OR* 47(3): 786–87; Rowland, *Jefferson Davis*, 9:334; Zebulon B. Vance, "Lecture—Last Days of the War," in Dowd, *Life of Vance*, 483.

41. B. F. Moore to K. Rayner, May 10, 1867, and K. Rayner to B. F. Moore, May 13, 1867, Kenneth Rayner Papers, SHC-UNC; Z. B. Vance to C. P. Spencer, February 17, 1866, Zebulon B. Vance to "My dear friend," January 8, 1867, and [R. H. Battle] to C. P. Spencer, February 26, 1866, Cornelia P. Spencer Papers, SHC-UNC; *OR* 47(3): 792; Vance, "Lecture—Last Days of the War," in Dowd, *Life of Vance*, 483; Hamilton and Williams, *Papers of William A. Graham*, 6:298. Vance recalled going to Johnston to seek his advice, but Rayner remembered being in Vance's office when Johnston called on the governor. If Rayner's recollection is correct, then Vance received Davis's message just before Johnston's arrival. Rayner's version is consistent with Vance's recollection that he sought Johnston's advice after receiving Davis's telegram.

42. K. Rayner to B. F. Moore, May 13, 1867, Kenneth Rayner Papers, SHC-UNC; [R. H. Battle] to C. P. Spencer, February 26, 1866, Cornelia P. Spencer Papers, SHC-UNC; *City of Raleigh*, 57; Amis, *Historical Raleigh*, 141.

43. Joseph Hamilton, *Correspondence of Jonathan Worth*, 1:371; *OR* 47(3):695–96, 789; Z. B. Vance to C. P. Spencer, February 17, 1866, and [R. H. Battle] to C. P. Spencer, February 26, 1866, Cornelia P. Spencer Papers, SHC-UNC; Spencer, *Last Ninety Days*, 146; Vance, "Lecture—Last Days of the War," in Dowd, *Life of Vance*, 483.

44. *OR* 47(3):788; Johnston, *Narrative*, 396; A. Toomer Porter, *Led On!*, 180–83.

45. Alfred T. Fielder Diary, April 12, 1865, Tennessee Historical Society Collection, TNSLA; Thomas L. Sullivan Account Book, April 11, 1865, Civil War Collection—Confederate, TNSLA. This building replaced North Carolina's original State House, which burned in 1831.

46. Alfred T. Fielder Diary, April 12, 1865, Tennessee Historical Society Collection, TNSLA.

47. *OR* 47(1):116; Floyd, *Seventy-fifth Indiana*, 383; William B. Miller Journal, April 11, 1865, INHS; Joseph F. Waring Diary, April 11, 1865, SHC-UNC; Orrin L. Ellis Diary, April 11, 1865, *CWTI* Collection, USAMHI; Jesse R. Sparkman Diary, April 11, 1865, Box 3, Diaries, Memoirs, Etc., TNSLA.

48. Floyd, *Seventy-fifth Indiana*, 383–84; Orrin L. Ellis Diary, April 11, 1865, *CWTI* Collection, USAMHI; Nichols, *Story of the Great March*, 292.

49. William B. Miller Journal, April 11, 1865, INHS; John L. Black, *Crumbling Defenses*, 117–18; Joseph F. Waring Diary, April 11, 1865, SHC-UNC; Orrin L. Ellis Diary, April 11, 1865, *CWTI* Collection, USAMHI; Jesse R. Sparkman Diary, April 11, 1865, Box 3, Diaries, Memoirs, Etc., TNSLA.

50. Ginger, "The 75th Ind."; William B. Miller Journal, April 11, 1865, INHS.

51. Ginger, "The 75th Ind."

52. Ibid.

53. Stormont, *Fifty-eighth Indiana*, 513–15; H[enry] to Mary, April 14, 1865, Henry Hitchcock Papers, LC; Hitchcock, *Marching with Sherman*, 296; Nichols, *Story of the Great March*, 292; Smithfield Methodist Church Sabbath School Record Book (photocopy), April 12, 1865, entry, JCPL.

54. *OR* 47(1):210, 700, 791, 811; *OR* 47(3):165; Alpheus S. Williams Diary, April 11, 1865, Alpheus S. Williams Papers, DPL; William H. McIntosh, "Annals of the 22d Wisconsin," 223, William H. McIntosh Papers, SHSW; Stormont, *Fifty-eighth Indiana*, 513–14; Wharton, *Smithfield as Seen*, 13; *Kenly (N.C.) News*, December 4, 1985.

55. *OR* 47(3): 163–64; Sherman, *General and Field Orders*, 226–27.

56. *OR* 47(3):171.

57. Ibid., 172.

58. *OR* 47(1):936; *OR* 47(3):173; *Annals of an American Family*, 203.

59. Geo[rge] to Sarah, April 17, 1865, George A. Collamore Letters, GHM; Furnas, *Forty-four Months*, 154.

60. *Annals of an American Family*, 207–8; Cox, *Military Reminiscences*, 2:458; *OR* 47(1):936.

61. *OR* 47(3):188–89; Cox, *Military Reminiscences*, 2:458.

62. Geo[rge] to Sarah, April 17, 1865, George A. Collamore Letters, GHM; Furnas, *Forty-four Months*, 155.

63. H. A. Gildersleeve to Fannie E. Gardner, February 8, 1892, and Affadavit of Judge H. A. Gildersleeve in U.S. House, *H.R. 8928*, 2–3; Stephens, "Frances Gardner," 17–18, JCPL; Alpheus S. Williams Diary, April 14, 1865, Alpheus S. Williams Papers, DPL; *Raleigh News and Observer*, March 31, 1980; *Smithfield Herald*, March 18, 1980.

64. Stephens, "Frances Gardner," 1–18, JCPL; Petition of Fannie E. Gardner, H. A. Gildersleeve to Fannie E. Gardner, February 8, 1892, and Affadavit of Judge H. A. Gildersleeve in U.S. House, *H.R. 8928*, 1–3.

65. Petition of Fannie E. Gardner, H. A. Gildersleeve to Fannie E. Gardner, February 8, 1892, and Affadavit of Judge H. A. Gildersleeve in U.S. House, *H.R. 8928*, 1–3; Stephens, "Frances Gardner," 18, JCPL.

66. Petition of Fannie E. Gardner in U.S. House, *H.R. 8928*, 1–2; Stephens, "Frances Gardner," 19–20, 30–34, JCPL.

67. Stephens, "Frances Gardner," 18; H[enry] to Mary, April 14, 1865, Henry Hitchcock Papers, LC; Hitchcock, *Marching with Sherman*, 296; *OR* 47(3):140, 177, 187.

68. Sherman, *Memoirs*, 2:344; Barrett, *Sherman's March*, 209–10; H[enry] to Mary, April 14, 1865, Henry Hitchcock Papers, LC; Hitchcock, *Marching with Sherman*, 295.

69. *OR* 47(1):603–4, 786; *OR* 47(3):140; J. Thayer to Wife, April 16, 1865, Federal Soldiers' Letters, SHC-UNC; H[enry] to Mary, April 14, 1865, Henry Hitchcock Papers, LC; Hitchcock, *Marching with Sherman*, 296.

70. Balloch, "Twentieth Corps"; Alpheus Williams Diary, April 12, 1865, Alpheus Williams Papers, DPL; Quaife, *From the Cannon's Mouth*, 381.

71. Furnas, *Forty-four Months*, 155; Ricks, "Carrying the News," 241–42; Charlie to "Mother & Etta," April 18, 1865, Charles S. Brown Papers, DU; Thompson, *112th*

Illinois, 316; Aten, *Eighty-fifth Illinois,* 303–4; Slocum, "Final Operations," 755; Cox, *March to the Sea,* 213–14; J. F. Woods to "My Dear Friends," April 14, 1865, J. F. Woods Papers, DU; *Cincinnati Daily Commercial,* May 2, 1865.

72. Ginger, "The 75th Ind."; William B. Miller Journal, April 12, 1865, INHS; *Cincinnati Daily Commercial,* May 4, 1865; Wills, *Army Life,* 368.

73. *Philadelphia Inquirer,* April 28, 1865; Manning F. Force Letterbook-Journal, April 13, 1865, Manning F. Force Papers, UWA.

74. *OR* 47(3):186, 794; Joseph F. Waring Diary, April 12, 1865, SHC-UNC; Orrin L. Ellis Diary, April 12, 1865, *CWTI* Collection, USAMHI; Jesse R. Sparkman Diary, April 11–12, 1865, Box 3, Diaries, Memoirs, Etc., TNSLA; Committee of the Regiment, *Ninety-second Illinois,* 235.

75. Wiley C. Howard, *Sketch of Cobb Legion,* 18; W. A. Russell, "Tragic Adventures," 401; Joseph F. Waring Diary, April 12, 1865, SHC-UNC; Committee of the Regiment, *Ninety-second Illinois,* 235. There is some confusion as to the correct spelling of the fallen Confederate's name. In his *Sketch of Cobb Legion,* Howard spelled his friend's name "Donahoo," yet according to the printout provided by Raleigh's Oakwood Cemetery—where the Georgian is buried—the name is "Donnahue." The cavalryman's descendants have since furnished the correct spelling of his name, which appears on his current headstone as "Dunnahoo." See Raleigh Cemetery Association, "List of Confederate Soldiers Buried in Oakwood Cemetery," 5.

76. Stalling's Station was also known as Clayton's Station and stood on what is now the town of Clayton. *OR* 47(1):116, 119, 120; *OR* (3):186; O. T. [Orville T. Chamberlain] to Father, April 21, 1865, Orville T. Chamberlain Letters, Dr. Joseph W. Chamberlain Papers, INHS; Eaton, "Diary of an Officer," 251; Kittinger, *Diary,* 203–4; Will to Brother, April 14, 1865, William C. Stevens Correspondence, BL-UMI; Committee of the Regiment, *Ninety-second Illinois,* 236.

77. Will to Brother, April 14, 1865, William C. Stevens Correspondence, BL-UMI; Committee of the Regiment, *Ninety-second Illinois,* 236.

CHAPTER FIVE

1. Spencer, *Last Ninety Days,* 143, 215; *Wilmington (N.C.) Daily Review,* March 6, 1885; Nichols, *Story of the Great March,* 298.

2. Spencer, *Last Ninety Days,* 143; *Wilmington (N.C.) Daily Review,* March 6, 1885; *OR* 47(3):178.

3. Z. B. Vance to C. P. Spencer, February 17, 1866, Cornelia P. Spencer Papers, SHC-UNC; J. Devereux to D. L. Swain, July 7, 1866, Walter Clark Papers, NCDAH; Zebulon B. Vance, "Lecture—Last Days of the War," in Dowd, *Life of Vance,* 483–84; Spencer, *Last Ninety Days,* 144–45; Warren, *A Doctor's Experiences,* 333–34; *Wilmington (N.C.) Daily Review,* March 2, 6, 1865; Ward, *Last Flag,* 9–10. State treasurer Jonathan Worth saw both Vance and Graham that morning and noted that the two men had misgivings about the mission to Sherman. According to Worth, Graham was reluctant to go because he feared being arrested as a Confederate senator. See Jonathan Worth to Br[other] Addison, April 22, 1865, Jonathan Worth Papers, SHC-UNC.

4. Spencer, *Last Ninety Days,* 144–45, 147; [R. H. Battle] to C. P. Spencer, Feb-

ruary 26, 1866, Cornelia P. Spencer Papers, SHC-UNC; Rowland, *Jefferson Davis,* 9:
332, 342.

5. Rowland, *Jefferson Davis,* 9:332. Maj. Gen. Robert F. Hoke reportedly visited
the governor on an errand similar to McRae's. Citing rumors that Vance intended
to surrender the state of North Carolina, Hoke asked the governor whether they
were true. Vance vigorously denied the rumors, saying, "All hell can't make me do
it." See J. J. Laughinghouse Reminiscence, Military Collection—Civil War, NCDAH,
and Robert F. Hoke Papers, NCDAH.

6. Rowland, *Jefferson Davis,* 9:332–34; *OR* 47(3):791; Z. B. Vance to Cornelia P.
Spencer, April 7, [1866], Cornelia P. Spencer Papers, SHC-UNC.

7. Ward, *Last Flag,* 10–11; Fred A. Olds, "How Sherman's Army Entered Raleigh,"
5, Box 9: "Historical File 1865," James D. and David R. Barbee Papers, LC; Fred A.
Olds, "Fiftieth Anniversary," *Raleigh Times,* April 13, 1915; Spencer, *Last Ninety Days,*
147; J. Devereux to D. L. Swain, July 7, 1866, Walter Clark Papers, NCDAH; *Wilmington (N.C.) Daily Review,* March 6, 1885.

8. Spencer, *Last Ninety Days,* 147–48; Ward, *Last Flag,* 11; J. Devereux to D. L.
Swain, July 7, 1866, Walter Clark Papers, NCDAH; *OR* 47(3):187, 791.

9. J. G. Burr to D. L. Swain, June 18, 1866, Walter Clark Papers, NCDAH; Ward,
Last Flag, 12; Warren, *A Doctor's Experiences,* 336; *Wilmington (N.C.) Daily Review,*
March 2, 1885; Spencer, *Last Ninety Days,* 148–49.

10. Will to Brother, April 14, 1865, William C. Stevens Correspondence, BL-UMI;
Committee of the Regiment, *Ninety-second Illinois,* 236–37; Spencer, *Last Ninety Days,*
149; J. Devereux to D. L. Swain, July 7, 1866, and J. G. Burr to D. L. Swain, June 18,
1866, Walter Clark Papers, NCDAH; Warren, *A Doctor's Experiences,* 336–37; *Wilmington (N.C.) Daily Review,* March 2, 1885; Ward, *Last Flag,* 12–13; Fred A. Olds, "How
Sherman's Army Entered Raleigh," 6–7, Box 9: "Historical File 1865," James D. and
David R. Barbee Papers, LC.

11. Spencer, *Last Ninety Days,* 149–50; J. G. Burr to D. L. Swain, June 18, 1866, and
J. Devereux to D. L. Swain, July 7, 1866, Walter Clark Papers, NCDAH.

12. Spencer, *Last Ninety Days,* 150; J. G. Burr to D. L. Swain, June 18, 1866, Walter
Clark Papers, NCDAH; *OR* 47(3):180, 186; Sherman, *General and Field Orders,* 228;
Special Field Order No. 54, April 12, 1865, Sylvester C. Noble Papers, YHS.

13. J. G. Burr to D. L. Swain, June 18, 1866, Walter Clark Papers, NCDAH; Warren, *A Doctor's Experiences,* 337–38; *Wilmington (N.C.) Daily Review,* March 2, 1885.

14. J. G. Burr to D. L. Swain, June 18, 1866, Walter Clark Papers, NCDAH; Warren, *A Doctor's Experiences,* 339.

15. Spencer, *Last Ninety Days,* 150–51; Ward, *Last Flag,* 13–14; J. Devereux to D. L.
Swain, July 7, 1866, Walter Clark Papers, NCDAH. Warren recalled traveling to Sherman's headquarters on a handcar, but this recollection differs from those of Swain,
Ward, and Devereux. See Warren, *A Doctor's Experiences,* 339–40; *Wilmington (N.C.)
Daily Review,* March 2, 1885.

16. Spencer, *Last Ninety Days,* 151; Sherman, *Memoirs,* 2:345; J. G. Burr to D. L.
Swain, June 18, 1866, and J. Devereux to D. L. Swain, July 7, 1866, Walter Clark
Papers, NCDAH.

17. Spencer, *Last Ninety Days,* 151–52; Sherman, *Memoirs,* 2:345; *OR* 47(3):178–
79; Joseph Hamilton, *Papers of Thomas Ruffin,* 4:28; W. T. Sherman to Z. B. Vance,

April 12, 1865 [two letters], and D. L. Swain to "My dear Sir" [Zebulon B. Vance], April 12, 1865, Letterbook, vol. 7, Zebulon B. Vance Papers, NCDAH.

18. Sherman, *Memoirs*, 2:137–40; U.S. Congress, "Sherman-Johnston," 3:6, 14.

19. Spencer, *Last Ninety Days*, 154–55; H[enry] to Mary, April 14, 1865, Henry Hitchcock Papers, LC; Hitchcock, *Marching with Sherman*, 297; Ward, *Last Flag*, 14.

20. Spencer, *Last Ninety Days*, 155; J. G. Burr to D. L. Swain, June 18, 1866, Walter Clark Papers, NCDAH.

21. J. G. Burr to D. L. Swain, June 18, 1866, Walter Clark Papers, NCDAH.

22. Ibid.; Spencer, *Last Ninety Days*, 153–55.

23. Spencer, *Last Ninety Days*, 155–56; H[enry] to Mary, April 14, 1865, Henry Hitchcock Papers, LC; Hitchcock, *Marching with Sherman*, 297; Vance, *Hon. David L. Swain*, 16. A similar coincidence involved Dr. Warren and Sherman's chief ordnance officer, Lt. Col. Thomas G. Baylor, who introduced himself as a friend of Warren's brother and invited the doctor to share his tent. See Warren, *A Doctor's Experiences*, 344; *Wilmington (N.C.) Daily Review*, March 2, 1885.

24. "Campaign Maps Showing the Line of March of the Army of Georgia from Goldsboro, N.C. to Avens Bridge, N.C.," H96, Map No. 3, RG 77, NACB; *OR Atlas*, pl. 138; John H. Ferguson Diary, April 15, 1865, Pfeiffer Library, MacMurray College, Jacksonville, Illinois; *OR* 47(1):90, 96, 98, 101; *OR* 47(3):180–87, 192.

25. *OR* 47(3):186.

26. *OR* 47(1):1083; *OR* 47(3):793; Ridley, *Battles and Sketches*, 457; John Johnson Diary, April 12, 1865, DU; Holmes, *Diary of Henry McCall Holmes*, 34; *OR Atlas*, pl. 138.

27. Clarke, "Sherman in Raleigh," 227–28; Manning F. Force Letterbook-Journal, April 14, 1865, Manning F. Force Papers, UWA.

28. William W. Gordon, "War Stories," 9–10, William W. Gordon Reminiscences, in Joseph F. Waring Papers, Georgia Historical Society, Savannah. On April 11, before his arrival in Raleigh, Captain Gordon had stopped at the house of a woman whose corn supply was taken from her by a detachment of Col. Charles C. Crews's Brigade of Wheeler's cavalry. See William W. Gordon Diary, April 11, 1865, Gordon Family Papers, SHC-UNC.

29. Charlotte E. Grimes Reminiscences, 22, Bryan Grimes Papers, SHC-UNC; Devereux, *Plantation Sketches*, 150; Clarke, "Sherman in Raleigh," 227–28; Battle, *Memories*, 191; K. P. Battle to D. H. Hill Jr., "Richmond in January 1865," December 2, 1916, 5–6, D. H. Hill Jr. Papers, NCDAH; [R. H. Battle] to C. P. Spencer, February 26, 1866, Cornelia P. Spencer Papers, SHC-UNC.

30. Joseph Hamilton, *Correspondence of Jonathan Worth*, 1:380; [R. H. Battle] to C. P. Spencer, February 26, 1866, Cornelia P. Spencer Papers, SHC-UNC; Daniel H. Reynolds Diary, April 8–12, 1865, Daniel H. Reynolds Papers, Special Collections Division, University of Arkansas, Fayetteville; Fred A. Olds, "How Sherman's Army Entered Raleigh," 1, Box 9: "Historical File 1865," James D. and David R. Barbee Papers, LC; Fred A. Olds, "Story of the Surrender," November 27, 1925, 1.

31. Spencer, *Last Ninety Days*, 158–59; Z. B. Vance to C. P. Spencer, February 17, 1866, Cornelia P. Spencer Papers, SHC-UNC; Vance, "Lecture—Last Days of the War," in Dowd, *Life of Vance*, 484–85; Z. B. Vance to W. T. Sherman, April 11 [12], 1865, Cornelia P. Spencer Papers, SHC-UNC. Page's (or Carey) Station stood on the site of present-day downtown Cary.

32. Z. B. Vance to C. P. Spencer, February 17, 1866, Cornelia P. Spencer Papers, SHC-UNC; *OR* 47(3):792. Vance later denied attempting to open peace negotiations with Sherman. "I sent a commission to him under a flag of truce to ask protection, not separate terms for the people of my State," Vance said in 1885. See *OR* 47(3):178; U.S. Congress, "Remarks of Hon. Z. B. Vance," 3; Vance, "Lecture—Last Days of the War," in Dowd, *Life of Vance*, 483.

33. Spencer, *Last Ninety Days*, 157; H[enry] to Mary, April 14, 1865, Henry Hitchcock Papers, LC; Hitchcock, *Marching with Sherman*, 297; J. Devereux to D. L. Swain, July 7, 1866, Walter Clark Papers, NCDAH; Ward, *Last Flag*, 15.

34. Amis, *Historical Raleigh*, 142; *Raleigh News and Observer*, April 13, 1934; Spencer, *Last Ninety Days*, 157; J. Devereux to D. L. Swain, July 7, 1866, Walter Clark Papers, NCDAH.

35. Spencer, *Last Ninety Days*, 157–60; J. G. Burr to D. L. Swain, June 18, 1866, Walter Clark Papers, NCDAH; Swain, *Early Times*, 8.

36. Swain, *Early Times*, 8; Spencer, *Last Ninety Days*, 160.

37. Swain, *Early Times*, 8–9; Spencer, *Last Ninety Days*, 160–61.

38. James T. Reeve Diary, Memorandum of April 13, 1865, SHSW; "Surrender of Raleigh," *Philadelphia Times*, March 9, 1885.

39. James T. Reeve Diary, Memorandum of April 13, 1865, SHSW; "Surrender of Raleigh," *Philadelphia Times*, March 9, 1885; Joseph F. Waring Diary, April 13, 1865, SHC-UNC.

40. James T. Reeve Diary, Memorandum of April 13, 1865, SHSW; "Surrender of Raleigh," *Philadelphia Times*, March 9, 1885; K. Rayner to B. F. Moore, May 13, 1867, and K. R[ayner] to Sir [B. F. Moore], May 20, 1867, Kenneth Rayner Papers, SHC-UNC; *Raleigh Daily Standard*, April 17, 1865; *City of Raleigh*, 58; Amis, *Historical Raleigh*, 142–43; Haywood, *Builders of the Old North State*, 198; *Raleigh News and Observer*, April 13, 1934; Murray, *Wake: Capital County*, 506.

41. James T. Reeve Diary, Memorandum of April 13, 1865, SHSW; "Surrender of Raleigh," *Philadelphia Times*, March 9, 1885; Spencer, *Last Ninety Days*, 160–61.

42. Williamson D. Ward Journal, April 13, 1865, INHS; *Detroit Advertiser and Tribune*, May 11, 1865; James T. Reeve Diary, Memorandum of April 13, 1865, SHSW; "Surrender of Raleigh," *Philadelphia Times*, March 9, 1885; Spencer, *Last Ninety Days*, 161; Kittinger, *Diary*, 204; *City of Raleigh*, 59–60; Amis, *Historical Raleigh*, 143–44; *Raleigh News and Observer*, April 28, 1885, June 6, 1907, and April 13, 1909; Fred A. Olds, "Fiftieth Anniversary," *Raleigh Times*, April 13, 1915; Murray, *Wake: Capital County*, 507–8; Raleigh Cemetery Association, "List of Confederate Soldiers in Oakwood Cemetery," 18; Swain, *Early Times*, 9. In his account of the incident, Maj. James T. Reeve spelled the Texan's name "Welsh."

43. *City of Raleigh*, 60–62; Amis, *Historical Raleigh*, 144–45; *Wilmington (N.C.) Daily Review*, March 6, 1885; "A War Incident," Stephen B. Weeks Scrapbooks, 2:149, NCC-UNC.

44. "A War Incident," Stephen B. Weeks Scrapbooks, 2:149, NCC-UNC.

45. McMakin, "Capturing Raleigh," "Joining Sherman," and "Not Quite Over"; Gilberg, "Another View of It."

46. McMakin, "Capturing Raleigh" and "Flag on the Raleigh Capitol"; Caldwell, "Planting the Flag at Raleigh"; Will to Brother, April 14, 1865, William C.

Stevens Correspondence, BL-UMI; Clarke, "Sherman in Raleigh," 230; K. Rayner to B. F. Moore, May 13, 1867, Kenneth Rayner Papers, SHC-UNC; George to Fannie, April 21, 1865, George Shuman Letters, Harrisburg Civil War Round Table Collection, USAMHI; Cornelius Baker Diary, April 13, 1865, Bennett Place State Historic Site, Durham, North Carolina; Rowell, *Yankee Cavalrymen*, 249; Spencer, *Last Ninety Days*, 162; *Philadelphia Inquirer*, April 26, 1865.

47. *Raleigh News and Observer*, April 13, 1909; James S. Thompson Journal, April 13, 1865, INHS; Kittinger, *Diary*, 204; G. B., "9th Michigan Cavalry," *Detroit Advertiser and Tribune*, May 11, 1865.

48. Will to Brother, April 14, 1865, William C. Stevens Correspondence, BL-UMI; Michael H. Fitch Diary, April 13, 1865, Michael H. Fitch Papers, SHSW; John H. Otto, "War Memories," 123, John H. Otto Papers, SHSW; Ward, *Last Flag*, 16.

49. *OR* 47(1):604; Stine, "What Troops Were the First?"; Alpheus S. Williams Diary, April 13, 1865, Alpheus S. Williams Papers, DPL; Quaife, *From the Cannon's Mouth*, 381–82; Circular No. 18, April 12, 1865, 1st Division, 20th Corps, Letters and Reports Sent, January 1863–June 1865, 20th Army Corps, E 5762, vol. 33, RG 393, NA.

50. John Langhans to Brother, June 9, 1865, John Langhans Letters, Michael Winey Collection, USAMHI; "Campaign Maps Showing the Line of March of the Army of Georgia from Goldsboro, N.C. to Avens Bridge, N.C.," H96, Map No. 4, RG 77, NACB; Michael H. Fitch Diary, April 13, 1865, Michael H. Fitch Papers, SHSW; "Journal of the Campaign from Goldsboro, North Carolina to Alexandria, Virginia," April 13, 1865, James D. Morgan Collection, HSQAC; Alpheus S. Williams Diary, April 13, 1865, Alpheus S. Williams Papers, DPL; Quaife, *From the Cannon's Mouth*, 382.

51. *OR* 47(1):162, 937; *OR* 47(3):191–96, 199.

52. H[enry] to Mary, April 14, 1865, Henry Hitchcock Papers, LC; Hitchcock, *Marching with Sherman*, 298; O. M. Poe to Wife, April 13, 1865, Orlando M. Poe Papers, LC; Swain, *Early Times*, 9–10; Spencer, *Last Ninety Days*, 162–63; J. G. Burr to D. L. Swain, June 18, 1866, Walter Clark Papers, NCDAH.

53. Swain, *Early Times*, 9–10; Spencer, *Last Ninety Days*, 162–63; W. T. Sherman to "All officers & soldiers of the U.S. Army" [safeguard for Governor Vance and other state and city officials], April 13, 1865, Letterbook, vol. 7, Zebulon B. Vance Papers, NCDAH; W. T. Sherman to "All officers and men" [safeguard for former governors Swain and Graham], April 13, 1865, Walter Clark Papers, NCDAH; Hamilton and Williams, *Papers of William A. Graham*, 6:299; Vett to Sis, April 13, 1865, Sylvester C. Noble Papers, YHS.

54. Joseph F. Waring Diary, April 13, 1865, SHC-UNC; McMakin, "Capturing Raleigh"; *OR* 47(1):1132; *OR* 47(3):197; "A Rousing Reunion"; Kittinger, *Diary*, 204; O. P. Hargis Reminiscences, 9, SHC-UNC; Hargis, "We Kept Fighting," 42; Robert A. McClellan Memorandum, April 14 [13], 1865, Robert A. McClellan Papers, DU.

55. *OR* 47(3):796–97; Murray, *Wake: Capital County*, 509; Williamson D. Ward Journal, April 13, 1865, INHS; Orrin L. Ellis Diary, April 13, 1865, *CWTI* Collection, USAMHI; Fallis, "Entering Raleigh"; Kittinger, *Diary*, 204; Ditty, "Entering Raleigh."

56. Kittinger, *Diary*, 202; *OR* 44:362, 369, 508; David Evans, *Sherman's Horsemen*, 339–40.

57. Kittinger, *Diary*, 204–5; William E. Sloan Diary, April 13, 1865, Civil War Collection—Confederate, TNSLA.

58. Fallis, "Entering Raleigh"; Rowell, *Yankee Cavalrymen*, 251; Daniel H. Reynolds Diary, April 8–12, 13, 1865, Daniel H. Reynolds Papers, Special Collections Division, University of Arkansas, Fayetteville; *OR* 47(3):198.

59. Orrin L. Ellis Diary, April 13, 1865, *CWTI* Collection, USAMHI; *OR* 47(1): 1132; *OR* 47(3):198; Williamson D. Ward Journal, April 13, 1865, INHS; Committee of the Regiment, *Ninety-second Illinois*, 240; Will to Brother, April 14, 1865, William C. Stevens Correspondence, BL-UMI; Robert Y. Woodlief Diary, April 13, 1865, USC.

60. *OR* 47(3):208–9; Sherman, *General and Field Orders*, 228–29; Sherman, *Memoirs*, 2:345–46.

61. Sherman, *Memoirs*, 2:346; *OR* 47(3):209; Sherman, *General and Field Orders*, 229.

62. Ridley, *Battles and Sketches*, 457; *OR* 46(3):733; *OR* 47(1):1083; *OR* 47(3):191, 198, 796.

63. Hendricks, "Imperiled City," 11.

CHAPTER SIX

1. T. H. Holmes to J. E. Johnston, April 10, 1865, and T. H. Holmes to S. Cooper, April 10, 1865, Military Departments: Telegrams Sent, Reserve Forces of North Carolina, chap. 2, vol. 354, RG 109, NA; *OR* 47(3):777–79, 790–91; *OR* 49(1):332; Spencer, *Last Ninety Days*, 199; Van Noppen, *Stoneman's Last Raid*, 37–38; Barrett, *Civil War in North Carolina*, 351, 353; Trelease, *North Carolina Railroad*, 192.

2. *OR* 49(1):324, 332, 345; Kirk, *Fifteenth Pennsylvania Cavalry*, 501–2, 538, 698; Stephen R. Mallory Recollections, 2:344–45, SHC-UNC; Anna H. Trenholm Diary, April 11, 1865, SHC-UNC; Spencer, *Last Ninety Days*, 197–98; William C. Davis, *Jefferson Davis*, 613–14; James C. Clark, *Last Train South*, 55; Van Noppen, *Stoneman's Last Raid*, 43–45; Trelease, *North Carolina Railroad*, 192; Barrett, *Civil War in North Carolina*, 355.

3. Kirk, *Fifteenth Pennsylvania Cavalry*, 502–3, 541–44, 545–49, 550–52, 553–55, 698–700; Mrs. John S. Welborn, "High Point during the Confederacy," 2–3, Mrs. John S. Welborn Papers, SHC-UNC; Spencer, *Last Ninety Days*, 197–98; Van Noppen, *Stoneman's Last Raid*, 45–46; Barrett, *Civil War in North Carolina*, 355; Trelease, *North Carolina Railroad*, 192–93.

4. Regarding Stoneman, Stanton wrote: "I think him one of the most worthless officers in the service and who has failed in everything intrusted to him." Grant replied: "I am not in favor of using officers who have signally failed when intrusted with commands in important places." Nevertheless, the general-in-chief suggested that Stanton send the order relieving Stoneman to Schofield and allow him to act as he saw fit. Schofield decided to withhold the order and retain Stoneman. See *OR* 45(2):54, 58–59.

5. Trelease, *North Carolina Railroad*, 193; Barrett, *Civil War in North Carolina*, 356.

6. *OR* 49(1):324, 333–34; Hartley, " 'Like an Avalanche,' " 83; Spencer, *Last Ninety Days*, 199; Amann, *Personnel*, 1:263, 325; Hoole, *Forty-sixth Alabama*, 39; Lindsley, *Military Annals of Tennessee*, 837–38; Barrett, *Civil War in North Carolina*, 357; Daniel, *Cannoneers in Gray*, 183–85, 195. The three Confederate batteries defending Salisbury were Van den Corput's Cherokee Artillery (Georgia), Marshall's Tennessee battery, and Beauregard's South Carolina battery, the last-named commanded by General Beauregard's son, René. The first two batteries were from Johnston's Battalion, and the third was from Cobb's Battalion, of the Army of Tennessee. They were commanded at Salisbury by Maj. John W. Johnston.

7. The number of captured field pieces is from General Gillem's report. General Stoneman reported only fourteen captured cannon. *OR* 49(1):324, 333–34; Kirk, *Fifteenth Pennsylvania Cavalry*, 503–4; Lindsley, *Military Annals of Tennessee*, 838–41; Hartley, " 'Like an Avalanche,' " 84; Spencer, *Last Ninety Days*, 199–200; Van Noppen, *Stoneman's Last Raid*, 62–64; Barrett, *Civil War in North Carolina*, 357–59; Trelease, *North Carolina Railroad*, 193.

8. *OR* 49(1):334; Grant, *Personal Memoirs*, 571; Trelease, *North Carolina Railroad*, 194.

9. Nellie R. Jones, "Guilford Under the Stars and Bars," 1, Guilford File, History— Civil War, NCC-GPL; *Annals of an American Family*, 217; "Statement of William C. McLean," 2, Guilford File, History—Civil War, NCC-GPL; Trelease, *North Carolina Railroad*, 187; Robert C. Black, *Railroads of the Confederacy*, 227–28; "A Bird's Eye View of Johnston's Surrender," in Cole, *Miscellany*, 9; Athos, "Greensboro in April, 1865," *Greensboro Patriot*, March 29, 1866; Mrs. Jacob H. Smith, *The Women of Greensboro*, North Carolina Biography File, NCC-UNC; M. A. Bogart, "Notes of the Times," Guilford File, History—Civil War, NCC-GPL; Aaron Thompson to W. P. Nixon, February 21, 1865, Thomas Nixon Papers, DU; Ford and Ford, *Life in the Confederate Army*, 63.

10. *OR* 47(3):742–45; Roman, *Military Operations of Beauregard*, 2:387; Herriot, "At Greensboro, N.C., in April, 1865," 101.

11. "A Bird's Eye View of Johnston's Surrender," in Cole, *Miscellany*, 10–11; Athos, "Greensboro in April, 1865," *Greensboro Patriot*, March 29, 1866.

12. *OR* 47(3):787–88; *Annals of an American Family*, 214; Jacob H. Smith Diary, April 11, 1865, SHC-UNC; Harrison, "Capture of Jefferson Davis," 132–33; Stephen R. Mallory Recollections, 2:344, SHC-UNC; Anna H. Trenholm Diary, April 11, 1865, SHC-UNC; [Walker], *Surrender in Greensboro*, 3; Nellie R. Jones, "Guilford Under the Stars and Bars," 16, Guilford File, History—Civil War, NCC-GPL; John Taylor Wood Diary, April 11, 1865, John Taylor Wood Papers, SHC-UNC; Arnett, *Confederate Guns*, 36.

13. Stephen R. Mallory Recollections, 2:343–44, SHC-UNC; Harrison, "Capture of Jefferson Davis," 132–33; Swallow, "Retreat of the Confederate Government," 600; Hanna, *Flight into Oblivion*, 26–29; James C. Clark, *Last Train South*, 55–56; Ballard, *A Long Shadow*, 76–77; William C. Davis, *Jefferson Davis*, 614; Ford and Ford, *Life in the Confederate Army*, 63; Roman, *Military Operations of Beauregard*, 2:387; Charles W. Hutson to Em, April 26, 1865, Charles W. Hutson Papers, SHC-UNC.

14. Roman, *Military Operations of Beauregard*, 2:387, 390; Alexander R. Chisolm, "Notes Personal of Lt. Col. Alex. Robt. Chisolm, Book No. 2," 83, Alexander R.

Chisolm Papers, Manuscript Department, New-York Historical Society, New York; Walmsley, "Last Meeting of the Confederate Cabinet," 340; *OR* 47(3):778–79.

15. Roman, *Military Operations of Beauregard,* 2:390; Swallow, "Retreat of the Confederate Government," 600.

16. Roman, *Military Operations of Beauregard,* 2:390–91.

17. Ibid., 392.

18. Johnston, *Narrative,* 396; Stephen R. Mallory Recollections, 2:342–43, SHC-UNC; Mallory, "Last Days," 239. Shortly after his arrival in Greensboro, Davis had sent a message proposing a meeting at Johnston's headquarters; he decided on Greensboro when he learned that Breckinridge was en route with news regarding Lee's army. See *OR* 47(3):787–88.

19. J. E. Johnston to "My dear General" [G. T. Beauregard], December 26, 1867, JO 187, Joseph E. Johnston Papers, HEHL; Johnston, *Narrative,* 396, and "My Negotiations," 185–86; Roman, *Military Operations of Beauregard,* 2:664–65.

20. Johnston, *Narrative,* 396; Roman, *Military Operations of Beauregard,* 2:394; Stephen R. Mallory Recollections, 2:337, SHC-UNC; Mallory, "Last Days," 240.

21. J. E. Johnston to "My dear General" [G. T. Beauregard], December 26, 1867, JO 187, Joseph E. Johnston Papers, HEHL; Roman, *Military Operations of Beauregard,* 2:394, 665; Johnston, *Narrative,* 396–97, and "My Negotiations," 186. According to Lt. Col. Alexander R. Chisolm, Johnston and Beauregard were so dissatisfied with the result of the April 12 conference that they discussed opening negotiations with Sherman in defiance of Davis. See Chisolm, "Notes Personal of Lieut. Col. Alex. Robt. Chisolm, Book No. 2," 83–85, Alexander R. Chisolm Papers, Manuscript Department, New-York Historical Society.

22. J. E. Johnston to "My dear General" [G. T. Beauregard], December 26, 1867, JO 187, Joseph E. Johnston Papers, HEHL; Johnston, *Narrative,* 397–98, and "My Negotiations," 186; Roman, *Military Operations of Beauregard,* 2:394–95, 665.

23. Attorney General Davis and Secretary of State Benjamin later stated that they were not present at this meeting, but their recollections differ from those of other participants. Moreover, President Davis and Secretary of the Navy Mallory recalled only one conference (which Mallory thought was at night), but the consensus is that there were two daytime conferences. J. P. Benjamin to "My dear friend" [Jefferson Davis], December 15, 1880, Jefferson Davis Papers, SHC-UNC; Rowland, *Jefferson Davis,* 8:504–6, 535–39; Jefferson Davis, *Rise and Fall,* 2:679–81; Reagan, *Memoirs,* 199; Stephen R. Mallory Recollections, 2:336–37, SHC-UNC; Mallory, "Last Days," 240; J. E. Johnston to "My dear General" [G. T. Beauregard], December 26, 1867, JO 187, Joseph E. Johnston Papers, HEHL; Johnston, *Narrative,* 398, and "My Negotiations," 187; Roman, *Military Operations of Beauregard,* 2:665.

24. Stephen R. Mallory Recollections, 2:336, SHC-UNC; Mallory, "Last Days," 240; Jefferson Davis, *Rise and Fall,* 2:679–80.

25. Jefferson Davis, *Rise and Fall,* 2:679–81; William C. Davis, *Jefferson Davis,* 614–15.

26. J. E. Johnston to "My dear General" [G. T. Beauregard], December 26, 1867, JO 187, Joseph E. Johnston Papers, HEHL; Johnston, *Narrative,* 398–99, and "My Negotiations," 187; Roman, *Military Operations of Beauregard,* 2:665; Stephen R. Mallory Recollections, 2:335–36, SHC-UNC; Mallory, "Last Days," 240–41. In a postwar

letter to former Confederate vice president Alexander H. Stephens, Johnston took issue with a portion of Mallory's recollection that has the commanding general saying that his troops were whipped and were deserting in large numbers, often stealing artillery horses to speed their homeward journey. Johnston insisted that Mallory was describing the condition of the army just before its surrender on April 26, not as it was on April 13. J. E. Johnston to A. H. Stephens, April 29, 1868, Alexander H. Stephens Papers, LC.

27. Stephen R. Mallory Recollections, 2:335, SHC-UNC; Mallory, "Last Days," 242; J. E. Johnston to "My dear General" [G. T. Beauregard], December 26, 1867, JO 187, Joseph E. Johnston Papers, HEHL; Johnston, *Narrative*, 399, and "My Negotiations," 187; Roman, *Military Operations of Beauregard*, 2:395, 665; Rowland, *Jefferson Davis*, 8:536.

28. J. E. Johnston to "My dear General" [G. T. Beauregard], December 26, 1867, Joseph E. Johnston Papers, JO 187, HEHL; J. E. Johnston to A. H. Stephens, April 29, 1868, Alexander H. Stephens Papers, LC; Johnston, *Narrative*, 399–400, and "My Negotiations," 187–88; Roman, *Military Operations of Beauregard*, 2:395, 665–66; Stephen R. Mallory Recollections, 2:334, SHC-UNC; Mallory, "Last Days," 242; Jefferson Davis, *Rise and Fall*, 2:681; *OR* 47(3):206–7.

29. Jefferson Davis, *Rise and Fall*, 2:681; Strode, *Jefferson Davis*, 152.

30. Welles, *Diary*, 2:280–83; Carpenter, *Six Months*, 292–93.

31. *OR* 47(1):80, 83, 90–101, 107, 111, 112, 117, 120–31, 139, 141, 144, 152–56, 160–64, 210, 937; *OR* 47(3):210–11, 213, 217–18; "Journal of the Campaign from Goldsboro, North Carolina to Alexandria, Virginia," April 14, 1865, James D. Morgan Collection, HSQAC; Alpheus S. Williams Diary, April 14, 1865, Alpheus S. Williams Papers, DPL; Redmond F. Laswell Diary, April 14, 1865, Military Archival Collection, ACHM; Hazen, *Narrative*, 369; Schafer, *Intimate Letters of Carl Schurz*, 333.

32. Geo[rge] to Sarah, April 17, 1865, George A. Collamore Letters, GHM; *Smithfield Herald* article, March 1924, reprinted in Mrs. Denton Farmer (Margaret) Lee, "History of the Finch Place," JCPL; *OR* 47(1):966–67; Pinney, *104th Ohio*, 81; Becker, "Campaigning with a Grand Army"; Whitaker, *Whitaker's Reminiscences*, 254.

33. Williamson D. Ward Journal, April 14, 1865, INHS; *OR* 47(1):147–48; *OR* 47(3):214–15; Will to Brother, April 14, 1865, William C. Stevens Correspondence, BL-UMI; Kittinger, *Diary*, 205; Committee of the Regiment, *Ninety-second Illinois*, 240.

34. *OR* 47(3):215.

35. Johnston, *Narrative*, 400–401; *OR* 47(3):798, 802.

36. Johnston, *Narrative*, 401; John Johnson Diary, April 14, 1865, DU; Thomas L. Sullivan Account Book, April 14, 1865, Civil War Collection—Confederate, TNSLA; James W. Brown Diary, April 14, 1865, Private Papers, Mf Drawer 187, Reel 13, GADAH; Alexander W. Marshall, "1865 Memoranda," April 14, 1865, Rachel Susan (Bee) Cheves Papers, DU; Charles W. Hutson, "My Reminiscences," 125, and Charles W. Hutson to Mother, April 7, 1865 [Journal-Letter, April 14, 1865], Charles W. Hutson Papers, SHC-UNC.

37. *OR* 47(1):1083, 1132; *OR* 47(3):797–99; Johnston, *Narrative*, 401; John Johnson Diary, April 14, 1865, DU; George W. F. Harper Diary, April 14, 1865, George W. F. Harper Papers, SHC-UNC; Thomas B. Roy Diary, April 15, 1865, photocopy

in the possession of N. C. Hughes Jr., Chattanooga, Tennessee; Holmes, *Diary of Henry McCall Holmes*, 34; Saunders, "Governor Z. B. Vance," 165; Jesse R. Sparkman Diary, April 14, 1865, Box 3, Diaries, Memoirs, Etc., TNSLA; William E. Sloan Diary, April 14, 1865, Civil War Collection—Confederate, TNSLA; Ridley, *Battles and Sketches*, 456–57; Alfred T. Fielder Diary, April 14, 1865, Tennessee Historical Society Collection, TNSLA; Norman D. Brown, *One of Cleburne's Command*, 163; Joseph F. Waring Diary, April 14, 1865, SHC-UNC.

38. Saunders, "Governor Z. B. Vance," 165; Spencer, *Last Ninety Days*, 163–64.

39. Saunders, "Governor Z. B. Vance," 165–66.

40. Ibid., 166; *OR* 47(3):798.

41. Spencer, *Last Ninety Days*, 163–64; Z. B. Vance to Cornelia P. Spencer, April 7, [1866], Cornelia P. Spencer Papers, SHC-UNC; Zebulon B. Vance to "My dear friend" [Cornelia P. Spencer], January 8, 1867, David L. Swain Papers, SHC-UNC. Vance later recalled that he received Davis's message while at Hillsborough, but he was probably referring to the telegram he received from Davis on April 11 while still at Raleigh. "I expected to visit you at Raleigh," the president wrote, "but am accidentally prevented from executing that design, and would be very glad to see you here [at Greensboro] if you can come at once, or to meet you elsewhere in North Carolina at a future time." In mid-April, Vance deemed it more prudent to see Davis than to return to Union-held Raleigh with Graham and Swain. See Zebulon B. Vance, "Lecture—Last Days of the War," in Dowd, *Life of Vance*, 485; *OR* 47(3):787.

42. Saunders, "Governor Z. B. Vance," 166.

43. Z. B. Vance to Cornelia P. Spencer, April 7, [1866], Cornelia P. Spencer Papers, SHC-UNC; Saunders, "Governor Z. B. Vance," 166; Spencer, *Last Ninety Days*, 164.

44. Wells, *Hampton and His Cavalry*, 421–22; Sherman, *Memoirs*, 2:346. The Confederates never offered an explanation as to why Davis's letter, written April 13, took more than a day to reach General Hampton. Given that Johnston left Greensboro on the evening of the 13th and arrived in Hillsborough the following morning, it would appear that someone intentionally delayed Davis's dispatch.

45. *OR* 47(3):206–7, 222, 230, 234, 235; Sherman, *Memoirs*, 2:346–47. In his *Memoirs*, Sherman erroneously states that he received Johnston's letter on the morning of April 14; in fact, he received it at midnight. In the *OR*, Sherman's reply is dated April 14, yet one of his clerks and two of his staff officers state that Johnston's letter did not arrive until April 15. Moreover, Sherman noted that he forwarded his dispatch to Kilpatrick at Durham's Station, but the Union cavalry commander did not arrive there until the morning of April 15. See *OR* 47(1):31; *OR* 47(3):206–7; H[enry] to Mary, April 15, 1865, Henry Hitchcock Papers, LC; Hitchcock, *Marching with Sherman*, 299; S. C. Noble to Sis, April 15, 1865, Sylvester C. Noble Papers, YHS; Nichols, *Story of the Great March*, 309.

On April 15, Major McCoy's train was preceded by a locomotive, the Walter Raleigh, to detect the presence of torpedoes on the track. The officer in charge, Col. D. T. Kirby of Blair's Seventeenth Corps staff, kept his revolver pointed at the head of the engineer. The locomotive was run in reverse with the coal tender in front, which proved to be a wise precaution, for the tender struck a torpedo about ten miles west of Raleigh. The explosion hurled the tender from the track, injuring several men.

The damaged track was repaired, McCoy was dropped off at Morrisville, and the locomotive arrived at Durham's Station on April 16 without further mishap. McCoy remained at Morrisville until April 16, when he returned to Raleigh. Meanwhile, the telegraph lines were repaired from Morrisville to Durham to expedite transmittal of Johnston's reply. See *OR* 47(3):229–30, 235; *Philadelphia Inquirer,* April 28, 1865.

46. Wells, *Hampton and His Cavalry,* 422–24.

47. *OR* 47(3):215, 225.

48. Ibid., 224, 234; *Cincinnati Daily Commercial,* April 27, 1865; Williamson D. Ward Journal, April 15, 1865, INHS; Kittinger, *Diary,* 205; Records Concerning the Conduct and Loyalty of Certain Union Army Officers, Civilian Employees of the War Department, and U.S. Citizens during the Civil War, 1861–1872, Box 2, "Statements dated 1872 concerning H. Judson Kilpatrick's affair with a woman during the Civil War," deposition of R[ichard] Blacknall, August 8, 1872, RG 107, NA; Boyd, *Story of Durham,* 35.

49. Committee of the Regiment, *Ninety-second Illinois,* 240; William D. Hamilton, *Recollections,* 203–6, and "In at the Death," 287–89; Will to Brother, April 14, 1865 [postdated April 19, 1865], William C. Stevens Correspondence, BL-UMI.

50. Committee of the Regiment, *Ninety-second Illinois,* 240; William D. Hamilton, *Recollections,* 200, 206–7, and "In at the Death," 288–89; Robert Y. Woodlief Diary, April 15, 1865, USC; *Detroit Advertiser and Tribune,* May 11, 1865.

51. Spencer, *Last Ninety Days,* 167; Guild, *Fourth Tennessee Cavalry,* 144–45; Baxter Smith Reminiscences, 32, Civil War Miscellaneous Collection, USAMHI; James Coffin, "Chapel Hill at the Close," 274.

52. Spencer, *Last Ninety Days,* 167–68.

53. Joseph F. Waring Diary, April 15, 1865, SHC-UNC; J. W. Evans, "With Hampton's Scouts," 470; Jesse R. Sparkman Diary, April 15, 1865, Box 3, Diaries, Memoirs, Etc., TNSLA.

54. *OR* 47(3):784, 788–89, 802; J. E. Johnston to "Comdg. Officer, Chester," [April] 10, 186[5], Joseph E. Johnston Papers, DU; J. J. McKay, "Some Recollections," Reminiscences, Diaries, and Letters of Confederate Soldiers, Georgia Division, UDC, 13:31–32, GADAH; D. E. H. Smith, *A Charlestonian's Recollections,* 106.

55. D. E. H. Smith, *A Charlestonian's Recollections,* 106.

56. *OR* 47(1):1083; Holmes, *Diary of Henry McCall Holmes,* 34; Walter Clark, *Histories,* 4:60; Worsham, *Old Nineteenth Tennessee,* 175; William E. Stoney quoted in Hagood, *Memoirs,* 368.

57. Walter Clark, *Histories,* 4:22, 32, 61.

58. Ibid., 60; William E. Stoney quoted in Hagood, *Memoirs,* 368.

59. Walter Clark, *Histories,* 4:60; Worsham, *Old Nineteenth Tennessee,* 175.

60. John Johnson Diary, April 15, 1865, DU; Alexander Marshall, "1865 Memoranda," April 15, 1865, Rachel Susan (Bee) Cheves Papers, DU; Thomas L. Sullivan Account Book, April 15, 1865, Civil War Collection—Confederate, TNSLA; George W. F. Harper Diary, April 15, 1865, George W. F. Harper Papers, SHC-UNC; Ridley, *Battles and Sketches,* 458; David G. McIntosh Diary, April 15, 1865, 1M1895a1, VAHS; "Map of Alamance County, North Carolina, 1893," ACHM.

61. D. E. H. Smith, *A Charlestonian's Recollections,* 105–6; Thomas L. Sullivan Account Book, April 15, 1865, Civil War Collection—Confederate, TNSLA; George

W. F. Harper Diary, April 15, 1865, George W. F. Harper Papers, SHC-UNC; William E. Stoney quoted in Hagood, *Memoirs*, 368.

62. Hendricks, "Imperiled City," 8, 166–67.

63. *OR* 47(3):799, 800; Alfred Iverson to Col. [George W. Brent], April 16, 1865, George W. Brent Papers, DU.

64. David G. McIntosh Diary, April 16, 1865, 1M1895a1, VAHS; George G. Dibrell, "Eighth Tennessee Cavalry," in Lindsley, *Military Annals of Tennessee*, 676; M. A. Bogart, "Notes of the Times," Guilford File, History—Civil War, NCC-GPL; Hezekiah M. McCorkle Diary, April 16, 1865, Civil War Miscellany—Personal Papers, Mf Drawer 283, Reel 32, GADAH; James W. Albright Autobiography, extract from diary, April 16, 1865, James W. Albright Diary and Reminiscences, SHC-UNC; J. A. Harvey to "Colonel" [John M. Otey], April 14, 1865, P. G. T. Beauregard Papers, EU; "A Bird's Eye View of Johnston's Surrender," in Cole, *Miscellany*, 12–13; Athos, "Greensboro in April, 1865," *Greensboro Patriot*, March 29, 1866; Robert A. Jenkins, "Endurin' the War," 61–62, Robert A. Jenkins Reminiscences, Gertrude Jenkins Papers, DU.

65. James Sloan to Z. B. Vance, April 21, 1865, Letterbook, vol. 7, Zebulon B. Vance Papers, NCDAH; Walter Clark, *Histories*, 3:78–79.

66. [John M. Otey?] to "General" [George G. Dibrell], April 14 [15?], 1865, Army Units: Wheeler's Cavalry Corps, Confederate States of America Archives, DU; Joseph Mullen Jr. Diary, April 15, 1865, Diary Collection, MOC; Harris, *Seventh North Carolina*, 61; James Sloan to Z. B. Vance, April 21, 1865, Letterbook, vol. 7, Zebulon B. Vance Papers, NCDAH; Dibrell, "Eighth Tennessee Cavalry," in Lindsley, *Military Annals of Tennessee*, 676; "A Bird's Eye View of Johnston's Surrender," in Cole, *Miscellany*, 12–13; Athos, "Greensboro in April, 1865," *Greensboro Patriot*, March 29, 1866; Herriot, "At Greensboro, N.C., in April, 1865," 101–2.

67. Joseph Mullen Jr. Diary, April 16, 1865, Diary Collection, MOC; R. Amos Jarman, "History of Company K, 27th Mississippi Infantry," 56, R. Amos Jarman Papers, MSDAH; "A Bird's Eye View of Johnston's Surrender," in Cole, *Miscellany*, 13–14; Athos, "Greensboro in April, 1865," *Greensboro Patriot*, March 29, 1866.

68. Athos, "Greensboro in April, 1865," *Greensboro Patriot*, March 29, 1866; "A Bird's Eye View of Johnston's Surrender," in Cole, *Miscellany*, 14; Z. B. Vance to Major Sloan, April 16, 1865, and James Sloan to Z. B. Vance, April 21, 1865, Letterbook, vol. 7, Zebulon B. Vance Papers, NCDAH.

69. John Taylor Wood Diary, April 15, 1865, John Taylor Wood Papers, SHC-UNC; Anna H. Trenholm Diary, April 15, 1865, SHC-UNC; Stephen R. Mallory Recollections, 2:333, SHC-UNC; Mallory, "Last Days," 242; Harrison, "Capture of Jefferson Davis," 134–35; Given Campbell Journal, April 15, 1865, LC; Dibrell, "Eighth Tennessee Cavalry," in Lindsley, *Military Annals of Tennessee*, 676–77; Ballard, *A Long Shadow*, 88–89.

70. Johnston, *Narrative*, 401, and "My Negotiations," 188; John Johnson Diary, April 16, 1865, DU; Roman, *Military Operations of Beauregard*, 666; *OR* 47(3):803.

71. Johnston, *Narrative*, 401, and "My Negotiations," 188; *OR* 47(3):804–5.

72. Robert A. McClellan Memorandum, April 16, 1865, Robert A. McClellan Papers, DU; James Coffin, "Chapel Hill at the Close," 274; Norvell W. Wilson Diary, April 16, 1865, Norvell W. Wilson Papers, SHC-UNC; Spencer, *Last Ninety Days*, 170.

73. Spencer, *Last Ninety Days*, 170–71; C. P. Mallett to Son [Journal-Letter],

April 18, 1865, Charles P. Mallett Letters, Charles B. Mallett Papers, SHC-UNC; A 10th Ohio Cavalryman, "Campaign through the Carolinas," May 12, 1892.

74. *OR* 47(3):233–34.

75. Ibid., 223, 231, 234; William T. Sherman Diary, April 16, 1865, Sherman Family Papers, UND; H[enry] to Mary, April 16, 1865, Henry Hitchcock Papers, LC; Hitchcock, *Marching with Sherman*, 301–2. Because Sherman's reply to Kilpatrick does not appear in the *OR*, I quote it here in full: "I have just received and read your communication from Lieutenant General Wade Hampton, proposing a meeting between General Johnston and myself at 10 A.M. to-morrow. You can make all necessary arrangements with General Hampton for the proposed meeting. You had better defer the meeting till 12 o'clock, M. Also say to General Hampton that I should be pleased to see Generals Hardee and Bragg." *Cincinnati Daily Commercial,* April 27, 1865.

76. Johnston, *Narrative,* 401–2, and "My Negotiations," 188; John Johnson Diary, April 16, 1865, DU; John Johnson, "An Incident Under the White Flag," 1, Folder J-525, Joseph E. Johnston Papers, MOC.

77. H[enry] to Mary, April 14, 1865, Henry Hitchcock Papers, LC; Hitchcock, *Marching with Sherman,* 295.

CHAPTER SEVEN

1. *Cincinnati Daily Commercial,* April 27, 1865; Theo Davis, "With Sherman," 205; Kirk, *Fifteenth Pennsylvania Cavalry,* 593; Hatcher, *Last Four Weeks,* 272; Sherman, *Memoirs,* 2:347–48; Murray, *Wake: Capital County,* 530; *OR* 47(1):33; *OR* 47(3):220–21; W. T. Sherman to John W. Draper, November 6, 1868, John W. Draper Papers, LC; Sherman, "To Execute the Terms," 36 (this is a verbatim transcript of the letter from Sherman to Draper dated November 6, 1868); Draper, *American Civil War,* 3:600. The version of the dispatch from Stanton to Sherman quoted here from *OR* 47(3): 220–21 is correctly dated April 15, 1865. Evidently a telegraph operator made a transmitting or decoding error in the date on the cipher dispatch, because Sherman referred to the date of Lincoln's assassination as April 11 instead of April 14 in his Special Field Orders No. 56 of April 17. See Sherman, *General and Field Orders,* 229; *OR* 47(1):33; *OR* 47(3):238.

2. Hatcher, *Last Four Weeks,* 285; Sherman, *Memoirs,* 2:348, 350; *Cincinnati Daily Commercial,* April 27, 1865; *Philadelphia Inquirer,* April 26, 1865; Cornelius Baker Diary, April 17, 1865, Bennett Place State Historic Site, Durham, North Carolina; W. T. Sherman to John W. Draper, November 6, 1868, John W. Draper Papers, LC; Sherman, "To Execute the Terms," 36; Nichols, *Story of the Great March,* 310. In his letter to Draper, Sherman stated that he revealed the news of Lincoln's murder to Logan on the morning of April 17, whereas in his *Memoirs* he noted that he waited until his return that afternoon to break the news to his subordinate.

My thanks to author Timothy J. Reese and publisher David E. Roth for identifying journalist Volney Hickox, whose byline was "V.H."

3. John Johnson Diary, April 17, 1865, DU; John Johnson, "An Incident Under the White Flag," 2, Folder J-525, Joseph E. Johnston Papers, MOC; Joseph F. War-

ing Diary, April 16–17, 1865, SHC-UNC; William T. Sherman Diary, April 17, 1865, Sherman Family Papers, UND.

4. *OR* 47(1):32; Sherman, *Memoirs*, 2:348–49; *Cincinnati Daily Commercial*, April 27, 1865; *New York Herald*, April 27, 1865.

5. Sherman, *Memoirs*, 2:348; W. T. Sherman to John W. Draper, November 6, 1868, John W. Draper Papers, LC; Sherman, "To Execute the Terms," 36–37; John Johnson, "An Incident Under the White Flag," 2–3, Folder J-525, Joseph E. Johnston Papers, MOC. In his letter to Draper, Sherman mentioned that he was angry at Hampton for abusing Federal prisoners at Fayetteville the month before, but the mutual dislike of the two men ran deeper than that. In his official report of the Carolinas campaign, Sherman blamed Hampton for the burning of Columbia, whereas the South Carolinian accused Sherman. And in the letters that the two men had exchanged in February 1865 on the subject of murdered Union foragers, Sherman had called foraging "a war right as old as history," to which Hampton had replied that there was a right "older . . . and more inalienable—the right that every man has to protect his home and to protect those who are dependent on him." Although Sherman was adept at polemics, Hampton bested him in this instance. See Sherman, *Memoirs*, 2:302; *OR* 47(1):21–22; *OR* 47(2):546, 596–97.

6. Sherman, *Memoirs*, 2:349; W. T. Sherman to John W. Draper, November 6, 1868, John W. Draper Papers, LC; Sherman, "To Execute the Terms," 37; Young, "Sherman on His Own Record," 296; Nichols, *Story of the Great March*, 310–11. Confusion over the spelling of the Bennett family name is understandable, given that James Bennett had spelled his name "Bennitt" prior to the war. By the 1860s, however, he used the more common spelling of "Bennett." For two examples of his use of the latter spelling, see James Bennett to Governor Holden, October 5, 1869, and January [?], 1870, Papers of Governor William W. Holden, Boxes 220 and 222, State Agency Records, NCDAH.

Confederate staff officer Maj. John Johnson recalled that when the flags of truce met, the Federals had already chosen a house a half-mile east of the Bennett farm. The house probably belonged to James Bennett's neighbor, Henry Neal. According to Major Johnson, Johnston deemed the Bennett house a better location, and Sherman yielded to his judgment. If Johnson's recollection of events is correct, then Henry Neal narrowly missed his moment in history. See John Johnson, "An Incident Under the White Flag," 2, Folder J-525, Joseph E. Johnston Papers, MOC. Henry Neal appears in the 1870 census for Orange County, as well as in Bennett's 1873 petition to the Southern Claims Commission. See U.S. Census Records, 1870, Orange County, North Carolina, 210, Microcopy M593, Microfiche 1153, NA, and Barred and Disallowed Case Files of the Southern Claims Commission, Claim No. 18945: James Bennett, Microcopy M1407, Microfiche 4311, RG 56, NA.

7. W. T. Sherman to John W. Draper, November 6, 1868, John W. Draper Papers, LC; Sherman, "To Execute the Terms," 37; Hatcher, *Last Four Weeks*, 300–301.

8. Although Sherman may not have mentioned Davis's name at the Bennett house, he did so in an April 23 dispatch to Johnston, which was prompted by Northern newspaper reports that John Wilkes Booth had received his instructions from Richmond. *OR* 47(3):287; Sherman, *Memoirs*, 2:349; W. T. Sherman to John W. Draper, November 6, 1868, John W. Draper Papers, LC; Sherman, "To Execute

the Terms," 37; Johnston, *Narrative,* 402, "My Negotiations," 188–89, and "Dalton-Atlanta Operations," 12.

9. Johnston, *Narrative,* 402, and "My Negotiations," 189; J. E. Johnston to "My dear General," March 30, 1868, P-28, Joseph E. Johnston Papers in the William P. Palmer Collection, WRHS; Johnston, "Dalton-Atlanta Operations," 12; Sherman, *Memoirs,* 2:349.

10. J. E. Johnston to "My dear General," March 30, 1868, P-28, Joseph E. Johnston Papers in the William P. Palmer Collection, WRHS; Johnston, *Narrative,* 403, and "My Negotiations," 189; *OR* 47(1):32; U.S. Congress, "Sherman-Johnston," 3: 4; Sherman, *Memoirs,* 2:349; W. T. Sherman to John W. Draper, November 6, 1868, John W. Draper Papers, LC; Sherman, "To Execute the Terms," 37–38.

11. Johnston, *Narrative,* 403, and "My Negotiations," 189–90; Sherman, *Memoirs,* 2:349–50.

12. Johnston, *Narrative,* 403–4, and "My Negotiations," 190; J. E. Johnston to A. H. Stephens, April 29, 1868, Alexander H. Stephens Papers, LC; Johnston, "Dalton-Atlanta Operations," 13; Sherman, *Memoirs,* 2:350; W. T. Sherman to John W. Draper, November 6, 1868, John W. Draper Papers, LC; Sherman, "To Execute the Terms," 38; *OR* 47(1):32.

13. U. R. Brooks, *Butler and His Cavalry,* 289; Buford, "Surrender of Johnston's Army," 170; Kirk, *Fifteenth Pennsylvania Cavalry,* 593; *Cincinnati Daily Commercial,* April 27, 1865; *New York Herald,* April 27, 1865; *Philadelphia Inquirer,* April 28, 1865; Kittinger, *Diary,* 205–6; John Johnson, "An Incident Under the White Flag," 4, Folder J-525, Joseph E. Johnston Papers, MOC; John Johnson Diary, April 17, 1865, DU; Joseph F. Waring Diary, April 17, 1865, SHC-UNC.

14. *Cincinnati Daily Commercial,* April 27, 1865; *New York Herald,* April 27, 1865; *Philadelphia Inquirer,* April 28, 1865; Conyngham, *Sherman's March,* 365; John Johnson, "An Incident Under the White Flag," 3–4, Folder J-525, Joseph E. Johnston Papers, MOC. One source had Hampton carrying a large saber, but Major Johnson emphasized that he carried only a switch.

15. *Cincinnati Daily Commercial,* April 27, 1865; *New York Herald,* April 27, 1865; *Philadelphia Inquirer,* April 28, 1865; Conyngham, *Sherman's March,* 365; H[enry] to Mary, April 25, 1865, Henry Hitchcock Papers, LC; Hitchcock, *Marching with Sherman,* 310; "A Rousing Reunion"; Henry B. McClellan, "The Campaign of 1863—A Reply to Kilpatrick," *Philadelphia Weekly Times,* February 7, 1880.

16. Sherman, *Memoirs,* 2:350; Keyes, "Lincoln's Assassination."

17. Sherman, *Memoirs,* 2:350; Edward A. Rowley Diary, April 17, 1865, USC. Sherman states that the Fifteenth Corps was encamped at Morrisville and Jones's Station. In actuality, Corse's division of the Fifteenth Corps was at Morrisville and Giles Smith's division of the Seventeenth Corps was at Jones's Station. The remainder of the two corps was encamped on the outskirts of Raleigh. See *OR* 47(1):104; *OR* 47(3): 232.

18. Manning F. Force Letterbook-Journal, April 17, 1865, and M. F. Force to "My Dear Mr. Kebler," April 18, 1865, Manning F. Force Papers, UWA; Wills, *Army Life,* 371; Hedley, *Marching through Georgia,* 426; James R. M. Gaskill Memoranda, April 17, 1865, Archives and Manuscripts Department, Chicago Historical Society. At least one man in Sherman's army was arrested, tried, and convicted for applaud-

ing the news of Lincoln's murder. See General Court-Martial Proceedings No. MM 1997, Frederick Bodmer, RG 153, NA.

19. Sherman, *Memoirs,* 2:350–51, and *General and Field Orders,* 229–30; *OR* 47(3): 238–39. In Sherman's *Memoirs,* the correct date of Lincoln's assassination—April 14 —is given, whereas the *General and Field Orders* reprints the incorrect date as shown on the original document. The *OR* reprints the incorrect date as well but inserts the correct date in brackets. The incorrect date is significant, because it led many of Sherman's men to believe that the report of Lincoln's assassination was a hoax.

20. Cox, *Military Reminiscences,* 2:465; Pinney, *104th Ohio,* 82; William T. Humphrey Diary, April 18, 1865, William T. Humphrey Papers, Special Collections, Chicago Public Library; George N. Compton Diary, April 17–18, 1865, George N. Compton Papers, Illinois State Historical Library, Springfield; Sherman, *Memoirs,* 2: 350–51; Marszalek, *Sherman,* 344.

21. Dawson, *Life and Services of John A. Logan,* 119–20; *City of Raleigh,* 64.

22. Dawson, *Life and Services of John A. Logan,* 120; *City of Raleigh,* 64; William B. Johnson, *Union to the Hub,* 106–7; Winther, *With Sherman to the Sea,* 166–67.

23. *City of Raleigh,* 63–64; Toombs, *Reminiscences,* 222; William C. Meffert Diary, April 18, 1865, SHSW; Battle, *Memories,* 194–95; Murray, *Wake: Capital County,* 521, 532; Pinney, *104th Ohio,* 82.

24. Andersen, *Diary of Allen Morgan Geer,* 214–15; Thomas J. Davis to Wife, April 19, 1865, Thomas J. Davis Papers, Archives Department, Michigan State University, East Lansing; Charles G. Michael Diary, April 18–19, 1865, INHS; C. C. Platter Diary, April 19, 1865, UGA; William B. Miller Journal, April 19, 1865, INHS; Levi N. Green Diary, April 18, 1865, Levi N. Green Papers, MNHS; Edmund J. Cleveland Diary, April 18–19, 22, 1865, SHC-UNC; *OR* 47(1):33; *Raleigh Daily Standard,* April 18, 1865; *Raleigh Daily Progress,* April 18, 1865. Even one week later, the Federals' anger regarding Lincoln's assassination had not abated. See Oscar to Parents, April 25, 1865, Edward O. Kimberly Papers, SHSW.

25. *Raleigh Daily Standard,* April 19, 1865; *Raleigh Daily Progress,* April 19, 1865; *OR* 47(1):937.

26. Sherman, *Memoirs,* 2:351–52; W. T. Sherman to John W. Draper, November 6, 1868, John W. Draper Papers, LC; Sherman, "To Execute the Terms," 38; *OR* 47(1): 32; Andrew H. Hickenlooper Reminiscences, 115, *CWTI* Collection, USAMHI; Andrew H. Hickenlooper, "Reminiscences, Vol. I," 338–39, Hickenlooper Family Collection, CINHS.

27. Because the movements of Vance, Breckinridge, and Reagan at this time were complicated, they bear recounting. Vance left Hillsborough on April 15 to meet with President Davis at Greensboro. The governor arrived in Greensboro on the morning of April 16, only to learn that Davis had left for Charlotte. Vance spent the next two days in Greensboro at the home of Congressman John A. Gilmer, waiting to see what Johnston would do. On the evening of April 16, Breckinridge received Johnston's dispatch summoning him to Greensboro. Leaving the Davis party near Lexington, Breckinridge and Postmaster General Reagan traveled all night to Greensboro, arriving on April 17. Later that day, Breckinridge received Johnston's request to meet with him at Hampton's headquarters near Hillsborough. The secretary of war then invited Vance to accompany Reagan and him to the conference. Johnston, *Narrative,*

404; Z. B. Vance to Cornelia P. Spencer, April 7, [1866], Cornelia P. Spencer Papers, SHC-UNC; Zebulon B. Vance, "Lecture—Last Days of the War," in Dowd, *Life of Vance*, 485–87; Spencer, *Last Ninety Days*, 183; John Taylor Wood Diary, April 16, 1865, John Taylor Wood Papers, SHC-UNC; Jefferson Davis, *Rise and Fall*, 2:683; *OR* 47(3):806; John C. Breckinridge to Z. B. Vance, April 17, 1865, Letterbook, vol. 7, Zebulon B. Vance Papers, NCDAH; Reagan, *Memoirs*, 201; Saunders, "Governor Z. B. Vance," 168.

28. *Cincinnati Daily Commercial*, April 27, 1865; *OR* 47(3):811, 816; Saunders, "Governor Z. B. Vance," 168. Vance did not name his accuser, but there were only three men at the Dickson house who, by virtue of rank or station, would have confronted him in such a manner: Johnston, Breckinridge, and Hampton. Johnston is eliminated because he was the man to whom Vance complained of shabby treatment at the hands of a third party. Breckinridge is also an unlikely candidate, for he had invited the governor to accompany him. That leaves Hampton, whose outspoken opposition to the surrender negotiations and the Graham-Swain mission makes him the most likely accuser.

Hampton was not the only Confederate general to voice strong disapproval of the Graham-Swain mission. According to Cornelia Phillips Spencer, a general in Hardee's Corps declared on a Chapel Hill street corner that Graham and Swain "were a couple of traitors and ought to be hung." See Spencer, *Last Ninety Days*, 165–66.

29. Saunders, "Governor Z. B. Vance," 167; *Cincinnati Daily Commercial*, April 27, 1865.

30. Saunders, "Governor Z. B. Vance," 168.

31. Johnston, *Narrative*, 404, and "My Negotiations," 190; Reagan, *Memoirs*, 201–2; Vance, "Lecture—Last Days of the War," in Dowd, *Life of Vance*, 487.

32. John Johnson Diary, April 18, 1865, DU; *Cincinnati Daily Commercial*, April 27, 1865.

33. *OR* 47(3):807–8; Holmes, *Diary of Henry McCall Holmes*, 34; William W. Gordon Diary, April 17, 1865, Gordon Family Papers, SHC-UNC; Thomas B. Roy Diary, April 17–18, 1865, photocopy in the possession of N. C. Hughes Jr., Chattanooga, Tennessee; W. H. Thomas to Wife, April 21, 1865, W. H. Thomas Papers, USC; William E. Stoney quoted in Hagood, *Memoirs*, 369.

34. William E. Stoney quoted in Hagood, *Memoirs*, 369.

35. *OR* 47(2):1424; Muster Rolls for Ellis's Battery (Co. A, 3rd N.C. Battalion), 1st N.C. Reserves, 2nd N.C. Reserves, 3rd N.C. Reserves, 1st Battalion N.C. Reserves, 36th N.C., and 40th N.C., Muster Rolls and Lists of Confederate Troops Paroled in North Carolina, Microcopy M1781, Roll 4 (mf), RG 109, NA.

36. William W. Gordon Diary, April 17, 1865, Gordon Family Papers, SHC-UNC.

37. Sherman, *Memoirs*, 2:352; *Cincinnati Daily Commercial*, April 27, 1865.

38. *Cincinnati Daily Commercial*, April 27, 1865; Tom to Jane, April 20, 1865, Thomas J. Jordan Letters, HSPA; Shipp, "Gens. Kilpatrick and Johnston"; W. J. L. Hughes, "The Bennett Farmhouse."

39. In his *Memoirs*, Sherman states that Johnston arrived at the Bennett house at 2:00 P.M., but all other relevant sources note that Johnston arrived at noon as scheduled. Perhaps with the passing of years, Sherman confused the time of Johnston's arrival on April 18 with his late arrival on April 26. Sherman also recalled seeing

Hampton on April 18, but his memory deceived him in this instance as well. Sherman, *Memoirs*, 2:352; *OR* 47(1):34; H[enry] to Mary, April 25, 1865, Henry Hitchcock Papers, LC; Hitchcock, *Marching with Sherman*, 311; Nichols, *Story of the Great March*, 312, 315; John Johnson Diary, April 18, 1865, DU; *Cincinnati Daily Commercial*, April 27, 1865.

40. Nichols, *Story of the Great March*, 315; Sherman, *Memoirs*, 2:352; U.S. Congress, "Sherman-Johnston," 3:4; W. T. Sherman to John W. Draper, November 6, 1868, John W. Draper Papers, LC; Sherman, "To Execute the Terms," 38; *OR* 47(1):32–33.

41. Johnston, *Narrative*, 404–5, and "My Negotiations," 190; U.S. Congress, "Sherman-Johnston," 3:4–5; Sherman, *Memoirs*, 2:352; W. T. Sherman to John W. Draper, November 6, 1868, John W. Draper Papers, LC; Sherman, "To Execute the Terms," 38; *Cincinnati Daily Commercial*, April 27, 1865.

42. Sherman, *Memoirs*, 2:352–53; U.S. Congress, "Sherman-Johnston," 3:5; Johnston, *Narrative*, 405, and "My Negotiations," 190.

43. Johnston, *Narrative*, 405, and "My Negotiations," 190; Wise, *End of an Era*, 449–53. John Goode, an erstwhile Confederate congressman from Virginia, tells a similar story in an article that appeared in the *Raleigh News and Observer*. See John Goode, "The Civilian Leaders of the Confederacy," *Raleigh News and Observer*, November 10, 1907, in Scrapbook Collection, North Carolina Division, UDC, Box 81, Military Collection—Civil War, NCDAH.

44. Sherman, *Memoirs*, 2:353; U.S. Congress, "Sherman-Johnston," 3:5; *OR* 47(1): 33; Johnston, *Narrative*, 405, "My Negotiations," 190–91, and "Dalton-Atlanta Operations," 13; *Cincinnati Daily Commercial*, April 27, 1865.

45. *OR* 47(3):244–45, 806–7.

46. Sherman, *Memoirs*, 2:356–57; Johnston, *Narrative*, 405–7; *OR* 47(3):243–44.

47. Sherman, *Memoirs*, 2:357; Johnston, *Narrative*, 407; *OR* 47(3):244.

48. U.S. Congress, "Sherman-Johnston," 3:4, 13, 15; *OR* 47(1):32–33; *OR* 47(3): 302; Sherman, *Memoirs*, 2:351, 353; W. T. Sherman to John W. Draper, November 6, 1868, John W. Draper Papers, LC; Sherman, "To Execute the Terms," 41–42; Royster, *Destructive War*, 348.

49. Johnston, *Narrative*, 405, and "My Negotiations," 190–91; J. E. Johnston to A. H. Stephens, April 29, 1868, Alexander H. Stephens Papers, LC.

50. Kirk, *Fifteenth Pennsylvania Cavalry*, 594; H[enry] to Mary, April 21, 25, 1865, Henry Hitchcock Papers, LC; Hitchcock, *Marching with Sherman*, 303, 311; *Cincinnati Daily Commercial*, April 27, 1865.

51. *Cincinnati Daily Commercial*, April 27, 1865; W. T. Sherman to John W. Draper, November 6, 1868, John W. Draper Papers, LC; Sherman, "To Execute the Terms," 37; Tom to Jane, April 21, 28, 1865, Thomas J. Jordan Letters, HSPA; O. M. Poe to Wife, April 19, 1865, Orlando M. Poe Papers, LC; Theo Davis, "With Sherman," 205; *Harper's Weekly*, May 27, 1865.

52. *Cincinnati Daily Commercial*, April 27, 1865; John Johnson Diary, April 18, 1865, DU; Sherman, *Memoirs*, 2:353–54; W. T. Sherman to John W. Draper, November 6, 1868, John W. Draper Papers, LC; Sherman, "To Execute the Terms," 38–39.

53. John Johnson Diary, April 17–18, 1865, DU; H[enry] to Mary, April 25, 1865, Henry Hitchcock Papers, LC; Hitchcock, *Marching with Sherman*, 311; *Cincinnati Daily Commercial*, April 27, 1865.

54. *Cincinnati Daily Commercial*, April 27, 1865; Kittinger, *Diary*, 206.

55. William T. Sherman Diary, April 18–19, 1865, Sherman Family Papers, UND; *Cincinnati Daily Commercial*, April 27, 1865; H[enry] to Mary, April 21, 1865, Henry Hitchcock Papers, LC; Hitchcock, *Marching with Sherman*, 303; Sherman, *Memoirs*, 2: 355–56; *OR* 47(1):33; *OR* 47(3):243; Sherman, *General and Field Orders*, 230–31.

56. *OR* 47(3):245; Sherman, *Memoirs*, 2:354–55; W. T. Sherman to Ellen [Sherman], April 18, 1865, Sherman Family Papers, UND.

57. Sherman, *Memoirs*, 2:354; Slocum, "Final Operations," 756; Bancroft, *Papers of Carl Schurz*, 1:253; Schurz, *Reminiscences*, 3:113–14; Harwell and Racine, *Fiery Trail*, 211, 213. In addition to Logan, Slocum, and Schurz, General Blair also believed that Sherman's terms would be rejected. See Andrew H. Hickenlooper Diary, April 19, 1865, Hickenlooper Family Collection, CINHS.

58. Sherman, *General and Field Orders*, 231–32; *OR* 47(3):250. In describing the truce line, Sherman mistakenly referred to "West Point on the Neuse River" instead of "West Point on the Eno."

59. Wills, *Army Life*, 372; John Mahon, "Letters of Samuel Mahon," 261; Jamison, *Recollections*, 327.

60. John Johnson Diary, April 18, 1865, DU; John Johnson to "Dear General" [Bradley T. Johnson], December 17, 1891, Bradley T. Johnson Papers, DU; [J. E. Johnston to P. G. T. Beauregard], "Synopsis of the Agreement Between Generals Johnston & Sherman," April 18, 1865, P-28, Joseph E. Johnston Papers in the William P. Palmer Collection, WRHS; Thomas Webb to Z. B. Vance, April 18, 1865, Letterbook, vol. 7, Zebulon B. Vance Papers, NCDAH.

61. *OR* 47(3):811; Thomas Webb to Z. B. Vance, April 18, 1865, Letterbook, vol. 7, Zebulon B. Vance Papers, NCDAH; Orrin L. Ellis Diary, April 18, 1865, *CWTI* Collection, USAMHI.

62. Thomas Webb to Z. B. Vance, April 18, 1865, and Z. B. Vance to Joseph E. Johns[t]on, April 19, 1865, Letterbook, vol. 7, Zebulon B. Vance Papers, NCDAH.

63. *OR* 47(3):811; *OR* 53:418.

64. *OR* 47(3):812.

65. Ibid., 816.

66. Ratchford, *Some Reminiscences*, 45.

67. *OR* 47(3):810, 813.

68. William E. Stoney quoted in Hagood, *Memoirs*, 369–70; Alexander W. Marshall, "1865 Memoranda," April 20, 1865, Rachel Susan (Bee) Cheves Papers, DU; J. M. J. Tolly to James A. Hall, April 22, 1865, Bolling Hall Collection, Hall Family Papers, ALDAH; W. A. Johnson, "Closing Days," June 5, 1902; James W. Brown Diary, April 19, 1865, Private Papers, Mf Drawer 187, Reel 13, GADAH; Joseph F. Waring Diary, April 19, 1865, SHC-UNC; Hezekiah M. McCorkle Diary, April 19, 1865, Civil War Miscellany—Personal Papers, Mf Drawer 283, Reel 32, GADAH.

CHAPTER EIGHT

1. C. P. Mallett to Son, April 18, 1865 [Journal-Letter, April 17–18, 1865], Charles P. Mallett Letters, Charles B. Mallett Papers, SHC-UNC; Norvell W. Wil-

son Diary, April 17, 1865, Norvell W. Wilson Papers, SHC-UNC; Cornelia P. Spencer Diary, April 17, 1865, Cornelia P. Spencer Papers, SHC-UNC; Robert Y. Woodlief Diary, April 17, 1865, USC; *Detroit Advertiser and Tribune,* May 11, 1865; Spencer, *Last Ninety Days,* 171–72.

2. Elliott B. McKeever, "Sketch of the 9th Ohio Cavalry," 28, Civil War Miscellaneous Collection, USAMHI; Will to Brother, April 14, 1865 [section dated April 19, 1865], William C. Stevens Correspondence, BL-UMI; C. P. Mallett to Son, April 18, 1865 [Journal-Letter, April 18–19, 25, 1865], Charles P. Mallett Letters, Charles B. Mallett Papers, SHC-UNC. Cornelia Phillips Spencer contradicts Mallett's account, claiming that most former slaves in Chapel Hill remained with their previous masters and continued to work on a voluntary basis. See Spencer, *Last Ninety Days,* 186–87.

3. Committee of the Regiment, *Ninety-second Illinois,* 245; Will to Brother, April 14, 1865 [section dated April 19, 1865], and Will to Sister, April 22, 1865 [section dated April 24, 1865], William C. Stevens Correspondence, BL-UMI; C. P. Mallett to Son, April 18, 1865 [Journal-Letter, April 19, 1865], Charles P. Mallett Letters, Charles B. Mallett Papers, SHC-UNC.

4. Lucy P. Russell, *A Rare Pattern,* 6–7; C. P. Mallett to Son, April 18, 1865 [Journal-Letter, April 19, 22, 1865], Charles P. Mallett Letters, Charles B. Mallett Papers, SHC-UNC; Norvell W. Wilson Diary, April 21–22, 1865, Norvell W. Wilson Papers, SHC-UNC.

5. Spencer, *Last Ninety Days,* 261–62; Battle, *University of North Carolina,* 1:746; Henderson, *Campus of the First State University,* 184; Lucy P. Russell, *A Rare Pattern,* 5; Delia White Woodward Civil War Memorandum, 1, Augustus W. Long Papers, DU; Walter Clark, *Histories,* 5:647; C. P. Mallett to Son, April 18, 1865 [Journal-Letter, April 21, 1865], Charles P. Mallett Letters, Charles B. Mallett Papers, SHC-UNC.

6. Spencer, *Last Ninety Days,* 178–81, 188; Norvell W. Wilson Diary, April 22–23, 1865, Norvell W. Wilson Papers, SHC-UNC; C. P. Mallett to Son, April 18, 1865 [Journal-Letter, April 19, 21, 26, 1865], Charles P. Mallett Letters, Charles B. Mallett Papers, SHC-UNC; *OR* 47(3):247–48.

7. *OR* 47(3):248, 279–80; Circular 17, April 20, 1865; Circular 19, April 24, 1865; Circular 24, May 1, 1865, Circulars and Letters Sent, Second Brigade, Third Cavalry Division, Cavalry Corps, Military Division of the Mississippi, vol. 61/162, RG 393, NA.

8. Hiram M. Austin to "father and mother," April 28, 1865, Hiram M. Austin Letters, Bentonville Battleground State Historic Site, Four Oaks, North Carolina; Will to Sister, April 22, 1865 [see also section dated April 24, 1865], William C. Stevens Correspondence, BL-UMI. At his headquarters near Raleigh, Union general Manning F. Force recorded that a squad of Wheeler's cavalry brought in some stragglers from his command. "The [Confederate] Sergeant in charge said that they and Kilpatrick's cavalry patrol together, under the same orders," Force wrote. See Manning F. Force Letterbook-Journal, April 22, 1865, Manning F. Force Papers, UWA.

9. Spencer, *Last Ninety Days,* 188–89; Tomlinson, *"Dear Friends,"* 189.

10. Delia White Woodward Civil War Memorandum, 1–2, Augustus W. Long Papers, DU; Bradbury Smith, "A Maine Boy," 21; C. P. Mallett to Son, April 18, 1865 [Journal-Letter, April 19, 23, 1865], Charles P. Mallett Letters, Charles B. Mallett Papers, SHC-UNC.

11. Will to Brother, April 14, 1865 [section dated April 19, 1865], Will to Father,

April 21, 1865, and Will to Sister, April 22, 1865, William C. Stevens Correspondence, BL-UMI.

12. Spencer, "Old Times in Chapel Hill," 216–17.

13. Ibid., 217.

14. C. P. Mallett to Son, April 18, 1865 [Journal-Letter, April 25, 1865], Charles P. Mallett Letters, Charles B. Mallett Papers, SHC-UNC; Spencer, "Old Times in Chapel Hill," 217; Committee of the Regiment, *Ninety-second Illinois*, 246–47. Professor Charles Phillips stated that Atkins also presented Eleanor Swain with his bill of sale for the horse to forestall the inevitable rumors. See Charles Phillips to "My Dear Sir" [E. J. Hale], June 14, 23, 1866, Edward J. Hale Papers, NCDAH.

15. Committee of the Regiment, *Ninety-second Illinois*, 247; Spencer, "Old Times in Chapel Hill," 217–18; Barrett, *Sherman's March*, 266; untitled poem by Cornelia P. Spencer, "written May 3, 1865, & inscribed to E[leanor] H. S[wain] on occasion of *General A[tkins]'s surrender*," Cornelia P. Spencer Papers, SHC-UNC; Henderson, *Campus of the First State University*, 186. According to Charles Phillips, Mrs. Swain told her daughter that "she would rather see her in her grave than Genl. A[tkins]'s wife." See Charles Phillips to "My Dear Sir" [E. J. Hale], June 14, 1866, Edward J. Hale Papers, NCDAH.

16. Records Concerning the Conduct and Loyalty of Certain Union Army Officers, Civilian Employees of the War Department, and Other U.S. Citizens during the Civil War, 1861–1872, Box 2, "Statements dated 1872 concerning H. Judson Kilpatrick's affair with a woman during the Civil War," deposition of R[ichard] Blacknall, August 8, 1872; deposition of Mrs. Robert F. Morris, n.d., RG 107, NA.

17. Paul, *History of Durham*, 25–26; Jean B. Anderson, *Durham County*, 126; C. P. Mallett to Son, April 18, 1865 [Journal-Letter, April 19, 22, 1865], Charles P. Mallett Letters, Charles B. Mallett Papers, SHC-UNC.

18. The Camerons were also among the largest slaveholders in the state, owning more than 1,000 in 1860. Jean B. Anderson, *Piedmont Plantation*, viii, ix, 116–17; Rebecca B[ennehan] A[nderson] to "Dear Aunt Maggie" [Margaret Mordecai], April 21, 1865, Folder 64, Thomas Ruffin Papers, SHC-UNC.

19. Rebecca B[ennehan] A[nderson] to "Dear Aunt Maggie" [Margaret Mordecai], April 21, 1865, Folder 64, Thomas Ruffin Papers, SHC-UNC; Jean B. Anderson, *Piedmont Plantation*, 118–19, 122; William H. Day to Mrs. [Anne] Ruffin, April 21, 22, 1865, Cameron Family Papers, SHC-UNC. Capt. William H. Day was General Kilpatrick's provost marshal.

20. Jonathan Worth to Son, May 4, 1865, Worth Family Papers, DU; Charles Manly to D[avid] L. Swain, May 16, 1865, and George W. Mordecai to D[avid] L. Swain, May 15, 1865, Walter Clark Papers, NCDAH; Spencer, *Last Ninety Days*, 173–77; Murray, *Wake: Capital County*, 525.

21. Jonathan Worth to Son, May 4, 1865, Worth Family Papers, DU; Charles Manly to D[avid] L. Swain, May 16, 1865, Walter Clark Papers, NCDAH; Charles Manly to Cornelia Spencer, April 25, 1866, Cornelia P. Spencer Papers, SHC-UNC; Murray, *Wake: Capital County*, 525.

22. *OR* 47(3):251, 281; *Raleigh Daily Progress*, April 22, 1865. On April 22, Howard issued an order to his inspector general directing that all wagons, tents, and knapsacks be searched for such contraband as women's clothing, watches, jewelry, shot-

guns, and silver plate. Howard stipulated that the inspections were to occur simultaneously and in the presence of a strong guard. The inspectors were to confiscate all unauthorized property.

Many North Carolinians received horses, mules, and rations from the Federals at Raleigh. See Edward E. Schweitzer Diary, April 20, 1865, Edward E. Schweitzer Diaries and Correspondence, *CWTI* Collection, USAMHI; David Brainard Whiting Reminiscences, 3, NCDAH; *Raleigh Daily Standard,* April 17, 1865.

The depredations of bummers in Franklin County led Howard to send a detachment after the raiders. Howard's order urged "all citizens beyond the lines . . . to afford our officers in charge of patrols and guards every possible facility for bringing to justice these marauders and stragglers, who are a disgrace to our army and to our country." See *OR* 47(3):280–81, 288; Anna L. Fuller Diary, April 20, 1865, Robbins Library, Louisburg College, Louisburg, North Carolina.

23. Wright, *Sixth Iowa,* 451; *Raleigh Daily Progress,* April 19, 1865; *Raleigh Daily Standard,* April 17, 1865; Circular, Headquarters Twentieth Army Corps, April 15, 1865, Regimental Records, 1st Regiment, Michigan Engineers and Mechanics, RG 94, NA; Boies, *Thirty-third Massachusetts,* 121; *OR* 47(1):700, 741; *OR* 47(3):240.

24. Eaton, "Diary of an Officer," 252; *OR* 47(3):240; Murray, *Wake: Capital County,* 522.

25. *OR* 47(1):937; anonymous Federal soldier in *Raleigh Daily Standard,* April 28, 1865; Osborn, *Trials and Triumphs,* 210–11; Underwood, *Thirty-third Mass.,* 292; William H. McIntosh, "Annals of the 22d Wisconsin," 226, William H. McIntosh Papers, SHSW; Toombs, *Reminiscences,* 221; C[hester] M. Slayton to "Brother Asa," April 26, 1865, Chester M. Slayton Letters, Slayton Family Papers, BL-UMI; Vett to Sis, April 13, 1865, Sylvester C. Noble Papers, YHS; Clason [Miller] to Mother, April 15, 1865, Box 5, Folder 20, Miller Family Collection, CINHS; George K. Collins, *149th New York,* 325; Pepper, *Personal Recollections,* 387–88; *Philadelphia Inquirer,* April 26, 29, 1865; Pinney, *104th Ohio,* 83; Furnas, *Forty-four Months,* 161.

26. Pepper, *Personal Recollections,* 387–88; *Philadelphia Inquirer,* April 26, 1865; Kittinger, *Diary,* 204; [Samuel] Merrill to Em, May 11, 1865 [Journal-Letter], Samuel Merrill Papers, INSL; Geo[rge] to Sarah, April 17, 1865, George A. Collamore Letters, GHM; Montgomery C. Meigs Diary, April 26, 1865, Montgomery C. Meigs Papers, LC.

27. *OR* 47(3):217; Murray, *Wake: Capital County,* 519; Round, "Last Signal Message of the War," 27–30, and "Last Signal Message."

28. Hedley, *Marching through Georgia,* 440–41; Dawson, *Life and Services of John A. Logan,* 119; Andy Hickenlooper to "My Dear Friend" [Maria Smith], April 16, 1865; Hickenlooper Family Collection, CINHS; Jackson, *Colonel's Diary,* 207; Lybarger, *Leaves from My Diary,* April 19–20, 1865; "J S R[obinson]" to "Friend Hunt," April 20, 1865, James S. Robinson Papers, OHS; *Cincinnati Daily Commercial,* April 27, 1865.

29. Wright, *Sixth Iowa,* 451–52; Jackson, *Colonel's Diary,* 208–9; Laura to Em, May 5, 1865, Craven-Pegram Papers, DU; Grunert, *One Hundred and Twenty-ninth Illinois,* 236–37; Tracie, *Nineteenth Ohio Battery,* 451.

30. Nathaniel L. Parmeter Diary, April 13, 1865, Nathaniel L. Parmeter Papers, OHS; Toombs, *Reminiscences,* 221; Halsey, *A Yankee Private's Civil War,* 198–200; U. H. Farr reminiscence in Merrill, *Seventieth Indiana,* 268–71; "Record of a Statement

Made to C. C. Crittenden . . . by Mrs. T. F. Maguire, Sr., . . . March 9, 1940," Allston Lavender Paper, NCDAH.

31. Nichols, *Story of the Great March,* 298.

32. Wright, *Sixth Iowa,* 450–51; C[hester] M. Slayton to "Brother Asa," April 26, 1865, Chester M. Slayton Letters, Slayton Family Papers, BL-UMI; Wilfred W. Black, "Marching with Sherman," 473; Henry G. Noble Diary, April 18, 1865, and Henry G. Noble to "My Own Dear Girl," April 28, 1865, Henry G. Noble Papers, BL-UMI; "Sly" quoted in Alonzo L. Brown, *Fourth Minnesota,* 407.

33. Burton, *Diary,* 75; Otis to Wife, April 26, 1865, Oliver O. Howard Papers, BC; Oliver O. Howard, *Autobiography,* 2:159; John H. Otto, "War Memories," 123, John H. Otto Papers, SHSW; Murray, *Wake: Capital County,* 534–35.

34. Sylvester, " 'Gone for a Soldier,' " 236; J. R. Stillwell to Wife, April 23, 1865, James R. Stillwell Letters, OHS; Edmund J. Cleveland Diary, April 15–17, 1865, SHC-UNC; C[hester] M. Slayton to "Brother Asa," April 26, 1865, Chester M. Slayton Letters, Slayton Family Papers, BL-UMI; Edgar to Frank, April 23, 1865, Correspondence 1865, Soldier 154th New York, Box 1028, Folder 37, GHM; Levi N. Green Diary, April 21, 1865, Levi N. Green Papers, MNHS; Andrew H. Hickenlooper Diary, April 28, 1865, Hickenlooper Family Collection, CINHS; Clarke, "Sherman in Raleigh," 231; Orville T. Chamberlain Diary, April 20, 1865, and O. T. [Orville T. Chamberlain] to Father, April 21, 1865, Orville T. Chamberlain Letters, Dr. Joseph W. Chamberlain Papers, INHS.

35. Spencer, *Last Ninety Days,* 247–48; Murray, *Wake: Capital County,* 520; Furnas, *Forty-four Months,* 156; *City of Raleigh,* 64–65.

36. *City of Raleigh,* 64–65.

37. *OR* 47(3):245, 249, 255–56, 257, 265–66, 267.

38. Ibid., 266.

39. Ibid., 246, 255, 267.

40. Sherman, *Memoirs,* 2:357; *OR* 47(1):31–32; *OR* (3):258, 279, 287–88; U.S. Congress, "Sherman-Johnston," 3:4; Vett to Mother, April 20, 1865 [April 22, 1865, portion], Sylvester C. Noble Papers, YHS; Harvey Reid Diary, April 19, 1865, Harvey Reid Papers, University Archives and Area Research Center, University of Wisconsin-Parkside, Kenosha. Establishing a truce as a means of gaining time to repair the railroad from Goldsboro was an explanation Sherman offered after the fact. At the time, the Union commander was convinced that his agreement would be approved in Washington, and he was therefore limiting the shipment of supplies from the coast. See *OR* 47(3):246.

41. *OR* 47(1):938; *OR* 47(3):251, 268–69; Circular No. 21, 1st Division, 20th Corps, April 21, 1865, Letters and Reports Sent, January 1863–June 1865, 12th Army Corps and 20th Army Corps, pt. 2, vol. 33/80, RG 393, NA; Alpheus S. Williams Diary, April 20–22, 1865, Alpheus S. Williams Papers, DPL; Vett to Mother, April 20, 1865 [April 22, 1865, portion], Sylvester C. Noble Papers, YHS; William T. Sherman Diary, April 20, 1865, Sherman Family Papers, UND; Sherman, *Memoirs,* 2:357; Slocum, "Final Operations," 757; *Raleigh Daily Progress,* April 21, 1865; *Philadelphia Inquirer,* April 28, 1865; Joseph F. Waring Diary, April 22, 1865, SHC-UNC; Furnas, *Forty-four Months,* 156–58; Ezra W. Button Diary, April 21, 1865, John B. Tripp Papers, SHSW.

42. Johnston, *Narrative*, 410; W. H. Andrews, "First Georgia Regulars at Johnston's Surrender," Lovic P. Thomas Scrapbooks, 1:38, Lovic P. Thomas Papers, AHS.

43. W. H. Andrews, "First Georgia Regulars at Johnston's Surrender," Lovic P. Thomas Scrapbooks, 1:38, Lovic P. Thomas Papers, AHS. Some units—such as Parker's and Wheaton's Batteries—maintained a high degree of discipline, but this was exceptional. See D. E. H. Smith, *A Charlestonian's Recollections*, 106–7; Charles C. Jones, *Chatham Artillery*, 216.

44. Cox, "Surrender of Johnston's Army," 252; *New York Herald*, May 9, 1865; *OR* 47(3):810–11, 815; Z. B. Vance to J. E. Johnston, April 16, 1865, Z. B. Vance to J. E. Johnston, April 19, 1865 [three letters], Z. B. Vance to J. E. Johnston, April 20, 1865 ["In your first note of yesterday"], Z. B. Vance to J. E. Johnston, April 21, 1865 [two letters], and Z. B. Vance to J. E. Johnston, April 22, 1865, Letterbook, vol. 7, Zebulon B. Vance Papers, NCDAH. Governor Vance also appealed to Secretary of War Breckinridge for restitution. See Z. B. Vance to John C. Breckenridge [*sic*], April 22, 1865, Letterbook, vol. 7, Zebulon B. Vance Papers, NCDAH.

45. J. E. Johnston to Z. B. Vance, April 19, 1865 ["I have just received the letter"], J. E. Johnston to Z. B. Vance, April 21, 1865, J. E. Johnston to Z. B. Vance, April 24, 1865 ["I have had the honour"], J. E. Johnston to Z. B. Vance, April 24, 1865 [". . . the only robberies you mentioned"], E. J. Harvie to Z. B. Vance, April 21, 1865, and Z. B. Vance to E. J. Harvie, April 21, 1865, Letterbook, vol. 7, Zebulon B. Vance Papers, NCDAH; E. J. Harvie to Z. B. Vance, April 21, 1865, and E. J. Harvie to Z. B. Vance, April 22, 1865, Army of Tennessee—Inspector General's Letterbook, chap. 2, no. 19 ¼, RG 109, NA.

46. Johnston, *Narrative*, 410, 417–18, and "My Negotiations," 192, 195.

47. Holmes, *Diary of Henry McCall Holmes*, 34; C. W. Hutson to Em, April 26, 1865, Charles W. Hutson Papers, SHC-UNC; W. H. Andrews, "First Georgia Regulars at Johnston's Surrender," Lovic P. Thomas Scrapbooks, 1:38, Lovic P. Thomas Papers, AHS; Andrews, *Footprints*, 180; Norman D. Brown, *One of Cleburne's Command*, 164, 166; R. M. Collins, *Chapters*, 294–97; Guild, *Fourth Tennessee Cavalry*, 147. General Johnston later stated that there were enough rations in North Carolina depots to feed his troops through the end of April. See Johnston, *Narrative*, 410.

Although rations and clothing were plentiful, forage for the horses and mules was scarce. Wheaton's Battery had to scour the countryside "for twenty-five miles round" to find sufficient fodder for their teams. The scarcity of forage compelled Johnston to spread his army from Hillsborough to Charlotte. See Charles C. Jones, *Chatham Artillery*, 216; *OR* 47(3):349.

48. Henry ——— to "Dear Sister Mollie," April 20, 1865, Army Miscellany: Officers' and Soldiers' Miscellaneous Letters, Confederate States of America Archives, DU; R. Amos Jarman, "History of Company K, 27th Mississippi Infantry," 57, R. Amos Jarman Papers, MSDAH; W. A. Johnson, "Closing Days," June 5, 1902; D. E. H. Smith, *A Charlestonian's Recollections*, 106; W. H. Andrews, "First Georgia Regulars at Johnston's Surrender," Lovic P. Thomas Scrapbooks, 1:38, Lovic P. Thomas Papers, AHS; Andrews, *Footprints*, 180; Thomas L. Sullivan Account Book, April 20, 1865, Civil War Collection—Confederate, TNSLA.

49. Ridley, *Battles and Sketches*, 459; Hawes, "Memoirs of Charles H. Olmstead," 153.

50. Albert Q. Porter Diary, April 25, 1865, Albert Q. Porter Collection, LC; Worsham, *Old Nineteenth Tennessee,* 193; W. A. Johnson, "Closing Days," June 5, 1902; W. A. Johnson, "Marching, Camping, Fighting," Lovic P. Thomas Scrapbooks, 2:155, Lovic P. Thomas Papers, AHS; Walter A. Clark, *Under the Stars and Bars,* 199; W. H. Rhea quoted in Marshall, *Life of Bate,* 171–73; Hezekiah M. McCorkle Diary, April 21, 1865, Civil War Miscellany—Personal Papers, Mf Drawer 283, Reel 32, GADAH.

51. William E. Sloan Diary, April 20, 1865, Civil War Collection—Confederate, TNSLA; William W. Gordon Diary, April 20, 1865, Gordon Family Papers, SHC-UNC.

52. Joseph F. Waring Diary, April 16, 1865, SHC-UNC; *OR* 47(3):813–14, 829–30. On April 22, Hampton learned that his letter had failed to reach Davis. He left his headquarters, hoping to see Davis at Salisbury. When Hampton reached Greensboro, however, he discovered that Davis was at Charlotte and that the railroad from Jamestown was virtually impassable. Hampton contented himself with writing a second missive to the president expressing the same sentiments as the first.

53. *OR* 47(3): 812, 814, 818, 819–20.

54. Ibid., 821–28, 830–31, 832–34; Jefferson Davis, *Rise and Fall,* 2:688–89.

55. Z. B. Vance to Cornelia P. Spencer, April 7, [1866], Cornelia P. Spencer Papers, SHC-UNC; Zebulon B. Vance, "Lecture—Last Days of the War," in Dowd, *Life of Vance,* 485–86; Spencer, *Last Ninety Days,* 184; *OR* 47(3):828, 831. In his April 7, 1866, letter to Spencer, Vance states that his visit to Davis in Charlotte occurred after the Sherman-Johnston agreement was reached, whereas in his later lecture, "The Last Days of the War," he implies that it occurred *before* the negotiations. The evidence indicates that Vance's visit to Davis occurred on or about April 25, 1865. In any event, Davis did not reach Charlotte until April 19 (*after* the initial negotiations), and telegraphic correspondence between the two men indicates that their conference occurred no earlier than April 23. See Rowland, *Jefferson Davis,* 9:558–59, 562.

56. Vance, "Lecture—Last Ninety Days of the War," in Dowd, *Life of Vance,* 486; Z. B. Vance to Cornelia P. Spencer, April 7, [1866], Cornelia P. Spencer Papers, SHC-UNC.

57. *OR* 47(3):287.

CHAPTER NINE

1. William T. Sherman Diary, April 18–19, 1865, Sherman Family Papers, UND; *OR* 47(1):33; *OR* 47(3):257; Sherman, *Memoirs,* 2:354; H[enry] to Wife, April 21, 1865, Henry Hitchcock Papers, LC; Hitchcock, *Marching with Sherman,* 303.

2. Hitchcock, *Marching with Sherman,* 4, 6–8.

3. H[enry] to Wife, April 21, 1865, Henry Hitchcock Papers, LC; Hitchcock, *Marching with Sherman,* 303; Simon, *Papers of Grant,* 14:397.

4. *OR* 47(3):263; Simon, *Papers of Grant,* 14:423; Thomas and Hyman, *Stanton,* 405–6; Welles, *Diary,* 2:294; Bates, *Lincoln in the Telegraph Office,* 395–97.

5. Welles, *Diary,* 2:294–95; Thomas and Hyman, *Stanton,* 406–7; Flower, *Stanton,* 265; Grant, *Personal Memoirs,* 569–70; *OR* 47(3):221, 243–44; *New York Times,* April 23, 1865; Sherman, *Official Account,* 195–96.

6. Welles, *Diary*, 2:294–95; Flower, *Stanton*, 265; *New York Times*, April 23, 1865.

7. Fellman, *Citizen Sherman*, 245; Randall, *Diary of Orville H. Browning*, 2:24.

8. *OR* 47(3):263–64; Simon, *Papers of Grant*, 14:424–25; Flower, *Stanton*, 265–66.

9. Simon, *Papers of Grant*, 14:428; H[enry] to Wife, April 21, 1865, Henry Hitchcock Papers, LC; Hitchcock, *Marching with Sherman*, 303.

10. The three staff officers were Maj. Edward M. Hudson, Maj. George K. Leet, and Capt. William M. Dunn Jr. Simon, *Papers of Grant*, 14:428; H[enry] to Mary, April 22, 1865, Henry Hitchcock Papers, LC; Hitchcock, *Marching with Sherman*, 304–5; Montgomery C. Meigs Diary, April 22, 1865, Montgomery C. Meigs Papers, LC; *Philadelphia Inquirer*, April 24, 1865.

11. *OR* 46(3):888–90, 892–95; *OR* 47(3):276–77.

12. H[enry] to Mary, April 22, 1865, and H[enry] to Mary, April 25, 1865, Henry Hitchcock Papers, LC; Hitchcock, *Marching with Sherman*, 305–6, 308; *Philadelphia Inquirer*, April 24, 1865.

13. *OR* 47(1):34; *OR* 47(3):287; H[enry] to Mary, April 25, 1865, Henry Hitchcock Papers, LC; Hitchcock, *Marching with Sherman*, 308; Montgomery C. Meigs Diary, April 23–24, 1865, Montgomery C. Meigs Papers, LC; Sherman, *Memoirs*, 2:357–58.

14. Sherman, *Memoirs*, 2:358–60; H[enry] to Mary, April 25, 1865, Henry Hitchcock Papers, LC; Hitchcock, *Marching with Sherman*, 308; Grant, *Personal Memoirs*, 570; *OR* 47(1):34; *OR* 47(3):263, 293; U.S. Congress, "Sherman-Johnston," 3:18.

15. H[enry] to Mary, April 25, 1865, Henry Hitchcock Papers, LC; Hitchcock, *Marching with Sherman*, 309.

16. *OR* 47(1):34; *OR* 47(3):293–94, 295, 298, 299; Sherman, *General and Field Orders*, 234–35.

17. Simon, *Papers of Grant*, 14:433; *OR* 47(1):34; *OR* 47(3):293.

18. Montgomery C. Meigs Diary, April 24–25, 1865, Montgomery C. Meigs Papers, LC; John H. Ferguson Diary, April 24, 1865, Pfeiffer Library, MacMurray College, Jacksonville, Illinois; Enos W. McKenney Diary, April 24, 1865, Bentonville Battleground State Historic Site, Four Oaks, North Carolina; Rood, *Company E, Twelfth Wisconsin*, 430–31; Furnas, *Forty-four Months*, 158; Jesse S. Bean Diary, April 24–25, 1865, SHC-UNC; George N. Compton Diary, April 25, 1865, George N. Compton Papers, Illinois State Historical Library, Springfield; Levi B. Aldrich Diary, April 25, 1865, Levi B. Aldrich Papers, MNHS; Wilfred W. Black, "Marching with Sherman," 472; Saunier, *Forty-seventh Ohio*, 441; Otis to Wife, April 26, 1865, Oliver O. Howard Papers, BC; Oliver O. Howard, *Autobiography*, 2:159, and "Campaign of the Carolinas," 30.

19. *OR* 47(3):302; Sherman, *Memoirs*, 2:360–61.

20. Sherman, *Memoirs*, 2:361–62; *OR* 47(3):303.

21. *OR* 47(3):302; Sherman, *Memoirs*, 2:362.

22. *OR* 47(1):90–99, 101, 104, 123, 125, 134, 144, 596, 604, 700, 786; *OR* 47(3):208–9, 295–98, 305–6, 308–9; Sherman, *General and Field Orders*, 228–29; H[enry] to Mary, April 25, 1865, Henry Hitchcock Papers, LC; Hitchcock, *Marching with Sherman*, 309.

23. *OR* 47(3):834–35; Johnston, *Narrative*, 410–11, and "My Negotiations," 193.

24. Jefferson Davis, *Rise and Fall,* 2:688–89, 692–93; *OR* 47(3):835; Johnston, *Narrative,* 411, and "My Negotiations," 193.

25. *OR* 47(3):836; John Johnson Diary, April 25, 1865, DU; Edward R. Archer Diary, April 25, 1865, Mss 5:1 Ar234:1, VAHS; Roman, *Military Operations of Beauregard,* 2:404; Ridley, *Battles and Sketches,* 464; Johnston, *Narrative,* 411, and "My Negotiations," 193.

26. *OR* 47(3):837–38, 840–41; Norman D. Brown, *One of Cleburne's Command,* 167–68; Ridley, *Battles and Sketches,* 464; William E. Stoney quoted in Hagood, *Memoirs,* 370–71.

27. *OR* 47(3):303–4.

28. *OR* 47(1):34; *OR* 47(3):303–4, 308, 313, 317, 841; H[enry] to Mary, April 25, 1865, and April 26, 1865 [addendum to April 25, 1865, letter], Henry Hitchcock Papers, LC; Hitchcock, *Marching with Sherman,* 314–15; John M. Schofield, "Narrative Part V: The Army of the Ohio. Closing Events of the War in North Carolina," 5–6, John M. Schofield Papers, LC; Schofield, *Forty-six Years,* 351; Otis to Wife, April 26, 1865, Oliver O. Howard Papers, BC; Oliver O. Howard, *Autobiography,* 2:158–59; Kirk, *Fifteenth Pennsylvania Cavalry,* 595. Sherman received a third dispatch from Johnston just minutes after the second, asking whether the truce would be extended for the negotiations. See *OR* 47(3):312.

29. Schofield, *Forty-six Years,* 351; Kirk, *Fifteenth Pennsylvania Cavalry,* 595; *New York Herald,* April 30, 1865. Sherman and Johnston left only brief accounts of the April 26 conference, and neither mentions Schofield's prominent role in the negotiations. See *OR* 47(1):34; Sherman, *Memoirs,* 2:362–63; Johnston, *Narrative,* 412–15, and "My Negotiations," 194–95.

30. Schofield, "Narrative Part V: The Army of the Ohio. Closing Events of the War in North Carolina," 6, John M. Schofield Papers, LC; Schofield, *Forty-six Years,* 351; Johnston, *Narrative,* 414.

31. *OR* 46(3):665; *OR* 47(3):313.

32. Kirk, *Fifteenth Pennsylvania Cavalry,* 595; Schofield, *Forty-six Years,* 351–52.

33. *OR* 47(3):321, 482; Schofield, *Forty-six Years,* 352.

34. Johnston, "My Negotiations," 187; Dowdey and Manarin, *Wartime Papers of R. E. Lee,* 938–39; Jefferson Davis, *Rise and Fall,* 2:692–93.

35. Paul, *History of Durham,* xv; U. R. Brooks, *Butler and His Cavalry,* 476; Lily Logan Morrill, "A Builder of the New South [Thomas M. Logan]," 66, manuscript in the possession of Alan and Nancy Bruns, Fredericksburg, Virginia; *Cincinnati Daily Commercial,* May 5, 1865; *New York Herald,* April 30, 1865.

36. Jesse R. Sparkman Diary, April 26, 1865, Box 3, Diaries, Memoirs, Etc., TNSLA; Kirk, *Fifteenth Pennsylvania Cavalry,* 595; Theo Davis, "With Sherman," 205; *Philadelphia Inquirer,* May 8, 1865.

37. James Bennett to Governor Holden, October 5, 1869, and January [?], 1870, Papers of Governor William W. Holden, Boxes 220 and 222, State Agency Records, NCDAH; Barred and Disallowed Case Files of the Southern Claims Commission, Claim No. 18945: James Bennett, Microcopy M1407, Microfiche 4311, RG 56, NA.

38. *OR* 47(3):305–6, 308, 317, 337; Alpheus S. Williams Diary, April 26, 1865, Alpheus S. Williams Papers, DPL; William E. Stoney quoted in Hagood, *Memoirs,* 371; Muster Rolls for the 1st N.C. Reserves, 2nd N.C. Reserves, 3rd N.C. Reserves,

1st Battalion N.C. Reserves, 8th N.C., 17th N.C., 31st N.C., 36th N.C., 40th N.C., 42nd N.C., 50th N.C., 51st N.C., 61st N.C., and 66th N.C., Muster Rolls and Lists of Confederate Troops Paroled in North Carolina, Microcopy M1781, Rolls 4 and 5 (mf), RG 109, NA; *OR* 47(3):246, 337.

39. *OR* 47(3):839; W. H. Andrews, "First Georgia Regulars at Johnston's Surrender," Lovic P. Thomas Scrapbooks, 1:38, Lovic P. Thomas Papers, AHS; Andrews, *Footprints,* 181.

40. *OR* 47(3):839; Jefferson Davis, *Rise and Fall,* 2:689; Anna H. Trenholm Diary, April 19, 26, 1865, SHC-UNC; Mrs. James A. Fore, "The Importance of Charlotte to the Confederacy," 6–7; Junius Davis to Mrs. J. A. Fore, October 1, 1913; W. W. Phifer to Mrs. James A. Fore, June 11, 1913; Mrs. James A. Fore, "Last Meeting of Confederate Cabinet Held in Charlotte," in *Raleigh State Journal,* March 2, 1917, all in Mrs. James A. Fore Papers, North Carolina Division, UDC, Military Collection— Civil War, Box 76, Folder 58, NCDAH; Ballard, *A Long Shadow,* 109–10.

41. *OR* 47(3):841; Hampton, "The Effort to Rescue Davis," 134; Wheeler, "An Effort," 85–86.

42. Samuel A. Ashe, "Some Reminiscences," 8, Military Collection—Civil War, Box 70, Folder 6, NCDAH; Richard Pollard to Mrs. E. S. Dudley, April 25, 1865, #26168, Archives Division, Virginia State Library, Richmond; Tench Tilghman Diary, April 26, 1865, Tench Tilghman Papers, SHC-UNC; Younger, *Inside the Confederate Government,* 207; John Taylor Wood Diary, April 24–25 [26?], 1865, John Taylor Wood Papers, SHC-UNC.

43. William T. Sherman Diary, April 26, 1865, Sherman Family Papers, UND; *OR* 47(1):34; *OR* 47(3):312; Sherman, *Memoirs,* 2:363; Cornelius Baker quoted in Rowell, *Yankee Cavalrymen,* 246.

44. H[enry] to Mary, April 26, 1865 [addendum to April 25, 1865, letter], Henry Hitchcock Papers, LC; Hitchcock, *Marching with Sherman,* 316; Furnas, *Forty-four Months,* 159.

45. Round, "Last Signal Message of the War," 33–34, and "Last Signal Message."

46. Hansell, "Surrender of Cobb's Legion," 463; Joseph F. Waring Diary, April 25, 1865, SHC-UNC.

47. Hansell, "Surrender of Cobb's Legion," 463; Joseph F. Waring Diary, April 26– 27, 1865, SHC-UNC; Jesse R. Sparkman Diary, April 26, 1865, Box 3, Memoirs, Diaries, Etc., TNSLA.

48. Hampton, "The Effort to Rescue Davis," 134–35; *OR* 47(3):841; Hansell, "Surrender of Cobb's Legion," 463.

49. Hansell, "Surrender of Cobb's Legion," 463; Hampton, "The Effort to Rescue Davis," 135; Joseph F. Waring Diary, April 27, 1865, SHC-UNC; Jesse R. Sparkman Diary, April 26 [27], 1865, Box 3, Diaries, Memoirs, Etc., TNSLA.

50. *OR* 47(3):844–46.

51. For Johnston's dispatches to Sherman on the subject of his deserting cavalry, see *OR* 47(3):336–37.

52. Ibid., 841, 844–46, 847, 854; J. E. Johnston to B. T. Johnson, September 30, 1887, Bradley T. Johnson Papers, DU. Breckinridge's April 28 dispatch permitting Hampton to join Davis's escort is in *OR* 47(3):851.

53. *OR* 47(3):846; Wheeler, "An Effort," 86; William E. Sloan Diary, April 28,

1865, Civil War Collection—Confederate, TNSLA; William W. Gordon Diary, April 28, 1865, Gordon Family Papers, SHC-UNC.

54. William E. Sloan Diary, April 29–30, 1865, Civil War Collection—Confederate, TNSLA.

55. Alfred Roman, "Inspection Report of Wheeler's Cavalry Corps," Alfred Roman Letterbooks, 1:20–22, Alfred Roman Papers, LC; Bradley, *Last Stand,* 84–85.

56. *OR* 47(3):843–44; Rennolds, *Henry County Commands,* 116; Ridley, *Battles and Sketches,* 465–66. Johnston also notified the governors of the four states comprising his command: North Carolina, South Carolina, Georgia, and Florida. See *OR* 47(3): 855.

57. *OR* 47(3):43, 355, 851; Samuel T. Fielder Diary, April 29, 1865, Tennessee Historical Society Collection, TNSLA; Thomas L. Sullivan Account Book, April 28, 1865, Civil War Collection—Confederate, TNSLA; Thomas B. Roy Diary, April 28, 1865, photocopy in the possession of N. C. Hughes Jr., Chattanooga, Tennessee; Hezekiah M. McCorkle Diary, April 29, 1865, Personal Papers, Mf Drawer 283, Reel 32, GADAH; W. A. Johnson, "Closing Days," June 5, 1902; W. A. Johnson, "Marching, Camping, Fighting," Lovic P. Thomas Scrapbooks, 2:155, Lovic P. Thomas Papers, AHS; John Johnson Diary, April 27–28, 1865, DU; C. W. Hutson to Em, April 26, 1865 [Journal-Letter, April 28, 1865], Charles W. Hutson Papers, SHC-UNC; William R. Talley, "Autobiography," 47, William R. Talley Reminiscences, KMNP; R. M. Collins, *Chapters,* 301; D. E. H. Smith, *A Charlestonian's Recollections,* 108; Charles C. Jones, *Chatham Artillery,* 220.

58. *OR* 47(3):850; Johnston, *Narrative,* 408–9, and "My Negotiations," 191–92; Jefferson Davis, *Rise and Fall,* 2:690–92; W. A. Johnson, "Marching, Camping, Fighting," Lovic P. Thomas Scrapbooks, 2:155, Lovic P. Thomas Papers, AHS; Alexander W. Marshall, "1865 Memoranda," April 27, 1865, Rachel Susan (Bee) Cheves Papers, DU; Thomas L. Sullivan Account Book, April 27, 1865, Civil War Collection—Confederate, TNSLA; Alfred T. Fielder Diary, April 28, 1865, Tennessee Historical Society Collection, TNSLA; William E. Stoney quoted in Hagood, *Memoirs,* 372; "Henry Daniel Hogan," in Elliot and Moxley, *Tennessee Veterans Questionnaires,* 3:1119; Holmes, *Diary of Henry McCall Holmes,* 34; Hawes, "Memoirs of Charles H. Olmstead," 154.

59. W. J. Hardee to Major Gen. [Robert F.] Hoke, September 8, 1865, and T. B. Roy to R. F. Hoke, September 8, 1865, William J. Hardee Papers, ALDAH.

60. Johnston, *Narrative,* 417–18, and "My Negotiations," 195; *OR* 47(3):320; Ridley, *Battles and Sketches,* 466.

61. *OR* 47(3):322, 336; Sherman, *General and Field Orders,* 236–37.

62. Sherman, *General and Field Orders,* 238–39; *OR* 47(3):323.

63. *OR* 47(3):330–31.

64. *Raleigh Daily Progress,* April 29, 1865, quoting extra edition of April 27, 1865; Pepper, *Personal Recollections,* 401; Edmund J. Cleveland Diary, April 27, 1865, SHC-UNC; William H. McIntosh, "Annals of the 22d Wisconsin," 229–30, William H. McIntosh Papers, SHSW; Murray, *Wake: Capital County,* 538–39.

65. James Milner to Sister, April 23, 1865, James R. Milner Papers, Western Historical Manuscripts Collection, Ellis Library, University of Missouri, Columbia; John H. Otto, "War Memories," 151–52, John H. Otto Papers, SHSW; Sanford Fort-

ner [?] Diary, April 28, 1865, Helen Floyd Carlin Collection, INHS; William B. Miller Journal, April 28, 1865, INHS; H. B. Waterman to Parents, April 29, 1865, Herbert B. Waterman Papers, DU; McAdams, *Every-Day Soldier Life*, 153; Fitch, *Echoes*, 272.

66. William T. Sherman Diary, April 27, 1865, Sherman Family Papers, UND; *OR* 47(1):35; *OR* 47(3):301–2; Grant, *Personal Memoirs*, 570.

67. *OR* 47(1):35; *OR* 47(3):337; W. T. Sherman to Ellen, April 28, 1865, Sherman Family Papers, UND; *New York Times*, April 23, 1865. Stanton's *Times* bulletin is reprinted in Sherman, *Official Account*, 191–96.

68. *New York Times*, April 23, 1865; *OR* 47(1):34.

69. *New York Times*, April 23, 1865; *OR* 47(3):334–35. In his bulletin to the *Times*, Stanton omitted the last sentence of Halleck's dispatch: "Would it not be well to put Sherman and all other commanding generals on their guard in this respect[?]" As a result, Stanton made Sherman appear to be a conspirator in Davis's escape. See *OR* 47(3):277.
Only one of Stoneman's three brigades was at Statesville during the April 17–18 negotiations. The other two were at Lenoir, forty-five miles west of Salisbury. Stoneman left his command on April 17 and returned to Greeneville, Tennessee. See *OR* 49(1):334.

70. *OR* 47(1):33, 35; *OR* 47(3):51; *New York Times*, April 23, 1865; W. T. Sherman to John W. Draper, November 6, 1868, John W. Draper Papers, LC; Sherman, "To Execute the Terms," 41.

71. Sherman, *Memoirs*, 2:368; Jacob D. Cox Diary, April 28, 1865, KMNP; Schurz, *Reminiscences*, 3:116–17.

72. Foraker, *Notes*, 1:65–67.

73. *Chicago Tribune*, April 24, 1865; *Cincinnati Daily Commercial*, April 24, 1865; *Detroit Free Press*, April 25, 1865; *New York Herald*, April 24, 1865; *New York Times*, April 24, 1865; *New York Tribune*, April 24, 1865; *Washington Daily Chronicle*, April 24, 1865; Sherman, *Official Account*, 196–99; Marszalek, *Sherman's Other War*, 190–93.

74. Ellen [Sherman] to Cump, April 26, 1865, Sherman Family Papers, UND; John Sherman to E. M. Stanton, April 27, 1865, Edwin M. Stanton Papers, LC.

75. *Cleveland Plain Dealer*, April 25, 1865; *Philadelphia Inquirer*, April 24, 29, 1865; *New York Times*, May 1, 1865; *Detroit Advertiser and Tribune*, May 1, 1865; *Detroit Free Press*, May 2, 1865; Marszalek, *Sherman's Other War*, 193–94; Royster, *Destructive War*, 349.

76. *Washington Chronicle*, May 25, 1865; *Cincinnati Daily Commercial*, April 26–29, May 1, 8, 1865; undated newspaper clipping from the *New York Evening Post* enclosed with letter from W. T. Cooke to John Sherman, May 8, 1865, John Sherman Letterbook, vol. 83, John Sherman Papers, LC; Frank P. Blair Jr. to "Judge" [Montgomery Blair], April 30, 1865, and Frank P. Blair Jr. to Father, May 4, 1865, Mf Reel 2, Blair Family Papers, LC; Charles Ewing to Father [Thomas Ewing], April [May] 4, 1865, Box 6, Charles Ewing Family Papers, LC; Frank H. Putney to Father, May 8, 1865, Frank H. Putney Papers, SHSW. Thomas Ewing's May 8 letter to the *Cincinnati Daily Commercial*, as well as a series of four *Commercial* editorials entitled "A Word for Sherman" and a pro-Sherman editorial from the *New York Leader*, appears in *Criticisms on the Surrender of Johnston's Army;* John Sherman's anonymous letter to the *Washington Chronicle* is reprinted in Sherman, *Official Account*, 201–8.

77. Dana, *Recollections*, 289; Sumner, *Diary of Cyrus B. Comstock*, 317; Julian, *Political Recollections*, 257–58; Randall, *Diary of Orville H. Browning*, 2:24; John Sherman, *Recollections*, 302–3; Welles, *Diary*, 2:296–97; W. T. Sherman to William M. McPherson, March 24, 1865, vol. 15, Letters Sent, Papers and Books, Maj. Gen. William T. Sherman, RG 94, NA.

78. *OR* 47(1):32–33; Sherman, *Memoirs*, 2:353.

79. William T. Sherman Diary, April 28, 1865, Sherman Family Papers, UND; *OR* 47(3):345–46. The letter Sherman asked Grant to send Stanton was comparatively tame, but Grant misunderstood and sent the Rawlins letter instead. For the letter that Grant should have sent, see *OR* 47(3):334–35.

80. William T. Sherman Diary, April 29–May 2, 1865, Sherman Family Papers, UND; *OR* 47(1):35–36; *OR* 47(3):311–12; Sherman, *Memoirs*, 2:368–69; *New York Times*, April 28, 1865. On the day that Halleck's dispatch appeared in the *Times*, "Old Brains" himself rendered it obsolete. On April 26, Grant had notified Halleck of Johnston's surrender and ordered him to recall Sheridan and halt Wright at Danville. Halleck received Grant's orders on April 28 and immediately complied. See *OR* 46(3):969, 991, 996–97; *OR* 47(3):312.

81. *OR* 38(5):791; *OR* 47(3):393, 399; Fellman, *Citizen Sherman*, 249.

82. Sherman, *Memoirs*, 2:373.

CHAPTER TEN

1. Arnett, *Confederate Guns*, 102; Nellie R. Jones, "Guilford Under the Stars and Bars," 18, Guilford File, History—Civil War, NCC-GPL; Z. B. Vance to W. T. Sherman, April 27, 1865 [two letters], Letterbook, vol. 7, Zebulon B. Vance Papers, NCDAH.

2. *OR* 47(3):848; Z. B. Vance to C. P. Spencer, April 7, [1866], Cornelia P. Spencer Papers, SHC-UNC.

3. "A Proclamation by the Governor of North Carolina," April 28, 1865, Letterbook, vol. 7, Zebulon B. Vance Papers, NCDAH; Yearns and Barrett, *North Carolina Civil War Documentary*, 340–41.

4. *OR* 47(3):336–37, 349, 354.

5. Ibid., 350, 858.

6. Ibid., 368, 376, 483, 856, 862. The nine staff officers who assisted Hartsuff were Majors S. M. Letcher, F. E. Wolcott, and T. J. Dow; Brevet Majors William A. Lord and George F. Towle; Captains Hobart Ford and John L. Dow; and Lieutenants William L. Halbert and F. E. Beardslee. See Special Field Orders No. 45, April 29, 1865, Letters Received by the Adjutant General's Office, 1801–1870, Papers Relating to the Surrender of Johnston's Army, Microcopy 619, Roll 381, RG 94, NA.

7. Raphael Semmes Diary, May 1, 1865, Raphael Semmes Papers, DU; Hoole, "Admiral on Horseback," 143; Semmes, *Memoirs*, 821–23; Hatcher, *Last Four Weeks*, 336; Arnett, *Confederate Guns*, 124.

8. Hoole, "Admiral on Horseback," 129–31, 138–39, 142; Raphael Semmes Diary, April 2–5, 26, 1865, Raphael Semmes Papers, DU; Semmes, *Memoirs*, 809–17; Coski, *Capital Navy*, 221–22.

9. Raphael Semmes Diary, April 14–26, 1865, Raphael Semmes Papers, DU; Hoole, "Admiral on Horseback," 140–42; Semmes, *Memoirs*, 819–20.

10. Semmes, *Memoirs*, 822–23; Raphael Semmes Diary, May 1, 1865, Raphael Semmes Papers, DU; Hoole, "Admiral on Horseback," 143; Muster Rolls and Lists of Confederate Troops Paroled in North Carolina, Microcopy M1781, Roll 2 (mf), RG 109, NA; Hatcher, *Last Four Weeks*, 336.

11. Raphael Semmes Diary, May 1, 1865, Raphael Semmes Papers, DU; Hoole, "Admiral on Horseback," 131, 143; Semmes, *Memoirs*, 823, 824–31. For correspondence from Semmes to Ulysses S. Grant and from William T. Sherman to Joseph E. Johnston on the subject of Semmes's arrest and imprisonment, see *OR* 8, ser. 2, 836–37, 842.

12. *Greensboro Patriot*, June 3, 1865; C. Irvine Walker Letter, May 1, 1865, C. Irvine Walker Letters, Regimental Papers of the Civil War, South Carolina, MSS 2152, Box 30, WRHS.

13. *OR* 47(3):367; James W. Albright Diary and Reminiscences, 299–300, SHC-UNC; Albright, *Greensboro, 1808–1904*, 83.

14. *OR* 47(3):366; Thomas B. Roy Diary, May 1–2, 1865, photocopy in the possession of N. C. Hughes Jr., Chattanooga, Tennessee; *New York Herald*, May 9, 1865; Hughes, *General William J. Hardee*, 296–97.

15. Jacob D. Cox Diary, May 1 [2], 1865, KMNP; Cox, "Surrender of Johnston's Army," 248–49; *New York Herald*, May 9, 1865.

16. Cox, "Surrender of Johnston's Army," 249–52; Jacob D. Cox Diary, May 1 [2], 1865, KMNP.

17. Cox, "Surrender of Johnston's Army," 252; Pinney, *104th Ohio*, 85; Becker, "Campaigning with a Grand Army"; Nellie R. Jones, "Guilford Under the Stars and Bars," 17, Guilford File, History—Civil War, NCC-GPL; *New York Herald*, May 9, 1865.

18. Cox, "Surrender of Johnston's Army," 252; Jacob D. Cox Diary, May 1 [2], 1865, KMNP; *New York Herald*, May 9, 1865.

19. Jacob D. Cox Diary, May 1 [2], 1865, KMNP; Cox, "Surrender of Johnston's Army," 253–54.

20. Cox, "Surrender of Johnston's Army," 254–55; Jacob D. Cox Diary, May 1 [2], 1865, KMNP; *OR* 47(3):864, 868; Special Orders No. 40, May 4, 1865, Letters Received by the Adjutant General's Office, 1801–1870, Papers Relating to the Surrender of Johnston's Army, Microcopy 619, Roll 381, RG 94, NA. As of May 3, 27,749 paroles had been issued, but this figure does not include Pettus's Brigade or several brigades of Wheeler's cavalry, which were stationed south of the main body. See *OR* 47(3):867.

21. Cox, "Surrender of Johnston's Army," 256–57; Jacob D. Cox Diary, May 1 [2], 1865, KMNP.

22. *OR* 47(1):1061.

23. Cox, "Surrender of Johnston's Army," 257–59; Jacob D. Cox Diary, May 1 [2], 1865, KMNP; Z. B. Vance to C. P. Spencer, April 7, [1866], Cornelia P. Spencer Papers, SHC-UNC; Hamilton and Williams, *Papers of William A. Graham*, 6:310.

24. Jacob D. Cox Diary, May 1 [2], 1865, KMNP; Pinney, *104th Ohio*, 85–86; Becker, "Campaigning with a Grand Army"; Gaskill, *Footprints through Dixie*, 179.

25. *OR* 47(3):866; Pinney, *104th Ohio*, 85–86; Becker, "Campaigning with a

Grand Army"; Myers, "In North Carolina"; Gaskill, *Footprints through Dixie,* 179–82; Will to Brother, May 6, 1865, William C. Stevens Correspondence, BL-UMI; W. A. Johnson, "Closing Days," June 5, 1902; W. A. Johnson, "Marching, Camping, Fighting," Lovic P. Thomas Scrapbooks, 2:155, Lovic P. Thomas Papers, AHS.

26. Jacob D. Cox Diary, May 2 [3], 1865, KMNP; *OR* 47(3):376; Pinney, *104th Ohio,* 86; W. A. Johnson, "Marching, Camping, Fighting," Lovic P. Thomas Scrapbooks, 2:155, Lovic P. Thomas Papers, AHS; W. A. Johnson, "Closing Days," June 5, 1902.

27. R. Amos Jarman, "History of Company K, 27th Mississippi Infantry," 57, R. Amos Jarman Papers, MSDAH; Thomas L. Sullivan Account Book, May 3, 1865, Civil War Collection—Confederate, TNSLA; William M. Pollard Diary, May 3, 1865, Civil War Collection—Confederate, TNSLA; Francis H. Nash Diary, May 3, 1865, UGA; I. V. Moore, "Diary," Reminiscences, Diaries, and Letters of Confederate Soldiers, Georgia Division, UDC, 6:32, GADAH; William E. Stoney quoted in Hagood, *Memoirs,* 372; Hezekiah M. McCorkle Diary, May 3, 1865, Drawer 283, Reel 32 (mf), GADAH; W. A. Johnson, "Closing Days," June 5, 1902; "Henry Daniel Hogan," in Elliott and Moxley, *Tennessee Veterans Questionnaires,* 3:1119; Norman D. Brown, *One of Cleburne's Command,* 173.

28. Fletcher, *Rebel Private,* 145–46.

29. Alfred T. Fielder Diary, May 4–5, 1865, Tennessee Historical Society Collection, TNSLA; I. V. Moore, "Diary," Reminiscences, Diaries, and Letters of Confederate Soldiers, Georgia Division, UDC, 6:32, GADAH; William M. Pollard Diary, May 4–5, 1865, Civil War Collection—Confederate, TNSLA; Hezekiah M. McCorkle Diary, May 4–5, 1865, Drawer 283, Reel 32 (mf); Norman D. Brown, *One of Cleburne's Command,* 173–74.

30. *New York Herald,* May 9, 1865; Hawes, "Memoirs of Charles H. Olmstead," 154; "Henry Daniel Hogan," in Elliott and Moxley, *Tennessee Veterans Questionnaires,* 3:1119; Inglesby, *First South Carolina Artillery,* 19–20; Guild, *Fourth Tennessee Cavalry,* 129; Henderson Deans Reminiscences, 11, SHC-UNC; R. M. Collins, *Chapters,* 301; *OR* 47(3):483; Cox, "Surrender of Johnston's Army," 260–61.

31. *OR* 47(3):871; [Walker], *Surrender in Greensboro,* 4; *New York Herald,* May 10, 1865.

32. Drake, *Ninth New Jersey,* 299–301; Runyan, *Eight Days,* 8–14; *OR* 47(1):160; *OR* 47(3):442, 490.

33. *OR* 47(3):442, 490; Drake, *Ninth New Jersey,* 301–2; Runyan, *Eight Days,* 14–20. For a Confederate's description of the chaotic conditions on the railroad between Greensboro and Charlotte, see Ford and Ford, *Life in the Confederate Army,* 66–68.

34. Runyan, *Eight Days,* 20–25; *OR* 47(3):490–91.

35. *OR* 47(3):491; Runyan, *Eight Days,* 28–29.

36. Runyan, *Eight Days,* 29.

37. Ibid., 29–30; Drake, *Ninth New Jersey,* 303. In reporting the Confederate War Department archives to Schofield, Johnston was less than candid when he stated on May 8 that he had just learned of their presence. On April 27, Gen. Samuel Cooper had informed Johnston that the Davis party had to abandon the archives at Charlotte. Johnston replied on April 28: "I do not know what to advise about the records." Johnston's reluctance to surrender the archives probably stemmed from fears that

they might serve as evidence in prosecuting former Confederates. See *OR* 47(3): 443, 483, 497, 842, 848.

In one instance, the turning over of Confederate records to "friendly hands" had disastrous results. Cheatham's chief of staff, Col. James D. Porter, entrusted a trunk-load of papers to a cousin in Salisbury. When the cousin heard a rumor that Porter was indicted for treason, she burned his papers, fearing that they might be used against him. The rumor proved false. Porter recalled the loss of the papers in 1909: "It was a great sorrow to me. I had in that box the material for a history of the Army of Tennessee, and many letters and reports that were invaluable to me and my friends." See James D. Porter to Irving A. Buck, July 14, 1909, Irving A. Buck Papers, MOC.

38. Runyan, *Eight Days*, 35; *OR* 47(3):491.

39. *OR* 47(3):431, 512, 521, 522; William D. Hamilton, *Recollections*, 213–14; Tracie, *Nineteenth Ohio Battery*, 452–53.

40. *OR* 47(3):632; G. G. Dickson, "Trailing the Treasure of the Confederacy," *Raleigh News and Observer*, April 29, 1928; Stokes, *Company Shops*, 46–48; Arnett, *Confederate Guns*, 149–50.

41. Thomas J. Jordan to Mrs. Pride Jones, May 9, 1865, Thomas J. Jordan Letters, HSPA; John W. Graham to D. L. Swain, June 11, 1866, Walter Clark Papers, NCDAH. John W. Graham, a son of William A. Graham, wrote Swain to assure him that his son-in-law, Smith Atkins, was not responsible for the theft of Jones's silver plate. Although untrue, the rumor implicating Atkins was believed by many North Carolinians, including Edward J. Hale, the former editor and publisher of the *Fayetteville Observer*. "[I]f I had heard the story I should not have doubted it," Hale wrote Swain, "for were not such things common from privates up to Sherman himself, during the 'Great March?'" Hale then admitted, "As to the [theft], I did hear that story, & did repeat it, not having a doubt of its truth." He also believed that it would have been "a great hazard for any of them [Atkins and other Yankees] to sue for defamation in any Court in N. C." Hale's bitterness is easily explained: the offices and presses of his newspaper were destroyed by Sherman's troops during their occupation of Fayetteville. See E. J. Hale to D. L. Swain, June 20, 1866, and E. J. Hale to D. L. Swain, July 5, 1866, Walter Clark Papers, NCDAH.

42. *OR* 47(3):430; Redmond F. Laswell Diary, May 5, 1865, Military Archival Collection, ACHM; Thompson, *112th Illinois*, 319; Jacob D. Cox Diary, May 8, 1865, KMNP; Cox, "Surrender of Johnston's Army," 265; [Walker], *Surrender in Greensboro*, 4–5; Jacob H. Smith Diary, May 4–5, 1865, SHC-UNC; Mrs. Jacob H. Smith, *The Women of Greensboro*, North Carolina Biography File, NCC-GPL; Arnett, *Confederate Guns*, 88.

43. Records Concerning the Conduct and Loyalty of Certain Union Army Officers, Civilian Employees of the War Department, and U.S. Citizens during the Civil War, 1861–1872, Box 2, "Statements dated 1872 concerning H. Judson Kilpatrick's affair with a woman during the Civil War," Deposition of Leddy Garrett, August 9, 1872; deposition of Mrs. Jane Dick, August 10, 1872; deposition of Eugene Eckels [n.d.]; deposition of Edmund Hill, August 9, 1872, RG 107, NA; Arnett, *Confederate Guns*, 85.

44. Redmond F. Laswell Diary, May 6–7, 9–10, 1865, Military Archival Collection, ACHM; *New York Herald*, May 10, 1865.

45. Jacob D. Cox Diary, May 2 [3], 1865, KMNP; Cox, "Surrender of Johnston's Army," 265–66, 272; *OR* 47(3):511; Kirwan and Splaine, *Seventeenth Massachusetts,* 391.

46. *OR* 47(1):5, 164; *OR* 47(3):396, 405, 406, 602, 646–47.

47. *OR* 47(1):78–83, 88, 90, 94, 99–104, 107, 108, 117, 120–27, 131, 134, 139, 141, 144, 210–11; *OR* 47(3):322, 324; Special Field Orders No. 102, April 27, 1865, Charles Reynolds Order Book, LC; Hazen, *Narrative,* 371–72; S[amuel] Merrill to Em, May 11, 1865, Samuel Merrill Papers, INSL; Bauer, *Soldiering,* 242; Saunier, *Forty-seventh Ohio,* 443; Andrew H. Hickenlooper, "Reminiscences, Vol. I," 343, Hickenlooper Family Collection, CINHS; Loop, "Rounding Up the Confederacy," July 4, 1901; John D. Inskeep Dairy, April 28–May 1, 1865, OHS; James E. Graham Diary, May 1, 1865, OHS; John N. Ferguson Diary, May 3, 1865, LC; Husband [Charles B. Tompkins] to Mollie, May 7, 1865, Charles B. Tompkins Papers, DU.

48. Anna Fuller Diary, May 1–2, 1865, Robbins Library, Louisburg College, Louisburg, North Carolina; Saunier, *Forty-seventh Ohio,* 444; Husband [Charles B. Tompkins] to Mollie, May 7, 1865, Charles B. Tompkins Papers, DU.

49. "Journal of the Campaign from Goldsboro, North Carolina to Alexandria, Virginia," May 1–May 7, 1865, James D. Morgan Collection, HSQAC; John W. Geary to Mary, May 10, 1865, John W. Geary Letters, HSPA; Halsey, *Yankee Private's Civil War,* 202–3; Andersen, *Diary of Allen Morgan Geer,* 219; Rood, *Company E, Twelfth Wisconsin,* 434–35; John Mahon, "Letters of Samuel Mahon," 261–62; McBride, *Thirty-third Indiana,* 183.

50. William T. Sherman Diary, May 3–4, 1865, Sherman Family Papers, UND; *OR* 47(1):38; *OR* 47(3):410–12; Sherman, *Memoirs,* 2:369, 373–74; Reid, *After the War,* 31–33.

51. William T. Sherman Diary, May 7, 1865, and W. T. Sherman to Ellen, May 8, 1865, Sherman Family Papers, UND; Sherman, *Memoirs,* 2:373–74; *OR* 47(3):435.

52. *OR* 47(1):29, 37, 40; *OR* 47(3):437–38, 446; Vett to Mother, May 12, 1865, Sylvester C. Noble Papers, YHS; Andrew H. Hickenlooper, "Reminiscences, Vol. I," 344–45, Hickenlooper Family Collection, CINHS; Sherman, *Memoirs,* 2:374–75; W. T. Sherman to Ellen, May 10, 1865, Sherman Family Papers, UND; Eli to "Mother & Sisters," May 10, 1865, and Eli to Mary, May 10, 1865, Eli S. Ricker Papers, Nebraska State Historical Society, Lincoln.

53. *OR* 47(3):437; Andrew H. Hickenlooper, "Reminiscences, Vol. I," 344, Hickenlooper Family Collection, CINHS; Throne, "History of Company D, Eleventh Iowa," 89; Glatthaar, *March to the Sea,* 180.

54. *OR* 47(3):454; Ambrose, *Halleck,* 201.

55. *OR* 47(3):454–55; W. T. Sherman to Ellen, May 10, 1865, Sherman Family Papers, UND.

56. Loop, "Rounding Up the Confederacy," July 4, 1901.

57. *OR* 47(1):605; Slocum, "Final Operations," 757; Toombs, *Reminiscences,* 225–26; Federico, *Letters of John H. Morse,* 189; Bauer, *Soldiering,* 244–45.

58. *OR* 47(3):530–32; W. T. Sherman to Ellen, May 8, 1865, Sherman Family Papers, UND; Sherman, *Memoirs,* 2:375.

59. W. T. Sherman to Ellen, May 10, 1865, Sherman Family Papers, UND; *OR* 47(3):526, 539–40.

60. Sherman, *Memoirs,* 2:375–76; John Sherman, *Recollections,* 303.

61. *OR* 47(3):546–47.

62. U.S. Congress, "Sherman-Johnston," 3:6, 13–14.

63. Naroll, "Lincoln and the Sherman Peace Fiasco," 477–79.

64. Sherman, *Memoirs,* 2:376; Slocum, "Final Operations," 758.

65. John Mahon, "Letters of Samuel Mahon," 263; Oliver O. Howard, *Autobiography,* 2:211, and "Marching through Georgia," March 26, 1896; Andrew H. Hickenlooper, "Reminiscences, Vol. I," 348, Hickenlooper Family Collection, CINHS; *New York Herald,* May 25, 1865; Hatcher, *Last Four Weeks,* 373, 377, 397.

66. *OR* 47(3):554–55; Oliver O. Howard, *Autobiography,* 2:211, and "Marching through Georgia," March 26, 1896. Sherman's and Howard's conduct no doubt surprised Logan. On May 20, "Black Jack" had written his wife: "Genl. Howard has been assigned to the 'Darkie' Bureau in Washington and I am told that I am to command the [A]rmy [of the Tennessee] but God only knows, I am sure I shall not ask it, as I have been so treated once before, I have nothing to expect at the hands of these men." See John A. Logan to Wife, May 20, 1865, John A. Logan and Family Papers, LC.

67. Hazen, *Narrative,* 375; Hatcher, *Last Four Weeks,* 377; Royster, *Destructive War,* 408–9; Sherman, *Memoirs,* 2:377; Keim, *Sherman: A Memorial,* 54.

68. *OR* 47(3):576; *New York Herald,* May 25, 1865; Royster, *Destructive War,* 406; Hatcher, *Last Four Weeks,* 379, 383, 401; Bauer, *Soldiering,* 247.

69. *New York Herald,* May 25, 1865; Hatcher, *Last Four Weeks,* 379, 381–82, 401–2; *OR* 47(3):555; Sherman, *Memoirs,* 2:378; Grant, *Personal Memoirs,* 579; Royster, *Destructive War,* 414.

70. *New York Herald,* May 25, 1865; Hatcher, *Last Four Weeks,* 380; Toombs, *Reminiscences,* 227–28; Sherman, *Memoirs,* 2:377–78; B. F. Fisher to Friend, May 21, 1865 [May 28 addition], Letterbook, Benjamin F. Fisher Papers, DU; John Sherman, *Recollections,* 303–4; H[enry] to Wife, May 26, 1865, Henry Hitchcock Papers, LC; Hitchcock, *Marching with Sherman,* 320; Thomas and Hyman, *Stanton,* 416. Assistant Secretary of War Charles A. Dana recalled that Stanton did not extend his hand to Sherman, but his recollection conflicts with nearly every other eyewitness account. See Dana, *Recollections,* 288–90.

71. *OR* 47(1):44–46.

72. Ibid., 134, 141, 142, 145; *OR* 47(3):589–90, 606, 639–40, 649; George to Wife, June 18, 1865, and reprint of letter to *Louisville Daily Journal,* June 15, 1865, George Lawson Correspondence, AHS. Lawson's letter to the *Journal* complaining of the soldiers' detention on "Mosquito Island" near Louisville resulted in his arrest by order of his division commander, Bvt. Maj. Gen. Mortimer D. Leggett. Lawson was released after eight days' imprisonment. See George to Wife, July 9, 1865, George Lawson Correspondence, AHS.

73. Bauer, *Soldiering,* 248–49.

74. Norman D. Brown, *One of Cleburne's Command,* 174–75.

75. Ibid., 174–78. For a somewhat different version of the Texans' encounter with black troops, see R. M. Collins, *Chapters,* 305–6.

76. Norman D. Brown, *One of Cleburne's Command,* 178–79.

77. Ibid., 179–81.

78. Ibid., 181–86.

79. Hamilton and Williams, *Papers of William A. Graham,* 6:308–9.

80. Ibid., 307–8.

81. Ibid., 309.

82. Ibid., 310–11.

83. Z. B. Vance to C. P. Spencer, April 7, [1866], Cornelia P. Spencer Papers, SHC-UNC; *OR* 47(3):440, 451; Yates, *Confederacy and Zeb Vance,* 121–22; Tucker, *Zeb Vance,* 411; Dowd, *Life of Vance,* 98–99; Miller, "With Sherman," 43–44.

84. Adler, "Zebulon B. Vance," 360; Tucker, *Zeb Vance,* 412–13; Dowd, *Life of Vance,* 96–97; Yates, *Confederacy and Zeb Vance,* 122.

85. Tucker, *Zeb Vance,* 414–15; Yates, *Confederacy and Zeb Vance,* 122; Adler, "Zebulon B. Vance," 361; Z. V[ance] to D. G. Fowle, May 16, 1865, Letterbook, vol. 7, Zebulon B. Vance Papers, NCDAH.

86. *OR* 47(3):453, 486, 489; *OR* 5, ser. 3, 37–39; Holden, *Memoirs,* 44–45, 48; Harris, "William Woods Holden," 357; *Raleigh Daily Standard,* April 27, May 9, 1865.

87. *Raleigh Daily Standard,* April 17, 1865; Elizabeth Collier Diary, May 9 [?], 1865, SHC-UNC; Crabtree and Patton, *"Journal of a Secesh Lady,"* 714.

88. Tucker, *Zeb Vance,* 429. Holden later claimed that he secured Vance's release when he learned of the illness of the former governor's wife. See Holden, *Memoirs,* 46.

89. *OR* 47(3):416; Jacob D. Cox Diary, May 12, 1865, KMNP. According to Schurz, at the end of April 1865 Schofield had still favored retaining Vance as governor of North Carolina. See C. Schurz to Charles Sumner, May 9, 1865, Carl Schurz Papers, LC.

90. Cox, "Surrender of Johnston's Army," 275–76.

EPILOGUE

1. Johnston, *Narrative,* 419–20; *OR* 47(3):560, 564, 615, 675; Govan and Livingood, *A Different Valor,* 377–78.

2. Johnston, *Narrative,* 372.

3. *OR* 47(3):827.

4. Ibid., 662–63, 668, 671, 677–78; *OR Atlas,* pl. 76, map 2.

5. At the time of the surrender, Johnston commanded the Department of North Carolina and the Department of South Carolina, Georgia, and Florida. Almost 90,000 Confederates were paroled under the terms of the April 26 convention. Of that number, 39,012 were under Johnston's immediate command. See *OR* 47(1): 1066.

BIBLIOGRAPHY

MANUSCRIPT SOURCES

Alexandria, Virginia
National Archives Cartographic and Architectural Branch
    Record Group 77: Records of the Office of the Chief of Engineers
        Dr. 143-35: "Map of the Rebel Lines at Raleigh, N.C., evacuated April 13, 1865, upon the approach of the Army commanded by Maj. Gen. W. T. Sherman, U.S.A. Reduced under the direction of Capt. O. M. Poe, Corps of Engineers, Bvt. Brig. Gen., U.S.A. & Chief Engineer, Mil. Div. Miss. From captured Rebel map. B. Drayton, Draughtsman."
        H95: "Survey of all the approaches to the City of Raleigh showing the Line of Intrenchments, made by order of His Excellency Z. B. Vance, Governor of the State of North Carolina. Oct. 26th, 1863. [Signed] H. T. Guion, Lt. Col., Arty. & Eng."
        H96: "Campaign Maps Showing the Line of March of the Army of Georgia from Goldsboro, N.C. to Avens Bridge, N.C."

Ann Arbor, Michigan
Bentley Historical Library, University of Michigan
    Henry G. Noble Papers
    Slayton Family Papers
        Chester Metcalf Slayton Letters
    William Collin Stevens Correspondence

Athens, Georgia
Hargrett Rare Book and Manuscript Library, University of Georgia
    Francis H. Nash Diary
    C. C. Platter Diary

Atlanta, Georgia
Library and Archives Room, McElreath Hall, Atlanta Historical Society
    George Lawson Correspondence
    Lovic P. Thomas Papers
Special Collections Department, Woodruff Library, Emory University
    Pierre Gustave Toutant Beauregard Papers
    James Appleton Blackshear Diaries

Alfred A. Rigby Diary
Georgia Department of Archives and History
   Civil War Miscellany—Personal Papers
      Hezekiah M. McCorkle Diary
   Private Papers
      James Welsman Brown Diary
   Reminiscences, Diaries, and Letters of Confederate Soldiers, Georgia Division,
      United Daughters of the Confederacy
      J. J. McKay Recollections
      I. V. Moore Diary

Austin, Texas
Center for American History, University of Texas
   William E. Stanton Letters

Brunswick, Maine
Special Collections, Hawthorne-Longfellow Library, Bowdoin College
   Oliver Otis Howard Papers

Burlington, North Carolina
Alamance County Historical Museum
   "Map of Alamance County, North Carolina, 1893"
   Military Archival Collection
      Redmond F. Laswell Diary

Carlisle Barracks, Pennsylvania
Archives Branch, United States Army Military History Institute
   Solon A. Carter Papers
   Civil War Miscellaneous Collection
      Thomas Y. Finley Diary
      Elliott B. McKeever, "Sketch of the 9th Ohio Cavalry Regiment"
      Aaron Overstreet Letters
      Baxter Smith Reminiscences
   Civil War Times Illustrated Collection
      Orrin L. Ellis Diary
      Andrew H. Hickenlooper Reminiscences
      Benjamin F. Hunter, "A Soldier's Reminiscence"
      Edward E. Schweitzer Diaries and Correspondence
   Harrisburg Civil War Round Table Collection
      David Nichol Papers
      George Shuman Letters
   Daniel Harvey Hill Papers
   Michael Winey Collection
      John Langhans Letters

Chapel Hill, North Carolina
Wilson Library, University of North Carolina
   North Carolina Collection

Harriet Cobb Lane Reminiscences
Stephen Beauregard Weeks Scrapbooks
Southern Historical Collection
James W. Albright Diary and Reminiscences
Edward W. Allen Papers
Jesse S. Bean Diary
William Calder Papers
Cameron Family Papers
Campbell Family Papers
Edmund J. Cleveland Diary
Elizabeth Collier Diary
David Thomas Copeland Papers
Joseph B. Cumming War Recollections
Burke Davis Papers
Jefferson Davis Papers
Henderson Deans Reminiscences
Federal Soldiers' Letters
    J. Thayer Letter
Gale and Polk Family Papers
Gordon Family Papers
Bryan Grimes Papers
    Charlotte E. Grimes Reminiscences
O. P. Hargis Reminiscences
George Washington Frederick Harper Papers
Charles Woodward Hutson Papers
Lafayette McLaws Papers
Charles Beatty Mallett Papers
    Charles Peter Mallett Letters
Stephen Russell Mallory Diary, Letterbook, and Recollections
Moore-Gatling Law Firm Papers
Kenneth Rayner Papers
Thomas Ruffin Papers
Jacob Henry Smith Diary
Augustine Thomas Smythe Papers
Cornelia Phillips Spencer Papers
David Lowry Swain Papers
John L. Swain Papers
Tench Tilghman Papers
Anna H. Trenholm Diary
Joseph Frederick Waring Diary
Louis H. Webb Diary
Mrs. John S. Welborn Papers
Norvell Winsboro Wilson Papers
John Taylor Wood Papers
Jonathan Worth Papers

Charleston, South Carolina
South Carolina Historical Society
    Edward Laight Wells Correspondence

Chattanooga, Tennessee
Personal collection of Nathaniel Cheairs Hughes Jr.
    Thomas Benton Roy Diary. Photocopy.

Chicago, Illinois
Archives and Manuscripts Department, Chicago Historical Society
    Isaac Newton Arnold Papers
    James R. M. Gaskill Memoranda
Special Collections, Chicago Public Library
    William T. Humphrey Papers

Cincinnati, Ohio
Research Library, Cincinnati Historical Society
    Hickenlooper Family Collection
    Miller Family Collection
    Thomas Edwin Smith and Family Collection

Cleveland, Ohio
Western Reserve Historical Society
    William David Evans Papers
    William Pendleton Palmer Collection
        Braxton Bragg Papers
        Joseph E. Johnston Papers
    Regimental Papers of the Civil War, South Carolina
        Cornelius Irvine Walker Letters

Columbia, Missouri
Western Historical Manuscripts Collection, Ellis Library, University of Missouri
    James R. Milner Papers
    Rhoderick R. Rockwood Diary

Columbia, South Carolina
South Caroliniana Library, University of South Carolina
    William H. Johnson Papers
    Edward Abijah Rowley Diary
    W. H. Thomas Papers
    Robert Y. Woodlief Diary

Columbus, Ohio
Archives and Research Center, Ohio Historical Society
    James E. Graham Diary
    Joseph Hoffhines Papers
    John D. Inskeep Diary
    Nathaniel L. Parmeter Papers
    William Henry Pittenger Diary

James Sidney Robinson Papers
James R. Stillwell Letters

Detroit, Michigan
Detroit Public Library
Alpheus Starkey Williams Papers

Durham, North Carolina
Bennett Place State Historic Site
Cornelius Baker Diary
Special Manuscripts Department, Perkins Library, Duke University
Ellen Aumack Papers
Joseph Fulton Boyd Papers
George William Brent Papers
Charles S. Brown Papers
William Calder Papers
Rachel Susan (Bee) Cheves Papers
Alexander W. Marshall, "1865 Memoranda"
Confederate States of America Archives
Army Miscellany: Officers' and Soldiers' Miscellaneous Letters
Henry ——— Letter
Army Units: Wheeler's Cavalry Corps
Craven-Pegram Papers
Benjamin Franklin Fisher Papers
Gertrude Jenkins Papers
Robert Alexander Jenkins Reminiscences
Bradley Tyler Johnson Papers
John Johnson Diary
Joseph Eggleston Johnston Papers
Augustus White Long Papers
Delia White Woodward Civil War Memorandum
Robert Anderson McClellan Papers
George P. Metz Papers
Thomas Nixon Papers
Aaron Thompson Letter
Raphael Semmes Papers
Tillinghast Family Papers
J. W. Norwood Letter
Charles Brown Tompkins Papers
Herbert Benjamin Waterman Papers
Benjamin S. Williams Papers
J. F. Woods Papers
Worth Family Papers

East Lansing, Michigan
Archives Department, Michigan State University
Thomas J. Davis Papers

Fayetteville, Arkansas
Special Collections Division, University of Arkansas
  Daniel Harris Reynolds Papers

Four Oaks, North Carolina
Bentonville Battleground State Historic Site
  Hiram M. Austin Letters
  Enos W. McKenney Diary

Fredericksburg, Virginia
Personal collection of Alan and Nancy Bruns
  Lily Logan Morrill, "A Builder of the New South"

Greensboro, North Carolina
Archives Department, Greensboro Historical Museum
  George Anthony Collamore Letters
  Correspondence 1865, Soldier 154th New York
    Edgar —— Letter
North Carolina Collection, Greensboro Public Library
  Greensboro File, History—Civil War
    M. A. Bogart, "Notes of the Times in Greensboro from '62 Until After the
      Surrender"
  Guilford File, History—Civil War
    Nellie Rowe Jones, "Guilford Under the Stars and Bars"
    "Statement of William C. McLean"
  North Carolina Biography File
    Mrs. Jacob Henry Smith, *The Women of Greensboro, N.C., 1861–1865*

Indianapolis, Indiana
Smith Memorial Library, Indiana Historical Society
  Helen Floyd Carlin Collection
    Sanford Fortner [?] Diary
  Dr. Joseph Wright Chamberlain Papers
    Orville T. Chamberlain Letters
  Charles Gottlieb Michael Diary
  William Bluffton Miller Journal
  James S. Thompson Journal
  Williamson D. Ward Journal
Manuscript Section—Indiana Division, Indiana State Library
  Hiram Matthew Letters
  Samuel Merrill Papers

Jackson, Mississippi
Mississippi Department of Archives and History
  Robert Amos Jarman Papers

Jacksonville, Illinois
Pfeiffer Library, MacMurray College
  John H. Ferguson Diary

Kenosha, Wisconsin
University Archives and Area Research Center, University of Wisconsin-Parkside
   Harvey Reid Papers

Lincoln, Nebraska
Nebraska State Historical Society
   Eli Seavey Ricker Papers

Louisburg, North Carolina
Robbins Library, Louisburg College
   Anna L. Fuller Diary

Madison, Wisconsin
State Historical Society of Wisconsin
   Peter Ege Papers
   Michael Hendrick Fitch Papers
   Julian Wisner Hinkley Papers
   Edward Oscar Kimberly Papers
   William H. McIntosh Papers
   William C. Meffert Diary
   John Henry Otto Papers
   Frank H. Putney Papers
   James Theodore Reeve Diary
   Samuel Glyde Swain Papers
   John B. Tripp Papers
     Ezra W. Button Diary

Marietta, Georgia
Research Library, Kennesaw Mountain National Park
   Jacob Dolson Cox Diary
   William Ralston Talley Reminiscences
   Lyman S. Widney Papers

Montgomery, Alabama
Alabama Department of Archives and History
   Civil War Soldiers' Letters
     M. J. Blackwell Letters
   Hall Family Papers
     Bolling Hall Collection
   William Joseph Hardee Papers
   Wheeler Family Papers

Nashville, Tennessee
Tennessee State Library and Archives
   Civil War Collection—Confederate
     D. G. Godwin Letters
     William Mebane Pollard Diary
     William Erskine Sloan Diary
     Thomas L. Sullivan Account Book

Diaries, Memoirs, Etc.
    Jesse Roderick Sparkman Diary
Tennessee Historical Society Collection
    Alfred Tyler Fielder Diary

New York, New York
Manuscript Department, New-York Historical Society
    Alexander Robert Chisolm Papers

Philadelphia, Pennsylvania
Historical Society of Pennsylvania
    John White Geary Letters
    Thomas Jefferson Jordan Letters

Quincy, Illinois
Historical Society of Quincy and Adams County
    James Dada Morgan Collection

Raleigh, North Carolina
North Carolina Division of Archives and History
    Archives Section
        Walter Clark Papers
        Edward Jones Hale Papers
        Daniel Harvey Hill Jr. Papers
        Robert Frederick Hoke Papers
        Allston Lavender Paper
        Military Collection—Civil War
            Samuel A'Court Ashe Reminiscence
            J. J. Laughinghouse Reminiscence
            North Carolina Division, United Daughters of the Confederacy
                Mrs. James A. Fore Papers
                Scrapbook Collection
        Joseph B. Starr Papers
        State Agency Records
            Papers of Governor William Woods Holden
            Papers of Governor Zebulon Baird Vance
        Zebulon Baird Vance Papers
        David Brainard Whiting Reminiscences
    Historic Sites Section
        Bennett Place State Historic Site File

Richmond, Virginia
Brockenbrough Library, Museum of the Confederacy
    Irving A. Buck Papers
    Diary Collection
        Joseph Mullen Jr. Diary
    Joseph Eggleston Johnston Papers

Virginia Historical Society
    Edward R. Archer Diary
    J. R. Hamilton Letter
    David G. McIntosh Diary
    Charles Jackson Paine Papers
Archives Division, Virginia State Library
    Richard Pollard Letter

St. Louis, Missouri
Library and Collections Center, Missouri Historical Society
    Henry Hitchcock Papers
    McEwen Family Papers

St. Paul, Minnesota
Minnesota Historical Society
    Levi Burrel Aldrich Papers
    William Franklin Allee, "A Civil War History"
    George T. Cambell and Family Papers
    Christie Family Papers
    Levi Nelson Green Papers
    Axel Hayford Reed Papers

San Marino, California
Huntington Library
    Joseph Eggleston Johnston Papers

Savannah, Georgia
Georgia Historical Society
    Joseph Frederick Waring Papers
        William Washington Gordon Reminiscences

Seattle, Washington
University of Washington Libraries
    Manning Ferguson Force Papers

Smithfield, North Carolina
Johnston County Room, Johnston County Public Library
    Mrs. Denton Farmer (Margaret) Lee, "The History of the Finch Place"
    Smithfield Methodist Church Sabbath School Record Book. Photocopy.
    David Stephens, "Frances Secor Mitchener Hastings Gardner"

South Bend, Indiana
Archives, University of Notre Dame
    Sherman Family Papers

Springfield, Illinois
Illinois State Historical Library
    George N. Compton Papers
    William E. Strong Papers

Washington, D.C.

Library of Congress

James D. and David R. Barbee Papers

Blair Family Papers

Breckinridge Family Papers

Given Campbell Journal

John William Draper Papers

Charles Ewing Family Papers

John N. Ferguson Diary

Henry Hitchcock Papers

W. C. Johnson, "Through the Carolinas to Goldsboro, N.C."

John Alexander Logan and Family Papers

Absalom H. Markland Papers

Rufus Mead Papers

Montgomery C. Meigs Papers

Orlando Metcalfe Poe Papers

Albert Quincy Porter Collection

David Dixon Porter Papers

Charles Reynolds Order Book

Alfred Roman Papers

Theodore Edgar St. John Papers

John McAllister Schofield Papers

Carl Schurz Papers

John Sherman Papers

William Tecumseh Sherman Papers

Edwin McMasters Stanton Papers

Alexander Hamilton Stephens Papers

Henry Clay Weaver Papers

Louis Trezevant Wigfall Papers

National Archives

Record Group 56: Records of the Department of the Treasury

Barred and Disallowed Case Files of the Southern Claims Commission.

Claim No. 18945: James Bennett. Microcopy M1407, Microfiche 4311.

Records of Claims Commissioners (Southern Claims), 1871–1880:

Consolidated Index of Claims

Record Group 94: Records of the Adjutant General's Office

Letters Received by the Adjutant General's Office, 1801–1870

Papers Relating to the Surrender of Gen. Joseph E. Johnston's Army to Gen. W. T. Sherman at Greensboro, N.C., Apr.–May 1865. Microcopy M-619, Roll 381.

Papers and Books, Maj. Gen. William T. Sherman

Regimental Records, 1st Regiment, Michigan Engineers and Mechanics

Record Group 107: Records of the Office of the Secretary of War

Records Concerning the Conduct and Loyalty of Certain Union Army Officers, Civilian Employees of the War Department, and U.S. Citizens during the Civil War, 1861–1872

Record Group 109: War Department Collection of Confederate Records
Army of Tennessee—Inspector General's Letterbook
Military Departments: Telegrams Sent, Reserve Forces of North Carolina
Miscellaneous Confederate Correspondence, 1864–1865
Muster Rolls and Lists of Confederate Troops Paroled in North Carolina,
Microcopy M1781.
Order Book, Co. C, 45th Alabama, and Co. C, 1st Alabama
Telegrams, Orders, Letters, and Court-Martial Proceedings, Department
and Army of Tennessee—Gen. Joseph E. Johnston
Record Group 153: Records of the Office of the Judge Advocate-General
General Court-Martial Proceedings
MM 1997—Frederick Bodmer
OO 3428—James Preble
Record Group 393: Records of U.S. Army Continental Commands, 1821–1920
Letters and Reports Sent, January 1863–June 1865, 12th Army Corps; 1st
Brigade, 1st Division, 14th Army Corps; 20th Army Corps
Circulars and Letters Sent, Second Brigade, Third Cavalry Division, Cavalry
Corps, Military Division of the Mississippi
U.S. Census Records, 1870
Orange County, North Carolina. Microcopy M593, Microfiche 1153

Williamsburg, Virginia
Manuscripts and Rare Book Department, Swem Library, College of William
and Mary
Joseph Eggleston Johnston Papers

Ypsilanti, Michigan
Ypsilanti Historical Society
Sylvester C. Noble Papers

OFFICIAL PUBLICATIONS

U.S. Congress. "Remarks of Hon. Z. B. Vance." In *Message of the President of the
United States, Transmitting, in Answer to Senate Resolution, January 13, 1885, Copy of
a Letter to the Secretary of War, by General W. T. Sherman, Dated January 6, 1885.*
Executive Document No. 36, 48th Cong., 2d sess. Washington, D.C.:
Government Printing Office, 1885.
———. "Sherman-Johnston." In *Report of the Joint Committee on the Conduct of the War,
at the Second Session, Thirty-eighth Congress,* 3:2–23. Washington, D.C.:
Government Printing Office, 1865.
———. House of Representatives. *H.R. 8928: A Bill for the Relief of Mrs. Fannie E.
Gardner.* 52d Cong., 1st sess., May 23, 1892. Washington, D.C.: Government
Printing Office, 1892.
U.S. War Department. *Atlas to Accompany the Official Records of the Union and
Confederate Armies.* Washington, D.C.: Government Printing Office, 1891–95.
———. *The War of the Rebellion: A Compilation of the Official Records of the Union and*

Confederate Armies. 128 vols. Washington, D.C.: Government Printing Office, 1880–1901.

NEWSPAPERS AND PERIODICALS

Chicago Tribune
Christian Recorder (Philadelphia)
Cincinnati Daily Commercial
Cleveland Plain Dealer
Detroit Advertiser and Tribune
Detroit Free Press
Fayetteville (N.C.) Observer
Frank Leslie's Illustrated Newspaper
Goldsboro (N.C.) News-Argus
Greensboro (N.C.) Patriot
Harper's Weekly
Hillsborough (N.C.) Recorder
Kenly (N.C.) News
National Tribune
New York Herald
New York Times
New York Tribune
North Carolina Times (New Bern)
Philadelphia Inquirer
Philadelphia Times
Raleigh Daily Confederate
Raleigh News and Observer
Raleigh Progress
Raleigh Standard
Raleigh Times
Raleigh Weekly Conservative
Smithfield (N.C.) Herald
Washington Daily Chronicle
Wilmington (N.C.) Daily Review

PUBLISHED PRIMARY SOURCES
(Autobiographies, Diaries, Journals, Memoirs, Reminiscences, and Unit Histories)

Agassiz, George R., ed. *Meade's Headquarters, 1863–1865: Letters of Colonel Theodore Lyman from the Wilderness to Appomattox.* Boston: Atlantic Monthly Press, 1922.
Albright, James W. *Greensboro, 1808–1904. Facts, Figures, Traditions and Reminiscences.* Greensboro: Joseph J. Stone and Company, 1904.
Andersen, Mary Ann, ed. *The Civil War Diary of Allen Morgan Geer, Twentieth Regiment, Illinois Volunteers.* Denver: Robert C. Appleman, 1977.

Andrews, W. H. *Footprints of a Regiment: A Recollection of the First Georgia Regulars, 1861–1865.* Edited by Richard M. McMurry. Marietta, Ga.: Longstreet Press, 1992.

Aten, Henry J. *History of the Eighty-fifth Regiment, Illinois Volunteer Infantry.* Hiawatha, Kans.: n.p., 1901.

Baker, Daniel B. *A Soldier's Experiences in the Civil War.* Long Beach, Calif.: Graves and Hersey, 1914.

Balloch, George W. "The Twentieth Corps." *National Tribune,* June 18, 1903.

Bancroft, Frederic, ed. *Speeches, Correspondence and Political Papers of Carl Schurz.* Vol. 1, *October 20, 1852–November 26, 1870.* New York: G. P. Putnam's Sons, 1913.

Barnard, George N. *Photographic Views of Sherman's Campaign.* New York: Dover Publications, 1977.

Barnes, John Sanford. "With Lincoln from Washington to Richmond in 1865." *Magazine of History with Notes and Queries* 41, no. 161 (1931): 37–56.

Bates, David Homer. *Lincoln in the Telegraph Office: Recollections of the United States Military Telegraph Corps during the Civil War.* 1907. Reprint, Lincoln: University of Nebraska Press, 1995.

Battle, Kemp Plummer. *Memories of an Old-Time Tar Heel.* Chapel Hill: University of North Carolina Press, 1945.

Bauer, K. Jack, ed. *Soldiering: The Civil War Diary of Rice C. Bull.* San Rafael, Calif.: Presidio Press, 1977.

Becker, L. F. "Campaigning with a Grand Army: Some of the 104th Ohio's Service in the Latter Part of the War." *National Tribune,* November 23, 1899.

Bircher, William. *A Drummer-Boy's Diary: Comprising Four Years of Service with the Second Minnesota Veteran Volunteers, 1861 to 1865.* St. Paul: St. Paul Book and Stationery Company, 1889.

Black, John Logan. *Crumbling Defenses; Or Memoirs and Reminiscences of John Logan Black, Colonel C.S.A.* Macon, Ga.: Eleanor D. McSwain, 1960.

Black, Wilfred W., ed. "Marching with Sherman through Georgia and the Carolinas: Civil War Diary of Jesse L. Dozer." *Georgia Historical Quarterly* 52 (September and December 1968): 308–36, 451–79.

Boies, Andrew J. *Record of the Thirty-third Massachusetts Volunteer Infantry from Aug. 1862 to Aug. 1865.* Fitchburg: Sentinel Printing Company, 1880.

Brant, J. E. *History of the Eighty-fifth Indiana Volunteer Infantry.* Bloomington: Cravens Brothers, 1902.

Branum, John Marshall. "Letters from the Field." *National Tribune,* May 24, June 21, 1900.

Brooks, Aubrey Lee, and Hugh Talmadge Lefler, eds. *The Papers of Walter Clark.* 2 vols. Chapel Hill: University of North Carolina Press, 1948.

Brooks, U. R., ed. *Butler and His Cavalry in the War of Secession.* Columbia, S.C.: The State Company, 1909.

Brown, Alonzo L. *History of the Fourth Regiment of Minnesota Infantry Volunteers.* St. Paul: Pioneer Press Company, 1892.

Brown, Norman D., ed. *One of Cleburne's Command: The Civil War Reminiscences and*

Diary of Capt. Samuel T. Foster, Granbury's Texas Brigade, CSA. Austin: University of Texas Press, 1980.

Bryant, Edwin E. *History of the Third Regiment of Wisconsin Veteran Volunteer Infantry, 1861–1865.* Cleveland: Arthur H. Clark Company, 1891.

Buford, M. M. "Surrender of Johnston's Army." *Confederate Veteran* 28 (May 1920): 170–72.

Burton, E. P. *Diary of E. P. Burton.* Des Moines: Historical Records Survey, 1939.

Caldwell, D. "Planting the Flag at Raleigh, N.C." *National Tribune,* June 18, 1885.

Calkins, William Wirt. *The History of the One Hundred and Fourth Regiment of Illinois Volunteer Infantry.* Chicago: Donohue and Henneberry, 1895.

Carpenter, F. B. *Six Months at the White House with Abraham Lincoln.* New York: Hurd and Houghton, 1866.

Clark, Olynthus B., ed. *Downing's Civil War Diary.* Des Moines: Historical Department of Iowa, 1916.

Clark, Walter, ed. *Histories of the Several Regiments and Battalions from North Carolina in the Great War 1861–'65. Written by Members of the Respective Commands.* 5 vols. Goldsboro, N.C.: Nash Brothers, 1901.

Clark, Walter A. *Under the Stars and Bars, or Memories of Four Years' Service with the Oglethorpes of Augusta, Georgia.* Augusta: Chronicle Printing Company, 1900.

Clarke, Mary Bayard. "General Sherman in Raleigh." *The Old Guard* 4 (April 1866): 226–32.

Coffin, Charles Carleton. *The Boys of '61; Or, Four Years of Fighting. Personal Observation with the Army and Navy, from the First Battle of Bull Run to the Fall of Richmond.* Boston: Estes and Lauriat, 1882.

Coffin, James. "Chapel Hill at the Close of the War." *North Carolina University Magazine* 31 (1901): 272–75.

Cole, James Reid. *Miscellany.* Dallas, Tex.: Press of Ewing B. Bedford, 1897.

Collins, George K. *Memoirs of the 149th Regiment, New York Volunteer Infantry, 3rd Brigade, 2nd Division, 12th and 20th Corps.* Syracuse, N.Y.: published by the author, 1891.

Collins, R. M. *Chapters from the Unwritten History of the War Between the States; Or, the Incidents in the Life of a Confederate Soldier in Camp, on the March, in the Great Battles, and in Prison.* St. Louis: Nixon Jones Printing Company, 1893.

Committee of the Regiment. *Ninety-second Illinois Volunteers.* Freeport, Ill.: Journal Steam Publishing House and Bookbindery, 1875.

Committee of the Regiment. *The Story of the Fifty-fifth Regiment, Illinois Volunteer Infantry, in the Civil War, 1861–1865.* Clinton, Mass.: W. J. Coulter, 1887.

Conyngham, David P. *Sherman's March through the South with Sketches and Incidents of the Campaign.* New York: Sheldon and Company, 1865.

Cook, S. G., and Charles E. Benton. *The "Dutchess County Regiment" (150th New York State Volunteer Infantry) in the Civil War. Its Story as Told by Its Members. Based upon the Writings of Rev. Edward O. Bartlett, D.D.* Danbury, Conn.: Danbury Medical Printing Company, 1907.

Cox, Jacob Dolson. *Military Reminiscences of the Civil War.* 2 vols. New York: Charles Scribner's Sons, 1900.

———. "Surrender of Johnston's Army and the Closing Scenes of the War in

North Carolina." In *Sketches of War History, 1861–1865. Papers Prepared for the Ohio Commandery of the Military Order of the Loyal Legion of the United States*, 2:247–76. Cincinnati: Robert Clarke and Company, 1888–1908.

Crabtree, Beth G., and James W. Patton, eds. *"Journal of a Secesh Lady": The Diary of Catherine Devereux Edmondston, 1860–1866*. Raleigh: North Carolina Division of Archives and History, 1979.

Criticisms on the Surrender of Johnston's Army with the "Memorandum" Thereon as Presented by the Executive. N.p., n.d.

Cumming, Joseph B. "How I Knew That the War Was Over." *Confederate Veteran* 9 (January 1901): 18–19.

Cuttino, George Peddy, ed. *Saddle Bag and Spinning Wheel, Being the Civil War Letters of George W. Peddy, M.D., and His Wife, Kate Featherston Peddy*. Macon, Ga.: Mercer University Press, 1981.

Dana, Charles A. *Recollections of the Civil War: With the Leaders at Washington and in the Field in the Sixties*. New York: D. Appleton and Company, 1898.

Darst, Maury, ed. "Robert Hughes, Jr.: Confederate Soldier." *East Texas Historical Journal* 9 (March 1971): 20–49.

Davis, Jefferson. *The Rise and Fall of the Confederate Government*. 2 vols. New York: D. Appleton and Company, 1881.

Davis, Theo R. "With Sherman in His Army Home." *The Cosmopolitan* 12 (December 1891): 195–205.

Devereux, Margaret. *Plantation Sketches*. Cambridge, Mass.: Riverside Press, 1906.

Dickert, D. Augustus. *History of Kershaw's Brigade, with Complete Roll of Companies, Biographical Sketches, Incidents, Anecdotes, Etc.* Newberry, S.C.: Elbert H. Aull Company, 1899.

Ditty, Jesse B. "Entering Raleigh." *National Tribune*, December 29, 1898.

Dowdey, Clifford, and Louis H. Manarin, eds. *The Wartime Papers of R. E. Lee*. New York: Bramhall House, 1961.

Drake, James Madison. *The History of the Ninth New Jersey Veteran Volunteers. A Record of Its Service from Sept. 13th, 1861, to July 12, 1865, with a Complete Official Roster, and Sketches of Prominent Members, with Anecdotes, Incidents and Thrilling Reminiscences*. Elizabeth, N.J.: Journal Printing House, 1889.

Eaton, Clement, ed. "Diary of an Officer in Sherman's Army Marching through the Carolinas." *Journal of Southern History* 9 (May 1943): 238–54.

Elliott, Colleen Morse, and Louise Armstrong Moxley, eds. *The Tennessee Civil War Veterans Questionnaires*. 5 vols. Easley, S.C.: Southern Historical Press, 1985.

Evans, J. W. "With Hampton's Scouts." *Confederate Veteran* 32 (December 1924): 470.

Fallis, Leroy S. "Entering Raleigh." *National Tribune*, February 16, 1899.

Federico, Bianca Morse, ed. *The Civil War Letters of John Holbrook Morse, 1861–1865*. Washington, D.C.: Federico, 1975.

Fitch, Michael H. *Echoes of the Civil War as I Hear Them*. New York: R. F. Fenno and Company, 1905.

Fleharty, S. F. *Our Regiment. A History of the 102d Illinois Infantry Volunteers with Sketches of the Atlanta Campaign, the Georgia Raid, and the Campaign of the Carolinas*. Chicago: Brewster and Hanscom, 1865.

Fletcher, William Andrew. *Rebel Private, Front and Rear.* 1908. Reprint, Austin: University of Texas Press, 1954.

Floyd, David Bittle. *History of the Seventy-fifth Regiment of Indiana Infantry Volunteers, Its Organization, Campaigns, and Battles.* Philadelphia: Lutheran Publication Society, 1893.

Foraker, Joseph Benson. *Notes of a Busy Life.* 2 vols. Cincinnati: Stewart and Kidd Company, 1916.

Force, Manning F. "Marching Across Carolina." In *Sketches of War History, 1861–1865. Papers Prepared for the Ohio Commandery of the Military Order of the Loyal Legion of the United States,* 1:1–18. Cincinnati: Robert Clarke and Company, 1888–1908.

Ford, Arthur P. "A March Across the Carolinas." *Philadelphia Weekly Times,* July 7, 1883.

Ford, Arthur P., and Marion J. Ford. *Life in the Confederate Army.* New York: Neale Publishing Company, 1905.

Freeman, Douglas Southall, ed. *Lee's Dispatches: Unpublished Letters of General Robert E. Lee, C.S.A., to Jefferson Davis and the War Department of the Confederate States of America, 1862–1865.* New York: G. P. Putnam's Sons, 1957.

Furnas, Adam J. *Forty-four Months at the Front.* Muscatine, Iowa: n.p., 1995.

Gage, M. D. *From Vicksburg to Raleigh, or a Complete History of the Twelfth Regiment, Indiana Volunteer Infantry, and the Campaigns of Grant and Sherman, with an Outline of the Great Rebellion.* Chicago: Clarke and Company, 1865.

Gaskill, J. W. *Footprints through Dixie: Everyday Life of the Man Under a Musket.* Alliance, Ohio: n.p., 1919.

"General Johnston's Effect on His Soldiers." *Confederate Veteran* 18 (May 1910): 207.

Gilberg, J. A. "Another View of It." *National Tribune,* February 16, 1899.

Ginger, Lew. "The 75th Ind. It Does the Last Fighting in Which Infantry Is Engaged in Sherman's Army." *National Tribune,* May 2, 1889.

Goodloe, Albert Theodore. *Some Rebel Relics from the Seat of War.* Nashville: Publishing House of the Methodist Episcopal Church, South, 1893.

Grant, Ulysses S. *Personal Memoirs.* New York: Da Capo Press, 1982.

Grunert, William. *History of the One Hundred and Twenty-ninth Regiment, Illinois Volunteer Infantry.* Winchester, Ill.: R. B. Dedman, 1866.

Guild, George B. *A Brief Narrative of the Fourth Tennessee Cavalry Regiment.* Nashville: n.p., 1913.

Hagood, Johnson. *Memoirs of the War of Secession, from the Original Manuscripts of Johnson Hagood.* Columbia, S.C.: The State Company, 1910.

Halsey, Ashley, ed. *A Yankee Private's Civil War by Robert Hale Strong.* Chicago: Henry Regnery Company, 1961.

Hamilton, Joseph Gregoire de Roulhac, ed. *The Correspondence of Jonathan Worth.* 2 vols. Raleigh: Edwards and Broughton, 1909.

———. *The Papers of Thomas Ruffin.* 4 vols. Raleigh: Edwards and Broughton, State Printers, 1920.

Hamilton, Joseph Gregoire de Roulhac, and Max R. Williams, eds. *The Papers of William Alexander Graham.* 7 vols. to date. Raleigh: North Carolina Division of Archives and History, 1957–.

Hamilton, William Douglas. "In at the Death, or the Last Shot at the Confederacy." In *Sketches of War History, 1861–1865. Papers Prepared for the Commandery of the State of Ohio, Military Order of the Loyal Legion of the United States,* 6:287–95. Cincinnati: Robert Clarke and Company, 1908.

———. *Recollections of a Cavalryman after Fifty Years.* Columbus, Ohio: F. J. Heer Printing Company, 1915.

Hampton, Wade. "The Battle of Bentonville." In *Battles and Leaders of the Civil War,* edited by Robert U. Johnson and Clarence C. Buel, 4:700–705. New York: Century Company, 1888.

———. "The Effort to Rescue Jefferson Davis." *Southern Historical Society Papers* 27 (1899): 132–36.

Hansell, Charles P. "Surrender of Cobb's Legion." *Confederate Veteran* 25 (October 1917): 463–64.

Hargis, O. P. "We Kept Fighting and Falling Back." *Civil War Times Illustrated* 7 (December 1968): 37–42.

Harris, J. S. *Historical Sketches of the Seventh Regiment, North Carolina Troops.* Mooresville, N.C.: Mooresville Printing Company, n.d.

Harrison, Burton N. "The Capture of Jefferson Davis." *Century Magazine* 27 (November 1883–April 1884): 130–45.

Harwell, Richard, and Philip N. Racine, eds. *The Fiery Trail: A Union Officer's Account of Sherman's Last Campaigns.* Knoxville: University of Tennessee Press, 1986.

Hatcher, Edmund N. *The Last Four Weeks of the War.* Columbus, Ohio: Co-operative Publishing Company, 1892.

Hawes, Lilla Miles, ed. "The Memoirs of Charles H. Olmstead." *Georgia Historical Quarterly* 45 (June 1961): 137–55.

Hazen, William Babcock. *A Narrative of Military Service.* Boston: Ticknor and Company, 1885.

Hedley, Fenwick Y. *Marching through Georgia: Pen-Pictures of Every-Day Life in General Sherman's Army from the Beginning of the Atlanta Campaign Until the Close of the War.* Chicago: R. R. Donnelly and Sons, 1887.

Herriot, Robert. "At Greensboro, N.C., in April, 1865." *Confederate Veteran* 30 (March 1922): 101–2.

Hitchcock, Henry. *Marching with Sherman: Passages from the Letters and Campaign Diaries of Henry Hitchcock.* Edited by M. A. DeWolfe Howe. Lincoln: University of Nebraska Press, 1995.

Holden, William Woods. *Memoirs of W. W. Holden.* Durham, N.C.: Seeman Printery, 1911.

Holmes, Alester G., Jr., ed. *Diary of Henry McCall Holmes, Army of Tennessee, Assistant Surgeon Florida Troops, with Related Letters, Documents, Etc.* State College, Miss.: n.p., 1968.

Hoole, William Stanley, ed. "Admiral on Horseback: The Diary of Brigadier General Raphael Semmes, February–May, 1865." *Alabama Review* 28 (April 1975): 129–50.

———. *History of the Forty-sixth Alabama Regiment Volunteer Infantry, 1862–1865, by Captain George Evans Brewer.* University, Ala.: Confederate Publishing Company, 1985.

Howard, Oliver O. *Autobiography of Oliver Otis Howard, Major General, United States Army.* 2 vols. New York: Baker and Taylor Company, 1907.

———. "The Campaign of the Carolinas." *Eleventh Annual Dinner Ohio Commandery, MOLLUS. Burnet House—Cincinnati, May 2nd, 1894,* 11:18–31. N.p., n.d.

———. "Marching through Georgia." *National Tribune,* March 19, 26, 1896.

Howard, Wiley C. *Sketch of Cobb Legion Cavalry and Some Incidents and Scenes Remembered.* Atlanta: Atlanta Camp 159, U.C.V., 1901.

Howe, Mark Antony DeWolfe, ed. *Home Letters of General Sherman.* New York: Charles Scribner's Sons, 1909.

Hughes, W. J. L. "The Bennett Farmhouse." *National Tribune,* October 3, 1912.

Inglesby, Charles. *Historical Sketch of the First Regiment of South Carolina Artillery. (Regulars).* N.p.: Walker, Evans and Cogswell Company, n.d.

Jackson, Oscar L. *The Colonel's Diary: Journals Kept Before and During the Civil War by the Late Colonel Oscar L. Jackson, Sometime Commander of the Sixty-third Regiment, Ohio Volunteer Infantry.* Sharon, Pa.: privately published, 1922.

Jamison, Matthew H. *Recollections of Pioneer and Army Life.* Kansas City, Mo.: Hudson Press, 1911.

Johnson, W. A. "Closing Days with Johnston." *National Tribune,* May 29, June 5, 1902.

Johnson, William Benjamin. *"Union to the Hub and Twice Around the Tire": Reminiscences of the Civil War.* Balboa, Calif.: n.p., 1950.

Johnston, Joseph E. "The Dalton-Atlanta Operations: A Review, in Part, of General Sherman's *Memoirs.*" *Annals of the Army of Tennessee and Early Western History* 1 (April 1878): 1–13.

———. "My Negotiations with General Sherman." *North American Review* 143 (August 1886): 183–97.

———. *Narrative of Military Operations during the Civil War.* New York: Da Capo Press, 1990.

Jones, Charles Colcock. *Historical Sketch of the Chatham Artillery during the Confederate Struggle for Independence.* Albany, N.Y.: Joel Munsell, 1867.

Julian, George W. *Political Recollections, 1840–1872.* Chicago: Jansen, McClurg and Company, 1884.

Kerr, Charles D. "From Atlanta to Raleigh." In *War Papers Read Before the Commandery of the State of Michigan, Military Order of the Loyal Legion of the United States,* 1:202–23. Detroit: Winn and Hammond, 1893.

Keyes, J. H. "Lincoln's Assassination: Reception of the News in Sherman's Army." *National Tribune,* January 13, 1910.

Kirk, Charles H., ed. *History of the Fifteenth Pennsylvania Volunteer Cavalry.* Philadelphia: n.p., 1906.

Kirwan, Thomas, and Henry Splaine. *Memorial History of the Seventeenth Regiment, Massachusetts Volunteer Infantry, in the Civil War from 1861–1865.* Salem, Mass.: Salem Press Company, 1911.

Kittinger, Joseph. *Diary, 1861–1865.* Buffalo, N.Y.: Kittinger Company, 1979.

Lindsley, John Berrien, ed. *The Military Annals of Tennessee. Confederate. First Series.* Nashville: J. M. Lindsley and Company, 1886.

Loop, M. B. "Rounding Up the Confederacy: Veteran Campaigns of the 68th Ohio." *National Tribune,* June 27, July 4, 1901.

Lybarger, Edwin L. *Leaves from My Diary.* Warsaw, Ohio: Edwin L. Lybarger, n.d.

McAdams, Francis M. *Every-Day Soldier Life, or a History of the One Hundred and Thirteenth Ohio Volunteer Infantry.* Columbus, Ohio: Charles M. Cott and Company, 1884.

McBride, John R. *History of the Thirty-third Indiana Veteran Volunteer Infantry.* Indianapolis: William B. Buford, 1900.

McClellan, H. B. "A Reply to General Kilpatrick." *Philadelphia Weekly Times,* February 7, 1880.

McClurg, Alexander. "The Last Chance of the Confederacy." *Atlantic Monthly* 50 (September 1882): 389–400.

McMakin, Lew. "Capturing Raleigh: Col. Michael Kerwin's Brigade Was the First to Enter the Capital of North Carolina." *National Tribune,* September 1, 1921.

———. "Flag on the Raleigh Capitol." *National Tribune,* March 23, 1911.

———. "Joining Sherman: An Interesting March after the 13th Pa. Cav." *National Tribune,* July 15, 1920.

———. "Not Quite Over." *National Tribune,* February 22, 1912.

Mahon, John K., ed. "The Civil War Letters of Samuel Mahon, Seventh Iowa Infantry." *Iowa Journal of History* 51 (July 1953): 233–66.

Mallory, Stephen R. "Last Days of the Confederate Government." *McClure's Magazine* 16 (1901): 239–48.

Merrill, Samuel. *The Seventieth Indiana Volunteer Infantry in the War of the Rebellion.* Indianapolis: Bowen-Merrill Company, 1900.

Miller, James C. "With Sherman through the Carolinas." *Civil War Times Illustrated* 8 (October 1969): 35–44.

Morhous, Henry C. *Reminiscences of the 123d Regiment, N.Y.S.V., Giving a Complete History of Its Three Years Service in the War.* Greenwich, N.Y.: People's Book and Job Office, 1879.

Mowris, J. A. *A History of the One Hundred and Seventeenth Regiment, New York Volunteers.* Hartford: Case, Lockwood and Company, 1866.

Mullen, James M. "Last Days of Johnston's Army." *Southern Historical Society Papers* 18 (January 1890): 97–113.

Myers, W. O. "In North Carolina: At the Wind-up of the Great Conflict." *National Tribune,* March 30, 1916.

Nichols, George Ward. *The Story of the Great March from the Diary of a Staff Officer.* New York: Harper and Brothers, 1866.

Osborn, Hartwell, and Others. *Trials and Triumphs. The Record of the Fifty-fifth Ohio Volunteer Infantry.* Chicago: A. C. McClurg and Company, 1904.

Outline of the Veteran Service of the Tenth Regiment of Michigan Veteran Volunteer Infantry. N.p., n.d.

Payne, Edwin W. *History of the Thirty-fourth Regiment of Illinois Volunteer Infantry.* Clinton, Iowa: Allen Printing Company, 1903.

Pepper, George W. *Personal Recollections of Sherman's Campaigns in Georgia and the Carolinas.* Zanesville, Ohio: Hugh Dunne, 1866.

Pinney, N. A. *History of the 104th Regiment, Ohio Volunteer Infantry, from 1862 to 1865.* Akron, Ohio: Werner and Lohmann, 1886.

Porter, A. Toomer. *Led On! Step by Step: Scenes from Clerical, Military, Educational, and Plantation Life in the South, 1828–1898.* 1898. Reprint, Miami: Mnemosyne Publishing Company, 1969.

Porter, David Dixon. *Incidents and Anecdotes of the Civil War.* New York: D. Appleton and Company, 1885.

———. *The Naval History of the Civil War.* New York: Sherman Publishing Company, 1886.

Porter, Horace. *Campaigning with Grant.* Edited by Wayne C. Temple. Bloomington: Indiana University Press, 1961.

Quaife, Milo M., ed. *From the Cannon's Mouth: The Civil War Letters of General Alpheus S. Williams.* Detroit: Wayne State University Press and the Detroit Historical Society, 1959.

Randall, James G., ed. *The Diary of Orville Hickman Browning. Collections of the Illinois State Historical Library. Volumes XX and XXII.* 2 vols. Springfield, Ill.: Jeffersons Printing and Stationery Company, 1933.

Ratchford, J. W. *Some Reminiscences of Persons and Incidents of the Civil War.* 1909. Reprint, Austin, Tex.: Shoal Creek Publishers, 1971.

Reagan, John H. *Memoirs, with Special Reference to Secession and the Civil War.* New York: Neale Publishing Company, 1906.

Redkey, Edwin S. "They Are Invincible." *Civil War Times Illustrated* 28 (April 1989): 32–37.

Reid, Whitelaw. *After the War: A Tour of the Southern States, 1865–1866.* Edited by C. Vann Woodward. New York: Harper and Row, 1965.

Rennolds, Edwin H. *A History of the Henry County Commands Which Served in the Confederate States Army, Including Rosters of the Various Companies Enlisted in Henry County, Tenn.* 1904. Reprint, Kennesaw, Ga.: Continental Book Company, 1961.

Ricks, Augustus J. "Carrying the News of Lee's Surrender to the Army of the Ohio." In *Sketches of War History, 1861–1865. Papers Prepared for the Ohio Commandery of the Military Order of the Loyal Legion of the United States,* 2:234–46. Cincinnati: Robert Clarke and Company, 1888–1908.

Ridley, Bromfield. *Battles and Sketches of the Army of Tennessee.* Mexico, Mo.: Missouri Printing and Publishing Company, 1906.

Roman, Alfred. *The Military Operations of General Beauregard in the War Between the States.* 2 vols. New York: Harper and Brothers, 1884.

Rood, Hosea W. *Story of the Service of Company E, and of the Twelfth Wisconsin Regiment, Veteran Volunteer Infantry.* Milwaukee: Swain and Tate Company, 1893.

Round, George C. "The Last Signal Message." *National Tribune,* July 23, 1903.

———. "The Last Signal Message of the War: By the One Who Sent It." In *Twenty-seventh Annual Reunion of the Signal Corps, U.S.A., Washington, D.C., October, 1902,* 26–34. Manassas, Va.: Journal Press, 1903.

"A Rousing Reunion. General Gregg Attended That of the 13th Pa. Cav., Which Was Exceptionally Interesting." *National Tribune,* November 3, 1898.

Rowland, Dunbar, ed. *Jefferson Davis, Constitutionalist: His Letters, Papers and Speeches.* 10 vols. Jackson: Mississippi Department of Archives and History, 1923.

Bibliography

Runyan, Morris C. *Eight Days with the Confederates and Capture of Their Archives, Flags, Etc., by Company "G," Ninth New Jersey Vol.* Princeton, N.J.: William C. Zapf, 1896.

Russell, Lucy Phillips. *A Rare Pattern.* Chapel Hill: University of North Carolina Press, 1957.

Russell, W. A. "Tragic Adventures as the War Closed." *Confederate Veteran* 22 (September 1914): 401–3.

Sargeant, Charles Sheldon. *Personal Recollections of the 18th Missouri Infantry in the War for the Union.* Unionville, Mo.: Stille and Lincoln, 1891.

Saunders, W. J. "Governor Z. B. Vance: Story of the Last Days of the Confederacy in North Carolina." *Southern Historical Society Papers* 32 (1904): 164–68.

Saunier, Joseph A. *A History of the Forty-seventh Regiment, Ohio Veteran Volunteer Infantry.* Hillsboro, Ohio: Lyle Printing Company, n.d.

Schafer, Joseph, ed. *Intimate Letters of Carl Schurz, 1841–1869.* Madison: State Historical Society of Wisconsin, 1928.

Schofield, John M. *Forty-six Years in the Army.* New York: Century Company, 1897.

Schurz, Carl. *The Reminiscences of Carl Schurz.* 3 vols. New York: McClure Company, 1908.

Semmes, Raphael. *Memoirs of Service Afloat, During the War Between the States.* Baltimore: Kelly, Piet and Company, 1869.

Sheridan, Philip Henry. *Personal Memoirs of P. H. Sheridan, General, United States Army.* 2 vols. New York: Charles L. Webster and Company, 1888.

Sherman, John. *John Sherman's Recollections of Forty Years in the House, Senate and Cabinet. An Autobiography.* Chicago: Werner Company, 1895.

Sherman, William T. *General and Field Orders, Campaigns of the Army of the Tennessee, Ohio and Cumberland, Maj. Gen. W. T. Sherman, Commanding, 1864–5.* St. Louis: R. F. Studley and Company, 1865.

———. *General Sherman's Official Account of the Great March through Georgia and the Carolinas.* New York: Bunce and Huntington, 1865.

———. "The Grand Strategy of the Last Year of the War." In *Battles and Leaders of the Civil War,* edited by Robert U. Johnson and Clarence C. Buel, 4:247–59. New York: Century Company, 1888.

———. *Memoirs.* 2 vols. in 1. New York: Da Capo Press, 1984.

———. "The Surrender of Gen. Johnston. Letter from General Sherman." *The Historical Magazine, and Notes and Queries, Concerning the Antiquities, History and Biography of America* 5, 2d ser. (May 1869): 333–34.

———. "To Execute the Terms of Surrender." *Civil War Times Illustrated* 15 (January 1977): 34–42.

[———]. "Unpublished Letters of General Sherman." *North American Review* 152 (1891): 371–75.

Shipp, Hezekiah. "Gens. Kilpatrick and Johnston." *National Tribune,* February 8, 1912.

Simon, John Y., ed. *The Papers of Ulysses S. Grant.* 22 vols. to date. Carbondale: Southern Illinois University Press, 1967–.

Simpson, Brooks D., and Jean V. Berlin, eds. *Sherman's Civil War: Selected Correspondence of William T. Sherman, 1860–1865.* Chapel Hill: University of North Carolina Press, 1999.

Slocum, Henry W. "Final Operations of Sherman's Army." In *Battles and Leaders of the Civil War,* edited by Robert U. Johnson and Clarence C. Buel, 4:754–58. New York: Century Company, 1888.

———. "Sherman's March from Savannah to Bentonville." In *Battles and Leaders of the Civil War,* edited by Robert U. Johnson and Clarence C. Buel, 4:681–95. New York: Century Publishing Company, 1888.

Smith, Bradbury. "A Maine Boy in the Tenth Ohio Cavalry." *Maine Bugle* 4 (January 1897): 11–21.

Smith, D. E. Huger. *A Charlestonian's Recollections, 1846–1913.* Charleston, S.C.: Carolina Art Association, 1950.

Sparks, David S., ed. *Inside Lincoln's Army: The Diary of Marsena Rudolph Patrick, Provost Marshal General, Army of the Potomac.* New York: Thomas Yoseloff, 1964.

Spencer, Cornelia Phillips. "Old Times in Chapel Hill, No. IX: Governor Swain." *North Carolina University Magazine* 7 (May 1888): 214–21.

Stine, A. D. "What Troops Were the First to Enter Raleigh, N.C.?" *National Tribune,* May 14, 1885.

Stormont, Gilbert R., ed. *History of the Fifty-eighth Regiment of Indiana Volunteer Infantry. Its Organization, Campaigns and Battles from 1861 to 1865. From the Manuscript Prepared by the Late Chaplain John J. Hight, During His Service with the Regiment in the Field.* Princeton, N.J.: Press of the Clarion, 1895.

Strode, Hudson, ed. *Jefferson Davis: Private Letters, 1823–1889.* New York: Harcourt, Brace and World, 1966.

Sumner, Merlin E., ed. *The Diary of Cyrus B. Comstock.* Dayton, Ohio: Morningside House, 1987.

Swain, David L. *Early Times in Raleigh: Addresses Delivered by the Hon. David L. Swain, L.L.D. at the Dedication of Tucker Hall.* Raleigh: Walters, Hughes and Company, 1867.

Swallow, W. H. "Retreat of the Confederate Government from Richmond to the Gulf." *Magazine of American History* 15 (January–June 1886): 596–608.

Sylvester, Lorna Lutes, ed. "'Gone for a Soldier': The Civil War Letters of Charles Harding Cox." *Indiana Magazine of History* 68 (September 1972): 181–239.

Tenth Ohio Cavalryman. "Campaign through the Carolinas." *National Tribune,* May 5, 12, 1892.

Thomas, Benjamin P., ed. *Three Years with Grant, as Recalled by War Correspondent Sylvanus Cadwallader.* New York: Alfred A. Knopf, 1955.

Thompson, B. F. *History of the 112th Regiment of Illinois Volunteer Infantry in the War of the Rebellion, 1862–1865.* Toulon, Ill.: Stark County News Office, 1885.

Throne, Mildred, ed. "A History of Company D, Eleventh Iowa Infantry [by William S. Fultz]." *Iowa Journal of History* 55 (January 1957): 35–90.

Tomlinson, Helyn W., ed. *"Dear Friends": The Civil War Letters and Diary of Charles Edwin Cort.* N.p.: Helyn W. Tomlinson, 1962.

Toombs, Samuel. *Reminiscences of the War, Comprising a Detailed Account of the Experiences of the Thirteenth Regiment, New Jersey Volunteers.* Orange, N.J.: Printed at the Journal Office, 1878.

Tracie, Theodore C. *Annals of the Nineteenth Ohio Battery, Volunteer Artillery.* Cleveland: J. B. Savage, 1878.

Bibliography

Underwood, Adin B. *The Three Years' Service of the Thirty-third Mass. Infantry Regiment, 1862–1865.* Boston: A. Williams and Company, 1881.

Vance, Zebulon B. *Life and Character of Hon. David L. Swain, Late President of the University of North Carolina.* Durham, N.C.: W. T. Blackwell and Company's Steam Presses, 1878.

[Walker, L. A.] *The Surrender in Greensboro.* N.p., n.d. Reprinted from the *Charlotte Observer*, January 11, 1901.

Ward, Dallas T. *The Last Flag of Truce.* Franklinton, N.C.: n.p., 1915.

Warren, Edward. *A Doctor's Experiences in Three Continents.* Baltimore: Cushings and Bailey, 1885.

Welles, Gideon. *Diary of Gideon Welles, Secretary of the Navy Under Lincoln and Johnson.* 3 vols. Boston: Houghton-Mifflin Company, 1911.

Wells, Edward Laight. *Hampton and His Cavalry in '64.* Richmond: B. F. Johnson, 1899.

Wheeler, Joseph. "An Effort to Rescue Jefferson Davis." *Century Magazine* 56 (1898): 85–91.

Whitaker, R. H. *Whitaker's Reminiscences, Incidents and Anecdotes.* Raleigh: Edwards and Broughton, 1905.

Widney, Lyman S. "From the Sea to the Grand Review." *National Tribune,* August 27, September 3, 1903.

Wills, Charles W. *Army Life of an Illinois Soldier.* Washington, D.C.: Globe Printing Company, 1906.

Winther, Oscar Ogburn, ed. *With Sherman to the Sea: The Civil War Letters, Diaries, and Reminiscences of Theodore F. Upson.* Baton Rouge: Louisiana State University Press, 1943.

Wise, John Sergeant. *The End of an Era.* Edited by Curtis Carroll Davis. New York: Thomas Yoseloff, n.d.

Woodward, C. Vann, ed. *Mary Chesnut's Civil War.* New Haven: Yale University Press, 1981.

Worsham, W. J. *The Old Nineteenth Tennessee Regiment.* Knoxville: Press of Paragon Printing Company, 1902.

Wright, Henry H. *A History of the Sixth Iowa Infantry.* Iowa City: State Historical Society of Iowa, 1923.

Yearns, W. Buck, and John G. Barrett, eds. *North Carolina Civil War Documentary.* Chapel Hill: University of North Carolina Press, 1980.

Young, Jared W., ed. "General Sherman on His Own Record: Some Unpublished Comments." *Atlantic Monthly* 108 (September 1911): 289–300.

Younger, Edward, ed. *Inside the Confederate Government: The Diary of Robert Garlick Hill Kean.* New York: Oxford University Press, 1957.

SECONDARY SOURCES

Adler, Selig. "Zebulon B. Vance and the 'Scattered Nation.'" *Journal of Southern History* 7 (August 1941): 357–77.

Amann, William Frayne, ed. *Personnel of the Civil War.* 2 vols. in 1. New York: Thomas Yoseloff, 1961.

Ambrose, Stephen E. *Halleck: Lincoln's Chief of Staff.* Baton Rouge: Louisiana State University Press, 1962.

Amis, Moses N. *Historical Raleigh; With Sketches of Wake County and Its Important Towns.* Raleigh: Commercial Printing Company, 1913.

Anderson, Jean Bradley. *Durham County.* Durham, N.C.: Duke University Press, 1990.

———. *Piedmont Plantation: The Bennehan-Cameron Family and Lands in North Carolina.* Durham, N.C.: Historic Preservation Society of Durham, 1985.

Anderson, Mrs. John Huske (Lucy London). *North Carolina Women of the Confederacy.* Fayetteville, N.C.: published by the author, 1926.

Angley, Wilson, Jerry L. Cross, and Michael Hill, eds. *Sherman's March through North Carolina: A Chronology.* Raleigh: North Carolina Division of Archives and History, 1995.

Annals of an American Family: A Chronicle of the Lives and Times of Successive Generations from Merging Pioneer Lines of the Richardson and Smith Families. Greensboro, N.C.: privately published, 1953.

Arnett, Ethel Stephens. *Confederate Guns Were Stacked at Greensboro, North Carolina.* Greensboro, N.C.: Piedmont Press, 1965.

Ballard, Michael B. *A Long Shadow: Jefferson Davis and the Final Days of the Confederacy.* Jackson: University Press of Mississippi, 1986.

Barefoot, Daniel W. *General Robert F. Hoke: Lee's Modest Warrior.* Winston-Salem, N.C.: John F. Blair, 1996.

Barrett, John G. *The Civil War in North Carolina.* Chapel Hill: University of North Carolina Press, 1963.

———. *Sherman's March through the Carolinas.* Chapel Hill: University of North Carolina Press, 1956.

Battle, Kemp Plummer. *History of the University of North Carolina.* 2 vols. Raleigh: Edwards and Broughton, 1907.

Bearss, Edwin C., and Chris Calkins. *The Battle of Five Forks.* Lynchburg, Va.: H. E. Howard, 1985.

Black, Robert C. *The Railroads of the Confederacy.* Chapel Hill: University of North Carolina Press, 1952.

Boatner, Mark Mayo, III. *The Civil War Dictionary.* New York: David McKay Company, 1959.

Boyd, William Kenneth. *The Story of Durham, City of the New South.* Durham, N.C.: Duke University Press, 1927.

Bradley, Mark L. *Last Stand in the Carolinas: The Battle of Bentonville.* Campbell, Calif.: Savas Woodbury Publishers, 1996.

Brady, James P. *Hurrah for the Artillery! Knap's Independent Battery "E," Pennsylvania Light Artillery.* Gettysburg, Pa.: Thomas Publications, 1992.

Burne, Alfred H. *Lee, Grant and Sherman: A Study in Leadership in the 1864–65 Campaign.* New York: Charles Scribner's Sons, 1939.

Castel, Albert. *Decision in the West: The Atlanta Campaign of 1864.* Lawrence: University Press of Kansas, 1992.

The City of Raleigh. Historical Sketches from Its Foundation. A Review of the City in All Its Varied Aspects — Commercial, Industrial, Statistical, Religious, Social, Etc. Raleigh: Edwards and Broughton, 1887.

Clark, James C. *Last Train South: The Flight of the Confederate Government from Richmond.* Jefferson, N.C.: McFarland and Company, 1984.

Coski, John M. *Capital Navy: The Men, Ships, and Operations of the James River Squadron.* Campbell, Calif.: Savas Woodbury Publishers, 1996.

Cox, Jacob Dolson. *The March to the Sea — Franklin and Nashville.* New York: Charles Scribner's Sons, 1882.

———. "The Sherman-Johnston Convention." *Scribner's* 28 (October 1900): 489–505.

Daniel, Larry J. *Cannoneers in Gray: The Field Artillery of the Army of Tennessee, 1861–1865.* University: University of Alabama Press, 1984.

Davis, William C. *Breckinridge: Statesman, Soldier, Symbol.* Baton Rouge: Louisiana State University Press, 1974.

———. *Jefferson Davis: The Man and His Hour.* New York: HarperCollins, 1991.

Dawson, George Francis. *Life and Services of General John A. Logan as Soldier and Statesman.* Washington, D.C.: National Tribune, 1884.

Dodson, William C. *Campaigns of Wheeler and His Cavalry, 1862–1865.* Atlanta: Hudgins Publishing Company, 1899.

Dowd, Clement. *Life of Zebulon B. Vance.* Charlotte, N.C.: Observer Printing and Publishing House, 1897.

Draper, John William. *History of the American Civil War.* 3 vols. New York: Harper and Brothers, 1870.

DuBose, John Witherspoon. *General Joseph Wheeler and the Army of Tennessee.* New York: Neale Publishing Company, 1912.

Dyer, Frederick H. *A Compendium of the War of the Rebellion.* Des Moines: Dyer Publishing Company, 1908.

Evans, David. *Sherman's Horsemen: Union Cavalry Operations in the Atlanta Campaign.* Bloomington: Indiana University Press, 1996.

Fellman, Michael. *Citizen Sherman.* New York: Random House, 1995.

Flower, Frank Abial. *Edwin McMasters Stanton: The Autocrat of Rebellion, Emancipation and Reconstruction.* New York: Western W. Wilson, 1915.

Fonvielle, Chris E., Jr. *Last Rays of Departing Hope: The Wilmington Campaign.* Campbell, Calif.: Savas Publishing Company, 1997.

Foote, Shelby. *The Civil War: A Narrative.* 3 vols. New York: Random House, 1958–74.

Gibson, John M. *Those 163 Days: A Southern Account of Sherman's March from Atlanta to Raleigh.* New York: Van Rees Press, 1961.

Glatthaar, Joseph T. *The March to the Sea and Beyond: Sherman's Troops in the Savannah and Carolinas Campaigns.* New York: New York University Press, 1985.

———. Untitled paper on Confederate soldier morale in the Army of Tennessee from September 1, 1864 to April 26, 1865. Photocopy in the author's possession.

Govan, Gilbert E., and James W. Livingood. *A Different Valor: The Story of General Joseph E. Johnston, C.S.A.* Indianapolis: Bobbs-Merrill Company, 1956.

"Governor Cox's Speech." In *Report of the Proceedings of the Society of the Army of the Tennessee at the Fourteenth Annual Meeting, Held at Cincinnati, Ohio, April 6th and 7th, 1881*, 113–16. Cincinnati: published by the Society, 1885.

Greco, Thomas A. "Individual Property Form for the Everitt P. Stevens House." North Carolina Division of Archives and History, Raleigh.

Grimsley, Mark. "Fighting a Lost War." Blue and Gray Education Society Lecture, Duke University, Durham, N.C., June 28, 1997.

———. *The Hard Hand of War: Union Military Policy toward Southern Civilians, 1861–1865*. Cambridge: Cambridge University Press, 1995.

Hanna, A. J. *Flight into Oblivion*. 1938. Reprint, Bloomington: Indiana University Press, 1959.

Harris, William C. "The Hampton Roads Peace Conference: A Final Test of Lincoln's Presidential Leadership." Photocopy in the author's possession.

———. "William Woods Holden: In Search of Vindication." *North Carolina Historical Review* 59 (October 1982): 354–72.

Hartley, Chris J. " 'Like an Avalanche': George Stoneman's 1865 Cavalry Raid." *Civil War Regiments* 6, no. 1 (1998): 74–92.

Haywood, Marshall DeLancey. *Builders of the Old North State*. Raleigh: Litho Industries, 1968.

Henderson, Archibald. *The Campus of the First State University*. Chapel Hill: University of North Carolina Press, 1949.

Hendricks, Howard O. "Imperiled City: The Movements of the Union and Confederate Armies toward Greensboro in the Closing Days of the Civil War in North Carolina." Master's thesis, University of North Carolina at Greensboro, 1987.

Hill, D. H., Jr. *North Carolina*. Vol. 5 of *Confederate Military History*, edited by Clement A. Evans. 1899. Reprint, Wilmington, N.C.: Broadfoot Publishing Company, 1987.

Hoar, Jay S. *The South's Last Boys in Gray, An Epic Prose Elegy: A Substudy of Sunset and Dusk of the Blue and the Gray*. Bowling Green, Ohio: Bowling Green State University Popular Press, 1986.

Hughes, Nathaniel Cheairs, Jr. *General William J. Hardee: Old Reliable*. Baton Rouge: Louisiana State University Press, 1965.

Johnson, Frontis. "Zebulon Baird Vance: A Personality Sketch." *North Carolina Historical Review* 30 (April 1953): 178–90.

Keim, DeB. Randolph, ed. *Sherman: A Memorial in Art, Oratory, and Literature by the Society of the Army of the Tennessee with the Aid of the Congress of the United States of America*. Washington, D.C.: Government Printing Office, 1904.

Krick, Robert K. *Lee's Colonels: A Biographical Register of the Field Officers of the Army of Northern Virginia*. Dayton, Ohio: Press of the Morningside Bookshop, 1979.

Lash, Jeffrey N. *Destroyer of the Iron Horse: General Joseph E. Johnston and Confederate Rail Transport, 1861–1865*. Kent, Ohio: Kent State University Press, 1991.

Lewis, Lloyd. *Sherman: Fighting Prophet*. New York: Harcourt, Brace and Company, 1932.

Losson, Christopher. *Tennessee's Forgotten Warriors: Frank Cheatham and His Confederate Division*. Knoxville: University of Tennessee Press, 1989.

Lucas, Marion Brunson. *Sherman and the Burning of Columbia.* College Station: Texas A&M University Press, 1976.

McGehee, Montford. *Life and Character of the Hon. William A. Graham: A Memorial Oration.* Raleigh: News Job Office and Book Bindery, 1877.

McMurry, Richard M. *John Bell Hood and the War for Southern Independence.* Lexington: University Press of Kentucky, 1982.

———. " 'A Policy So Disastrous': Joseph E. Johnston's Atlanta Campaign." In *The Campaign for Atlanta,* edited by Theodore P. Savas and David A. Woodbury, 223–50. Campbell, Calif.: Savas Woodbury Publishers, 1994.

McNeil, William James. "The Stress of War: The Confederacy and William Tecumseh Sherman during the Last Year of the War." Ph.D. diss., Rice University, 1973.

McPherson, James M. *Battle Cry of Freedom: The Civil War Era.* New York: Oxford University Press, 1988.

Manarin, Louis H., and Weymouth T. Jordan Jr., eds. *North Carolina Troops, 1861–1865: A Roster.* 13 vols. to date. Raleigh: North Carolina Division of Archives and History, 1968–.

Marshall, Park. *A Life of William B. Bate: Citizen, Soldier and Statesman.* Nashville: Cumberland Press, 1908.

Marszalek, John F. *Sherman: A Soldier's Passion for Order.* New York: Free Press, 1993.

———. *Sherman's Other War: The General and the Civil War Press.* Memphis: Memphis State University Press, 1981.

Martin, Samuel J. *"Kill-Cavalry," Sherman's Merchant of Terror: The Life of Union General Hugh Judson Kilpatrick.* Madison, N.J.: Fairleigh Dickinson University Press, 1996.

Menius, Arthur C., III. "A Beginning to Reconstruction: The Surrender of J. E. Johnston to W. T. Sherman." Master's thesis, University of North Carolina at Chapel Hill, 1982.

———. "The Bennett Place." North Carolina Department of Cultural Resources, Division of Archives and History, 1979.

Murray, Elizabeth Reid. *Wake: Capital County of North Carolina.* Raleigh: Capital County Publishing Company, 1983.

Naroll, Raoul S. "Lincoln and the Sherman Peace Fiasco—Another Fable?" *Journal of Southern History* 20 (November 1954): 459–83.

Nevins, Allan. *The Organized War, 1863–1864, and The Organized War to Victory, 1864–1865.* Vol. 4 of *Ordeal of the Union.* New York: Collier Books, 1992.

Olds, Fred A. "Story of the Surrender of Raleigh to Federal Army." *Orphans' Friend and Masonic Journal* 50, no. 28 (November 27, 1925): 1, 8, and no. 29 (December 4, 1925): 1, 7–8.

Paul, Hiram V. *History of the Town of Durham, N.C.* Raleigh: Edwards, Broughton and Company, 1884.

Pfanz, Donald C. *The Petersburg Campaign: Abraham Lincoln at City Point, March 20–April 9, 1865.* Lynchburg, Va.: H. E. Howard, 1989.

Powell, William S., ed. *Dictionary of North Carolina Biography.* 6 vols. Chapel Hill: University of North Carolina Press, 1979–96.

Price, Charles Lewis. "The Railroads of North Carolina during the Civil War." M.A. thesis, University of North Carolina at Chapel Hill, 1951.

Raleigh Cemetery Association. List of Confederate Soldiers Buried in Oakwood Cemetery, Raleigh, North Carolina.

Reid, Whitelaw. *Ohio in the War: Her Statesman, Her Generals and Soldiers.* 2 vols. Cincinnati: Moore, Wistach and Baldwin, 1868.

Rowell, John W. *Yankee Cavalrymen: Through the Civil War with the Ninth Pennsylvania Cavalry.* Knoxville: University of Tennessee Press, 1971.

Royster, Charles. *The Destructive War: William Tecumseh Sherman, Stonewall Jackson and the Americans.* New York: Alfred A. Knopf, 1991.

Sears, Stephen W. *To the Gates of Richmond: The Peninsula Campaign.* New York: Ticknor and Fields, 1992.

Spencer, Cornelia Phillips. *The Last Ninety Days of the War in North Carolina.* 1866. Reprint, Wilmington, N.C.: Broadfoot Publishing Company, 1993.

Stokes, Durward T. *Company Shops: The Town Built by a Railroad.* Winston-Salem, N.C.: John F. Blair, 1981.

Symonds, Craig L. *Joseph E. Johnston: A Civil War Biography.* New York: W. W. Norton and Company, 1992.

Thomas, Benjamin P., and Harold M. Hyman. *Stanton: The Life and Times of Lincoln's Secretary of War.* New York: Alfred A. Knopf, 1962.

Trelease, Allen W. *The North Carolina Railroad, 1849–1871, and the Modernization of North Carolina.* Chapel Hill: University of North Carolina Press, 1991.

Trudeau, Noah Andre. *Out of the Storm: The End of the Civil War, April–June 1865.* Baton Rouge: Louisiana State University Press, 1994.

Tucker, Glenn. *Zeb Vance: Champion of Personal Freedom.* Indianapolis: Bobbs-Merrill Company, 1965.

Van Noppen, Ina Woestemeyer. *Stoneman's Last Raid.* Raleigh: North Carolina State College Print Shop, 1961.

Vatavuk, William M. *Dawn of Peace: The Bennett Place State Historic Site.* N.p.: Bennett Place Support Fund, 1989.

Walmsley, James Elliott. "The Last Meeting of the Confederate Cabinet." *Mississippi Valley Historical Review* 6 (December 1919): 336–49.

Warner, Ezra J. *Generals in Blue: Lives of the Union Commanders.* Baton Rouge: Louisiana State University Press, 1964.

———. *Generals in Gray: Lives of the Confederate Commanders.* Baton Rouge: Louisiana State University Press, 1959.

Wharton, Don. *Smithfield as Seen by Sherman's Soldiers.* Smithfield, N.C.: Smithfield Herald Publishing Company, 1977.

Woodworth, Steven E. *Jefferson Davis and His Generals: The Failure of Confederate Command in the West.* Lawrence: University Press of Kansas, 1990.

Yates, Richard E. *The Confederacy and Zeb Vance.* Tuscaloosa, Ala.: Confederate Publishing Company, 1958.

———. "Governor Vance and the End of the War in North Carolina." *North Carolina Historical Review* 18 (October 1941): 315–38.

———. "Zebulon B. Vance as War Governor of North Carolina, 1862–1865." *Journal of Southern History* 3 (February–November 1937): 43–75.

INDEX

Atkins's brigade, 106, 116, 145, 149, 184, 246, 259

Atlanta, Ga., 4, 52, 64, 75, 138, 232

Atlanta campaign, 30, 64, 65, 87, 128, 133

Atlantic and North Carolina Railroad, 3

Auburn, N.C., 110

Augusta, Ga., 2, 5, 10, 63

Aven's Ferry, N.C., 145, 156, 192, 213, 265

Averasboro, N.C., 15, 16, 18, 221

Averasboro, Battle of, 16–17, 31

Bachman's Battery, 135

Baird, Bvt. Maj. Gen. Absalom, 98

Baker, Daniel B., 72

Balloch, George W., 103

Bate, Maj. Gen. William B., 80, 202

Battle, Kemp P. 117–18

Battle, William H., 185

Battle's Bridge, 88, 90, 106, 116, 126

Beauregard, Gen. Pierre G. T., 10, 64, 65, 68, 95, 153, 154, 168, 180, 213, 220, 235; commands forces opposing Sherman's march, 5–8; briefs J. Davis, 137–39; confers with J. Davis and J. E. Johnston, 140–42

Beauregard, Capt. Rene T., 330 (n. 6)

"Beautiful Raleigh, City of Oaks," (anonymous poem), 192

Beckwith, Bvt. Brig. Gen. Amos, 30, 33, 50

Benham, Capt. Daniel W., 121

Benjamin, Judah P., 137, 140, 142, 203

Bennett, James, 159, 218, 219, 337 (n. 6)

Bennett, Nancy, 159

Bennett farm, 158, 167, 169–70, 176, 214–15, 218–19, 231

Bensell, Pvt. John, 86

Bentonville, N.C., 15, 16, 18, 19, 20, 33, 52, 57, 71, 86–87, 105, 221, 263, 265

Bentonville, Battle of, 20–25, 26–27, 31, 34, 61, 80, 86, 135, 156, 229

Bircher, Pvt. William, 53

Black, Col. John Logan, 84, 97

Black Creek, 100

Blacknall, Richard, 149, 188

Black River, 17

Blackshear, Capt. James A., 92

Blair, Maj. Gen. Frank P., Jr., 30, 115, 179, 214, 230, 342 (n. 57)

Bloody Angle, 250

Bloomington, N.C., 242

Blue Ridge Mountains, 256

Boozer, Marie, 306 (n. 38)

Bragg, Gen. Braxton, 6, 17, 18, 19, 21–22, 63; communicates with J. Davis, 12, 62; fights Battle of Wise's Forks, 13

Bragg, Thomas, 109, 156

Brandy Station, Battle of, 218

Brantly, Brig. Gen. William F., 154

Brantly's Brigade, 154

Branum, Lt. John Marshall, 20

Breckinridge, John C., 8, 13–14, 68, 79, 140–41, 154, 165, 177, 178, 180, 181, 203, 204, 213, 222, 229; and Dickson house conference, 167; and Bennett Place negotiations, 170–72

Breckinridge, Col. William C. P., 65, 67, 220

Brink, Capt. Edwin R., 244

Britton House hotel, 234

Brown, Lt. Charles S., 39, 105

Brown, Lt. Col. James W., 78, 91, 183

Brown, Joseph E., 75, 114, 115, 173, 252

Bryan, Capt. George P., 118

Buffalo Creek, 133

Bull, Sgt. Rice C., 27, 250–51, 256

Buncombe County, N.C., 74

Burke's Station, Va., 43, 45, 55, 71

Burlington, N.C., 152

Burnside, Maj. Gen. Ambrose E., 250

Burr, Col. James G., 108–9, 113, 119, 127

Bush Hill, N.C., 242

Butler, Maj. Gen. Matthew C., 6, 214, 218

visits Guilford Court House battlefield, 262

Cox's Bridge, 20, 26–27, 31; skirmish at, 35

Craven, Laura, 193

Crews, Col. Charles C., 128

Crews's Brigade, 128, 326 (n. 28)

Crockett, Pvt. William C., 105

Cumberland River, 257

Cumming, Maj. Joseph B., 89–90, 315 (n. 15), 321 (n. 24)

Danville, Va., 6, 11, 48, 64, 68, 69, 71, 79, 87, 130, 135, 209, 235, 263

Davis, George, 137, 140, 220, 264

Davis, Jefferson, 5, 6–8, 10, 12, 33, 46–47, 62, 68, 79, 90, 91, 95, 109, 118–19, 131, 132, 147, 160, 161, 165, 167, 171–72, 178, 204, 213–14, 217, 224, 225, 228, 235, 264, 318 (n. 64); arrives at Greensboro, 136–37; confers with P. G. T. Beauregard, 137–39; confers with J. E. Johnston, 140–43; opens communications with W. T. Sherman, 143; leaves Greensboro, 154; considers Sherman-Johnston agreement, 203–4; leaves North Carolina, 220

Davis, Bvt. Maj. Gen. Jefferson C. Davis, 20, 125, 191

Davis, Theodore R., 176–77

Davis, Col. Zimmerman, 168

Day, Capt. William H., 122, 125, 219

Dayton, Maj. Lewis M., 104

Deep River, 133, 203

Department of North Carolina, C.S., 12, 62

Department of North Carolina, U.S., 4

Department of South Carolina, Georgia, and Florida, C.S., 8

Department of the Ohio, U.S., 133

Department of the South, U.S., 198

Devereux, Maj. John, 108–9, 114, 119

Devereux, Margaret, 117

Dewey, H. M., 39

Dibrell, Brig. Gen. George G., 153, 220

Dibrell's Division, 20–21, 153–54; detached as J. Davis's escort, 154

Dick, Robert P., 245

Dickson house, 156, 180, 222; Confederate conference at, 165–67

Dinwiddie Court House, Va., 44

District of Beaufort, U.S., 246

District of East Tennessee, U.S. 133

District of Wilmington, U.S., 246

DuBose, Capt. James R., 200

Duke, Brig. Gen. Basil W. Duke, 220

Dunnahoo, Lt. Tom, 106

Durham's Station, N.C., 116, 149, 157–58, 162, 169, 177, 180, 188, 213, 214, 219, 238, 245, 265; description of, 189

Easton, Bvt. Brig. Gen. Langdon C., 30, 33, 50, 193

Eckels, Alexander P., 245

Edgeworth Seminary, 135

Edmondston, Catherine, 69, 261

Ege, Lt. Col. Peter, 70, 85

Elevation, N.C., 18, 71

Eleventh Corps, U.S., 250

Elliott, Brig. Gen. Stephen, 16

Elliott's Brigade, 16, 91, 183

Ellis, John W., 73

Emancipation Proclamation, 231

Eno River, 146, 180

Estes, Maj. L. G., 114, 149, 161, 188

Evans, J. W., 151

Evans, Pvt. William D., 29

Everittsville, N.C., 55

Ewing, Brig. Gen. Charles, 230

Ewing, Thomas, 49–50, 173, 230, 255

Faison's Depot, N.C., 34, 86

Farr, U. H., 28

Fayetteville, N.C., 12, 14–15, 61, 92, 115

Ferguson, Brig. Gen. Samuel W., 220

Fielder, Capt. Alfred T., 91, 96, 242

Fifteenth Corps, U.S., 4, 51–52, 83, 126, 144, 211–12, 213, 247, 253

Finch, Elizabeth, 145

Fleischmann, Capt. Franz, 86

118, 125, 130–31, 132, 145, 149, 151, 156, 165, 168, 169, 178, 179, 180–82, 184, 199, 200–1, 202, 204, 211, 213–14, 220–29 passim, 235, 243–44, 248–49, 251, 254, 265; assumes command of forces opposing Sherman, 8, 305 (n. 17); attempts to check Sherman's advance, 11–14, 17–20; at Battle of Bentonville, 21–25; encamps near Smithfield, 58; communicates with R. E. Lee, 58–59, 65; reacts to Hood's report for Atlanta and Tennessee campaigns, 64–65, 316 (n. 19); receives news of fall of Richmond, 68; reorganizes Army of Tennessee, 80; reacts to news of R. E. Lee's surrender, 90–91; summoned to Greensboro, 95, 139; confers with J. Davis, 140–43, 331 (n. 21), 332 (n. 26); arranges conference with Sherman, 154; descriptions of, 158–59, 239; and Bennett Place negotiations, 159–61, 170–77, 215–18; and Dickson house conference, 167; communicates with Sherman, 198; and "Supplementary Terms," 217; announces surrender to army, 224; communicates with Schofield, 234; meets Schofield and Cox, 238–39; issues farewell address, 239; assessment of, 263–64

Johnston County, N.C., 61

Johnston County Court House, 98

Joint Committee on the Conduct of the War (U.S. Congress), 251, 252

Jones, Cadwallader, 166

Jones, Rebecca, 245

Jones's Crossroads, 144, 213

Jones's Station, N.C., 163, 213

Jordan, Bvt. Brig. Gen. Thomas J., 128, 170, 176, 245

Jordan, Lt. Col. William J., 240

Jordan's (Thomas J.) brigade, 128, 145, 149, 170, 189, 246

Junior Reserves Brigade, 13, 60, 63, 67, 78, 91–92, 151–52, 219

Kennedy, Brig. Gen. John D., 240

Kennedy's Brigade, 67, 89, 240

Kentucky troops, U.S.: 3rd Cavalry, 128, 169; 16th Infantry, 71

Kerwin, Col. Michael, 123

Kerwin's brigade, 123–25, 145, 149, 158, 189

Keyes, Pvt. J. R., 162

Kille, Lt. David, 243

Kilpatrick, Bvt. Maj. Gen. Judson, 2, 19, 71, 86, 100, 107, 114, 116, 119, 122, 123, 127, 145, 148–49, 155–56, 158, 166, 170, 178, 185, 188, 190, 218, 244–45, 306 (n. 38); and Battle of Monroe's Crossroads, 14–15; receives Graham and Swain, 111–13; and skirmish at Morrisville, 128–29; and confrontation with Hampton, 161–62

Kilpatrick's cavalry division (Third Cavalry Division), 2, 4, 12, 15, 16, 34, 52, 55, 86, 105–6, 116, 121, 129, 184, 213, 226, 240, 245, 246; occupies Raleigh, 123–25

Kinston, N.C., 12–13, 34, 51

Kittinger, Lt. Joseph, 128–29, 178

Knoxville, Tenn., 257

Laswell, Lt. Redmond F., 87, 245–46

Lavender, Allston, 193–94

Law, Brig. Gen. Evander M., 128, 146, 150, 154, 214

Law's Brigade, 60

Lawson, George, 359 (n. 72)

Lee, Maj. Gen. Fitzhugh, 79

Lee, Gen. Robert E., 1, 6, 11–12, 13, 17, 27, 33, 43, 45–49, 55–56, 63, 65, 68, 69, 71, 72, 78–79, 87, 92, 103, 113, 132, 141, 148, 150, 160, 170, 173, 207, 211, 212, 216, 228, 265; restores J. E. Johnston to command, 8; assesses strategic situation, 59–60; advises J. Davis to capitulate, 217

Lee, Lt. Gen. Stephen D., 6, 63, 80, 88, 116, 146, 152, 182, 315 (n. 15)

Lee's Corps, 6, 88, 116, 130, 145, 151, 152

Minnesota troops: 1st Battery, 28, 163; 2nd Infantry, 53; 4th Infantry, 196

Mississippi River, 43, 257

Mississippi troops: 9th Consolidated Infantry, 96, 202; Jeff Davis Legion, 106, 146, 151, 158, 183, 203, 223

Missouri troops: 1st Engineers, 72; 18th Infantry, 29; 29th Mounted Infantry, 116

Mitchell, Brig. Gen. John G., 70, 81, 85

Mitchell's brigade, 81, 85

Mitchener, Agrippa, 102

Mitchener, Fannie Secor, 102–3

Mitchener's Station, N.C., 58, 116

Mobile, Ala., 138, 214, 217, 236

Moccasin Creek/Swamp, 83, 97, 101, 103; skirmishes at, 84–86

Monroe's Crossroads, Battle of, 14–15, 19, 41, 100, 107, 116, 149, 162, 306 (n. 38)

Montgomery, Ala., 138

Moore, Bartholomew F., 60, 92, 93, 94–95, 109, 127, 165

Moore, John, 31, 32

Moore, Maj. W. E., 201

Mordecai, George, 190

Morehead, John Motley, 136, 240, 243

Morehead City, N.C., 30, 33–34, 40–41, 51, 56, 206, 209, 210, 248

Morgan, Brig. Gen. James D., 16, 38, 85–86

Morgan's division, 16, 20, 22, 85

Morris (Reddick) farm, 21, 22

Morrisville, N.C., 116, 145, 148, 156, 157, 163; skirmish at, 128–29

Mount Olive, N.C., 34, 86, 188

Mower, Maj. Gen. Joseph A., 23–24, 191, 265; promoted to command of Twentieth Corps, 52

Mower's division, 23–24

Mowris, James A., 87

Murfreesboro, Tenn., 257

Nahunta, N.C., 83

Nance, James, 243

Nashville, Tenn., 3, 96, 257

Nashville, Battle of, 9

Nelson, Lt. William J., 234

Neuse River, 18, 26–27, 51, 60, 66, 71, 88, 90, 97, 99, 116, 126, 196, 199

New Bern, N.C., 4, 12, 40, 50, 210, 219, 244

New Bern, Battle of, 74

Newburry, Pvt. J. B., 31–32

New Hope Creek, 149–50

New Jersey troops: 9th Infantry, 39–40, 240, 243–44

New Orleans, La., 217, 257

New Salem, N.C., 154

New York troops: 23rd Battery, 106, 127, 128–29, 178; 12th Cavalry, 53; 123rd Infantry, 27, 81, 83–85, 250, 256; 141st Infantry, 83–84; 117th Infantry, 87; 154th Infantry, 126

Nichols, Maj. George W., 158

Noble, Pvt. Sylvester C. "Vett," 51, 127, 200, 248

North Carolina capitol, 95–96, 108–9, 118, 119–21, 122, 123, 192–93, 221

North Carolina Home Guard, 133, 135, 153

North Carolina Railroad, 13, 48, 58, 63–64, 71, 88, 95, 106, 133, 135, 136, 140, 234, 238, 312 (n. 70)

North Carolina troops: Ellis's Battery (Co. A, 3rd Battalion), 169; 3rd Regiment, 123; 5th Regiment, 73; 7th Regiment, 153; 17th Regiment, 62; 26th Regiment, 74; 36th Regiment (2nd Artillery), 219; 40th Regiment (3rd Artillery), 219; 58th Regiment, 152; 65th Regiment (6th Cavalry), 84

Norwood, J. W., 60

Nottoway Court House, Va., 130

O'Brien, Lt. Col. William, 97, 105

Ohio River, 257

Ohio troops: 5th Cavalry, 125, 162, 306 (n. 38); 9th Cavalry, 149–50; 10th Cavalry, 155, 244–45, 259; 17th Infantry, 50; 27th Infantry, 29; 33rd

Reid, Whitelaw, 248
Rennolds, Lt. Edwin H., 224
Revolutionary War, 262
Reynolds, Brig. Gen. Daniel H., 129
Rhett, Col. Alfred M., 16
Rhett's Brigade, 16
Richardson, Pharaoh, 58, 89–90
Richardson, W. R., 196–98
Richmond, Va., 1, 11, 17, 33, 43, 55–56, 58–59, 68–71, 169, 234, 248, 249–50, 265, 266
Richmond and Danville Railroad, 41, 43, 45, 55
Ridley, Capt. Bromfield, 57, 66–67, 68, 91, 202, 214, 224
Rigby, Pvt. Alfred A., 39
River Queen, 5, 42, 45, 49, 252
Roanoke River, 11, 43, 59, 69
Robinson, Brig. Gen. James S., 52
Rogers, Col. James C., 83, 85
Roman, Col. Alfred, 10, 224
"Rough and Ready Guards," 74
Round, Lt. George C., 193, 221–22
Rowley, Pvt. Edward A., 163
Roy, Lt. Col. Thomas B., 10, 238
Ruffin's Mill, 146, 151
Rundell, Capt. Frank, 144
Runyan, Capt. Morris C., 243–44

Safely, Capt. John J., 37
St. Mary's School, 91, 125, 212
St. Stephen's Depot, S.C., 11
Salem, N.C., 132
Salisbury, N.C., 13, 63–64, 95, 129, 130, 137–38, 145, 146, 201, 203, 214, 223, 228, 242, 243, 260; Stoneman's capture of, 133–35
Salisbury prison, 133
Salkehatchie River, 6
Saunders, Maj. William J., 146–48, 158, 167
Savannah, Ga., 1, 4, 25, 33, 127, 212, 228, 232, 264, 266
Savannah River, 2
Schofield, Maj. Gen. John M., 6, 11, 14, 15, 18, 20, 29, 39, 40, 41, 46, 54, 59,

71, 86, 102, 103, 133, 145, 179, 214, 226–27, 233, 244–45, 262; transferred to North Carolina, 4; assumes command of Army of the Ohio, 51–52; drafts "Terms of a Military Convention," 215–16, 350 (n. 29); drafts "Supplemental Terms," 217; appointed occupation commander, 226; stipulates paroling procedures to J. E. Johnston, 234; and Cox travel to Greensboro, 238–40; returns to Raleigh, 240; as occupation commander, 246–47
Schurz, Maj. Gen. Carl, 144, 179–80, 193
Scott, Levi M., 233
Scott, W. L., 233
Selfridge, Col. James L., 52, 81, 83
Selfridge's brigade, 81
Selma, Ala., 69, 138
Semmes, Rear Adm. and Brig. Gen. Raphael, 234, 237; background of, 234–35; receives parole, 235–36
Seven Days campaign, 73
Seventeenth Corps, U.S., 4, 23, 30, 51–52, 83, 105, 126, 144, 211, 213, 249, 250
Seward, William H., 207
Shannon, Capt. A. M., 35–36
Sharpsburg, Battle of (Antietam), 73
Sheldon, Col. Charles, 29
Sheridan, Maj. Gen. Philip H., 41, 43–44, 45, 46, 103, 130, 145, 209, 232, 265
Sherman, Ellen, 30, 49, 229, 255
Sherman, John, 41, 50, 51, 229–30, 251, 255
Sherman, Thomas E. "Tom," 255
Sherman, Maj. Gen. William Tecumseh, 8, 9, 12–14, 15, 18, 19, 20, 21, 29, 30, 32–33, 37–38, 51, 58–59, 62, 63, 68, 69, 72, 86, 87, 92, 93, 95, 108, 110–11, 118, 125, 131, 137, 143, 144, 145, 147, 149, 165, 166, 167, 168, 169, 181–82, 184, 194–96, 197–98, 202, 209, 218–27 passim, 233,

247, 264, 311 (n. 53), 311 (n. 57);
plans for Carolinas campaign, 1–5;
and Johnston's return to command,
11, 305 (n. 22); and Battle of Averasboro, 16–17; and Battle of Bentonville, 22–25; critique of, 33–34; travels to City Point, 40–45; descriptions
of, 44–45, 51, 158–59; confers with
Lincoln, 46–49, 312 (n. 74); returns
to Goldsboro, 50; reorganizes army,
51–52; plans spring campaign,
55–56; revises plan, 70–71; occupies
Smithfield, 99–100; announces Lee's
surrender, 103–4, 113; and Graham-
Swain peace mission, 114–15; establishes headquarters, 126–27; plans
next stage of campaign, 129–30;
agrees to meet J. E. Johnston, 148,
155–56, 333 (n. 45), 336 (n. 75);
informed of Lincoln's assassination,
157, 336 (n. 1); and Bennett Place
negotiations, 159–61, 170–77, 214–
18; protects Raleigh, 163; communicates with Grant and Halleck, 178–
79; establishes truce line, 180, 342
(n. 58); and Swain, 186; communicates with J. E. Johnston, 199, 204–5,
211; reviews army, 199–200, 211–12;
confers with Grant, 210–11; writes
Grant and E. M. Stanton, 212; pre-
pares to resume campaign, 213;
reacts to E. M. Stanton, 228–29, 232;
army's support of, 230; reacts to Halleck, 232; returns to army, 248–49;
snubs Halleck, 249–50; arrives at
Washington, 251; testifies before
Joint Committee, 252; and Grand
Review, 252–55; and farewell address
to army, 255; snubs E. M. Stanton,
255, 359 (n. 70); assessment of,
264–66
— "Memorandum or Basis of Agreement," 171–73, 203, 207–9, 228–29;
Northern reaction to, 229–30; critique of, 231
Shiloh, Battle of, 70

Shuman, Maj. George, 125
Sister's Ferry, Ga., 2
Sixth Corps, U.S., 209
Sloan, Maj. James, 153, 154
Sloan, Capt. Thomas S., 84
Sloan, Sgt. William E., 202–3, 224
Slocum, Maj. Gen. Henry W., 2, 15, 16,
    20–21, 22, 34, 40, 51, 71, 81, 86, 99,
    105, 125, 145, 179–80, 200, 226;
    attempts to ease civilian hardships,
    191–92
Smith, Col. Baxter, 150, 168
Smith, Pvt. Daniel E. H., 151, 152
Smith, Gen. E. Kirby Smith, 139, 204,
    217, 257
Smith, Bvt. Maj. Gen. Giles A., 105, 163
Smith, Maj. Gen. Gustavus W., 65
Smith, Jacob Henry, 245
Smithfield, N.C., 15, 17, 18, 19, 24, 48,
    55–69 passim, 71, 72, 73, 79, 83, 84,
    86, 87, 96–97, 100, 101, 126, 167,
    264; Federal occupation of, 97–99
Smithville, N.C., 15
Smythe, Augustine T., 62
Society of the Army of the Tennessee,
    193
South Carolina troops: 1st Artillery
    (Regulars), 57, 68; 2nd Artillery, 78;
    Beauregard's Battery, 330 (n. 6);
    Parker's Battery (Marion Light
    Artillery), 151, 152; Stuart's Battery
    (Beaufort Light Artillery), 57, 62,
    89, 91; 1st Cavalry, 84; 3rd Cavalry,
    133; 5th Cavalry, 168; 2nd Infantry,
    67, 91, 183; 3rd Infantry, 62; 19th
    Infantry (Battalion), 237
Southern Claims Commission, 219
South Mountain, Battle of, 73
South Side Railroad, 41, 43, 45, 55
Spencer, Cornelia Phillips, 150, 155,
    184, 186, 188, 343 (n. 2)
Spotsylvania Court House, Va., 250
Springfield, Ill., 207
Stalling's Station, 106
Stanton, Edwin L., 50, 51
Stanton, Edwin M., 50, 133, 144, 157,

Index

Index